With Liberty and Justice for All?

With Liberty and Justice for All?

The Constitution in the Classroom

Edited by
STEVEN A. STEINBACH
MAEVA MARCUS
ROBERT COHEN

Foreword by
JUSTICE RUTH BADER GINSBURG

OXFORD
UNIVERSITY PRESS

OXFORD
UNIVERSITY PRESS

Oxford University Press is a department of the University of Oxford. It furthers
the University's objective of excellence in research, scholarship, and education
by publishing worldwide. Oxford is a registered trade mark of Oxford University
Press in the UK and certain other countries.

Published in the United States of America by Oxford University Press
198 Madison Avenue, New York, NY 10016, United States of America.

Library of Congress Control Number: 2021057247

ISBN 978–0–19–751630–0 (pbk.)
ISBN 978–0–19–751631–7 (hbk.)

DOI: 10.1093/oso/9780197516317.001.0001

To the memory of Ruth Bader Ginsburg

Contents

Foreword

Justice Ruth Bader Ginsburg

The United States is not old among the world's nations, but its Constitution is the oldest written constitution still in force. Drafted in 1787, a terse Bill of Rights was added four years later. Thereafter, our fundamental instrument of government has been amended on only seventeen occasions. Most of the world's nations have constitutions written since 1970. What accounts for our Constitution's longevity?

Characteristics of our governance system, established at the start, have worked well for us, three most prominently. First, Article II describes a chief executive who is not answerable to the legislature as chief executives are under parliamentary systems to which most nations adhere. Second, in our federal union, legislative authority is divided between a national Congress with powers enumerated in Article I, Section 8, and state governments, which retain authority not committed exclusively to Congress. Finally, our nation's hallmark and pride, we have an independent federal judiciary, a third branch of government, the subject of Article III, with authority to declare laws passed by Congress or executive orders decreed by the President unconstitutional.

For most of our history, our courts were alone in exercising judicial review for constitutionality. Elsewhere, parliaments had the last word. Particularly since the end of the Second World War, however, other nations have installed constitutional review by independent tribunals of justice as one check against return to dictatorial governments of the kind that spawned the Holocaust Kingdom in Germany.

This book, with its concentration on citizenship and rights, captures what seems to me the genius of our Constitution, and accounts for its staying power more than anything else. The document's Preamble opens with the words: "We the People of the United States, in order to form a more perfect Union . . . ." Who counted among those entitled "We the People" in 1787 and decades thereafter? Only white, property-owning men. Left out were people held in human bondage, Native Americans, certain newcomers to our shores, and women, who composed half the population.

Yes, in the course of well over two sometimes turbulent centuries, "We the People" grew to become ever more embracive. Constitutional amendments and court decisions tell part of the story of today's political constituency. But changes wrought always begin with a concerned public. Prime examples are the long-standing abolitionists' demand for the demise of slavery and all its badges and indicia, and the suffragist movement enduring for more than seventy years, culminating in the ratification of the Nineteenth Amendment in 1920. Later movements for change were similarly sparked. They are described in the informative essays introducing each chapter of *With Liberty and Justice for All?*

Celebrated constitutional law scholar Paul Freund presciently observed about the bearing of social change on Justices' opinions: The Supreme Court should never be swayed by the weather of the day, but inevitably, the Court will be influenced by the climate of the era. And renowned jurist Learned Hand cautioned: "Liberty lies in the hearts of men and women; when it dies there, no constitution, no law, no court can save it . . . ." That is why it is of vital importance for young people growing up today to learn about and value their citizenship in the USA and the hard-won rights attending their inclusion in "We the People."

Introduction

Effective teachers of history and civics know that engaging students in their classrooms involves analysis and debate about the American past. And getting students to care about the past means going beyond names and dates by motivating them to think critically about history and its links to the present. Our students today have grown up in a society riven by political divisions and a host of heated arguments that they can readily track with a glance at their phones. So today more than ever, teachers need historical materials that can both illuminate current disputes and introduce their students to weighty controversies throughout United States history about liberty, security, freedom, justice, equality, and rights. At a time, moreover, when the US history curriculum is often front-page news (and even the subject of acrimony in state legislatures), we believe the need for a balanced, open-ended, and open-minded assessment of our nation's constitutional heritage is all the more essential. We need to teach our students that political disagreements in a democracy can and must be discussed rationally and respectfully.

This volume is designed to assist teachers and students by deepening their understanding of a part of history that has generated and reflected the most focused and intense disagreements about rights and wrongs: constitutional history. Controversies involving constitutional claims often begin in the streets and are reported in the press, but they almost always end up in courtrooms, litigated in a setting where evidence, reason, and the Constitution itself are supposed to help resolve them and bring the nation closer to its ideal of "liberty and justice for all." Contention is embedded in the very structure of legal advocacy—with two sides disputing each other in court—and is equally present in congressional, media, and grass-roots arguments about the relationship between the Constitution and competing claims of rights. That is why we are convinced that constitutional history, explored here through succinct and probing essays by leading scholars, lively primary sources, and focused discussion questions, can assist teachers and students alike. We hope to demonstrate that—beyond the few historic court cases that commonly appear on standardized tests—the world of controversy surrounding the Constitution can and should be taught, studied, discussed, and debated far more in our nation's classrooms.

With Liberty and Justice for All?. Edited by Steven A. Steinbach, Maeva Marcus, and Robert Cohen, Oxford University Press. © Oxford University Press 2022. DOI: 10.1093/oso/9780197516317.001.0001

The more closely one looks at constitutional history and its contentious-ness, the more it seems ideal for sparking lively classroom discussions about the meaning of the United States and its republican experiment. Did the Constitution, as written, interpreted, and applied, promote liberty and justice for all? This question can be examined in every era since the founding of the re-public. Controversy has been so much a part of constitutional history that heated discord raged even when the newly independent nation was still governed in the early and mid-1780s under its first constitution, the Articles of Confederation. Indeed, there was far from a national consensus at the time about the need to replace the Articles. Generations of historians (from the time of John Fiske's *The Critical Period of American History* (1888) to our own century, as in Michael Klarman's *The Framers' Coup* (2016)) have continued to argue whether the new Constitution was intended to save the country from political and economic col-lapse or instead to protect elites from advocates of the more democratic ideals of the American Revolution.

Even as the framers wrote the document we now know as the Constitution, they quarreled vigorously among themselves about issues of representation, leadership, accountability, and power—and the results of those arguments had lasting implications for constitutional disputes over the course of more than two centuries. The fight over whether to ratify the Constitution—reflected in *The Federalist*, Antifederalist writings, and the Bill of Rights itself—left a legacy that is very much alive today, which is why teachers often center class sessions on discussing and even reenacting that historic event. An exploration of consti-tutional history can open students up to other arguments of equal significance. Americans have continually fought about what the Constitution permits or requires (or does not), and what values and ideals it enshrines (or does not)—in-deed, who is to be included (or not) in the very definition of "We the People."

Over the many years of the republic, perspectives offered on the Constitution have ranged from glorification to denunciation. The work of the Philadelphia Convention has been lauded as a "miracle" by presidents, Supreme Court justices, historians, and originalists, contributing to literature now known as "Founders Chic," but also criticized by presidents, judges, historians, grass-roots reformers, and radicals as unworkable, outdated, or worse. The same text has been viewed as democratic by some and antidemocratic by others. Abolitionist Frederick Douglass praised the Constitution as an antislavery document, while his aboli-tionist comrade William Lloyd Garrison denounced it as a proslavery pact with the devil, even as the slavocracy's champions, including John C. Calhoun, fer-vently invoked certain (but not all) of the Constitution's provisions. Generations of Americans, including our own, have argued over whether the Constitution enshrined "liberty and justice for all" or neglected racial and ethnic minorities, women, Native Americans, gays, aliens, workers, and the poor. Depending on the issue and the circumstances, constitutional provisions are either invoked by or scorned by the Left (and, conversely, by the Right)—and similar praise or contempt is ladled on Supreme Court decisions interpreting those clauses. Because the Constitution, which includes both specific and vague provisions in its text, continues as the framework under which the nation governs itself, US history can be told, in large measure, as the story of the collective reading, use, and misuse of the Constitution over time, from early disputes about liberty and property to more recent quarrels over equality and dignity.

Of the many areas of constitutional history, we have chosen in this book to focus upon the nature of citizenship and the foundational rights that Americans have come to enjoy.

- *Citizenship*—Who gets to be an American? Or, to use the language of the Constitution itself, who exactly constitutes "We the People"?
- *Rights*—What does it mean to be an American? To borrow again from the Constitution, what are the "Blessings of Liberty" that Americans possess?

Our choice is grounded in practical, historical, and pedagogical considerations. We can probe the lived American constitutional experience with more depth and meaning by examining vital questions of rights and citizenship than would be possible if we tried to cover every historical episode giving rise to a constitutional dispute. So we have elected to minimize (alas) other areas of contention, including separation of powers, federalism, economic regulation, war powers, and the appropriate roles of the legislative and executive branches. We hope thereby to avoid the "full coverage" model of textbooks, which often leads to encyclopedia-style mentioning of topics rather than a reckoning with historical problems that promotes critical thinking. Our concentration on questions of rights and citizenship also derives from an understanding that these are among the most engaging topics for students who have been raised in a society shaped by what historian James Patterson has aptly termed "the rights revolution," which erupted, beginning with the civil rights movement, in the second half of the twentieth century. The political culture of the United States, from the schoolhouse to the White House, has been transformed by a focus on constitutional claims and constitutional rights, and students already understand and speak this language.

The purpose of our book, then, is to provide teachers and students of US history, civics, and government classes with resources to explore specific moments of conflict about the Constitution and its meaning. Our objective is to build bridges between the world of schools and the world of academic historians and legal scholars. At the same time, we hope that everyone who shares a passion for the story of the American past will find this work helpful in exposing them to some of the complexities of more than two centuries of constitutional dialogue.

About this Book

How did this book come about? Two related concerns motivated us as editors. First, despite the work of dedicated yet inadequately supported teachers, recent times have witnessed a decline (at least in many jurisdictions) in the amount of classroom time devoted to the teaching of civics, government, and the Constitution in our nation's schools. It is perhaps not unrelated to this profound curricular trend that an increasing number of Americans can no longer identify even the most basic facts about our structure of government or our core rights and liberties. Even as some state education boards and local school districts have deemphasized the teaching of civics education at the high school level, virtually all schools still teach and require a standard US history survey class in one form or another. While the particular content of these courses is far from uniform nationwide, we believe that all teachers of US history survey courses have the means to infuse more constitutional history—and thus more civics education—into their day-to-day classroom experiences. To be sure, the "decline in civics" trend is far from universal, and civics education—often coupled with active service-learning programs—is on the rebound in many parts of the nation. And many high school and college students are quite politically conscious, astute, and active. All the more reason why it is time, in our view, for the US history curriculum to catch up and make use of such enthusiasm to promote constitutional literacy.

Which brings us to our second motivation. If, as we believe, more focus in the classroom on constitutional controversies would benefit both pedagogy and civil society, who teaches teachers about constitutional history? With rare exceptions, not history or political science departments, or education schools, or law schools, or existing textbooks or curriculum standards.

Hence, this project. This book arises from our direct experience in working with teachers on constitutional history. One of the editors has spent a career researching and teaching constitutional history, another editor's academic work has focused on assisting and improving the teaching of history by public school teachers and student teachers, and another editor practiced as an attorney for many years before becoming a high school history teacher. Over the past decade, each of us in various ways has participated—along with constitutional scholars, history teachers, students, nonprofit organizations, and even Supreme Court justices—in planning and promoting Constitution-themed workshops and other events. At these sessions, we have witnessed a hunger among teachers (and students) to use constitutional learning and disputes to bring history to life in their classrooms.

We are eager to foster dialogue about the Constitution—and even more eager to assist teachers in injecting the energy and engagement that flow from the study of our nation's past. Toward that end, we link constitutional scholarship with teaching practice—which is why we have sought essays from distinguished constitutional scholars, assembled a cornucopia of primary source documents, identified thought-provoking discussion topics, and consulted with teachers in putting this book together. In the pages that follow, we do not offer a cookie-cutter compendium of lesson plans for teachers—but rather rich historical content that creative teachers can shape and adapt in their own ways and by their own lights for their own classrooms.

The Book's Scope

Any survey course in US history would surely begin with the hemisphere's indigenous history and continue with the arrival of Europeans, the significance of 1619 and other milestones in the history of slavery, and the legacy of the colonial and revolutionary eras. We have chosen to begin in 1776 and 1787 not because we see this earlier history as of lesser importance but because the era of the American Revolution is when constitutional history—our past and continuing disputation over the meaning and purpose of the Constitution—commenced. In so doing, of course, we do not mean to suggest that the whole of "the American story" began at this point. In fact, whether the Constitution was a deliberate continuation of colonial norms with respect to slavery, gender, and Native Americans or whether it was a break with the past remains a subject of intense disagreement.

Using this Book

One need not be a lawyer or a constitutional scholar to teach constitutional history in the classroom. This book has been structured to enable teachers to add to their curriculum, perhaps bit by bit over the years, background information and primary sources regarding some of the formative—and fascinating—constitutional battles in our nation's past (and present).

Each chapter begins with a panoramic essay written by a prominent constitutional scholar. The essay highlights selected constitutional moments during the historical era in question, examining how these constitutional controversies arose, how they were resolved, why they mattered at the time, and (often) their continuing relevance in more recent years.

A generous selection of excerpts from primary source documents follows each essay. The sources of constitutional history are found not only in court cases but also in politics broadly conceived, so we have included a variety of documents that expand our collective recognition of constitutionally protected rights. The primary sources reflect a diverse array of speakers and perspectives relating to constitutional law. We have edited the documents for clarity and ease of classroom use—particularly Supreme Court opinions, which can often appear (at least from a nonspecialist's perspective) overlong and full of legalese. We place the excerpts within explanatory narratives in an effort to tell an understandable "story." Primary sources covering two or three different topics per chapter are included in this book, and additional primary source documents, concerning additional subjects, are available on the companion website.

Each set of document excerpts is followed by a series of questions that are intended to stimulate classroom discussions and generate ideas for out-of-class assignments (whether through debate topics, potential essay assignments, suggestions for individual research projects, etc.). Perhaps it goes without saying, but there are not necessarily "right" answers for many of the suggested discussion questions. The goal is to provide teachers with ideas to permit students to continue their exploration of the constitutional controversies highlighted in the chapter.

Finally, each chapter concludes with a brief list of a variety of other constitutional topics—not directly related to our themes of citizenship and rights—that might prove fruitful for further exploration by teachers and students in conjunction with any study of US history.

A Few Caveats

Spelling, capitalization, and punctuation in the primary sources have been edited to conform to modern usage and to achieve consistency. Most internal quotations, cross references, and footnotes have been omitted, especially in Supreme Court decisions.

A word about bias: Our contemporary political scene is fraught with bitter partisan sniping—although no more so than during James Madison's time or Abraham Lincoln's. But the cable news and social media blogosphere can be so totalistic and ideologically isolating that millions of Americans in our high-tech society seem to have reached a terrifying low in actual political dialogue with those from competing political orientations. To help counter such narrow-mindedness, in assembling the primary sources and discussion questions for this book, we have presented both (or all) sides of the constitutional controversies that are explored. Students will confront conservative, moderate, liberal, and radical constitutional arguments and can discuss their strengths and weaknesses. After all, constitutional history by its very nature involves analysis and argument, conflict and debate—it invites consideration and evaluation of diverse viewpoints—it provides an open forum for those in the majority and the minority alike. Our goal is to help teachers motivate their students to think and speak critically, even passionately, about court cases and legal history. Such exchanges are aimed not at closing minds but at opening them to multiple perspectives and to dialogue across political and ideological lines. In our own era of tribalism and right- and left-wing bubbles, the courtroom is still a place where civil discussion, logic, and evidence matter. Supreme Court justices might not agree with each other, but they aspire to communicate with each other, and with society at large, through reasoned argument. Ideally, the classroom can be a similar space.

Steven A. Steinbach
Maeva Marcus
Robert Cohen

About the Companion Website

Numerous additional primary source excerpts and related discussion questions—not published in this text because of space limitations—can be found in the companion website that accompanies this book. These resources are available free of charge to teachers and students. The website will be updated periodically by the editors to provide additional documents and resources, particularly in light of ongoing constitutional developments.

The companion website is located at:

www.oup.com/us/libertyandjustice

Constitutional controversies addressed in the companion website include:

Chapter 1   Antifederalist Critics of the Constitution
Scholarly and Popular Criticism of the Constitution

Chapter 2   Popular Sovereignty

Chapter 3   Alien and Sedition Acts
Slavery, Race, and the Nation
"Democracy in America"

Chapter 4   Secession and the Right to Rebel
Slavery and the Thirteenth Amendment

Chapter 5   Birthright Citizenship
Native Americans

Chapter 6   Free Speech during World War I
Eugenics

Chapter 7   Voting Rights
Student Speech Rights

Chapter 8   Affirmative Action and Diversity
"New" Rights: Guns and Property
Immigration

Contributors

Mary Sarah Bilder, Founders Professor at Boston College Law School, received the Bancroft Prize in American History and Diplomacy for *Madison's Hand: Revising the Constitutional Convention*. She teaches in the areas of property, trusts and estates, and American legal and constitutional history and is the author of *Female Genius: Eliza Harriot and George Washington at the Dawn of the Constitution*.

Robert Cohen, Professor, Department of Teaching & Learning, New York University, has written or edited more than a dozen books about United States history, including *Rethinking America's Past: Howard Zinn's* A People's History of the United States *in the Classroom and Beyond*. He is co-founder of the NYU-Steinhardt-NYU School of Law Constitution in the Schools Partnership program.

Sam Erman, Associate Professor at the University of Southern California Gould School of Law, focuses on citizenship, race, empire, and constitutional change, especially during the late nineteenth and early twentieth centuries. His most recent book is *Almost Citizens: Puerto Rico, the U.S. Constitution, and Empire*.

Eric Foner, DeWitt Clinton Professor Emeritus of History at Columbia University, won the Bancroft Prize, the Pulitzer Prize for History, and the Lincoln Prize for his many works about the Civil War-Reconstruction era. His most recent book is *The Second Founding: How the Civil War and Reconstruction Remade the Constitution*.

Ruth Bader Ginsburg was an Associate Justice of the Supreme Court from 1993 until her death in September 2020. She was a law professor, first at Rutgers, then at Columbia; co-founded the American Civil Liberties Union's Women's Rights Project; argued before the Supreme Court; and served as a judge of the United States Court of Appeals for the District of Columbia Circuit from 1980 to 1993. A collection of her writings and speeches, published in 2016, is titled *My Own Words*. A subsequent collection, *Justice, Justice, Thou Shalt Pursue*, was published in 2021.

Annette Gordon-Reed, the Carl M. Loeb University Professor at Harvard University, won the Pulitzer Prize in History for *The Hemingses of Monticello: An American Family*. Her most recent book is *On Juneteenth*.

Linda Greenhouse, Senior Research Scholar at Yale Law School, served as the Supreme Court correspondent for the *New York Times* for thirty years, receiving a Pulitzer Prize for her work. Among other books, she is the author of *The U.S. Supreme Court: A Very Short Introduction* and *Justice on the Brink: The Death of Ruth Bader Ginsburg, the Rise of Amy Coney Barrett, and Twelve Months that Transformed the Supreme Court*.

Laura Kalman, Distinguished Research Professor at the University of California, Santa Barbara, is a past president of the American Society for Legal History. She is the author of *Abe Fortas: A Biography*, *The Strange Career of Legal Liberalism*, *The Long Reach of the Sixties: LBJ, Nixon, and the Making of the Contemporary Supreme Court*, and other books.

Maeva Marcus, a past president of the American Society for Legal History, is Research Professor of Law and Director of the Institute for Constitutional Studies at The George Washington University Law School. She serves as the General Editor of the Oliver Wendell Holmes Devise History of the Supreme Court of the United States. Author of *Truman and the Steel Seizure Case: The Limits of Presidential Power*, she also edited the eight-volume series *The Documentary History of the Supreme Court of the United States, 1789–1800* and *Origins of the Federal Judiciary: Essays on the Judiciary Act of 1789*.

Melissa Murray is Frederick I. and Grace Stokes Professor of Law at New York University School of Law, where she teaches constitutional law, family law, criminal law, and reproductive rights and justice. Her writing has appeared in a range of legal and lay publications, including the *Harvard Law Review*, the *Yale Law Journal*, and the *New York Times*. Most recently, she co-edited *Reproductive Rights and Justice Stories*.

Steven A. Steinbach teaches United States History and American Government courses and has served as History Department Chair at Sidwell Friends School in Washington, DC. Previously he was a partner in the Washington, DC, law firm of Williams & Connolly LLP, where he specialized in criminal and civil litigation.

Julie C. Suk is Professor of Law, Fordham University School of Law, and Visiting Professor of Law at Yale Law School. She is the author of *We the Women: The Unstoppable Mothers of the Equal Rights Amendment*, and dozens of scholarly articles on comparative constitutional law, equality, women's rights, and constitutional change.

1

The Foundations of
Constitutional History

The purpose of this book is to explore disagreements over the text, implications, and applicability of the Constitution—our "constitutional history"—that have changed the course of US history. The Constitution, an old document, is at the center of an ongoing process in which judicial thought interacts with American politics and society. Recognizing how and why "constitutional moments" arise and evolve over time is integral to a more complete appreciation of our nation's past.

But any focus on constitutional history should be grounded in the basics: How do constitutional controversies arise? What role do the courts play in defining and enforcing the meaning of the Constitution? How has the Supreme Court emerged as the ultimate authority in interpreting the Constitution? Why does the Supreme Court change its mind so frequently about how the Constitution should be interpreted—because of new justices, or the persuasive force of earlier dissents, or in response to public opinion? How is constitutional history actually made in this country? To what extent is constitutional history shaped by the Supreme Court versus political and social forces, electoral politics, and popular expectations?

The Constitution has been characterized as a framework, a structure, a set of guidelines, a rulebook, a procedural manual, and a cookbook. It tells us how to make laws (Article I, Section 7) but not which laws to make. It outlines who is in charge of what (Article I, Section 8, for Congress; Article II, Section 2, for the president) but not the policies that should be pursued. It sets out over-arching, open-ended, and arguably contradictory goals (the Preamble). It apportions power and responsibilities among the branches (Articles I, II, and III) and between the national government and the states (Article I, Section 10, and Article IV). It attempts to limit government power (Article I, Section 9) and secure individual and collective rights (the Bill of Rights and various subsequent amendments). It was ratified (indirectly) by the people (Article VII), and it can be altered (Article V). But the Constitution originally came without a Bill of Rights; it embraced a far from universal understanding of "We the People," and it failed to enshrine fundamental values now taken for granted, including democracy, equality, and individual autonomy.

With Liberty and Justice for All?. Edited by Steven A. Steinbach, Maeva Marcus, and Robert Cohen, Oxford University Press. © Oxford University Press 2022. DOI: 10.1093/oso/9780197516317.003.0001

What exactly is this document—and why is its study so essential to an understanding of US history? Is the Constitution, big picture, more deserving of praise or criticism? Should the Constitution and its authors be venerated, as President Ronald Reagan claimed on its bicentennial, for putting wind in the sails of freedom? Or regarded as badly flawed because of its omissions and failures, as Justice Thurgood Marshall suggested several months later? What does it mean to say that the Constitution is "the supreme law of the land"? How was the Constitution actually made in Philadelphia? Through what means and methods has the Constitution changed over time? And why do we—or why should we—still govern ourselves by the Constitution's requirements and norms?

Teachers of US history (no less than law school professors) have long been fascinated with the story of *Marbury v. Madison*—of how the Supreme Court girded itself with the extraordinary power to nullify laws passed by Congress. But Chief Justice John Marshall did not invent judicial review; it had been discussed at the Constitutional Convention, debated during the ratification process by Federalists and Antifederalists, and invoked and applied in other court cases prior to its dramatic emergence in 1803. Nor did the Supreme Court's self-announced authority go unchallenged thereafter—by Thomas Jefferson, Andrew Jackson, Abraham Lincoln, and Southern segregationists, among others. As a result of judicial review, the Supreme Court has issued thousands of decisions interpreting, expounding, expanding, minimizing, and all but rewriting constitutional provisions (as well as its own previous opinions), in ways that have influenced the course of American history. Studying this process offers the opportunity to debate fundamental questions about the influence of the courts: Why do (unelected) judges have so much power? Is this power excessive? What reforms, if any, should be made to limit (or enhance) the influence of the Court?

Then there are crucial questions about how best to interpret the Constitution. Should judges and others be guided (or even constrained) by the "original" understandings of its authors? Or should they be free to refashion the meaning of the Constitution to reflect changing societal values? The Constitution does not tell us how to answer these questions. Given the abundance of ambiguous phrases in the Constitution, thinking about the method of constitutional interpretation provides the opportunity to reflect on the malleable nature of constitutional law.

Many history teachers already craft classroom exercises intended to probe the disagreements between Federalists and Antifederalists that emerged during the Constitution's ratification struggle. The wide-ranging, iconoclastic criticisms of the Constitution made by Antifederalists yield lively discussions. Considering some of today's heated and partisan constitutional controversies, were the Antifederalists prescient in their concerns and fears? Or has the Constitution largely withstood the test of time? Judgments from a host of constitutional critics, both distant and recent, serve to highlight the Constitution's glories, shortcomings, and continuing relevance.

Shaping the Constitution

Linda Greenhouse
Senior Research Scholar, Yale Law School

A mail-order catalogue recently offered—along with refrigerator magnets, assorted colored pens, and coffee mugs with clever sayings—a pocket-sized "US Constitution Leatherbound Keepsake," described as "a great gift for anyone who cares about the past (and future) of our nation." The price tag of $27, with an additional $16 for personalization with three initials on the "soft navy calfskin leather" cover, suggested that this would be an acquisition of some significance. By contrast, copies of the Constitution are commonly available at no cost from civic organizations, and from the US Government Printing Office for $1.50 each.

Despite its anomalous placement amid a collection of stocking-stuffers, there was something familiar about this diminutive booklet and the claim the catalogue's copywriters made for it: read it, and revere it, and thou shalt know the truth. The country's past, perhaps even its future, will stand revealed.

We have, after all, become accustomed to the Constitution as an object of civic worship, perhaps best exemplified by the forty-foot-long replica of a parchment scroll that marchers carried through the streets of Philadelphia on September 17, 1987, to mark the Constitution's bicentennial. In 2004, under the sponsorship of Senator Robert Byrd, a West Virginia Democrat who during a sixty-year congressional career was never without his pocket Constitution, Congress designated September 17 as Constitution Day and required all schools and colleges that receive federal funds to provide an educational program about the Constitution on or near that date or face loss of their federal dollars. A minieducational industry sprang up as a result.

So we know how to honor the Constitution, whether out of habit, legal obligation, or in appreciation of how remarkable an achievement it represents. In the more than two centuries since its ratification in 1788, some 220 states and countries have produced 900 constitutions. The US Constitution, including its twenty-seven amendments, contains 7,600 words—the length of a book chapter or long magazine article. Many of the world's other constitutions have been much longer. Most survive only in memory, if at all.

But the fact is that the formal Constitution, whether on parchment at the National Archives or in a senator's pocket, whether downloaded from the Web or read aloud at a Constitution Day ceremony, is not the Constitution as the country lives it today. Today's Constitution—the actual working Constitution—is the product of the judicial interpretations that fill nearly six hundred volumes of Supreme Court decisions, the official *United States Reports*. It is the result of social movements that have attached new meanings to old words. Political forces have given the Constitution shape even as constitutional debate continues to drive our politics.

The thirty-nine white men of property who signed the Constitution's final draft on September 17, 1787—a document providing in Article I that, for purposes of political apportionment, a slave would count for three-fifths of a free person—would not have imagined that "We the People" would come to include not only non-white men but also women of all races. And the framers of the post-Civil War amendments (the Thirteenth, Fourteenth, and Fifteenth) that marked what Eric Foner labels a "second founding" did not anticipate the near century-long erasure by states of the former Confederacy of the right of African Americans to vote. The words were there in the amended Constitution for all to see; it was political will, on the one hand, and political power, on the other, that were lacking.

Who and what the Constitution constitutes—who it includes and what rights it conveys—are questions at the very heart of the American story, and the answers are inextricably rooted in American history. American history *is* constitutional history; there is no separating the two. The mail-order catalogue was therefore not mistaken to offer its Constitution as "a great gift for anyone who cares about the past." The offer was simply incomplete. We need to know constitutional history in order to understand not only the past but the present. We need to understand the Constitution not as *object* but as *process*. It is in the contest over constitutional meaning through which American history has unfolded and American identity has been forged.

The Supreme Court has by no means been the only player in the struggle over constitutional meaning. But it has left the most tangible record, beginning with the celebrated case of *Marbury v. Madison* (1803).[1] In that unanimous opinion by the fourth chief justice, John Marshall, the Court invalidated an act of Congress. In doing so, it asserted for the federal judiciary the power of judicial review, a power that the Constitution's framers had discussed and even assumed, but that the text itself had not explicitly bestowed on the courts.

John Marshall was near the beginning of his Supreme Court tenure, which began in 1801 and lasted until his death in 1835. An ally of President John Adams, whom he had served first as a floor leader in the House of Representatives and then as secretary of state, Marshall was immersed in Federalist Party politics, and *Marbury v. Madison* was an exquisitely political decision. It is worth describing in some detail because it illustrates that from the country's earliest days, constitutional interpretation was no abstract exercise but anchored firmly in the political context that shaped the particular dispute and propelled it to the courts.

The hotly contested election of 1800 plunged the young country into a political crisis. The Federalists lost both the White House and Congress. The incumbent president, John Adams, suffered a bitter defeat. But the months between the November election and Thomas Jefferson's inauguration as president the following March offered the Federalists an opportunity to legislate a hold on power. This was the Judiciary Act of 1801, passed by the lame-duck Congress to reduce the number of Supreme Court justices from six to five, so that President Jefferson would have fewer seats at his disposal, while creating sixteen new judgeships for President Adams to fill on a new layer of federal courts between the trial courts and the Supreme Court.[2] These new courts would relieve the Supreme Court justices of the need to "ride circuit" in order to serve as intermediate-court judges themselves, an onerous duty they were eager to shed.

Adams named, and the Senate confirmed, loyal Federalists for these important new courts. He also had forty-two new slots to fill for the minor but politically desirable municipal position of justice of the peace for the District of Columbia. William Marbury, a well-connected Maryland tax collector, received one of these political plums. The resignation of Chief Justice Oliver Ellsworth gave Adams the opportunity to name a new chief justice. His selection of John Marshall was promptly confirmed by the Senate. Taking office in February 1801, Marshall agreed to stay on as secretary of state for the remaining month of Adams's presidency. In that capacity, one of his duties was to administer judicial appointments, including signing, sealing, and delivering new judges' commission papers. But by the time of Jefferson's inauguration, Marbury's commission, although properly signed and sealed, was still sitting, undelivered, along with three others in the secretary of state's office. Jefferson, deeply resentful of the Federalists' "midnight judges," ordered his secretary of state, James Madison, not to deliver the four commissions.

In December 1801, a lawyer for the four men (Charles Lee, who had served as attorney general under both Washington and Adams) sued in the Supreme Court for a writ of mandamus—a form of legal directive—ordering Madison to deliver the commissions. The Court scheduled a hearing for the following June. But in March 1802, the new Republican Congress passed a new Judiciary Act.[3] It not only repealed the Act of 1801, meaning that the new judgeships were abolished and the justices would have to go back to riding circuit, but it also cancelled the Supreme Court's scheduled sessions for the remainder of 1802, eliminating the opportunity for prompt Supreme Court action. The Court would not sit again until February 1803, and then in a renewed atmosphere of crisis; the Federalists were now claiming that the abolition of the new appellate judgeships was an unconstitutional assault on judicial independence. A case challenging the constitutionality of the new Judiciary Act of 1802, *Stuart v. Laird* (1803),[4] was on the Court's docket when the justices convened to hear the case of the undelivered commissions.

The two cases placed the Supreme Court in a delicate, even dangerous position. None of the "midnight judges" sought reinstatement to the abolished positions, so unlike Marbury's case, *Stuart v. Laird* did not concern the rights of individuals. It posed the structural question of Congress's ability to reshape the federal judiciary to its liking. That the Republican-controlled Congress had acted so quickly to repeal the 1801 Act and return the justices to their detested circuit-riding duties could only be seen as a message to the Supreme Court, still controlled by Federalists, that it could pay an even higher price if it displeased those newly in power. The new president and the new chief justice were distant cousins and political enemies. What would happen if Jefferson defied a court order to give Marbury and the others their promised jobs? The Supreme Court, even the entire judiciary, described by Alexander Hamilton in *Federalist No. 78* as "the least dangerous branch,"[5] could emerge from such a clash even weaker than the framers had intended.

Marshall's solution to this dilemma was to assert the Court's power without directly exercising it. While Marbury was entitled to his commission, the Court held it was powerless to give him the remedy he sought. The jurisdictional basis for Marbury's suit was section 13 of the Judiciary Act of 1789, which gave the Supreme Court authority to issue writs of mandamus as original actions (i.e., as cases brought directly to the Justices rather than as appeals from lower courts). But Article III of the Constitution, establishing the judicial branch, limited the Supreme Court's "original jurisdiction" to "all cases affecting Ambassadors, other public Ministers and Consuls, and those in which a State shall be a Party." Writs of mandamus were not on that list. Congress had no authority to expand Article III by conferring original mandamus jurisdiction on the Supreme Court, Marshall wrote. Section 13 was unconstitutional, and Marbury's right to his commission was vindicated—but it was a right without a remedy. He never got the job.

The winner in *Marbury v. Madison* was the Supreme Court itself. Marshall's declaration that "it is emphatically the province and duty of the judicial department to say what the law is" became foundational, the bulwark of the Supreme Court's authority. Hardly a term of the Supreme Court goes by to this day without at least one justice quoting the line in at least one opinion.

An interesting footnote: A week after deciding *Marbury*, the Court issued its decision in *Stuart v. Laird* (1803), the case challenging the constitutionality of the Judiciary Act of 1802.[6] Marshall recused himself because he had sat on the case in the lower court. The Federalist Supreme Court, having asserted its power a week earlier, now withdrew. It stayed its hand and upheld the Republican law. The justices went back to riding circuit, a duty they retained until 1891, when Congress established the modern federal circuit courts in the Evarts Act.[7]

"We are not final because we are infallible, but we are infallible only because we are final." Justice Robert Jackson wrote those words in 1953, in a concurring opinion in *Brown v. Allen* (1953), a decision asserting the federal courts' juris-diction to review certain state criminal convictions.[8] This oft-quoted line might seem a bookend to John Marshall's even more famous line in *Marbury* as a claim to judicial supremacy. But history says otherwise. The Warren Court's decision in *Brown v. Allen* would prove far from final. In *Stone v. Powell* (1976),[9] a more con-servative Supreme Court, more considerate of state prerogatives, partially repu-diated *Brown v. Allen* and has continued to whittle away at it ever since.[10]

The Supreme Court has explicitly overturned its own precedents nearly 250 times, and it has reinterpreted its precedents—limiting or expanding them—at least as often. How can that be? How could the Supreme Court have ruled in 1940 that Jehovah's Witnesses children were obliged to violate the rule of their religion and recite the Pledge of Allegiance (*Minersville School District v. Gobitis* (1940)[11]), only to rule a mere three years later in *West Virginia State Board of Education v. Barnette* (1943) that for school officials to compel saluting the US flag violates the First Amendment's protection of freedom of speech?[12]

How could the Court have held in *Bowers v. Hardwick* (1986) that the claim of gay men and lesbians to constitutional protection against prosecution for their intimate behavior was "at best, facetious,"[13] only to rule seventeen years later in *Lawrence v. Texas* (2003) that the guarantee of liberty in the Fourteenth Amendment's Due Process Clause prevents the state from criminalizing people's private sexual activity?[14]

How could the Court have found in the Second Amendment an individual right to own a gun, in *District of Columbia v. Heller* (2008),[15] after having long rejected that interpretation so definitively that a conservative Chief Justice, Warren Burger, could declare in a nationally televised interview after his retire-ment that the claim of an individual right under the Second Amendment was one of the "greatest pieces of fraud" in his lifetime?[16]

There are particular answers to each of these questions but all point in the same direction: Constitutional meaning is the product of many forces, and meaning inevitably changes as society changes. Not all meaning, of course; Article II requires the president to have attained the age of thirty-five, a provision not open to interpretation. But consider, by contrast, the Fourteenth Amendment's "nor shall any State deprive any person of life, liberty, or property without due pro-cess of law." While some argue that courts are limited to interpreting those open-ended terms according to whatever eighteenth-century meaning can be ascribed to them, constitutional history has taken a different course. Justice Anthony Kennedy wrote the majority opinion in *Lawrence v. Texas*, the 2003 decision that declared that *Bowers v. Hardwick* "was not correct when it was decided, and it is not correct today." Acknowledging at the end of his opinion that the Constitution's framers would not have reached the same result, Kennedy went on to explain why that was in fact the point: "They knew times can blind us to certain truths and later generations can see that laws once thought necessary and proper in fact serve only to oppress. As the Constitution endures, persons in every generation can invoke its principles in their own search for greater freedom."[17]

It is also worth noting that although only seventeen years separated the two decisions, social attitudes toward homosexuality had changed substantially during that time. Many states had either repealed their criminal sodomy statutes or had permitted the laws to go unenforced. Although gay rights lawyers correctly sensed that the time was ripe to bring the issue back to the Supreme Court, they had trouble finding a plaintiff who had actually been prosecuted and whose conviction they might appeal, as law professor Dale Carpenter documented in an illuminating book.[18]

Just as social and political forces shape how issues reach the Supreme Court, the Court itself is shaped by electoral politics. The six justices in the majority in *Stone v. Powell*, the 1976 decision that limited the force of *Brown v. Allen*, included four justices who had been named to the Court by President Richard Nixon. Nixon had run for office on a platform attacking the Warren Court as "soft on crime." Chief Justice Warren Burger, Nixon's first appointee to the Court, fully embraced the new president's criminal law agenda; it was a principal reason Nixon chose him to succeed Chief Justice Earl Warren.

William Rehnquist, another of the Nixon appointees, also shared the president's views on crime. As a justice, he took every occasion to criticize *Miranda v. Arizona* (1966),[19] a landmark of the Warren Court's criminal procedure revolution. And yet something unexpected happened in 2000, when the Court took up a case brought by a leading critic of *Miranda* who argued that the landmark decision should be overturned. Rehnquist, by then the chief justice, wrote the majority opinion for the Court in *Dickerson v. United States* (2000) upholding the old precedent and its "*Miranda* warnings" which, Rehnquist explained, "have become part of our national culture."[20]

Was Chief Justice Rehnquist finally persuaded that *Miranda* had been correctly decided? Almost certainly not, although having led the Court in weakening the 1966 decision by creating exceptions to its rules, he undoubtedly preferred the version that existed in 2000 to the original. Rehnquist by then had been on the Court for nearly thirty years. He had developed a good sense of what the public expected from the Supreme Court and of how far it was prudent to push his own deeply conservative preferences. A presidential election year, with the Court in a quadrennial spotlight, was not the time to take the symbolically potent leap of overturning *Miranda*.

There is no doubt that public opinion influences the Supreme Court and its members, although despite political scientists' best efforts, the effect cannot be quantified. Lee Epstein and Andrew Martin, prominent scholars of judicial behavior, published an article titled "Does Public Opinion Influence the Supreme

Court? Possibly Yes (But We're Not Sure Why)."[21] It is perhaps more useful to listen to judges themselves than to scholars trying to understand what judges do.

In 1986, shortly before he became chief justice, William Rehnquist gave a lecture titled "Constitutional Law and Public Opinion." "It would be very wrong to say that judges are not influenced by public opinion," the then-associate justice said. He added that although judges, especially Supreme Court justices, spend their days in an insulated atmosphere, "these same judges go home at night and read the newspapers or watch the evening news on television; they talk to their family and friends about current events. Somewhere 'out there,' beyond the walls of the courthouse, run currents and tides of public opinion which lap at the courthouse door."[22]

Whether consciously or not, Rehnquist was echoing an observation made decades earlier by Benjamin Cardozo in *The Nature of the Judicial Process*, a classic account of how judges think and act. It was published in 1921 when Cardozo, not yet a Supreme Court justice, was serving on New York State's highest court. Judges "do not stand aloof on these chill and distant heights," he wrote, "and we shall not help the cause of truth by acting and speaking as if they do." He added: "The great tides and currents which engulf the rest of men do not turn aside in their course and pass the judges by."[23]

Cardozo observed that John Marshall himself had claimed the contrary when he wrote in *Osborn v. Bank of the United States* (1824) that "Judicial power is never exercised for the purpose of giving effect to the will of the judge; always for the purpose of giving effect to the will of the legislature; or in other words, to the will of the law."[24] Marshall's words had a "lofty sound," Cardozo wrote, but were negated by the very fact that "our constitutional law is what it is because he molded it while it was still plastic and malleable in the fire of his own intense convictions."[25]

To the extent that Supreme Court justices do care how the public will react to the Court's decisions, they have often done a poor job of anticipating the public's response. The *Gobitis* case, the first of the two flag-salute cases, was decided by a vote of 8–1, with only Justice Harlan Fiske Stone dissenting. The year was 1940; World War II was engulfing Europe and patriotic fervor was rising at home. In ruling that the Jehovah's Witnesses children had to recite the Pledge of Allegiance or be expelled from school, the justices had no idea that the public would understand them to have labeled the Witnesses as traitors. The decision unleashed a torrent of religious bigotry against the peaceable sect. Across the country, the Jehovah's Witnesses saw their houses of worship burned and their children thrown out of school.

The Court's abrupt reversal in the 1943 *Barnette* case is attributable in part to changes on the Court itself: President Franklin D. Roosevelt had named two new justices, Robert H. Jackson and Wiley Rutledge and elevated Justice Stone to the chief justiceship. But there is little doubt that the ugly public response to *Gobitis* impelled the Court to revisit the issue. Three justices who had joined the *Gobitis* majority, Hugo Black, William O. Douglas, and Frank Murphy, repudiated their earlier votes, joining the two new justices plus Chief Justice Stone to form a 6–3 majority in *Barnette*. Justice Jackson's majority opinion contained one of the most powerful declarations in constitutional history of the meaning of free speech: "If there is any fixed star in our constitutional constellation, it is that no official, high or petty, can prescribe what shall be orthodox in politics, nationalism, religion, or other matters of opinion, or force citizens to confess by word or act their faith therein."[26]

Roe v. Wade (1973), where the Court first recognized a constitutional right to an abortion,[27] is often depicted as an example of the Court misjudging the public mood and creating a backlash. The real story is more complex. Support for reform of the regime of criminal abortion laws had been growing for more than a decade, led initially by the public health profession, which viewed the estimated one million illegal abortions a year as a public health crisis that put women's health and even lives at risk. The public health doctors were joined in their calls for reform by the American Law Institute, a prestigious group of lawyers, academics, and judges, and eventually by the American Medical Association, which a century earlier had helped lead the drive for abortion's criminalization.

While feminists soon added their voices to the reform effort and framed their arguments in terms of women's equality, theirs were not the voices that Justice Harry Blackmun's opinion for a 7–2 majority reflected. Rather, the justices were clearly attentive to the views of their professional peers that treating abortion as a crime was bad public policy. They were also likely aware of public opinion on the issue. In the summer of 1972, newspapers around the country carried George Gallup's syndicated column reporting on his organization's poll on abortion. The poll asked people whether the question of abortion should be left to a woman and her doctor. Majorities of all groups—Democrats, Republicans, men, women, Protestants, Roman Catholics—answered yes.

In the immediate aftermath of *Roe*, public support for the right to abortion actually increased. The so-called backlash built gradually over the following decade as Republican strategists deemed it in their interest to use opposition to legalized abortion as a wedge issue that could draw urban ethnic Catholics, who traditionally voted Democratic, into the Republican camp. A platform of opposition to abortion also attracted evangelical voters who had been mobilized by opposition to the Equal Rights Amendment and acute unease with the social revolutions that were reshaping family life and sexual behavior. In 1980, the Republican platform for the first time called for the appointment of judges who opposed the right to abortion. Understanding this history is essential to understanding the constitutional trajectory of the abortion issue.[28] That three of President Nixon's four

Supreme Court appointees joined the majority in *Roe* strikes modern audiences as scarcely believable, but that fact demonstrates the power of constitutional politics to shape and reshape constitutional law.

That observation brings us back to the Court's 2008 decision in *District of Columbia v. Heller*, interpreting the Second Amendment as conveying an individual right to "bear arms."[29] Decided by a vote of 5–4, *Heller* came sixty-nine years after the Court ruled in *United States v. Miller* (1939) that an individual right to gun ownership was limited to only those weapons that would serve the Second Amendment's stated purpose of maintaining a "well-regulated Militia."[30] The *Miller* decision lay quiescent for many years while a gun rights movement grew in social acceptance and political power, finding fertile but not exclusive ground in the Republican Party. Both sides in the debate over limitations on gun ownership claimed fealty to the original meaning of the Second Amendment. But what was that meaning, and what gave the Court the authority in the early years of the twenty-first century to reject the meaning that an earlier Court had derived from the same words?

Scholars point to the *Heller* decision as a leading example of "democratic constitutionalism," in which constitutional meaning is forged in popular debate, using the tools of social and political mobilization to shape public understanding. As Reva B. Siegel pointed out in an influential article, while Justice Antonin Scalia's majority opinion claimed authority from the Second Amendment's original meaning, the years of popular debate and political intervention preceding the decision had in fact shifted that meaning. Professor Siegel noted that by the time *Heller* was decided, "almost all significant opinions written by federal judges in the late twentieth century that recognize or remark favorably upon an individual right to bear arms appear to have been written by judges whom President Reagan appointed."[31]

It was Justice Clarence Thomas, an appointee of President George H. W. Bush, who in 1997 injected the individual-right argument into a Supreme Court case. The case was *Printz v. United States* (1997), in which the Court held unconstitutional, on states'-rights grounds, a law that required state law enforcement officials to perform background checks on gun buyers to assure compliance with federal regulations.[32] The Second Amendment did not play a role in the case. But in a brief concurring opinion, Justice Thomas suggested that it might well have. "This Court has not had recent occasion to consider the nature of the substantive right safeguarded by the Second Amendment," he wrote. And then, citing a half dozen recent law review articles, he added: "Marshaling an impressive array of historical evidence, a growing body of scholarly commentary indicates that the 'right to keep and bear arms' is, as the Amendment's text suggests, a personal right."[33] Thomas wrote only for himself, and his opinion did not make public waves. But stakeholders in the gun rights debate recognized it immediately for what it was: an invitation to present exactly those historical claims to the Court and, in doing so, perhaps to change constitutional history.

Constitutional moments do not always announce themselves. They become obvious only in retrospect, as history adjusts its gaze. *Reed v. Reed* (1971), the decision holding that a state's automatic preference for men over women as administrators of estates violated the Fourteenth Amendment's guarantee of equal protection, was a twelve-paragraph unanimous opinion.[34] Its author, the conservative Warren Burger, spent the next several years minimizing its significance whenever one of his more liberal colleagues cited it for a broad constitutional principle of sex equality. "The author of *Reed* never remotely considered such a broad concept but then a lot of people sire offspring unintended," Burger, referring to himself in the third person, wrote in a memo complaining about a draft opinion in a subsequent case in which Justice William Brennan was seeking to use *Reed* as the foundation for raising the constitutional bar against sex discrimination.[35]

We can now see how, from this modest beginning, the Supreme Court went on to construct a robust jurisprudence of sex equality under the guidance of Ruth Bader Ginsburg, first as a women's rights advocate and later as a justice. When asked to account for her notable success arguing before the Burger Court when the more liberal Warren Court had never ruled that the Fourteenth Amendment had anything to do with sex discrimination, Justice Ginsburg often explained that times had changed, and that the nine men of the Burger Court were ready to listen to arguments that their predecessors were unable to hear. History provided a different context that enabled the Constitution to move in a new direction, based on a new appreciation of women's role in society.

Sometimes, by contrast, what looks like a constitutional moment arrives with bells on but significant or lasting change fails to follow. In 1995, the Rehnquist Court ruled in *United States v. Lopez* that Congress lacked authority under the Commerce Clause to prohibit people from possessing guns in school zones.[36] *Lopez* marked the first time since the early New Deal that the Court found the commerce power insufficient to support a congressional goal. The decision appeared to be the opening shot in what some called a "federalism revolution." Indeed, over the next few years, the Court did strike down several federal statutes as beyond the authority of Congress and treading too far onto territory the Constitution reserved for the states. But the public never took up the call to arms, and the "revolution" petered out before it could alter the fundamental allocation of power between the states and the federal government.

History notices the constitutional moments that prove to matter—not the near misses or might-have-beens. Yet these failed constitutional moments are also the products of history. If Richard Nixon's four Supreme Court appointees had not all taken their seats by the time the Court decided *San Antonio Independent School*

District v. Rodriguez (1973),[37] chances are good that the constitutional attack on the property-tax based system of financing local schools in that case would have prevailed instead of being sent to a 5–4 defeat. We would have looked back on that decision as the constitutional moment that changed the face of public education.

Today, without the slightest doubt, there are constitutional moments in the making. As always, history will be the judge—and not only of the performance of the Supreme Court. It will be our judge too.

Five Questions about the Constitution—Primary Sources

All things considered, is the Constitution deserving of veneration or censure? Opening perspectives are offered from Ronald Reagan and Thurgood Marshall. What exactly is a "constitution"? Reflections on this question from John Marshall and Alexander Hamilton focus in particular on the significance of the Supremacy Clause in Article VI of the Constitution. How did the Constitution come about? The views of George Washington and James Madison are counterposed with the perhaps less idealistic observations of modern observers. How does the Constitution get changed? It certainly should not be immune from revision, counseled John Jay. Should the Constitution be substantially reformed—or even ignored or abandoned? The opinions of a variety of contemporary critics are presented, followed by a dialogue between Madison and Thomas Jefferson on the need for constitutional reverence.

To begin with a big-picture question: Is the Constitution praiseworthy or objectionable?

Ronald Reagan's Perspective on the Constitution (1987)

It was the 200th birthday of the Constitution. Appearing before a joint session of Congress to deliver his State of the Union Address, Ronald Reagan invoked the wisdom and spirit of the framers.

> May I congratulate all of you who are Members of this historic 100th Congress of the United States of America. In this 200th anniversary year of our Constitution, you and I stand on the shoulders of giants—men whose words and deeds put wind in the sails of freedom. However, we must always remember that our Constitution is to be celebrated not for being old, but for being young—young with the same energy, spirit, and promise that filled each eventful day in Philadelphia's statehouse. We will be guided tonight by their acts, and we will be guided forever by their words. . . .

We're entering our third century now, but it's wrong to judge our nation by its years. The calendar can't measure America because we were meant to be an endless experiment in freedom—with no limit to our reaches, no boundaries to what we can do, no end point to our hopes. The United States Constitution is the impassioned and inspired vehicle by which we travel through history. It grew out of the most fundamental inspiration of our existence: that we are here to serve Him by living free—that living free releases in us the noblest of impulses and the best of our abilities; that we would use these gifts for good and generous purposes and would secure them not just for ourselves and for our children but for all mankind.

Over the years . . . nothing has been so heartwarming to me as speaking to America's young, and the little ones especially, so fresh-faced and so eager to know. Well, from time to time I've been with them—they will ask about our Constitution. And I hope you Members of Congress will not deem this a breach of protocol if you'll permit me to share these thoughts again with the young people who might be listening or watching this evening. I've read the constitutions of a number of countries, including the Soviet Union's. Now, some people are surprised to hear that they have a constitution, and it even supposedly grants a number of freedoms to its people. Many countries have written into their constitution provisions for freedom of speech and freedom of assembly. Well, if this is true, why is the Constitution of the United States so exceptional?

Well, the difference is so small that it almost escapes you, but it's so great it tells you the whole story in just three words: We the people. In those other constitutions, the government tells the people of those countries what they're allowed to do. In our Constitution, we the people tell the government what it can do, and it can do only those things listed in that document and no others. Virtually every other revolution in history has just exchanged one set of rulers for another set of rulers. Our revolution is the first to say the people are the masters and government is their servant. And you young people out there, don't ever forget that. Someday you could be in this room, but wherever you are, America is depending on you to reach your highest and be your best—because here in America, we the people are in charge.[38]

Thurgood Marshall's Perspective on the Constitution (1987)

Several months later, a justice of the Supreme Court—the 96th justice in the nation's history, in fact, but the first who was not a white male—struck a discordant note. Thurgood Marshall maintained that far from being worthy of celebration, the Constitution should be memorialized as a fatally flawed document that—eventually, over time—became somewhat more inclusive and egalitarian, but only as the result of struggle by those who at the beginning—and indeed, long thereafter—were not considered to be a part of "We the People."

1987 marks the 200th anniversary of the United States Constitution. . . . Like many anniversary celebrations, the plan for 1987 takes particular events and holds them up as the source of all the very best that has followed. Patriotic feelings will surely swell, prompting proud proclamations of the wisdom, foresight, and sense of justice shared by the framers and reflected in a written document now yellowed with age. This is unfortunate—not the patriotism itself, but the tendency for the celebration to oversimplify and overlook the many other events that have been instrumental to our achievements as a nation. The focus of this celebration invites a complacent belief that the vision of those who debated and compromised in Philadelphia yielded the "more perfect Union" it is said we now enjoy.

I cannot accept this invitation, for I do not believe that the meaning of the Constitution was forever "fixed" at the Philadelphia Convention. Nor do I find the wisdom, foresight, and sense of justice exhibited by the framers particularly profound. To the contrary, the government they devised was defective from the start, requiring several amendments, a civil war, and momentous social transformation to attain the system of constitutional government and its respect for the individual freedoms and human rights we hold as fundamental today. When contemporary Americans cite "The Constitution," they invoke a concept that is vastly different from what the framers barely began to construct two centuries ago. . . .

New constitutional principles have emerged to meet the challenges of a changing society. The progress has been dramatic, and it will continue. The men who gathered in Philadelphia in 1787 could not have envisioned these changes. They could not have imagined, nor would they have accepted, that the document they were drafting would one day be construed by a Supreme Court to which had been appointed a woman and the descendent of an African slave. "We the People" no longer enslave, but the credit does not belong to the framers. It belongs to those who refused to acquiesce in outdated notions of "liberty," "justice," and "equality," and who strived to better them.

And so we must be careful, when focusing on the events which took place in Philadelphia two centuries ago, that we not overlook the momentous events which followed, and thereby lose our proper sense of perspective. Otherwise, the odds are that for many Americans the bicentennial celebration will be little more than a blind pilgrimage to the shrine of the original document now stored in a vault in the National Archives. If we seek, instead, a sensitive understanding of the Constitution's inherent defects, and its promising evolution through two-hundred years of history, the celebration of the "Miracle at Philadelphia" . . . will, in my view, be a far more meaningful and humbling experience. We will see that the true miracle was not the birth of the Constitution, but its life—a life nurtured through two turbulent centuries of our own making, and a life embodying much good fortune that was not.

Thus, in this bicentennial year, we may not all participate in the festivities with flag-waving fervor. Some may more quietly commemorate the suffering, struggle, and sacrifice that has triumphed over much of what was wrong with the original document, and observe the anniversary with hopes not realized and promises not fulfilled. I plan to celebrate the bicentennial of the Constitution as a living document, including the Bill of Rights and the other amendments protecting individual freedoms and human rights.[39]

The contrasting perspectives offered by President Reagan and Justice Marshall serve as an effective backdrop when considering several other big-picture questions about the Constitution of the United States.

John Marshall on the "Written" Constitution (1803)

A second overarching question about the Constitution arises from its claim to be "the supreme law of the land." What does that mean? How does a written constitution differ from an ordinary law? The excerpts that follow suggest that the Constitution is meant to set out a "great outline" intended to be "paramount" or "fundamental"—that is, "supreme." But, as will be seen, such answers raise difficult questions about enforcement.

The Constitution is a written document—a fact which is far from unimportant, as recognized by Chief Justice John Marshall. A written constitution serves to limit the power of government by setting out "fundamental" boundary lines that cannot be transgressed.

The powers of the legislature are defined and limited; and that those limits may not be mistaken or forgotten, the Constitution is written. To what purpose are powers limited, and to what purpose is that limitation committed to writing, if these limits may, at any time, be passed by those intended to be restrained? . . . Certainly all those who have framed written constitutions contemplate them as forming the fundamental and paramount law of the nation. . . . What we have deemed the greatest improvement on political institutions [is] a written constitution.[40]

John Marshall on the Constitution as an "Outline" (1819)

At the same time, however, precisely because the Constitution is far from a detailed script, its textual provisions can be broadly interpreted, consistent with its stated purposes. Again, in the words of Chief Justice Marshall:

A constitution, to contain an accurate detail of all the subdivisions of which its great powers will admit, and of all the means by which they may be carried into execution, would partake of the prolixity of a legal code, and could scarcely be embraced by the human mind. It would probably never be understood by the public. Its nature, therefore, requires that only its great outlines should be marked, its important objects designated, and the minor ingredients which compose those objects be deduced from the nature of the objects themselves. That this idea was entertained by the framers of the American Constitution is not only to be inferred from the nature of the instrument, but from the language. . . . It is also in some degree warranted by their having omitted to use any restrictive term which might prevent its receiving a fair and just interpretation. In considering this question, then, we must never forget that it is *a constitution* we are expounding. . . .
   [The] Constitution [is] intended to endure for ages to come, and consequently [is] to be adapted to the various crises of human affairs. . . .
   We admit, as all must admit, that the powers of the government are limited, and that its limits are not to be transcended. But we think the sound construction of the Constitution must allow to the national legislature that discretion with respect to the means by which the powers it confers are to be carried into execution which will enable that body to perform the high duties assigned to it in the manner most beneficial to the people. Let the end be legitimate, let it be within the scope of the Constitution, and all means which are appropriate, which are plainly adapted to that end, which are not prohibited, but consist with the letter and spirit of the Constitution, are constitutional.[41]

The Supremacy Clause (1787)

The Constitution, moreover, to use Chief Justice Marshall's word, is "paramount." By its own terms, it purports to be "the supreme Law of the Land."

This Constitution, and the laws of the United States which shall be made in Pursuance thereof; and all Treaties made, or which shall be made, under the Authority of the United States, shall be the supreme Law of the Land; and the Judges in every State shall be bound thereby, any Thing in the Constitution or Laws of any State to the Contrary notwithstanding. The Senators and Representatives before mentioned, and the Members of the several State Legislatures, and all executive and judicial Officers, both of the United States and of the several States, shall be bound by Oath or Affirmation, to support this Constitution. . . . [Article VI, Sections 2 and 3]

Alexander Hamilton and James Madison on the Supremacy Clause (1788)

Alexander Hamilton was later to make the bold claim that the Supremacy Clause was not necessary—that the Constitution would have been just fine, thank you very much, had nothing ever been mentioned on this matter.

> The constitutional operation of the intended government would be precisely the same, if [this clause] were entirely obliterated. [It is] only declaratory of a truth which would have resulted by necessary and unavoidable implication from the very act of constituting a federal government. . . . The clause which declares the supremacy of the laws of the Union . . . only declares a truth which flows immediately and necessarily from the institution of a federal government.[42]

James Madison's contrary assertion was more convincing. Absent the supremacy provision, the Constitution would have been "evidently and radically defective," because the states would have claimed superiority, resulting in "a monster in which the head was under the direction of its members."[43]

How exactly the Supremacy Clause was to be enforced raised an entirely different set of problems. Article VI itself posited at least some good-faith reliance on an officeholder's "oath or affirmation." But Madison insisted that self-denying constraints based on honor or virtue—"neither moral nor religious motives"— could never be counted on to restrain selfish interests.[44] In the final analysis, the authors of *The Federalist* looked to the federal courts to provide a "constitutional mode" for "enforcing the observance" of the Constitution by pronouncing actions "contrary to the supreme law of the land [to be] unconstitutional and void."[45] Out of this conception was to emerge the doctrine of judicial review.

George Washington on the Constitutional Convention (1787)

A third foundational question: How did the Constitution happen? George Washington, who presided over the Constitutional Convention, maintained that its delegates made decisions solely in order to promote "the greatest interest of every true American."

> In all our deliberations on this subject we kept steadily in our view that which appears to us the greatest interest of every true American, the consolidation of our union in which is involved our prosperity, felicity, safety, [and] perhaps our national existence. This important consideration seriously and deeply impressed on our minds led each state in the Convention to be less rigid on points of inferior magnitude than might have been otherwise expected. And thus the Constitution which we now present is the result of a spirit of amity and of that mutual deference and concession which the peculiarity of our political situation rendered indispensable. That it will meet the full and entire approbation of every state is not perhaps to be expected. But each will doubtless consider that had her interests been alone consulted the consequences might have been particularly disagreeable or injurious to others. That it is liable to as few exceptions as could reasonably have been expected we hope and believe. That it may promote the lasting welfare of that country so dear to us all and secure her freedom and happiness is our most ardent wish.[46]

James Madison on the Constitutional Convention (1788)

In much the same vein, James Madison attempted to explain the "wonderful" result of the Philadelphia Convention:

> The real wonder is that so many difficulties should have been surmounted; and surmounted with a unanimity almost as unprecedented as it must have been unexpected. It is impossible for any man of candor to reflect on this circumstance without partaking of the astonishment. It is impossible for the man of pious reflection not to perceive in it a finger of that Almighty hand which has been so frequently and signally extended to our relief in the critical stages of the revolution. . . .
>
> The history of almost all the great councils and consultations held among mankind for reconciling their discordant opinions, assuaging their mutual jealousies, and adjusting their respective interests, is a history of factions, contentions, and disappointments, and may be classed among the most dark and degrading pictures which display the infirmities and depravities of the human character. If in a few scattered instances a brighter aspect is presented, they serve only as exceptions to admonish us of the general truth; and by their luster to darken the gloom of the adverse prospect to which they are contrasted.

In revolving the causes from which these exceptions result, and applying them to the particular instance before us, we are necessarily led to two important conclusions. The first is that the convention must have enjoyed in a very singular degree an exemption from the pestilential influence of party animosities—the disease most incident to deliberative bodies and most apt to contaminate their proceedings. The second conclusion is that all the deputations composing the convention were satisfactorily accommodated by the final act, or were induced to accede to it by a deep conviction of the necessity of sacrificing private opinions and partial interests to the public good, and by a despair of seeing this necessity diminished by delays or by new experiments.[47]

Michael Klarman on the Constitutional Convention (2016)

Perhaps Washington and Madison were right. Perhaps patriotism and compromise carried the day. But it is not exactly unpatriotic to discount divine inspiration or unselfish altruism as explanations for what happened in Philadelphia and rather instead to examine the political, economic, and social motivations that guided decision-making by the delegates.

> The compromises undertaken in Philadelphia illustrate the extent to which the Constitution was a product of clashing interests rather than dispassionate political philosophizing. . . . While these were remarkable men, their interests were rather ordinary. As Benjamin Franklin keenly observed, any assembly of men, no matter how talented, bring with them "all their prejudices, their passions, their errors of opinion, their local interests and their selfish views." One need not deny that the framers . . . had "the purest intentions" in order to believe that—inevitably—they also had interests. Unsurprisingly, supporters of the Constitution preferred to believe that they were disinterested, while their opponents were motivated by selfish concerns. . . . Yet while the Federalists considered themselves disinterested, in reality they simply held different interests than their political opponents.[48]

Over the years, legions of constitutional historians (including Klarman) have explored the proceedings of the Constitutional Convention, along with the wellsprings of each of the Constitution's many operative provisions. Whether the delegates—as well as their Antifederalist opponents—were driven primarily by economic self-interest (including the preservation of slavery) or by a desire to resist and corral democratic and populist forces, or by an ideology consistent with the radicalism of the American Revolution, or by fear of the consequences of disunion, or by any of a host of other possible motivations remains very much the subject of vigorous debate.

Changing the Constitution

A fourth preliminary question: How does the Constitution change? The Constitution is not etched in stone. In can be changed, formally or informally, by at least four different methods. First and most obviously, as has already occurred more than two dozen times in the nation's history, amendments can be added to the Constitution following the route set forth in Article V—amendments that are "valid to all Intents and Purposes, as Part of this Constitution." The Thirteenth Amendment, for example, abolished chattel slavery in 1865. Second, the scope and meaning of various constitutional provisions can change over time—even dramatically—depending on their interpretation by the judiciary. In *Plessy v. Ferguson* (1896), for example, the Supreme Court held that racial segregation was permissible despite the "equal protection" provision in the Fourteenth Amendment.[49] In *Brown v. Board of Education* (1954), however, the Supreme Court ruled that segregated schools were unconstitutional.[50] Third, the Constitution—or at least its practical application—can evolve through custom, practice, and tradition. For example, the crucial power of judicial review is not to be located in Article III but rather has developed over time. Finally, Article V provides for the possibility of a "second" Philadelphia—that is, another "Convention for proposing Amendments"—that, at least in theory, could throw out the baby with the bathwater and start afresh.

John Jay on the Constitution as an "Experiment" (1790)

That the Constitution is not etched in stone—that it can indeed be changed in a variety of ways—is not a concept that would be at all upsetting to the framers. George Washington himself expected that future generations, with "the aid of experience on their side," would craft "alterations and amendments" to the Constitution, "for I do not conceive that we are more inspired—have more wisdom—or possess more virtue than those who will come after us."[51] And John Jay, the nation's first chief justice, put things this way:

> Providence has been pleased to bless the people of this country with more perfect opportunities of choosing, and more effectual means of establishing their own government, than any other nation has hitherto enjoyed.... The institution of general and state governments, their respective conveniences and defects in

practice, and the subsequent alterations made in some of them, have operated as useful experiments, and conspired to promote our advancement in this interesting science. It is pleasing to observe that the present national government already affords advantages, which the [Articles of Confederation] proved too feeble and ill constructed to produce. How far it may be still distant from the degree of perfection to which it may possibly be carried time only can decide. It is a consolation to reflect that the good sense of the people will be enabled by experience to discover and correct its imperfections, especially while they continue to retain a proper confidence in themselves.[52]

Sanford Levinson (and Others): Reform the Constitution (2006)

Fifth, one might inquire whether the Constitution has become an outdated relic. Much like a sacred religious text, the Constitution is enshrined in its place of honor in the National Archives, the nation's secular temple. In the eyes of many observers, however, the Constitution—far from being sacrosanct—is desperately in need of reform. Both the problems faced and the values shared by most contemporary Americans differ greatly from those of the late eighteenth-century founders. Does it really make sense to continue to be governed by procedures and restrictions more than 230 years old?

Constitutional scholar Sanford Levinson has urged the adoption of a series of what he believes to be long-overdue constitutional reforms.

Many structural provisions of the Constitution place almost insurmountable barriers in the way of any acceptable notion of democracy. . . . It is increasingly difficult to construct a theory of democratic constitutionalism, *applying our own twenty-first-century norms*, that vindicates the Constitution under which we are governed today. Our eighteenth-century ancestors had little trouble integrating slavery and the rank subordination of women into their conception of a "republican" political order. *That* vision of politics is blessedly long behind us, but the Constitution is not. It does not deserve rote support from Americans who properly believe that majority rule, even if tempered by the recognition of minority rights, is integral to "consent of the governed." . . .

[Examples of antiquated and dangerous constitutional provisions include: equality of states in the Senate; the Electoral College system; extraordinary presidential powers; lifetime tenure for Supreme Court justices; the difficulty of passing constitutional amendments]. . . . *We must recognize that a substantial responsibility for the defects of our polity lies in the Constitution itself.* A number of wrong turns were taken at the time of the initial drafting of the

Constitution, even if for the best of reasons given the political realities of 1787. Even the most skilled and admirable leaders may not be able to overcome the barriers to effective government constructed by the Constitution. . . .

If I am correct that the Constitution is both insufficiently democratic, in a country that professes to believe in democracy, and significantly dysfunctional, in terms of the quality of government that we receive, then it follows that we should no longer express our blind devotion to it. . . . It is a human creation open to criticism and even to rejection.[53]

Levinson is part of a long line of critics who have maintained that the Constitution is in need of drastic reform. For example, political scientist Larry Sabato has offered no fewer than twenty-three "proposals to revitalize our Constitution and make America a fairer country."[54] Even a former Supreme Court justice, John Paul Stevens, got in on the act by calling for the urgent passage of six constitutional amendments concerning the death penalty, gun control, campaign finance laws, and the like.[55]

Louis Michael Seidman: Ignore, Disobey the Constitution (2012)

Constitutional law scholar Louis Michael Seidman would push the boundaries of reform even further. He contends that whenever the Constitution makes no sense in terms of the needs of a modern, democratic society, its provisions should simply be ignored.

Why should *anyone*, on the Left, the Right, or in the center, renounce positions of policy and principle that she favors simply because those policies and principles are inconsistent with the Constitution? The standard answer, of course, is that the Constitution, in the words of its preamble, was adopted by "We the People." . . . Because "We the People" chose to be bound by this text, "We the People" are now obligated to obey it.

Unfortunately, there are many things wrong with this story. We can start with the awkward fact that the Constitution itself was born of disobedience. The delegates were summoned to Philadelphia to amend the existing Articles of Confederation, not to displace it. . . . Why should we feel obligated to obey their handiwork when they themselves disobeyed the legal limits on their power? . . .

The problem is compounded by the fact that many people were not considered "people" in late eighteenth-century America. No women, African Americans, or Indians and few individuals without property were allowed to cast votes. More significantly, no one alive today had anything to do with the ratification process. . . .

> These are all reasons that ought to give us pause about the Constitution's binding force.... The test for constitutional obligation arises when one thinks that, all-things-considered, the right thing to do is X, but the Constitution tells us to do not-X.... It is only then that if we obey the Constitution, we are doing so for the sole reason that we are bound to obey. But who in their right mind would do this? If we are convinced after taking everything into account that one course of action is right, why should we take another course of action just because of words written down on a piece of paper more than two hundred years ago?[56]

Lest this seem a radical approach, Seidman contends that throughout the country's history, the Constitution's mandates have been effectively ignored: by John Adams in endorsing the Sedition Act; by Thomas Jefferson in purchasing the Louisiana Territory; by abolitionists who denounced the document's proslavery clauses; by Abraham Lincoln when he fashioned the Emancipation Proclamation; by Franklin Roosevelt during the New Deal; and by the Supreme Court, repeatedly, when it has announced new constitutional rights—among other instances.

Thomas Jefferson on the Need for Frequent Constitutional Conventions (1788)

Dissatisfaction with being governed by—or, as some would argue, being bound by—the constraints of our constitutional system is far from a modern concern. Thomas Jefferson and James Madison were close friends. They both hailed from privileged Virginia backgrounds; they shared numerous political and social values; they worked together in opposition to Alexander Hamilton's economic programs; they jointly conspired to found the nation's first organized political party; they wrote, respectively, the Kentucky and Virginia Resolutions in protest of the Alien and Sedition Acts; Madison served as Jefferson's secretary of state for eight years and then followed him as president for two terms; there was even a "Madison Room" at Monticello to accommodate the frequent visits of James and Dolley. Yet the two founders disagreed—profoundly—on the extent to which one generation could (or should) bind the next by means of an ancient (Jefferson would have said hoary) and difficult-to-alter constitutional scripture. Jefferson got the ball rolling with his proposal to amend Virginia's state constitution by calling popular conventions to resolve constitutional gridlock and enact needed reforms.

> Any two of the three branches of government concurring in opinion, each by the voices of two-thirds of their whole existing number, that a convention is necessary for altering this constitution, or correcting breaches of it, they shall

be authorized to issue writs to every county for the election of so many delegates as they are authorized to send to the general assembly, which elections shall be held, and writs returned, as the laws shall have provide[d] in the case of elections of delegates to assembly . . . and the said delegates shall meet at the usual place of holding assemblies, three months after the date of such writs, and shall be acknowledged to have equal powers with this present convention.[57]

James Madison on the Dangers of Frequent "Appeal to the People" (1788)

Madison found Jefferson's proposal horrifying, precisely because it would have undermined those foundations of veneration Madison believed were necessary to support a stable republican government—and especially because Americans did not routinely approach political questions with "enlightened reason." Jefferson's idea, he conceded, "like everything from the same pen, marks a turn of thinking original, comprehensive and accurate." But:

> As the people are the only legitimate fountain of power, and it is from them that the constitutional charter, under which the several branches of government hold their power, is derived, it seems strictly consonant to the republican theory to recur to the same original authority, not only whenever it may be necessary to enlarge, diminish, or new-model the powers of government, but also whenever any one of the departments may commit encroachments on the chartered authorities of the others. . . . There is certainly great force in this reasoning, and it must be allowed to prove that a constitutional road to the decision of the people ought to be marked out, and kept open, for certain great and extraordinary occasions. But there appear to be insuperable objections against the proposed recurrence to the people as a provision in all cases for keeping the several departments of power within their constitutional limits. . . .
>
> It may be considered as an objection inherent in the principle that as every appeal to the people would carry an implication of some defect in the government, frequent appeals would in great measure deprive the government of that veneration which time bestows on everything, and without which perhaps the wisest and freest governments would not possess the requisite stability. . . . In a nation of philosophers, this consideration ought to be disregarded. A reverence for the laws would be sufficiently inculcated by the voice of an enlightened reason. But a nation of philosophers is as little to be expected as the philosophical race of kings wished for by Plato. And in every other nation, the most rational government will not find it a superfluous advantage to have the prejudices of the community on its side.

The danger of disturbing the public tranquility by interesting too strongly the public passions is a still more serious objection against a frequent reference of constitutional questions to the decision of the whole society. Notwithstanding the success which has attended the revisions of our established forms of government, and which does so much honor to the virtue and intelligence of the people of America, it must be confessed that the experiments are of too ticklish a nature to be unnecessarily multiplied. We are to recollect that all the existing constitutions were formed in the midst of a danger which repressed the passions most unfriendly to order and concord; of an enthusiastic confidence of the people in their patriotic leaders, which stifled the ordinary diversity of opinions on great national questions; of a universal ardor for new and opposite forms, produced by a universal resentment and indignation against the ancient government; and whilst no spirit of party, connected with the changes to be made or the abuses to be reformed, could mingle its leaven in the operation. The future situations in which we must expect to be usually placed do not present any equivalent security against the danger which is apprehended.[58]

Thomas Jefferson: No Constitution Should Be Perpetual (1789)

The Jefferson-Madison debate over the dangers of frequent constitutional reform continued in their private correspondence. Jefferson threw down the initial gauntlet.

The question whether one generation of men has a right to bind another, seems never to have been started either on this or our side of the water. Yet it is a question of such consequences as not only to merit decision, but place also among the fundamental principles of every government. . . . I set out on this ground, which I suppose to be self-evident, *"that the earth belongs in usufruct to the living"*; that the dead have neither powers nor rights over it. The portion occupied by any individual ceases to be his when himself ceases to be, and reverts to the society. . . .

No society can make a perpetual constitution, or even a perpetual law. The earth belongs always to the living generation. They may manage it then, and what proceeds from it, as they please, during their usufruct. They are masters too of their own persons and consequently may govern them as they please. But persons and property make the sum of the objects of government. The constitution and the laws of their predecessors extinguished then in their natural course, with those who gave them being. This could preserve that being till it ceased to be itself, and no longer. Every constitution then, and every law, naturally expires at the end of nineteen years [i.e., a single generation]. If it be enforced longer, it is an act of force, and not of right. It may be said that the succeeding generation exercising in fact the power of repeal, this leaves them as free as if the constitution or law had been expressly limited to nineteen years.[59]

James Madison on the Dangers of Constitutional Instability (1790)

Madison, ever the pragmatic realist, wanted no part of any scheme of continual constitutional upheaval. That way madness lies, he must have thought, echoing Shakespeare.

However applicable in theory the doctrine may be to a constitution, [it] seems liable in practice to some very powerful objections. Would not a government so often revised become too mutable to retain those prejudices in its favor which antiquity inspires, and which are perhaps a salutary aid to the most rational government in the most enlightened age? Would not such a periodical revision engender pernicious factions that might not otherwise come into existence? Would not, in fine, a government depending for its existence beyond a fixed date, on some positive and authentic intervention of the society itself, be too subject to the casualty and consequences of an actual interregnum? . . .

Unless such laws should be kept in force by new acts regularly anticipating the end of the term, all the rights depending on positive laws, that is, most of the rights of property, would become absolutely defunct; and the most violent struggles be generated between those interested in reviving and those interested in new-modelling the former state of property. Nor would events of this kind be improbable. The obstacles to the passage of laws which render a power to repeal inferior to an opportunity of rejecting, as a security against oppression, would here render an opportunity of rejecting, an insecure provision against anarchy. Add that the possibility of an event so hazardous to the rights of property could not fail to depreciate its value; that the approach of the crisis would increase this effect; that the frequent return of periods superseding all the obligations depending on antecedent laws and usages, must by weakening the reverence for those obligations, co-operate with motives to licentiousness already too powerful; and that the uncertainty incident to such a state of things would on one side discourage the steady exertions of industry produced by permanent laws, and on the other, give a disproportionate advantage to the more, over the less, sagacious and enterprising part of the society.

I find no relief from these consequences but in the received doctrine that a tacit assent may be given to established constitutions and laws, and that this assent may be inferred where no positive dissent appears.[60]

Thomas Jefferson: Each Generation Deserves Its Own Constitution (1816)

Jefferson got the last word in this high-level constitutional debate—if only because his final letter on the subject was addressed to someone other than James Madison.

Some men look at constitutions with sanctimonious reverence, and deem them like the Ark of the Covenant, too sacred to be touched. They ascribe to the men of the preceding age a wisdom more than human and suppose what they did to be beyond amendment. I knew that age well; I belonged to it and labored with it. It deserved well of its country. It was very like the present, but without the experience of the present; and forty years of experience in government is worth a century of book-reading; and this they would say themselves, were they to rise from the dead.

I am certainly not an advocate for frequent and untried changes in laws and constitutions. I think moderate imperfections had better be borne with; because, when once known, we accommodate ourselves to them and find practical means of correcting their ill effects. But I know also that laws and institutions must go hand in hand with the progress of the human mind. As that becomes more developed, more enlightened, as new discoveries are made, new truths disclosed, and manners and opinions change with the change of circumstances, institutions must advance also and keep pace with the times. We might as well require a man to wear still the coat which fitted him when a boy, as civilized society to remain ever under the regimen of their barbarous ancestors. It is this preposterous idea which has lately deluged Europe in blood. Their monarchs, instead of wisely yielding to the gradual change of circumstances, of favoring progressive accommodation to progressive improvement, have clung to old abuses, entrenched themselves behind steady habits, and obliged their subjects to seek through blood and violence rash and ruinous innovations, which, had they been referred to the peaceful deliberations and collected wisdom of the nation, would have been put into acceptable and salutary forms. Let us follow no such examples, nor weakly believe that one generation is not as capable as another of taking care of itself and of ordering its own affairs. Let us, as our sister states have done, avail ourselves of our reason and experience to correct the crude essays of our first and unexperienced, although wise, virtuous, and well-meaning councils. And lastly, let us provide in our constitution for its revision at stated periods.

What these periods should be, nature herself indicates. By the European tables of mortality, of the adults living at any one moment of time, a majority will be dead in about nineteen years. At the end of that period, then, a new majority is come into place; or, in other words, a new generation. Each generation is as independent as the one preceding, as that was of all which had gone before. It has then, like them, a right to choose for itself the form of government it believes most promotive of its own happiness; consequently, to accommodate to the circumstances in which it finds itself that received from its predecessors; and it is for the peace and good of mankind that a solemn opportunity of doing this every nineteen or twenty years should be provided by the constitution; so that it may be handed on, with periodical repairs, from generation to generation, to the end of time, if anything human can so long endure.[61]

Jefferson might have been surprised (and perhaps even distressed) by the lasting endurance of the Constitution. But he carried his point, at least to this extent: despite more than two centuries of experience, We the People continue to reflect on whether—and, if so, how—the Constitution can be "updated" to achieve "a more perfect Union."

Discussion Questions

1. The Constitution can be read, from beginning to end, in about half an hour. Is it clear and easy to understand, or arcane and complicated? Does it read like poetry or more like something written in a foreign language? Does the Constitution contain too many details (it's too long), or not enough specificity (it's too short)?
2. What does Linda Greenhouse mean when she suggests that the Constitution is not an object but a process?
3. Compare the remarks of Ronald Reagan and Thurgood Marshall on the Constitution. Is there any common ground between their perspectives?
4. Chief Justice John Marshall placed a great deal of weight on the fact that the Constitution is written. What difference does that make? Great Britain's "constitution" is unwritten, consisting of centuries of shared traditions and understandings; Great Britain is no less of a democracy. What is gained (or lost) by reducing the "fundamental law" of a nation to writing?
5. In *Federalist No. 48*, James Madison seemed to doubt the capacity of written rules to prevent wrongdoing. In the context of discussing the

separation of powers among the branches of the national government, he observed that "a mere demarcation on parchment of the constitutional limits of the several departments is not a sufficient guard against those encroachments which lead to a tyrannical concentration of all the powers of government in the same hands."[62] Separately, in *Federalist No. 41*, he suggested that even the strongest of "constitutional barriers" might be ignored due to "the impulse of self-preservation" when the survival of the nation was at stake.[63] Does the fact that the Constitution is a written document provide any additional security against a tyrannical government or an oppressive majority?

6. What does it mean to say that the Constitution is "the supreme law of the land"? Hamilton and Madison disagreed as to whether the Supremacy Clause was necessary or not. Who was right? How exactly is the provision to be enforced?

7. Both George Washington and James Madison maintained that the Constitution was, in effect, a miracle: Everyone who participated in its drafting set aside their selfish interests and compromised for the general welfare. How likely or reasonable is this explanation?

8. How important was it that the proceedings of the Constitutional Convention were closed to the public? Had the delegates not pledged themselves to secrecy, what might have happened? Given today's environment of "open government" and "sunshine" laws, would it be possible to privately debate and draft something like the Constitution?

9. Although Madison did his best in *Federalist No. 40* to defend the legitimacy of the Constitutional Convention,[64] it has been argued that the delegates acted illegally: (a) They were authorized only to propose amendments to the Articles of Confederation, yet they abandoned it. (b) Any amendments to the Articles were required to be approved unanimously, yet the Constitution became effective after ratification by only nine states. (c) The proposed Constitution was submitted to popular "conventions" for approval instead of state legislatures. Did the ends justify the means?

10. Is it too difficult to amend the Constitution (two-thirds of the House of Representatives plus two-thirds of the Senate plus three-fourths of the states)? In reality, it requires an overwhelming political consensus to amend the Constitution. Especially during times of polarization and intense partisanship and gridlock, when it is difficult to harness slim majorities even to pass legislation, is it conceivable to expect significant constitutional change? Is that good or bad?

11. When considering changes to the Constitution, is too much focus placed on the process of formal constitutional amendment? The courts

play an enormous role in enforcing and interpreting the Constitution. Does the evolving process of constitutional litigation provide a healthy "safety valve" in light of the difficulty in securing new constitutional amendments? Or, is it somehow less legitimate to achieve "constitutional rewrites" through the courts (and unelected judges) instead of through formal amendments?

12. Consider efforts to abolish slavery, or to secure the right to vote for women, or to end segregation. When reflecting on the history of the United States, is it not important to recognize that constitutional change has originated from activists and ordinary citizens, from protests, petitions, and even civil disobedience, as well as from amendments and courts?

13. Should we start over? Should a new constitutional convention be held? Pursuant to the terms of Article V of the Constitution, "the Legislatures of two thirds of the several States" can call for a "Convention for proposing Amendments." Would a "second Philadelphia" be a good (fabulous) idea, or a bad (dangerous) idea?

14. Should we simply ignore (or even disobey) the Constitution, as Louis Michael Seidman suggests?

Judicial Review—Primary Sources

Article III of the Constitution, which describes the judicial system, is far shorter—far less fleshed out—than its legislative (Article I) and executive (Article II) branch counterparts. Nothing in Article III sets forth the structure of the federal court system (apart from specifying "one supreme Court" and "such inferior Courts as the Congress may from time to time ordain and establish"), or even the number of "Judges" on the Supreme Court. The jurisdiction of the federal courts to entertain lawsuits brought against states was the subject of immediate controversy and soon enough resulted in the Eleventh Amendment. But most significantly, nothing in Article III indicated that the courts would possess the power of "judicial review"—that is, the ability to "review" laws passed by Congress and state legislatures (as well as acts undertaken by executive officials and agencies) and declare them to be at odds with the Constitution—and therefore null and void, or "unconstitutional."

Judicial Review at the Constitutional Convention (1787, 1788)

Contrary to popular belief, the concept of judicial review did not emerge out of thin air in *Marbury v. Madison*. Indeed, several delegates to the Constitutional

Convention and during the subsequent state ratification debates spoke affirmatively about the expected ability of the federal courts to enforce the constitutional structure, particularly in response to legislative overreach and oppression—if necessary, by declaring laws unconstitutional. For example:

> *Luther Martin* [Maryland]: As to the constitutionality of laws, that point will come before the judges in their proper official character. In this character they have a negative on the laws.[65]

> *George Mason* [Virginia]: Notwithstanding the precautions taken in the Constitution of the legislature, it would so much resemble that of the individual states, that it must be expected frequently to pass unjust and pernicious laws. . . . The judges were joined in this check on the laws. . . . They could declare an unconstitutional law void.[66]

> *James Madison* [Virginia]: A law violating a constitution established by the people themselves would be considered by the judges as null and void.[67]

> *Oliver Ellsworth* [Connecticut]: This Constitution defines the extent of the powers of the general government. If the general legislature should at any time overleap their limits, the judicial department is a constitutional check. If the United States go beyond their powers, if they make a law which the Constitution does not authorize, it is void; and the judicial power, the national judges, who to secure their impartiality, are to be made independent, will declare it to be void.[68]

Federalist No. 78 on the Need for Judicial Independence (1788)

A good place to turn for additional explication is *Federalist No. 78*, authored by Alexander Hamilton. The essay was intended to respond to Antifederalist concerns about lifetime tenure for federal judges—or, more accurately, the continued service by judges in "their Offices during good Behaviour" (Article III, Section 1). Hamilton maintained that open-ended terms of office were essential if judges were to be divorced from political pressures. And why was that crucial? Because judges needed to be sufficiently independent in order, if necessary, to issue unpopular rulings—specifically, rulings that guarded the Constitution against encroachment by the legislative branch. This necessarily required that courts have the ability and the means to set aside any legislative acts that went beyond "the limits assigned to their authority" under the Constitution.

The complete independence of the courts of justice is peculiarly essential in a limited Constitution. By a limited Constitution, I understand one which contains certain specified exceptions to the legislative authority; such, for instance, as that it shall pass no bills of attainder, no ex post facto laws, and the like. Limitations of this kind can be preserved in practice no other way than through the medium of courts of justice, whose duty it must be to declare all acts contrary to the manifest tenor of the Constitution void. Without this, all the reservations of particular rights or privileges would amount to nothing. . . .

The courts were designed to be an intermediate body between the people and the legislature, in order, among other things, to keep the latter within the limits assigned to their authority. The interpretation of the laws is the proper and peculiar province of the courts. A constitution is, in fact, and must be regarded by the judges, as a fundamental law. It therefore belongs to them to ascertain its meaning, as well as the meaning of any particular act proceeding from the legislative body. If there should happen to be an irreconcilable variance between the two, that which has the superior obligation and validity ought, of course, to be preferred; or, in other words, the Constitution ought to be preferred to the statute, the intention of the people to the intention of their agents. . . . Accordingly, whenever a particular statute contravenes the Constitution, it will be the duty of the judicial tribunals to adhere to the latter and disregard the former. . . .

If, then, the courts of justice are to be considered as the bulwarks of a limited Constitution against legislative encroachments, this consideration will afford a strong argument for the permanent tenure of judicial offices, since nothing will contribute so much as this to that independent spirit in the judges which must be essential to the faithful performance of so arduous a duty.[69]

Federalist No. 78 on the Need for Judicial Review (1788)

But judicial review was essential for an additional reason, argued Hamilton: to protect the people from themselves. Inevitably, "occasional ill humors in the society" will entice a popular majority to ignore the Constitution or the rights of those in the minority. In such circumstances, courts—staffed with lifetime, "independent" judges—would be expected to guard the rights of the weak against the "designs" of the strong.

This independence of the judges is equally requisite to guard the Constitution and the rights of individuals from the effects of those ill humors, which the arts of designing men, or the influence of particular conjunctures, sometimes disseminate among the people themselves, and which, though they speedily give place to better information and more deliberate reflection, have a tendency, in the meantime, to occasion dangerous innovations in the government, and serious oppressions of the minor party in the community.

Though I trust the friends of the proposed Constitution will never concur with its enemies in questioning that fundamental principle of republican government, which admits the right of the people to alter or abolish the established Constitution whenever they find it inconsistent with their happiness, yet it is not to be inferred from this principle that the representatives of the people, whenever a momentary inclination happens to lay hold of a majority of their constituents, incompatible with the provisions in the existing Constitution, would, on that account, be justifiable in a violation of those provisions; or that the courts would be under a greater obligation to connive at infractions in this shape, than when they had proceeded wholly from the cabals of the representative body. Until the people have, by some solemn and authoritative act, annulled or changed the established form, it is binding upon themselves collectively, as well as individually; and no presumption, or even knowledge, of their sentiments can warrant their representatives in a departure from it prior to such an act. But it is easy to see that it would require an uncommon portion of fortitude in the judges to do their duty as faithful guardians of the Constitution where legislative invasions of it had been instigated by the major voice of the community.

But it is not with a view to infractions of the Constitution only that the independence of the judges may be an essential safeguard against the effects of occasional ill humors in the society. These sometimes extend no farther than to the injury of the private rights of particular classes of citizens by unjust and partial laws. Here also the firmness of the judicial magistracy is of vast importance in mitigating the severity and confining the operation of such laws. It not only serves to moderate the immediate mischiefs of those which may have been passed, but it operates as a check upon the legislative body in passing them; who, perceiving that obstacles to the success of iniquitous intention are to be expected from the scruples of the courts, are in a manner compelled, by the very motives of the injustice they meditate, to qualify their attempts. This is a circumstance calculated to have more influence upon the character of our governments, than but few may be aware of. The benefits of the integrity and moderation of the judiciary have already been felt in more states than one; and though they may have displeased those whose sinister expectations they may have disappointed, they must have commanded the esteem and applause of all the virtuous and disinterested. Considerate men of every description ought to prize whatever will tend to beget or fortify that temper in the courts, as no man can be sure that he may not be tomorrow the victim of a spirit of injustice, by which he may be a gainer today. And every man must now feel that the inevitable tendency of such a spirit is to sap the foundations of public and private confidence, and to introduce in its stead universal distrust and distress.[70]

Antifederalist Objections to Judicial Review (1788)

Hamilton's empowerment of the judiciary was expressly antimajoritarian. He envisioned judicial review as a means to protect not only the constitutional structure but also the outvoted minority from "dangerous innovations" and "serious oppressions" stemming from "the arts of designing men." This antidemocratic streak did not escape unnoticed at the time. Especially given the silence of the Constitution on the subject, it was a huge leap to suggest that acts of Congress could be overturned by some unelected and lifetime "higher power." "Brutus," the prominent Antifederalist (whose exact identity is unknown), took direct issue with such a notion of paramount—indeed, potentially tyrannical—judicial authority.

The Supreme Court under this Constitution would be exalted above all other power in the government, and subject to no control. The business of this paper will be to illustrate this and to show the danger that will result from it. I question whether the world ever saw, in any period of it, a court of justice invested with such immense powers and yet placed in a situation so little responsible. Certain it is that in England and in the several states, where we have been taught to believe the courts of law are put upon the most prudent establishment, they are on a very different footing.

The judges in England, it is true, hold their offices during their good behavior, but then their determinations are subject to correction by the House of Lords; and their power is by no means so extensive as that of the proposed Supreme Court of the union. I believe they in no instance assume the authority to set aside an act of Parliament under the idea that it is inconsistent with their constitution. They consider themselves bound to decide according to the existing laws of the land, and never undertake to control them by adjudging that they are inconsistent with the constitution—much less are they vested with the power of giving an equitable construction to the constitution.

The judges in England are under the control of the legislature, for they are bound to determine according to the laws passed under them. But the judges under this Constitution will control the legislature, for the Supreme Court are authorized in the last resort to determine what is the extent of the powers of the Congress. They are to give the Constitution an explanation, and there is no power above them to set aside their judgment. . . .

[The authors of the Constitution] have made the judges independent, in the fullest sense of the word. There is no power above them to control any of their decisions. There is no authority that can remove them, and they cannot be controlled by the laws of the legislature. In short, they are independent of the people, of the legislature, and of every power under heaven. Men placed in this situation will generally soon feel themselves independent of heaven itself. . . .

The Supreme Court then has a right, independent of the legislature, to give a construction to the Constitution and every part of it, and there is no power provided in this system to correct their construction or do it away. If, therefore, the legislature pass any laws inconsistent with the sense the judges put upon the Constitution, they will declare it void; and therefore in this respect their power is superior to that of the legislature.[71]

Judicial Review in the Early Republic

It is often suggested—erroneously—that the practice of judicial review originated with the Supreme Court's decision of *Marbury v. Madison* (1803). In fact, the understanding that courts could and would review statutes for their consistency with the Constitution was accepted from the earliest days of the new nation. The notion is explicit in section 25 of the Judiciary Act of 1789, which provided for review by the Supreme Court whenever a state court decided against "the validity of a statute . . . on the ground of [its] being repugnant to the Constitution . . . of the United States" (or vice versa).[72] The Invalid Pensions Act, passed by Congress in 1792, was deemed unconstitutional by Justice James Wilson and several of his brethren sitting as circuit court judges.[73] In *Hylton v. United States* (1796), the justices expressly rejected a constitutional challenge to a federal tax on carriages, thereby implicitly suggesting that they also held the authority to have voided the statute.[74] All told, federal and state judges invoked the power to declare laws unconstitutional on numerous occasions prior to *Marbury*.[75]

Marbury v. Madison—Background (1803)

Despite these antecedents, popular culture continues to trace the dawn of judicial review to the opinion of John Marshall, the nation's fourth chief justice, in *Marbury v. Madison*. During his thirty-five years in office, Marshall worked to ensure the supremacy of the national government (vis-à-vis the states) and the authority of the courts (vis-à-vis the political branches). And even if Marshall did not invent judicial review, *Marbury v. Madison* was a masterstroke.

William Marbury, who had been appointed by President John Adams to serve as a justice of the peace in the District of Columbia, was denied the right to perform his job by the new administration, led by President Thomas Jefferson and Secretary of State James Madison, because Marbury's judicial commission (certificate) had accidentally not been delivered to him. Marbury contested Jefferson's continued withholding of the commission by filing a lawsuit directly in the Supreme Court, seeking from the justices a "writ of mandamus" (an order to compel government action, in this case delivery of the commission). The first two-thirds of Chief Justice Marshall's unanimous opinion doubtless gave Marbury confidence in his likely victory.

1. Has the applicant [Marbury] a right to the commission he demands? . . . It is therefore decidedly the opinion of the Court that, when a commission has been signed by the president, the appointment is made, and that the commission is complete when the seal of the United States has been affixed to it by the secretary of state. . . . Mr. Marbury, then, since his commission was signed by the president [John Adams] and sealed by the secretary of state, was appointed, and as the law creating the office gave the officer a right to hold for five years independent of the executive, the appointment was not revocable, but vested in the officer legal rights which are protected by the laws of his country. To withhold the commission, therefore, is an act deemed by the Court not warranted by law, but violative of a vested legal right. . . .

2. If he has a right, and that right has been violated, do the laws of his country afford him a remedy? The very essence of civil liberty certainly consists in the right of every individual to claim the protection of the laws whenever he receives an injury. One of the first duties of government is to afford that protection. In Great Britain, the king himself is sued in the respectful form of a petition, and he never fails to comply with the judgment of his court. . . . Having this legal title to the office, [Marbury] has a consequent right to the commission, a refusal to deliver which is a plain violation of that right, for which the laws of his country afford him a remedy.

It remains to be inquired whether, 3. . . . if they do afford him a remedy, is it a mandamus issuing from this Court?[76]

Judiciary Act (1789)

At this point, Chief Justice Marshall unexpectedly delivered a curve ball—much to the surprise of Marbury (and Jefferson), and much to the empowerment of the Supreme Court. He declared Marbury to be the loser, and Jefferson the winner, because Marbury had *begun* his lawsuit in the Supreme Court, thereby invoking that Court's (very limited) "original Jurisdiction," instead of its (much broader, and much more common) "appellate Jurisdiction." (The text of Article III, Section 2 requires litigants to appeal to the Supreme Court from a lower court decision, except in a handful of rare instances—for example, when one state sues another—that can be brought initially in the Supreme Court itself.) In other words, Marbury erred by not beginning in the lower federal courts; his case should only have reached the Supreme Court through an appeal from a lower court ruling. And why had Marbury (or his counsel) been so dense as to proceed in the first instance in the Supreme Court? Because an act of Congress—specifically, section 13 of the Judiciary Act of 1789—authorized litigants to seek writs of mandamus *directly* from the Supreme Court.

> Section 13. . . . The Supreme Court . . . shall have power to issue . . . writs of mandamus in cases warranted by the principles and usages of law, to any courts appointed, or persons holding office, under the authority of the United States.[77]

Marbury v. Madison—Holding (1803)

In other words, Marbury (and his lawyer) had simply followed the procedures set forth in a law passed by Congress.[78] But that law—which told Marbury he could go straight to the Supreme Court to seek a writ of mandamus—appeared to be in direct conflict with the text of the Constitution—which limited the Supreme Court's "original Jurisdiction" to a handful of situations that Marbury clearly did not fit. Now what should happen? Here, Marshall delivered his surprising *coup de grace*.

> The act to establish the judicial courts of the United States [i.e., the Judiciary Act of 1789] authorizes the Supreme Court "to issue writs of mandamus, in cases warranted by the principles and usages of law, to any courts appointed, or persons holding office, under the authority of the United States." . . . The authority, therefore, given to the Supreme Court by the act establishing the judicial courts of the United States to issue writs of mandamus to public officers appears not to be warranted by the Constitution, and it becomes necessary to inquire whether a jurisdiction so conferred can be exercised.
>
> The question whether an act repugnant to the Constitution can become the law of the land is a question deeply interesting to the United States, but, happily, not of an intricacy proportioned to its interest. It seems only necessary to recognize certain principles, supposed to have been long and well established, to decide it. . . .

The powers of the legislature are defined and limited; and that those limits may not be mistaken or forgotten, the Constitution is written. To what purpose are powers limited, and to what purpose is that limitation committed to writing, if these limits may at any time be passed by those intended to be restrained? The distinction between a government with limited and unlimited powers is abolished if those limits do not confine the persons on whom they are imposed, and if acts prohibited and acts allowed are of equal obligation. It is a proposition too plain to be contested that the Constitution controls any legislative act repugnant to it, or that the legislature may alter the Constitution by an ordinary act.

Between these alternatives there is no middle ground. The Constitution is either a superior, paramount law, unchangeable by ordinary means, or it is on a level with ordinary legislative acts, and, like other acts, is alterable when the legislature shall please to alter it. If the former part of the alternative be true, then a legislative act contrary to the Constitution is not law; if the latter part be true, then written constitutions are absurd attempts on the part of the people to limit a power in its own nature illimitable.

Certainly all those who have framed written constitutions contemplate them as forming the fundamental and paramount law of the nation, and consequently the theory of every such government must be that an act of the legislature repugnant to the Constitution is void. . . . If an act of the legislature repugnant to the Constitution is void, does it, notwithstanding its invalidity, bind the courts and oblige them to give it effect? Or, in other words, though it be not law, does it constitute a rule as operative as if it was a law? This would be to overthrow in fact what was established in theory, and would seem, at first view, an absurdity too gross to be insisted on. It shall, however, receive a more attentive consideration.

It is emphatically the province and duty of the judicial department to say what the law is. Those who apply the rule to particular cases must, of necessity, expound and interpret that rule. If two laws conflict with each other, the courts must decide on the operation of each. So, if a law be in opposition to the Constitution, if both the law and the Constitution apply to a particular case, so that the court must either decide that case conformably to the law, disregarding the Constitution, or conformably to the Constitution, disregarding the law, the court must determine which of these conflicting rules governs the case. This is of the very essence of judicial duty. If, then, the courts are to regard the Constitution, and the Constitution is superior to any ordinary act of the legislature, the Constitution, and not such ordinary act, must govern the case to which they both apply. Those, then, who controvert the principle that the Constitution is to be considered in court as a paramount law are reduced to the necessity of maintaining that courts must close their eyes on the Constitution and see only the law.

This doctrine would subvert the very foundation of all written constitutions. It would declare that an act which, according to the principles and theory of our government is entirely void, is yet, in practice, completely obligatory. It would declare that, if the legislature shall do what is expressly forbidden, such act, notwithstanding the express prohibition, is in reality effectual. It would be giving to the legislature a practical and real omnipotence with the same breath which professes to restrict their powers within narrow limits. It is prescribing limits, and declaring that those limits may be passed at pleasure. . . .

It is declared that "no Tax or Duty shall be laid on Articles exported from any State." Suppose a duty on the export of cotton, of tobacco, or of flour, and a suit instituted to recover it. Ought judgment to be rendered in such a case? Ought the judges to close their eyes on the Constitution, and only see the law? The Constitution declares that "no Bill of Attainder or ex post facto Law shall be passed." If, however, such a bill should be passed and a person should be prosecuted under it, must the court condemn to death those victims whom the Constitution endeavors to preserve? "No Person," says the Constitution, "shall be convicted of Treason unless on the Testimony of two Witnesses to the same overt Act, or on Confession in open Court." Here, the language of the Constitution is addressed especially to the courts. It prescribes, directly for them, a rule of evidence not to be departed from. If the legislature should change that rule, and declare one witness, or a confession out of court, sufficient for conviction, must the constitutional principle yield to the legislative act? From these and many other selections which might be made, it is apparent that the framers of the Constitution contemplated that instrument as a rule for the government of *courts*, as well as of the legislature. . . .

It is also not entirely unworthy of observation that, in declaring what shall be the *supreme* law of the land, the *Constitution* itself is first mentioned, and not the laws of the United States generally, but those only which shall be made in pursuance of the Constitution, have that rank.

Thus, the particular phraseology of the Constitution of the United States confirms and strengthens the principle, supposed to be essential to all written constitutions, that a law repugnant to the Constitution is void, and that courts, as well as other departments, are bound by that instrument.[79]

Long story short, Marbury lost (and Jefferson prevailed) because a law passed by Congress conflicted with the Constitution. For the first time in the nation's history, the Supreme Court had declared such a law to be unconstitutional.

Thomas Jefferson's Reactions to *Marbury v. Madison* (1804–23)

Back in the days when Jefferson was fighting for a bill of rights to be added to the Constitution, he had proposed something very much like judicial review in a letter to Madison.[80] But now he was president, his political party controlled Congress, and he worried about how a hostile Supreme Court might wield this self-granted constitutional power. Indeed, Jefferson fumed about this issue for the rest of his life.

Jefferson in 1804: You seem to think it devolved on the judges to decide on the validity of the sedition law, but nothing in the Constitution has given them a right to decide for the executive, more than to the executive to decide for them. Both magistracies are equally independent in the sphere of action assigned to them. The judges, believing the law constitutional, had a right to pass a sentence of fine and imprisonment, because that power was placed in their hands by the Constitution. But the executive, believing the law to be unconstitutional, was bound to remit the execution of it, because that power has been confided to him by the Constitution. That instrument meant that its coordinate branches should be checks on each other. But the opinion which gives to the judges the right to decide what laws are constitutional, and what not, not only for themselves in their own sphere of action, but for the legislature and executive also in their spheres, would make the judiciary a despotic branch.[81]

Jefferson in 1807: I observe that the case of *Marbury v. Madison* has been cited, and I think it material to stop at the threshold the citing that case as authority and to have it denied to be law.... The Constitution intended that the three great branches of the government should be coordinate and independent of each other. As to acts therefore which are to be done by either, it has given no control to another branch.... I have long wished for a proper occasion to have the gratuitous opinion in *Marbury v. Madison* brought before the public and denounced as not law.[82]

Jefferson in 1819: In denying the right [judges] usurp of exclusively explaining the Constitution I go further than you do, if I understand rightly your quotation from *The Federalist* of an opinion that the judiciary is the last resort in relation to the other departments of the government, but not in relation to the right of the parties to the compact under which the judiciary is derived.... [The Constitution is intended] to establish three departments, coordinate and independent, that they might check and balance one another. It has given according to this opinion, to one of them alone the right to prescribe rules for the government of the others; and to that one too which is unelected by, and independent of, the nation.... The Constitution, on this hypothesis, is a mere thing of wax in the hands of the judiciary which they may twist and shape in to any form they please. . . . My construction of the Constitution is very different from that you quote. It is that each department is truly independent of the others, and has an equal right to decide for itself what is the meaning of the Constitution in the cases submitted to its action; and especially where it is to act ultimately and without appeal.[83]

Jefferson in 1820: To consider the judges as the ultimate arbiters of all constitutional questions [is] a very dangerous doctrine indeed and one which would place us under the despotism of an oligarchy. Our judges are as honest as other men, and not more so. They have, with others, the same passions for party, for power, and the privileges of their corps. . . . Their power [is] the more dangerous as they are in office for life, and not responsible, as the other functionaries are, to the elective control. The Constitution has erected no such single tribunal knowing that, to whatever hands confided, with the corruptions of time and party its members would become despots. It has more wisely made all the departments co-equal and co-sovereign within themselves.[84]

Jefferson in 1823: But the chief justice says "there must be an ultimate arbiter somewhere." True, there must: but does that prove it is either party? The ultimate arbiter is the people of the Union, assembled by their deputies in convention, at the call of Congress, or of two-thirds of the states. Let them decide to which they meant to give an authority claimed by two of their organs. And it has been the peculiar wisdom and felicity of our Constitution to have provided this peaceable appeal where that of other nation[s] is at once to force.[85]

Andrew Jackson on the Limits of the Supreme Court's Authority (1832)

Jefferson was not alone in calling into question—or even rejecting—the power claimed by the Supreme Court in *Marbury v. Madison*. President Andrew Jackson vetoed a bill renewing the charter of the Second Bank of the United States because he believed the institution to be unconstitutional—even though the Supreme Court had already upheld the bank's constitutionality in *McCulloch v. Maryland* (1819).[86] Jackson was decidedly unimpressed (and undeterred) by the Court's earlier constitutional pronouncement.

It is maintained by the advocates of the bank that its constitutionality in all its features ought to be considered as settled by precedent and by the decision of the Supreme Court. To this conclusion I cannot assent. Mere precedent is a dangerous source of authority, and should not be regarded as deciding questions of constitutional power except where the acquiescence of the people and the states can be considered as well settled. So far from this being the case on this subject, an argument against the bank might be based on precedent. One Congress, in 1791, decided in favor of a bank; another, in 1811, decided against it. One Congress, in 1815, decided against a bank; another, in 1816, decided in its favor. Prior to the present Congress, therefore, the precedents drawn from that source were equal. If we resort to the states, the expressions of legislative, judicial, and executive opinions against the bank have been probably to those in its favor as four to one. There is nothing in precedent, therefore, which, if its authority were admitted, ought to weigh in favor of the act before me.

If the opinion of the Supreme Court covered the whole ground of this act, it ought not to control the coordinate authorities of this government. The Congress, the executive, and the Court must each for itself be guided by its own opinion of the Constitution. Each public officer who takes an oath to support the Constitution swears that he will support it as he understands it, and not as it is understood by others. It is as much the duty of the House of Representatives, of the Senate, and of the president to decide upon the constitutionality of any bill or resolution which may be presented to them for passage or approval as it is of the supreme judges when it may be brought before them for judicial decision. The opinion of the judges has no more authority over Congress than the opinion of Congress has over the judges, and on that point the president is independent of both. The authority of the Supreme Court must not, therefore, be permitted to control the Congress or the executive when acting in their legislative capacities, but to have only such influence as the force of their reasoning may deserve.[87]

The Supreme Court as the Ultimate Interpreter of the Constitution (1952, 1958, 1962)

Abraham Lincoln questioned the necessity of abiding by the Supreme Court's decision to strike down the Missouri Compromise as unconstitutional in the *Dred Scott* case. A century later, many Southerners railed against the Supreme Court in the aftermath of *Brown v. Board of Education*. But, for the most part, "We the People" have come to accept the power of the Supreme Court to declare laws to be unconstitutional—which has now happened to almost two hundred acts of Congress, not to mention numerous state statutes.[88] Americans may not like the outcome in any particular case, but few question the authority of the Court to dispense, Olympus-like, its constitutional thunderbolts.

And few Americans (or constitutional theorists) take issue with the Supreme Court's repeated pronouncements that it (the Supreme Court) is the final arbiter on the meaning and applicability of the Constitution. Witness:

> Article VI of the Constitution makes the Constitution the "supreme Law of the Land." In 1803, Chief Justice Marshall, speaking for a unanimous Court, referring to the Constitution as "the fundamental and paramount law of the nation," declared in the notable case of *Marbury v. Madison* that "It is emphatically the province and duty of the judicial department to say what the law is." This decision declared the basic principle that the federal judiciary is supreme in the exposition of the law of the Constitution, and that principle has ever since been respected by this Court and the country as a permanent and indispensable feature of our constitutional system.[89]

> Deciding whether a matter has in any measure been committed by the Constitution to another branch of government, or whether the action of that branch exceeds whatever authority has been committed, is itself a delicate exercise in constitutional interpretation, and is a responsibility of this Court as ultimate interpreter of the Constitution.[90]

> The judicial process [is] the ultimate authority in interpreting the Constitution.[91]

Richard Nixon on the Supreme Court as the Final Constitutional Authority (1974)

The "ultimate authority" of the Supreme Court has been recognized even in extraordinary circumstances. At the height of the Watergate crisis, the Supreme Court ruled (unanimously) in *United States v. Nixon* (1974) that President Richard Nixon was required to turn over his (incriminating) Oval Office tape recordings.[92] Even though complying with the Court's order was to cost him the presidency, Nixon acceded.

> My challenge in the courts to the subpoena of the special prosecutor was based on the belief it was unconstitutionally issued and on my strong desire to protect the principle of presidential confidentiality in a system of separation of powers. While I am, of course, disappointed in the result, I respect and accept the Court's decision, and I have instructed [my attorney] to take whatever measures are necessary to comply with that decision in all respects.[93]

Al Gore on the Supreme Court as the Final Constitutional Authority (2000)

A generation later, at the height of an electoral crisis, the Supreme Court ruled (5–4) in *Bush v. Gore* (2000) that Florida's vote recount process violated the Constitution, effectively making George W. Bush the winner.[94] Even though complying with the Court's order was to cost him the presidency, Al Gore conceded.

> Over the library of one of our great law schools is inscribed the motto: "Not under man, but under God and law." That's the ruling principle of American freedom, the source of our democratic liberties. I've tried to make it my guide throughout this contest, as it has guided America's deliberations of all the complex issues of the past five weeks. Now the US Supreme Court has spoken. Let there be no doubt, while I strongly disagree with the Court's decision, I accept it. I accept the finality of this outcome. . . . And tonight, for the sake of our unity as a people and the strength of our democracy, I offer my concession.[95]

The Limits of Judicial Power—*Federalist No. 78* (1788)

To be sure, there are many limits, formal and practical, on "the judicial Power of the United States" established under Article III of the Constitution. Courts and judges cannot command troops; they do not disburse money; their very membership is determined by the executive and legislative branches; they decide only those cases and controversies brought to them; their structure, jurisdiction, and powers can be regulated by Congress; their statutory interpretations can be overturned by legislatures and their constitutional decisions can be overturned by amendment; and in the final analysis, their decisions achieve respect and obedience largely through popular acceptance. For all such reasons, Hamilton maintained that the federal judiciary was the "least dangerous" branch of the new government.

> Whoever attentively considers the different departments of power must perceive that in a government in which they are separated from each other, the judiciary, from the nature of its functions, will always be the least dangerous to the political rights of the Constitution; because it will be least in a capacity to annoy or injure them. The executive not only dispenses the honors, but holds the sword of the community. The legislature not only commands the purse, but prescribes the rules by which the duties and rights of every citizen are to be regulated. The judiciary, on the contrary, has no influence over either the sword or the purse; no direction either of the strength or of the wealth of the society; and

can take no active resolution whatever. It may truly be said to have neither *force* nor *will*, but merely judgment. . . .

This simple view of the matter suggests several important consequences. It proves incontestably, that the judiciary is beyond comparison the weakest of the three departments of power; that it can never attack with success either of the other two; and that all possible care is requisite to enable it to defend itself against their attacks. It equally proves that though individual oppression may now and then proceed from the courts of justice, the general liberty of the people can never be endangered from that quarter. . . . Liberty can have nothing to fear from the judiciary alone.[96]

Discussion Questions

1. How does the Constitution differ from an ordinary law?
2. If a law passed by Congress (or a state legislature) conflicts with the Constitution, then that law must be declared void by the courts—so decreed Chief Justice Marshall and his colleagues in *Marbury v. Madison*. But *why* should a law passed by a majority of the people's elected representatives "lose" in such a showdown with unelected judges?
3. Is it appropriate for the Supreme Court to exercise judicial review, if that important power is not mentioned in Article III?
4. Should the other branches of government have coequal authority to interpret the Constitution, as "Brutus" and Andrew Jackson suggested? Must the president, or the Congress, or the states, or "We the People" accept the judgments of the Supreme Court as "ultimate" and "supreme"?
5. The Supreme Court does not simply review the actions of the other branches of government; it also reviews its own previous decisions. And, as Linda Greenhouse points out, the Court has reversed itself on at least several hundred occasions.[97] How and why does this occur? Should it give us comfort, or concern, that the Court changes its mind—and thus the meaning of the Constitution—from time to time?
6. Was Hamilton right about the judiciary being the "least dangerous" branch?
7. Was Hamilton right that "the general liberty of the people can never be endangered from that quarter [i.e., the judiciary]?" What about *Dred Scott v. Sandford*? What about *Plessy v. Ferguson*? What about *Buck v. Bell* and *Korematsu v. United States*?
8. What standards should govern the judicial confirmation process?
9. Using some examples from Greenhouse's essay, is the better view that the Supreme Court is (or should be) "above" politics—or instead that the

Supreme Court does (or should) engage in dialogue with the political branches, and does (or should) respond to public sentiment?

Interpreting the Constitution—Primary Sources

Nothing in the Constitution tells a judge (or, for that matter, a president or a member of Congress) how to interpret the Constitution. What tools and resources should judges use? What perspectives should they bring to the effort? Even the briefest of constitutional phrases ("the right of the people to keep and bear Arms"; "nor shall private property be taken for public use") are seemingly open to multiple, equal, and opposite constructions. In recent years, two overarching—and largely contrasting—approaches to constitutional interpretation have been prominently discussed. They are far from the only methods of constitutional adjudication—others include the judge's own values, natural law, neutral principles, reason, tradition, consensus, and predicting progress[98]—and few judges have openly committed to following only one approach at the expense of others. Still, there is much to be gleaned from comparing the doctrine of "originalism"—favored by Justices Antonin Scalia and Neil Gorsuch, for example—with the concept of a "living Constitution" that is "still being perfected"—as propounded by Justice Stephen Breyer among others.

James Madison on Constitutional Interpretation (1824)

Nearly two hundred years ago, James Madison posited an approach to interpreting the Constitution that attempted to identify, first and foremost, the "sense" of what particular words in question meant at the time they were written and approved.

I entirely concur in the propriety of resorting to the sense in which the Constitution was accepted and ratified by the nation. In that sense alone it is the legitimate Constitution. And if that be not the guide in expounding it, there can be no security for a consistent and stable, more than for a faithful exercise of its powers. If the meaning of the text be sought in the changeable meaning of the words composing it, it is evident that the shape and attributes of the government must partake of the changes to which the words and phrases of all living languages are constantly subject. What a metamorphosis would be produced in the code of law if all its ancient phraseology were to be taken in its modern sense. And that the language of our Constitution is already undergoing interpretations unknown to its founders, will I believe appear to all unbiased enquirers into the history of its origin and adoption.[99]

Neil Gorsuch on "Originalism" (2019)

In more recent times, the judicial approach of interpreting constitutional texts by seeking to ascertain their "original" meaning has been attributed to (former) Justice Antonin Scalia, (current) Justice Neil Gorsuch, and (former) Judge Robert Bork, among other adherents. "Originalists" take the position that judges err when they take into account anything other than the text and its original public meaning when interpreting and applying the provisions of the Constitution—rejecting, to cite an example from the Supreme Court's Eighth Amendment jurisprudence, "the evolving standards of decency that mark the progress of a maturing society."[100]

Originalists believe that the Constitution should be read in our time the same way it was read when adopted. . . . The Constitution's meaning was fixed at its ratification and the judge's job is to discern and apply that meaning to the people's cases and controversies. . . .

While the Constitution doesn't speak directly to the proper mode of its interpretation, a careful inspection of its terms and structure shows that originalism is anticipated and fairly commanded by its terms. Start with what the Constitution says about itself: "This Constitution . . . [is] the supreme Law of the Land." Underscoring its status as "supreme Law," the Constitution requires "all . . . judicial Officers . . . [to] be bound by Oath or Affirmation, to support" it. In England, of course, the constitution was largely a set of unwritten customs. Our founders deliberately rejected that model when they decided to adopt a written Constitution. And the Constitution's self-conscious language emphasizing its written-ness, its status as a law, and the judge's duty to abide its terms tell us some important things about the judge's job. It tells us that the Constitution's express limitations on the scope of governmental action are not merely aspirational or customary or advisory. Or at least that they are not supposed to be. It tells us that the Constitution is itself a law, the supreme law. It tells us, too, that only the terms of this written document and nothing else, not any unreferenced norm or custom, constitutes that supreme law. And it tells us that judges are bound to enforce this law before any other. . . .

[The founders assumed] that judges would resolve ambiguity using neutral and well-known rules of interpretation, not their own "living" and "evolving" values. Life tenure makes little sense if judges are supposed to be nothing more than politicians wearing robes. Insulating the federal judiciary from the political process—and exempting judges from the procedural safeguards placed on the exercise of legislative power—cannot be easily explained if you expect them to make value judgments on policy grounds. . . .

Originalism fits with the framers' design. It respects the line between making new law and the far more modest judicial power of interpreting law according to neutral principles. Consider first the goal of originalism: to ascertain the ordinary and public meaning of the Constitution's text at the time of ratification. Notice that originalism can describe a judge's goal in interpretation without reference to any value judgments or subjective preferences. The goal is not to "do justice" as the judge personally may see it, but to enforce the Constitution as written.[101]

Stephen Breyer on "Active Liberty" (2005)

A contrasting approach to judicial decision-making begins with the premise that the language of the Constitution itself is often unspecific, open-ended, and arguably even aspirational. In the view of (former) Justice Felix Frankfurter, "The words of the Constitution . . . are so unrestricted by their intrinsic meaning or by their history or by tradition or by prior decisions that they leave the individual justice free, if indeed they do not compel him, to gather meaning not from reading the Constitution but from reading life."[102] This judicial mindset maintains that the Constitution's meaning should not be rigidly fixed to the priorities and prejudices of the (white, male, wealthy, slaveholding) persons who wrote it centuries ago. Rather, interpretation of the document should purposely reflect, incorporate, and embrace developing societal norms. Justice Stephen Breyer, who has been on the Supreme Court for more than twenty-five years, has written extensively about what he considers the obligation of judges to make decisions relying not only on the text of the Constitution but also on its motivating purposes—what Breyer refers to as the Constitution's core principle of "active liberty."

> A judge's "agreement or disagreement" about the wisdom of a law "has nothing to do with the right of a majority to embody their opinions in law." . . . Even if a judge knows "what the just result should be," that judge "is not to substitute even his juster will" for that of "the people." In a constitutional democracy "a deep-seated conviction on the part of the people . . . is entitled to great respect."
>
> That tradition sees texts as driven by *purposes*. . . . The judge should read constitutional language "as the revelation of the great purposes which were intended to be achieved by the Constitution" itself, a "framework for" and a

"continuing instrument of government." The judge should recognize that the Constitution will apply to "new subject matter . . . with which the framers were not familiar." Thus, the judge . . . should "reconstruct the past solution imaginatively in its setting and project the purposes which inspired it upon the concrete occasions which arise for their decision." Since law is connected to life, judges, in applying a text in light of its purpose, should look to *consequences*, including "contemporary conditions, social, industrial, and political, of the community to be affected." And since "the purpose of construction is the ascertainment of meaning, nothing that is logically relevant should be excluded." . . .

Active liberty, the principle of participatory self-government, was a primary force shaping the system of government that [the Constitution] creates. . . . From a historical perspective, one can reasonably view the Constitution as focusing upon active liberty, both as important in itself and as a partial means to help secure individual (modern) freedom. . . . Our constitutional history has been a quest for workable government, workable democratic government, workable democratic government protective of individual personal liberty. Our central commitment has been to "government of the people, by the people, for the people." . . . This constitutional understanding helps interpret the Constitution—in a way that helps to resolve problems related to *modern* government.[103]

Antonin Scalia Rejects a "Living Constitution" (1997)

Not surprisingly, the proponents of each approach to judicial interpretation of the Constitution find shortcomings and faults in the methodology of their adversaries. Supporters of originalism, for example, insist that judges who believe in a "living Constitution" are simply imposing their own personal, value-laden preferences and constraints on the people's democratic choices, despite never having been elected themselves.

Perhaps the most glaring defect of Living Constitutionalism, next to its incompatibility with the whole antievolutionary purpose of a constitution, is that there is no agreement, and no chance of agreement, upon what is to be the guiding principle of the evolution. . . . What is it that the judge must consult to determine when, and in what direction, evolution has occurred? Is it the will of the majority, discerned from newspapers, radio talk shows, public opinion polls, and chats at the country club? Is it the philosophy of Hume, or of John Rawls, or of John Stuart Mill, or of Aristotle? As soon as the discussion goes beyond the issue of whether the Constitution is static, the evolutionists divide into as many camps as there are individual views of the good, the true, and the beautiful. I think that is inevitably so, which means that evolutionism is simply not a practicable constitutional philosophy. . . .

The American people have been converted to belief in The Living Constitution, a "morphing" document that means, from age to age, what it ought to mean. And with that conversion has inevitably come the new phenomenon of selecting and confirming federal judges, at all levels, on the basis of their views regarding a whole series of proposals for constitutional evolution. If the courts are free to write the Constitution anew, they will, by God, write it the way the majority wants; the appointment and confirmation process will see to that. This, of course, is the end of the Bill of Rights, whose meaning will be committed to the very body it was meant to protect against: the majority. By trying to make the Constitution do everything that needs doing from age to age, we shall have caused it to do nothing at all.[104]

Stephen Breyer Rejects Originalism (2005)

In his turn, Justice Breyer condemns "the unsatisfactory nature" of originalism, calling into question its supposed neutrality, as well as (in his opinion) its counterproductive consequences.

First . . . "originalist" judges cannot appeal to the Framers themselves in support of their interpretive views. The Framers did not say specifically what factors judges should take into account when they interpret statutes or the Constitution. . . . Why would the Framers have preferred (1) a system of interpretation that relies heavily on linguistic canons to (2) a system that seeks more directly to find the intent of the legislators who enacted the statute [or the Constitution]?

Second . . . judges who reject literalism [do not] necessarily open the door to subjectivity. . . . Third, "subjectivity" is a two-edged criticism, which the literalist himself cannot escape. The literalist's tools—language and structure, history and tradition—often fail to provide objective guidance in those truly difficult cases. . . . Fourth, I do not believe that textualist or originalist methods of interpretation are more likely to produce clear, workable legal rules. . . . Fifth, textualist and originalist doctrines may themselves produce seriously harmful consequences—outweighing whatever risks of subjectivity or uncertainty are inherent in other approaches.[105]

Richard Posner Criticizes Originalism (2012)

Richard Posner, a former federal judge and a vocal critic of the originalist approach to constitutional interpretation, further questions the ability of judges ever truly to divine "original" understandings.

> The decisive objection to the quest for original meaning, even when the quest is conducted in good faith, is that judicial historiography rarely dispels ambiguity. Judges are not competent historians. Even real historiography is frequently indeterminate, as real historians acknowledge. To put to a judge a question that he cannot answer is to evoke "motivated thinking," the form of cognitive delusion that consists of credulously accepting the evidence that supports a preconception and of peremptorily rejecting the evidence that contradicts it.[106]

Jack Rakove on the Appeal—and the Peril—of Originalism (1996)

Original Meanings, Stanford professor Jack Rakove's comprehensive historical account of James Madison's political thought and its evolution and application in the context of the Constitutional Convention, grapples with this central question: "What authority should [the Constitution's] 'original meaning' (or 'original intention' or 'understanding') enjoy in its ongoing interpretation?" Rakove advances a nuanced answer.

> Why, then, in a society not otherwise known to defer to past wisdom, do appeals to the original meanings of the Constitution and the original intentions of its framers still play a conspicuous role in our political and legal discourse? The short answer might be that originalist appeals are used for instrumental purposes alone. They offer a form of argument to be employed whenever rhetorical convenience or the imperatives of law-office history and its political variants promise some tangible advantage. . . .
>
> Yet there is another reason why an anti-patriarchal society may find this appeal attractive. For better or worse, the Revolutionary era provides Americans with the one set of consensual political symbols that come closest to universal acceptance. . . . Reaffirming them, even for superficial purposes, may accordingly have some value in preserving "that veneration which time bestows on every thing, and without which perhaps the wisest and freest governments would not possess the requisite stability." So Madison wrote in *Federalist 49.* . . .
>
> [But having] learned so much from the experience of a mere decade of self-government, and having celebrated their own ability to act from "reflection and

choice," would [the framers] not find the idea that later generations could not improve upon their discoveries incredible? How could those who wrote the Constitution possibly understand its meaning better than those who had the experience of observing and participating in its operation? It is one thing to rail against the evils of politically unaccountable judges enlarging constitutional rights beyond the ideas and purposes of their original adopters; another to explain why morally sustainable claims of equality should be held captive to the extraordinary obstacles of Article V or subject to the partial and incomplete understandings of 1789 or 1868.

Yet language, or at least the language constitutive of a polity, cannot be infinitely malleable. If nothing in the text of the Constitution literally constrains or even instructs us to read it as its framers and ratifiers might have done, we may still have soundly Madisonian reasons for attempting to recover its original meanings. But then we also have to ask why we are doing so. Is it because we truly believe that language can only mean now what it meant then? Or is it because the meditations about popular government that we encounter there remain more profound than those that the ordinary politics of our endless democratic present usually sustains?[107]

Excerpts from *Scalia/Ginsburg*: An Opera by Derrick Wang

Fundamental differences about approaches to constitutional decision-making are important; their effects are far-reaching. Which is not to say that they cannot, at the same time, be examined in a more artistic vein. As proof, we turn to the libretto of a modern opera, written by composer Derrick Wang[108] and featuring two singing Supreme Court justices.

SCALIA: This court's so changeable—
           As if it's never, ever known the law!

           The Justices are blind!
           How can they possibly spout this—?
           The Constitution says absolutely nothing about this,

           This right that they've enshrined—
           When did the document sprout this?
           The Framers wrote and signed
           Words that endured without this;
           The Constitution says absolutely nothing about this!

We all know well what the Framers did say,
And (with certain amendments) their wording will stay,
And these words of our Fathers limit us,
For we are unelected,
And thus, when we interpret them,
Rigor is expected.

Oh, Ruth, can you read? You're aware of the text,
Yet so proudly you've failed to derive its true meaning,
And never were so few
Rights made so numerous—
It's almost humorous
What you construe!

Oh, well; oh, well; oh, well; oh, well:
You are the reason I have to rebel!

Though you are all aligned
In your decision to flout this,
The Constitution says absolutely nothing about this—
So, though you have combined,
You would do well not to doubt this:
Since I have not resigned,
I will proceed to shout this:
"The Constitution says absolutely nothing about this!"

* * *

GINSBURG: How many times must I tell you,
Dear Mister Justice Scalia:
You'd spare us such pain
If you'd just entertain
This idea . . . (Then you might relax your rigid posture.)

You are searching in vain for a bright-line solution
To a problem that isn't so easy to solve—
But the beautiful thing about our Constitution
Is that, like our society, it can evolve.

For our Founders, of course, were great men with a vision,
But their culture restricted how far they could go,

So, to us, I believe, they bequeath the decision
To allow certain meanings to flourish—and grow . . .

For the law of the land in that era was grounded
In the notion that justice was just for the few,
But the Founders' assumption was wholly unfounded,
So we've had to subject it to further review.

So we're freeing the people we used to hold captive,
Who deserve to be more than just servants or wives.
If we hadn't been willing to be so adaptive,
Can you honestly say we'd have led better lives?

And we can't wait for slow legislation
To catch up with the lives that we already lead;
We have rights, and they need preservation,
And we have to remember this if we intend to succeed:

Though we won't be afraid of forgiving,
We must not stop in our mission to right every wrong—
Not until We the People and our Constitution are living
In a nation, in a place
That, regardless of station or race,
Is a nation where all of us truly belong!

So, until every person is treated as equal
Well beyond what the Founders initially saw,
Let our past and our present be merely the prequel
To a future enlightened by flexible law!

Alexis de Tocqueville on the Responsibility of Judges (1835)

It might not be surprising to learn that barrels of academic ink have been spilled debating the merits of "originalism" versus a "living Constitution." The point of this brief introduction is not to descend into the scholarly thickets—or to endorse one approach as opposed to another—but rather to state a simple truth: There is no fixed, generally accepted, "correct" way to interpret the Constitution. As a result, judicial opinions issued over the course of the nation's history have not only produced a wide array of substantive results, they have also reflected, at least to some degree, different ideas about the role and the work of a judge. Stepping back somewhat from this spirited debate, it might not be unwise to give the last word to that unusually prescient observer of American politics, Alexis de Tocqueville, who—long before the concepts of "originalism" and "active liberty" were given voice—had this to say about the proper spirit of the judiciary within our constitutional framework.

> The peace, the prosperity, and the very existence of the Union are vested in the hands of the seven judges [the number of Supreme Court justices at the time]. Without their active cooperation the Constitution would be a dead letter: the executive appeals to them for assistance against the encroachments of the legislative powers; the legislature demands their protection from the designs of the executive; they defend the Union from the disobedience of the states, the states from the exaggerated claims of the Union, the public interest against the interests of private citizens, and the conservative spirit of order against the fleeting innovations of democracy. Their power is enormous, but it is clothed in the authority of public opinion. They are the all-powerful guardians of a people which respects law, but they would be impotent against popular neglect or popular contempt. . . . Federal judges must not only be good citizens, and men possessed of that information and integrity which are indispensable to magistrates, but they must be statesmen—politicians, not unread in the signs of the times, not afraid to brave the obstacles which can be subdued, nor slow to turn aside such encroaching elements as may threaten the supremacy of the Union and the obedience which is due to the laws.[109]

Discussion Questions

1. How should a justice or judge resolve questions of constitutional interpretation? What approach should be adopted and what tools should be used: historical research, linguistic analysis, judicial precedent, legislative intent, overarching constitutional principles, contemporary concerns, evolving standards of behavior, popular opinion, etc.?
2. What are the strengths and weaknesses of "originalism"? What are the strengths and weaknesses of the "living Constitution" methodology? Is it a virtue or a defect that there is no single, agreed-upon, "correct" way of interpreting the Constitution?
3. The Constitution is full of provisions that require at least some degree of judicial interpretation: "to declare War"; "necessary and proper"; "The executive Power"; "natural born citizen"; "high Crimes and Misdemeanors"; "freedom of speech"; "the right of the people to keep and bear Arms"; "unreasonable searches and seizures"; "cruel and unusual punishment"; "privileges or Immunities of citizens"; "the equal protection of the laws."

But, arguably, the most ambiguous portion of the Constitution is the Preamble:

> We the People of the United States, in Order to form a more perfect Union, establish Justice, insure domestic Tranquility, provide for the common defence, promote the general Welfare, and secure the Blessings of Liberty to ourselves and our Posterity do ordain and establish this Constitution for the United States of America.

What do those terms mean? Are they enforceable, or merely aspirational? And what if several of these laudable constitutional goals are in conflict with each other?

Additional Primary Source Documents

Primary source document excerpts covering the following topics are located on the website accompanying this book:

Antifederalist Critics of the Constitution

Scholarly and Popular Criticism of the Constitution

Notes

1. 5 U.S. 137 (1803).
2. An act to provide for the more convenient organization of the courts of the United States, ch. 4; 2 Stat. 89 (February 13, 1801), govtrackus.s3.amazonaws.com/legislink/pdf/stat/2/STATUTE-2-Pg89.pdf.
3. An act to repeal certain acts respecting the organization of the courts of the United States, ch. 8, 2 Stat. 132 (March 8, 1802), govtrackus.s3.amazonaws.com/legislink/pdf/stat/2/STATUTE-2-Pg132a.pdf.
4. 5 U.S. 299 (1803).
5. The Federalist No. 78 (Alexander Hamilton) (May 28, 1788), guides.loc.gov/federalist-papers/text-71-80#s-lg-box-wrapper-25493470.
6. 5 U.S. 299.
7. An act to establish circuit courts of appeals and to define and regulate in certain cases the jurisdiction of the courts of the United States, ch. 517, 26 Stat. 826 (March 3, 1891), govtrackus.s3.amazonaws.com/legislink/pdf/stat/26/STATUTE-26-Pg826.pdf.
8. Brown v. Allen, 344 U.S. 443 (1953) (Jackson, J., concurring).

9. 428 U.S. 465 (1976).

10. See, e.g., Coleman v. Thompson, 501 U.S. 722 (1991).

11. 310 U.S. 586 (1940).

12. West Virginia State Bd. of Educ. v. Barnette, 319 U.S. 624 (1943).

13. Bowers v. Hardwick, 478 U.S. 186 (1986).

14. Lawrence v. Texas, 539 U.S. 558 (2003).

15. 554 U.S. 570 (2008).

16. Warren E. Burger, quoted in Nina Totenberg, *From "Fraud" to Individual Right, Where Does the Supreme Court Stand on Guns?* NPR (March 5, 2018), www.npr.org/2018/03/05/590920670/from-fraud-to-individual-right-where-does-the-supreme-court-stand-on-guns.

17. Lawrence v. Texas, 539 U.S. 558 (2003).

18. Dale Carpenter, *Flagrant Conduct: The Story of* Lawrence v. Texas (New York: W.W. Norton, 2012).

19. 384 U.S. 436 (1966).

20. Dickerson v. United States, 530 U.S. 428 (2000).

21. Lee Epstein and Andrew D. Martin, "Does Public Opinion Influence the Supreme Court? Possibly Yes (But We're Not Sure Why)," *University of Pennsylvania Journal of Constitutional Law* 13, no. 2 (2010): 263–82, scholarship.law.upenn.edu/jcl/vol13/iss2/2/.

22. William H. Rehnquist, "Constitutional Law and Public Opinion," *Suffolk University Law Review* 20, no. 4 (1986): 751–69; see also "Required Reading: Judicial Isolation," *New York Times*, April 17, 1986, www.nytimes.com/1986/04/17/us/required-reading.html.

23. Benjamin N. Cardozo, *The Nature of the Judicial Process* (New Haven, CT: Yale University Press, 1921), 168, xroads.virginia.edu/~Hyper/CARDOZO/CarNatIV.html.

24. Osborn v. Bank of the United States, 22 U.S. 738 (1824).

25. Cardozo, *Nature of Judicial Process*, 169–70.

26. West Va. State Bd. of Educ. v. Barnette, 319 U.S. 624 (1943).

27. Roe v. Wade, 410 U.S. 113 (1973).

28. See generally Linda Greenhouse and Reva B. Siegel, "Backlash to the Future? From *Roe* to *Perry*," *UCLA Law Review Discourse* 60 (2013): 240–46, www.uclalawreview.org/pdf/discourse/60-17.pdf.

29. District of Columbia v. Heller, 554 U.S. 570 (2008).

30. United States v. Miller, 307 U.S. 174 (1939).

31. Reva B. Siegel, "Dead or Alive: Originalism as Popular Constitutionalism in *Heller*," *Harvard Law Review* 122 (2008): 191–245, at 222 n.154, digitalcommons.law.yale.edu/cgi/viewcontent.cgi?article = 2132&context = fss_papers.

32. Printz v. United States, 521 U.S. 898 (1997).

33. *Id.* (Thomas, J., concurring).

34. Reed v. Reed, 404 U.S. 71 (1971).

35. Warren Burger to William Brennan, March 7, 1973, supremecourtopinions.wustl.edu/files/opinion_pdfs/1972/71-1694.pdf.

36. United States v. Lopez, 514 U.S. 549 (1995).

37. 411 U.S. 1 (1973).

38. Ronald Reagan, "State of the Union Address" (January 27, 1987), www.presidency. ucsb.edu/documents/address-before-joint-session-congress-the-state-the-union-1.

39. Thurgood Marshall, "The Constitution's Bicentennial: Commemorating the Wrong Document?" *Vanderbilt Law Review* 40, no. 6 (November 1987): 1337–42, scholar-ship.law.vanderbilt.edu/cgi/viewcontent.cgi?article = 2686&context = vlr.

40. Marbury v. Madison, 5 U.S. 137 (1803).

41. McCulloch v. Maryland, 17 U.S. 316 (1819).

42. The Federalist No. 33 (Alexander Hamilton) (January 3, 1788), guides.loc.gov/ federalist-papers/text-31-40#s-lg-box-wrapper-25493387.

43. The Federalist No. 44 (James Madison) (January 25, 1788), guides.loc.gov/federalist-papers/text-41-50#s-lg-box-wrapper-25493408.

44. The Federalist No. 10 (James Madison) (November 22, 1787), guides.loc.gov/ federalist-papers/text-1-10#s-lg-box-wrapper-25493273.

45. The Federalist No. 80 (Alexander Hamilton) (June 21, 1788), guides.loc.gov/ federalist-papers/text-71-80#s-lg-box-wrapper-25493472; The Federalist No. 16 (Alexander Hamilton) (December 4, 1787), guides.loc.gov/federalist-papers/ text-11-20#s-lg-box-wrapper-25493287.

46. George Washington to the President of Congress, September 17, 1787, founders. archives.gov/documents/Washington/04-05-02-0306.

47. The Federalist No. 37 (James Madison) (January 11, 1788), guides.loc.gov/federalist-papers/text-31-40#s-lg-box-wrapper-25493391.

48. Michael J. Klarman, *The Framers' Coup: The Making of the United States Constitution* (New York: Oxford University Press, 2016), 600.

49. Plessy v. Ferguson, 163 U.S. 537 (1896).

50. Brown v. Board of Educ., 347 U.S. 483 (1954).

51. George Washington to Bushrod Washington, November 9, 1787, founders.archives. gov/GEWN-04-05-02-0388.

52. John Jay, "Charge to the Grand Jury of the Circuit Court for the District of New York," April 12, 1790, in *The Documentary History of the Supreme Court of the United States, 1789-1800: Volume Two, The Justices on Circuit, 1790-1794*, ed. Maeva Marcus (New York: Columbia University Press, 1988), 25–30.

53. Sanford Levinson, *Our Undemocratic Constitution: Where the Constitution Goes Wrong (and How We the People Can Correct It)* (New York: Oxford University Press, 2006), 6–9; see also the blog maintained by Cynthia Levison and Sanford Levinson, *Fault Lines in the Constitution*, faultlinesintheconstitution.com/.

54. Larry J. Sabato, *A More Perfect Constitution* (New York: Walker & Co., 2007).

55. John Paul Stevens, *Six Amendments: How and Why We Should Change the Constitution* (New York: Little, Brown, 2014).

56. Louis Michael Seidman, *On Constitutional Disobedience* (New York: Oxford University Press, 2012), 5–7.

57. Thomas Jefferson, *Notes on the State of Virginia* (Philadelphia, 1788), App. No. 2.

58. The Federalist No. 49 (James Madison) (February 5, 1788), guides.loc.gov/federalist-papers/text-41-50#s-lg-box-wrapper-25493416.

59. Thomas Jefferson to James Madison, September 6, 1789, founders.archives.gov/documents/Madison/01-12-02-0248.

60. James Madison to Thomas Jefferson, February 4, 1790, founders.archives.gov/documents/Madison/01-13-02-0020.

61. Thomas Jefferson to Samuel Kercheval, July 12, 1816, founders.archives.gov/documents/Jefferson/03-10-02-0128-0002.

62. The Federalist No. 48 (James Madison) (February 1, 1788), guides.loc.gov/federalist-papers/text-41-50#s-lg-box-wrapper-25493415.

63. The Federalist No. 41 (James Madison) (January 19, 1788), guides.loc.gov/federalist-papers/text-41-50#s-lg-box-wrapper-25493405.

64. The Federalist No. 40 (James Madison) (January 18, 1788), guides.loc.gov/federalist-papers/text-31-40#s-lg-box-wrapper-25493396.

65. Luther Martin (July 21, 1787), in Max Farrand, *The Records of the Federal Convention of 1787* (New Haven, CT: Yale University Press, 1911), 2:76. Note: Farrand's *Records* can be searched online courtesy of the Library of Congress, memory.loc.gov/ammem/amlaw/lwfr.html, Liberty Fund, oll.libertyfund.org/title/farrand-the-records-of-the-federal-convention-of-1787-3vols, and Quill Project at Pembroke College, Oxford, www.quillproject.net/resources/resource_collections/3.

66. George Mason (July 21, 1787), in Farrand, *Records of the Federal Convention*, 2:78.

67. James Madison (July 23, 1787), in Farrand, *Records of the Federal Convention*, 2:93.

68. Oliver Ellsworth, Connecticut Ratifying Convention Debate (January 7, 1788), in Farrand, *Records of the Federal Convention*, 3:240–41.

69. The Federalist No. 78 (Alexander Hamilton) (May 28, 1788), guides.loc.gov/federalist-papers/text-71-80#s-lg-box-wrapper-25493470.

70. *Id.*

71. Brutus, "Essay No. XV," March 20, 1788; in *The Antifederalists*, ed. Cecelia M. Kenyon (Indianapolis, IN: Bobbs-Merrill, 1966), 350–52, 355, www.consource.org/document/brutus-xv-1788-3-20/.

72. An act to establish the Judicial Courts of the United States, ch. 20, 1 Stat. 73 (September 24, 1789), memory.loc.gov/cgi-bin/ampage?collId = llsl&fileName = 001/llsl001.db&recNum = 208.

73. James Wilson et al., Circuit Court for the District of Pennsylvania to the President of the United States, April 18, 1792, quoted in *Hayburn's Case*, 2 U.S. 409 (1792).

74. Hylton v. United States, 3 U.S. 171 (1796).

75. See Maeva Marcus, "Judicial Review in the Early Republic," in *Launching the "Extended Republic": The Federalist Era*, ed. Ronald Hoffman and Peter J. Albert (Charlottesville: University of Virginia Press, 1997); Saikrishna B. Prakash and John C. Yoo, "The Origins of Judicial Review," *University of Chicago Law Review* 70 (2003): 887–982, chicagounbound.uchicago.edu/cgi/viewcontent.cgi?article = 5220&context = uclrev.

76. Marbury v. Madison, 5 U.S. 137 (1803).

77. An act to establish the Judicial Courts of the United States, ch. 20; 1 Stat. 73 (September 24, 1789), memory.loc.gov/cgi-bin/ampage?collId = llsl&fileName = 001/llsl001.db&recNum = 208.

78. Marbury and his lawyer also arguably followed precedent, as the Supreme Court had entertained such writs without voicing any objection on jurisdictional grounds

in several earlier cases. See Susan Low Bloch and Maeva Marcus, "John Marshall's Selective Use of History in *Marbury v. Madison*," *Wisconsin Law Review* 1986, no. 2 (1986): 301–37, repository.law.wisc.edu/s/uwlaw/media/17094.

79. *Marbury*, 5 U.S. 137 (1803).

80. Thomas Jefferson to James Madison, March 15, 1789, founders.archives.gov/documents/Jefferson/01-14-02-0410.

81. Thomas Jefferson to Abigail Adams, September 11, 1804, founders.archives.gov/documents/Jefferson/99-01-02-0348.

82. Thomas Jefferson to George Hay, June 2, 1807, founders.archives.gov/documents/Jefferson/99-01-02-5683.

83. Thomas Jefferson to Spencer Roane, September 6, 1819, founders.archives.gov/documents/Jefferson/03-15-02-0014.

84. Thomas Jefferson to William Jarvis, September 28, 1820, founders.archives.gov/documents/Jefferson/98-01-02-1540.

85. Thomas Jefferson to Justice William Johnson, June 12, 1823, founders.archives.gov/documents/Jefferson/98-01-02-3562.

86. 17 U.S. 316 (1819).

87. Andrew Jackson, "Veto Message Regarding the Bank of the United States," July 10, 1832, millercenter.org/the-presidency/presidential-speeches/july-10-1832-bank-veto.

88. Keith E. Whittington, *Repugnant Laws: Judicial Review of Acts of Congress from the Founding to the Present* (Lawrence: University Press of Kansas, 2019).

89. Cooper v. Aaron, 358 U.S. 1 (1958).

90. Baker v. Carr, 369 U.S. 186 (1962).

91. Youngstown Sheet & Tube Co. v. Sawyer, 343 U.S. 579 (1952) (Frankfurter, J., concurring).

92. United States v. Nixon, 418 U.S. 683 (1974).

93. Richard Nixon, "Statement Announcing Intention to Comply with Supreme Court Decision Requiring Production of Presidential Tape Recordings" (July 24, 1974), www.presidency.ucsb.edu/documents/statement-announcing-intention-comply-with-supreme-court-decision-requiring-production.

94. Bush v. Gore, 531 U.S. 98 (2000).

95. Al Gore, "Text of Gore's Concession Speech," *New York Times*, December 13, 2000, www.nytimes.com/2000/12/13/politics/text-of-goreacutes-concession-speech.html.

96. The Federalist No. 78 (Alexander Hamilton) (May 28, 1788), guides.loc.gov/federalist-papers/text-71-80#s-lg-box-wrapper-25493470.

97. See also Ramos v. Louisiana, 590 U.S. ___ (2020) (Kavanaugh, J., concurring) (identifying thirty of "the Court's most notable and consequential decisions [that] have entailed overruling precedent").

98. John Hart Ely, *Democracy and Distrust: A Theory of Judicial Review* (Cambridge, MA: Harvard University Press, 1980), 43–70. Another set of possible interpretative approaches might include textualism, judicial precedent, pragmatism, moral reasoning, national identity, structuralism, and historical practices; see Brandon J. Murrill, "Modes of Constitutional Interpretation," *Congressional Research Service* (March 15, 2018), www.fas.org/sgp/crs/misc/R45129.pdf.

99. James Madison to Henry Lee, June 25, 1824, founders.archives.gov/documents/Madison/04-03-02-0333.

100. Rhodes v. Chapman, 452 U.S. 337 (1981).

101. Neil M. Gorsuch with Jane Nitze and David Feder, *A Republic, If You Can Keep It* (New York: Crown Forum, 2019), 110, 116–17, 123. Used by permission of Crown Forum, an imprint of Random House, a division of Penguin Random House LLC. All rights reserved.

102. Felix Frankfurter, "The Supreme Court," *Parliamentary Affairs* 3, no. 1 (Winter 1949): 55–71, academic.oup.com/pa/article-abstract/III/1/55/1495984?redirectedFrom = fulltext.

103. Stephen Breyer, *Active Liberty: Interpreting Our Democratic Constitution* (New York: Alfred A. Knopf, 2005), 17–18, 21, 32, 34. Used by permission of Alfred A. Knopf, an imprint of the Knopf Doubleday Publishing Group, a division of Penguin Random House LLC. All rights reserved.

104. Antonin Scalia, *A Matter of Interpretation: Federal Courts and the Law* (Princeton, NJ: Princeton University Press, 1997), 44–45, 47.

105. Breyer, *Active Liberty*, 117–29.

106. Richard A. Posner, "The Incoherence of Antonin Scalia," *The New Republic*, August 24, 2012, newrepublic.com/article/106441/scalia-garner-reading-the-law-textual-originalism.

107. Jack N. Rakove, *Original Meanings: Politics and Ideas in the Making of the Constitution* (New York: Random House, 1996), 366–68. Used by permission of Alfred A. Knopf, an imprint of the Knopf Doubleday Publishing Group, a division of Penguin Random House LLC. All rights reserved.

108. Derrick Wang [composer and librettist], *Scalia/Ginsburg* [opera]. Copyright © 2012–2021 by Derrick Wang. All rights reserved. The excerpt herein is used by permission of Consequent Music on behalf of the author. Please contact info@ derrickwang.com for inquiries regarding the licensing, performance, or other use of this work or any portion thereof. For more information, please visit www. derrickwang.com. The excerpt herein is from an early version of the full libretto published by permission of the author as Derrick Wang, *Scalia/Ginsburg: A (Gentle) Parody of Operatic Proportions*, libretto reprinted in *Columbia Journal of Law and the Arts* 38, no. 2 (2015): 237–92, journals.library.columbia.edu/index.php/ lawandarts/article/view/2119;   www.derrickwang.com/blog/category/read-the-complete-text-of-derrick-wangs-opera-scaliaginsburg. Wang's opera, which he describes as "inspired by the opinions of U.S. Supreme Court Justices Ruth Bader Ginsburg and Antonin Scalia and by the operatic precedent of Händel, Mozart, Verdi, Bizet, Sullivan, Puccini, Strauss, et al.," is accompanied by more than two hundred footnotes, which provide detailed citations to his legal and musical references.

109. Alexis de Tocqueville, *Democracy in America*, Vol. 1 (1835), www.gutenberg.org/ files/815/815-h/815-h.htm.

2

The Founding (1776–91)

Teachers and students of US history devote extensive class time to the meetings in Philadelphia that announced the birth of a new nation and produced its charter of government. The events, personalities, controversies, successes, and failures of the founding era merit this attention. But of equal importance are the shifting attitudes toward authority, forms of government, representation, sovereignty, and rights that characterized this founding era. After Americans declared their separation from Great Britain, who exactly was in charge—who was "sovereign"—in the new nation: the colonies-turned-states, the "United States," or "the People"? Profound transformations in ideas about self-government produced the Constitution of 1787, as amended by the Bill of Rights of 1791. Everything was up for grabs, including the very idea of what exactly a constitution was—or what it was supposed to do—or whom it purported to represent (or exclude)—or which rights it was intended to protect.

Thinking about these foundational concepts permits appreciation of the triumphs and tragedies of the founding years and their continuing relevance. In today's America, no less than in the years following the Revolution, questions abound as to who gets represented and excluded, what rights are to be protected and for whom, and whether liberty and justice exist for all. Concentrating on the Constitution—how it works, whom it serves, and what it means—helps to broaden the focus from the events of the 1770s and 1780s to the present. Concentrating on the opening words of the Constitution permits consideration of the meaning, contours, and limitations of the doctrine of popular sovereignty embedded in the language of "We the People."

Two additional features of the Constitution as originally written cry out for truly meaningful engagement in today's classrooms. The early nation had been handed a constitutional charter that was both fatally flawed and radically incomplete—flawed because of the "wrongs" enshrined in the document and incomplete because of the "rights" it omitted.

The Constitution's treatment of slavery provides abundant opportunities for dialogue about the framers' intentions, evasions, and tragic compromises. Students can explore the antebellum debates about whether the Constitution was a pro- or antislavery document. Why were the words "slave" and "slavery" absent from the Constitution? Abraham Lincoln, among others, maintained that this absence reflected a firm disposition on the part of the Constitution's

With Liberty and Justice for All?. Edited by Steven A. Steinbach, Maeva Marcus, and Robert Cohen, Oxford University Press. © Oxford University Press 2022. DOI: 10.1093/oso/9780197516317.003.0002

authors to prevent slavery's expansion to new territories. But his conclusion was rejected by the slavocracy. Did the three-fifths clause, adopted for purposes of determining a state's representation in the House of Representatives, unjustly reward slaveholders? Was the twenty-year window permitted for continued slave importations a victory for slave traders or a grudging concession that eventually ended US participation in the international slave trade? Was the Constitution's provision for suppressing rebellions included to suppress slave uprisings? Could that same power be used—as abolitionist leader Frederick Douglass predicted—to suppress revolts by lawless slave owners? By examining the text of the Constitution, the Convention debates, *The Federalist*, and the writings of abolitionists, students can engage in the very debates that rent the nation during the decades between Philadelphia and Appomattox—leading to a better appreciation of how a Constitution that purported to secure the "Blessings of Liberty" nonetheless enabled slavery's expansion while simultaneously permitting the abolitionist movement to grow, thus creating a "house divided" that paved the way for secession and civil war.

So enamored are contemporary Americans with the Bill of Rights that it sounds heretical even to pose the question that dominated the ratification debates: Was it necessary for the Constitution to contain a bill of rights? The delegates at Philadelphia unanimously rejected the inclusion of any such listing of liberties. Leading proponents of the Constitution—Alexander Hamilton and James Madison—argued that a bill of rights was not needed, counterproductive, and even dangerous. How could this be? By immersing themselves in the particulars of this dispute, students gain perspective on why credit for the Bill of Rights belongs to the Constitution's Antifederalist critics who prevailed on this issue, and why the transcendent collection of privileges and liberties in the first ten amendments have proved to be even more important and revered in twentieth- and twenty-first-century America.

The Age of the Constitution

Mary Sarah Bilder
Founders Professor at Boston College Law School

What was the Constitution? Today, we know what we mean when we say "the Constitution." We mean a written document that establishes a government in the name of the people, delegates authority to three government branches, delineates powers between national and state governments, guarantees rights, and is interpreted by a judiciary as the supreme law. To us, the Constitution is four pages of parchment in a bulletproof case at the National Archives. We capitalize

Constitution as a proper noun. But that meaning of "constitution" only slowly and tentatively developed in the founding period. "Constitution" continued to mean the frame of government, the history and ideas about authority that gave meaning to that frame, and the people who were included and empowered by the frame. The late eighteenth century was the Age of the Constitution.

In 1776, by contrast, no one would have thought "Constitution" meant one particular written document. By 1791, some people were beginning to think that "constitution" meant a specific written document, drafted in 1787 and ratified in 1788. But—and this is a big but—important aspects of our understanding of American constitutionalism remained far in the future. The constitution emerged as a new type of legal document with the rules and conventions yet to be established. What did English people on the eve of the Revolution mean when they spoke of their constitution? What did they mean after the Revolution? Why do historians sometimes capitalize Constitution and other times do not? Is the American Constitution the written document drafted in 1787, or is it that document with its amendments, or is it the entire constitutional system?

Many excellent analyses exist of the period between independence and the ratification of the first ten amendments to the Constitution. One approach focuses on the people. In these versions, brilliant but imperfect men invent a new form of government in one brief summer. The men may be "founding fathers," or "founders," or "framers." Historians prefer "framers" to "founders" because the United States was not founded in 1776 by a small group of men but rather framed, or more precisely reframed, under altered structures of government. But even in focusing on framers, the narrative approach often privileges the men in the room and excludes from view the people whom they politically represented and those whose lives they affected. The people who literally drafted the words were all men, all white, all property owners of some sort. Some owned people; indeed, some owned a great many people, and they avoided acknowledging that they owned people by calling the enslaved people "slaves." All the drafters had the luxury of knowing they would not be owned and that, as men, their marriages did not erase their legal status. But the constitution survived because it spoke in a vocabulary drawn from many Americans and claimed authority derived from all the people. A way to expand the lens is to think of a "framing generation," which recognizes the distance between the drafters and our modern political community. A "framing generation" emphasizes that the ideas underlying the constitution arose from, were discussed and debated by, and intended for a larger community.

People do not live their lives the way historians think of periodization. Thus, to define a period is to make an argument about a crucial development— here, American constitutionalism. The year 1776, in which the Declaration of Independence and first state constitutions were written, focuses on the struggle to define governance structures, the problem of authority and sovereignty, and boundaries of the political community. The year 1791 represents the transition to the ordinary operation of the new government. The First Congress (1789–91) came to an end, and with it came the first peaceful transition pursuant to the Constitution as members changed in the House of Representatives. Federal judicial review began with the first case heard by the Supreme Court, *West v. Barnes* (1791).[1] And 1791 marked the ratification of ten of the twelve proposed amendments to the Constitution. The year would also be the last moment before the rise of two political parties—the Federalists and the Democratic-Republicans—altered government political processes. Only at the end of this period does the document that established a constitution begin to become "the" Constitution.

The People: Reform, Revolution, Republic

The American story fits within a larger transatlantic story in which the late eighteenth century was the Age of the Constitution. It was a moment when political reformers across the British Empire came to believe that their constitution needed to be reformed. Sometimes they spoke in the language of reform—reforming the constitution to ensure that the people were more perfectly represented; sometimes they spoke in the language of restoration—restoring the ancient constitution in which the people had been more perfectly represented. They shared a belief that legitimate government arose from the people. To these reformers, this idea that government arose from the people and was for the people was not simply a theoretical claim; it was an idea by which one could criticize the existing constitution and the foundational principle for a reconstructed constitution.

In 1776, Thomas Paine wrote in *Common Sense* that the American colonies had a "constitution without a name."[2] For most of the eighteenth century, "constitution" did not refer to a specific document. The term encompassed laws, principles, customs, and political institutions. It alluded to an organic body politic that was imagined as existing over time. Historians sometimes call this idea the small-c constitution, but at the time, spelling conventions meant that it was usually capitalized. The British Constitution continues today to represent this conception of a constitution.

Under the British Empire, this constitution expanded to accommodate colonies. This transatlantic constitution accepted the reality of dual authorities, England and the colony. Specific written instruments called charters authorized the colonies to legislate for themselves within the boundaries set by two principles: repugnancy and divergence. Colonial law could not be repugnant (i.e., contrary) to the laws of England. But because law and government should relate to the people and place, colonial laws could diverge for local circumstance. They had to be only "as near" or "agreeable" to English laws as made sense given the nature and constitution of the people and place.

London authorities enforced this transatlantic constitution by various mechanisms. The "negative" required that colonial laws be sent to the Privy Council where they would be reviewed and possibly disallowed. (Rhode Island and Connecticut had charters that exempted them from this requirement.) Cases from colonial courts could be appealed to and reviewed by the Privy Council. The Crown appointed most colonial governors and gave detailed instructions about governance. In many colonies, the Crown-appointed governor also appointed judges. This constitution contained the types of dual authorities that came to embody modern federalism. And this constitution also included an idea of judging legislation against a boundary. Both ideas became critical to our modern notion of the Constitution.

Although logically this dual-authority structure violated the principle of an absolute sovereign authority in the Crown, colonial and English officials tried to avoid creating irreconcilable conflict. The Privy Council presumed its ultimate authority while acknowledging the reality of colonial governance. The colonial legislatures operated by self-governance while acknowledging the theoretical authority of the Crown, Privy Council, and royal governors. For a century and a half that constitution worked across the vast distance of the Atlantic Ocean.

During the 1770s, people in the American colonies, in London, in Ireland, and in Scotland began to feel that the British Constitution should be more representative of "the people." Government was a power delegated from the people for the people. What precisely "the people" meant, particularly in terms of actual political participation, differed among reformers. Because British constitutional government limited political participation and officeholding in England to a very small group, mostly defined by landed property and membership in the Church of England, a rather extensive consensus arose on expanding representation of the people without much thought having to be given as to whether religion, gender, race, or class would still remain relevant. Reformers often used words like "man" and "mankind" in their gender-neutral sense, and so from our perspective it is difficult to be certain of the boundaries of their ideal political community.

The American Revolution arose from this larger Age of the Constitution as a means of achieving a better and more representative constitution. Independence was not the initial goal of American political reform. For a decade before 1776, American politicians and writers advocated an improved constitution in which the people in the colonies would be directly represented. Revolution was a means to achieve a more representative constitution.

Revolution necessitated the framing of a new constitution. In fact, the first steps toward a new constitutional structure, a Congress, predated the revolution. In 1774, for two months a "Continental Congress" of eleven colonies and the three lower counties of the Delaware, self-described subjects of his Majesty in Great Britain, met in Philadelphia. In 1775–76, a Congress again met and drafted and approved the Declaration and drafted a governance structure, later known as the Articles of Confederation. In turn, in 1787, the Articles were revised into a radically modified structure as a new constitution and sent by Congress for ratification by the states. Thus Congress formed a fundamental national continuity in the name of self-governance by the people.

Congress's continuity had two important consequences. First, a national decision-making body existed throughout the pre-Revolution, Revolution, and post-Revolution period. There was no power vacuum; there was no confusion about pretenders or coups. The continued existence of Congress gave Americans the luxury of trying to improve and legitimize a constitutional structure, not to impose a new one.

Second, the voting practice within Congress had lasting consequences. In the Continental Congress, the practice arose of each delegation casting a single vote. The political community represented by that vote was less than clear. Initially, there were colonies and the three Delaware counties. In the Confederation Congress, each "state" was given a vote and Canada was also offered an automatic in. The vote represented something like a "state," but not a predefined political entity. Vermont, despite self-authorizing itself as a state by 1777, was not admitted as an official state until March 1791. In Philadelphia, in 1787, this practice of each state having one vote in Congress (equal state suffrage) would prove too politically difficult to alter.

Although the Age of the Constitution did not begin with the intention of ending monarchy, in the United States that proved to be the result. The abandonment of a monarchical government was signaled by the key term "republic." The Constitution uses the term "republican form of government." The term "republic" had multiple meanings, building on teachings about ancient classical republics and critiques of British monarchical constitutionalism. At a theoretical level, monarchy imagined authority flowing from God to the monarch, whose subjects were the people. Republican thought instead grounded legitimacy and authority in "the people." There were no subjects. Thus in *Common Sense*, Paine declared: "For as in absolute governments the King is law, so in free countries the law ought to be King; and there ought to be no other."[3]

As a key term, "republic" meant many things to the framing generation. Significant historical writing, particularly surrounding the bicentennial in 1976, explored the meaning of "republicanism." It represented a constellation of beliefs, some of which, not surprisingly, were inconsistent and even hypo-critical. Republican thought often used words like "slavery" as applied to the subordinate status of the colonists in the British Empire without applying the same critique to the race-based slavery in the colonies. Republican thought demanded "liberty" and "equality" without insisting on the application of those concepts beyond propertied white men.

Sovereignty: People, Colonies, States, Congress, United States

The Age of the Constitution recast sovereignty. The root of the word "sovereignty" is "sovereign"—originally meaning above or supreme—and came to be synony-mous with the monarch. Constitutional reform imagining the people as sover-eign and delegating power to government was the critical element of American constitutionalism. The transformation began in 1766 when the dual authorities that characterized the colonial transatlantic constitution came to an abrupt halt. That year, Parliament passed the Declaratory Act, stating that "in all cases what-soever" Parliament could make laws binding on the colonies.[4] The Declaratory Act represented a dramatic shift in the transatlantic relationship between Great Britain and the American colonies by repudiating colonial authority and reconceptualizing the colonies through the lens of subordination and depend-ence. Almost every word denied that people in the colonies had equal political representation to those in England. Over the next decade, the people in the colo-nies debated the fundamental question: who represented the people of America?

A decade later, the Declaration of Independence spoke of "one people" as-suming "the separate and equal station." The "former Systems of Government" were to be altered. The long enumeration of complaints was made against the monarch, "King of Great Britain." In the place of the monarch was a new au-thority: Congress. On the engrossed original parchment, although the docu-ment was signed by the delegations from north to south as they sat in Congress, the names of the states were not included. The first printing followed suit, be-ginning with "In Congress, July 4, 1776" and in large letters twice stated, "UNITED STATES OF AMERICA." The "United Colonies" were "FREE AND INDEPENDENT STATES," but "state" meant a political body, not a legal cat-egory. "State" was a word to deny and replace "colony." The sole signature was that of "John Hancock" who signed "By Order and in behalf of the Congress." Mary Katherine Goddard, the Baltimore printer, above the bold printing of her own name, produced the first version which arranged the signatures under state labels. By altering the title to the "Thirteen United States of America," her version suggested a sovereignty arising from each state.

In 1776, Thomas Paine proposed a "Continental Charter, or Charter of the United Colonies." In mid-June, the Continental Congress created a committee, led by John Dickinson, to draft "the form of confederation to be entered into between these colonies."[5] The draft was controversial and not sent to the states until November 1777. Disagreements existed over the nature of representation in a unicameral Congress (proposed equal state suffrage or representation based on population), the distribution of taxation (proposed inhabitants of "every age, sex, and quality" or only "white inhabitants"), and the authority to draw state boundaries (proposed congressional authority or state authority over western lands under charters to the "South Sea").[6] Only in the spring of 1781 was the document ratified.

The Articles[7] foregrounded the political entity of the "state" in a "firm league of friendship." In Congress, each state retained an equal vote with important matters requiring nine states to agree. Executive power rested with a committee of Congress, whose chair was "president." There was no separate judiciary. Amending the Articles required unanimous consent. Revenue was to be supplied to the treasury by the states based on the "proportion to the value of all land." Military requisitions were based on the "number of white inhabitants." Canada was given an automatic right of entry, presumably as a state. Although the "United States in Congress assembled" was described as the authority, Congress had no coercive power over the states. The states agreed to "abide" by the determinations of Congress and ensure that the "union shall be perpetual." The Articles contained a central tension between the "sovereignty, freedom and independence" retained by the states unless expressly delegated and the overall insistence on a union as the United States.

As the "federal constitution," the Articles faced persistent operational difficulties arising from the states' divergent interests. The absence of a financing mechanism made acquiring foreign credit difficult and complicated efforts to pay soldiers. In 1783, Congress sought to solve the lack of revenue. A new proposal shifted the apportionment of revenue from land to population. This shift raised the issue of how to count enslaved people. James Madison proposed a three-fifths ratio: revenue contributions would be calculated by equating five enslaved persons to three free persons. This calculation became known as the federal ratio. The revenue plan failed as a constitutional amendment but was adopted as legislation in 1786. The three-fifths ratio revealed Congress's willingness to distinguish free and enslaved inhabitants.

In 1787, the drafted document again reshuffled sovereignty. A bicameral Congress reduced the direct power of the states as political entities and increased the power of the people. Congress's power was diminished by the creation of two coequal branches: an executive and a judiciary. National power expanded with the abandonment of explicit enumeration, the inclusion of the broad term "general welfare," and the addition of the necessary and proper clause. The states appeared as distinct political entities, permitted to join the national union only under delineated rules. A supremacy clause placed this new constitutional government above the United States and state officers. As the preamble insisted, the sovereignty of this Constitution lay in the people. "We the People"—"ourselves and our posterity"—reflected the overarching theory that the Constitution was by and for the people.

State Constitutions: Charters, Frames of Government, Declarations of Rights

Beginning in 1776, colonial political leaders reimagined their governmental structures in dialogue with Congress. In January, New Hampshire was "reduced to the necessity of establishing A FORM OF GOVERNMENT" after loyalists fled.[8] The cursory document was nonetheless technically the first state constitution. In May, Congress advised the colonies to form new governments. By the summer of 1777, eleven states had drafted documents establishing new constitutions of government. Massachusetts wrote two documents—the first one in 1778 failed to be approved by the towns; the second in 1780 proved a powerful model. Vermont, not yet recognized as a state, wrote one in 1777 and again in 1786. These documents described their authority as coming from the people.

The importance of recasting American government as the delegated authority of the people explains why two colonies did not write new documents. Rhode Island and Connecticut held charters granted by the Crown in the 1660s. Under these charters, colonial voters elected the legislature, and the legislature appointed the governor and judges. Both states deleted references to the Crown but otherwise left the charters intact. As far as the two states were concerned, the constitutions under which they had governed for over a century embodied representation by the people. Only in 1818 (Connecticut) and 1842 (Rhode Island) did written constitutions become so ubiquitous that the states replaced the charters with constitutions.

Although historical collections place "Constitution" as the title of these state documents, contemporary printings reveal that "constitution" meant a plan of government. In 1780, Massachusetts described a "Constitution or Frame of Government." The constitution usually followed a pattern used in Virginia in 1776: a Declaration of Rights of Inhabitants followed by a Plan or Frame of Government. Prefatory material—a flowery preface or words similar to the Declaration of Independence—also often appeared.

These frames of government focused on legislatures. Bicameral models dominated with only Pennsylvania and Georgia adopting unicameral legislatures.

Legislatures selected the governors (or presidents) in more than half the states; in the remaining ones, voters did so. Judges rarely occupied a coequal branch and were appointed in diverse ways. Of these constitutions, the 1780 Massachusetts constitution came closest to three separated powers.

These documents did not worry about persuasively claiming supreme legal authority. Eight were written by the legislatures. A few simply declared their fundamentality over ordinary statute law. Only with the rejected 1778 Massachusetts constitution did the ratification model develop. The 1780 process created the illusion that the sovereignty in the people was delegated to the constitution: a convention was called of specially selected delegates, and the resulting document was reviewed by the towns. Ironically, ratification produced extensive debate but, as long as the voters approved, did not require actual alteration. Indeed, few of these documents addressed amendment procedures, two of which gave that power to the legislature. As written constitutions became common, ratification and amendment processes became specific.

Rights proved a difficult problem in the early constitutions. No one agreed on where they came from, which ones were needed, what they were good for, and whether and how they were to be enforced. The Virginia decision to place the Declaration of Rights before the frame of government was a powerful model, again placing the people above the state. Yet the Declaration of Rights declared large principles of political theory rather than judicially enforced guarantees. The first half focused on political processes and the principles underlying them. The verb "ought" appeared repeatedly rather than "shall." The term "right" appeared most often in conjunction with criminal protections. Most other issues were stated as propositions: "that the freedom of the press is one of the great bulwarks of liberty, and can never be restrained but by despotic governments."[9]

Six states (and Vermont) wrote documents with separate bills of rights. Four did not include a separate declaration of rights (New Hampshire, South Carolina, New Jersey, and New York). A wide diversity of items were listed and many seemingly obvious rights omitted. At the core, however, the rights associated with the Magna Carta repeatedly appeared—due process and jury trial in criminal cases—and rights relating to religious conscience or free exercise. Two rights relating to political disagreement also recurred, relating to the press and the freedom to petition. Massachusetts and New Hampshire included language that would be interpreted by state courts as abolishing slavery: "all men are born free and equal"; the Virginia constitution had similar language but drafters imagined it unenforceable. Vermont—then not yet a state—explicitly abolished slavery.

The experience of using written documents to create state constitutions emphasized the inherent difficulties. There was no perfect document; a piece of paper could not solve every problem. This insight appeared in James Madison's most important ratification essay, *Federalist No. 37*.[10] Referring to the federal Constitution of 1787, Madison explained that the document was not written by "an ingenious theorist" planning "in his closet or his imagination." The Convention tried to "avoid the errors suggested by the past experience" and provide a mode of "rectifying their own errors, as future experience may unfold them." There was an "unavoidable inaccuracy" in the use of terms because they had required new concepts. No document could perfectly "discriminate and define" the powers or branches. Madison cautioned against assuming "artificial structure and regular symmetry." At the time, in 1787, Madison had not even seen what would turn out to become a shift in the very understanding of "Constitution" itself: in 1787, he referred to the Convention's plan to revise the former "federal Constitution"—only years, possibly decades, later did he revise this description of the pre-1787 United States to refer to it as only "the federal system of Government," implicitly without a Constitution.[11]

Persons: Slavery, People of Color, Women, Citizens

The Constitution refers repeatedly to a category it describes as "Person." The word appears more than twenty times. Far less often, but also importantly, the Constitution refers to "Citizen." To be a president, senator, or representative, one must be a Person and a Citizen. But who is a "Person"? And who is a "Citizen"? These two words are at the center of over two centuries of debate about the Constitution's relationship to slavery, to people of color, to women, to members of the Indian Nations, and to those people who live in the United States without the security of formal documentation.

Slavery and the status of people of color under the Constitution is one of the most debated topics in the framing period. In the nineteenth century, abolitionists divided over whether the Constitution was a bargain with slavery which emboldened a white supremacist slave power, or should be interpreted, in the words of Frederick Douglass, as a "glorious liberty document" which should be used to abolish slavery and ensure the full and equal citizenship of people of color.

As a system of government, the Constitution seemingly accepted the existence of slavery and empowered those who wanted it to expand. Greater political power was allocated to white representatives from slave states and that imbalance meant that national power tilted in favor of protecting and extending slavery. Soon after the Convention, James Madison began to insist on a narrative in which there had been an inevitable compromise to allow slavery so that South Carolina and Georgia delegates would remain. As a Virginia slaveholder who did not free a single person at his death, Madison's allocation of blame might be viewed with some suspicion. This compromise narrative has a pernicious legacy, absolving the various delegates from a decision they made to consider the claims of people of color as less worthy than those of white Americans and also suggesting that the nation had no choice.

And yet, at the same time, the document never explicitly referred to slaves or slavery. Interpreted against the backdrop of abolition or intention of abolition in various states, this omission was significant. Read literally, the Constitution did not recognize *slave* as a category. The document empowered the national government to end the slave trade and, theoretically, to abolish slavery. Each of us will reach a different conclusion as to whether these silences were grudging concessions designed to disguise a proslavery government from the people or reflected an idealistic hope that if the document described only persons, then the United States could be forced to guarantee that reality.

The framing generation was well aware of the tension between the Revolution's rhetoric of liberty and equality and the presence of legalized slavery. People of color advocated publicly and privately for freedom, submitted petitions, and seized opportunities to deny enslaved categorization. Efforts were made to free people of color who had fought in the war. Some individual "owners" took legal steps to manumit people. In 1780, Pennsylvania passed an act for the gradual abolition of slavery: it freed no living person and applied only to children born to enslaved people after the act and consigned them to serve as indentured servants until age twenty-eight. In 1784, Rhode Island and Connecticut adopted similar acts. Slavery was legally abolished by the Vermont constitution. Massachusetts appeared to have done so by 1783 through judicial interpretation of the clause "all men are born free and equal." New Hampshire had a similar clause. Even in Virginia, a 1782 act permitted the private manumission of enslaved people, although not until 1791 was a person actually manumitted.

But most of the people enslaved in the United States lived in Virginia, which held nearly half of the enslaved population. The 1790 census showed 292,627 persons denoted as "slaves." Maryland, South Carolina, and North Carolina each had slightly more than 100,000 persons so listed. Although Georgia held comparatively fewer people in slavery (nearly 30,000), they represented almost 35 percent of the state's population. Conceptions of the political community based on racist ideas circulated. Perhaps most prominently, Thomas Jefferson proposed racialist distinctions and inevitable hierarchy between Black and white persons in *Notes on the State of Virginia*. Indeed, while the Convention met in Philadelphia, one magazine published the Marquis de Chastellux's plan for abolishing slavery with his suggestion that Black men should be deported to Africa while Black women would marry white men so that over time their descendants would become white.

For people of color, the rights and legal privileges of free status were uncertain and differed across the states. Their status, like that of women, was not yet clearly subordinate as a matter of constitutional law. Free people of color argued for their inclusion in political life. But after 1791, federal statutes began to create a white male world of constitutional participation. In May 1792, the new federal militia act established federal standards for local militias by stating that "each and every free able-bodied white male citizen" between eighteen and forty-five was to be enrolled.[12]

Slavery intertwined with political power in the drafting of the 1787 constitution. Who were the people? Who counted for proportional representation? Alexander Hamilton wanted "the number of free inhabitants." Instead, initially the Convention used an "equitable ratio of representation" for the first branch: "the whole number of white and other free citizens and inhabitants of every age, sex, and condition including those bound to servitude for a term of years, and three fifths of all other persons not comprehended in the foregoing description, except Indians, not paying taxes in each State."[13] The explicit language alluded to women and people of color considered citizens with political privileges. "Citizens" and "inhabitants" and "persons" might or might not be different categories. "Indians, not paying taxes" acknowledged the considerable presence of members of Indian Nations. But the final version deleted "white," "citizens," "inhabitants," "age," and "sex," leaving a distinction between "free Persons" and "all other Persons."

The Convention reached two controversial conclusions relating to slavery together in mid-July. One protected slavery by including the three-fifths clause in representation and ensured that slaveholding states received representatives for that interest; the other by ensuring that the states were represented in one house of Congress. The dynamic that linked the two was not inevitable but the result of the fight over whether both houses would be based on proportional representation. Proportional representation plus the three-fifths clause in the House and Senate offered Virginia future political dominance and any state with slavery greater voting power. James Madison raised fears about the future status of slavery to try to secure this result through a coalition between the three large states and the three most Southern states. Instead, he clarified a sectional line of division. Madison even proposed that the number of House members be calculated based on free inhabitants, and the Senators—to ensure the "guardianship of the rights of property"—based on population "counting the slaves as free."[14] The Senate would favor the South; the House, the North; and Congress would be unable to abolish slavery. Although Madison's proposal failed, the three-fifths clause nonetheless built the national government on a foundation of enslavement.

Two other provisions also embedded slavery in the constitutional body politic. Antislavery activism focused on the slave trade. With the exception of three Southern states (Georgia, South Carolina, and North Carolina), the states had banned the foreign slave trade. The Convention presumed the foreign slave trade would end but barred abolishing it before 1808. Moreover, the document barred any amendment altering this section. The twenty-year extension resulted in approximately one hundred thousand additional people enslaved.

Equally significantly, in the fugitive slave clause, a person "held to service or labour" who escaped to a free state was not to be discharged by the free state but "delivered up." This clause mirrored a clause in the recently passed Northwest Ordinance. The Ordinance abolished slavery but simultaneously prevented the territory from becoming a haven for freedom by requiring people of color to be returned rather than freed. The clause implicitly accepted slavery as a legitimate argument rather than insisting that people were born free and equal.

Because the Constitution did not use the word "slave" but "persons," as soon as the document appeared people began to argue about the future of slavery. In early 1790, petitions from Quakers and from Benjamin Franklin and the Pennsylvania Society for Promoting the Abolition of Slavery forced Congress to debate congressional power to emancipate. The committee report concluded that Congress was "restrained from interfering in the emancipation of slaves" by "a fair construction of the Constitution."[15] That is, the Constitution was not explicit as to slavery but required interpretation.

And the Constitution did not define the rights and privileges of "Persons." Thus began a larger discussion about who would be included in the constitutional state. Who was a "Person" for the purposes of political participation? After the Revolution, some state constitutions referred to the people permitted to vote using broad language ("all inhabitants" or "freeholders"), while other states described "male inhabitants" or "male white inhabitants." States included additional age, property, or residency restrictions. In New Jersey, the state constitution permitted women and people of color to vote on the same terms as white men. Gradually, state constitutions and laws would move to explicitly enfranchise white men regardless of property and gradually disenfranchise women and people of color. With respect to tribal members of the many Indian Nations, the Constitution was largely silent. Congressional representation was determined by excluding "Indians not taxed," but the words offered no hint of the myriad possible relationships of tribal, state, and national citizenship. Finally, because many of the drafters of the Constitution and significant political leaders were themselves immigrants, the Constitution ensured that every office other than the president could be held by a person not born in the United States.

Rights: Enumeration, Incorporation, Amendments

We think of rights in terms of the Bill of Rights, the first ten amendments to the Constitution. Our focus on this addition leads us to overlook that the Constitution of 1787 contained rights. The document included rights associated with the Magna Carta: trial by jury in criminal cases and the right of habeas corpus. Congressional members were protected from arrest in attending Congress and could not be questioned about debates. Legislative action against the individual was barred with provisions to prevent bills of attainder, ex post facto laws, and corruption of blood for treason. No titles of nobility were permitted. Religious tests for offices were prohibited. And affirmation was protected, ensuring that non-oath takers could serve in government. In sum, the document protected against the most grievous aspects of English political culture. The document also guaranteed to all citizens an unspecified body of state "privileges and immunities."

The document, however, contained no explicit enumeration of rights. In the waning days of the Convention, a motion was made for a committee to write a bill of rights. That motion lost unanimously. In part, the motion may have seemed an effort to undermine the document. For others, the rationale for bills of rights— that they represented the people's insistence on rights against the Crown—made no sense where power was delegated from the people. Moreover, on September 12, when the motion arose, delegates wanted to be done.

The absence of a bill of rights became a persistent complaint among opponents of the Constitution during the ratification process. Although the most common complaint involved the taxing structure, the absence of a bill of rights struck a chord with the Federalist defenders. Some initially attempted to argue that the government was one of only enumerated powers and could not infringe on rights. But as opponents were quick to point out, the general welfare clause, the necessary and proper clause, and discretionary power with respect to means suggested broad unenumerated powers. The defenders fell back on arguing that bills of rights were "parchment barriers" that rarely proved protective.[16]

As the states ratified the Constitution, their conventions sent suggestions for amendments to Congress. Some suggestions were so significant as to gut the Constitution. Others recommended the addition of rights. These suggestions began to alter the mind of James Madison. Madison had never "thought the omission a material defect." Nonetheless, in correspondence with Thomas Jefferson, Madison decided rights could become "incorporated with the national sentiment" and become "fundamental maxims of free Government."[17] Jefferson added that it would provide a "legal check" for the judiciary.[18] Madison also believed that rights would help persuade North Carolina and Rhode Island finally to ratify and join the union.

In June 1789, Madison offered a lengthy list of amendments. His draft placed each amendment where it belonged in the text of the 1787 document. Some amendments were declaratory (e.g., power derived from the people); others altered congressional representation and compensation. Congressional powers were to be limited by a series of rights held by "the people." Criminal protections were given to the individual "person" or "the accused." Madison also added that "no state shall violate the equal rights of conscience, or the freedom of the press, or the trial by jury in criminal cases." He believed "independent tribunals of justice" would consider themselves "in a peculiar manner the guardians of those rights."[19] Worrying that the enumeration of rights would suggest that unenumerated rights were left insecure, Madison drafted language that insisted on the "just importance of other rights retained by the people."[20]

Over the summer, Congress debated and altered Madison's proposal. The language was repeatedly simplified and made less specific. The prohibitions on the states were abandoned. Most significant, Madison's belief that the document should be revised was voted down. Roger Sherman successfully argued that the amendments should be made supplemental to the document—that is, tacked on at the end. With this 1789 decision, the original 1787 document began to acquire special status.

By the time Congress sent the amendments to the states for ratification, they had been reduced to twelve amendments. The first and second amendments related to Congress: the first altering the allocation of representatives and the second barring Congress from altering compensation until after an election. The third amendment began, "Congress shall make no law. . . ." The eleventh amendment stated that the enumeration "shall not be construed to deny or disparage others retained by the people." By 1791, ten amendments were ratified. The first two did not receive sufficient approval, although compensation would be technically ratified in 1992 as the Twenty-seventh Amendment.

Ratification of the amendments produced the text that we would come to call "the Constitution." Judicial review was not mentioned, although the framers understood the Supreme Court—created in 1789 with six justices—would review legislation for conformity to the Constitution. The importance of that review in interpreting the Constitution lay in the future.

We the People

In January 1792, an anonymous essay appeared in the *National Gazette*. The title was "Charters," the author was the future so-called Father of the Constitution, James Madison. Madison described American "instruments" as "constitutional charters." They were "charters of power granted by liberty" and represented a "revolution in the practice of the world." These governments, "delineated in the *great charters*," derived from the "legitimate authority of the people" instead of the usurped power of kings.[21] Never once did Madison call the instrument "the Constitution."

Even the Convention had not thought of the Constitution in the way that we understand it. The Convention sent a letter to Congress, along with the document.[22] That letter is the only official explanation and appeared with the Constitution in contemporary printings. Throughout the deliberations, the Convention kept an unpublished record of formal motions and decisions. Some delegates kept sporadic private notes. James Madison kept the most complete set of notes, likely composed several times a week from rough notes during the session. His notes, however, are not a transcript but the topics and debates that interested him. His own speeches as he recalled them reflect hindsight. And the final section of the notes after the third week of August was likely completed by Madison only after the fall of 1789 with the aid of the formal record and the recognition of a growing interest in the text of the Constitution.

At the end of September 1787, the "Constitution" was still a constitution—a frame of government. The Convention's letter referred to "that Constitution," not "the" Constitution. The purposes of that Constitution were broad. The "consolidation of our Union" was to ensure "prosperity, felicity, safety, and perhaps our national existence" and secure the country's "freedom and happiness."[23] These purposes echoed the first words of the document, the Preamble.

The Preamble embodied the Age of the Constitution. The iconic first words, "We the People of the United States," insisted on the sovereignty of the people. The people's purpose was to form "a more perfect Union." To that end, the people established justice, promoted the general welfare, and secured the "Blessings of Liberty," as well as ensuring domestic tranquility and common defense. The object was "ourselves and our Posterity"—the People broadly conceived, existing over time. And what did they ordain and establish? "This Constitution"—a frame of government written on a piece of paper. This Constitution eventually became the Constitution.

Constitutional Provisions Regarding Slavery—Primary Sources

When the delegates met in Philadelphia to fashion the Constitution, they gave almost no consideration to restricting slavery, much less to abolishing it. No doubt this was partially explained by the fact that many of the delegates (not quite half) owned slaves themselves. But beyond this, slavery had long been a matter subject to the differing domestic laws of each colony (and later, each state). While several Northern states had taken tentative steps to gradually end slavery within their jurisdictions, the institution remained entrenched in other states, and no efforts were made in Philadelphia to alter that state of affairs.

But even if slavery were a matter for each state to manage on its own, at least some limited national rules were nonetheless needed. What would happen, for example, if an enslaved person "escaped" to a state that had abolished slavery? To what extent would the power of Congress to "regulate Commerce with foreign Nations" permit it to superintend (or tax, or eliminate) the transatlantic slave trade? Could states appeal to each other or to Congress for assistance in suppressing slave uprisings? And, most important, were enslaved persons to be counted as part of a state's total population for the purpose of representation (or taxation)? In many significant respects, then, questions about slavery were front and center in Philadelphia—resulting not only in divisive debates at the Convention but in unending controversy over whether the Constitution should be deemed a "proslavery" or an "antislavery" document.

The Constitution's provisions touched directly on slavery in at least four important aspects: representation and taxation, continued importation from Africa, fugitivity, and insurrection. With respect to each of these matters, the text of the Constitution will be presented, followed (where applicable) by excerpts from debates at the Convention;[24] explication of the particular clause in *The Federalist*; and, finally, contrasting interpretations of the Constitution's language and purpose offered several decades later by two prominent abolitionists, William Bowditch (who adhered to the Constitution-promotes-slavery line of William Lloyd Garrison) and Frederick Douglass (whose position evolved over time to embrace the Constitution as an antislavery document[25]).

Euphemisms for Slavery: Abraham Lincoln (1860)

As has been often noted, the text of the Constitution that issued from Philadelphia did not include any explicit mention of slavery. (Indeed, the word "slavery" appeared in the Constitution for the first time only after the Civil War—in the Thirteenth Amendment, which abolished chattel slavery.) In his Cooper Union address of February 1860, Abraham Lincoln argued that the omission was deliberate—and that it reflected a consensus among the framers that slavery did not deserve constitutional protection.

> Neither the word "slave" nor "slavery" is to be found in the Constitution, nor the word "property" even, in any connection with language alluding to the things slave, or slavery; and that wherever in that instrument the slave is alluded to, he is called a "person"—and wherever his master's legal right in relation to him is alluded to, it is spoken of as "service or labor which may be due"—as a debt

payable in service or labor. . . . This mode of alluding to slaves and slavery, instead of speaking of them, was employed on purpose to exclude from the Constitution the idea that there could be property in man.[26]

Euphemisms for Slavery: Convention Debates (1787)

Lincoln elevated semantics over substance. In fact, the Constitution was far from silent on the subject of slavery, even if the word itself did not appear in its text. Instead, various euphemisms were employed—such as "all other Persons" or "Person[s] held to Service or Labour"—to refer to enslaved persons and the institution of slavery. During the debate at the Convention on the slave importation clause, for example, the following exchanges occurred:

Gouverneur Morris [Pennsylvania] was for making the clause read at once, "importation of slaves into North Carolina, South Carolina, and Georgia" (shall not be prohibited etc.). . . .

George Mason [Virginia] was not against using the term "slaves" but [against] naming North Carolina, South Carolina, and Georgia, lest it should give offense to the people of those states.

Roger Sherman [Connecticut] liked a description better than the terms proposed, which had been declined by the old Congress and were not pleasing to some people. *George Clymer* [Pennsylvania] concurred with Mr. Sherman. . . .

The first part of the report was then agreed to, amended as follows: "The migration or importation of such persons as the several States now existing shall think proper to admit, shall not be prohibited by the Legislature prior to the year 1808."

James Madison [Virginia] thought it wrong to admit in the Constitution the idea that there could be property in men.[27]

Euphemisms for Slavery: Subsequent Explanations (1787, 1798, 1819)

Several members of the Constitutional Convention subsequently offered explanations as to the absence of the word "slave" in this and other constitutional provisions.

James Wilson [Pennsylvania]: Much fault has been found with the mode of expression used in the first clause of [Article I, Section 9]. I believe I can assign a reason why that mode of expression was used and why the term slave was not directly admitted in this Constitution. . . . These were the very expressions used in 1783 [by Congress under the Articles of Confederation]. . . . It was natural, sir, for the late convention . . . to use the expression which they found had been received as unexceptionable before.[28]

Luther Martin [Maryland]: The design of this clause is to prevent the general government from prohibiting the importation of slaves; but the same reasons which caused them [in other contexts] to strike out the word "national," and not admit the word "stamps," influenced them here to guard against the word "slaves." They anxiously sought to avoid the admission of expressions which might be odious in the ears of Americans, although they were willing to admit into their system those things which the expressions signified.[29]

Jonathan Dayton [New Jersey]: The sole reason assigned for changing ["slaves" to "such persons"] was that it would be better not to stain the constitutional code with such a term, since it could be avoided by the introduction of other equally intelligible words, as had been done in the former part of the same instrument, where the same sense was conveyed by the circuitous expression of "three-fifths of all other persons."[30]

James Madison [Virginia]: But some of the states were not only anxious for a constitutional provision against the introduction of slaves. They had scruples against admitting the term "slaves" into the instrument. Hence the descriptive phrase "migration or importation of persons."[31]

Representation and Taxation

The number of seats in the House of Representatives a state was to receive once the new government was up and running would depend on its total population. This led to an extended debate between Northern and Southern delegates at the Convention: Should slaves be counted as persons for purposes of representation? In order to maximize their representation in Congress, and hence their political clout, Southerners insisted that slaves be counted as whole persons for this purpose (despite the fact, of course, that enslaved persons were deemed "property" and enjoyed no rights); Northerners took the opposite position. Eventually, the delegates defaulted to the same "three-fifths" formulation that had been devised to allocate revenue burdens under the Articles of Confederation (and eventually the same proportion came to be used to determine a state's population for purposes of direct taxation). This so-called compromise remained in effect until after the Civil War.

Representation: Text of the Constitution (1787)

Representatives and direct Taxes shall be apportioned among the several States which may be included within this Union, according to their respective Numbers, which shall be determined by adding to the whole Number of free Persons, including those bound to Service for a Term of Years, and excluding Indians not taxed, three fifths of all other Persons. [Article I, Section 2]

Representation: Debates at the Convention (1787)

William Paterson [New Jersey]: What is the true principle of representation? It is an expedient by which an assembly of certain individuals chosen by the people is substituted in place of the inconvenient meeting of the people themselves. If such a meeting of the people was actually to take place, would the slaves vote? They would not. Why then should they be represented?

James Madison [Virginia] ... suggested as a proper ground of compromise, that in the first branch the states should be represented according to their number of free inhabitants; and in the second which had for one of its primary objects the guardianship of property, according to the whole number, including slaves.[32]

Resolved That in order to ascertain the alterations that may happen in the population and wealth of the several states a census shall be taken of the free inhabitants of each state, and three-fifths of the inhabitants of other description on the first year after this form of government shall have been adopted—and afterwards on every term of ____ years.[33]

Pierce Butler [South Carolina] and *Charles Cotesworth Pinckney* [South Carolina] insisted that blacks be included in the rule of representation, equally with the whites (and for that purpose moved that the words "three-fifths" be struck out).

Elbridge Gerry [Massachusetts] thought that three-fifths of them was to say the least the full proportion that could be admitted.

Nathaniel Gorham [Massachusetts]: The ratio was fixed by Congress [under the Articles of Confederation] as a rule of taxation. Then it was urged by delegates representing the states having slaves that the blacks were still more inferior to freemen. At present when the ratio of representation is to be established, we are assured that they are equal to freemen. The arguments on the former occasion had convinced him that three-fifths was pretty near the just proportion and he should vote according to the same opinion now.

Pierce Butler [South Carolina] insisted that the labor of a slave in South Carolina was as productive and valuable as that of a freeman in Massachusetts, that as wealth was the great means of defense and utility to the nation they were equally valuable to it with freemen; and that consequently an equal representation ought to be allowed for them in a government which was instituted principally for the protection of property, and was itself to be supported by property.

George Mason [Virginia]: It was certain that the slaves were valuable, as they raised the value of land, increased the exports and imports, and of course the revenue, would supply the means of feeding and supporting an army, and might in cases of emergency become themselves soldiers. As in these important respects they were useful to the community at large, they ought not to be excluded from the estimate of representation. He could not however regard them as equal to freemen and could not vote for them as such.

Hugh Williamson [North Carolina] reminded Mr. Gorham that if the Southern states contended for the inferiority of blacks to whites when taxation was in view, the Eastern states on the same occasion contended for their equality. He did not however either then or now concur in either extreme but approved of the ratio of three-fifths.

Rufus King [Massachusetts] being much opposed to fixing numbers as the rule of representation, was particularly so on account of the blacks. He thought the admission of them along with whites at all would excite great discontents among the states having no slaves.

James Wilson [Pennsylvania] did not see well on what principle the admission of blacks in the proportion of three-fifths could be explained. Are they admitted as citizens? Then why are they not admitted on an equality with white citizens? Are they admitted as property? Then why is not other property admitted into the computation? These were difficulties however which he thought must be overruled by the necessity of compromise.[34]

Gouverneur Morris [Pennsylvania]: Upon what principle is it that the slaves shall be computed in the representation? Are they men? Then make them citizens and let them vote. Are they property? Why then is no other property included? The houses in this city (Philadelphia) are worth more than all the wretched slaves which cover the rice swamps of South Carolina. The admission of slaves into the representation when fairly explained comes to this: that the inhabitant of Georgia and South Carolina who goes to the coast of Africa, and in defiance of the most sacred laws of humanity tears away his fellow creatures from their dearest connections and damns them to the most cruel bondages, shall have more votes in a government instituted for protection of the rights of mankind than the citizen of Pennsylvania or New Jersey who views with a laudable horror so nefarious a practice.[35]

Representation: *Federalist No. 54* (1788)

Does it follow, from an admission of numbers for the measure of representation, or of slaves combined with free citizens as a ratio of taxation, that slaves ought to be included in the numerical rule of representation? Slaves are considered as property, not as persons. They ought therefore to be comprehended in estimates of taxation which are founded on property, and to be excluded from representation which is regulated by a census of persons. This is the objection, as I understand it, stated in its full force. I shall be equally candid in stating the reasoning which may be offered on the opposite side.

"We subscribe to the doctrine," might one of our Southern brethren observe, "that representation relates more immediately to persons, and taxation more immediately to property, and we join in the application of this distinction to the case of our slaves. But we must deny the fact that slaves are considered merely as property, and in no respect whatever as persons. The true state of the case is that they partake of both these qualities: being considered by our laws in some respects as persons, and in other respects as property. In being compelled to labor not for himself but for a master; in being vendible by one master to another master; and in being subject at all times to be restrained in his liberty and chastised in his body by the capricious will of another, the slave may appear to be degraded from the human rank and classed with those irrational animals which fall under the legal denomination of property. In being protected, on the other hand, in his life and in his limbs against the violence of all others, even the master of his labor and his liberty; and in being punishable himself for all violence committed against others, the slave is no less evidently regarded by the law as a member of the society, not as a part of the irrational creation; as a moral person, not as a mere article of property. The federal Constitution, therefore, decides with great propriety on the case of our slaves when it views them in the mixed character of persons and of property. This is in fact their true character. . . .

"Let the compromising expedient of the Constitution be mutually adopted, which regards them as inhabitants, but as debased by servitude below the equal level of free inhabitants, which regards the slave as divested of two-fifths of the man."[36]

More succinctly, Alexander Hamilton defended the Convention's decision as one of necessity: "[The] clause which allows a representation for three-fifths of the negroes . . . was one result of the spirit of accommodation which governed the Convention; and without this indulgence no union could possibly have been formed."[37]

Representation: William Bowditch vs. Frederick Douglass (1849, 1860)

William Bowditch: By this section, persons are divided into those who are free and those who are slaves; for to the whole number of free persons are to be added three-fifths of all other persons, that is, persons not free, or slaves. If we adopt the plain, obvious, and common meaning of the words as their true meaning, this conclusion is incontrovertible. . . . This article, therefore, recognizes slavery as explicitly as if the word *slave* itself had been used, and gives to the free persons in a slave state, solely because they are slaveholders, a larger representation, and consequently greater political power, than the same number of free persons in a free state. *A bounty on slaveholding!*[38]

Frederick Douglass: Let us grant for the sake of the argument that [this provision], referring to the basis of representation and taxation, does refer to slaves. We are not compelled to make this admission, for it might fairly apply, and indeed was intended to apply, to aliens and others living in the United States but who were not naturalized. But giving the provision the very worse construction—that it applies to slaves—what does it amount to? I answer: . . . It is in itself a downright disability imposed upon the slave system of America, one which deprives the slaveholding states of at least two-fifths of their natural basis of representation. A black man in a free state is worth just two-fifths more than a black man in a slave state, as a basis of political power under the Constitution. Therefore, instead of encouraging slavery, the Constitution encourages freedom, by holding out to every slaveholding state in the inducement of an increase of two-fifths of political power by becoming a free state. So much for the three-fifths clause; taking it at its worst, it still leans to freedom, not to slavery.[39]

Despite Douglass's clever argument, no Southern state ever chose to liberate its slaves in order to increase its political representation in the House. (Nor did Congress ever enact a "direct" tax, which, because slaves were partially counted, would have hit Southern states harder.) But there can be no doubt that until it was finally abolished by the Fourteenth Amendment, the three-fifths clause bestowed disproportionate political power upon the slaveholding states—not only in the House of Representatives but also in the Electoral College (allocated on the basis of House plus Senate seats), thereby further exaggerating the slavocracy's influence over the executive and judicial branches.

Importation

The Convention also needed to reach a consensus about the transatlantic slave trade, because that practice (like other "Commerce with foreign Nations") would be subject to national rules. While some delegates favored the outright abolition of the Middle Passage, representatives from South Carolina and Georgia made retention of the practice an absolute condition for joining the new union. Once again, a muddled compromise was reached.

Importation: Text of the Constitution (1787)

The Migration or Importation of such Persons as any of the States now existing shall think proper to admit, shall not be prohibited by the Congress prior to the Year one thousand eight hundred and eight, but a Tax or duty may be imposed on such Importation, not exceeding ten dollars for each Person. [Article I, Section 9]

Importation: Debates at the Convention (1787)

Luther Martin [Maryland] proposed . . . a prohibition or tax on the importation of slaves. As five slaves are to be counted as three free men in the apportionment of representatives, such a clause would leave an encouragement to this traffic. Slaves weakened one part of the Union which the other parts were bound to protect; the privilege of importing them was therefore unreasonable.

It was inconsistent with the principles of the Revolution and dishonorable to the American character to have such a feature in the Constitution.

John Rutledge [South Carolina]: Religion and humanity had nothing to do with this question. Interest alone is the governing principle with nations. The true question at present is whether the Southern states shall or shall not be parties to the Union. If the Northern states consult their interest, they will not oppose the increase of slaves which will increase the commodities of which they will become the carriers.

Oliver Ellsworth [Connecticut]: Let every state import what it pleases. The morality or wisdom of slavery are considerations belonging to the states themselves. What enriches a part enriches the whole, and the states are the best judges of their particular interest. The old confederation had not meddled with this point.

Charles Pinckney [South Carolina]: South Carolina can never receive the plan if it prohibits the slave trade. . . . If the states be all left at liberty on this subject, South Carolina may perhaps by degrees do of herself what is wished, as Virginia and Maryland have already done.[40]

Roger Sherman [Connecticut] disapproved of the slave trade; yet as the states were now possessed of the right to import slaves, as the public good did not require it to be taken from them, and as it was expedient to have as few objections as possible to the proposed scheme of government, he thought it best to leave the matter as we find it.

George Mason [Virginia]: Maryland and Virginia . . . had already prohibited the importation of slaves expressly. North Carolina had done the same in substance. All this would be in vain if South Carolina and Georgia be at liberty to import. The Western people are already calling out for slaves for their new lands, and will fill that country with slaves if they can be got through South Carolina and Georgia. . . . As to the states being in possession of the right to import, this was the case with many other rights, now to be properly given up. . . . The general government should have power to prevent the increase of slavery.

Charles Cotesworth Pinckney [South Carolina] declared it to be his firm opinion that if himself and all his colleagues were to sign the Constitution and use their personal influence, it would be of no avail towards obtaining the assent of their constituents. South Carolina and Georgia cannot do without slaves. As to Virginia she will gain by stopping the importations. Her slaves will rise in value, and she has more than she wants. It would be unequal to require South Carolina and Georgia to confederate on such unequal terms. . . . The importation of slaves would be for the interest of the whole Union. The more slaves, the more produce to employ the carrying trade. The more consumption also, and the more of this, the more of revenue for the common treasury.

John Dickinson [Delaware]: The true question was whether the national happiness would be promoted or impeded by the importation, and this question ought to be left to the national government not to the states particularly interested. . . . He could not believe that the Southern states would refuse to confederate on the account apprehended.

Hugh Williamson [North Carolina]: He thought the Southern states could not be members of the Union if the clause [prohibiting interference with the international slave trade] should be rejected, and that it was wrong to force anything down not absolutely necessary, and which any state must disagree to.

John Rutledge [South Carolina]: If the Convention thinks that North Carolina, South Carolina, and Georgia will ever agree to the plan, unless their right to import slaves be untouched, the expectation is vain. The people of those states will never be such fools as to give up so important an interest.[41]

Importation: *Federalist No. 42* (1788)

It were doubtless to be wished that the power of prohibiting the importation of slaves had not been postponed until the year 1808, or rather that it had been suffered to have immediate operation. But it is not difficult to account either for this restriction on the general government or for the manner in which the whole clause is expressed. It ought to be considered as a great point gained in favor of humanity that a period of twenty years may terminate forever, within these states, a traffic which has so long and so loudly upbraided the barbarism of modern policy; that within that period it will receive a considerable discouragement from the federal government, and may be totally abolished, by a concurrence of the few states which continue the unnatural traffic, in the prohibitory example which has been given by so great a majority of the Union. Happy would it be for the unfortunate Africans if an equal prospect lay before them of being redeemed from the oppressions of their European brethren!

Attempts have been made to pervert this clause into an objection against the Constitution, by representing it on one side as a criminal toleration of an illicit practice, and on another as calculated to prevent voluntary and beneficial emigrations from Europe to America. I mention these misconstructions not with a view to give them an answer, for they deserve none, but as specimens of the manner and spirit in which some have thought fit to conduct their opposition to the proposed government.[42]

Subsequently, at the Virginia ratifying convention in 1788, Madison elaborated on the rationale underlying the Convention's importation decision.

I should conceive this clause to be impolitic if it were one of those things which could be excluded without encountering greater evils. The Southern states would not have entered into the union of America without the temporary permission of that trade. And if they were excluded from the union, the consequences might be dreadful to them and to us. . . . The union in general is not in a worse situation. Under the Articles of Confederation, [importation] might be continued forever. But by this clause an end may be put to it after twenty years. . . . Great as the evil is, a dismemberment of the union would be worse.[43]

Importation: William Bowditch vs. Frederick Douglass (1849, 1860)

William Bowditch: By this clause, therefore, Congress was prevented during twenty years from prohibiting the foreign slave trade with any state that pleased to allow it. But by Article I, Section 8, Congress had the general power "to regulate commerce with foreign nations." Consequently, the slave trade was excepted from the operation of the general power, with a view to place the slave trade during twenty years under the control of the slave states. It could not be wholly stopped, so long as one state wished to continue it. It is a clear compromise in favor of slavery. True, the compromise was a temporary one; but it will be noticed that Congress, even after 1808, was not obliged to prohibit the trade.[44]

Frederick Douglass: This part of the Constitution of the United States expired by its own limitation no fewer than fifty-two years ago. . . . I ask, is the Constitution of the United States to be condemned to everlasting infamy because of what was done fifty-two years ago? But there is still more to be said about this provision of the Constitution. At the time the Constitution was adopted, the slave trade was regarded as the jugular vein of slavery itself, and it was thought that slavery would die with the death of the slave trade. . . . The theory was: cut off the stream, and of course the pond or lake would dry up. Cut off the stream flowing out of Africa, and the slave-trade in America and the colonies would perish. . . . The men who framed the Constitution . . . said to the slave states: if you would purchase the privileges of this union, you must consent that the humanity of this nation shall lay its hand upon this traffic at least in twenty years after the adoption of the Constitution. . . . The Constitution is anti-slavery, because it looked to the abolition of slavery rather than to its perpetuity.[45]

After the twenty-year window of protection provided to the international slave trade as a result of this clause finally expired, Congress abolished the infamous practice, effective January 1, 1808.

Fugitive Slaves

The Convention also grappled with an additional slavery-related question that could not be left solely to each state but rather required some sort of national rule: what policy would govern "runaway" slaves? Only minimal debate occurred, however, as the delegates elected to replicate language adopted several months earlier by the Articles of Confederation Congress. The Northwest Ordinance had provided that any such "fugitive may be lawfully reclaimed and conveyed to the person claiming his or her labor or service."[46]

Fugitives: Text of the Constitution (1787)

No Person held to Service or Labour in one State, under the Laws thereof, escaping into another, shall, in Consequence of any Law or Regulation therein, be discharged from such Service or Labour, but shall be delivered up on Claim of the Party to whom such Service or Labour may be due. [Article IV, Section 2]

Fugitives: Debates at the Convention (1787, 1788)

Pierce Butler [South Carolina] and *Charles Pinckney* [South Carolina] moved "to require fugitive slaves and servants to be delivered up like criminals."

James Wilson [Pennsylvania]: This would oblige the executive of the state to do it, at the public expense.

Roger Sherman [Connecticut] saw no more propriety in the public seizing and surrendering a slave or servant, than a horse.[47]

Pierce Butler [South Carolina] moved to insert after article XV, "If any person bound to service or labor in any of the states shall escape into another state, he or she shall not be discharged from such service or labor, in consequence of any regulations subsisting in the state to which they escape, but shall be delivered up to the person justly claiming their service or labor," which was agreed to [without dissent].[48]

Two slaveholding members of the Convention later maintained that this provision significantly enhanced the rights of Southern slaveholders.

Charles Cotesworth Pinckney [South Carolina]: We have obtained a right to recover our slaves in whatever part of America they may take refuge, which is a right we had not before.[49]

James Madison [Virginia]: Another clause secures us that property which we now possess. At present, if any slave elopes to any of those states where slaves are free, he becomes emancipated by their laws. For the laws of the states are uncharitable to one another in this respect. But in this Constitution [quotes Article IV, Section 2]. This clause was expressly inserted to enable owners of slaves to reclaim them. This is a better security than any that now exists.[50]

Fugitives: *The Federalist*

This provision of the Constitution was not discussed in *The Federalist*.

Fugitives: William Bowditch vs. Frederick Douglass (1849, 1860)

William Bowditch: By this section, therefore, it is provided that no person held as a slave in one state under the laws thereof, escaping into another, shall, in consequence of any law or regulation therein, be discharged from his slavery, but shall be delivered up on claim of his owner. The laws of one state, whether they support slavery or any other institution, have no power in another state. Consequently, if a slave escapes into a free state, he becomes free. This is the general rule of law. . . . But this section declares that he shall not thereby become free but shall be delivered up. Again, the Constitution makes an exception from a general rule of law in favor of slavery. It gives to slaveholders, and slave laws, a power which the general rule of law does not give. It enables a South Carolina slaveholder to drag from the soil of Massachusetts a person whom the general rule of law pronounces free, solely because South Carolina laws declare the contrary. It makes the whole Union a vast hunting ground for slaves![51]

Frederick Douglass: The plain reading of this provision shows that it applies, and that it can only properly and legally apply, to persons "bound to service." Its object plainly is to secure the fulfillment of contracts for "service and labour." It applies to indentured apprentices and any other persons from whom service and labour may be due. The legal condition of the slave puts him beyond the operation of this provision. He is not described in it. He is a simple article of property. He does not owe and cannot owe service. He cannot even make a contract. It is impossible for him to do so. He can no more make such a contract than a horse or an ox can make one. This provision, then, only respects persons who owe service, and they only can owe service who can receive an equivalent and make a bargain. The slave cannot do that and is therefore exempted from the operation of this fugitive provision.[52]

The status of escaped "fugitive" slaves riled the new nation almost from the time of its inception until the firing upon Fort Sumter.

Insurrection and Rebellion

In light of Shays's Rebellion, the Constitution certainly should grant the new Congress power to assist in the suppression of domestic insurrections and rebellions, thought the delegates in Philadelphia. But to what extent could the language ultimately adopted in this connection be used to repress potential uprisings by slaves?

Rebellion: Text of the Constitution (1787)

The Congress shall have Power . . . To provide for calling forth the Militia to execute the Laws of the Union, suppress Insurrections and repel Invasions. . . . The United States shall . . . protect [every State] . . . against domestic Violence. [Article I, Section 8; Article IV, Section 4]

Rebellion: Debates at the Convention (1787)

Rufus King [Massachusetts]: The importation of slaves could not be prohibited—exports could not be taxed. Is this reasonable? What are the great objects of the general system? 1. defense against foreign invasion. 2. against internal sedition. Shall all the states then be bound to defend each, and shall each be at liberty to introduce a weakness which will render defense more difficult? Shall one part of the United States be bound to defend another part, and that other part be at liberty not only to increase its own danger, but to withhold the compensation for the burden?

Gouverneur Morris [Pennsylvania]: What is the proposed compensation to the Northern states for a sacrifice of every principle of right, of every impulse of humanity? They are to bind themselves to march their militia for the defense of the Southern states; for their defense against those very slaves of whom they complain. . . . The Southern states are not to be restrained from importing fresh supplies of wretched Africans, at once to increase the danger of attack and the difficulty of defense.[53]

Rebellion: *Federalist No. 43* (1788)

Protection against domestic violence is added [to the Constitution] with equal propriety. . . . It will be much better that the violence in such cases should be repressed by the superintending power [i.e., the national government] than that the majority [in a state] should be left to maintain their cause by a bloody and obstinate contest. [A number of hypothetical violent situations are mentioned.] I take no notice of an unhappy species of population abounding in some of the states who, during the calm of regular government, are sunk below the level of men; but who, in the tempestuous scenes of civil violence may emerge into the human character, and give a superiority of strength to any party with which they may associate themselves.[54]

Rebellion: William Bowditch vs. Frederick Douglass (1849, 1860)

William Bowditch: To constitute an insurrection within the meaning of the Constitution, there must be a rising against those laws which are recognized as such by the Constitution. . . . [If slaves] rise in rebellion, or commit acts of violence contrary to the laws which hold them in slavery, their rising constitutes an insurrection; such acts are acts of violence within the meaning of the Constitution, and consequently must be suppressed by the national power. And what insurrections were more likely to happen and more to be dreaded than slave insurrections, and therefore more likely to have been provided for? . . . In sober truth, then, we are a nation of slaveholders! For we have bound our whole national strength to the slaveowners, to aid them, if necessary, in holding their slaves in subjection![55]

Frederick Douglass: I go to the "slave insurrection" clause, though, in truth, there is no such clause. The one which is called so has nothing whatever to do with slaves or slaveholders any more than your laws for suppression of popular outbreaks has to do with making slaves of you and your children. It is only a law for suppression of riots or insurrections. But I will be generous here, as well as elsewhere, and grant that it applies to slave insurrections. Let us suppose that an anti-slavery man is president of the United States (and the day that shall see this the case is not distant) and this very power of suppressing slave insurrections would put an end to slavery. The right to put down an insurrection carries with it the right to determine the means by which it shall be put down. If it should turn out that slavery is a source of insurrection, that there is no security from insurrection while slavery lasts, why, the Constitution would be best obeyed by putting an end to slavery, and an anti-slavery Congress would do that very thing.[56]

Summary: The Constitution's Treatment of Slavery

The Constitution's clauses concerning slavery could be interpreted in very different ways. While Southerners aggressively defended "the peculiar institution" on constitutional grounds, abolitionists differed as to whether the charter produced in Philadelphia actively assisted—or affirmatively discouraged—the continuation of slavery. In the former camp, in addition to Bowditch, was William Lloyd Garrison, who denounced the Constitution as a "covenant with death" and an "agreement with Hell" while burning a copy of it on the Fourth of July, 1854. On the other side, not only Frederick Douglass (post-1850) but other prominent "antislavery constitutionalists" (such as Gerrit Smith, Lysander Spooner, William Goodell, Robert Rantoul, Jr., James G. Birney, and Joel Tiffany) maintained that the Constitution, by its terms and consistent with its purposes, subversively recognized a radical abolitionist agenda.[57] Occupying somewhat of a middle ground, Free Soilers and (later) Republicans such as John Fremont, William Seward, Samuel P. Chase, and Lincoln argued that although the Constitution did not permit interference with slavery in the states, Congress was empowered to prohibit its expansion into the territories. Disagreements over what the text of the Constitution actually meant, and what the framers of the Constitution actually intended, reached fever pitch in the decades prior to the Civil War.

Discussion Questions

1. Relying on the same words, observers drew diametrically opposed conclusions as to whether the Constitution was pro- or antislavery. Is that because the text of the Constitution was ambiguous—perhaps because its authors intended it to be so—or is this an example of reading and interpreting the Constitution to support a predetermined point of view?

2. Were William Bowditch and William Lloyd Garrison right to condemn the Constitution as proslavery? Or did Frederick Douglass—after he broke with Garrison on this question—have the better of the constitutional argument?[58]

3. Lincoln repeatedly took the position that neither Congress nor the president had the power to interfere with (abolish, restrict, regulate, etc.) the institution of slavery in those states where it already existed. Was that a correct reading of the Constitution? Was it the only possible reading of the Constitution?

4. Recognizing that hindsight is twenty-twenty, what should the delegates at the Constitutional Convention have done about slavery? Was an explicitly antislavery Constitution possible in 1787? Or was a compromise of some sort with the Southern states "necessary" in order to avoid the formation of two (or more) separate new nations? Does the fact that the Constitution's evasions and compromises on slavery paved the way for the Civil War suggest that the framers failed to set the new nation on a firm foundation?

5. Barack Obama has suggested that the original Constitution, however much flawed because of its compromises over slavery, nonetheless inherently contained the seeds of abolition:

   The document they produced was eventually signed but ultimately unfinished. It was stained by this nation's original sin of slavery, a question that divided the colonies and brought the convention to a stalemate until the founders chose to allow the slave trade to continue for at least twenty more years, and to leave any final resolution to future generations. Of course, the answer to the slavery question was already embedded within our Constitution—a Constitution that had at its very core the ideal of equal citizenship under the law; a Constitution that promised its people liberty, and justice, and a union that could be and should be perfected over time.[59]

Is this a fair, or an unduly optimistic, interpretation of the original Constitution?

6. Great Britain ended slavery peacefully by act of Parliament. The serfs were freed in Russia peacefully by czarist decree. What was it about the Constitution and the form of government it established that made it impossible for the United States to end slavery short of a civil war?

7. Was it a shameful evasion, or an act of inspired genius, not to use the words "slave" or "slavery" in the Constitution? Was the use of euphemisms demeaning, dehumanizing, or deceitful? Or was the refusal to acknowledge the legitimacy of slavery in the Constitution arguably an act of prudence, or even a confession of embarrassment?

8. Why did Southerners at the Constitutional Convention, who believed enslaved persons were property, nonetheless argue that they should be counted as whole persons for purposes of representation? Why did Northern delegates, at least some of whom opposed slavery, contend that slaves should not be counted at all? Were both sides being principled or hypocritical? How satisfying (or not) is Madison's praise in *Federalist No. 54* of the "compromising expedient of the Constitution" in light of (in his words) the slaves' "mixed character of persons and of property"?

9. The three-fifths clause, in its operation, gave slaveholding states disproportionate weight not only in Congress (because of extra seats in the House of Representatives) but also in picking a president (because the number of a state's Electoral College votes is determined by its total of House and Senate members)—which in turn gave slave states disproportionate weight in the executive and judicial branches (whose members are nominated by the president). What alternatives to the three-fifths clause were or might have been considered?[60]

10. The Constitution sanctioned the continuation of the African slave trade for twenty years but also permitted Congress to abolish the practice after that window had expired. Was this a pro- or an antislavery provision?

A Bill of Rights?—Primary Sources

By the time of the Convention, many state constitutions contained a "bill of rights" of some sort. Most protected the same core rights—to speech and petition, to religious protection and practice, and to trial by jury—and most had been designed to restrain both executive and legislative authority.[61] Yet the Constitution that emerged from Philadelphia contained no bill of rights.

After a perfunctory debate toward its close, the Convention voted not to include a bill of rights. Criticisms of this omission were voiced initially by Thomas Jefferson and then stridently by various Antifederalists. Its absence came close to jeopardizing the ratification process. Alexander Hamilton, James Madison, and (perversely) Charles Pinckney argued against the need for a bill of rights in the Constitution. But eventually Madison, urged on by George Washington, altered course and drafted a series of proposed amendments designed to protect fundamental liberties against governmental abuse. By 1791, the Constitution had been significantly rewritten.

Discussions at the Constitutional Convention (1787)

Only toward the very end of the Philadelphia assembly was any consideration given to the possible inclusion in the Constitution of a list of protected liberties. Less than a week before the delegates adjourned, the concept of a "Bill of Rights" was first proposed—but then defeated, unanimously.

George Mason [Virginia]: He wished the plan had been prefaced with a bill of rights, and would second a motion if made for the purpose. It would give great quiet to the people; and with the aid of the state declarations, a bill might be prepared in a few hours.

Elbridge Gerry [Massachusetts] concurred in the idea and moved for a committee to prepare a bill of rights. Col. Mason seconded the motion.

Roger Sherman [Connecticut] was for securing the rights of the people where requisite. The state declarations of rights are not repealed by this Constitution; and being in force are sufficient. . . . The legislature may be safely trusted.

George Mason [Virginia]: The laws of the United States are to be paramount to state bills of rights.

On the question for a committee to prepare a bill of rights. . . . Ayes—0; noes—10; absent—1.[62]

As James Wilson of Pennsylvania later recalled, the possibility of annexing a bill of rights to the Constitution "never struck the mind of any member in the late convention till, I believe, within three days of the dissolution of that body, and even then of so little account was the idea that it passed off in a short conversation, without introducing a formal debate."[63]

Thomas Jefferson Complains about the Absence of a Bill of Rights (1787)

About a month after the Convention ended, James Madison informed Thomas Jefferson—who was serving during 1787 as America's Minister to France—that "Col. Mason left Philadelphia in an exceeding ill humor indeed. . . . He returned to Virginia with a fixed disposition to prevent the adoption of the plan if possible. He considers the want of a bill of rights as a fatal objection."[64] But once Jefferson had a chance to review the Constitution, he expressed a similar concern to Madison. After praising certain features in the proposed new frame of government, Jefferson observed:

> I will now add what I do not like. First the omission of a bill of rights providing clearly and without the aid of sophisms for freedom of religion, freedom of the press, protection against standing armies, restriction against monopolies, the eternal and unremitting force of the habeas corpus laws, and trials by jury in all matters of fact triable by the laws of the land and not by the law of nations. To say . . . that a bill of rights was not necessary because all is reserved in the case of the general government which is not given, while in the particular ones all is given which is not reserved, [is unconvincing]. . . . Let me add that a bill of rights is what the people are entitled to against every government on earth, general or particular, and what no just government should refuse or rest on inference.[65]

Jefferson Reiterates His Concern (1789)

In a subsequent letter further expounding on the need for some sort of bill of rights, Jefferson responded to Madison's contention that "a positive declaration of some essential rights could not be obtained" in the existing political climate. Jefferson suggested—in a preview of what would eventually emerge over the course of US history as a bedrock source of protection for individual rights—that a bill of rights would provide the courts with a legitimate basis for recognizing and enforcing fundamental liberties.

> Half a loaf is better than no bread. If we cannot secure all our rights, let us secure what we can. . . . There is a remarkable difference between the characters

of the inconveniencies which attend a declaration of rights, and those which attend the want of it. The inconveniences of the declaration are that it may cramp government in its useful exertions. But the evil of this is short-lived, moderate, and reparable. The inconveniencies of the want of a declaration are permanent, afflicting, and irreparable: they are in constant progression from bad to worse. The executive in our governments is not the sole, it is scarcely the principal object of my jealousy. The tyranny of the legislatures is the most formidable dread at present. . . .

In the arguments in favor of a declaration of rights . . . one which has great weight with me [is] the legal check which it puts into the hands of the judiciary. This is a body, which if rendered independent and kept strictly to their own department, merits great confidence for their learning and integrity.[66]

Antifederalist Objections to the Constitution's Lack of a Bill of Rights (1787, 1788)

As it turned out, George Mason and Thomas Jefferson were far from alone in their worries and objections on this score. In fact, the absence of a declaration of rights in the proposed Constitution would prove to be one of the most serious of the Antifederalist concerns. Opponent after opponent in state after state pointed to the lack of a "charter of liberties" as the ultimate proof of the Federalists' supposedly aristocratic, power-centralizing intentions. Some examples:

Report of Pennsylvania Minority: The first consideration that this review suggests is the omission of a bill of rights, ascertaining and fundamentally establishing those unalienable and personal rights of men, without the full, free, and secure enjoyment of which there can be no liberty, and over which it is not necessary for a good government to have the control. The principal of which are the rights of conscience, personal liberty by the clear and unequivocal establishment of the writ of habeas corpus, jury trial in criminal and civil cases, by an impartial jury of the vicinage or county, with the common law proceedings, for the safety of the accused in criminal prosecutions, and the liberty of the press, that scourge of tyrants and the grand bulwark of every other liberty and privilege; the stipulations heretofore made in favor of them in the state constitutions are entirely superseded by this Constitution.[67]

"Agrippa" (James Winthrop) [Massachusetts]: I know it is often asked against whom in a government by representation is a bill of rights to secure us? I answer that such a government is indeed a government by ourselves; but as a just government protects all alike, it is necessary that the sober and

industrious part of the community should be defended from the rapacity and violence of the vicious and idle. A bill of rights therefore ought to set forth the purposes for which the compact is made, and serves to secure the minority against the usurpation and tyranny of the majority. It is a just observation of his excellency doctor [John] Adams in his learned defense of the American constitutions that unbridled passions produce the same effect, whether in a king, nobility, or a mob. The experience of all mankind has proved the prevalence of a disposition to use power wantonly. It is therefore as necessary to defend an individual against the majority in a republic, as against the king in a monarchy.[68]

Richard Henry Lee [Virginia]: There are certain unalienable and fundamental rights, which in forming the social compact, ought to be explicitly ascertained and fixed—a free and enlightened people, in forming this compact, will not resign all their rights to those who govern, and they will fix limits to their legislators and rulers, which will soon be plainly seen by those who are governed as well as by those who govern; and the latter will know they cannot be passed unperceived by the former, and without giving a general alarm. These rights should be made the basis of every constitution, and if a people be so situated, or have such different opinions that they cannot agree in ascertaining and fixing them, it is a very strong argument against their attempting to form one entire society, to live under one system of laws only. I confess, I never thought the people of these states differed essentially in these respects; they having derived all these rights from one common source, the British systems; and having in the formation of their state constitutions, discovered that their ideas relative to these rights are very similar. However, it is now said that the states differ so essentially in these respects, and even in the important article of the trial by jury, that when assembled in convention, they can agree to no words by which to establish that trial, or by which to ascertain and establish many other of these rights, as fundamental articles in the social compact. If so, we proceed to consolidate the states on no solid basis whatever.[69]

"Brutus" [New York]: When a building is to be erected which is intended to stand for ages, the foundation should be firmly laid. The Constitution proposed to your acceptance is designed not for yourselves alone but for generations yet unborn. The principles, therefore, upon which the social compact is founded, ought to have been clearly and precisely stated, and the most express and full declaration of rights to have been made. But on this subject there is almost an entire silence. . . . In forming government on its true principles, the foundation should be laid . . . by expressly reserving to the people such of

their essential rights as are not necessary to be parted with. . . . The powers, rights, and authority granted to the general government by this Constitution are as complete, with respect to every object to which they extend, as that of any state government—it reaches to everything which concerns human happiness—life, liberty, and property are under its control. There is the same reason, therefore, that the exercise of power, in this case, should be restrained within proper limits as in that of the state governments. . . . So clear a point is this that I cannot help suspecting that persons who attempt to persuade people that such reservations were less necessary under this Constitution than under those of the states are willfully endeavoring to deceive and to lead you into an absolute state of vassalage.[70]

Luther Martin [Maryland]: The more the system advanced the more was I impressed with the necessity of not merely attempting to secure a few rights, but of digesting and forming a complete bill of rights, including those of states and of individuals, which should be assented to and prefixed to the Constitution, to serve as a barrier between the general government and the respective states and their citizens; because the more the system advanced the more clearly it appeared to me that the framers of it did not consider that either states or men had any rights at all, or that they meant to secure the enjoyment of any to either the one or the other. . . . And from the best judgment I could form while in Convention, I then was, and yet remained, decidedly of the opinion that ambition and interest had so far blinded the understanding of some of the principal framers of the Constitution, that while they were laboring to erect a fabric by which they themselves might be exalted and benefited, they were rendered insensible to the sacrifice of the freedom and happiness of the states and their citizens, which must inevitably be the consequence. I most sacredly believe their object is the total abolition and destruction of all state governments, and the erection on their ruins of one great and extensive empire, calculated to aggrandize and elevate its rulers and chief officers far above the common herd of mankind, to enrich them with wealth, and to encircle them with honors and glory, and which according to my judgment, on the maturest reflection, must inevitably be attended with the most humiliating and abject slavery of their fellow citizens, by the sweat of whose brows and by the toil of whose bodies it can only be effected.[71]

Federalist No. 84: Bills of Rights Unnecessary (1788)

Despite these numerous and strident attacks—which the Federalists initially interpreted as disguised efforts to protect the states against the new, stronger national government—supporters of the Constitution, during much of the

THE FOUNDING (1776–91)   103

ratification process, continued to defend ardently the absence of a bill of rights. They resisted, as simply unnecessary, calls for any amendments to be added to the Constitution. Consider, for example, Hamilton's extended discussion of the subject in *Federalist No. 84*. "The most considerable of the remaining objections [to the Constitution] is that the plan of the convention contains no bill of rights," Hamilton's second-to-last *Federalist* essay began. After noting that several states (including New York) "are in a similar predicament" in that their state constitutions, too, lacked formal declarations of rights, and after outlining various provisions in the proposed Constitution that in fact guarded individual liberties (such as the restrictions on congressional power in Article I, Section 9, and the trial by jury and treason clauses in Article III), Hamilton advanced three lines of argument in response to Antifederalist concerns. First, Hamilton maintained that a bill of rights was unnecessary in a republic, whose foundations rested on the sovereignty of the people.

> Bills of rights are, in their origin, stipulations between kings and their subjects, abridgments of prerogative in favor of privilege, reservations of rights not surrendered to the prince. Such was Magna Carta . . . the Petition of Right assented to by Charles I . . . [and] the Declaration of Right [of 1688]. It is evident, therefore, that, according to their primitive signification, they have no application to constitutions professedly founded upon the power of the people and executed by their immediate representatives and servants. Here, in strictness, the people surrender nothing; and as they retain everything they have no need of particular reservations. "We, the People of the United States, to secure the blessings of liberty to ourselves and our posterity, do ordain and establish this Constitution for the United States of America." Here is a better recognition of popular rights than volumes of those aphorisms which make the principal figure in several of our state bills of rights, and which would sound much better in a treatise of ethics than in a constitution of government.[72]

Federalist No. 84: Bills of Rights Dangerous (1788)

Next, Hamilton maintained that enumerating various "rights" and adding them to the text of the Constitution was an undertaking fraught with danger, particularly since it implicitly suggested that the government inherently possessed virtually unlimited reservoirs of power unless specifically constrained.

> I go further, and affirm that bills of rights, in the sense and to the extent in which they are contended for, are not only unnecessary in the proposed Constitution, but would even be dangerous. They would contain various

exceptions to powers not granted; and on this very account would afford a colorable pretext to claim more than were granted. For why declare that things shall not be done which there is no power to do? Why, for instance, should it be said that the liberty of the press shall not be restrained when no power is given by which restrictions may be imposed? I will not contend that such a provision would confer a regulating power; but it is evident that it would furnish, to men disposed to usurp, a plausible pretense for claiming that power. They might urge with a semblance of reason that the Constitution ought not to be charged with the absurdity of providing against the abuse of an authority which was not given, and that the provision against restraining the liberty of the press afforded a clear implication that a power to prescribe proper regulations concerning it was intended to be vested in the national government. This may serve as a specimen of the numerous handles which would be given to the doctrine of constructive powers by the indulgence of an injudicious zeal for bills of rights.[73]

Federalist No. 84: Constitution Itself Effectively a Bill of Rights (1788)

Finally—although perhaps not quite as persuasively—Hamilton contended that the Constitution, by specifying the structure of the government and each citizen's place therein, itself amounted to the equivalent of a bill of rights.

The truth is, after all the declamations we have heard, that the Constitution is itself, in every rational sense and to every useful purpose, a bill of rights. The several bills of rights in Great Britain form its Constitution, and conversely the constitution of each state is its bill of rights. And the proposed Constitution, if adopted, will be the bill of rights of the Union. Is it one object of a bill of rights to declare and specify the political privileges of the citizens in the structure and administration of the government? This is done in the most ample and precise manner in the plan of the convention; comprehending various precautions for the public security which are not to be found in any of the state constitutions. Is another object of a bill of rights to define certain immunities and modes of proceeding which are relative to personal and private concerns? This we have seen has also been attended to, in a variety of cases, in the same plan. Adverting therefore to the substantial meaning of a bill of rights, it is absurd to allege that it is not to be found in the work of the convention. It may be said that it does not go far enough, though it will not be easy to make this appear; but it can with no propriety be contended that there is no such thing.[74]

James Madison Opposes Adding a Declaration of Rights (1788, 1789)

Other Federalists advanced additional arguments denying the need for—or the danger of—or the impossibility of—adding a bill of rights. "Enumerate all the rights of men! I am sure, sir, that no gentleman in the late convention would have attempted such a thing," declared James Wilson.[75] In a similar vein, James Madison observed:

> It has been objected also against a bill of rights that, by enumerating particular exceptions to the grant of power, it would disparage those rights which were not placed in that enumeration; and it might follow, by implication, that those rights which were not singled out were intended to be assigned into the hands of the general government, and were consequently insecure. This is one of the most plausible arguments I have ever heard urged against the admission of a bill of rights into this system.[76]

Madison also suggested that in the final analysis, a bill of rights—like all such "parchment barriers" (see *Federalist No. 48*)—would be ineffective in preventing a determined majority, no less than a despotic government, from achieving its will.

> Experience proves the inefficacy of a bill of rights on those occasions when its control is most needed. Repeated violations of these parchment barriers have been committed by overbearing majorities in every state. In Virginia I have seen the bill of rights violated in every instance where it has been opposed to a popular current. Notwithstanding the explicit provision contained in that instrument for the rights of conscience, it is well known that a religious establishment would have taken place in that state if the legislative majority had found, as they expected, a majority of the people in favor of the measure. . . . Wherever the real power in a government lies, there is the danger of oppression. In our governments the real power lies in the majority of the community, and the invasion of private rights is chiefly to be apprehended not from acts of government contrary to the sense of its constituents, but from acts in which the government is the mere instrument of the major number of the constituents.[77]

Charles Pinckney's Argument against a Bill of Rights (1788)

One of the more unusual—although brutally honest—arguments against a bill of rights came from Charles Cotesworth Pinckney of South Carolina.

Another reason weighed particularly with the members from this state against the insertion of a bill of rights. Such bills generally begin with declaring that all men are by nature born free. Now, we should make that declaration with a very bad grace, when a large part of our property consists in men who are actually born slaves.[78]

Madison Promises to Add an Enumeration of Rights (1789)

Over time (especially as a result of state ratifying conventions, particularly in Massachusetts and Virginia), it became clear to the Federalists that some accommodation on this issue was necessary politically. Madison made it known in 1789 during his campaign for a seat in the House of Representatives that once the new government was up and running, he would seek to secure the addition of a declaration of rights to the new Constitution.

[While] it remained unratified and it was necessary to unite the states in some one plan, I opposed all previous alterations as calculated to throw the states into dangerous contentions, and to furnish the secret enemies of the Union with an opportunity of promoting its dissolution. Circumstances are now changed: The Constitution is established on the ratifications of eleven states and a very great majority of the people of America; and amendments, if pursued with a proper moderation and in a proper mode, will be not only safe, but may serve the double purpose of satisfying the minds of well-meaning opponents, and of providing additional guards in favor of liberty. Under this change of circumstances, it is my sincere opinion that the Constitution ought to be revised, and that the first Congress meeting under it ought to prepare and recommend to the states for ratification the most satisfactory provisions for all essential rights, particularly the rights of conscience in the fullest latitude, the freedom of the press, trials by jury, security against general warrants, etc.[79]

George Washington Calls for Protection of Rights (1789)

Consistent with this strategy, in his initial Inaugural Address, delivered in April 1789, George Washington urged Congress to consider amending the Constitution to incorporate some version of a bill of rights, in order to protect the "rights of freemen" and to secure "public harmony."

Besides the ordinary objects submitted to your care, it will remain with your judgment to decide how far an exercise of the occasional power delegated by

the fifth Article of the Constitution is rendered expedient at the present junc-
ture by the nature of objections which have been urged against the system, or
by the degree of inquietude which has given birth to them. Instead of undertaking particular recommendations on this subject, in which I could be guided
by no lights derived from official opportunities, I shall again give way to my
entire confidence in your discernment and pursuit of the public good: For I
assure myself that whilst you carefully avoid every alteration which might endanger the benefits of a united and effective government, or which ought to
await the future lessons of experience; a reverence for the characteristic rights
of freemen, and a regard for the public harmony, will sufficiently influence your
deliberations on the question how far the former can be more impregnably for-
tified, or the latter be safely and advantageously promoted.[80]

James Madison Seeks to Reconcile Opponents to the Constitution (1789)

Madison spent the next few months drafting and then shepherding through
Congress the amendments that had been promised. When he first introduced his
proposals on the floor of the House of Representatives, he began by discussing
the political justifications.

The applications for amendments come from a very respectable number of
our constituents, and it is certainly proper for Congress to consider the subject in order to quiet that anxiety which prevails in the public mind. . . . I wish,
among other reasons why something should be done, that those who have
been friendly to the adoption of this Constitution may have the opportunity of
proving to those who were opposed to it that they were as sincerely devoted to
liberty and a republican government, as those who charged them with wishing
the adoption of this Constitution in order to lay the foundation of an aristocracy or despotism. It will be a desirable thing to extinguish from the bosom
of every member of the community any apprehensions that there are those
among his countrymen who wish to deprive them of the liberty for which they
valiantly fought and honorably bled. And if there are amendments desired of
such a nature as will not injure the Constitution, and they can be ingrafted so
as to give satisfaction to the doubting part of our fellow citizens, the friends
of the federal government will evince that spirit of deference and concession
for which they have hitherto been distinguished. . . . There is a great body of
the people falling under this description, who at present feel much inclined to
join their support to the cause of federalism, if they were satisfied in this one
point. We ought not to disregard their inclination, but, on principles of amity

and moderation, conform to their wishes and expressly declare the great rights of mankind secured under this Constitution.[81]

James Madison: An Enumeration of Rights Protects the Minority from the Majority (1789)

Madison proceeded to offer a ringing defense of the role that might be played by a bill of rights in securing the blessings of liberty (ignoring or recanting arguments he had previously made to the opposite effect). A declaration of rights would guard not only against the excesses of the government but would also serve as a bulwark against majoritarian tyranny.

The great object in view is to limit and qualify the powers of government, by excepting out of the grant of power those cases in which the government ought not to act, or to act only in a particular mode. They point these exceptions sometimes against the abuse of the executive power, sometimes against the legislative, and, in some cases, against the community itself; or, in other words, against the majority in favor of the minority.

In our government it is, perhaps, less necessary to guard against the abuse in the executive department than any other; because it is not the stronger branch of the system, but the weaker. It therefore must be levelled against the legislative, for it is the most powerful and most likely to be abused, because it is under the least control. Hence, so far as a declaration of rights can tend to prevent the exercise of undue power, it cannot be doubted but such declaration is proper. But I confess that I do conceive that in a government modified like this of the United States, the great danger lies rather in the abuse of the community than in the legislative body. The prescriptions in favor of liberty ought to be levelled against that quarter where the greatest danger lies, namely, that which possesses the highest prerogative of power. But this is not found in either the executive or legislative departments of government, but in the body of the people, operating by the majority against the minority.

It may be thought that all paper barriers against the power of the community are too weak to be worthy of attention. I am sensible they are not so strong as to satisfy gentlemen of every description who have seen and examined thoroughly the texture of such a defense; yet, as they have a tendency to impress some degree of respect for them, to establish the public opinion in their favor, and rouse the attention of the whole community, it may be one means to control the majority from those acts to which they might be otherwise inclined. . . .

[If a bill of rights is] incorporated into the Constitution, independent tribunals of justice will consider themselves in a peculiar manner the guardians of those rights; they will be an impenetrable bulwark against every assumption of power in the legislative or executive; they will be naturally led to resist every encroachment upon rights expressly stipulated for in the Constitution by the declaration of rights. Besides this security, there is a great probability that such a declaration in the federal system would be enforced; because the state legislatures will jealously and closely watch the operations of this government, and be able to resist with more effect every assumption of power, than any other power on earth can do; and the greatest opponents to a federal government admit the state legislatures to be sure guardians of the people's liberty. I conclude, from this view of the subject, that it will be proper in itself, and highly politic, for the tranquility of the public mind and the stability of the government, that we should offer something, in the form I have proposed, to be incorporated in the system of government as a declaration of the rights of the people.[82]

Constitutional Amendments Are Proposed and Ratified (1789, 1791)

In September 1789, the first Congress transmitted to the states for their consideration a dozen proposed constitutional amendments along with the following explanation:

The conventions of a number of the states, having at the time of their adopting the Constitution, expressed a desire, in order to prevent misconstruction or abuse of its powers, that further declaratory and restrictive clauses should be added: And as extending the ground of public confidence in the government, will best ensure the beneficent ends of its institution.[83]

Ten of the proposed amendments were ultimately ratified by the requisite number of states, effective December 1791, and eventually became known as the Bill of Rights.

Discussion Questions

1. The Federalists and Antifederalists disagreed profoundly on whether the Constitution needed a bill of rights—and whether it should be defeated

because it lacked one. How persuasive were the Federalist arguments that a bill of rights was not necessary (because the Constitution itself already protected numerous rights) or even dangerous (by effectively not protecting any rights that happened not to be named)? Obviously, from a practical, political viewpoint, the Antifederalists "won" the argument, as the Federalists found it necessary and expedient to add the Bill of Rights to the Constitution. But which side had the better argument?

2. Over the years, Woody Holton has asked students in his American history classes to shout out specific clauses of the Constitution they most appreciate.

> Students are often struck by the same thing that astonished me when I first began this study of the origins of America's founding document: the vast majority of the most popular constitutional clauses are not actually in the Constitution that the framers signed on September 17, 1787. Nearly all of the stirring phrases that Americans most cherish are actually in the Bill of Rights or in later amendments. . . . There is irony in the fact that most of the best-loved portions of the Constitution appear in the first ten amendments.[84]

Would we think of the Constitution in the same way—and would it have been as long-lasting and effective—had it never been supplemented with the Bill of Rights?

3. Early in the country's history, the Supreme Court ruled in *Barron v. Baltimore* (1833) that the Bill of Rights constrained only Congress and the national government; it was not meant to apply to the states.[85] *Barron* serves as a textbook example of how constitutional history affects the course of US history, inasmuch as the decision greatly lessened federal and judicial oversight of state actions. Not until well into the twentieth century did the Supreme Court commence the steady process of "incorporation," that is, holding that provisions of the Bill of Rights were also applicable against the states. Even today, several portions of the Bill of Rights (e.g., requirements for grand juries and civil jury trials) still apply only to the national government. Should the Bill of Rights constrain only the national government or the states too? If the latter, should its authors have made that clear?

4. In 1944, President Franklin Roosevelt called for a "second Bill of Rights."[86] Is the Bill of Rights outdated or incomplete? If a "second Bill of Rights" were to be written today, what should it include?

Additional Primary Source Documents

Primary source document excerpts covering the following topics are located on the website accompanying this book:

Popular Sovereignty: What Does "We the People" Mean?—including the Declaratory Act; the Declaration of Independence; the Articles of Confederation; the Preamble; "checks" on the people.

Other "Constitutional Moments" during This Era

- The "inalienable rights" of the Declaration of Independence—including the English Bill of Rights (1689); John Locke's *Second Treatise on Government* (1690); Thomas Paine's *Common Sense* (1776).
- "Form of government"—including state constitutions; factions and representation (*Federalist No. 10*); separation of powers and checks and balances (*Federalist Nos. 47–48, 51*); states and federalism (*Federalist Nos. 17, 41–46, 82*); House of Representatives (*Federalist Nos. 52–61*); Senate (*Federalist Nos. 62–66*); executive branch (*Federalist Nos. 67–77*); and judiciary (*Federalist Nos. 78–83*).
- Equality of voting and representation in the Senate—including debates at the Constitutional Convention; Article V; *Federalist No. 62.*
- Ratification of the Constitution—including Article VII; *Federalist Nos. 38–40*; and debates at the state ratifying conventions.
- Election of the president—including Article II, Section 1; Twelfth Amendment. Subsequently: Twenty-second Amendment; Twenty-third Amendment; Twenty-fifth Amendment; contested presidential elections of 1800, 1824, 1876, 2000, and 2020; *Chiafalo v. Washington*, 591 U.S. ___ (2020) ("faithless electors"); and National Popular Vote Interstate Compact (proposed).
- Role of the First Congress in organizing the new government—including Oaths Act (1789); Judiciary Act (1789); Treasury Act (1789); Census Act (1790); Naturalization Act (1790); Crimes Act (1790); First Bank of the United States (1791); Whiskey Act (1791); and congressional investigation of St. Clair military defeat (1792).
- Removal by the president of executive branch officers—including Article II, Section 2; section 2 of the Foreign Affairs Act (1789). Subsequently: Tenure of Office Act (1867) and Andrew Johnson impeachment (1868); *Myers*

v. United States, 272 U.S. 52 (1926); *Humphrey's Executor v. United States*, 295 U.S. 602 (1935); and *Selia Law LLC v. Consumer Financial Protection Bureau*, 591 U.S. ___ (2020).

Notes

1. West v. Barnes, 2 U.S. 401 (1791).
2. Thomas Paine, *Common Sense* (Philadelphia, 1776), www.gutenberg.org/files/147/ 147-h/147-h.htm.
3. Paine, *Common Sense*.
4. Great Britain Parliament, "The Declaratory Act" (March 18, 1766), avalon.law.yale. edu/18th_century/declaratory_act_1766.asp.
5. 5 Journals of the Continental Congress 433 (June 12, 1776), memory.loc.gov/cgi-bin/ ampage?collId = lljc&fileName = 005/lljc005.db&recNum = 17&itemLink = r%3Fa mmem%2Fhlaw%3A%40field%28DOCID%2B%40lit%28jc0051%29%29%2300500 01&linkText = 1.
6. 5 Journals of the Continental Congress 546–54 (July 12, 1776) (Dickerson draft), av-alon.law.yale.edu/18th_century/contcong_07-12-76.asp.
7. Articles of Confederation of 1781, www.consource.org/document/articles-of-confederation-1777-11-15/.
8. N.H. Const. (January 5, 1776), avalon.law.yale.edu/18th_century/nh09.asp.
9. Virginia Declaration of Rights (June 12, 1776), avalon.law.yale.edu/18th_century/ virginia.asp.
10. The Federalist No. 37 (James Madison) (January 11, 1788), guides.loc.gov/federalist-papers/text-31-40#s-lg-box-wrapper-25493391.
11. See Mary Sarah Bilder, *Madison's Hand: Revising the Constitutional Convention* (Cambridge, MA: Harvard University Press, 2015).
12. An act more efficiently to provide for the National Defense by establishing a Uniform Militia throughout the United States, ch. 33, 1 Stat. 271 (May 8, 1792), govtrackus. s3.amazonaws.com/legislink/pdf/stat/1/STATUTE-1-Pg271.pdf.
13. The Virginia Plan as Amended in Committee (June 13, 1787), in Max Farrand, *The Records of the Federal Convention of 1787* (New Haven, CT: Yale University Press, 1911), 1:229.
14. James Madison (June 30, 1787), in Farrand, *Records of the Federal Convention*, 1:486.
15. H. R. Comm. Rep. No. 13, "Abolition of Slavery," 1st Cong., 2d Sess. (March 5, 1790), memory.loc.gov/cgi-bin/ampage?collId = llsp&fileName = 037/llsp037. db&recNum = 19.
16. James Madison to Thomas Jefferson, October 17, 1788, founders.archives.gov/ documents/Madison/01-11-02-0218.
17. James Madison to Thomas Jefferson, October 17, 1788, founders.archives.gov/ documents/Madison/01-11-02-0218.

18. Thomas Jefferson to James Madison, March 15, 1789, founders.archives.gov/documents/Jefferson/01-14-02-0410.

19. James Madison, House of Representatives Debate (June 8, 1789), www.consource.org/document/the-congressional-register-1789-6-8/.

20. James Madison, Resolutions for Amendments to the Constitution (June 8, 1789), www.consource.org/document/madisons-resolution-for-amendments-to-the-constitution-1789-6-8/.

21. James Madison, "Charters," *National Gazette*, January 18, 1792, founders.archives.gov/documents/Madison/01-14-02-0172.

22. George Washington to the President of Congress, September 17, 1787, founders.archives.gov/documents/Washington/04-05-02-0306.

23. *Id.*

24. As Mary Bilder explains at the conclusion of her essay, no stenographic record was made of the Convention debates. The excerpts that follow should be considered in that cautionary light. There is evidence, for example, that James Madison revised (and rerevised) his *Notes* over the years prior to their publication, arguably to reflect his changing political views. See Bilder, *Madison's Hand.*

25. Robert Cohen, "Was the Constitution Pro-Slavery? The Changing View of Frederick Douglass," *Social Education* 72, no. 5 (September 2008): 246–50, www.socialstudies.org/social-education/72/5. James Oakes, "Frederick Douglass Changed My Mind about the Constitution," *Social Education* 72, no. 5 (September 2008): 251–52, www.socialstudies.org/publications/socialeducation/september2008/frederick-douglass-changed-my-mind-about-the-constitution.

26. Abraham Lincoln, "Cooper Union Address" (speech, New York, February 27, 1860), www.nytimes.com/2004/05/02/nyregion/full-text-abraham-lincolns-cooper-union-address.html.

27. Gouverneur Morris, George Mason, Roger Sherman, and James Madison (August 25, 1787), in Farrand, *Records of the Federal Convention*, 2:415–17.

28. James Wilson, Pennsylvania Ratifying Convention Debate (December 3, 1787), in Farrand, *Records of the Federal Convention*, App. A, CXLVIII, 3:160.

29. Luther Martin, *General Information, Delivered to the Legislature of the State of Maryland* (November 29, 1787), in Farrand, *Records of the Federal Convention*, App. A, CLVIII, 3:210.

30. Jonathan Dayton, House of Representatives Debate (June 16, 1798), in Farrand, *Records of the Federal Convention*, App. A, CCLXXX, 3:377.

31. James Madison to Robert Walsh (November 27, 1819), in Farrand, *Records of the Federal Convention*, App. A, CCCXXXII, 3:436, founders.archives.gov/documents/Madison/04-01-02-0504.

32. William Patterson and James Madison (July 9, 1787), in Farrand, *Records of the Federal Convention*, 1:561–62.

33. Journal (July 11, 1787), in Farrand, *Records of the Federal Convention*, 1:575.

34. Pierce Butler, Elbridge Gerry, Nathaniel Gorham, George Mason, Hugh Williamson, Rufus King, and James Wilson (July 11, 1787), in Farrand, *Records of the Federal Convention*, 580–81, 586–87.

35. Gouverneur Morris (August 8, 1787), in Farrand, *Records of the Federal Convention*, 2:222.
36. The Federalist No. 54 (James Madison) (February 12, 1788), guides.loc.gov/federalist-papers/text-51-60#s-lg-box-wrapper-25493430.
37. Alexander Hamilton, New York Ratifying Convention Debate (June 20, 1788), in Farrand, *Records of the Federal Convention*, App. A, CCXVI, at 3:333.
38. William Ingersoll Bowditch, *Slavery and the Constitution* (Boston, 1849), 120–21.
39. Frederick Douglass, "The American Constitution and the Slave" (speech, Glasgow, March 26, 1860), in *The Speeches of Frederick Douglass: A Critical Edition*, ed. John R. McKivigan, Julie Husband, and Heather L. Kaufman (New Haven, CT: Yale University Press, 2018), 168.
40. Luther Martin, John Rutledge, Oliver Ellsworth, and Charles Pinckney (August 21, 1787), in Farrand, *Records of the Federal Convention*, 2:364–65.
41. Roger Sherman, George Mason, Charles Cotesworth Pinckney, John Dickinson, Hugh Williamson, and John Rutledge (August 22, 1787), in Farrand, *Records of the Federal Convention*, 2:369–73.
42. The Federalist No. 42 (James Madison) (January 22, 1788), guides.loc.gov/federalist-papers/text-41-50#s-lg-box-wrapper-25493406.
43. James Madison, Virginia Ratifying Commission Debate (June 17, 1788), in Farrand, *Records of the Federal Convention*, App. A, CCXII, 3:325.
44. Bowditch, *Slavery and the Constitution*, 121–22.
45. Douglass, "American Constitution and the Slave," 169–70.
46. An ordinance for the government of the Territory of the United States northwest of the River Ohio, art. 6 (July 13, 1787), avalon.law.yale.edu/18th_century/nworder.asp.
47. Pierce Butler, James Wilson, and Roger Sherman (August 28, 1787), in Farrand, *Records of the Federal Convention*, 2:443.
48. Pierce Butler (August 29, 1787), in Farrand, *Records of the Federal Convention*, 2:453–54.
49. Charles Cotesworth Pinckney, speech in South Carolina House (January 1788), in Farrand, *Records of the Federal Convention*, App. A, CLXXI, 3:254.
50. James Madison, Virginia Ratifying Convention Debate (June 17, 1788), in Farrand, *Records of the Federal Convention*, App. A, CCXII, 3:325.
51. Bowditch, *Slavery and the Constitution*, 125.
52. Frederick Douglass, *The Constitution of the United States: Is It Pro-Slavery or Anti-Slavery?* (1860),, in *The Antislavery Argument*, ed. William H. Pease and Jane H. Pease (Indianapolis, IN: Bobbs-Merrill, 1965), 354.
53. Rufus King and Gouverneur Morris (August 8, 1787), in Farrand, *Records of the Federal Convention*, 2:220, 222.
54. The Federalist No. 43 (James Madison) (January 23, 1788), guides.loc.gov/federalist-papers/text-41-50#s-lg-box-wrapper-25493407.
55. Bowditch, *Slavery and the Constitution*, 125–26.
56. Douglass, *Constitution of the United States*, 351–52.
57. See William M. Wiecek, *The Sources of Antislavery Constitutionalism in America, 1760-1848* (Ithaca, NY: Cornell University Press, 1977).

58. The debate whether the original Constitution was a proslavery or an antislavery document rages to this day. Compare the scholarly analyses of David Waldstreicher and Paul Finkelman (both in the camp that thinks the Constitution was proslavery) with the contrasting views of Sean Wilentz and Allen Guelzo, for example. David Waldstreicher, *Slavery's Constitution: From Revolution to Ratification* (New York: Hill and Wang, 2009); Paul Finkelman, *Slavery and the Founders: Race and Liberty in the Age of Jefferson*, 3rd ed. (New York: Routledge, 2014); Paul Finkelman, *Defending Slavery: Proslavery Thought in the Old South* (Boston: Bedford/St. Martin's, 2003); Sean Wilentz, *No Property in Man: Slavery and Antislavery at the Nation's Founding* (Cambridge, MA: Harvard University Press, 2018); Allen C. Guelzo, "How Slavery Is and Isn't in the Constitution," *Public Discourse: The Journal of the Witherspoon Institute*, November 8, 2018, www.thepublicdiscourse.com/2018/11/42658/; Allen C. Guelzo, "The Constitution Was Never Pro-Slavery," *National Review*, May 6, 2019, www.nationalreview.com/magazine/2019/05/06/the-constitution-was-never-pro-slavery/.

59. Barack Obama, "Speech on Race" (speech, Philadelphia, March 18, 2008), www.nytimes.com/2008/03/18/us/politics/18text-obama.html.

60. Akhil Amar has suggested, for example, that the framers could have adopted a "sliding-scale" approach, reducing the three-fifths fraction to zero-fifths over the course of several decades. Akhil Reed Amar, *America's Constitution: A Biography* (New York: Random House, 2005), 95–96.

61. See generally Gordon S. Wood, *The Creation of the American Republic, 1776-1787* (Chapel Hill: North Carolina University Press, 1969), 271–73.

62. George Mason, Elbridge Gerry, Roger Sherman, and George Mason (September 12, 1787), in Farrand, *Records of the Federal Convention*, 2:587–88.

63. James Wilson, Pennsylvania Ratifying Convention Debate (November 28, 1787), in Farrand, *Records of the Federal Convention*, App. A, CXLV, 3:143.

64. James Madison to Thomas Jefferson, October 24, 1787, founders.archives.gov/documents/Jefferson/01-12-02-0274.

65. Thomas Jefferson to James Madison, December 20, 1787, founders.archives.gov/documents/Madison/01-10-02-0210.

66. Thomas Jefferson to James Madison, March 15, 1789, founders.archives.gov/documents/Jefferson/01-14-02-0410.

67. "The Address and Reasons of Dissent of the Minority of the Convention of Pennsylvania to Their Constituents" (December 18, 1787), in *The Antifederalists* ed. Cecelia M. Kenyon (Indianapolis, IN: Bobbs-Merrill, 1966),. 46–47, www.consource.org/document/the-dissent-of-the-minority-of-the-pennsylvania-convention-pennsylvania-packet-1787-12-18/.

68. Agrippa, "To the Massachusetts Convention, No. XVIII" (February 5, 1788), in Paul Leicester Ford, *Essays on the Constitution of the United States: Published during Its Discussion by the People, 1787-1788* (Brooklyn, 1892), 120, www.gutenberg.org/files/31891/31891-pdf.pdf.

69. Richard Henry Lee, "Federal Farmer Letters to the Republican, No. II" (October 9, 1787), in *The Antifederalists*, ed. Cecelia M. Kenyon (Indianapolis, IN: Bobbs-Merrill,

1966),   211,   www.consource.org/document/federal-farmer-letters-to-the-republican-ii-1787-10-9/.

70. Brutus, "To the Citizens of the State of New York, No. II" (November 1, 1787), in *The Complete Anti-Federalist*, ed. Herbert J. Storing (Chicago: University of Chicago Press, 1981), 2:372–76, www.consource.org/document/brutus-ii-1787-11-1/.

71. Luther Martin, Reply to the Landholder (March 19, 1788), in Farrand, *Records of the Federal Convention*, App. A, CXCII, 3L:290-91, www.consource.org/document/luther-martins-reply-to-the-landholder-1788-3-19/.

72. The Federalist No. 84 (Alexander Hamilton) (July 16, 1788), guides.loc.gov/federalist-papers/text-81-85#s-lg-box-wrapper-25493491.

73. The Federalist No. 84 (Alexander Hamilton) (July 16, 1788), guides.loc.gov/federalist-papers/text-81-85#s-lg-box-wrapper-25493491.

74. The Federalist No. 84 (Alexander Hamilton) (July 16, 1788) guides.loc.gov/federalist-papers/text-81-85#s-lg-box-wrapper-25493491.

75. James Wilson, Pennsylvania Ratifying Convention Debate (December 4, 1787), in Farrand, *Records of the Federal Convention*, App. A, CXLIX, 3:162.

76. James Madison, H.R. debate, Cong. Reg. (June 8, 1789), www.consource.org/document/the-congressional-register-1789-6-8/.

77. James Madison to Thomas Jefferson, October 17, 1788, founders.archives.gov/documents/Madison/01-11-02-0218.

78. Charles Cotesworth Pinckney, South Carolina House of Representatives speech (January 18, 1788), in Farrand, *Records of the Federal Convention*, App. A, CLXXIII, 3:256.

79. James Madison to George Eve, January 2, 1789, founders.archives.gov/documents/Madison/01-11-02-0297.

80. George Washington, First Inaugural Address, April 30, 1789, www.archives.gov/exhibits/american_originals/inaugtxt.html.

81. James Madison, H.R. debate, Cong. Reg. (June 8, 1789), www.consource.org/document/the-congressional-register-1789-6-8/.

82. James Madison, H.R. debate, Congr. Reg. (June 8, 1789), www.consource.org/document/the-congressional-register-1789-6-8/.

83. 1st   Cong.,   1st   Sess.   (September   1789),   www.loc.gov/resource/rbc0001.2010madison38253/?sp=2.

84. Woody Holton, *Unruly Americans and the Origins of the Constitution* (New York: Hill and Wang, 2007), x.

85. Barron v. Baltimore, 32 U.S. 243 (1833).

86. Franklin Delano Roosevelt, "State of the Union Message to Congress," January 11, 1944, www.fdrlibrary.marist.edu/archives/pdfs/state_union.pdf.

3

The Constitution in the New Nation
(1789–1848)

The first decades of the new American nation witnessed numerous constitutional controversies. Alexander Hamilton, Thomas Jefferson, and James Madison disagreed about the authority of Congress to establish a national bank, consistent with the Constitution. Differences of opinion about the interplay of state sovereignty and judicial authority led to the overturning of the Supreme Court's decision in *Chisholm v. Georgia* (1793)[1] and the adoption of the Eleventh Amendment (protecting states against certain types of lawsuits). A Twelfth Amendment followed shortly thereafter, in response to the unhappy reality of a president and vice president aligned with different party ideologies (as candidates ran as individuals, not on a party ticket). Jay's Treaty, Washington's Neutrality Proclamation, and Jefferson's purchase of Louisiana all raised significant constitutional issues about foreign policy. The Alien and Sedition Act controversy pushed the boundaries of the young country's commitment to free speech and political dissent. And in *Barron v. Baltimore* (1833),[2] the Supreme Court ruled that the Bill of Rights would constrain only the national government, not states.

Underlying all these constitutional disputes was an even more fundamental question: Exactly which persons were meant to be included—or not—in the new national polity? Slaves, free Blacks, Native Americans, immigrant aliens, indentured servants, and women were excluded in whole or in part from the rights of equal citizenship—at the same time that the nation became a far more participatory polity for white males (by ending most property qualifications for voting). What accounted for the sizable gap that emerged between the lofty democratic ideals of the republic and the sobering realties of Jeffersonian-Jacksonian America?

In considering this era, classroom dialogue can profitably be focused on the centrality of institutionalized slavery, particularly at the state level. While a few textual provisions in the original Constitution directly concerned slavery (permitting Congress eventually to end the international slave trade and exclude slavery from certain territories), for the most part the Convention's decisions left slavery matters in the hands of individual states. Above the Mason-Dixon Line, states used this autonomy to enact the gradual emancipation of slavery. But also

With Liberty and Justice for All?. Edited by Steven A. Steinbach, Maeva Marcus, and Robert Cohen, Oxford University Press. © Oxford University Press 2022. DOI: 10.1093/oso/9780197516317.003.0003

under the antebellum Constitution, Southern states, where the vast majority of slaves lived, were free to write tyrannical slave codes and to enforce them vigorously in state courts. Federal authorities deferred to the slavocracy throughout the first half of the 1800s even when slave states interfered with distinctly national responsibilities within the constitutional structure, such as delivery of the mails and the freedom of interstate travel. Left virtually alone by the Constitution and fueled by the westward expansion of the young nation, slavery thrived in the South—and white Southern attitudes toward it hardened, even as abolitionist sentiment grew in Northern states. In retrospect, what should be history's verdict on the framers' decision in Philadelphia to leave the future of slavery in the United States largely to the states themselves?

Despite concerted efforts to confine the regulation of slavery to the state level, from time to time—like "a fire bell in the night," in Jefferson's words[3]—national comity and unity were endangered over slavery-related disputes. For example, Quaker petitions to abolish slavery submitted to Congress in its very first session threatened almost immediately to unravel the awkward consensus reached at Philadelphia. Subsequently, when the Constitution's twenty-year prohibition on outlawing US participation in the international slave trade was set to expire, Congress moved to bar further slave importation—but at the same time took no steps to limit the continued domestic purchase and sale of enslaved Blacks, paving the way for a second middle passage, as more than a million were uprooted to facilitate the westward expansion of the Cotton South. By the mid-1830s, members of the House of Representatives adopted a "gag rule" to suppress abolitionist petitions to Congress. And a highly charged Supreme Court case involved the killing in self-defense of Cuban slave traders by their African captives on the high seas.

And what about Native American peoples[4]—who, from the Constitution's perspective, were neither citizens nor sovereign? Soon enough, tentative national policies of separate self-governance and/or gradual assimilation gave way to forced "Indian removal"—the Jacksonian era's antiseptic euphemism for the deportation of Native Americans who lived in the path of ever-expanding white settlers. The Supreme Court lacked the legal creativity to articulate, and the political influence to enforce, any bright-line demarcation between national and state authority and tribal autonomy.

The nation experienced a further defining constitutional moment in its early years. Already riven by rancorous partisanship, a foreign crisis with France plunged the United States into one of the most dangerous threats to civil liberties it would ever experience, as Federalists used a new criminal law (the Sedition Act) to prosecute and imprison their political rivals, the Democratic-Republicans. James Madison and Thomas Jefferson responded with states' rights clarion calls, the Virginia and Kentucky Resolutions, which effectively amounted to constitutional rebellion. Even after the Alien and Sedition crisis had receded, however, smoldering partisan animosities propelled the Republicans to launch an attack on judicial independence and the Supreme Court. The failed impeachment of Justice Samuel Chase serves as an instructive coda to the Sedition Act controversy: it offers students abundant opportunity to reflect on the intense polarization in the new republic—and on the dangers such divisions pose to personal liberties and political institutions.

Creating "We the People"

Annette Gordon-Reed
Carl M. Loeb University Professor, Harvard University

The Preamble to the Constitution of the United States begins with the words "We the People," to signify the creation of a republic from colonies that had once been part of an empire run under a monarchy. But just who were "the People" who were supposed to constitute the government of the United States and who were to be protected under the newly written charter? The question was extremely important for determining the rights and responsibilities of all those who lived within the confines of the new nation. During the years in which the Constitution was written and ratified, the population of the country—just under four million—included Native Americans, people of European descent, and people of African descent. Native Americans were, by and large, treated as members of their own nations. The vast majority of people of African descent were enslaved, and thus out of civil and civic society. In the wake of the Revolution, a number of Northern states instituted gradual emancipation statutes that began a process of ending slavery over a period of years. Several New England states, in which few Black people lived, ended slavery more abruptly. Some Southern states, most notably Virginia, liberalized their emancipation laws, resulting in the creation of a class of free Blacks who were deemed to be "denizens," not actual citizens.[5] They lived in various states but did not have all of the civic rights and protections of either the state or the federal Constitution. Not everyone who lived within the boundaries of the United States was part of "the People" to whom the Constitution referred.

One of the first acts by the new government under the Constitution was to set rules about who could come to the United States and join the American experiment. The choices made give an idea about what those who initially ran the country thought about who was eligible to become part of "the people." Under Article I, Section 8, Clause 4 of the Constitution, Congress was given the power to set the terms by which those not born in the United States can come to the country and become a citizen. Acting under this power, Congress passed the Naturalization Act of 1790 (also referred to as the Nationality Act of 1790). On the question of what type of person could become a citizen, the Act provided in pertinent part:

> Any alien, being a free white person, who shall have resided within the limits and under the jurisdiction of the United States for the term of two years, may be admitted to become a citizen thereof, on application to any common law court of record in any one of the states wherein he shall have resided for the term of one year at least, making proof to the satisfaction of such court, that he is a person of good character, and taking the oath or affirmation prescribed by law, to support the Constitution of the United States.[6]

The language of the statute specifically excluded nonwhite people and indentured servants of any color. Women, operating under legal disabilities (e.g., their inability to vote) generally were not subject to the Act's provisions, which changed in the decade after passage, and at various points throughout the nineteenth century (usually with respect to the length of residency requirements). The language of the Act suggests that for purposes of federal law, nonwhites were not seen as citizens, though some Northern states treated people of African descent as citizens of their state.

The fledgling United States found itself in the midst of a turbulent world that it had a hand in roiling with its own revolution. The American Revolution had been followed by the French Revolution and the Haitian Revolution, both world-shattering events. What had happened in France, in particular, influenced the American political scene just as it was getting started. During the 1790s, Americans lined up on both sides of the divide about the events in France. Many felt close to the French, as they had been the colonists' first ally, playing a pivotal role in the conflict with Great Britain. Indeed, the intervention of France had made American victory possible. The French Revolution proclaimed the "Rights of Man," offering hope that entrenched hierarchies would be upended and those who had lived under the oppression of elites would be liberated to have decent lives. This seemed in keeping with the spirit of 1776. On the other hand, the chaos in France frightened many Americans. The king and queen had been beheaded; the Catholic Church attacked, as the revolutionaries sought to put "reason" in the place of religion. Those wary of the French Revolution saw the rise of "the people" as the rise of "the mob," and feared that mob rule could come in their new country. The split among the populace helped give rise to the formation of political parties—which were not mentioned in the Constitution and not welcomed by its authors—with "Democratic-Republicans" seen generally as pro-French Revolution and the "Federalists" seen as anti-French Revolution.

The Haitian Revolution and its aftermath sent a flood of refugees into the United States, who settled largely in Philadelphia, New York, and Virginia. Although some Americans were sympathetic to their plight, the émigrés' determination to become involved in politics became a cause for concern. White Southerners were also frightened that the enslaved people who had been brought to the United States by their enslavers would bring the "contagion of liberty" to the American mainland, inciting African Americans to fight for their freedom. Those fears came to pass in 1800 in Virginia when a man named Gabriel emerged as the leader of a plotted slave rebellion, with some of the participants speaking of the Haitian Revolution as an inspiration.[7] Concerns about émigrés from Europe and Haiti led to the passage of another version of the Naturalization Act, in 1795.[8] This legislation lengthened the time of residency for establishing citizenship from two years to five years.

In the midst of a flare-up between Great Britain and revolutionary France in the late 1790s, the United States found itself in conflict with its oldest ally. The "Quasi-War" with France, which people feared would result in more refugees coming into the country, increased American anxieties about foreigners even more. The law regarding naturalization was changed yet again in 1798, extending the period of residence to fourteen years, among other provisions designed to make it harder to become a citizen.[9] At the same time, the Congress, led by Federalists, also passed a law to punish sedition, aimed at writings by immigrants in the political newspapers that proliferated in the 1790s.[10] These measures, known as the Alien and Sedition Acts, galvanized public opinion and further deepened the split between what had become the Democratic-Republican Party and the Federalist Party, as many immigrants supported the former.[11] Prominent Democratic-Republican journalists and even a sitting congressman were prosecuted and jailed. Political passions became so intense that even Thomas Jefferson and James Madison, through the Kentucky and Virginia Resolutions they drafted, called upon state governments to declare the federal laws unconstitutional. Eventually, immigrants who were eligible to vote joined with other Americans to turn the Federalists out of office and helped elect Thomas Jefferson president in 1800. The Naturalization Act of 1798 was repealed in 1802.

Jefferson would later refer to his election as the "Revolution of 1800." He believed, as did many of his supporters, that he had rescued the American Revolution and put "the people," with him as their representative, in power. This was, he thought, in keeping with the spirit of '76. The election was close—a tie in fact—and had to be decided in the House of Representatives. Jefferson took office in an extremely partisan atmosphere that he had helped to create. The partisanship continued with early fights over the composition of, and powers of, the judicial branch, which led to the famous case of *Marbury v. Madison* (1803)[12] and attempts by Republicans to impeach Samuel Chase, a Federalist-leaning member of the Supreme Court. This serious threat to judicial independence was narrowly averted only because several Republican senators abandoned the quest to oust Justice Chase. Members of the founding generation had not anticipated that the pull of "party," or "faction" as Madison called it in *Federalist No. 10*, would take hold so quickly and thoroughly. But by the time Jefferson took office, most Americans had been participating in the political system as a member of one party or another.

One event united nearly all Americans at the turn of the nineteenth century. Perhaps the signal achievement of the Jefferson presidency was the 1803 purchase from France of Louisiana for $15 million. The acquisition of the territory, or actually the acquisition of the right to deal with the indigenous population about the fate of the territory, doubled the country's size and opened a large swath of the middle of the continent to the United States. Eventually fourteen states would be carved out of the land. Contrary to the way it is often portrayed, the Louisiana Territory was not empty. Native Americans, white settlers, and enslaved people were already there when the deal was made. European settlers, developing their own understanding of citizenship, were interested in land, which they saw as a necessary precursor to independence. If one owned land, one was not dependent upon others, as farmers could grow their own food and sell surpluses to others. But thinking about the nation's future raised this question: Would the process of realizing citizenship be carried out on family farms, or on farms that relied on enslaved labor?

The question of slavery took on greater urgency after the Louisiana Purchase. The "compromise" that had been reached during the Constitutional Convention left slavery to be regulated by the states—and Southern states used that authority to promulgate increasingly strict slave codes, to issue judicial opinions that affirmed the violence of the enslaver-enslaved relationship, and even to censor delivery of the federal mails and to prevent free Black sailors from leaving their ships in Southern ports. Some members of the founding generation had expressed the view that slavery was a dying system and postponed reckoning with the institution. But white settlers' determination to move west put further pressure on the slavery question. The Northwest Ordinance, drafted in 1784 by Thomas Jefferson, was the first attempt to set the standard for admission of territories as states in the land north of the Ohio River. Article VI of the Ordinance forbade the extension of slavery into the area that would become Ohio, Illinois, Indiana, and Michigan. The redone Ordinance, passed in 1787, kept the provision, though some enslaved people were already in the area. Crucially, the Southwest Ordinance of 1790 did not contain the prohibition of slavery in the territories below the Ohio River. As a result, new states that formed in this region could have slavery.

The balance between states with slavery and those without remained relatively stable throughout the first two decades of the nineteenth century. From the time of the ratification of the Constitution, there had been evidence of a growing regional divide over the issue of slavery. But other political issues during the Jefferson administration, and then the War of 1812 during the Madison administration, became the center of attention. The (arguable) victory over Great Britain and the electoral demise of the Federalist Party, which dampened political conflict and left the Republican Party in ascendancy, brought a general sense of unity to the country—so much so that the Monroe presidency is often referred to as the "Era of Good Feelings." Nationalism was the order of the day, bolstered by rulings from the Supreme Court, led by Chief Justice John Marshall, that increased the power of the federal government over commerce (especially in *Gibbons v. Ogden* (1824)[13]) and vis-à-vis the states and state courts (in a series of decisions beginning with *Fletcher v. Peck* (1810)[14]).

Cracks in the façade of the relative calm of this period began to appear in 1819 with the arrival of important crises. First, the nation suffered a depression that devastated the economy for several years. The "Panic of 1819" brought the always controversial issue of the role of banks into view, as banking policy had made the situation worse. The question of the efficacy and indeed the constitutionality of a national bank, heatedly debated at the time Congress approved the First Bank of the United States, had been very much a political question. Citizens argued that a strict construction of the Constitution required a constitutional amendment for the creation of the bank, while others held that the "necessary and proper" clause of the Constitution could be interpreted to allow for a federally created bank. This issue had been divisive from the beginning of the republic, driving the conflict between Jefferson and Alexander Hamilton when they served in the Washington administration. The initial National Bank's charter was permitted to lapse in 1811, but financial problems during the War of 1812 led to an approval of the Second Bank in 1816. Although the Supreme Court upheld the constitutionality of the bank in *McCulloch v. Maryland* (1819),[15] the "Panic" revived political conflict over the issue, and Andrew Jackson eventually used constitutional arguments, along with others, to bring about the demise of the institution.

In addition to economic turmoil, the sectional crisis over slavery came to the fore around the same time, raising the question of what kind of nation the United States would be. Debates at the national level over slavery had arisen previously: for example, when a group of Quakers from Pennsylvania filed antislavery petitions, or at the time Congress voted to end the international slave trade. But in 1819, inhabitants of the Missouri Territory applied to become a state, and tensions over slavery erupted. The territory had slavery, and its admission as a slave state would have upset the numerical balance among the states, putting the states with slavery ahead of those without. New York Representative James

Tallmadge suggested that Missouri be admitted only if no additional enslaved people could be brought into the state and that children born after a certain date would be freed at the age of twenty-five, a proposal reminiscent of the Northern gradual emancipation statutes. The proposal incensed many Missourians and other Southerners, as they saw it as an attack on the institution and their rights as citizens to enslave people.

The crisis was a broad hint of how serious the regional divide over slavery had become. Jefferson, now ten years retired to Monticello, wrote that the crisis was like a "fire bell in the night,"[16] warning of a deep conflict that could result in the dissolution of the American Union. A proposed compromise forestalled the fight: Missouri would be admitted as a "slave" state and Maine would be admitted as a "free" state, thus keeping the balance between the two types of states in the Union. This "Missouri Compromise" was accepted with an additional drawing of a latitude line: slavery would be allowed in states below latitude 36° 30', the border of Missouri, and would be disallowed in new states formed above that latitude. The worst was averted, but the underlying problem of a nation with two vastly different labor systems, and two different conceptions of morality, did not go away. Nor did the debate over slavery in Congress cease after the Missouri crisis had been resolved. To the contrary, sectional discord became so vehement that by 1836 the House of Representatives imposed upon itself a "gag rule" prohibiting further speech or debate about the subject.

By the time the nation faced the Missouri crisis, the political landscape was changing, for the majority of white males could vote. This was the beginning of what has been called the "Era of the Common Man"—or, in the words of Alexis de Tocqueville, a visitor from France, "Democracy in America"—a period that saw the rise of Andrew Jackson, the hero of the Battle of New Orleans in the War of 1812. Jackson, as a senator from Tennessee, ran for president in 1824 against a crowded field. He won a mere plurality of the popular vote and the Electoral College votes, and the election went to the House of Representatives. Ultimately, John Quincy Adams of Massachusetts was chosen as president. Like his father, John Adams, John Quincy, a proponent of a strong and active federal government that would, among other things, promote internal improvements (nationally funded infrastructure projects), was destined to be a one-term president. Adams, chilly and patrician, though clearly one of the most prepared and intelligent presidents the nation has ever produced, never managed to become popular. Jackson and his supporters regrouped and won the election of 1828, an achievement of significant cultural importance because Jackson was the first president who did not come from the highest rungs of the elite. His relatively humble background fit perfectly with the spirit of the times. He was the very embodiment of what "Jacksonian democracy" was supposed to be about: a system that was to give an equal chance for white men to rise, no matter what the circumstances of their birth. Jackson's inaugural party, in which the President's House was opened to the public, was a rowdy affair that also seemed to symbolize the form of democracy he had helped to unleash.

For all the efforts at equalizing the franchise among white males and talk of social equality among whites, it was clear that Jacksonian democracy, in the federal and state contexts, was to be about creating a "white man's government." The voting rights of free Black Americans were actually curtailed during this time. Over the course of the 1830s, states—like Jackson's Tennessee—that had not written racial requirements into voting rules changed the laws to explicitly state that only white men were allowed to vote. Even Pennsylvania, which had enacted the first gradual emancipation statute in 1780 and had allowed Black voting, revoked Black males' suffrage rights at a constitutional convention held in 1838.[17] The notion that Blacks were mere inhabitants of the country, not true citizens, first suggested in the Naturalization Act of 1790, was confirmed in the 1830s (and, of course, would eventually be embraced by the Supreme Court two decades later in the *Dred Scott* decision[18]). When taken with the compromise over slavery, allowing millions of inhabitants of the country to hold the status of chattel, and thousands of free African Americans to be treated as second-class citizens, the message about who was fully American was clear.

Constitutional issues roiled the Jacksonian era. Although he had extremely devoted followers, his presidency was contentious. There were, among other things, battles over the extension of the charter of the Second National Bank (Jackson was opposed to it), over tariffs, and over the Nullification Crisis, stoked by Vice President John C. Calhoun and his supporters who talked of disunion, which Jackson adamantly opposed. Jackson also played a pivotal role in national policy regarding Native Americans. In a State of the Union address he called for the "voluntary" removal of Indians from the southeastern part of the United States to make way for more white settlement.[19] Although he styled it as a benevolent measure, designed to protect Native Americans who had to contend with aggressive white settlers, the main goal was to replace the Native American population with a white population, including whites who would bring enslaved people into the area. Congress responded to his call, passing the Indian Removal Act of 1830,[20] which Jackson enthusiastically signed into law. This eventually put in motion the "Trail of Tears" in which Native Americans, along with the Black people whom they enslaved, were forced to leave the southeastern part of the United States to move across the Mississippi River to land designated as Indian Territory.

Although Jackson's Indian policy was controversial among many Americans, the objections appeared to be more about process rather than the ultimate substantive outcome—the opening of the West to white settlement. There was a general consensus that the land was to be taken from Native Americans—acquired by sale or treaty, or through the abrogation of treaties, or by force. After all, a similar policy had taken place along the eastern seaboard from the moment the English settlers had landed in the Chesapeake and in New England. The thinking early on was that the United States would gain control over the land from the Atlantic to the Pacific.

It was natural that a country that styled itself as a "government of law" would turn to law in an attempt to set the terms of, or in some cases, justify the project. Along with the executive and legislative branches, the Supreme Court, led by Chief Justice John Marshall, dealt with the question of how Native Americans would fit into the United States in three important cases from 1823 to 1832, often called "the Marshall Trilogy." In the first case, *Johnson and Graham's Lessee v. McIntosh* (1823),[21] Marshall presented his version of the history between the Native Americans and the European colonists, referring, at one point, to Europeans' aggression and their "pretense" at having discovered a place that was already inhabited. Though Marshall spoke with seeming sympathy for the indigenous population, the Court ultimately decided that the United States had the ownership interest in the land in its territory and that the Native Americans had a mere "right of occupancy." The Native Americans, therefore, lacked the power to sell their land to anyone but the federal government. The government had the sole right to convey the property to white settlers. Both Jeffersonian and Jacksonian democracy proclaimed that "the people of the United States" constituted the true sovereign government, and this decision gave a clear message about to whom the country belonged.

The Court next addressed the Native American question in *Cherokee Nation v. Georgia* (1831).[22] In this case, the Court held that Indian nations were not foreign nations but were instead "domestic dependent nations" under the jurisdiction and stewardship of the federal government. As a result, the states could not make policy with respect to them. Finally, *Worcester v. Georgia* (1832)[23] repeated the pronouncement that Indians were a dependent nation and held that the federal government, not state governments, had the authority to deal with Indian nations. Legislation, court decisions, executive orders, and the actions of white settlers effectively sealed the fate of the various Native American groups. The process played itself out over the course of the nineteenth century until indigenous people were consigned to reservations, no longer in control of the land their ancestors had lived on for generations before the arrival of Europeans.

While the fates of enslaved people and Native American peoples in the new United States became issues for open political dispute and argument during the end of the eighteenth century and the first decades of the nineteenth century, arguments about the status of women were not as prominent. Relations between males and females were seen as a matter of "nature," not politics. While both slavery and family relationships were deemed to involve "domestic" affairs and were said to be in the province of individual states, provisions in the Constitution regarding slavery, like the Fugitive Slave Clause, made clear that some aspects of the institution were of national import. That was not true of marriage and family life. For the most part, women were seen as living under the protection and direction of their male relatives: father to daughter, husband to wife. The political rights gained in the new republic would be conveyed to women through their fathers or their husbands. Immediately after the American Revolution, certain classes of women in New Jersey were allowed to vote. But that right to vote was revoked in 1807.

Scholars have suggested that in the immediate aftermath of the Revolution, there was a backlash against efforts to change the status of women, in consideration of the fact that women had been active participants in the effort against Great Britain.[24] Women participated in boycotts of British goods, helped make ammunition for the guns used against British forces, and kept farms and households going in the absence of their husbands and fathers. Some even disguised themselves as men in order to fight in battles. But the notion of the equality of all mankind meant that women were "equal" in their separate space, fulfilling their "natural" role as wives and mothers. The concept of Republican Motherhood suggested that women could best serve the new country by raising children who would function well in the new society.

Despite being effectively barred from political power, the status of American white women did begin to change in the decades after the Revolution. Educational opportunities expanded for elite white women in the early American republic with the opening of many "academies" that helped broaden their horizons with training beyond the domestic sphere. With the opening of textile mills in Lowell, Massachusetts, non-elite white women left farms to work in the factories where some education was provided for the women who lived in dormitories close to the mills.

The movement for abolition of slavery, seen as having moral and religious bases, gave women an opportunity to become involved in a social movement that was actually deeply political. As they pondered the plight of the enslaved—their status as legal chattel, and enslaved women who had no right to refuse consent to sex and no right to control the lives of their children—they began to think of the status of women in relationship to men. Women, no matter what their race or marital status, could not vote. Under the doctrine of coverture, married women lost the right to control property and to make contracts. They had no legal right to refuse to have sex with their husbands, the marriage contract having created perpetual consent. Children of a marriage were seen as belonging to the husband. Given the rhetoric about equality, why, many asked, should women be kept in a second-class status?

Women such as Lucretia Mott—who in 1833 with William Lloyd Garrison founded the American Anti-Slavery Society (AASS)—her sister Martha Coffin Wright, and Elizabeth Cady Stanton became leaders of the women's suffrage movement after learning about organizing and persuasion from their participation in the abolitionist movement. Not everyone was happy about the open and vigorous involvement of women in this very intense social movement. There were strong taboos against women speaking in public and engaging in what were seen as "masculine" activities. Concerns about the propriety of women taking too strong a role in the movement led the AASS to splinter. Mott and Stanton became even more adamant about women's rights and were the driving force behind the Seneca Falls Convention, held in 1848 in Seneca Falls, New York, to promote the cause of women's equality.

Stanton drafted a "Declaration of Sentiments and Grievances" that was modeled on Jefferson's construction of the Declaration of Independence. To make the point clear, the Declaration of Sentiments added "and women" to the famous phrase, so that it became "self-evident" that all "men and women" are created equal.[25] Stanton, who gave the speech opening the convention, stated explicitly that women were living under "a form of government, existing without the consent of the governed," and they were declaring women's "right to be free as man is free, to be represented in the government which we are taxed to support."[26] This language echoed some of the complaints and grievances enunciated by the American patriots in the 1760s and 1770s in the run-up to the American Revolution. Equality was a universal principle that should apply to people, period. That logic made both slavery and discrimination against women abhorrent.

The women and men who convened in upstate New York did so in a society that had been changing on many fronts, not just in the growing insistence on the need to abolish slavery and give equal rights for women. Americans also had an interest in reforming the way prisons were run; they attempted to deal with the problems caused by alcoholic consumption through the temperance movement. There was a great interest among many in working to make society better. Technological advances—the invention of the telegraph and the daguerreotype— helped transform life in the United States. But it was the Mexican War, declared in 1846 and won in 1848, that reignited the issue of slavery and westward expansion. The American victory in the war brought California and the New Mexico Territory under the control of the United States. Earlier, in 1845, after much controversy, Texas had entered the Union as a slave state. Some, but not all, Americans had come to believe that it was the country's "Manifest Destiny" to take control of North America and spread American values. One of the values that animated many Americans was that of slaveholding, which after the rise of King Cotton brought great wealth to the South. By 1848, it was clear to many that there might be no constitutional or legal solution to the question of whether the United States would be a nation of slavery or a nation of free labor. The answer to that question would come only after the total breakdown of law and the deaths of many Americans.

Slavery, Race, and the States—Primary Sources

The Constitution written in Philadelphia mostly left slavery as a matter to be dealt with by the individual states. As a consequence, for generations of enslaved Africans, almost all aspects of the master-slave relationship—as well as almost all other matters concerning race and slavery—were subject to the laws of the states and the discretion of state officials, with little federal involvement or oversight. Whereas Northern states, over time, enacted emancipation policies, in Southern states control over the institution of slavery was manifested in many ways, including through slave codes; judicial rulings that offered unflinching support for slave masters; the suppression of interstate travel and free speech; and the force of public opinion, which soon enough declared slavery to be a "positive good."

Slave Codes

Even before the rebellion against Great Britain, many of the colonies had adopted slave codes governing slavery and race relations. These laws were expanded and intensified in the early decades of the nation's history. Slaves not only were legally treated as property belonging to their masters under these slave codes, they were denied civil and human rights, including the right to own property, secure literacy or education, marry, travel, assemble, or act in self-defense. Many of the slave codes also imposed restrictions on free Blacks and even whites in order to guard against possible interference with the slave system. And because of the decisions made at the Philadelphia Convention, none of these state laws violated the US Constitution.

Georgia Slave Code (1848)

Some representative examples from the laws of Georgia:

1. The following shall be considered as capital offenses, when committed by a slave or free person of color: insurrection, or an attempt to excite it; committing a rape, or attempting it on a free white female; murder of a free white person, or murder of a slave or free person of color, or poisoning of a human being; every and each of these offences shall, on conviction, be punished with death.

2. And the following also shall be considered as capital offenses, when committed by a slave or free person of color: assaulting a free white person with

intent to murder, or with a weapon likely to produce death; maiming a free white person; burglary, or arson of any description; also, any attempt to poison a human being; every and each of these offenses shall, on conviction, be punished with death. . . .

4. If any slave shall presume to strike any white person, such slave upon trial and conviction before the justice or justices, according to the direction of this act, shall for the first offense suffer such punishment as the said justice or justices shall in his or their discretion think fit, not extending to life or limb; and for the second offense, suffer death: but in case any such slave shall grievously wound, maim, or bruise any white person, though it shall be only the first offense, such slave shall suffer death. . . .

9. If any free person of color commits the offense of inveigling or enticing away any slave or slaves for the purpose of, and with the intention to aid and assist such slave or slaves leaving the service of his or their owner or owners, or in going to another state, such person so offending shall, for each and every such offense, on conviction, be confined in the penitentiary at hard labor for one year. . . .

11. If any slave, Negro, or free person of color, or any white person, shall teach any other slave, Negro, or free person of color, to read or write either written or printed characters, the said free person of color or slave shall be punished by fine and whipping.

12. If any slave or slaves, or free persons of color shall purchase or buy [certain] commodities from any slave or slaves, he, she, or they . . . shall receive on his, her, or their bare back or backs, thirty-nine lashes. . . .

16. No person of color, whether free or slave, shall be allowed to preach to, exhort, or join in any religious exercise with any persons of color, either free or slave, there being more than seven persons of color present.[27]

South Carolina Slave Code (1840)

Further representative examples of punitive statutes regulating slavery were to be found in the slave code of South Carolina.

I. [All existing slaves] are hereby declared to be, and remain forever hereafter, absolute slaves, and shall follow the condition of the mother, and shall be deemed, held, taken, reputed, and adjudged in law, to be chattels personal, in the hands of their owners and possessors. . . .

III. No person whatsoever shall permit or suffer any slave under his or their care or management . . . to go out of the plantation to which such slave belongs . . . without a letter . . . or a ticket in the words following. . . .

VII. [Constables are authorized and directed] to disperse any assembly or meeting of slaves which may disturb the peace or endanger the safety . . . and to search all suspected places for arms, ammunition or stolen goods. . . .

XXIII. It shall not be lawful for any slave, unless in the presence of some white person, to carry or make use of firearms, or any offensive weapons whatsoever. . . .

XXXVI. As it is absolutely necessary for the safety of this province that all due care be taken to restrain the wanderings and meetings of Negroes and other slaves, at all times, and more especially on Saturday nights, Sundays, and other holidays, and their using and carrying wooden swords and other mischievous and dangerous weapons, or using or keeping of drums, horns, or other loud instruments, which may call together or give sign or notice to one another of their wicked designs and purposes. . . .

XXXVII. And whereas cruelty is not only highly unbecoming those who profess themselves Christians, but is odious in the eyes of all men who have any sense of virtue of humanity; therefore, to restrain and prevent barbarity being exercised towards slaves . . . if any person or persons whosoever shall willfully murder his own slave, or the slave of any other person, every such person shall, upon conviction thereof, forfeit and pay the sum of seven hundred pounds. . . . And if any person shall on sudden heat or passion, or by undue correction, kill his own slave, or the slave of any other person, he shall forfeit the sum of three hundred and fifty pounds. . . . And in case any person or persons shall willfully cut out the tongue, put out the eye, castrate, or cruelly scald, burn, or deprive any slave of any limb or member, or shall inflict any other cruel punishment, other than by whipping or beating with a horsewhip, cowskin, switch, or small stick, or by putting irons on, or confining or imprisoning such slave, every such person shall, for every such offense, forfeit the sum of one hundred pounds.[28]

Judicial Enforcement

Slave codes were diligently—and sometimes ruthlessly—enforced by state courts, confirming Frederick Douglass's observation that masters committed crimes against their slaves "with almost as much impunity as upon the deck of a pirate ship."[29] Nothing in the US Constitution prevented state courts from reaching such decisions.

State v. Mann (1829)

One such notorious judicial decision was issued by Thomas Ruffin, the chief justice of the North Carolina Supreme Court. The facts of the case were simple and disturbing. John Mann hired, on a temporary basis, an enslaved woman named Lydia from her master. Lydia "committed some small offense." When Mann attempted to punish her, Lydia "ran off." Mann "called upon her to stop, which being refused, he shot at and wounded her." Mann's conviction in the lower courts was overturned on appeal by Justice Ruffin.

> Arguments drawn from the well-established principles, which confer and restrain the authority of the parent over the child, the tutor over the pupil, the master over the apprentice, have been pressed on us. The court does not recognize their application. There is no likeness between the cases. They are in opposition to each other, and there is an impassable gulf between them. The difference is that which exists between freedom and slavery—and a greater cannot be imagined. In the one, the end in view is the happiness of the youth, born to equal rights with that governor, on whom the duty devolves of training the young to usefulness, in a station which he is afterwards to assume among freemen. To such an end, and with such a subject, moral and intellectual instruction seem the natural means; and for the most part, they are found to suffice. Moderate force is superadded only to make the others effectual. If that fail, it is better to leave the party to his own headstrong passions, and the ultimate correction of the law, than to allow it to be immoderately inflicted by a private person. With slavery it is far otherwise. The end is the profit of the master, his security and the public safety; the subject, one doomed in his own person and his posterity to live without knowledge and without the capacity to make anything his own, and to toil that another may reap the fruits. . . . Such services can only be expected from one who has no will of his own; who surrenders his will in implicit obedience to that of another. . . . The power of the master must be absolute to render the submission of the slave perfect. . . . It must be so. There is no remedy. This discipline belongs to the state of slavery. . . .
>
> We cannot allow the right of the master to be brought into discussion in the courts of justice. The slave, to remain a slave, must be made sensible that there is no appeal from his master; that his power is in no instance usurped; but is conferred by the laws of man at least, if not by the law of God. The danger would be great, indeed, if the tribunals of justice should be called on to graduate the punishment appropriate to every temper and every dereliction of menial duty. No man can anticipate the many and aggravated provocations of the master, which the slave would be constantly stimulated by his own passions or the instigation of others to give; or the consequent wrath of the master, prompting him

to bloody vengeance upon the turbulent traitor—a vengeance generally practiced with impunity, by reason of its privacy. The court therefore disclaims the
power of changing the relation in which these parts of our people stand to each
other. . . .

The protection already afforded by several statutes, that all-powerful motive,
the private interest of the owner, the benevolences towards each other, seated
in the hearts of those who have been born and bred together, the frowns and
deep execrations of the community upon the barbarian who is guilty of excessive and brutal cruelty to his unprotected slave, all combined, have produced a
mildness of treatment and attention to the comforts of the unfortunate class of
slaves, greatly mitigating the rigors of servitude and ameliorating the condition
of the slaves. . . . This result, greatly to be desired, may be much more rationally
expected from the events above alluded to and now in progress than from any
rash expositions of abstract truths by a judiciary tainted with a false and fanatical philanthropy, seeking to redress an acknowledged evil by means still more
wicked and appalling than even that evil. . . .

This dominion is essential to the value of slaves as property, to the security
of the master, and the public tranquility, greatly dependent upon their subordination; and in fine, as most effectually securing the general protection and
comfort of the slaves themselves.[30]

State of Missouri v. Celia, a Slave (1855)

Or consider the case of State of Missouri v. Celia, a Slave. Celia was indicted for
murder in 1855 after she killed her owner, Robert Newsom, as he was attempting
to rape her, which he had done on previous occasions. At trial, Celia's attorney
asked the judge to give a self-defense instruction to the jury.

If the jury believe from the evidence that Celia did kill Newsom, but that the
killing was necessary to protect herself against a forced sexual intercourse with
her, on the part of said Newsom, and there was imminent danger of such forced
sexual connection being accomplished by Newsom, they will not find her guilty
of murder in the first degree.[31]

Rejecting her claim of self-defense, however, Judge William Hall instead
instructed the jury as follows:

If Newsom was in the habit of having intercourse with the defendant who was his
slave and went to her cabin on the night he was killed to have intercourse with her
or for any other purpose and while he was standing on the floor talking to her she

struck him with a stick which was a dangerous weapon and knocked him down and struck him again after he fell, and killed him by either blow, it is murder in the first degree. Defendant had no right to kill him because he came to her cabin and was talking to her about having sexual intercourse with her or anything else.[32]

Celia was convicted by the jury of first-degree murder; she was sentenced to death by Judge Hall; and she was hung by the state of Missouri on December 21, 1855. "Thus has closed one of the most horrible tragedies ever enacted in our county," concluded a report from Missouri published in the *New York Times* shortly after Celia's execution—referring to the crime, not the hanging.[33] The *Mann* and *Celia* cases suggest that judicial doctrines, no less than legislative codes, were distorted by courts in slaveholding states in an effort to protect and support the institution of slavery.

Negro Seamen Acts: South Carolina Law (1822)

The Negro Seamen laws passed by South Carolina and seven other states pro-vided a further example of the consequences of vesting virtually all control over slavery and racial matters at the state level. In the aftermath of Denmark Vesey's alleged slave revolt plot in Charleston in 1822, South Carolina re-quired all free Black sailors who arrived on ships docking in the state's harbors to be jailed for the duration of their vessel's visit.

> An act for the better regulation of free negroes and persons of color. . . . That if any vessel shall come into any port or harbor of this state from any other state or foreign port, having on board any free negroes or persons of color, as cooks, stewards, or mariners, or in any other employment on board said vessels, such free negroes or persons of color shall be liable to be seized and confined in jail until said vessel shall clear out and depart from this state; and that when said vessel is ready to sail the captain of said vessel shall be bound to carry away the said free negro, or free person of color, and to pay the expenses of his detention; and in case of his neglect or refusal to do so . . . such free negroes or persons of color shall be deemed and taken as absolute slaves and sold.[34]

Elkison v. Deliesseline (1823)

The law's purpose was to prevent transitory free Blacks from mingling with—and presumably assisting or inciting—local slaves. US Supreme Court Justice William Johnson (sitting as a circuit justice) concluded that South Carolina's statute inter-fered with interstate and foreign commerce, in violation of the Constitution.

On the unconstitutionality of the law under which this man is confined, it is not too much to say that it will not bear argument; and I feel myself sanctioned in using this strong language from considering the course of reasoning by which it has been defended. Neither of the [lawyers for South Carolina] has attempted to prove that the power therein assumed by the state can be exercised without clashing with the general powers of the United States to regulate commerce. . . . [One lawyer for South Carolina] concluded his argument with the declaration that, if a dissolution of the Union must be the alternative, he was ready to meet it. . . . [Another South Carolina attorney insisted that] South Carolina was a sovereign state when she adopted the Constitution; a sovereign state cannot surrender a right of vital importance; South Carolina, therefore, either did not surrender this right, or still possesses the power to resume it. . . . [But this argument] leads to a dissolution of the Union and implies a direct attack upon the sovereignty of the United States. . . . It is in effect a repeal of the laws of the United States . . . converting a right into a crime. . . . Where is this to land us? Is it not asserting the right in each state to throw off the federal Constitution at its will and pleasure? If it can be done as to any particular article it may be done as to all; and, like the old confederation, the Union becomes a mere rope of sand.[35]

Justice Johnson further criticized South Carolina's law on three additional grounds: because it applied to sailors from foreign nations (indeed, Elkison was British), because it was not designed to achieve its desired purposes, and because it sought to regulate freemen as opposed to slaves.

The object of this law, and it has been so acknowledged in argument, is to prohibit ships coming into this port employing colored seamen, whether citizens or subjects of their own government or not. But if this state can prohibit Great Britain from employing her colored subjects (and she has them of all colors on the globe), or if at liberty to prohibit the employment of her subjects of the African race, why not prohibit her from using those of Irish or of Scottish nativity? If the color of his skin is to preclude the Lascar or the Sierra Leone seaman, why not the color of his eye or his hair exclude from our ports the inhabitants of her other territories? In fact it amounts to the assertion of the power to exclude the seamen of the territories of Great Britain or any other nation altogether. . . .

But if the policy of this law was to keep foreign free persons of color from holding communion with our slaves, it certainly pursues a course altogether inconsistent with its object. One gentleman likened the importation of such persons to that of clothes infected with the plague, or of wild beasts from Africa; the other to that of firebrands set to our own houses only to escape by the light. But surely if the penalty inflicted for coming here is in its effect that of being domesticated by being sold here, then we ourselves inoculate our community with the plague, we ourselves turn loose the wild beast in our streets, and we put the firebrand under our own houses. If there are evil persons abroad who would steal to this place in order to do us this mischief (and the whole provisions of this act are founded in that supposition), then this method of disposing of offenders by detaining them here presents the finest facilities in the world for introducing themselves lawfully into the very situation in which they would enjoy the best opportunities of pursuing their designs. . . . I am firmly persuaded that the legislature of South Carolina must have been surprised into the passing of this act. . . .

This act operates only as to freemen—free persons of color—and not as to slaves. . . . We do not pretend to a right to encroach on the power of the state over its slave population. The power remains unimpaired. But under a state law this man is recognized as a freeman, and in that view if in no other we are fully authorized to treat him as such.[36]

Notably, however, Justice Johnson did not rule the law unconstitutional on the grounds of its racially discriminatory infringement on the rights of free Blacks—but rather on interstate and foreign commerce grounds. Even more important, Justice Johnson's opinion had no discernable impact: it was ignored in South Carolina and elsewhere in the South; the practice of imprisoning Black seamen continued; and the federal government took no effective action to protect its own interstate commerce authority, much less the rights of free Black sailors.[37] Some historians regard this as the first act of nullification, preceding as it did by several years South Carolina's fight over the tariff.

Refusal to Deliver Abolitionist Mail

About a decade later, similar interference by the states with constitutional rights and federal power went unremedied—once again to protect slaveholders and their "property." In 1835, Northern abolitionists, led by the AASS, began a campaign of mailing antislavery newspapers and literature into the South, which local postmasters elected not to deliver. Some of the mail was seized from post offices and burned by angry mobs.[38]

Postmaster General Amos Kendall Refuses to Intervene (1835)

Appeals were made to federal officials, but to no avail. Amos Kendall, the US Postmaster General, sided with the states in their efforts to prevent the entry of "incendiary" publications into their midst.

A new question has arisen in the administration of this department. A number of individuals have established an association in the Northern and Eastern states and raised a large sum of money, for the purpose of effecting the immediate abolition of slavery in the Southern states. One of the means resorted to has been the printing of a large mass of newspapers, pamphlets, tracts, and almanacs containing exaggerated and in some instances false accounts of the treatment of slaves, illustrated with [pictures] calculated to operate on the passions of the colored men and produce discontent, assassination, and servile war. These they attempted to disseminate throughout the slaveholding states by the agency of the public mails. . . .

Our states are united only for certain purposes. There are interests in relation to which they are believed to be as independent of each other as they were before the Constitution was formed. The interest which the people of some of the states have in slaves is one of them. No state obtained by the union any right whatsoever over slavery in any other state, nor did any state lose any of its power over it, within its own borders. On this subject . . . the states are still independent and may fence round and protect their interest in slaves by such laws and regulations as in their sovereign will they deem expedient. Nor have the people of one state any more right to interfere with this subject in another state than they have to interfere with the internal regulations, rights of property, or domestic police of a foreign nation. . . .

Some of the states have passed laws prohibiting under heavy penalties the printing or circulation of papers like those in question within their respective territories. . . . It would be an extraordinary construction of the powers of the general government to maintain that they are bound to afford the agency of their mails and post offices, to counteract the laws of the states, in the circulation of papers calculated to produce domestic violence.[39]

Georgia's Law against Circulating Abolitionist Writings (1848)

As Kendall observed, some slave states passed laws forbidding the circulation of abolitionist literature, with violations punishable by death. Georgia's law provided:

If any slave, Negro, mestizo, or free person of color, or any other person shall circulate, bring, or cause to be circulated or brought into this state, or aid or assist in any manner, or be instrumental in aiding or assisting in the circulation or bringing into this state, or in any manner concerned in any written or printed pamphlet, paper, or circular, for the purpose of exciting to insurrection, conspiracy, or resistance among the slaves, Negroes, or free persons of color of this state, against their owners or the citizens of this state, the said person or persons offending against this section of this act shall be punished with death.[40]

Andrew Jackson Denounces Abolitionist Mailings (1835)

As the controversy continued, President Andrew Jackson—invoking the "compromises of the Constitution upon which the Union is founded"—urged Congress to enact legislation protecting slaveholding states from being forced to deliver "incendiary" and "wicked" abolitionist mailings.

In connection with these provisions in relation to the Post Office Department, I must also invite your attention to the painful excitement produced in the South by attempts to circulate through the mails inflammatory appeals addressed to the passions of the slaves, in prints and in various sorts of publications, calculated to stimulate them to insurrection and to produce all the horrors of a servile war. There is doubtless no respectable portion of our countrymen who can be so far misled as to feel any other sentiment than that of indignant regret at conduct so destructive of the harmony and peace of the country, and so repugnant to the principles of our national compact and to the dictates of humanity and religion. Our happiness and prosperity essentially depend upon peace within our borders, and peace depends upon the maintenance in good faith of those compromises of the Constitution upon which the Union is founded. It is fortunate for the country that the good sense, the generous feeling, and the deep-rooted attachment of the people of the non-slaveholding states to the Union and to their fellow citizens of the same blood in the South have given so strong and impressive a tone to the sentiments entertained against the proceedings of the misguided persons who have engaged in these unconstitutional and wicked attempts, and especially against the emissaries from foreign parts who have dared to interfere in this matter, as to authorize the hope that those attempts will no longer be persisted in. But if these expressions of the public will shall not be sufficient to effect so desirable a result, not a doubt can be entertained that the non-slaveholding states, so far from countenancing the slightest interference with the constitutional rights of the South, will be prompt to exercise their authority in suppressing so far as in them lies whatever is calculated to produce this evil.

In leaving the care of other branches of this interesting subject to the state authorities, to whom they properly belong, it is nevertheless proper for Congress to take such measures as will prevent the Post Office Department, which was designed to foster an amicable intercourse and correspondence between all the members of the confederacy, from being used as an instrument of an opposite character. The general government, to which the great trust is confided of preserving inviolate the relations created among the states by the Constitution, is especially bound to avoid in its own action anything that may disturb them. I would therefore call the special attention of Congress to the subject, and respectfully suggest the propriety of passing such a law as will prohibit, under severe penalties, the circulation in the Southern states through the mail of incendiary publications intended to instigate the slaves to insurrection.[41]

Congress never passed Jackson's proposed legislation. But neither did federal authorities take any steps to overcome interference by slave states with delivery of the US mails. In fact, in 1857, the US attorney general issued an official opinion concluding that postmasters had no obligation to deliver through the mails any publications that might "promote insurrection" within a slave state.[42]

Attitudes toward Slavery: Jefferson's Evolving View (1781, 1820)

An additional consequence of the constitutional compromise in Philadelphia that ceded almost all control over slavery to the states was the hardening over time of Southern attitudes in defense of slavery. In 1781, Jefferson could write: "The whole commerce between master and slave is a perpetual exercise of the most boisterous passions, the most unremitting despotism on the one part, and degrading submissions on the other. . . . I tremble for my country when I reflect that God is just."[43] But by 1820, Jefferson saw despotism as arising rather from Northerners attempting to interfere with the institution of slavery (or at least prevent its spread), in violation of supposedly agreed-upon constitutional bounds. "If Congress once goes out of the Constitution to arrogate a right of regulating the conditions of the inhabitants of the states, its majority may and probably will next declare that the condition of all men within the US shall be that of freedom, in which case all the whites south of the Potomac and Ohio must evacuate their states, and most fortunate those who can do it first."[44]

Charles Pinckney on the Happiness of Slaves (1820)

As slaveholders reacted to what they perceived as deliberate efforts by Northerners (especially abolitionists) to undermine the unilateral power over slavery they maintained they had been granted by the Constitutional Convention, many Southerners increasingly came to speak of slavery as a "positive good" for the enslaved no less than for the slaveowner, and for the nation no less than for the South. For example, during the heated debates in the House of Representatives over the potential admission of Missouri, Charles Pinckney of South Carolina (who had attended the Philadelphia Convention) resisted attempts to prevent the spread of the institution to the territories in part by praising the care and treatment taken by owners of their slaves.

> Certainly the present mild treatment of our slaves is most honorable to that part of the country where slavery exists. Every slave has a comfortable house, is well fed, clothed, and taken care of; he has his family about him, and in sickness has the same medical aid as his master, and has a sure and comfortable retreat in old age to protect him against the infirmities and weakness. During the whole of his life he is free from care, that canker of the human heart, which destroys at least one-half of the thinking part of mankind, and from which a favored few, very few, if indeed any, can be said to be free. Being without education and born to obey, to persons of that description moderate labor and discipline are essential. The discipline ought to be mild, but still, while slavery is to exist, there must be discipline. In this state they are happier than they can possibly be if free. A free black can only be happy where he has some share of education, and has been bred to a trade or some kind of business. The great body of slaves are happier in their present situation than they could be in any other, and the man or men who would attempt to give them freedom would be their greatest enemies.[45]

John Calhoun: Slavery as a "Positive Good" (1837)

Senator John Calhoun, also of South Carolina, defended the practice of slavery on moral and humanitarian grounds; indeed, Calhoun found slavery to be a necessary component of a civilized, self-governing democracy.

> The peculiar institution of the South—that, on the maintenance of which the very existence of the slaveholding states depends—is pronounced to be sinful and odious in the sight of God and man; and this with a systematic design of rendering us hateful in the eyes of the world—with a view to a general crusade against us and our institutions. . . .
> But I take higher ground. I hold that in the present state of civilization, where two races of different origin and distinguished by color and other physical differences as well as intellectual are brought together, the relation now existing in the slave-holding states between the two is, instead of an evil, a good—a positive good. . . .
> There never has yet existed a wealthy and civilized society in which one portion of

the community did not, in point of fact, live on the labor of the other. Broad and general as is this assertion, it is fully borne out by history. . . . I might well challenge a comparison between [other societies and nations] and the more direct, simple, and patriarchal mode by which the labor of the African race is, among us, commanded by the European. I may say with truth that in few countries so much is left to the share of the laborer, and so little exacted from him; or where there is more kind attention paid to him in sickness or infirmities of age. Compare his condition with the tenants of the poor houses in the more civilized portions of Europe—look at the sick, and the old and infirm slave, on one hand, in the midst of his family and friends, under the kind superintending care of his master and mistress, and compare it with the forlorn and wretched condition of the pauper in the poor house.

But I will not dwell on this aspect of the question; I turn to the political; and here I fearlessly assert that the existing relation between the two races in the South, against which these blind fanatics are waging war, forms the most solid and durable foundation on which to rear free and stable political institutions. It is useless to disguise the fact. There is and always has been in an advanced stage of wealth and civilization a conflict between labor and capital. The condition of society in the South exempts us from the disorders and dangers resulting from this conflict; and which explains why it is that the political condition of the slaveholding states has been so much more stable and quiet than that of the North.[46]

George Fitzhugh on the "Rights" of the Enslaved (1856)

By 1856, Southerners such as George Fitzhugh had gone even further—by not only defending the practice of slavery as positive and beneficial but by advancing a full-throated denunciation of Jefferson's pronouncement that "all men are created equal."

The negro slaves of the South are the happiest, and, in some sense, the freest people in the world. The children and the aged and infirm work not at all and yet have all the comforts and necessaries of life provided for them. They enjoy liberty because they are oppressed neither by care nor labor. The women do little hard work and are protected from the despotism of their husbands by their masters. The negro men and stout boys work, on the average, in good weather, not more than nine hours a day. The balance of their time is spent in perfect abandon. . . . [By contrast, the] free laborer must work or starve. He is more of a slave than the negro, because he works longer and harder for less allowance than the slave, and has no holiday, because the cares of life with him begin when its labors end. . . . Free laborers have not a thousandth part of the rights and liberties of negro slaves. Indeed, they have not a single liberty, unless it be the right or liberty to die. . . .

We agree with Mr. Jefferson that all men have natural and inalienable rights. To violate or disregard such rights is to oppose the designs and plans of Providence.... The order and subordination observable in the physical, animal, and human world show that some are formed for higher, others for lower stations—the few to command, the many to obey. We conclude that about nineteen out of every twenty individuals have "a natural and inalienable right" to be taken care of and protected, to have guardians, trustees, husbands, or masters; in other words, they have a natural and inalienable right to be slaves. The one in twenty are as clearly born or educated or some way fitted for command and liberty. Not to make them rulers or masters is as great a violation of natural right as not to make slaves of the mass.[47]

Public expressions by slaveholders about slavery evolved dramatically over the decades of the nineteenth century—from an embarrassed defense of the institution to its righteous and indignant justification. The transformation was driven, in part, by perceptions in the South that the North had reneged on the promise it had made in Philadelphia to leave slavery alone.

Discussion Questions

1. Annette Gordon-Reed notes that, particularly in the aftermath of the Haitian and French Revolutions, slaveholders came to fear the "contagion of liberty." Indeed, a fear that the enslaved might work to secure their self-liberation underlay many of the repressive measures adopted by the states (slave codes, judicial rulings, restrictions against visitors and mailings). To what extent can each of these measures be attributed to the Constitution written in Philadelphia?

2. The US system of government is often venerated for federalism, which allows for significant decentralization of authority and more local control over matters closer to home. Federalism helps to guard against tyranny, promised *The Federalist*: "the society itself will be broken into so many parts, interests, and classes of citizens that the rights of individuals or of the minority will be in little danger from interested combinations of the majority."[48] Especially in light of slave codes and judicial decisions such as *State v. Mann*, what must an enslaved person have thought of a system of government that left virtually all control over slavery to the slave states themselves?

3. South Carolina essentially ignored Justice Johnson's decision striking down the Negro Seamen statute in *Elkison v. Deliesseline*. What does this suggest about the practical importance of judicial orders interpreting

the Constitution if they are not backed up by the executive branch and Congress?

4. Postmaster General Kendall contended that states were entitled to "fence round and protect their interest in slaves by laws and regulations"—and that the people of other states had no "right to interfere" with these "internal regulations" regarding slavery. Over the first half of the nineteenth century, Southerners often portrayed themselves as the aggrieved party: it was the North, the abolitionists, who were violating the letter of the Constitution and the spirit of the Philadelphia Convention. How should we assess this argument?

5. White Southerners complained that by mailing abolitionist literature into their communities, outside agitators were disseminating offensive viewpoints that threatened domestic tranquility and undermined the rule of law. The Post Office agreed. What position should the Postal Service adopt today with respect to the mailing of racist, misogynistic, or anti-Semitic publications? Or publications that promote what the government describes as "illegal" or "terroristic" acts?

Native American Policy—Primary Sources

United States policies toward Native American peoples and tribes culminated in Andrew Jackson's "voluntary removal" program, which in turn resulted in the Trail of Tears. But prior to Jackson, George Washington, Thomas Jefferson, and the Supreme Court (in *Worcester v. Georgia* and other cases) struggled to identify an acceptable, workable approach to US-Native American relations.

Native Americans under the New Constitution (1787)

The Constitution ambiguously suggested that Native Americans (or at least most of them) would be (somehow) outside the jurisdiction of the United States. Indians were not to be included for purposes of representation and taxation under Article I, Section 2. In Article I, Section 8, Congress was granted the authority "to regulate Commerce" not only "with foreign Nations" and "among the several States," but also "with the Indian Tribes"—suggesting that Native Americans possessed some sort of nebulous status other than foreigner or citizen. While *The Federalist* at one point referred in passing to "Indian war[s]" and "Indian hostilities," it did not otherwise discuss how the people of the Native American nations were intended to fit within the new constitutional structure.[49]

George Washington and Henry Knox on Native Policy (1789)

As the first president, George Washington announced that "the government of the United States are determined that their administration of Indian affairs shall be directed entirely by the great principles of justice and humanity." Washington's overall policy was to "negotiat[e] and conclud[e] treaties of peace with the independent tribes or nations of Indians within the limits of the United States."[50] His Secretary of War, Henry Knox, outlined the basis of that approach.

In examining the question how the disturbances on the frontiers are to be quieted two modes present themselves by which the object may be effected. The first of which is by raising an army and extirpating the refractory tribes entirely. Or secondly by forming treaties of peace with them, in which their rights and limits should be explicitly defined and the treaties observed on the part of the United States with the most rigid justice by punishing the whites who should violate the same.

In considering the first mode, an enquiry would arise whether under the existing circumstances of affairs, the United States have a clear right, consistently with the principles of justice and the laws of nature, to proceed to the destruction or expulsion of the savages on the Wabash, supposing the force for that object easily attainable. It is presumable that a nation solicitous of establishing its character on the broad basis of justice would not only hesitate at, but reject every proposition to benefit itself by the injury of any neighboring community, however contemptible and weak it might be either with respect to its manners or power. When it shall be considered that the Indians derive their subsistence chiefly by hunting, and that according to fixed principles their population is in proportion to the facility with which they procure their food, it would most probably be found that the expulsion or destruction of the Indian tribes have nearly the same effect. For if they are removed from their usual hunting ground they must necessarily encroach on the hunting of another tribe, who will not suffer the encroachment with impunity—hence they destroy each other.

The Indians being the prior occupants possess the right of the soil, it cannot be taken from them unless by their free consent, or by the right of conquest in case of a just war. To dispossess them on any other principle would be a gross violation of the fundamental laws of nature and of that distributive justice which is the glory of a nation.... The principle of the Indian right to lands they possess being thus conceded, the dignity and interest of the nation will be advanced by making it the basis of the future administration of justice towards the Indian tribes.[51]

Despite his magnanimous official policy, Washington took few active steps to prevent American settlers from further encroaching on Native American lands; nor did he hesitate to dispatch US military forces to engage in "wars" and "hostilities" against Native American tribes, often with disastrous results for all involved.[52]

Thomas Jefferson Urges Assimilation (1805)

Thomas Jefferson hoped and anticipated that Native Americans would abandon their traditional lifestyles—or what he called their "prejudices"—and fully incorporate themselves into the national fabric. Jefferson outlined his overall perspective toward Indians in his Second Inaugural Address.

The aboriginal inhabitants of these countries I have regarded with the commiseration their history inspires. Endowed with the faculties and the rights of men, breathing an ardent love of liberty and independence, and occupying a country which left them no desire but to be undisturbed, the stream of overflowing population from other regions directed itself on these shores; without power to divert, or habits to contend against, they have been overwhelmed by the current, or driven before it; now reduced within limits too narrow for the hunter's state, humanity enjoins us to teach them agriculture and the domestic arts; to encourage them to that industry which alone can enable them to maintain their place in existence, and to prepare them in time for that state of society, which to bodily comforts adds the improvement of the mind and morals. We have therefore liberally furnished them with the implements of husbandry and household use; we have placed among them instructors in the arts of first necessity; and they are covered with the aegis of the law against aggressors from among ourselves.

But the endeavors to enlighten them on the fate which awaits their present course of life, to induce them to exercise their reason, follow its dictates, and change their pursuits with the change of circumstances, have powerful obstacles to encounter; they are combated by the habits of their bodies, prejudice of their minds, ignorance, pride, and the influence of interested and crafty individuals among them, who feel themselves something in the present order of things, and fear to become nothing in any other. These persons inculcate a sanctimonious reverence for the customs of their ancestors; that whatsoever they did must be done through all time; that reason is a false guide, and to advance under its counsel in their physical, moral, or political condition is perilous innovation; that their duty is to remain as their Creator made them, ignorance being safety, and knowledge full of danger. In short, my friends, among them is seen the action and counteraction of good sense and bigotry; they, too, have their anti-philosophers, who find an interest in keeping things in their present state, who dread reformation, and exert all their faculties to maintain the ascendency of habit over the duty of improving our reason and obeying its mandates.[53]

Thomas Jefferson Covets Native Lands (1803)

But—iron fist in velvet glove—Jefferson also urged his military and diplomatic personnel to engage in an aggressive land acquisition policy from Native American tribes, backed by calculation and force, in order to expand the nation's possessions.

We bend our whole views to the purchase and settlement of the country on the Mississippi, from its mouth to its northern regions, that we may be able to present as strong a front on our western as on our eastern border, and plant on the Mississippi itself the means of its own defense. We now own [certain territory] and hope this summer to purchase what belongs to the Choctaws from the Yazoo up to their boundary. . . . The Cahokias being extinct, we are entitled to their country by our paramount sovereignty. The Piorias, we understand, have all been driven off from their country, and we might claim it in the same way; but as we understand there is one chief remaining who would, as the survivor of the tribe, sell the right, it is better to give him such terms as will make him easy for life, and take a conveyance from him. . . . [etc.]

Our system is to live in perpetual peace with the Indians, to cultivate an affectionate attachment from them by everything just and liberal which we can do for them within the bounds of reason, and by giving them effectual protection against wrongs from our own people. The decrease of game rendering their subsistence by hunting insufficient, we wish to draw them to agriculture, to spinning and weaving. . . . When they withdraw themselves to the culture of a small piece of land, they will perceive how useless to them are their extensive forests, and will be willing to pare them off from time to time in exchange for necessaries for their farms and families. To promote this disposition to exchange lands, which they have to spare and we want, for necessaries, which we have to spare and they want, we shall push our trading uses, and be glad to see the good and influential individuals among them run in debt, because we observe that when these debts get beyond what the individuals can pay, they become willing to lop them off by a cession of lands. . . .

In this way our settlements will gradually circumscribe and approach the Indians, and they will in time either incorporate with us as citizens of the United States or remove beyond the Mississippi. The former is certainly the termination of their history most happy for themselves; but in the whole course of this, it is essential to cultivate their love. As to their fear, we presume that our strength and their weakness is now so visible that they must see we have only to shut our hand to crush them, and that all our liberalities to them proceed from motives of pure humanity only. Should any tribe be foolhardy enough to take up the hatchet at any time, the seizing the whole country of that tribe, and driving them across the Mississippi as the only condition of peace, would be an example to others and a furtherance of our final consolidation.[54]

Andrew Jackson Rejects Self-Government for Native Tribes (1829)

Shortly after coming to the presidency, Andrew Jackson—with a long history of fighting Indians on behalf of the US military already under his belt—proposed a new national policy toward Native Americans. He was specifically focused on Native American nations located in Georgia and Alabama, who had asserted a right to govern themselves through tribal authorities, as opposed to submitting to the jurisdiction of the states in which they resided. Jackson rejected Native American claims to any separate or independent territorial sovereignty.

The condition and ulterior destiny of the Indian tribes within the limits of some of our states have become objects of much interest and importance. It has long been the policy of government to introduce among them the arts of civilization, in the hope of gradually reclaiming them from a wandering life. This policy has, however, been coupled with another wholly incompatible with its success. Professing a desire to civilize and settle them, we have at the same time lost no opportunity to purchase their lands and thrust them farther into the wilderness. By this means they have not only been kept in a wandering state, but been led to look upon us as unjust and indifferent to their fate. Thus, though lavish in its expenditures upon the subject, government has constantly defeated its own policy, and the Indians in general, receding farther and farther to the west, have retained their savage habits. A portion, however, of the southern tribes, having mingled much with the whites and made some progress in the arts of civilized life, have lately attempted to erect an independent government within the limits of Georgia and Alabama. These states, claiming to be the only sovereigns within their territories, extended their laws over the Indians, which induced the latter to call upon the United States for protection.

Under these circumstances the question presented was whether the general government had a right to sustain those people in their pretensions. The Constitution declares that "no new state shall be formed or erected within the jurisdiction of any other state" without the consent of its legislature. If the general government is not permitted to tolerate the erection of a confederate state within the territory of one of the members of this Union against her consent, much less could it allow a foreign and independent government to establish itself there. . . . Would the people of Maine permit the Penobscot tribe to erect an independent government within their state? . . .

Actuated by this view of the subject, I informed the Indians inhabiting parts of Georgia and Alabama that their attempt to establish an independent government would not be countenanced by the executive of the United States, and advised them to emigrate beyond the Mississippi or submit to the laws of those states.[55]

Andrew Jackson Calls for "Voluntary" Emigration (1829)

Jackson's "advice" that the Native Americans "emigrate beyond the Mississippi" became the central feature in his new federal policy regarding Native American tribes. Although Jackson cloaked his proposal in humanitarian language, Indians were to be given a stark choice: move or face assimilation, if not extinction.

Our conduct toward these people is deeply interesting to our national character. Their present condition, contrasted with what they once were, makes a most powerful appeal to our sympathies. Our ancestors found them the uncontrolled possessors of these vast regions. By persuasion and force they have been made to retire from river to river and from mountain to mountain, until some of the tribes have become extinct and others have left but remnants to preserve for a while their once terrible names. Surrounded by the whites with their arts of civilization, which by destroying the resources of the savage doom him to weakness and decay, the fate of the Mohegan, the Narragansett, and the Delaware is fast overtaking the Choctaw, the Cherokee, and the Creek. That this fate surely awaits them if they remain within the limits of the states does not admit of a doubt. Humanity and national honor demand that every effort should be made to avert so great a calamity. It is too late to inquire whether it was just in the United States to include them and their territory within the bounds of new states, whose limits they could control. That step cannot be retraced. A state cannot be dismembered by Congress or restricted in the exercise of her constitutional power. But the people of those states and of every state, actuated by feelings of justice and a regard for our national honor, submit to you the interesting question whether something cannot be done, consistently with the rights of the states, to preserve this much-injured race.

As a means of effecting this end I suggest for your consideration the propriety of setting apart an ample district west of the Mississippi, and without the limits of any state or territory now formed, to be guaranteed to the Indian tribes as long as they shall occupy it, each tribe having a distinct control over the portion designated for its use. There they may be secured in the enjoyment of governments of their own choice, subject to no other control from the United States than such as may be necessary to preserve peace on the frontier and between the several tribes. There the benevolent may endeavor to teach them the arts of civilization and, by promoting union and harmony among them, to raise up an interesting commonwealth, destined to perpetuate the race and to attest the humanity and justice of this government.

This emigration should be voluntary, for it would be as cruel as unjust to compel the aborigines to abandon the graves of their fathers and seek a home in a distant land. But they should be distinctly informed that if they remain within the limits of the states they must be subject to their laws. In return for their obedience as individuals they will without doubt be protected in the enjoyment of those possessions which they have improved by their industry. But it seems to me visionary to suppose that in this state of things claims can be allowed on tracts of country on which they have neither dwelt nor made improvements, merely because they have seen them from the mountain or passed them in the chase. Submitting to the laws of the states and receiving, like other citizens, protection in their persons and property, they will ere long become merged in the mass of our population.[56]

Indian Removal Act (1830)

With all this as background, in 1830, at Jackson's urging, Congress passed the Indian Removal Act, the goal of which was to persuade or force all Native American tribes east of the Mississippi River to relocate to the west.

Be it enacted . . . that it shall and may be lawful for the president of the United States to cause so much of any territory belonging to the United States, west of the river Mississippi, not included in any state or organized territory . . . as he may judge necessary, to be divided into a suitable number of districts, for the reception of such tribes or nations of Indians as may choose to exchange the lands where they now reside and remove there. . . .

Section 3. . . . That in the making of any such exchange or exchanges, it shall and may be lawful for the president solemnly to assure the tribe or nation with which the exchange is made that the United States will forever secure and guaranty to them and their heirs or successors the country so exchanged with them.[57]

Memorial of the Cherokee Nation (1829)

The debate on the Indian Removal Act, in both Congress and throughout the country, was intense, partisan, and often furious—what historian Daniel Walker Howe characterized as "the strongest nationwide democratic protest movement the country had yet witnessed."[58] During the course of the controversy, Congress received a direct appeal from the Cherokee tribe.

By the will of our Father in heaven, the governor of the whole world, the red man of America has become small and the white man great and renowned. When the ancestors of the people of these United States first came to the shores of America, they found the red man strong—though he was ignorant and savage, yet he received them kindly and gave them dry land to rest their weary feet. They met in peace and shook hands in token of friendship. Whatever the white man wanted and asked of the Indian, the latter willingly gave. At that time the Indian was the lord and the white man the suppliant. But now the scene has changed. . . .

Brothers . . . we now make known to you our grievances. We are troubled by some of your own people. Our neighbor, the state of Georgia, is pressing hard upon us and urging us to relinquish our possessions for her benefit. We are told if we do not leave the country, which we dearly love, and betake ourselves to the western wilds, the laws of the state will be extended over us. . . . When we first heard of this we were grieved and appealed to our father, the president, and begged that protection might be extended over us. But [we learned] . . . our father the president had refused us protection, and that he had decided in favor of the extension of the laws of the state over us. This decision induces us to appeal to the immediate representatives of the American people. . . .

The land on which we stand we have received as an inheritance from our fathers, who possessed it from time immemorial as a gift from our common father in heaven. . . . This right of inheritance we have never ceded nor ever forfeited. Permit us to ask, what better right can a people have to a country than the right of inheritance and immemorial peaceable possession? . . . What crime have we committed whereby we must forever be divested of our country and rights? . . . In addition . . . we have the faith and pledge of the United States, repeated over and over again, in treaties made at various times. By these treaties our rights as a separate people are distinctly acknowledged and guarantees given that they shall be secured and protected. . . .

> To the land of which we are now in possession we are attached—it is our fathers' gift—it contains their ashes—it is the land of our nativity and the land of our intellectual birth. We cannot consent to abandon it for another far inferior and which holds out to us no inducements.[59]

Theodore Frelinghuysen Opposes the Indian Removal Act (1830)

The Indian Removal Act was also strenuously opposed by the National Republican (or Anti-Jackson) Party, which included Senator Theodore Frelinghuysen of New Jersey (who later ran for vice president on the Whig ticket). Frelinghuysen's impassioned speech against removal lasted more than six hours over three days.

> Our ancestors found these people, far removed from the commotions of Europe, exercising all the rights and enjoying the privileges of free and independent sovereigns of this new world. . . . The white men, the authors of all their wrongs, approached them as friends. . . . The Indian yielded a slow but substantial confidence; granted to the colonists an abiding place; and suffered them to grow up to man's estate beside him. He never raised the claim of elder title; as the white man's wants increased, he opened the hand of his bounty wider and wider. By and by conditions are changed. His people melt away; his lands are constantly coveted; millions after millions are ceded. The Indian bears it all meekly. He complains, indeed, as well he may, but suffers on. And now he finds that his neighbor, whom his kindness had nourished, has spread an adverse title over the last remains of his patrimony, barely adequate to his wants, and turns upon him and says, "Away! We cannot endure you so near us! These forests and rivers, these groves of your fathers, these firesides and hunting grounds are ours by the right of power and the force of numbers." . . .
>
> The end, however, is to justify the means. "The removal of the Indian tribes to the west of the Mississippi is demanded by the dictates of humanity." This is a word of conciliating import. . . . Who urges this plea? Those who covet the Indian lands —who wish to rid themselves of a neighbor that they despise.[60]

Andrew Jackson Summarizes His "Removal" Policy (1830)

Because of vehement opposition both in and out of Congress, the Indian Removal Act passed by only a slim majority. But Jackson had won his victory, and his administration proceeded over the next several years to attempt to persuade various Native Americans (primarily in the Southeast) to consent to being

"removed" from their tribal lands. At the end of 1830, he reported on his progress—and his overall philosophy—to Congress.

> It gives me pleasure to announce to Congress that the benevolent policy of the
> government, steadily pursued for nearly thirty years, in relation to the removal
> of the Indians beyond the white settlements is approaching to a happy con-
> summation. Two important tribes have accepted the provision made for their
> removal at the last session of Congress, and it is believed that their example will
> induce the remaining tribes also to seek the same obvious advantages.
>
> The consequences of a speedy removal will be important to the United States,
> to individual states, and to the Indians themselves. The pecuniary advantages
> which it promises to the government are the least of its recommendations. It
> puts an end to all possible danger of collision between the authorities of the
> general and state governments on account of the Indians. It will place a dense
> and civilized population in large tracts of country now occupied by a few
> savage hunters. . . . It will separate the Indians from immediate contact with
> settlements of whites; free them from the power of the states; enable them to
> pursue happiness in their own way and under their own rude institutions; will
> retard the progress of decay, which is lessening their numbers, and perhaps
> cause them gradually, under the protection of the government and through the
> influence of good counsels, to cast off their savage habits and become an inter-
> esting, civilized, and Christian community. . . .
>
> Humanity has often wept over the fate of the aborigines of this country, and
> philanthropy has been long busily employed in devising means to avert it, but
> its progress has never for a moment been arrested, and one by one have many
> powerful tribes disappeared from the earth. To follow to the tomb the last of his
> race and to tread on the graves of extinct nations excite melancholy reflections.
> But true philanthropy reconciles the mind to these vicissitudes as it does to the
> extinction of one generation to make room for another. . . . Philanthropy could
> not wish to see this continent restored to the condition in which it was found
> by our forefathers. What good man would prefer a country covered with forests
> and ranged by a few thousand savages to our extensive republic, studded with
> cities, towns, and prosperous farms, embellished with all the improvements
> which art can devise or industry execute, occupied by more than twelve mil-
> lion happy people, and filled with all the blessings of liberty, civilization, and
> religion? . . .
>
> Doubtless it will be painful to leave the graves of their fathers. But what do
> they more than our ancestors did or than our children are now doing? To better
> their condition in an unknown land our forefathers left all that was dear in
> earthly objects. Our children by thousands yearly leave the land of their birth
> to seek new homes in distant regions. Does humanity weep at these painful

separations from every thing, animate and inanimate, with which the young heart has become entwined? Far from it. . . . And is it supposed that the wandering savage has a stronger attachment to his home than the settled, civilized Christian? Is it more afflicting to him to leave the graves of his fathers than it is to our brothers and children? Rightly considered, the policy of the general government toward the red man is not only liberal, but generous. . . . To save him from this alternative or perhaps utter annihilation, the general government kindly offers him a new home and proposes to pay the whole expense of his removal and settlement. . . .

May we not hope, therefore, that all good citizens, and none more zealously than those who think the Indians oppressed by subjection to the laws of the states, will unite in attempting to open the eyes of those children of the forest to their true condition, and by a speedy removal to relieve them from all the evils, real or imaginary, present or prospective, with which they may be supposed to be threatened.[61]

Worcester v. Georgia (1832)

Many Native Americans objected to efforts by both state governments and the national government to deprive them of their traditional homelands. Two appeals eventually reached the highest court. In *Cherokee Nation v. Georgia* (1831), the justices initially ducked the issue, ruling that they lacked jurisdiction to hear the case.[62] But in *Worcester v. Georgia*, Chief Justice John Marshall opined that Samuel Worcester, a white missionary, had been wrongly convicted and jailed by Georgia for not having obtained a license from the governor to live in the Cherokee settlement. The legal question before the Court was whether states (such as Georgia) possessed authority to regulate affairs within Indian communities (such as the Cherokees). Chief Justice Marshall answered this question in the negative: Native American tribes were "distinct communities" and therefore could only be bound by treaties they had entered into with the national government.

> We must inquire and decide whether the act of the legislature of Georgia under which [Worcester] has been prosecuted and condemned be consistent with or repugnant to the Constitution, laws, and treaties of the United States. . . .
>
> The Indian nations had always been considered as distinct, independent political communities, retaining their original natural rights as the undisputed possessors of the soil from time immemorial, with the single exception of that imposed by irresistible power, which excluded them from intercourse with any other European potentate than the first discoverer of the coast of the particular region claimed. . . . The very term "nation," so generally applied to them, means "a people distinct from others." The Constitution, by declaring treaties

already made, as well as those to be made, to be the supreme law of the land, has adopted and sanctioned the previous treaties with the Indian nations, and consequently admits their rank among those powers who are capable of making treaties....

The Cherokee Nation, then, is a distinct community occupying its own territory with boundaries accurately described, in which the laws of Georgia can have no force, and which the citizens of Georgia have no right to enter but with the assent of the Cherokees themselves or in conformity with treaties and with the acts of Congress. The whole intercourse between the United States and this nation is, by our Constitution and laws, vested in the government of the United States....

The acts of Georgia are repugnant to the Constitution, laws, and treaties of the United States. They interfere forcibly with the relations established between the United States and the Cherokee Nation, the regulation of which, according to the settled principles of our Constitution are committed exclusively to the government of the Union.[63]

The Supreme Court Is Ignored

"John Marshall has made his decision, now let him enforce it." So Andrew Jackson is reported to have said, although perhaps apocryphally.[64] Whatever his words, the sentiment proved to be accurate: Both Jackson and Georgia simply ignored the Court's ruling that Georgia was to keep its hands off Native American territories. Nor was the Supreme Court's enunciation of the constitutional and legal status of Native Americans of any effect or relevance in stopping what soon became known as the "Trail of Tears," a military program of forced (as opposed to "voluntary") removal and migration of Native Americans westward—from their homes, farms, and hunting grounds to what was then referred to as "The Great American Desert." Thousands died.

Chief John Ross Describes "Voluntary Removal" (1836)

Three contemporary observers reflected on these events. John Ross, who was Principal Chief of the Cherokee Nation, wrote of the dislocation he witnessed in 1836.

[We] are despoiled of our private possessions, the indefeasible property of individuals. We are stripped of every attribute of freedom and eligibility for legal self-defense. Our property may be plundered before our eyes; violence may be committed on our persons; even our lives may be taken away, and there is none to regard our complaints. We are denationalized; we are disenfranchised. We are deprived of membership in the human family! We have neither land nor home nor resting place that can be called our own. . . . We are overwhelmed! Our hearts are sickened, our utterance is paralyzed, when we reflect on the condition in which we are placed by the audacious practices of unprincipled men.[65]

John Quincy Adams on the Barbarity of National Policy (1841)

John Quincy Adams, who after serving as the nation's sixth president had been elected to the House of Representatives, declined to become head of the congressional committee responsible for Indian affairs, for reasons he explained in his diary.

I was excused from that service at my own request, from a full conviction that its only result would be to keep a perpetual harrow upon my feelings, with a total impotence to render any useful service. The policy, from Washington to myself, of all the presidents of the United States had been justice and kindness to the Indian tribes—to civilize and preserve them. With the Creeks and Cherokees it had been eminently successful. Its success was their misfortune. The states within whose borders their settlements were took the alarm, broke down all the treaties which had pledged the faith of the nation. Georgia extended her jurisdiction over them, took possession of their lands, houses, cattle, furniture, negroes, and drove them out from their own dwellings. All the Southern states supported Georgia in this utter prostration of faith and justice; and Andrew Jackson, by the simultaneous operation of fraudulent treaties and brutal force, consummated the work. . . . All resistance against this abomination is vain. It is among the heinous sins of this nation, for which I believe God will one day bring them to judgment—but at His own time and by His own means. I turned my eyes away from this sickening mass of putrefaction, and asked to be excused from serving as chairman of the committee.[66]

Alexis de Tocqueville Reflects on the Trail of Tears (1835)

Finally, a visitor from France, Alexis de Tocqueville, offered his own observations—and sobering prediction—as the tragedy of the Trail of Tears unfolded.

None of the Indian tribes which formerly inhabited the territory of New England—the Narragansetts, the Mohicans, the Pequots—have any existence but in the recollection of man. The Lenapes, who received William Penn a hundred and fifty years ago upon the banks of the Delaware, have disappeared; and I myself met with the last of the Iroquois, who were begging alms. The nations I have mentioned formerly covered the country to the seacoast; but a traveler at the present day must penetrate more than a hundred leagues into the interior of the continent to find an Indian. Not only have these wild tribes receded, but they are destroyed; and as they give way or perish, an immense and increasing people fills their place. . . . I believe that the Indian nations of North America are doomed to perish; and that whenever the Europeans shall be established on the shore of the Pacific Ocean, that race of men will be no more.[67]

Discussion Questions

1. In summarizing centuries of history involving relationships between Native Americans and whites in North America, historian Thomas King (himself a Native American) concludes, "The issue has always been land."[68] To what extent is this a valid conclusion or not, in light of the policies pursued by the federal government from the administrations of George Washington to Andrew Jackson?

2. In 1830, Congress passed the Indian Removal Act. The term "Indian removal"—which is how most historians have referred to these events ever since—almost sounds antiseptic, like spot removal. Historian James Merrell expressed concern about a "whole catalog of . . . noxious words that still foul everyday [historical] parlance." He has suggested that "removal," a "soft" word, should "give way to a hard alternative, 'ethnic cleansing.'"[69] Historian Claudio Saunt has labeled Jackson's policies as "deportation."[70] Should historians—and students—use or alter nomenclature from the past in discussing historical events?

3. Evaluate Andrew Jackson's policy toward Native Americans as well as his defense of his policy. Was he being magnanimous and humanitarian or hypocritical and arguably even genocidal?[71] In light of this history, what are the reasons Jackson should still be depicted on—or be removed from—the twenty-dollar bill?

4. Considering Annette Gordon-Reed's essay and the excerpts from *Worcester v. Georgia*, what exactly was the Supreme Court's position regarding the civic status and the territorial rights of Native Americans? Especially in light of prevailing attitudes at the time, was the Supreme Court's characterization of Native American tribes as "domestic dependent nations" a bold step forward or an act of paternal condescension?

5. Historian Lewis Perry suggested that efforts by missionaries and others to resist Georgia's assertion of sovereignty over Cherokee territory (ultimately giving rise to *Worcester v. Georgia*) constituted one of the first episodes of civil disobedience in US history.[72] The founders, of course, never enshrined civil disobedience into the Constitution, as they were looking for obedience to the law. Considering the protests against Native American removal—as well as other events in American history, such as the Underground Railroad, Susan B. Anthony's illegal attempt to vote, Fred Korematsu's decision not to report to a Japanese American detention camp, and civil rights protesters such as Rosa Parks, sit-in students, and Martin Luther King Jr.—what is the relationship between civil disobedience and political and constitutional change?

Additional Primary Source Documents

Primary source document excerpts covering the following topics are located on the website accompanying this book:

Alien and Sedition Acts—including the Virginia and Kentucky Resolutions; Justice Chase's impeachment; *New York Times v. Sullivan*, 376 U.S. 254 (1964).

Slavery, Race, and the Nation—including Quaker antislavery petitions; abolition of the international slave trade; the House of Representatives gag rule; *United States v. The Amistad*. 40 U.S. 518 (1841).

"Democracy in America"—including the observations of Alexis de Tocqueville.

Other "Constitutional Moments" during this Era

- Women and their place in the new constitutional order—including state laws governing marriage, divorce, and property; *Martin v. Commonwealth of Massachusetts*, 1 Mass. Reports 348 (1805); Seneca Falls Convention and Declaration of Sentiments.
- The National Bank controversy—including written opinions submitted to Washington on the bank's constitutionality; Bank Bill (1791); establishment of the Second Bank (1816); *McCulloch v. Maryland*, 17 U.S. 316 (1819); Jackson veto of the bank's charter renewal.
- The rise of presidential power over foreign policy—including the Neutrality Proclamation; Jay's Treaty; the Quasi-War with France; Jefferson's purchase

of the Louisiana Territory; the Embargo of 1807; the Hartford Convention's complaints.

- The growth of judicial power—including the Judiciary Act of 1801 and "midnight judges"; the Judiciary Act of 1802; *Marbury v. Madison*, 5 U.S. 137 (1803); *Stuart v. Laird*, 5 U.S. 299 (1803); the Burr treason trial; the Marshall Court.

- Supreme Court authority over state laws—including *Fletcher v. Peck*, 10 U.S. 87 (1810) (state laws); *Martin v. Hunter's Lessee*, 14 U.S. 304 (1816) (state civil cases); *Cohens v. Virginia*, 19 U.S. 264 (1821) (state criminal cases); *Barron v. Baltimore*, 32 U.S. 243 (1833) (Bill of Rights not binding on states).

- Regulation of commerce, contracts, and state police power—including *Dartmouth College v. Woodward*, 17 U.S. 518 (1819) (Contracts Clause); *Gibbons v. Ogden*, 22 U.S. 1 (1824) (interstate commerce); *Charles River Bridge v. Warren Bridge*, 36 U.S. 420 (1837) (Contracts Clause); *New York v. Miln*, 36 U.S. 102 (1837) (state police power).

- Presidential veto power—including Madison's veto of internal improvements fund; Jackson's vetoes of the Maysville Road and the National Bank extension.

- Nullification doctrine—including Calhoun's *Disquisition on Government*; Webster-Hayne debate; South Carolina nullification of tariff.

- Constitutional issues arising from the acquisition of new territory—including the Louisiana Purchase; the annexation of Texas; territory acquired after the Mexican-American War.

Notes

1. 2 U.S. 419 (1793).
2. 32 U.S. 243 (1833).
3. Thomas Jefferson to John Holmes, April 22, 1820, founders.archives.gov/documents/Jefferson/03-15-02-0518.
4. In this volume, consistent with prevailing practice, we refer to "Native Americans," although Indigenous scholars have recently suggested the use instead of "Native," "Indigenous," or "Native Nations." See Joy Harjo, "Introduction," in *When the Light of the World Was Subdued, Our Songs Came Through: A Norton Anthology of Native Nations Poetry*, ed. Joy Harjo with LeAnne Howe and Jennifer Elise Foerster (New York: W.W. Norton, 2020), 3–4.
5. Douglas Bradburn, *The Citizenship Revolution: Politics and the Creation of the American Union, 1774-1804* (Charlottesville: University of Virginia Press, 2009), 235.
6. An Act to establish an uniform Rule of Naturalization, ch. 3, 1 Stat. 103 (March 26, 1790), govtrackus.s3.amazonaws.com/legislink/pdf/stat/1/STATUTE-1-Pg103.pdf.

7. James Sidbury, *Ploughshares into Swords: Race, Rebellion, and Identity in Gabriel's Virginia, 1730-1810* (Cambridge, UK: Cambridge University Press, 1997), 39–42.

8. 1795 Naturalization Act ("An act to establish a uniform rule of naturalization"), ch. 20, 1 Stat. 414 (January 29, 1795), govtrackus.s3.amazonaws.com/legislink/pdf/stat/1/STATUTE-1-Pg414a.pdf.

9. 1798 Naturalization Act (An act supplementary to and to amend the act entitled "An Act to establish a uniform rule of naturalization"), ch, 54, 1 Stat. 566 (June 18, 1798), memory.loc.gov/cgi-bin/ampage?collId = llsl&fileName = 001/llsl001.db&recNum = 689.

10. An Act in addition to the Act entitled "An Act for the Punishment of Certain Crimes against the United States," ch. 74, 1 Stat. 596 (July 14, 1798), memory.loc.gov/cgi-bin/ampage?collId = llsl&fileName = 001/llsl001.db&recNum = 719.

11. Jeffrey L. Pasley, *"The Tyranny of Printers": Newspaper Politics in the Early American Republic* (Charlottesville: University of Virginia Press, 2001), 105–31.

12. 5 U.S. 137 (1803).

13. 22 U.S. 1 (1824).

14. 10 U.S. 87 (1810).

15. 17 U.S. 316 (1819).

16. Thomas Jefferson to John Holmes, April 22, 1820, founders.archives.gov/documents/Jefferson/03-15-02-0518.

17. Gary B. Nash, *Forging Freedom: The Formation of Philadelphia's Black Community, 1720-1840* (Cambridge, MA: Harvard University Press, 1988), 246–80.

18. Dred Scott v. Sandford, 60 U.S. 393 (1857).

19. Andrew Jackson, "First Annual Message to Congress" (December 8, 1829), millercenter.org/the-presidency/presidential-speeches/december-8-1829-first-annual-message-congress.

20. Indian Removal Act (An act to provide for an exchange of lands with the Indians residing in any of the states or territories, and for their removal west of the river Mississippi), ch. 158, 4 Stat. 411 (May 28, 1830), memory.loc.gov/cgi-bin/ampage?collId = llsl&fileName = 004/llsl004.db&recNum = 458.

21. 21 U.S. 543 (1823).

22. 30 U.S. 1 (1831).

23. 31 U.S. 515 (1832).

24. Rosemarie Zagarri, *Revolutionary Backlash: Women and Politics in the Early American Republic* (Philadelphia: University of Pennsylvania Press, 2007), 1–10; Jan Ellen Lewis, "Rethinking Women's Suffrage in New Jersey, 1776-1807," *Rutgers Law Journal* 63, no. 3 (2011): 1017–35, www.rutgerslawreview.com/wp-content/uploads/archive/vol63/Issue3/Lewis.pdf.

25. "Declaration of Sentiments," Seneca Falls Convention (July 29, 1848), www.nps.gov/wori/learn/historyculture/declaration-of-sentiments.htm.

26. Elizabeth Cady Stanton, "Keynote Address" (speech, Seneca Falls, NY, July 19, 1848), www.loc.gov/item/today-in-history/july-19.

27. "Crimes, Offenses, and Penalties," *Codification of the Statute Law of Georgia*, 2nd ed. (Augusta, GA, 1848), academic.udayton.edu/Race/02rights/slavelaw.htm#4.

28. David J. McCord, ed., *The Statutes at Large of South Carolina, Vol. 7 Containing the Acts Relating to Charleston, Courts, Slaves, and Rivers* (Columbia, SC, 1840), 397, digital.scetv.org/teachingAmerhistory/pdfs/Transciptionof1740SlaveCodes.pdf.

29. Frederick Douglass, *My Bondage and My Freedom* (New York, 1855), 65.

30. State v. Mann, 13 N.C. 263 (1 Dev.) (1829).

31. Martha S. Jones, "#Sayhername: Black Women and State Violence in the Case of *Missouri v. Celia, A Slave*" (lecture, State Historical Society of Missouri, March 23, 2016), shsmo.org/lecture-series/african-american-experience/lecture-2.

32. *Id.*

33. "Hanging a Negress—Celia," *New York Times*, January 16, 1856, timesmachine.nytimes.com/timesmachine/1856/01/16/76451883.pdf.

34. South Carolina Negro Seamen Act (An act for the better regulation of free negroes and persons of color, and for other purposes), December 1822, quoted in *Elkison v. Deliesseline*, 8 F. Cas. 493 (C.C.D.S.C. 1823) (No. 4,366), law.resource.org/pub/us/case/reporter/F.Cas/0008.f.cas/0008.f.cas.0493.4.pdf.

35. Elkison v. Deliesseline, 8 F. Cas. 493 (C.C.D.S.C. 1823) (No. 4,366).

36. *Id.*

37. Philip M. Hamer, "Great Britain, the United States, and the Negro Seamen Acts, 1822–1848," *Journal of Southern History* 1 (February 1935): 3–28, www.jstor.org/stable/2191749?seq=1#metadata_info_tab_contents.

38. Nancy Pope, "America's First Direct Mail Campaign," *Smithsonian National Postal Museum* (blog) (July 29, 2010), postalmuseum.si.edu/node/1912.

39. Amos Kendall, "Report of the Postmaster General," Cong. Globe, 24th Cong., 2d Sess. (December 1, 1835), App. 8-9, memory.loc.gov/cgi-bin/ampage?collId=llcg&fileName=112/llcg112.db&recNum=18&itemLink=r%3Fammem%2Fhlaw%3A%40field%28DOCID%2B%40lit%28cg1121%29%29%231120003&linkText=1.

40. "Crimes, Offenses, and Penalties," *Codification of the Statute Law of Georgia*, 2nd ed. (Augusta, GA, 1848).

41. Andrew Jackson, "Seventh Annual Message to Congress" (December 8, 1835), www.presidency.ucsb.edu/documents/seventh-annual-message-2.

42. Caleb Cushing, "Yahoo City Post Office Case," 8 *Official Opinions of the Attorney General of the United States* 489 (March 2, 1857), babel.hathitrust.org/cgi/pt?id=mdp.35112101351593&view=1up&seq=455&q1=mail.

43. Thomas Jefferson, *Notes on the State of Virginia* (Philadelphia, 1788), Query XVIII, Manners.

44. Thomas Jefferson to Albert Gallatin, December 26, 1820, founders.archives.gov/documents/Jefferson/98-01-02-1705.

45. Charles Pinckney, House of Representatives Debate, Cong. Globe, 16th Cong., 1st Sess. (February 1820), archive.oah.org/special-issues/teaching/2008_06/sources/ex4_a1.html.

46. John C. Calhoun, Senate Debate (February 6, 1837), in *Speeches of John C. Calhoun, Delivered in the House of Representatives and in the Senate of the United States*, ed. Richard R. Cralle (New York, 1853), 625–33.

47. George Fitzhugh, *Cannibals All! or, Slaves Without Masters*, ed. C. Vann Woodward (Cambridge, MA: Harvard University Press 1960), 18–19, 69, 200.

48. The Federalist No. 51 (James Madison) (February 6, 1788), guides.loc.gov/federalist-papers/text-51-60#s-lg-box-wrapper-25493427.

49. The Federalist No. 3 (John Jay) (November 3, 1787), guides.loc.gov/federalist-papers/text-1-10#s-lg-box-wrapper-25493266.

50. George Washington, "To the Commissioners to the Southern Indians," August 29, 1789, founders.archives.gov/documents/Washington/05-03-02-0326.

51. Henry Knox, "Enclosure," June 15, 1789, founders.archives.gov/documents/Washington/05-02-02-0357-0002.

52. See Colin G. Calloway, *The Indian World of George Washington: The First President, The First Americans, and the Birth of the Nation* (New York: Oxford University Press, 2018).

53. Thomas Jefferson, Second Inaugural Address (March 4, 1805), millercenter.org/the-presidency/presidential-speeches/march-4-1805-second-inaugural-address.

54. Thomas Jefferson to William Henry Harrison, February 27, 1803, founders.archives.gov/documents/Jefferson/01-39-02-0500.

55. Andrew Jackson, "First Annual Message to Congress" (December 8, 1829), millercenter.org/the-presidency/presidential-speeches/december-8-1829-first-annual-message-congress.

56. Andrew Jackson, "First Annual Message to Congress" (December 8, 1829), millercenter.org/the-presidency/presidential-speeches/december-8-1829-first-annual-message-congress.

57. Indian Removal Act (An act to provide for an exchange of lands with the Indians residing in any of the states or territories, and for their removal west of the river Mississippi), ch. 158, 4 Stat. 411 (May 28, 1830), memory.loc.gov/cgi-bin/ampage?collId = llsl&fileName = 004/llsl004.db&recNum = 458.

58. Daniel Walker Howe, *What Hath God Wrought: The Transformation of America, 1815-1848* (New York: Oxford University Press, 2007), 342–57.

59. Cherokee Nation, "Memorial of the Cherokee Indians," *Niles Register*, March 13, 1830, 53–54, babel.hathitrust.org/cgi/pt?id = pst.000055571425&view = 1up&seq = 67.

60. Theodore Frelinghuysen, Senate Debate, *Gales and Seaton's Register of Debates in Congress*, 6, pt. 1, 21st Cong., 1st Sess. 312–18 (April 9, 1830), memory.loc.gov/cgi-bin/ampage?collId = llrd&fileName = 008/llrd008.db&recNum = 315.

61. Andrew Jackson, "Second Annual Message to Congress" (December 6, 1830), millercenter.org/the-presidency/presidential-speeches/december-6-1830-second-annual-message-congress.

62. Cherokee Nation v. Georgia, 30 U.S. 1 (1831).

63. Worcester v. Georgia, 31 U.S. 515 (1832).

64. Stephen Breyer, "University of Pennsylvania Law School, Commencement Remarks" (speech, Philadelphia, May 19, 2003), www.supremecourt.gov/publicinfo/speeches/viewspeech/sp_05-19-03; see generally David S. Reynolds, *Waking Giant: America in the Age of Jackson* (New York: HarperCollins, 2008), 93.

65. John Ross, *The Papers of Chief John Ross*, ed. Gary E. Moulton, Vol. 1, 1807–1830 (Norman: University of Oklahoma Press, 1985), 459.

66. John Quincy Adams, June 30, 1841, in *Memoirs of John Quincy Adams: Comprising Portions of His Diary From 1795 to 1848*, Vol. 10 (Philadelphia, 1874), 492, babel. hathitrust.org/cgi/pt?id = hvd.32044013643937&view = 1up&seq = 508.

67. Alexis de Tocqueville, *Democracy in America*, Vol. 1 (1835), www.gutenberg.org/ files/815/815-h/815-h.htm.

68. Thomas King, *The Inconvenient Indian: A Curious Account of Native People in North America* (Minneapolis: University of Minnesota Press, 2013).

69. James H. Merrell, "Second Thoughts on Colonial Historians and American Indians," *The William and Mary Quarterly* 69, no. 3 (July 2012): 451–512, at 509, www.jstor. org/stable/pdf/10.5309/willmaryquar.69.3.0451.pdf?refreqid=excelsior%3A0385 74ab7721402db0e944d135d16eaf; James H. Merrell, "Some Thoughts on Colonial Historians and American Indians," *The William and Mary Quarterly* 46, no. 1 (January 1989): 94–119, mvlindsey.files.wordpress.com/2015/09/william-and-mary-quarterly-merrell-1989.pdf.

70. Claudio Saunt, *Unworthy Republic: The Dispossession of Native Americans and the Road to Indian Territory* (New York: W.W. Norton, 2020).

71. For the former view, see Jackson's own statements, quoted above. For the latter perspective, see Michael Paul Rogin, *Fathers and Children: Andrew Jackson and the Subjugation of the American Indian* (New York: Knopf, 1975).

72. Lewis Perry, *Civil Disobedience: An American Tradition* (New Haven, CT: Yale University Press, 2013).

4

The Constitution in Crisis (1848–77)

The study of the Civil War and its aftermath appropriately focuses on issues central to the nation's legacy of freedom and unfreedom: how and why discord over slavery led to an irreconcilable sectional schism, whether the Civil War might somehow have been avoided, who or what was most responsible for attaining emancipation for enslaved peoples, the successes and the failures of the postwar years. But the Civil War and Reconstruction also raise profound questions about rights, citizenship, and the Constitution. More so perhaps than during any other period of our history, this era witnessed a mix of highly charged constitutional disputes, the implications of which continue to resonate today. While its causes and consequences can be presented compellingly through a political, military, or social lens, the Civil War is also the story of how the founders' Constitution broke—and then how that document was dramatically rewritten. In fact, five major constitutional crises dominated the years before and after the first shots at Fort Sumter.

Over time, enforcement of the Constitution's language about fugitive slaves proved unacceptable, for very different reasons, to both slave and free states. The Fugitive Slave Act (1850) led to even more sectional conflict, as Northerners, denouncing slave hunters as kidnappers, passed "personal liberty" laws intended to hinder the return of runaways, which slave owners termed a grievous violation of their property rights. Radical calls by abolitionists for civil disobedience competed with disputes about the appropriate breadth of national government powers. The swirling controversy raised questions far from time bound: How have constitutional "compromises" arrived at in Congress and ratified by courts constricted the liberties of Americans (in this case, escaped slaves and Northerners who refused to assist in their forced return to slavery)? How much power should the national government have to enforce laws in the face of intense state and local opposition? When is civil disobedience justifiable in a nation committed to the rule of law?

Questions about constitutional power—and civil disobedience—were also at the heart of the anguished Northern reaction to the *Dred Scott* decision. That case remains definitive proof that constitutional interpretations matter. The Supreme Court used its powers to strip Blacks of the possibility of citizenship, elevated slaveholding to a near-fundamental constitutional right, and voided acts of Congress designed to prevent slavery's spread. Where does the Supreme Court

With Liberty and Justice for All?. Edited by Steven A. Steinbach, Maeva Marcus, and Robert Cohen, Oxford University Press. © Oxford University Press 2022. DOI: 10.1093/oso/9780197516317.003.0004

get such power? How much power should courts have? What deference should be accorded to the Supreme Court in setting the nation's legal—and moral— standards? Under our constitutional system, must decisions such as *Dred Scott* be obeyed? Abraham Lincoln, who loathed the *Dred Scott* decision, offered a textbook example of how not to accept—indeed, how to affirmatively undermine and resist—an intolerable Supreme Court ruling.

The 1860s began with a third constitutional disagreement: Did aggrieved Southern states have the authority to withdraw from the Union in order to form a separate nation, complete with its own constitution that expressly protected race-based slavery? Eleven states argued that the Constitution vested them with the right to secede—a "right" supposedly grounded in the right of rebellion embedded in the Declaration of Independence. The Supreme Court eventually declared secession to be at odds with the Constitution—but only after this constitutional dispute had been effectively resolved on the Civil War battlefields.

During the Civil War, the nation further struggled with how slavery could be abolished consistent with the Constitution. As thousands of enslaved African Americans fled to the safety of Union lines, first Congress (with two Confiscation Acts) and then President Lincoln (with the Emancipation Proclamation) responded with substantial—but only partial—emancipation measures. Doubts about the legal validity of such efforts to abolish slavery were ended only upon passage of the first constitutional amendment in more than sixty years. "A king's cure for all the evils," Lincoln called the Thirteenth Amendment.[1]

The Civil War not only ended secession and slavery, it also propelled a historic democratization of the Constitution. The final dramatic constitutional consequence of the Civil War was the passage of new amendments that guaranteed equal rights to all and prohibited race-based infringements on voting. But a crucial series of Supreme Court decisions late in the nineteenth century effectively eviscerated the Fourteenth and Fifteenth Amendments, leading to decades of racial segregation and disenfranchisement.

In this era in particular, then, debates over the reach and meaning of the Constitution played a pivotal role. Teachers and students can reflect on the process through which constitutional changes occur—from the top down, the bottom up, and as the result of a multiplicity of factors and influences. Yes, revisions to the Constitution are sometimes made through a formal process (witness the Thirteenth, Fourteenth, and Fifteenth Amendments). But the meaning and applicability of the Constitution also depend on the interpretation given to its provisions by judges, who themselves are influenced by political forces and who in turn respond to arguments raised by private litigants in unique factual settings (as in *Dred Scott* and the various Reconstruction-era decisions). Constitutional change also results from the actions of Congress (such as the Confiscation Acts), of presidents (such as the Emancipation Proclamation), and of "ordinary" Americans (such as those who resisted the Fugitive Slave law; or themselves escaped from the confines of slavery; or insisted on or rejected the "right" to secede; or fought and ultimately prevailed through force of arms).

The Civil War, Reconstruction, and the Constitutional Revolution

Eric Foner

DeWitt Clinton Professor Emeritus of History, Columbia University

The Civil War, which profoundly affected so many areas of American life, transformed the Constitution. Three amendments—the Thirteenth, Fourteenth, and Fifteenth—irrevocably abolished slavery, established a new definition of American citizenship and the rights it entailed, and extended the right to vote to African American men. These amendments both reflected and reinforced a new era of individual rights consciousness among Americans of all races and backgrounds and transformed the relationship between individual Americans and the national state. Together with far-reaching congressional legislation meant to secure the basic rights of the former slaves and protect them against violence, these amendments, ratified during the postwar era of Reconstruction, were crucial in creating the world's first biracial democracy.

So profound were these changes that the amendments should be seen not simply as an alteration of an existing structure but as a second founding that created a fundamentally new document. The Republican leader Carl Schurz spoke of a "constitutional revolution," which "found the rights of the individual at the mercy of the states . . . and placed them under the shield of national protection." For the first time, he continued, "the liberty and rights of every citizen in every state [became] a matter of national concern."[2] Reconstruction was an era of popular constitutionalism, in which debates over these amendments, and the basic principles of American democracy, spread far beyond the halls of Congress, engaging Americans, as Elizabeth Cady Stanton later recalled, "at every fireside."[3]

The word "slavery" does not appear in the original Constitution. The founders used circumlocutions—"Persons held to Service or Labour," "other Persons"—to refer to slaves. But even though the document began by announcing that its purpose was to "secure the Blessings of Liberty," it included important protections for slavery. It provided that three-fifths of the enslaved population would be counted in apportioning membership in the House of Representatives, thereby enhancing the political power of the Southern states. It allowed the importation of slaves from abroad, by then widely recognized as a crime against humanity, to continue for at least twenty years. And it required that fugitive slaves be returned to their owners. Although the Constitution does not state this explicitly, a "federal consensus" soon emerged that the national government lacked the power to take direct action against slavery in the states.[4] Whether Congress had the constitutional authority to regulate slavery in the nation's territories before they became states would become a focal point of political debate, especially after the United States acquired vast new lands in the Mexican-American War of 1846–48.

Some of the Constitution's framers hoped that slavery might slowly die out. Instead, thanks to the burgeoning world demand for cotton, the key raw material of the early industrial revolution, the institution expanded rapidly in the young republic. By 1860, the slave population—700,000 when the Constitution was ratified—had grown to nearly four million. Slave owners dominated the national government for most of the period from George Washington's inauguration to the Civil War. As a result, the definition of American citizenship quickly took on a racial dimension. The Naturalization Act of 1790 limited to "white" immigrants the ability to become American citizens.[5] What of persons born in the United States? The Constitution mentions "citizens" in several places but does not define who they are. Its language suggests that citizens' rights are determined by the individual states. In the 1790s and early nineteenth century, the federal government issued certificates of citizenship to Black sailors to prevent their impressment by the British navy. Yet as time went on, more and more states refused to recognize free African Americans as citizens and subjected them to restrictions not applicable to whites. By the eve of the Civil War, Black men enjoyed the right to vote on the same basis as whites only in five New England states with minuscule Black populations. A number of states, in both North and South, prohibited free Black persons from entering their territory. Yet an alternative definition of citizenship also emerged in these years. The abolitionist movement called not only for an end to slavery but for the severing of citizenship from race, to encompass all persons born in the United States. Gatherings of free Blacks who demanded equal rights called themselves conventions of "colored citizens." Their claim to a status the nation increasingly denied them would be incorporated into the Constitution in the aftermath of the Civil War.

The antislavery movement divided over whether the Constitution should be considered a proslavery document "null and void before God"[6] (the position of William Lloyd Garrison and his followers, who insisted that abolitionists could not vote under such a document) or one that, because it did not explicitly recognize property in man, opened the door to political action against the institution. Frederick Douglass, who began his career as a follower of Garrison, concluded in the 1850s that the Constitution was in fact a "glorious liberty document."[7] Clashing interpretations of the Constitution also played a major role in mainstream politics as the slavery controversy developed.

One key issue revolved around fugitive slaves. The Constitution required their return but does not say whether the state or federal governments are responsible for enforcement. In *Prigg v. Pennsylvania* (1842),[8] the Supreme Court declared that the federal government, not the states, had this responsibility. This led to a proliferation of "personal liberty" laws in the North that barred local officials from participating in the rendition of fugitives and required a jury trial before the alleged runaway was returned to bondage. As the abolitionist movement grew, increasing numbers of Northerners offered assistance to fugitive slaves. As part of the Compromise of 1850, Congress enacted a draconian new Fugitive Slave Act that invalidated the "personal liberty" laws and empowered federal marshals to arrest runaways and federal commissioners to determine their fate in hearings that did not allow the testimony of the accused individual. The law made it a federal crime to assist a fugitive or to refuse to participate in their capture. Because slavery was created and protected by state law, the Southern states generally adhered to a "state sovereignty" interpretation of the Constitution. But the Fugitive Slave Act was the most expansive exercise of national power over the states in the entire antebellum era. When it came to protecting slavery, white Southerners were happy to employ vigorous national power.

The debate over the constitutional status of slavery and the citizenship rights of Black Americans culminated in *Dred Scott v. Sandford* (1857).[9] Scott, a slave, had been taken by his owner from the slave state Missouri into Illinois, where slavery was prohibited by local law, and the Wisconsin Territory, where it had been barred by Congress in the Missouri Compromise of 1820. Scott later sued for his freedom because of his residence on free soil. The Supreme Court rejected his plea. Chief Justice Roger B. Taney declared that under the Constitution, citizenship was reserved for whites alone. The framers, he insisted, had believed that Blacks had "no rights which the white man was bound to respect." Moreover, Taney continued, Congress lacked the constitutional power to bar slavery from any territory. Thus, the political platform of the Republican Party, which had recently been created with the aim of barring slavery from spreading westward, was unconstitutional. Taney thought his decision would settle the sectional conflict. Instead, denounced in the North as evidence that the "slave power" controlled the federal government, it became a key milestone on the road to war.

The Civil War preserved the nation, destroyed slavery, and placed the question of the future status of the former slaves on the national agenda. The three amendments sought to place in the Constitution the victorious Union's understanding of these outcomes. The first was the Thirteenth, ratified in 1865, which abolished slavery throughout the United States (introducing the word "slavery" for the first time into the Constitution). Of course, slavery was already in its death throes. On January 1, 1863, in the Emancipation Proclamation,[10] President Lincoln had declared free more than three million slaves. But the Proclamation was a war measure, issued under the president's authority as commander-in-chief of the armed forces. Its constitutional status once the war ended was in doubt. The Proclamation, moreover, left in bondage three-quarters of a million in the four border slave states that remained in the Union and in certain portions of the Confederacy. Even after issuing it, Lincoln continued to promote his favored policy of state-by-state abolition. Given the high bar to ratification of an amendment, this route seemed more attainable. Lincoln's Proclamation of Amnesty and Reconstruction of December 1863 required rebellious states to abolish slavery as a condition of readmission to the Union.[11]

The amendment's language was taken almost word for word from the Northwest Ordinance of 1787,[12] to which it had migrated from Thomas Jefferson's Land Ordinance of 1784: "Neither slavery nor involuntary servitude, except as a punishment for crime whereof the party shall have been duly convicted, shall exist within the United States, or any place subject to their jurisdiction." The provision allowing involuntary servitude for those convicted of crime is an excellent illustration of the aphorism that historians write with one eye (at least) fixed on the present. For decades, scholars writing about the Thirteenth Amendment paid no attention to it. But with mass incarceration and the widespread use of prison labor being national issues today, it has attracted considerable discussion. Scholars have been unable to explain why Jefferson devised this wording in the first place, except to note that he felt that labor helped build character and would assist in rehabilitating criminals. But similar language was included in most of the constitutions of free states that entered the Union, beginning with Ohio in 1803, and was so familiar by 1865 that almost no one in Congress mentioned it when the amendment was under consideration. Inadvertently, the amendment created a loophole that would later allow for the widespread leasing of convict labor, in highly oppressive conditions, on plantations and in industries in the South, and the use of prison labor by businesses down to the present. The courts have consistently ruled that involuntary labor by prisoners does not violate the Thirteenth Amendment.

Abolitionists saw the amendment as the beginning of an even deeper transformation, what today might be called "regime change"—the transformation of a proslavery regime into one committed to the ideal of equality. Most Republicans were not abolitionists. But they agreed on certain principles: slavery had caused the war and the death of three-quarters of a million Americans. It had deprived its victims of the basic rights to which all persons were entitled. It had done more than oppress slaves; it was a cancer that degraded white labor and threatened all Americans' essential liberties, such as freedom of speech and the press. The amendment intended to change all this and more. Unlike the Emancipation Proclamation, the Thirteenth Amendment applied to the entire country and for the first time made the abolition of slavery an essential part of the nation's legal order. In one respect it was truly revolutionary—it abolished the largest concentration of property in the United States without monetary compensation.

"The one question of the age is *settled*," declared one congressman of the Thirteenth Amendment.[13] But if it resolved the fate of slavery, it opened a host of other issues. What, exactly, was being abolished? Property in man? The racial inequality inseparable from slavery? What would be the status of the former slaves and who would determine it? What did it mean to be a free person in postwar America? These were questions on which the politics of Reconstruction persistently turned.

White Southerners had their own answers, as became clear when Lincoln was assassinated and Andrew Johnson became president. Once lionized as a heroic defender of the Constitution against the Radical Republicans, Johnson today has a strong claim to being considered the worst president in American history. He was deeply racist, had no sense of Northern public opinion, and lacked the ability to work with Congress. Johnson set up new governments in the South in the months after the Civil War controlled entirely by white Southerners. These governments enacted a series of laws called the Black Codes to define the freedom African Americans now enjoyed. The laws gave Blacks virtually no civil or political rights. They required all adult Black men at the beginning of each year to sign a labor contract to go to work for a white employer or be deemed a vagrant and sold off to somebody who would pay the fine.

The Black Codes convinced the Republican Party, which controlled Congress, that the South was trying to restore slavery in all but name. Most Republicans agreed that the Thirteenth Amendment empowered Congress to ensure, as one senator put it, "that the man made free by the Constitution . . . is a freeman indeed."[14] In 1866, relying on the new amendment, it passed one of the most important laws in American history, the Civil Rights Act of 1866,[15] the first law to declare who are free citizens of the United States and what rights they are to enjoy.

The Civil Rights Act states that anybody born in the United States—except "Indians not taxed"—is automatically a citizen. This principle, known as birthright citizenship, is an affirmation that anyone can be a loyal American—race, religion, and national origin do not matter, nor does the legal status of one's parents. The law went on to declare that all these citizens must enjoy basic legal equality. States cannot pass one set of laws for Black people and another for white people. The Civil Rights Act said nothing about the right of Black men to vote, still very controversial in the North as well as the South. But it guaranteed equality of civil rights, specifically the right to sign contracts, own property, testify in court, sue, and be sued. These are the rights of free labor, necessary to compete in the economic marketplace. No state, or "custom," could deprive any citizen of these basic rights. The law's enforcement mechanisms were borrowed from the Fugitive Slave Act of 1850. Both laws sought to use federal power to protect a constitutional right—in 1850, the right of an owner to retrieve a fugitive slave; in 1866, the right of former slaves to genuine freedom. As one congressman declared, the Civil Rights Act turned "the artillery of slavery upon itself," wielding "the weapons which slavery has placed in our hands . . . in the holy cause of liberty."[16]

Andrew Johnson vetoed the Civil Rights Bill and it became the first important law in American history enacted over a veto. The veto message denounced the law for what today is called reverse discrimination: "The distinction of race and color is by the bill made to operate in favor of the colored and against the white race."[17] Indeed, in the idea that expanding the rights of nonwhites somehow punishes the white majority, the ghost of Andrew Johnson still haunts our discussions of race.

But a law can always be repealed, so very soon Congress put these principles into the Fourteenth Amendment, the most important change in the Constitution since the Bill of Rights. The amendment is long and complicated—the longest amendment ever added to the Constitution. It deals with specific, immediate problems such as the Confederate and Union debts. It contains a convoluted clause depriving states of part of their representation in the House of Representatives if they denied the right to vote to any group of male citizens. This section arose, in part, from an unusual consequence of the end of slavery. Previously, three-fifths of the slave population had been counted in apportioning representation. Now, as free persons, all would be counted, resulting in a significant increase in the number of members of Congress (and electoral votes) from the South. But if the Southern states denied Black men the right to vote, they would not enjoy this bounty. The section was a compromise between Republicans who favored Black suffrage and wanted the amendment to guarantee it and those who feared the idea was too unpopular to win ratification. It raised an outcry among the era's feminist movement because for the first time it introduced a gender distinction, the word "male," into the Constitution. Unlike men, there would be no penalty if states denied women, white or Black, the right to vote, as all of them at this point in our history did.

The heart of the Fourteenth Amendment, however, is the first section. This constitutionalizes the principle of birthright citizenship, except for persons not "subject to the jurisdiction" of the United States—that is, Native Americans, still considered members of their tribal sovereignties. It goes on to bar states from abridging the "privileges or immunities" of citizens, or denying to any person (a larger category, including both citizens and aliens) the equal protection of the law, or depriving them of life, liberty, or property without due process of law. Unlike the Civil Rights Act, the amendment is written in terms of general principles, not specific rights. It leaves it to future congresses and the courts to breathe meaning into these abstract phrases.

Congressman John A. Bingham, with whom most of the wording of Section One originated, intentionally couched a radical transformation of the Constitution in familiar terms. "I did imitate the framers," he said[18]; "every word . . . is today in the Constitution of our country."[19] This was not entirely correct. The word "equal" is not in the original Constitution (except for a provision about what happens if candidates for president or vice president receive an equal number of electoral votes). The Fourteenth Amendment makes the Constitution, for the first time, a vehicle through which aggrieved individuals and groups who believe that they are being denied equality can take their claims to federal court. The language is race neutral, which has had enormous consequences in our own time. In recent decades, the courts have used this amendment to expand the legal rights of numerous groups—most recently gay men and lesbians barred by state laws from marrying. Of course, declared Justice Anthony Kennedy's majority opinion in *Obergefell v. Hodges* (2015),[20] those who wrote the Fourteenth Amendment were not thinking of gay marriage. But our definitions of liberty and equality expand over time, and today reach into the most intimate areas of life—an illustration of the jurisprudence of a "living Constitution."

Despite enduring controversy over the precise meaning of its language, the first section of the Fourteenth Amendment fundamentally transformed Americans' relationship to their government. It asserted federal authority to create a new, uniform definition of citizenship and announced that being a citizen—or, in some cases, simply residing in the country—carried with it rights the states could not abridge. It proclaimed that everyone in the United States must enjoy a modicum of equality, protected by the national government. All in all, to borrow a phrase from the editor George William Curtis, the amendment changed a Constitution "for white men" into one "for mankind."[21]

All three of the postwar amendments also marked a significant change in the federal system. They not only put the concept of equal rights into the Constitution but empowered the federal government to enforce it. The Civil War had crystallized in the minds of Northerners the idea of a powerful national state protecting the rights of citizens. It is instructive to compare the Reconstruction amendments to the Bill of Rights, the first ten amendments, which protect our basic civil liberties. The Bill of Rights was based on the idea that the main danger to liberty was a too-powerful national state. It begins with the words "Congress shall make no law" and then lists the rights the federal government cannot abridge. It does not restrict the state governments. But all three postwar amendments end by declaring that Congress "shall have power" of enforcement. Now the federal government is seen as the protector of individual rights and the states as more likely to violate them. The three amendments made the federal government for the first time, in the words of Senator Charles Sumner, "the custodian of freedom."[22]

The Fourteenth Amendment said nothing directly about the suffrage, but, to guarantee state enforcement of the principle of equal citizenship, Congress in 1867 required that new governments be set up in the South, with Black men having the right to vote. And in the Fifteenth Amendment, ratified in 1870, Black male suffrage was extended to the entire nation. The amendment bars states from depriving any citizen of the right to vote because of race. This wording outraged the women's rights movement, for it allowed discrimination based on sex to continue. Even regarding men, Radical Republicans preferred a positive statement that all male citizens age twenty-one had the right to vote. But the tradition of state control of voting was deeply rooted, and many Northern states did not want to surrender that power. California barred the Chinese from voting. Rhode Island set different qualifications for immigrants than for native-born citizens. The Fifteenth Amendment's wording left open the possibility of voting requirements that could deprive Blacks of the right to vote without explicitly mentioning race. Unlike in the debates on the Thirteenth Amendment, Congress was aware of this loophole. Some members warned that states in the future might enact poll taxes, literacy tests, and other ostensibly nonracial requirements that would primarily affect Blacks. This indeed happened in the 1890s and early twentieth century, when the Southern states disenfranchised the vast majority of Black voters. Even today, voting qualifications vary widely among the fifty states. Many states have recently enacted laws that deprive significant numbers of Americans of the right to vote.

The advent of Black male suffrage inaugurated the period we call Radical Reconstruction, when new biracial governments came to power in the South. These governments had many accomplishments. They created the region's first public education systems. They began the process of rebuilding the Southern economy. They tried to protect the rights of Black laborers. Black men held office in Reconstruction at every level of government from the first two Black US senators to members of Congress and state legislatures, down to justices of the peace, sheriffs, and school board officials. Most power in Reconstruction remained in the hands of white Republicans, but the fact that perhaps two thousand African American men held public office was a revolutionary change in the American body politic.

This political revolution was dramatic enough that it inspired a wave of violence in the South by the Ku Klux Klan and kindred groups. At the same time, many Northerners began to retreat from the ideal of equality that had been written into the Constitution. One by one the Reconstruction governments fell by the wayside until, by 1877, the entire South was back under the political control of white supremacist Democrats, who would dominate it until the era of the civil rights revolution, sometimes called the Second Reconstruction. During the next generation, a new racial system was put in place in the South. Its pillars included racial segregation, denial of Black men's right to vote, a severe cutback in public funding of Black education, a segmented labor market in which most good jobs were reserved for whites, and widespread lynching.

Did not this racial system violate the Reconstruction amendments? With the conclusion of the second founding came the battle over its meaning. Ultimately, it fell to the Supreme Court to construe the constitutional amendments. And over time, the Court played a crucial role in the long retreat from the ideals of Reconstruction. The process was gradual and the outcome never total, and each decision involved its own laws, facts, and legal precedents. Recent scholars have attributed the retreat not simply to judicial racism but also to the persistence of federalism—fear among the justices that too great an expansion of nationally enforceable rights would undermine the legitimate powers of the states. For African Americans, however, the practical consequences were the same. The broad conception of constitutional rights with which they and their allies attempted to imbue the abolition of slavery proved tragically insecure.

A series of interconnected constitutional questions cried out for resolution. How substantially had the amendments altered the federal system? Did the Thirteenth Amendment prohibit only chattel bondage or extend to the "badges and incidents" of slavery, and what exactly were these? What did key provisions of the Fourteenth, including the "privileges or immunities" of citizens and the "equal protection of the laws," mean, and did this language apply only to Blacks or to all Americans? Did that amendment protect African Americans against violation of their rights by private individuals and businesses or only by state laws and the actions of public officials—the so-called state action doctrine—or did it also encompass what Blacks called "public rights," such as equal treatment by transportation companies and public accommodations? Did the Fifteenth Amendment's prohibition of disfranchisement "on account of race" prohibit laws, race-neutral on their face but clearly intended to limit African Americans' right to vote? On all of these issues, even though alternative understandings were readily available, the Court chose to restrict the scope of the second founding. By the early twentieth century, the Fourteenth and Fifteenth Amendments had become dead letters throughout the South. When the Court in 1903 threw up its hands and said there was nothing it could do if whites in Alabama chose to disfranchise the state's Black voters, a Northern newspaper declared, "We are brought face to face with the consideration that the Constitution may be violated with impunity."[23]

In the long train of Supreme Court decisions that eviscerated the postwar amendments, a few stand out as having the greatest impact. In the *Slaughterhouse Cases* (1873),[24] the justices defined the "privileges or immunities" of American citizens so narrowly that the phrase ceased to have substantive meaning. In *Bradwell v. Illinois* (1873),[25] they ruled that state measures discriminating against women (in this case barring them from practicing law) did not violate the equal protection of the laws. *United States v. Cruikshank* (1876)[26] overturned the few convictions the federal government had obtained of men responsible for the Colfax Massacre, when dozens of Black men were murdered in cold blood in Louisiana, seriously impeding national enforcement of Blacks' basic rights. In the *Civil Rights Cases* (1883),[27] the Court declared unconstitutional the Civil Rights Act of 1875, which barred racial discrimination by private businesses including transportation companies, theaters, and public accommodations. The Fourteenth Amendment, it declared, only applied to actions by state laws and officials. *Plessy v. Ferguson* (1896)[28] declared that state laws requiring racial segregation did not violate the equal protection of the law. And *Williams v. Mississippi* (1898)[29] and *Giles v. Harris* (1903)[30] allowed states to deny Black men the right to vote. While severely limiting the reach of the second founding when it came to the former slaves, the Court increasingly interpreted it as protecting business enterprises, ruling that state laws regulating working conditions and railroad rates violated the "due process" rights of corporations as legal "persons" under the Fourteenth Amendment.

In the late nineteenth century, however, an alternative, rights-based constitutionalism emerged among Black activists and their allies, one that rejected the key tenets of Supreme Court jurisprudence. In 1889, in the midst of the constitutional retreat, a group of Black lawyers and ministers in Baltimore calling themselves the Brotherhood of Liberty published *Justice and Jurisprudence*, the first sustained critique of Supreme Court rulings interpreting the Reconstruction amendments.[31] Its anonymous author proposed an alternative reading of the amended Constitution based on a broad conception of federal enforcement power. The book offered a different view of the rights "public and private" that constituted the privileges and immunities of American citizens, which the amendments were meant to protect. These included not only equal treatment by state authorities and in public accommodations, transport, and places of amusement but the rights of free labor, broadly defined. The book assailed employment discrimination, housing segregation, exclusion of Blacks from labor unions, and lack of access to education, insisting that citizenship carried with it the promise of economic opportunity. "Can a citizen," it asked, "be daily excluded from the paths of industrial progress . . . and yet be a citizen of the United States?"[32] Overall, as one reviewer of *Justice and Jurisprudence* wrote, the book demonstrated that too many rights had been lost as soon as they reached "that grave of liberty, the Supreme Court of the United States."[33] Despite the wholesale retreat from equality, however, the Reconstruction amendments remained in the Constitution, "sleeping giants," to borrow a phrase from Charles Sumner,[34] who would be awakened in the mid-twentieth century.

Today, the country has gone a long way toward fulfilling the agenda of Reconstruction. The states are now required to abide by virtually all the provisions of the Bill of Rights. Yet paradoxically, the recent history of the amendments reveals their ongoing expansion to protect the rights of new groups of Americans but a restricted application to questions involving race, especially affirmative action and limitations on the right to vote. This reflects both current political tendencies and the enduring impact of earlier decisions limiting the scope of the second founding. In a legal environment that relies so heavily on precedent, key decisions of the retreat from Reconstruction, with what Justice John Marshall Harlan, who dissented in many of these rulings, called the Court's "narrow and artificial"[35] understanding of the Thirteenth, Fourteenth, and Fifteenth Amendments, remain undisturbed. With the exception of repudiating *Plessy v. Ferguson*, even the Warren Court of the 1950s and 1960s did not directly confront the long train of decisions that restricted national power over citizens' basic rights. The justices could not bring themselves to say that for eighty years or more the Court had been wrong.

If this piece of our history proves anything, it is that the Constitution is not self-enforcing. Rights can be gained, and rights can be taken away. Yet however flawed, the era that followed the Civil War, and its great legacy, the Thirteenth, Fourteenth, and Fifteenth Amendments, can serve as an inspiration for those striving to achieve a more just society.

Fugitive Slave Act—Primary Sources

"Personal liberty" laws and practices adopted by Northern states, despite (or arguably because of) the Supreme Court's ruling in *Prigg v. Pennsylvania*, led to extended debates in Congress and ultimately produced, in 1850, a vastly strengthened Fugitive Slave Act. But as escapes via the Underground Railroad continued, and as Northern resistance to the new law intensified, the nation became even more divided over runaway slaves, revealing an unbridgeable chasm.

Fugitive Slave Act (1793)

In 1793, Congress passed legislation to enforce the Constitution's Fugitive Slave Clause (Article IV, Section 2). The statute permitted slave owners and their agents to cross state borders in order to "seize or arrest," and then to seek a federal court order requiring the return of, any "fugitive from labor." Fines could be imposed upon "any person who shall knowingly and willingly obstruct or hinder such claimant, his agent, or attorney in so seizing or arresting such fugitive from labor, or shall rescue such fugitive from such claimant . . . or shall harbor or conceal such person." The law was short, if not sweet: all of four paragraphs.[36]

Pennsylvania "Personal Liberty" Law (1826)

By the middle decades of the 1800s, controversies over "runaway" slaves had emerged as a major flashpoint between proponents and opponents of slavery. A number of Northern states had passed "personal liberty" laws that effectively nullified the federal law—for example, by prohibiting state and local officials from assisting in the process of apprehending fugitives, by refusing to prosecute residents who harbored or transported escaped slaves, or by providing attorneys and jury trials to captured runaways. Pennsylvania's 1826 statute, which established cumbersome procedures and proof requirements for slave owners seeking return of their "property" in the state courts, also authorized criminal penalties for slave owners who attempted to proceed extrajudicially.

> An act to give effect to the provisions of the Constitution of the United States relative to fugitives from labor, for the protection of free people of color, and prevent kidnapping.
>
> Section I. If any person or persons shall, from and after the passing of this act, by force and violence, take and carry away . . . any negro or mulatto, from any part or parts of this commonwealth to any other place or places whatsoever out of this commonwealth, with a design and intention of selling and disposing of, or of causing to be sold, or of keeping and detaining, or of causing to be kept and detained, such negro or mulatto, as a slave or servant for life or for any term whatsoever, every such person or persons, his or their aiders or abettors, shall on conviction thereof in any court of this commonwealth having competent jurisdiction be deemed guilty of a felony.[37]

Prigg v. Pennsylvania (1842)

The Supreme Court had little difficulty in striking down Pennsylvania's law—which, after all, was a direct and intentional interference with both the Constitution and an act of Congress.

> Historically, it is well known that the object of [Article IV, Section 2] was to secure to the citizens of the slaveholding states the complete right and title of ownership in their slaves, as property, in every state in the Union into which they might escape from the state where they were held in servitude. The full

recognition of this right and title was indispensable to the security of this species of property in all the slaveholding states, and indeed was so vital to the preservation of their domestic interests and institutions that it cannot be doubted that it constituted a fundamental article without the adoption of which the Union could not have been formed. Its true design was to guard against the doctrines and principles prevalent in the non-slaveholding states, by preventing them from intermeddling with, or obstructing, or abolishing the rights of the owners of slaves. . . .

We are of opinion that the act of Pennsylvania . . . is unconstitutional and void. It purports to punish as a public offense against that state the very act of seizing and removing a slave by his master which the Constitution of the United States was designed to justify and uphold.[38]

But the *Prigg* decision contained the seeds of a significant loophole: Because the process for capturing fugitives was deemed by the Court to be "exclusively" a federal responsibility, states arguably had no obligation to assist in any enforcement efforts. After *Prigg*, "personal liberty" laws at the state level multiplied—and contention between the North and the South over the issue intensified.

Congress Debates Whether to Strengthen the Fugitive Slave Act (1850)

In 1850, Congress debated a package of bills that included—in addition to the admission of California, rules about slavery for the new territories acquired after the war with Mexico, and a ban on slave trading in the District of Columbia—a plan to strengthen the fugitive slave law. Two titans of the Senate, Henry Clay of Kentucky and Daniel Webster of Massachusetts, spoke in favor of the proposed legislation.

> *Henry Clay:* [The Constitution] imposes an obligation upon the states—free or slaveholding—it imposes an obligation upon the officers of government, state or federal—and I add upon the people of the United States, under particular circumstances—to assist in the recovery and surrender of fugitive slaves from their masters. . . .
>
> I think that the whole class of legislation, beginning in the Northern states, and extending to some of the Western states, by which obstructions and impediments have been thrown in the way of the recovery of fugitive slaves are unconstitutional, and have originated in a spirit which I trust will correct itself when these states come to consider calmly the nature of their duty. . . .

I think that the existing laws for the recovery of fugitive slaves and the restoration and delivering of them to their owners, being often inadequate and ineffective, it is incumbent upon Congress—[and] I hope it will be regarded by the free states themselves as a part of their duty—to assist in allaying this subject, so irritating to the peace of this Union. . . . It is our duty to make the laws more effective, and I will go with the furthest senator from the South in this body to make penal laws, to impose the heaviest sanctions upon the recovery of fugitive slaves and the restoration of them to their owners.[39]

Daniel Webster: I wish to speak today, not as a Massachusetts man, nor as a Northern man, but as an American. . . .

In the excited times in which we live, there is found to exist a state of crimination and recrimination between the North and the South. There are lists of grievances produced by each; and those grievances, real or supposed, alienate the minds of one portion of the country from the other, exasperate the feelings, and subdue the sense of fraternal affection and patriotic love and mutual regard. . . . I begin with complaints of the South. . . [especially one] which has in my opinion just foundation; and that is that there has been found at the North, among individuals and among legislators of the North, a disinclination to perform fully their constitutional duties in regard to the return of persons bound to service who have escaped into the free states. In that respect, it is my judgment that the South is right and the North is wrong.

Every member of every Northern legislature is bound by oath, like every other officer in the country, to support the Constitution of the United States; and the article of the Constitution which says to these states, they shall deliver up fugitives from service is as binding in honor and conscience as any other article. No man fulfills his duty in any legislature who sets himself to find excuses, evasions, escapes from this constitutional obligation. . . . When it is said that a person escaping into another state, and coming therefore within the jurisdiction of that state, shall be delivered up, it seems to me the import of the passage is that the state itself, in obedience to the Constitution, shall cause him to be delivered up. . . .

I desire to call the attention of all sober-minded men, of all conscientious men, of all men in the North who are not carried away by any fanatical idea . . . to their constitutional obligations. I put it to all the sober and sound minds at the North as a question of morals and a question of conscience. What right have they, in their legislative capacity or any other [capacity], to endeavor to get round this Constitution or embarrass the free exercise of the rights secured by the Constitution to the persons whose slaves escape from them? None at all; none at all. Neither in the forum of conscience, nor before the face of the Constitution, are they justified, in my opinion. . . .

Here is a ground of complaint against the North, . . . which ought to be removed, which it is now in the power of the different departments of this government to remove; which calls for the enactment of proper laws authorizing the judicature of this government in the several states to do all that is necessary for the recapture of fugitive slaves and for the restoration of them to those who claim them.[40]

Opposing the proposed 1850 compromise package, John Calhoun of South Carolina contended that the North's refusal to enforce already existing fugitive slave laws revealed its rank hypocrisy with respect to the sanctity of the Constitution and the Union.

How can the Union be saved? To this I answer, there is but one way by which it can be, and that is by adopting such measures as will satisfy the states belonging to the Southern section that they can remain in the Union consistently with their honor and their safety. There is, again, only one way by which that can be effected, and that is by removing the causes by which this belief has been produced. . . . But how stands the profession of devotion to the Union by our assailants, when brought to this test? Have they abstained from violating the Constitution? Let the many acts passed by the Northern states to set aside and annul the clause of the Constitution providing for the delivery up of fugitive slaves answer. . . . Let them show a single instance during this long period in which they have denounced the agitators or their attempts to effect what is admitted to be unconstitutional.[41]

Fugitive Slave Act (1850)

The resulting Fugitive Slave Act of 1850 (which formed part of the Compromise of 1850) in fact greatly strengthened the law governing the capture and return of runaway slaves. Among other provisions: Northerners could now be personally compelled to search for escaped slaves (section 5); due process and proof requirements were streamlined, to the benefit of slaveholders (section 6); and persons who actively assisted runaways or otherwise interfered with their capture were subject to prosecution and imprisonment (section 7).

Section 5. And be it further enacted that it shall be the duty of all marshals and deputy marshals to obey and execute all warrants and precepts issued under the provisions of this act, when to them directed; . . . and the better to enable the said commissioners when thus appointed to execute their duties faithfully and efficiently, in conformity with the requirements of the Constitution of the

United States and of this act, they are hereby authorized and empowered ... to summon and call to their aid the bystanders, or posse comitatus of the proper county, when necessary to ensure a faithful observance of the clause of the Constitution referred to, in conformity with the provisions of this act; and all good citizens are hereby commanded to aid and assist in the prompt and efficient execution of this law, whenever their services may be required. ...

Section 6. And be it further enacted that when a person held to service or labor in any state or territory of the United States has heretofore or shall hereafter escape into another state or territory of the United States, the person or persons to whom such service or labor may be due, or his, her, or their agent or attorney, duly authorized ... may pursue and reclaim such fugitive person ... by taking, or causing such person to be taken, forthwith before such court, judge, or commissioner whose duty it shall be to hear and determine the case ... and upon satisfactory proof being made ... to take and remove such fugitive person back to the state or territory whence he or she may have escaped. ... In no trial or hearing under this act shall the testimony of such alleged fugitive be admitted in evidence.

Section 7. And be it further enacted that any person who shall knowingly and willingly obstruct, hinder, or prevent such claimant, his agent or attorney, or any person or persons lawfully assisting him, her, or them from arresting such a fugitive from service or labor ... or shall rescue, or attempt to rescue, such fugitive from service or labor from the custody of such claimant, his or her agent or attorney, or other person or persons lawfully assisting ... or shall aid, abet, or assist such person so owing service or labor ... to escape ... or shall harbor or conceal such fugitive ... shall, for either of said offenses, be subject to a fine not exceeding $1,000 and imprisonment not exceeding six months.[42]

In Praise of the New Fugitive Slave Act (1850)

Some Northerners praised the new law as consistent with a duty to follow and support the Constitution.

The willful harboring of a fugitive slave is a grave offense in morals as well as law, and those who commit this offense can exculpate themselves upon no other ground than the recognition of a higher authority than the Constitution and laws of the Union, the benefits of which they are continually enjoying, and which in all other matters they seek for their own protection. I freely admit that among the few abolitionists in our community are to be found the most exemplary men in private life, but their purity of character is of no value when they jeopard[ize] all that is dear to us. The present Fugitive Bill should be honestly carried out by the judicial authority of the country, and the exercise of that power should be strengthened by public opinion. This is the issue; if we do not cheerfully concede this ground, we violate the original federal compact and give the South just ground of complaint. I have no respect for the intelligence or motives of the man who will attempt to evade this question and say there is no danger and that the free states can continue to do so as they have done and preserve the Union.[43]

Abraham Lincoln Supports the Fugitive Slave Act (1854)

Abraham Lincoln, soon to emerge as a leader of the newly founded Republican Party, defended the Fugitive Slave Act as the necessary price to pay to hold the nation together.

> Stand with anybody that stands right. . . . Stand with the abolitionist in restoring the Missouri Compromise; and stand against him when he attempts to repeal the fugitive slave law. In the latter case you stand with the Southern disunionist. What of that? You are still right. In both cases you are right. In both cases you oppose the dangerous extremes. In both you stand on middle ground and hold the ship level and steady. In both you are national and nothing less than national.[44]

Harriet Tubman and the Underground Railroad (1850s)

But the enhanced Fugitive Slave Law did little to quell controversy in both the North and the South over the recapture of runaway slaves. Efforts to liberate slaves from the South continued apace, including via the Underground Railroad.[45] Harriet Tubman's endeavors in this regard are deservedly the stuff of legend. Of her, Frederick Douglass once remarked: "Excepting John Brown—of sacred memory—I know of no one who has willingly encountered more perils and hardships to serve our enslaved people."[46] An early biographical account of Tubman's remarkable deeds was published shortly after the end of the Civil War.

> Harriet Tubman—known at various times and in various places by many different names, such as "Moses," in allusion to her being the leader and guide to so many of her people in their exodus from the Land of Bondage; "the Conductor of the Underground Railroad;" and "Moll Pitcher," for the energy and daring by which she delivered a fugitive slave who was about to be dragged back to the

South—was for the first twenty-five years of her life a slave on the eastern shore of Maryland. . . .

It will be impossible to give any connected account of the different journeys taken by Harriet for the rescue of her people, as she herself has no idea of the dates connected with them or of the order in which they were made. She thinks she was about twenty-five when she made her own escape, and this was in the last year of James K. Polk's administration. From that time till the beginning of the war, her years were spent in these journeyings back and forth, with intervals between, in which she worked only to spend the avails of her labor in providing for the wants of her next party of fugitives. By night she traveled, many times on foot, over mountains, through forests, across rivers, mid perils by land, perils by water, perils from enemies, "perils among false brethren." Sometimes members of her party would become exhausted, foot-sore, and bleeding, and declare they could not go on, they must stay where they dropped down, and die; others would think a voluntary return to slavery better than being overtaken and carried back and would insist upon returning; then there was no remedy but force; the revolver carried by this bold and daring pioneer would be pointed at their heads . . . and so she compelled them to drag their weary limbs on their northward journey. . . .

And so by night travel, by hiding, by signals, by threatening, she brought the people safely to the land of liberty. But after the passage of the Fugitive Slave law, she said, "I wouldn't trust Uncle Sam wid my people no longer; I brought 'em all clar off to Canada."[47]

Northern Resistance to the Revised Fugitive Slave Act (1850s)

Enforcement of the new Fugitive Slave Act by the national government during the 1850s caused enormous controversy in the North. As Southern slave owners—ironically—called upon the enhanced enforcement powers of the central government to obtain return of their "property," tensions flared, often leading to substantial violence and civil disobedience. An appropriately named political tract, *The Fugitive Slave Law and Its Victims*, recounted more than 120 incidents of successful—and unsuccessful—recapture efforts, which were almost invariably resisted in the North by local citizens and sometimes by mobs.

The remainder of this tract will be devoted to a record, as complete as circumstances enable us to make, of the victims of the Fugitive Slave Law. It is a terrible record, which the people of this country should never allow to sleep in oblivion until the disgraceful and bloody system of slavery is swept from our land, and with it all compromise bills, all constitutional guarantees to slavery, all Fugitive Slave Laws.[48]

The Plight of Anthony Burns (1854)

Far and away the most celebrated of these episodes involved Anthony Burns and took place in Boston in 1854.

Anthony Burns, arrested in Boston, May 24, 1854, as the slave of Charles F. Suttle of Alexandria, Virginia, who was present to claim him, accompanied by a witness from Richmond, Virginia, named William Brent. Burns was arrested on a warrant granted by United States Commissioner Edward Greeley Loring, taken to the courthouse in Boston, ironed, and placed in an upper story room under a strong guard. . . . On [May 26], an attack was made upon the courthouse by a body of men, with the evident design of rescuing Burns; a door was forced in and one of the marshal's special guard (named Batchelder) was killed, whether by the assailants or by one of his own party is uncertain, it being quite dark. . . . During the trial Burns was continually surrounded by a numerous bodyguard (said to be at least 125 men) selected by Watson Freeman, United States marshal, from the vilest sinks of scoundrelism, corruption, and crime in the city to be deputy marshals for the occasion. These men, with every form of loathsome impurity and hardened villainy stamped upon their faces, sat constantly around the prisoner while in the courtroom, the handles of pistols and revolvers visibly protruding from their breast pockets. A company of United States troops from the Navy Yard occupied the courthouse and guarded all avenues to the United States courtroom. . . . The United States District Attorney Benjamin F. Hallett was in regular telegraphic communication with the president of the United States (F. Pierce) at Washington. . . .

On Friday morning, June 2nd, Commissioner Loring gave his decision . . . ordering him to be delivered up to [Suttle]. . . . Troops, which had been called out by the mayor, Jerome V.C. Smith, were marched to the scene of the kidnapping and so placed as to guard every street, lane, and other avenue. . . . All preparations being made, Watson Freeman . . . issued forth from the courthouse with his prisoner, who walked with a firm step, surrounded by the bodyguard of criminals before mentioned, with drawn United States sabers in their hands and followed by United States troops with the aforesaid piece of artillery. . . . The prisoner was taken on board a steam towboat and conveyed down the harbor to the United States Revenue Cutter *Morris*; in which he was transported to Virginia.

It may not be amiss to have given, in a single instance, this somewhat detailed account of the process of seizing, trying, and delivering up a man into
slavery, whose only crime was that he had fled from a bondage "one hour of
which is fraught with more misery than ages of that which our fathers rose in
rebellion to throw off," Thomas Jefferson, the Virginian slaveholder, himself
being witness.

Anthony Burns, having been sold into North Carolina, was afterwards purchased with money subscribed in Boston and vicinity for the purpose and
returned to Boston.[49]

Uncle Tom's Cabin (1852)

The Fugitive Slave Act of 1850 and the discord it generated persuaded Harriet
Beecher Stowe to write Uncle Tom's Cabin, one of the most influential books in
American history. In the novel's final chapter, Stowe revealed her motivation in
putting pen to paper.

> For many years of her life, the author avoided all reading upon or allusion to
> the subject of slavery, considering it as too painful to be inquired into, and one
> which advancing light and civilization would certainly live down. But since the
> legislative act of 1850, when she heard, with perfect surprise and consternation,
> Christian and humane people actually recommending the remanding escaped
> fugitives into slavery as a duty binding on good citizens—when she heard on
> all hands from kind, compassionate, and estimable people in the free states of
> the North deliberations and discussions as to what Christian duty could be on
> this head—she could only think, these men and Christians cannot know what
> slavery is; if they did, such a question could never be open for discussion. And
> from this arose a desire to exhibit it in a living dramatic reality. She has endeav-
> ored to show it fairly, in its best and its worst phases. In its best aspect, she has,
> perhaps, been successful; but, oh! who shall say what yet remains untold in that
> valley and shadow of death that lies the other side?[50]

Henry David Thoreau Condemns the Fugitive Law (1854)

Abolitionist William Lloyd Garrison burned a copy of the Fugitive Slave Act of
1850 (along with a copy of the Constitution) in Framingham, Massachusetts at
a Fourth of July "Anti-Slavery Celebration" in 1854. Henry David Thoreau also
spoke at that event.

> Much has been said about American slavery, but I think that we do not even
> yet realize what slavery is. If I were seriously to propose to Congress to make

mankind into sausages, I have no doubt that most of the members would smile at my proposition, and if any believed me to be in earnest, they would think that I proposed something much worse than Congress had ever done. But if any of them will tell me that to make a man into a sausage would be much worse— would be any worse—than to make him into a slave—than it was to enact the Fugitive Slave Law—I will accuse him of foolishness, of intellectual incapacity, of making a distinction without a difference. The one is just as sensible a proposition as the other. . . .

The judges and lawyers . . . consider not whether the Fugitive Slave Law is right, but whether it is what they call constitutional. Is virtue constitutional, or vice? Is equity constitutional, or iniquity? In important moral and vital questions like this, it is just as impertinent to ask whether a law is constitutional or not as to ask whether it is profitable or not. They persist in being the servants of the worst of men and not the servants of humanity. The question is not whether you or your grandfather, seventy years ago, did not enter into an agreement to serve the devil, and that service is not accordingly now due; but whether you will not now, for once and at last, serve God . . . by obeying that eternal and only just constitution, which He, and not any Jefferson or Adams, has written in your being. . . .

I am surprised to see men going about their business as if nothing had happened. . . . No prudent man will build a stone house under these circumstances or engage in any peaceful enterprise which it requires a long time to accomplish. . . . It is not an era of repose. We have used up all our inherited freedom. If we would save our lives, we must fight for them.

I walk toward one of our ponds; but what signifies the beauty of nature when men are base? We walk to lakes to see our serenity reflected in them; when we are not serene, we go not to them. Who can be serene in a country where both the rulers and the ruled are without principle? The remembrance of my country spoils my walk. My thoughts are murder to the state, and involuntarily go plotting against her.[51]

New "Personal Liberty" Efforts (1857)

In response to the 1850 legislation, an additional raft of new "personal liberty" laws issued from the North. In 1857, for example, Ohio passed a statute to prevent "kidnapping in Ohio."

Section 3. If any person shall seize or arrest . . . or shall use any force or fraud for the purpose of holding, detaining, controlling, or influencing any other person with intent to carry or remove such person out of this state . . . in order that such person may be taken, held, or controlled as a slave in some other state, territory, or jurisdiction, such person so offending shall be deemed guilty of kidnapping and shall be punished by imprisonment in the penitentiary at hard labor, not less than three years.[52]

The Supreme Court of Wisconsin went even further, declaring the Fugitive Slave Act to be unconstitutional—a decision that was subsequently overturned by the Supreme Court in *Abelman v. Booth* (1859).[53]

Jefferson Davis on the Fugitive Slave Controversy (1881)

Years later, former Confederate president Jefferson Davis reflected on the controversy surrounding implementation, enforcement, and (in his view) evasion of the revised federal fugitive law.

> It was reasonably argued that, as the legislatures of fourteen of the [Northern] states had enacted what were termed "personal liberty laws," which forbade the cooperation of state officials in the rendition of fugitives from service and labor, it became necessary that the general government should provide the requisite machinery for the execution of the law. The result proved what might have been anticipated—that those communities which had repudiated their constitutional obligations, which had nullified a previous law of Congress for the execution of a provision of the Constitution, and had murdered men who came peacefully to recover their property, would evade or obstruct, so as to render practically worthless, *any* law that could be enacted for that purpose. In the exceptional cases in which it might be executed, the event would be attended with such conflict between the state and federal authorities as to produce consequent evils greater than those it was intended to correct.[54]

President Lincoln Pledges to Enforce the Fugitive Slave Act (1861)

During his campaign for president, Abraham Lincoln repeatedly pledged to enforce the Fugitive Slave Act "because the Constitution requires us."[55] He repeated that vow during his First Inaugural Address.

> There is much controversy about the delivering up of fugitives from service or labor. The clause I now read is as plainly written in the Constitution as any other of its provisions.... It is scarcely questioned that this provision was intended by those who made it for the reclaiming of what we call fugitive slaves; and the intention of the lawgiver is the law. All members of Congress swear their support

to the whole Constitution—to this provision as much as to any other. . . . I take the official oath today with no mental reservations and with no purpose to construe the Constitution or laws by any hypercritical rules; and while I do not choose now to specify particular acts of Congress as proper to be enforced, I do suggest that it will be much safer for all, both in official and private stations, to conform to and abide by all those acts which stand unrepealed.[56]

Georgia's Secession Resolution (1861)

Lincoln might pledge, but the South still fulminated. The alleged failure of Northern states to live up to their obligations under the Fugitive Slave Act was often "Exhibit A" in the South's list of grievances justifying rebellion, as demonstrated by Georgia's secession resolution.

> The Constitution requires them to surrender fugitives from labor. This provision [was one of] our main inducements for confederating with the Northern states. Without [it] . . . we would have rejected the Constitution. In the fourth year of the republic, Congress passed a law to give full vigor and efficiency to this important provision. This act depended to a considerable degree upon the local magistrates in the several states for its efficiency. The non-slaveholding states generally repealed all laws intended to aid the execution of that act and imposed penalties upon those citizens whose loyalty to the Constitution and their oaths might induce them to discharge their duty. Congress then passed the act of 1850, providing for the complete execution of this duty by federal officers. This law, which their own bad faith rendered absolutely indispensable for the protection of constitutional rights, was instantly met with ferocious revilings and all conceivable modes of hostility. . . . [The Fugitive Slave Act] stands today a dead letter for all practicable purposes in every non-slaveholding state in the Union.[57]

The controversy over the Fugitive Slave Act truly was, in the words of one historian, "the war before the war."[58]

Discussion Questions

1. The controversy over fugitive slaves raises important questions about federalism and states' rights. As Eric Foner notes, white Southerners insisted on states' rights and a limited role for the central government, but, ironically, they complained about the lack of enforcement by the national

government of the Fugitive Slave Act prior to 1850 and the lack of compliance by Northern states with the enhanced law after 1850. Likewise, slave owners repeatedly insisted on the right to practice slavery by their own rules and without any outside interference, yet they refused to recognize an analogous desire by Northerners to enact "personal liberty" laws to protect citizens who did not want to assist in returning runaway slaves. Conversely, many Northerners welcomed the use of congressional power to prohibit the expansion of slavery into the territories but not to enforce the fugitivity clause of the Constitution. Explain whether it is good or bad that people's attitudes toward the Constitution and its interpretation and applicability—then and now—often depend on their political viewpoints.

2. How was the refusal of Northerners to enforce the Fugitive Slave Act during the 1850s similar to (or different from) South Carolina's refusal to enforce the Tariff of Abominations during the 1830s? Why might Northerners in this time period believe that some laws could be nullified but others could not?

3. Far from being a historical anachronism, one can readily posit a modern-day analog to the fugitive slave controversy. Some US citizens and organizations have taken steps to shelter undocumented immigrants from Immigration and Customs Enforcement authorities. Similarly, despite federal law to the contrary,[59] some state and local officials have pledged not to cooperate with federal agents seeking to obtain information about, or apprehend and deport, undocumented immigrants residing in their communities. In fact, hundreds of localities (by one estimate) have pronounced themselves "sanctuary cities," adopting various policies designed to resist federal efforts to enforce immigration laws.[60] To what extent does this present-day controversy mirror the discord over the Fugitive Slave Act? What constitutional arguments can be invoked to support either side of this debate?

4. The fugitive slave controversy also raises key questions about morality and ethics. What should happen when a person's moral judgment conflicts with a law? That question has arisen repeatedly in US history, from opponents of slavery and the fugitive slave laws to civil rights and antiwar protesters over the years to antiabortion activists in recent times. Henry David Thoreau's answer was straightforward: follow your conscience. When, if ever, is it acceptable for people to disobey laws that they believe are morally wrong? What effect might this have on the nation as a whole?

5. In the same vein, must public officials—duly elected to office, and duly sworn to "preserve, protect and defend the Constitution of the United States"[61]—abide by and enforce a law that they deem morally abhorrent?

Was Lincoln's pledge to uphold the Fugitive Slave Act required or immoral? What should be a judge's obligation to follow and apply an "unjust" law?[62]

Dred Scott—Primary Sources

Dred Scott v. Sandford is one of the Supreme Court's most famous cases—and certainly its most infamous. Chief Justice Roger Taney, who authored the 7–2 decision, intended to settle, definitively, various slavery-related debates that had roiled the nation and that the political branches had been unable to resolve. The Court did nothing of the sort, instead only accelerating the approaching crisis. Dred Scott's significance—and its explosiveness—is best understood in light of several questions: What did the Court conclude, both directly and implicitly? How was the ruling received at the time? And—using Lincoln's reaction as a guidepost—what does the case say about the role of the Supreme Court in our constitutional system?

The Decision: Dred Scott Not a Citizen (1857)

Dred Scott, a slave from Missouri, was taken by his owner to live first in the (free) state of Illinois and thereafter in the (free) then-territory of Wisconsin. Having been brought back to Missouri, he sued for his freedom. The Supreme Court held that Scott had no right to litigate in federal court because he was not a citizen— and he was not a citizen, and could never hope to become a citizen, because he was not white.

The question is simply this: Can a negro whose ancestors were imported into this country and sold as slaves become a member of the political community formed and brought into existence by the Constitution of the United States, and as such become entitled to all the rights, and privileges, and immunities guaranteed by that instrument to the citizen, one of which rights is the privilege of suing in a court of the United States in the cases specified in the Constitution? ...

The words "people of the United States" and "citizens" are synonymous terms and mean the same thing. They both describe the political body who, according to our republican institutions, form the sovereignty and who hold the power and conduct the government through their representatives. They are what we familiarly call the "sovereign people." . . . The question before us is whether [Dred Scott and all other persons of African ancestry] compose a portion of this people and are constituent members of this sovereignty? We think they are not, and that they are not included, and were not intended to be included, under the word "citizens" in the Constitution, and can therefore claim none of the rights and privileges which that instrument provides for and secures to citizens of the United States. On the contrary, they were at that time considered as a subordinate and inferior class of beings who had been subjugated by the dominant race, and, whether emancipated or not, yet remained subject to their authority and had no rights or privileges but such as those who held the power and the government might choose to grant them. . . .

[At the time of the Declaration of Independence, they] had for more than a century before been regarded as beings of an inferior order, and altogether unfit to associate with the white race either in social or political relations, and so far inferior that they had no rights which the white man was bound to respect, and that the negro might justly and lawfully be reduced to slavery for his benefit. He was bought and sold and treated as an ordinary article of merchandise and traffic whenever a profit could be made by it. This opinion was at that time fixed and universal in the civilized portion of the white race. . . .

"We hold these truths to be self-evident: that all men are created equal." . . . The general words above quoted would seem to embrace the whole human family. . . . But it is too clear for dispute that the enslaved African race were not intended to be included and formed no part of the people who framed and adopted this declaration, for if the language as understood in that day would embrace them, the conduct of the distinguished men who framed the Declaration of Independence would have been utterly and flagrantly inconsistent with the principles they asserted. . . .

The brief preamble [of the Constitution] . . . declares that it is formed by the people of the United States . . . and its great object is declared to be to secure the blessings of liberty to themselves and their posterity. . . . It does not define what description of persons are intended to be included under these terms, or who shall be regarded as a citizen and one of the people. . . . But there are two clauses in the Constitution which point directly and specifically to the negro race as a separate class of persons, and show clearly that they were not regarded as a portion of the people or citizens of the government then formed. . . . [The slave importation clause and the fugitive slave clause] show conclusively that neither the description of persons therein referred to nor their descendants were embraced in any of the other provisions of the Constitution, for certainly these two clauses were not intended to confer on them or their posterity the blessings of liberty or any of the personal rights so carefully provided for the citizen. . . .

Upon a full and careful consideration of the subject, the Court is of opinion that . . . Dred Scott was not a citizen of Missouri within the meaning of the Constitution of the United States, and not entitled as such to sue in its courts.[63]

Justice Benjamin Curtis Dissents (1857)

In holding that Dred Scott—and others in his "subordinate and inferior class"—were not (and never could be) among the Declaration's "all [equally created] men" or the Constitution's "We the People," the Court strongly suggested, even if it did not flatly say so, that all free Blacks throughout the United States were similarly ineligible to be considered "citizens" of the United States. (Taney himself later wrote that the Court's decision was meant to apply to all members of "the African or negro race . . . whether their ancestors were held in slavery or not."[64]) Justice Benjamin Curtis, who dissented, pointed out the incongruity between the Court's holding and the fact that at the time of the Constitution's adoption, free Blacks in at least five states (including North Carolina) were not only considered to be citizens but could even cast votes.

> These colored persons were not only included in the body of "the people of the United States" by whom the Constitution was ordained and established, but in at least five of the states they had the power to act, and doubtless did act, by their suffrages upon the question of its adoption. It would be strange if we were to find in that instrument anything which deprived of their citizenship any part of the people of the United States who were among those by whom it was established. . . .
>
> It has been often asserted that the Constitution was made exclusively by and for the white race. It has already been shown that in five of the thirteen original states, colored persons then possessed the elective franchise, and were among those by whom the Constitution was ordained and established. If so, it is not true, in point of fact, that the Constitution was made exclusively by the white race. And that it was made exclusively for the white race is, in my opinion, not only an assumption not warranted by anything in the Constitution, but contradicted by its opening declaration that it was ordained and established by the people of the United States, for themselves and their posterity. And as free colored persons were then citizens of at least five states, and so in every sense part of the people of the United States, they were among those for whom and whose posterity the Constitution was ordained and established.[65]

Dred Scott: Slavery a Constitutionally Protected Right (1857)

Chief Justice Taney and his fellow concurring justices then proceeded to declare that even if Scott had a right to sue (which they had already determined he did not), he would have lost anyway. Scott did not become free when his master took him to reside in a free state. (By implication, this suggested that states in the North that had already abolished slavery might not be able to keep slaveholders and their enslaved laborers from residing in their midst.) Nor did Scott become entitled to his freedom by reason of having lived in a territory expressly declared by Congress to be off limits to slavery. Congress had no constitutional power to restrict slavery in federal territories, said Taney, because that would infringe upon a slaveholder's Fifth Amendment right to "property" in his slave. (By implication, this suggested that states in the North that had already abolished slavery might also have violated the Fifth Amendment "property" rights of owners.)

> The rights of private property have been guarded with equal care [in the Bill of Rights]. Thus, the rights of property are united with the rights of person and placed on the same ground by the Fifth Amendment to the Constitution, which provides that no person shall be deprived of life, liberty, and property without due process of law. . . . If the Constitution recognizes the right of property of the master in a slave, and makes no distinction between that description of property and other property owned by a citizen, no tribunal acting under the authority of the United States, whether it be legislative, executive, or judicial, has a right to draw such a distinction or deny to it the benefit of the provisions and guarantees which have been provided for the protection of private property against the encroachments of the government. . . .
>
>   It is the opinion of the Court that the act of Congress which prohibited a citizen from holding and owning property of this kind in the territory of the United States north of the line [established by the Missouri Compromise] is not warranted by the Constitution, and is therefore void, and that neither Dred Scott himself nor any of his family were made free by being carried into this territory, even if they had been carried there by the owner with the intention of becoming a permanent resident.[66]

In his concurring opinion, Justice John Catron went even further, insisting that by prohibiting (in the Missouri Compromise) slaveholders from bringing only "one species of property" into certain portions of the Louisiana Territory, Congress had violated "the most leading feature of the Constitution—a feature on which the Union depends, and which secures to the respective States and their citizens an entire EQUALITY of rights, privileges, and immunities."[67]

Dred Scott: Congress Violated the Constitution (1857)

In ruling that Congress had no power to legislate with respect to slavery in the territories, moreover, the Supreme Court—for only the second time in the nation's history (the first being *Marbury v. Madison*)—declared a law passed by Congress to be unconstitutional and unenforceable: in this case, in fact, two laws, the Missouri Compromise (explicitly) and the Kansas-Nebraska Act (by implication).

> Congress was [not] authorized to pass this law under any of the powers granted to it by the Constitution; [and] if the authority is not given by that instrument, it is the duty of this Court to declare it void and inoperative, and incapable of conferring freedom upon anyone who is held as a slave under the laws of any one of the States.[68]

The Reaction: Southerners Embrace *Dred Scott* (1857)

Reactions to the *Dred Scott* ruling from white Southerners were predictable. The Court had both vindicated their long-held views as to the legitimacy of slavery under the Constitution and struck a deadly blow against efforts of Republicans and abolitionists to interfere with the institution, whether in the states where it existed or in the territories into which it might spread. A Virginia newspaper, for example, celebrated "the authentic annunciation of the grave and deliberate decision" of the Supreme Court, "that august body."

> Thus has a politico-legal question, involving others of deep import, been decided emphatically in favor of the advocates and supporters of the Constitution and the Union, the equality of the states, and the rights of the South, in contradistinction to and in repudiation of the diabolical doctrines inculcated by factionists and fanatics; and that too by a tribunal of jurists as learned, impartial, and unprejudiced as perhaps the world has ever seen. A prize for which the athletes of the nation have often wrestled in the halls of Congress has been awarded at last, by the proper umpire, to those who have justly won it. The nation has achieved a triumph, sectionalism has been rebuked, and abolitionism has been staggered and stunned. . . . And thus it is that reason and right, justice and truth, always triumph over passion and prejudice, ignorance and envy, when submitted to the deliberations of honest and able men.[69]

Jefferson Davis Praises *Dred Scott* (1881)

Even decades later, Jefferson Davis pointed to the *Dred Scott* ruling when attempting to justify both his actions and the Confederate cause.

In 1854 a case (the well-known *Dred Scott* case) came before the Supreme Court of the United States, involving the whole question of the status of the African race and the rights of citizens of the Southern states to migrate to the territories, temporarily or permanently, with their slave property, on a footing of equality with the citizens of other states with their property of any sort. This question . . . had already been the subject of long and energetic discussion without any satisfactory conclusion. All parties, however, had united in declaring that a decision by the Supreme Court of the United States—the highest judicial tribunal in the land—would be accepted as final. After long and patient consideration of the case in 1857, the decision of the Court was pronounced in an elaborate and exhaustive opinion delivered by Chief Justice Taney—a man eminent as a lawyer, great as a statesman, and stainless in his moral reputation— seven of the nine judges who composed the Court concurring in it. The salient points established by this decision were:

1. That persons of the African race were not, and could not be, acknowledged as "part of the people," or citizens, under the Constitution of the United States;
2. That Congress had no right to exclude citizens of the South from taking their negro servants, as any other property, into any part of the common territory, and that they were entitled to claim its protection therein;
3. And, finally, as a consequence of the principle just above stated, that the Missouri Compromise of 1820, insofar as it prohibited the existence of African servitude north of a designated line, was unconstitutional and void.

   . . .

Instead of accepting the decision of this then august tribunal—the ultimate authority in the interpretation of constitutional questions—as conclusive of a controversy that had so long disturbed the peace and was threatening the perpetuity of the Union, it was flouted, denounced, and utterly disregarded by the Northern agitators, and served only to stimulate the intensity of their sectional hostility. What resource for justice—what assurance of tranquility—what guarantee of safety—now remained for the South?[70]

Stephen A. Douglas Endorses *Dred Scott*'s Reading of the Declaration (1858)

Northern reactions to the *Dred Scott* ruling were less uniform. Even though his own pet project of "popular sovereignty" had been severely undermined by the Court's reasoning, Illinois Senator Stephen A. Douglas shed no tears over the holding that Dred Scott (and all others like him) was debarred from citizenship status. As Douglas declaimed during his third senatorial debate with Abraham Lincoln:

> Mr. Lincoln objects to [the *Dred Scott*] decision first and mainly because it deprives the negro of the rights of citizenship. I am as much opposed to his reason for that objection as I am to the objection itself. I hold that a negro is not and never ought to be a citizen of the United States. (Good, good, and tremendous cheers.) I hold that this government was made on the white basis, by white men, for the benefit of white men and their posterity forever and should be administered by white men and none others. I do not believe that the Almighty made the negro capable of self-government. I am aware that all the abolition lecturers that you find traveling about through the country are in the habit of reading the Declaration of Independence to prove that all men were created equal and endowed by their Creator with certain inalienable rights, among which are life, liberty, and the pursuit of happiness. Mr. Lincoln is very much in the habit of . . . reading that part of the Declaration of Independence to prove that the negro was endowed by the Almighty with the inalienable right of equality with white men. Now I say to you, my fellow citizens, that in my opinion, the signers of the Declaration had no reference to the negro whatever when they declared all men to be created equal. They desired to express by that phrase white men, men of European birth and European descent, and had no reference either to the negro, the savage Indians, the Fejee, the Malay, or any other inferior and degraded race when they spoke of the equality of men.[71]

Horace Greeley Denounces *Dred Scott* (1857)

Other Northerners, though, were aghast at the *Dred Scott* decision and its potential consequences. The *New York Tribune*, Horace Greeley's newspaper, editorialized vociferously against the ruling.

> It is impossible to exaggerate the importance of the recent decision of the Supreme Court . . . [and] the great fact which it establishes—the fact that slavery is national; and that until that remote period when different judges, sitting in this same Court, shall reverse this wicked and false judgment, the Constitution of the United States is nothing better than the bulwark of inhumanity and oppression.
>
> It is most true that this decision is bad law; that it is based on false historical premises and wrong interpretations of the Constitution; that it does not at all represent the legal or judicial opinion of the nation; that it is merely a

Southern sophism clothed with the dignity of our highest Court. Nevertheless there it is; the final action of the national judiciary, established by the founders of the republic to interpret the Constitution and to embody the ultimate legal conclusions of the whole people—an action proclaiming that in the view of the Constitution slaves are property.[72]

Frederick Douglass on *Dred Scott* (1857)

Frederick Douglass also vehemently condemned the Supreme Court decision, which he referred to as "this last and most shocking of all pro-slavery devices."

This infamous decision of the slaveholding wing of the Supreme Court maintains that slaves are, within the contemplation of the Constitution of the United States, property; that slaves are property in the same sense that horses, sheep, and swine are property; that the old doctrine that slavery is a creature of local law is false; that the right of the slaveholder to his slave does not depend upon the local law, but is secured wherever the Constitution of the United States extends; that Congress has no right to prohibit slavery anywhere; that slavery may go in safety anywhere under the star-spangled banner; that colored persons of African descent have no rights that white men are bound to respect; that colored men of African descent are not and cannot be citizens of the United States.

You will readily ask me how I am affected by this devilish decision—this judicial incarnation of wolfishness? My answer is, and no thanks to the slaveholding wing of the Supreme Court, my hopes were never brighter than now. I have no fear that the national conscience will be put to sleep by such an open, glaring, and scandalous tissue of lies as that decision is and has been over and over shown to be. The Supreme Court of the United States is not the only power in this world. It is very great, but the Supreme Court of the Almighty is greater. Judge Taney can do many things, but he cannot perform impossibilities. He cannot bail out the ocean, annihilate the firm old earth, or pluck the silvery star of liberty from our Northern sky. He may decide and decide again; but he cannot reverse the decision of the Most High. He cannot change the essential nature of things—making evil good, and good evil. Happily for the whole human family, their rights have been defined, declared, and decided in a court higher than the Supreme Court....

Come what will, I hold it to be morally certain that, sooner or later, by fair means or foul means, in quiet or in tumult, in peace or in blood, in judgment or in mercy, slavery is doomed to cease out of this otherwise goodly land, and liberty is destined to become the settled law of this republic. I base my sense of the certain overthrow of slavery, in part, upon the nature of the American government, the

Constitution, the tendencies of the age, and the character of the American people; and this notwithstanding the important decision of Judge Taney....

I have a quarrel with those who fling the supreme law of this land between the slave and freedom. It is a serious matter to fling the weight of the Constitution against the cause of human liberty, and those who do it take upon them a heavy responsibility. Nothing but absolute necessity shall or ought to drive me to such a concession to slavery.... "We, the people"—not we, the white people—not we, the citizens, or the legal voters—not we, the privileged class and excluding all other classes but we, the people; not we, the horses and cattle, but we the people—the men and women, the human inhabitants of the United States, do ordain and establish this Constitution, etc. I ask, then, any man to read the Constitution and tell me where, if he can, in what particular that instrument affords the slightest sanction of slavery? Where will he find a guarantee for slavery? Will he find it in the declaration that no person shall be deprived of life, liberty, or property, without due process of law? Will he find it in the declaration that the Constitution was established to secure the blessing of liberty? Will he find it in the right of the people to be secure in their persons and papers, and houses, and effects? Will he find it in the clause prohibiting the enactment by any state of a bill of attainder? These all strike at the root of slavery, and any one of them, but faithfully carried out, would put an end to slavery in every state in the American Union....

It may be said that it is quite true that the Constitution was designed to secure the blessings of liberty and justice to the people who made it, and to the posterity of the people who made it, but was never designed to do any such thing for the colored people of African descent. This is Judge Taney's argument ... but it is not the argument of the Constitution. The Constitution imposes no such mean and satanic limitations upon its own beneficent operation. . . . The Constitution knows all the human inhabitants of this country as "the people." . . . All I ask of the American people is that they live up to the Constitution, adopt its principles, imbibe its spirit, and enforce its provisions. When this is done, the wounds of my bleeding people will be healed, the chain will no longer rust on their ankles, their backs will no longer be torn by the bloody lash, and liberty, the glorious birthright of our common humanity, will become the inheritance of all the inhabitants of this highly favored country.[73]

Abraham Lincoln's "Reverence for the Laws" (1838)

And what about Abraham Lincoln? Lincoln was a lawyer and therefore almost by definition was pledged to uphold the rule of law. In one of his earliest speeches, given shortly after an angry mob's murder of abolitionist Elijah Lovejoy, he had insisted on law-abidingness as our "political religion" and had urged "a reverence for the Constitution and laws."

> Let reverence for the laws be breathed by every American mother to the lisping babe that prattles on her lap—let it be taught in schools, in seminaries, and in colleges; let it be written in primers, spelling books, and in almanacs—let it be preached from the pulpit, proclaimed in legislative halls, and enforced in courts of justice.[74]

The *Dred Scott* decision must have posed a constitutional (and perhaps also a psychological) crisis for Lincoln: what to do about a fundamentally abhorrent Supreme Court pronouncement?

Stephen A. Douglas: *Dred Scott* Is "Law of the Land" (1858)

During his debates with Lincoln, Stephen A. Douglas rammed the point home. Douglas argued that the Supreme Court had settled the slavery question once and for all—and that therefore all Americans, regardless of their personal views about slavery, were obligated to fall into line.

> The *Dred Scott* decision was pronounced by the highest tribunal on earth. From that decision there is no appeal this side of heaven. Yet Mr. Lincoln says he is going to reverse that decision. By what tribunal will he reverse it? Will he appeal to a mob? Does he intend to appeal to violence, to lynch law? Will he stir up strife and rebellion in the land and overthrow the Court by violence? . . .
>
> I choose to abide by the decisions of the Supreme Court as they are pronounced. . . . [When I was a lawyer], I appealed until I got to the Supreme Court, and then if that court, the highest tribunal in the world, decided against me, I was satisfied, because it is the duty of every law-abiding man to obey the constitutions, the laws, and the constituted authorities. . . . It is enough for me to know that the Constitution of the United States created the Supreme Court for the purpose of deciding all disputed questions touching the true construction of that instrument, and when such decisions are pronounced they are the law of the land, biding on every good citizen.[75]

Abraham Lincoln's Multiple Responses to *Dred Scott* (1857)

Lincoln rejected the idea of direct disobedience or violent resistance to *Dred Scott*. "We do not propose that when Dred Scott has been decided to be a slave by the Court, we, as a mob, will decide him to be free."[76] The Supreme Court was entitled to respect for its constitutional pronouncements. Yet, in a June 1857 speech pondering the decision and its ramifications, Lincoln advanced no fewer than five lines of arguments aimed at undermining *Dred Scott*'s legitimacy.

First, Lincoln expressed the hope that the decision—someday, somehow—would be overturned.

> We believe as much as Judge Douglas (perhaps more) in obedience to, and respect for the judicial department of government. We think its decisions on constitutional questions, when fully settled, should control not only the particular cases decided but the general policy of the country, subject to be disturbed only by amendments of the Constitution as provided in that instrument itself. More than this would be revolution. But we think the *Dred Scott* decision is erroneous. We know the Court that made it has often overruled its own decisions, and we shall do what we can to have it to overrule this.[77]

Second, Lincoln attempted to minimize the opinion's legal authority.

> If this important decision had been made by the unanimous concurrence of the judges, and without any apparent partisan bias, and in accordance with legal public expectation, and with the steady practice of the departments throughout our history, and had been in no part based on assumed historical facts which are not really true; or, if wanting in some of these, it had been before the Court more than once, and had there been affirmed and re-affirmed through a course of years, it then might be, perhaps would be, factious, nay, even revolutionary, to not acquiesce in it as a precedent. But when, as it is true, we find it wanting in all these claims to the public confidence, it is not resistance, it is not factious, it is not even disrespectful, to treat it as not having yet quite established a settled doctrine for the country.[78]

Third, Lincoln maintained that the "acquiescence of the people and the states" was also necessary before constitutional questions could be fully settled. To support this claim, Lincoln (ironically) invoked a precedent set by Andrew Jackson.

> Why this same Supreme Court once decided a national bank to be constitutional; but General Jackson, as president of the United States, disregarded the decision and vetoed a bill for a re-charter partly on constitutional ground, declaring that each public functionary must support the Constitution "as he understands it." But hear the General's own words. Here they are, taken from his veto message: "It is maintained by the advocates of the bank that its constitutionality, in all its features, ought to be considered as settled by precedent and

by the decision of the Supreme Court. To this conclusion I cannot assent. Mere precedent is a dangerous source of authority and should not be regarded as deciding questions of constitutional power, except where the acquiescence of the people and the states can be considered as well settled."[79]

Fourth, Lincoln further suggested that the Supreme Court's decision might be ignored in good faith by government officials acting to uphold their own constitutional oaths. Once again, he quoted from Andrew Jackson's veto message concerning the national bank.

"If the opinion of the Supreme Court covered the whole ground of this act, it ought not to control the co-ordinate authorities of this government. The Congress, the executive, and the Court must each for itself be guided by its own opinion of the Constitution. Each public officer who takes an oath to support the Constitution swears that he will support it as he understands it, and not as it is understood by others."[80]

In other words, regardless of its precedent as a matter of law, the *Dred Scott* decision need not be considered binding—or obeyed—as a "political rule." As Lincoln put it in a subsequent speech: "If I were in Congress, and a vote should come up on a question whether slavery should be prohibited in a new territory, in spite of the *Dred Scott* decision I would vote that it should."[81]

As a fifth and final response to the *Dred Scott* ruling, Lincoln invoked our "better angels"—namely, the Declaration of Independence (in contrast to Roger Taney's judicial opinion)—as the true embodiment of the nation's values.

In [earlier] days, our Declaration of Independence was held sacred by all and thought to include all; but now, to aid in making the bondage of the negro universal and eternal, it is assailed, and sneered at, and construed, and hawked at, and torn, till, if its framers could rise from their graves, they could not at all recognize it. All the powers of earth seem rapidly combining against him. Mammon is after him; ambition follows, and philosophy follows, and the theology of the day is fast joining the cry. They have him in his prison house; they have searched his person and left no prying instrument with him. One after another they have closed the heavy iron doors upon him, and now they have him, as it were, bolted in with a lock of a hundred keys, which can never be unlocked without the concurrence of every key; the keys in the hands of a hundred different men, and they scattered to a hundred different and distant places; and they stand musing as to what invention, in all the dominions of mind and matter, can be produced to make the impossibility of his escape more complete than it is. . . .

Chief Justice Taney [and Senator Douglas] . . . argue that the authors of [the Declaration of Independence] did not intend to include negroes. . . . [But] I think the authors of that notable instrument intended to include all men, but they did not intend to declare all men equal in all respects. They did not mean to say all were equal in color, size, intellect, moral developments, or social capacity. They defined with tolerable distinctness in what respects they did consider all men created equal—equal in "certain inalienable rights, among which are life, liberty, and the pursuit of happiness." This they said, and this meant. They did not mean to assert the obvious untruth that all were then actually enjoying that equality, nor yet that they were about to confer it immediately upon them. In fact they had no power to confer such a boon. They meant simply to declare the right, so that the enforcement of it might follow as fast as circumstances should permit. They meant to set up a standard maxim for free society which should be familiar to all and revered by all; constantly looked to, constantly labored for, and even though never perfectly attained, constantly approximated, and thereby constantly spreading and deepening its influence and augmenting the happiness and value of life to all people of all colors everywhere.[82]

In sum, while continuing to respect the rule of law—and refusing to follow a John Brown-like path of rebellion—Abraham Lincoln did all he could to undercut the legitimacy and the authority of the Supreme Court's constitutional pronouncement in *Dred Scott*. And he did so by relying on the Declaration of Independence as an alternative vision of the American creed.

Discussion Questions

1. Chief Justice Roger Taney wrote the majority opinion in *Dred Scott*, which is today widely viewed as the worst decision in the Supreme Court's history. Yet Taney had emancipated his own slaves. He also led the nation's highest court for almost thirty years and before that had served as secretary of the treasury, attorney general, and secretary of war, as well as Maryland's attorney general. A visitor to the US Capitol can find Taney's bust in the courtroom where he announced the *Dred Scott* ruling (although Congress is debating its removal); across the street, another bust of Taney rests on a marble pedestal in the Great Hall of the Supreme Court building. In 2017, Maryland removed a statue of Taney from its statehouse grounds, where it had stood for 145 years. What is the appropriate way to recognize (or not) Roger Taney's legacy?

2. Compare the excerpts reacting to the *Dred Scott* ruling from the Richmond and New York newspapers. Does one's view of the validity of a Supreme

Court decision largely depend on one's political preferences? Can that be avoided? Even now (and perhaps especially now), is it all too easy to embrace the Supreme Court when we agree with the outcome of a case—a product of "reason and right, justice and truth," to echo the *Richmond Enquirer*—and denounce the Court and its justices—as "wicked and false," in the words of the *New York Tribune*—when the result displeases us?

3. Frederick Douglass's reaction to *Dred Scott* was to appeal beyond the Supreme Court to "the Supreme Court of the Almighty." But this was the same Frederick Douglass who had argued throughout the 1850s that the Constitution was an antislavery document. Yet it was that very constitutional text upon which Chief Justice Taney and his colleagues had relied to banish any possibility of citizenship for African Americans, let alone any congressional regulation of slavery. Still, despite it all, Douglass returned to the Constitution—and particularly to his assertion that "We the People" included *all* the people. Under the circumstances, was Douglass right to have kept his faith in the Constitution?

4. Given his five-pronged attempt to undermine the *Dred Scott* decision, what conclusions can be drawn about Abraham Lincoln's fidelity to the rule of law? In the final analysis, did he accept the legitimacy of the Supreme Court as our constitutional oracle, or not? What if everyone who disagreed with a Supreme Court decision followed Lincoln's approach? On the other hand, is Lincoln's approach preferable to direct disobedience, or simply acquiescing in the decision?

5. Though Roger Taney believed his *Dred Scott* opinion would end the nation's divisions over slavery, the opposite occurred. *Dred Scott* converted slavery from a matter of state law to a national right of property under the Constitution. What conclusions can be drawn about the Supreme Court's role in helping to bring about the Civil War?

6. *Dred Scott* was only the second Supreme Court decision to overturn a federal law. In light of the decision, what should one think about the wisdom, and the dangers, of judicial review? How much faith and reliance do "We the People" want to put in the Supreme Court to define and interpret the Constitution?[83]

Interpretation of the Fourteenth and Fifteenth Amendments—Primary Sources

By their terms, the Fourteenth and Fifteenth Amendments wrought astounding changes to the Constitution in the aftermath of the Civil War. The Fourteenth Amendment not only protected the "privileges and immunities" of all citizens and guaranteed "due process of law" and "the equal protection of the laws" to all persons but also overturned the *Dred Scott* decision, established birthright citizenship, and abolished the three-fifths clause.[84] The Fifteenth Amendment prohibited any race-based denial or abridgement of the franchise (at least for men). In order to give teeth to these new constitutional provisions, Congress also enacted several sweeping civil rights enforcement laws during the dozen years of Reconstruction. Viewed through the hindsight of history, however, it becomes abundantly clear that the rights supposedly guaranteed by the Fourteenth and Fifteenth Amendments amounted only to paper promises—at least until the civil rights revolution of the mid-twentieth century.

The emasculation of the Reconstruction amendments can be attributed to a confluence of historical events and attitudes: the restoration of Democratic ("Redeemer") regimes in the South; the violence of the Klan and other vigilante, white supremacist groups; the gradual end of the disenfranchisement of Confederate soldiers and sympathizers; the steady withdrawal of federal troops from the South; the absence of land reform or other economic assistance to benefit former slaves; the collapse of the nation's economy in 1873; the prevalence of Social Darwinist theories and racist attitudes in the North no less than in the South; political and moral exhaustion among Northerners after decades of abolitionism and war and occupation; and the contested election of 1876. In this instance, at least, failure had a thousand fathers.

But a far from unimportant part of this story involves constitutional law. In considering how the soaring assurances of the Fourteenth and Fifteenth Amendments were watered down almost beyond recognition, it is worthwhile to focus on a series of Supreme Court decisions rendered during the final decades of the 1800s.

Slaughter-House Cases (1873)

The justices first considered the scope of the Fourteenth Amendment in the *Slaughter-House Cases*. New Orleans butchers, aggrieved over a city ordinance that regulated their business practices for sanitary purposes, protested that they had been denied the "privileges and immunities" promised to them under the newly amended Constitution. No, said Justice Samuel Miller, writing for the majority: all three of the Reconstruction amendments had been intended to protect the rights only of the former slaves.

> On the most casual examination of the language of these amendments, no one can fail to be impressed with the one pervading purpose found in them all, lying at the foundation of each, and without which none of them would

have been even suggested; we mean the freedom of the slave race, the security
and firm establishment of that freedom, and the protection of the newly made
freeman and citizen from the oppressions of those who had formerly exercised
unlimited dominion over him.[85]

But the Court then proceeded to sketch the universe of those "privileges and
immunities" of US citizens, now extended to the former slaves, in an extremely crabbed manner: the right to travel to the seat of government to assert a claim, the right to peaceably assemble and to petition, habeas corpus,
protection on the high seas, the right to use navigable waters, and privileges
secured for Americans by treaties with foreign nations. Beyond these, any
other "rights" derived from and depended upon one's state citizenship—as
to which the Fourteenth Amendment (and the rest of the Constitution) was
irrelevant.

> Of the privileges and immunities of the citizen of the United States, and
> of the privileges and immunities of the citizen of the state . . . it is only the
> former which are placed by this clause under the protection of the federal
> Constitution, and that the latter, whatever they may be, are not intended to
> have any additional protection by this paragraph of the amendment. . . . The
> latter must rest for their security and protection where they have heretofore
> rested, for they are not embraced by this paragraph of the Amendment. . . .
> [It was not] the purpose of the Fourteenth Amendment, by the simple dec-
> laration that no state should make or enforce any law which shall abridge the
> privileges and immunities of citizens of the United States, to transfer the se-
> curity and protection of all the civil rights which we have mentioned from the
> states to the federal government. . . .[86]

Slaughter-House Cases—Dissent (1873)

Four members of the Court dissented, in an opinion authored by Justice
Stephen Field.

> The question presented is, therefore, one of the gravest importance not merely
> to the parties here but to the whole country. It is nothing less than the question
> whether the recent amendments to the federal Constitution protect the citizens
> of the United States against the deprivation of their common rights by state
> legislation. In my judgment, the Fourteenth Amendment does afford such pro-
> tection and was so intended by the Congress which framed and the states which
> adopted it. . . .

A citizen of a state is now only a citizen of the United States residing in that state. The fundamental rights, privileges, and immunities which belong to him as a free man and a free citizen now belong to him as a citizen of the United States, and are not dependent upon his citizenship of any state. . . .

The Amendment does not attempt to confer any new privileges or immunities upon citizens, or to enumerate or define those already existing. It assumes that there are such privileges and immunities which belong of right to citizens as such, and ordains that they shall not be abridged by state legislation. If this inhibition . . . only refers, as held by the majority of the Court in their opinion, to such privileges and immunities as were before its adoption specially designated in the Constitution or necessarily implied as belonging to citizens of the United States, it was a vain and idle enactment, which accomplished nothing and most unnecessarily excited Congress and the people on its passage.[87]

The *Slaughter-House Cases* constituted the first circumscription of the Fourteenth Amendment by the Supreme Court: Virtually all of one's "privileges and immunities" (whatever they might happen to be) were subject to grant or regulation or limitation or denial by the states.

Thomas Morris Chester Reacts to the Colfax Massacre (1873)

Then came the *Cruikshank* decision. On Easter Sunday of 1873, more than 150 African Americans were massacred by white paramilitary forces in Colfax, Louisiana, in what amounted to the deadliest single such incident during the Reconstruction era. Thomas Morris Chester, a prominent Black newspaperman, reported from the scene that many of the victims had been gunned down mercilessly. Chester appealed directly to the federal government for help.

There can be no war of races in this country between the blacks and the whites, but there may occur in the future, as in the past, an indiscriminate carnage of our men, women, and children by the spirit of slavery, quickened by the plausible and hypocritical [Democrats] who, with their facilities and means, hasten to justify the infamy by falsely designating it as a war of races. . . .

We have never arrayed ourselves against our white fellow citizens, unless voting the Republican ticket constitutes that offense. We were loyal to the government and fought for liberty, for which the rebels have never forgiven us, and never will as long as one of the present generation is left to poison the current of public sentiment. It is useless to disguise the fact that they are our vindictive and covert enemies and would, if not restrained and deterred in their stupid attachment and devotion for the relic of barbarism, heap up hecatombs of colored bodies.

Our only hope and safety is in the federal government's realizing the situation and acting with that promptitude and vigor which would in the future protect the innocent and deter the guilty. Should we in our fidelity to principles and patriotism—in the exercise of our manhood and citizenship—continue to incur the wrath of our oppressors without invoking from the national government a corresponding degree of protection, our annihilation is a foregone conclusion.[88]

United States v. Cruikshank (1876)

In the Enforcement Act of 1870, Congress had authorized federal prosecutions against individuals who violated (or conspired to violate) the civil rights and voting rights of former slaves. Relying on this statute (as well as acting consistently with Chester's plea), federal officials brought criminal charges and secured convictions against several of the Colfax malefactors. But the Supreme Court reversed the convictions in *United States v. Cruikshank*. The Enforcement Act exceeded congressional powers, the Court declared, because under the Fourteenth Amendment the national government itself could only reach and punish discriminatory actions by states, and not by individuals.

The people of the United States resident within any state are subject to two governments. . . . The powers which one possesses the other does not. They are established for different purposes and have separate jurisdictions. Together they make one whole and furnish the people of the United States with a complete government, ample for the protection of all their rights at home and abroad. . . .

[The defendants were convicted of conspiracy to deprive the victims] "of their respective several lives and liberty of person without due process of law." This is nothing else than alleging a conspiracy to falsely imprison or murder citizens of the United States, being within the territorial jurisdiction of the state of Louisiana. . . . The very highest duty of the states, when they entered into the Union under the Constitution, was to protect all persons within their boundaries in the enjoyment of these "unalienable rights with which they were endowed by their Creator." Sovereignty for this purpose rests alone with the states. . . .

The Fourteenth Amendment prohibits a state from denying to any person within its jurisdiction the equal protection of the laws; but this provision does not . . . add anything to the rights which one citizen has under the Constitution against another. The equality of the rights of citizens is a principle of republicanism. Every republican government is in duty bound to protect all its citizens in the enjoyment of this principle, if within its power. That duty was originally assumed by the states, and it still remains there. The only obligation resting upon the United States is to see that the states do not deny the right. This the Amendment guarantees, but no more.[89]

In other words, if one person violated the civil rights of another—or, as in this case, even murdered him—that was solely within the discretion of the state government to prosecute and punish (which, in this instance, Louisiana never did).

United States v. Reese (1876)

The third blow struck by the Supreme Court against a broad interpretation of the Reconstruction Amendments came a year later in *United States v. Reese*, a case that involved the Fifteenth Amendment. This time, the Court voided federal charges brought against two state election officials who had refused to let an African American vote. The Court began by acknowledging that Congress possessed the power under the Fifteenth Amendment to punish the denial of vote on the basis of race.

The Fifteenth Amendment does not confer the right of suffrage upon anyone. It prevents the states, or the United States, however, from giving preference, in this particular, to one citizen of the United States over another on account of race, color, or previous condition of servitude. Before its adoption, this could be done. It was as much within the power of a state to exclude citizens of the United States from voting on account of race etc., as it was on account of age, property, or education. Now it is not. If citizens of one race having certain qualifications are permitted by law to vote, those of another having the same qualifications must be.[90]

But it was not enough simply to prove that an African American had been denied the right to vote, said the Court. Instead, the government was obligated to establish that the individual was prevented from voting because, and only because, of his race. But Congress had written the law in question to punish general acts of election misbehavior that arguably might not be connected to race—and it had no power under the Constitution to do so.

It has not been contended, nor can it be, that the Amendment confers authority to impose penalties for every wrongful refusal to receive the vote of a qualified elector at state elections. It is only when the wrongful refusal at such an election is because of race, color, or previous condition of servitude that Congress can interfere and provide for its punishment.[91]

Once again, federal convictions were reversed—and with the state unwilling to proceed, the deprivation of voting rights went unremedied. See also *Williams v. Mississippi* (1898), where the Supreme Court upheld a literacy test and a poll tax for voting because they were required of all members of all races,[92] and *Giles v. Harris* (1903), where the Court declined to determine whether such voting requirements were being discriminatorily applied by state officials. Indeed, in the last paragraph of *Giles*, Justice Oliver Wendell Holmes concluded that even where "the great mass of the white population intends to keep the blacks from voting," the judiciary was powerless to prevent such "a great political wrong" in the absence of relief from "the legislative and political department of the government of the United States."[93]

Civil Rights Act (1875)

The Supreme Court next declared the Civil Rights Act of 1875 unconstitutional. This pathbreaking law, passed by Congress in the death throes of Reconstruction, outlawed racial segregation in public accommodations, transportation, and theaters, among other businesses.

> Whereas it is essential to just government we recognize the equality of all men before the law, and hold that it is the duty of government in its dealings with the people to mete out equal and exact justice to all, of whatever nativity, race, color, or persuasion, religious or political; and it being the appropriate object of legislation to enact great fundamental principles into law: therefore,
>
> Section 1. Be it enacted by the Senate and House of Representatives of the United States of America in Congress assembled, that all persons within the jurisdiction of the United States shall be entitled to the full and equal enjoyment of the accommodations, advantages, facilities, and privileges of inns, public conveyances on land or water, theaters, and other places of public amusement; subject only to the conditions and limitations established by law, and applicable alike to citizens of every race and color, regardless of any previous condition of servitude.
>
> Section 2. That any person who shall violate the foregoing section by denying to any citizen . . . the full enjoyment of any of the accommodations, advantages, facilities, or privileges . . . shall for every offense [pay money damages to the aggrieved person and] be deemed guilty of a misdemeanor,

and upon conviction thereof shall be fined not less than $500 nor more than $1,000 or shall be imprisoned not less than thirty days nor more than one year.[94]

Civil Rights Cases (1883)

But employing the Fourteenth Amendment to prohibit racial discrimination by one private individual against another was a bridge way too far for Congress, Justice Joseph Bradley declared on behalf of a nearly unanimous Supreme Court.

Has Congress constitutional power to make such a law? . . .

It is state action of a particular character that is prohibited [by the Fourteenth Amendment]. Individual invasion of individual rights is not the subject matter of the Amendment. . . . [The Fourteenth Amendment] does not invest Congress with power to legislate upon subjects which are within the domain of state legislation, but to provide modes of relief against state legislation, or state action, of the kind referred to. It does not authorize Congress to create a code of municipal law for the regulation of private rights, but to provide modes of redress against the operation of state laws and the action of state officers executive or judicial when these are subversive of the fundamental rights specified in the Amendment. . . . Legislation cannot properly cover the whole domain of rights appertaining to life, liberty, and property, defining them and providing for their vindication. That would be to establish a code of municipal law regulative of all private rights between man and man in society. It would be to make Congress take the place of the state legislatures and to supersede them. . . .

When a man has emerged from slavery and, by the aid of beneficent legislation, has shaken off the inseparable concomitants of that state, there must be some stage in the progress of his elevation when he takes the rank of a mere citizen and ceases to be the special favorite of the laws, and when his rights as a citizen or a man are to be protected in the ordinary modes by which other men's rights are protected. There were thousands of free colored people in this country before the abolition of slavery, enjoying all the essential rights of life, liberty, and property the same as white citizens, yet no one at that time thought that it was any invasion of his personal status as a freeman because he was not admitted to all the privileges enjoyed by white citizens, or because he was subjected to discriminations in the enjoyment of accommodations in inns, public conveyances, and places of amusement. Mere discriminations on account of race or color were not regarded as badges of slavery.[95]

Civil Rights Cases—Dissent (1883)

Justice John Marshall Harlan (alone) dissented. The country, he warned, was entering "upon an era of constitutional law when the rights of freedom and American citizenship cannot receive from the nation that efficient protection which heretofore was unhesitatingly accorded to slavery and the rights of the master."

> My brethren say that when a man has emerged from slavery and by the aid of beneficent legislation has shaken off the inseparable concomitants of that state, there must be some stage in the progress of his elevation when he takes the rank of a mere citizen, and ceases to be the special favorite of the laws, and when his rights as a citizen or a man are to be protected in the ordinary modes by which other men's rights are protected. It is, I submit, scarcely just to say that the colored race has been the special favorite of the laws. The statute of 1875, now adjudged to be unconstitutional, is for the benefit of citizens of every race and color. What the nation through Congress has sought to accomplish in reference to that race is what had already been done in every state of the Union for the white race—to secure and protect rights belonging to them as freemen and citizens, nothing more . . . The difficulty has been to compel a recognition of the legal right of the black race to take the rank of citizens and to secure the enjoyment of privileges belonging, under the law, to them as a component part of the people for whose welfare and happiness government is ordained. At every step in this direction, the nation has been confronted with class tyranny. . . .
>
> The supreme law of the land has decreed that no authority shall be exercised in this country upon the basis of discrimination, in respect of civil rights, against freemen and citizens because of their race, color, or previous condition of servitude. To that decree—for the due enforcement of which, by appropriate legislation, Congress has been invested with express power—everyone must bow, whatever may have been, or whatever now are, his individual views as to the wisdom or policy either of the recent changes in the fundamental law or of the legislation which has been enacted to give them effect.[96]

Plessy v. Ferguson (1896)

And then came *Plessy v. Ferguson*, where the state itself (as opposed to the owner of a private business) mandated the physical separation of its residents on the basis of race.[97] Once again the Supreme Court determined that the Fourteenth

Amendment was powerless to ensure equality for nonwhites in their daily lives. The vote was 7-1, with Justice Henry Brown writing for the majority.

> The object of the [Fourteenth] Amendment was undoubtedly to enforce the absolute equality of the two races before the law, but, in the nature of things, it could not have been intended to abolish distinctions based upon color, or to enforce social, as distinguished from political, equality, or a commingling of the two races upon terms unsatisfactory to either. Laws permitting and even requiring their separation in places where they are liable to be brought into contact do not necessarily imply the inferiority of either race to the other, and have been generally if not universally recognized as within the competency of the state legislatures in the exercise of their police power.... [A state legislature] is at liberty to act with reference to the established usages, customs, and traditions of the people, and with a view to the promotion of their comfort and the preservation of the public peace and good order....
>
> We consider the underlying fallacy of [Homer Plessy's] argument to consist in the assumption that the enforced separation of the two races stamps the colored race with a badge of inferiority. If this be so, it is not by reason of anything found in the act, but solely because the colored race chooses to put that construction upon it.... The argument also assumes that social prejudices may be overcome by legislation and that equal rights cannot be secured to the negro except by an enforced commingling of the two races. We cannot accept this proposition. If the two races are to meet upon terms of social equality, it must be the result of natural affinities, a mutual appreciation of each other's merits, and a voluntary consent of individuals.... Legislation is powerless to eradicate racial instincts or to abolish distinctions based upon physical differences, and the attempt to do so can only result in accentuating the difficulties of the present situation. If the civil and political rights of both races be equal, one cannot be inferior to the other civilly or politically. If one race be inferior to the other socially, the Constitution of the United States cannot put them upon the same plane.[98]

Plessy v. Ferguson—Dissent (1896)

Once again, Justice Harlan dissented, alone.

> Such legislation as that here in question is inconsistent not only with that equality of rights which pertains to citizenship, national and state, but with the personal liberty enjoyed by everyone within the United States....

The white race deems itself to be the dominant race in this country. And so it is in prestige, in achievements, in education, in wealth and in power. So, I doubt not, it will continue to be for all time if it remains true to its great heritage and holds fast to the principles of constitutional liberty. But in view of the Constitution, in the eye of the law, there is in this country no superior, dominant, ruling class of citizens. There is no caste here. Our Constitution is color-blind and neither knows nor tolerates classes among citizens. In respect of civil rights, all citizens are equal before the law. The humblest is the peer of the most powerful. The law regards man as man, and takes no account of his surroundings or of his color when his civil rights as guaranteed by the supreme law of the land are involved. It is therefore to be regretted that this high tribunal, the final expositor of the fundamental law of the land, has reached the conclusion that it is competent for a state to regulate the enjoyment by citizens of their civil rights solely upon the basis of race. In my opinion, the judgment this day rendered will, in time, prove to be quite as pernicious as the decision made by this tribunal in the *Dred Scott* case . . . .

Sixty millions of whites are in no danger from the presence here of eight millions of blacks. The destinies of the two races in this country are indissolubly linked together, and the interests of both require that the common government of all shall not permit the seeds of race hate to be planted under the sanction of law. What can more certainly arouse race hate, what more certainly create and perpetuate a feeling of distrust between these races, than state enactments which, in fact, proceed on the ground that colored citizens are so inferior and degraded that they cannot be allowed to sit in public coaches occupied by white citizens. . . . The sure guarantee of the peace and security of each race is the clear, distinct, unconditional recognition by our governments, national and state, of every right that inheres in civil freedom, and of the equality before the law of all citizens of the United States, without regard to race. . . .

If laws of like character should be enacted in the several states of the Union, the effect would be in the highest degree mischievous. Slavery as an institution tolerated by law would, it is true, have disappeared from our country, but there would remain a power in the states, by sinister legislation, to interfere with the full enjoyment of the blessings of freedom to regulate civil rights, common to all citizens, upon the basis of race, and to place in a condition of legal inferiority a large body of American citizens now constituting a part of the political community called the People of the United States, for whom and by whom, through representatives, our government is administered. Such a system is inconsistent with the guarantee given by the Constitution. . . .[99]

Upon the close of the Civil War, "We the People" amended the Constitution thrice over. Congress also passed a series of unprecedented laws—laws that sought to ensure at least some degree of equality and rights for all Americans, regardless of race. The Supreme Court—with its decidedly narrow construction of the constitutional amendments and its aggressive narrowing of the congressional statutes—was far from the only reason why the former slaves failed to secure "a new birth of freedom" (to use Lincoln's words). But the Supreme Court played an outsized role.

Discussion Questions

1. The *Slaughter-House Cases* and *Cruikshank* show that the rights Americans enjoyed—and just as important, who was responsible for enforcing those rights—often turned on questions of federalism: who was in charge, the national government or the states? How did the Supreme Court's reliance on principles of federalism and states' rights undermine the promises of the Fourteenth and Fifteenth Amendments?

2. Eric Foner used the following subtitle for his most recent book: *How the Civil War and Reconstruction Remade the Constitution*. One of his earlier books about Reconstruction was subtitled: *America's Unfinished Revolution*.[100] Which subtitle would best describe the Supreme Court's interpretations of the Fourteenth and Fifteenth Amendments in the last half of the nineteenth century?

3. In the *Civil Rights Cases*, on what basis did the Supreme Court conclude that former slaves had become "the special favorite of the laws"? On what basis did the Supreme Court conclude that prior to the abolition of slavery "no one" thought free Blacks should enjoy the same "privileges" as white citizens?

4. What exactly is (or should be) the nature of the "equal protection of the laws" promised by the Fourteenth Amendment? Does that phrase mandate (or promise) only "civil and political" equality, or should it also encompass "social" equality? And "equal[ity]" of what—opportunity or outcome? On what basis was the Supreme Court able to conclude in *Plessy v. Ferguson* that enforced separation of the races on public transportation did not offend "civil and political" equality—and that segregation itself imposed a "badge of inferiority" upon members of a race only if they "[chose] to put that construction upon it"?

5. Writing in dissent in *Plessy v. Ferguson*, Justice John Marshall Harlan intoned that "our Constitution is color-blind. . . . The law regards man as man, and takes no account of his surroundings or of his color when his civil rights as guaranteed by the supreme law of the land are involved." Adopting this perspective, would it *ever* be permissible to take race into account

when legislating? The question might arise, for example, with respect to affirmative action or in considering possible reparations for slavery.

6. As Foner observes, because of its open-ended language, because its protections were not limited only to matters of race, and because it applies to all "persons" (not only citizens), the Fourteenth Amendment has been used over time to expand the constitutional rights of numerous persons and groups—most recently in the context of same-sex marriage. How have individuals and groups cited the Equal Protection Clause in their struggles for rights and recognition since 1868?

Additional Primary Source Documents

Primary source document excerpts covering the following topics are located on the website accompanying this book:

Secession and the Right to Rebel—including the South Carolina secession resolution; Buchanan and Lincoln's responses; *Texas v. White*, 74 U.S. 700 (1869).

Slavery and the Thirteenth Amendment—including the Confederate Constitution; Crittenden Compromise; Confiscation Acts; Emancipation Proclamation; Thirteenth Amendment.

Other "Constitutional Moments" during this Era

- Civil liberties during wartime—including suspension of habeas corpus (in both North and South); *Ex parte Merryman*, 17 F. Cas. 144 (1861); conscription acts (in both North and South); arrest of Clement Vallandigham; *Ex parte Milligan*, 71 U.S. 2 (1866).
- Nonslavery provisions in the Constitution of the Confederate States of America—including its explicit invocation of "Almighty God"; federal funds prohibited for "internal improvement intended to facilitate commerce"; two-thirds majority requirement for congressional appropriations; line-item veto for president; six-year presidential term, without eligibility for reelection; state impeachment of certain federal officers; two-thirds vote by Congress to add new states; no role for Congress in proposing constitutional amendments; only two-thirds of states needed to ratify constitutional amendments.
- 1864 election—holding an election during wartime (also in 1812, 1944, 1952, 1968, 1972, and 2004).

- Struggles over control of Reconstruction policy between the executive and legislative branches—including Wade-Davis Bill and Lincoln's veto; Freedman's Bureau; Sherman's Field Order No. 15; conditions for readmission of Southern states and representatives; Andrew Johnson's numerous vetoes; Tenure in Office Act; Johnson's impeachment.
- Congressional limits on judicial power—including *Ex parte McCardle*, 74 U.S. 506 (1868); *Ex parte Yerger*, 75 U.S. 85 (1869).
- Other provisions of the Fourteenth Amendment—including birthright citizenship; "due process of law"; disqualification of rebels from office holding; prohibition on compensation for former slaveholders.

Notes

1. Abraham Lincoln, "Response to a Serenade" (speech, Washington, DC, February 1, 1865), in *Abraham Lincoln: Speeches and Writings, 1859–1865*, ed. Don E. Fehrenbacher (New York: Library of America, 1989), 670.
2. Carl Schurz, Senate Debates, Cong. Globe, 41st Cong., 2d Sess. 3608 (May 19, 1870), memory.loc.gov/cgi-bin/ampage?collId = llcg&fileName = 092/llcg092.db&recNum = 779.
3. Elizabeth Cady Stanton, *Eighty Years and More: Reminiscences 1815–1897* (New York, 1898), 241, digital.library.upenn.edu/women/stanton/years/years.html.
4. Sean Wilentz, *No Property in Man: Slavery and Antislavery at the Nation's Founding* (Cambridge, MA: Harvard University Press, 2018), 162–63.
5. An Act to establish an uniform Rule of Naturalization, ch. 3, 1 Stat. 103 (March 26, 1790), govtrackus.s3.amazonaws.com/legislink/pdf/stat/1/STATUTE-1-Pg103.pdf.
6. William Lloyd Garrison, "Address of the Executive Committee of the American Anti-Slavery Society to the Friends of Freedom and Emancipation in the United States," *The Anti-Slavery Examiner, Part 4 of 4* (New York, 1845), www.gutenberg.org/files/11274/11274-h/11274-h.htm.
7. Frederick Douglass, "What to the Slave Is the Fourth of July?" (speech, Rochester, NY, July 5, 1852), in *The Speeches of Frederick Douglass: A Critical Edition*, ed. John R. McKivigan, Julie Husband, and Heather L. Kaufman (New Haven, CT: Yale University Press, 2018), 88.
8. 41 U.S. 539 (1842).
9. 60 U.S. 393 (1857).
10. Abraham Lincoln, "Emancipation Proclamation" (January 1, 1863), www.ourdocuments.gov/print_friendly.php?flash=false&page=transcript&doc=34&title=Transcript+of+Emancipation+Proclamation+%281863%29.
11. Abraham Lincoln, "A Proclamation" (December 8, 1863), www.presidency.ucsb.edu/documents/proclamation-108-amnesty-and-reconstruction.

12. Articles of Confederation Congress, An Ordinance for the Government of the Territory of the United States North-West of the River Ohio, July 13, 1787, avalon.law. yale.edu/18th_century/nworder.asp.

13. Cornelius Cole, *Memoirs of Cornelius Cole: Ex-Senator of the United States from California* (New York: McLoughlin Bros., 1908), 220.

14. Henry Wilson, Senate Debates, Cong. Globe, 39th Cong., 1st Sess. 111 (December 21, 1865), memory.loc.gov/cgi-bin/ampage?collId = llcg&fileName = 070/llcg070. db&recNum = 216.

15. Civil Rights Act of 1866 (An act to protect all Persons in the United States in their Civil Rights, and furnish the Means of their Vindication), ch. 31, 14 Stat. 27 (April 9, 1866), govtrackus.s3.amazonaws.com/legislink/pdf/stat/14/STATUTE-14-Pg27.pdf.

16. James Wilson, House of Representatives Debates, Cong. Globe, 39th Cong., 1st Sess. 1117–18 (March 1, 1866), memory.loc.gov/cgi-bin/ ampage?collId = llcg&fileName = 071/llcg071.db&recNum = 158.

17. Andrew Johnson, Veto Message, March 27, 1866, www.presidency.ucsb.edu/ documents/veto-message-438.

18. John Bingham, House of Representative Debates, Cong. Globe, App., 42d Cong., 1st Sess. 84 (March 31, 1871), memory.loc.gov/cgi-bin/ampage?collId = llcg&fileName = 100/ llcg100.db&recNum = 437.

19. John Bingham, House of Representative Debates, Cong. Globe, 39th Cong., 1st Sess. 1034 (February 26, 1866), memory.loc.gov/cgi-bin/ampage?collId = llcg&fileName = 071/ llcg071.db&recNum = 75.

20. 576 U.S. 644 (2015).

21. George William Curtis, *Orations and Addresses of George William Curtis*, ed. Charles Eliot Norton (New York, 1894), 1:172.

22. Eric Foner, *Reconstruction: America's Unfinished Revolution, 1863–1877* (New York: Harper & Row, 1988), 24.

23. *Springfield Daily Republican*, May 2, 1903.

24. 83 U.S. 36 (1873).

25. 83 U.S. 130 (1873).

26. 92 U.S. 542 (1876).

27. 109 U.S. 3 (1883).

28. 163 U.S. 537 (1896).

29. 170 U.S. 213 (1898).

30. 189 U.S. 475 (1903).

31. The Brotherhood of Liberty, *Justice and Jurisprudence: Inquiry Concerning the Constitutional Limitations of the Thirteenth, Fourteenth, and Fifteenth Amendments* (Philadelphia: J.B. Lippincott, 1889).

32. Brotherhood of Liberty, *Justice and Jurisprudence*, 38.

33. Thaddeus B. Wakeman, *Science: A Weekly Newspaper of All the Arts and Sciences* (January 10, 1890), 26–27, science.sciencemag.org/content/ns-15/362/26.

34. Charles Sumner, Senate Debates, Cong. Globe, App., 40th Cong., 1st Sess. 614 (July 12, 1867), memory.loc.gov/cgi-bin/ampage?collId = llcg&fileName = 078/llcg078. db&recNum = 136.

35. Civil Rights Cases, 109 U.S. 3 (1883) (Harlan, J., dissenting).
36. An Act respecting fugitives from justice, and persons escaping from the service of their masters, ch. 7, 1 Stat. 302 (February 12, 1793), govtrackus.s3.amazonaws.com/legislink/pdf/stat/1/STATUTE-1-Pg302.pdf.
37. An Act to Give Effect to the Provisions of the Constitution of the United States, Relative to Fugitives from Labor, for the Protection of Free People of Color, and to Prevent Kidnapping,, 1825 Pa. Laws 150, ch. 50 (March 25, 1826) (quoted in Prigg v. Pennsylvania, 41 U.S. 539 (1842)); see William R. Leslie, "The Pennsylvania Fugitive Slave Act of 1826," *Journal of Southern History* 18, no. 4 (November 1952): 429–45, www.jstor.org/stable/2955218?seq=1#metadata_info_tab_contents.
38. Prigg v. Pennsylvania, 41 U.S. 539 (1842).
39. Henry Clay, Senate Debate, Cong. Globe, 31st Cong., 1st Sess. 123 (February 6, 1850), memory.loc.gov/cgi-bin/ampage?collId=llcg&fileName=024/llcg024.db&recNum=142.
40. Daniel Webster, Senate Debate, Cong. Globe, 31st Cong., 1st Sess. 269, 274–75 (March 7, 1850), memory.loc.gov/cgi-bin/ampage?collId = llcg&fileName = 024/llcg024.db&recNum = 288.
41. John Calhoun, Senate Debate, Cong. Globe, 31st Cong., 1st Sess. 453 (March 4, 1850), memory.loc.gov/cgi-bin/ampage?collId=llcg&fileName=022/llcg022.db&recNum=538.
42. An Act to amend and supplementary to [the Fugitive Slave Act of 1793], ch. 60, 9 Stat. 462 (September 13, 1850), govtrackus.s3.amazonaws.com/legislink/pdf/stat/9/STATUTE-9-Pg462.pdf.
43. Joseph Randall, "Extract from the Proceedings of the Union Meeting held at Philadelphia" (November 21, 1850), in Union Safety Committee, *Selections from the Speeches and Writings of Prominent Men in the United States on the Subject of Abolition and Agitation and in Favor of the Compromise Measures of the Last Session of Congress* (New York, 1851), 22.
44. Abraham Lincoln, "Speech on Kansas-Nebraska Act" (speech, Peoria, IL, October 16, 1854), www.nps.gov/liho/learn/historyculture/peoriaspeech.htm.
45. See William Still, *The Underground Railroad: A Record of Facts, Authentic Narratives, Letters, etc.* (Philadelphia, 1872), www.gutenberg.org/files/15263/15263-h/15263-h.htm.
46. Frederick Douglass to Harriet Tubman, August 29, 1868, in Sarah H. Bradford, *Some Scenes in the Life of Harriet Tubman* (Auburn, NY, 1869), 7, www.gutenberg.org/files/57821/57821-h/57821-h.htm.
47. Bradford, *Some Scenes in the Life of Harriet Tubman* 9, 24–25, 27, www.gutenberg.org/files/57821/57821-h/57821-h.htm.
48. American Anti-Slavery Society, *The Fugitive Slave Law and Its Victims (Anti-Slavery Tract No. 18)* (New York, 1856), www.gutenberg.org/files/13990/13990-h/13990-h.htm.
49. American Anti-Slavery Society, *Fugitive Slave Law and Its Victims.*
50. Harriet Beecher Stowe, *Uncle Tom's Cabin* (Boston, 1852), ch. XLV ("Concluding Remarks"), www.gutenberg.org/files/203/203-h/203-h.htm.

51. Henry David Thoreau, "Slavery in Massachusetts" (speech, Framingham, MA, July 4, 1854), en.wikisource.org/wiki/Slavery_in_Massachusetts.

52. An Act to prevent Slaveholding and Kidnapping in Ohio, April 17, 1857, in Acts of the State of Ohio 54 (Columbus, OH, 1857), 186.

53. 62 U.S. 506 (1859).

54. Jefferson Davis, *The Rise and Fall of the Confederate Government* (New York, 1881), Vol. 1, 16–17, www.gutenberg.org/files/19831/19831-h/19831-h.htm.

55. Abraham Lincoln, "Address" (speech, Cincinnati, OH, September 17, 1859); in *Abraham Lincoln: Speeches and Writings, 1859-1865*, 87.

56. Abraham Lincoln, First Inaugural Address (March 4, 1861), avalon.law.yale.edu/19th_century/lincoln1.asp. Significantly, though, Lincoln also insisted in his First Inaugural on due process rights for those accused of being runaway slaves: "In any law upon this subject ought not all the safeguards of liberty known in civilized and humane jurisprudence to be introduced, so that a free man be not in any case surrendered as a slave?"

57. Republic of Georgia, "Resolution of Secession" (January 29, 1861), avalon.law.yale.edu/19th_century/csa_geosec.asp.

58. Andrew Delbanco, *The War before the War: Fugitive Slaves and the Struggle for America's Soul from the Revolution to the Civil War* (New York: Penguin Press, 2018).

59. See 8 U.S.C. § 1373(a) ("Notwithstanding any other provision of federal, state, or local law, a federal, state, or local government entity or official may not prohibit, or in any way restrict, any government entity or official from sending to, or receiving from, the Immigration and Naturalization Service information regarding the citizenship or immigration status, lawful or unlawful, of any individual."), www.govinfo.gov/content/pkg/USCODE-2011-title8/pdf/USCODE-2011-title8-chap12-subchapII-partIX-sec1373.pdf. See also Exec. Order 13,768, "Enhancing Public Safety in the Interior of the United States" (January 25, 2017) (denying "federal grants" to "sanctuary jurisdictions"), www.govinfo.gov/content/pkg/DCPD-201700072/html/DCPD-201700072.htm.

60. See generally Loren Collingwood and Benjamin Gonzalez O'Brien, *Sanctuary Cities: The Politics of Refuge* (New York: Oxford University Press, 2019).

61. U.S. Const., art. II, § 1 (oath for president). Members of Congress are required by oath to "support and defend the Constitution of the United States," 5 U.S.C. § 3331; judges swear to discharge their duties under "the Constitution and laws of the United States," 28 U.S.C. § 453.

62. See generally Robert M. Cover, *Justice Accused: Antislavery and the Judicial Process* (New Haven, CT: Yale University Press, 1975).

63. Dred Scott v. Sandford, 60 U.S. 393 (1857). See generally Don E. Fehrenbacher, *The Dred Scott Case: Its Significance in American Law and Politics* (New York: Oxford University Press, 1978).

64. Roger Taney, "Supplement to the *Dred Scott* Opinion" (September 1858), in Samuel Tyler, *Memoir of Roger Brooke Taney* (Baltimore, 1872), 579, babel.hathitrust.org/cgi/pt?id = uiug.30112100467783&view = 1up&seq = 11&skin = 2021.

65. *Dred Scott*, 60 U.S. 393 (Curtis, J., dissenting).

66. *Dred Scott*, 60 U.S. 393.

67. *Id.* (Catron, J., concurring).

68. *Dred Scott*, 60 U.S. 393.

69. "The *Dred Scott* Case," *Richmond Enquirer*, March 10, 1857, chroniclingamerica.loc. gov/lccn/sn84024735/1857-03-10/ed-1/seq-2/.

70. Davis, *Rise and Fall of the Confederate Government*, 83–85.

71. Stephen A. Douglas, Third Debate (Jonesboro, IL, September 15, 1858), www.nps. gov/liho/learn/historyculture/debate3.htm.

72. *New York Tribune*, March 11, 1857, en.wikisource.org/wiki/New_York_Tribune_editorial_on_the_Dred_Scott_case.

73. Frederick Douglass, "The *Dred Scott* Decision" (speech, Rochester, NY, May 14, 1857), www.loc.gov/resource/mfd.21039/?sp=2&st=list.

74. Abraham Lincoln, "The Perpetuation of Our Political Institutions" (speech, Young Men's Lyceum of Springfield, IL, January 27, 1838); in *Abraham Lincoln: Speeches and Writings, 1832-1858*, ed. Don E. Fehrenbacher (New York: Library of America, 1989), 32.

75. Stephen A. Douglas, Sixth Debate (Quincy, IL, October 13, 1858), www.nps.gov/liho/learn/historyculture/debate6.htm.

76. Abraham Lincoln, Sixth Debate (Quincy, IL, October 13, 1858), www.nps.gov/liho/learn/historyculture/debate6.htm.

77. Abraham Lincoln, "Speech on *Dred Scott* Decision" (speech, Springfield, IL, June 26, 1857), in *Abraham Lincoln: Speeches and Writings, 1832-1858*, 392–93. In response, Stephen A. Douglas accused Lincoln of trying to politicize the judiciary: "He is going to appeal to the people to elect a president who will appoint judges who will reverse the *Dred Scott* decision. . . . Suppose you get a Supreme Court composed of such judges, who have been appointed by a partisan president upon their giving pledges how they would decide a case before it arose, what confidence would you have in such a Court? . . . It is a proposition to make that Court the corrupt, unscrupulous tool of a political party. . . . The very proposition carries with it the demoralization and degradation destructive of the judicial department of the federal government." Stephen A. Douglas (speech, Springfield, IL, July 17, 1858), www.perseus.tufts.edu/hopper/text?doc=Perseus%3Atext%3A2001.05.0024%3Achapter%3D5.

78. Lincoln, "Speech on *Dred Scott* Decision," in *Abraham Lincoln: Speeches and Writings, 1832-1858*, 393.

79. Lincoln, "Speech on *Dred Scott* Decision," in *Abraham Lincoln: Speeches and Writings, 1832-1858*, 393–94.

80. Andrew Jackson, quoted in Lincoln, "Speech on *Dred Scott* Decision," in *Abraham Lincoln: Speeches and Writings, 1832-1858*, 394.

81. Abraham Lincoln, "Speech at Chicago" (speech, Chicago, July 10, 1858), in *Abraham Lincoln: Speeches and Writings, 1832-1858*, 450–51.

82. Lincoln, "Speech on *Dred Scott* Decision," in *Abraham Lincoln: Speeches and Writings, 1832-1858*, 396–98.

83. For a wide-ranging consideration of the *Dred Scott* decision within the larger context of US and constitutional history, see Jack M. Balkin and Sanford Levinson, "Thirteen Ways of Looking at *Dred Scott*," *Chicago-Kent Law Review* 82 (2007): 49–95, digitalcommons.law.yale.edu/cgi/viewcontent.cgi?referer= https://www.google.com/&httpsredir=1&article=1228&context=fss_papers.

84. Other important provisions of the Fourteenth Amendment penalized states for disenfranchising Black males, barred Confederate leaders and sympathizers from returning to political power, forbade the payment of any debt incurred in support of "insurrection or rebellion," and prohibited any compensation "for the loss or emancipation of any slave."

85. Slaughter-House Cases, 83 U.S. 36 (1873). See generally Ronald M. Labbe and Jonathan Lurie, *The* Slaughterhouse Cases: *Regulation, Reconstruction, and the Fourteenth Amendment* (Lawrence: University Press of Kansas, 2003).

86. Slaughter-House Cases, 83 U.S. 36 (1873).

87. *Id.* (Field, J., dissenting).

88. Thomas Morris Chester, "Speech to Meeting of Colored Men in New Orleans," in *Horrible Massacre in Grant Parish, Louisiana* (New Orleans, 1873), 11–12.

89. United v. Cruikshank, 92 U.S. 542 (1876). See generally Charles Lane, *The Day Freedom Died: The Colfax Massacre, the Supreme Court, and the Betrayal of Reconstruction* (New York: Henry Holt, 2008).

90. United States v. Reese, 92 U.S. 214 (1876).

91. *Id.*

92. Williams v. Mississippi, 170 U.S. 213 (1898).

93. Giles v. Harris, 189 U.S. 475 (1903).

94. Civil Rights Act of 1875 (An Act to protect all citizens in their civil and legal rights), ch. 114, 18 Stat. 335 (March 1, 1875), govtrackus.s3.amazonaws.com/legislink/pdf/ stat/18/STATUTE-18-Pg335a.pdf.

95. Civil Rights Cases, 109 U.S. 3 (1883).

96. *Id.* (Harlan, J., dissenting).

97. Even before *Plessy*, the Supreme Court had unanimously upheld an Alabama criminal law that imposed prison terms of up to seven years on persons of different races engaging in sexual relations. Pace v. Alabama, 106 U.S. 583 (1883).

98. Plessy v. Ferguson, 163 U.S. 537 (1896).

99. *Id.* (Harlan, J., dissenting). In January 2022, Homer Plessy was granted a posthumous pardon by the governor of Louisiana.

100. See Eric Foner, *The Second Founding: How the Civil War and Reconstruction Remade the Constitution* (New York: W.W. Norton, 2019); Eric Foner, *Reconstruction: America's Unfinished Revolution, 1863–1877*, updated ed. (New York: Harper, 2014).

5

The Constitution at Home and Abroad
(1877–1917)

In the five decades following the Civil War, the United States experienced startling economic growth and became a dominant industrial power. The nation acquired territories far beyond its continental borders as the result of wars fought against Spain and in the Philippines. The era was characterized by corporate behemoths, unregulated urbanization, Gilded Age "robber barons," mass immigration, imperialism, political corruption, vast inequality, Populist discontent, and Progressive reform. For teachers and students alike, constitutional history can help unify this sprawling age of excess. To whom—immigrants? territorial inhabitants? African Americans? workers? Native Americans? corporate entities?—was the Constitution's promise of citizenship and rights extended, or not?

This deceptively straightforward question embraced a host of substantial constitutional tensions. For example, did Congress have the power, in the Chinese Exclusion Act of 1882 (and subsequent iterations), to exclude persons from entry into the country solely because of their national origin (in this instance, the Chinese—described by one Supreme Court justice as "them," in contrast to "our people"[1])? Could persons legally present in the country be prevented, on the basis of their national origin, from ever gaining citizenship? What about radicals? Could anarchists be barred from entering the country or be deported on account of their political beliefs, as decreed by Congress in 1903? On the other hand, did every person born in the United States automatically become a citizen, no matter what, by reason of the language of the Fourteenth Amendment? Even if so, did this concept of "birthright citizenship" also apply to Native Americans? The United States continued its centuries-old tradition of "othering" Native Americans. The Dawes Act and a series of Supreme Court decisions suggested that Congress faced no constitutional limitations in designing Indian policy. At bottom, each of these intricate, interconnected constitutional questions concerned inclusion and exclusion—questions and concepts that teachers and students will recognize to be no less relevant today.

These manifold constitutional controversies ultimately coalesced into a more restrictive notion of constitutional rights—indeed, a "constitutional counterrevolution"—brought about in large measure by the need to govern far-flung territories acquired as the result of war. To what extent would "liberty and justice for

With Liberty and Justice for All?. Edited by Steven A. Steinbach, Maeva Marcus, and Robert Cohen, Oxford University Press. © Oxford University Press 2022. DOI: 10.1093/oso/9780197516317.003.0005

all" be made available to the residents of these new possessions—Puerto Ricans; Filipinos; Samoans? In the end, the Supreme Court in the *Insular Cases* answered this question by ducking it—or, more precisely, by affording Congress carte blanche power to bestow—or, more accurately, to withhold—whatever constitutional protections it deemed appropriate to govern this expanding empire.

Judges played a crucial role in applying and interpreting the Constitution throughout this unsettling period. The Supreme Court upheld race-based immigration rules intended to bar persons of Chinese ancestry from entry into the country or gaining citizenship. It permitted Congress to break up and redistribute communally held Native American lands. During these same years, the Court endorsed the intentional disenfranchisement and segregation of African Americans by Southern states; empowered business entities with constitutional rights, albeit with few corollary protections for laborers; and prevented Mormons from practicing polygamy in accordance with their religious teachings. And, as the country's boundaries enlarged, it created new doctrinal lingo—"unincorporated territories," "noncitizen nationals"—to sanction new nonequal realities and relationships. In the end, the former slaves were not the only victims of the broken promises of the Reconstruction Amendments.

From the Reconstruction Constitution to Empire

Sam Erman

Associate Professor of Law, University of Southern California Gould School of Law

A constitutional counterrevolution took place in the United States between 1877 and 1917. After the Civil War, new amendments to the Constitution expanded citizenship, guaranteed its privileges and immunities, protected voting rights, and demanded equality and inclusion. This Reconstruction Constitution was visionary, praiseworthy, and tragically vulnerable. Over the next forty years, however, much of the Reconstruction Constitution unraveled. Losses were greatest for those most intended to be helped: former slaves and their descendants. But many others also lost rights and access to citizenship. By contrast, large, powerful institutions such as the federal government, state governments, and corporations gained authority.

There are many vantage points from which this story could be told, including those of African Americans, American Indians, ethnic Chinese, other immigrants, women, religious minorities, and wage laborers. While the experiences of all these groups deserve sustained attention, the so-called imperial turn of the United States—its late nineteenth-century acquisition of island territories to be governed as colonies—is worthy of particular focus. This approach illuminates a central dynamic of the period: how the fight over the legal legacy of the Civil War and Reconstruction and that over the constitutional future of empire were always one and the same.

The National Constitutional Conflict over African Americans

After 1877, a national conflict raged over what the Constitution permitted the federal government to do. On one side were Southern white-supremacist Democrats. They had lost the Civil War and with it the power to enslave Americans of African descent. They now wanted to tip the scales as far back in their favor as they could. They aimed to reverse African Americans' post-1860 legal and political gains by establishing permanent control over Southern politics and constraining the freedom of former slaves and their descendants. To isolate African Americans in the South from federal officials, Democrats argued that the Constitution limited the power of the federal government to intervene in state affairs. (Today, by contrast, Republicans win most Southern whites' votes and tend to favor Southern states' rights.)

Northern Republicans were on the other side. They had won the Civil War and now generally controlled the national government. They understood the Constitution to grant the federal government wide power to act, including within states. They acted accordingly, including to guarantee African American rights. This was often a matter of principle, but it was also political common sense. African American votes were crucial to the party's success (as they are to the Democratic Party today).

Constitutional conflict was less intense when Republican officials in the national government acted outside the states. Southern Democrats saw a less direct threat. The Supreme Court repeatedly declared such federal exertions to be constitutional. That was not a big surprise. Most of the Supreme Court justices were appointed by Republican presidents.

Congress's Plenary Power beyond State Borders

During the last quarter of the nineteenth century, the national government exercised what the Supreme Court called a "plenary" power over territories, national borders, foreign lands, aliens, and American Indians. Plenary means full or complete. The Court only rarely imposed limits on Congress's attempts to legislate in these areas. Even when it did impose limits, they generally amounted to little. The plenary power could usually overpower individuals' rights. That was the experience of the Mormon majority in the Territory of Utah.

Despite its name, the United States has never been made up only of states. It has always contained territories as well. In 1877, most people expected that all territories would eventually become states, and most already had. But not Utah; it was still a territory. Its residents had all the individual rights guaranteed in the Constitution. But they did not vote for president, for Congress, or on constitutional amendments.

Utah was unique among the territories because it was dominated by members of the Mormon religious faith, which encouraged polygamy (specifically, families with multiple wives and a single husband). Congress condemned the practice as a form of slavery and criminalized it. Federal prosecutions followed. Defendants asserted their constitutionally guaranteed individual rights in response, but generally to little avail. In *Reynolds v. United States* (1879),[2] for instance, the Supreme Court rejected the claim that George Reynolds's constitutional right to "free exercise" of his Mormon faith protected him from prosecution for his plural marriage. Mormon leaders could stem the federal onslaught only by abandoning their support for polygamy, which they soon did. Congress and its plenary power prevailed.

Federal officials also had broad power in foreign places and over foreign people. The Supreme Court's decision in *In re Ross* (1891)[3] denied the constitutional right of a jury trial to a US citizen who was tried for murder by a US official under US law. The reason was that the crime and the trial both occurred overseas, in a Japanese harbor. In the Court's words, "The Constitution can have no operation in a foreign country."

The plenary power extended to immigration, which the Court framed as the movement of alien bodies across international borders. *Chae Chan Ping v. United States* (1889)[4] and *Fong Yue Ting v. United States* (1893)[5] involved a series of virulently anti-Chinese federal laws known as the Chinese Exclusion Acts. These statutes flatly forbade naturalization of Chinese aliens and sharply limited the presence of such Chinese nationals in the United States. The Supreme Court rejected constitutional challenges to these racist laws. It declared that Congress had plenary power to remove and bar foreigners from US territory.

Still, aliens who reached the United States did have important legal protections. In *United States v. Wong Kim Ark* (1898),[6] the Supreme Court reaffirmed the Fourteenth Amendment's guarantee that "all persons born . . . in the United States and subject to the jurisdiction thereof, are citizens of the United States." If subjects of China had children in the United States, those children were US citizens. The justices rejected the race-based claim that birth to such parents was birth outside US jurisdiction.

Even as the Supreme Court interpreted the Constitution to permit Congress to exclude Chinese immigrants, Congress was simultaneously welcoming settlers from more favored regions. For instance, federal law permitted European immigrants to become US citizens through a relatively quick and easy method. Congress thought this was good policy. More people would immigrate if citizenship were easily available. And once such immigrants became citizens, their sole allegiance would be to the United States, not to their country of origin.

Congress's Plenary Power over American Indians

Within US borders, American Indians faced a type of domestic imperialism. In the 1870s, the United States stopped interacting with tribes as it did with foreign nations, by entering into treaties with them. Instead, Congress began governing Native peoples directly. In *United States v. Kagama* (1886),[7] the Supreme Court approved of that policy. It declared that Congress had plenary power over American Indians.

During the same years, the United States engaged in military campaigns to subdue recalcitrant Indians. By the time the Army massacred hundreds of Lakota at Wounded Knee in 1890, American Indians' military power no longer posed a credible threat to US dominance. Having reduced Indians to dependent wards, Congress set about transforming them into autonomous US citizens. It enacted the 1887 Dawes Act,[8] which let federal officials take lands held by a whole tribe and break them up into parcels to be distributed to the tribe's individual members. The project was based on the assumption that US ways of living were superior to those of American Indians. The statute promised US citizenship and all its "rights, privileges, and immunities" to Indians who lived "separate and apart from any tribe of Indians" and "adopted the habits of civilized life."

The results were disastrous. Federal officials dissolved tribal governments, divided tribal lands, enforced distributions that culminated in massive Native land loss, and used coercive education to weaken Native American cultures. Indians received citizenship that lacked many rights. States subjected them to discriminatory laws.

The Rollback of Reconstruction

In 1877, many gains of Reconstruction remained. The Supreme Court permitted the federal government to prevent or remedy much public race discrimination. Federal law barred race discrimination in voting, by government officials, and in many commercial settings. US attorneys prosecuted people for preventing African Americans from voting. Former slaves and their descendants voted in large numbers.

As federal power outside states grew, however, Republican support for African Americans declined dramatically. White-supremacist Democrats seized the opportunity to subordinate former slaves and their descendants. By 1906, white-supremacist Democrats held a stranglehold on Southern state governments and Northern Republicans were doing little to impede their racist designs. The shift had occurred in stages. In the South, white supremacists had used terrorism, violence, intimidation, and fraud to drive former slaves and their descendants from the polls. Southern states thereby became reliably Democratic, reducing the electoral benefits to Republicans of guaranteeing African Americans' rights. Members of the Republican Party had long debated whether African American rights should be their top priority. Finally, in the early 1890s, the Republican Party essentially gave up enforcing voting rights in the South.

The Supreme Court then greenlighted racial segregation and disfranchisement of African Americans. *Plessy v. Ferguson* (1896)[9] involved a law segregating white and Black passengers into separate railway cars. The Court saw no inconsistency between such segregation and either the equal protection of the laws or the privileges and immunities of citizenship that the Fourteenth Amendment guaranteed. *Giles v. Harris* (1903)[10] concerned voting rules that the state of Alabama had tailor-made to prevent African American voting. The Court declined to find a violation of the Fifteenth Amendment's prohibition of race discrimination in voting. Both decisions displayed a solicitousness for the powerful and a disregard of the vulnerable that was marked in the Court's decisions in other areas.

Law and the Constitution in the Service of Big Business

Just as law helped federal and state governments increase their reach, it contributed to the growth of business's power. By the century's end, corporations had won recognition as rights-bearing "people." This was a big victory because people enjoy Fourteenth Amendment rights to equal treatment and due process. It was also a mind-bending one, since corporations have no existence outside of the people who form them. The corporation is a legal fiction. It permits a group of people to act in the group's name, as though the group existed separate and apart from the people who formed it.

The path by which the Supreme Court recognized corporate personhood was appropriately tangled and unorthodox. First, railroads sought to expand their rights by bringing a series of judicial actions that their lawyers termed "test cases." When they sought to win recognition of corporations as people in

Santa Clara County v. Southern Pacific Railroad (1886),[11] the Supreme Court declined to address the issue. But the publisher of the Court's decision added an introductory note falsely asserting that all the justices thought that corporations were people. Then in *Minneapolis & St. Louis Railroad Co. v. Beckwith* (1889),[12] Justice Stephen Field wrote an opinion for the Court in which he cited *Santa Clara County* as evidence that the Court had already decided that corporations were people. Afterward, the Court treated the question it had never decided as already-settled law.

Business lawyers also invented organizational forms capable of bundling companies within an industry together into a single "trust." By eliminating competition among the companies, the trust could raise prices and increase profits at consumers' expense. Of course, the trusts had to follow the laws of the state in which they were incorporated. But when one state outlawed them, they could reincorporate in a new state. New Jersey ran a lucrative trade collecting incorporation fees after it enacted laws that gave corporations free hands in organizing themselves.

Organized Labor Constrained by Law

As organized labor began to emerge as a potent force in the late nineteenth century, law helped business contain the threat. Rapid industrialization brought growing numbers of Americans into wage work at large factories. One employee's complaint about work conditions was now likely to be shared by many coworkers. The resultant solidarity was fertile ground for labor organizing and labor activism, as attested to by the growing numbers of workers who joined labor organizations and went on strike. Because strikes could cripple businesses and industries, they were a powerful tool for labor and a significant threat to corporate profits.

Employers struck back with a legal tool known as the antilabor injunction. These were judicial orders that barred workers and labor leaders from a variety of strike activities. They gained prominence in 1894 when a federal judge ended the nationwide Pullman railroad strike by issuing an injunction ordering workers back to work. The Supreme Court upheld that injunction a year later in *In re Debs* (1895).[13] Across the ensuing quarter century, workers' privileges and immunities as citizens did not shield them from this devastatingly effective antilabor tool. Judges turned similarly deaf ears to complaints that injunctions infringed constitutionally protected expressive freedoms and violated the Thirteenth Amendment ban on slavery.

The Reconstruction Constitution as a Constraint on Empire

As governmental and corporate power grew after 1877, formal US expansion ground to an unprecedented halt. From the founding through the acquisition of Alaska in 1867, the United States never had let fifteen years pass without expanding its borders. But after 1867, thirty years came and went without any change to its international boundaries.

A key reason was the Constitution. Between 1867 and 1898, US officials considered acquiring each of what is today the Dominican Republic, American Samoa, Hawai'i, and the US Virgin Islands. These lands all contained majority nonwhite populations. Stateside opponents defeated each annexation project by railing against citizenship, rights, and eventual statehood for such people. US officials preferred stable borders to these constitutional consequences of expansion. In the words of the eminent naval strategist Alfred T. Mahan, the chief obstacle to annexation was "the constitutional lion in the path."[14]

Three constitutional principles that emerged from the Civil War and Reconstruction worked together to make citizenship, rights, and statehood the constitutional consequences of annexation:

- *All Americans other than some Indians were US citizens.* Under federal law, one became an American by being naturalized or by being born within the United States. Naturalization always brought citizenship. And the Fourteenth Amendment guaranteed citizenship to all born as Americans within the United States. The sole exception was for those not born "subject to the jurisdiction" of the United States (i.e., American Indians born owing primary allegiance to a tribe).
- *Citizenship carried substantial rights that potentially included voting.* The Fourteenth Amendment guaranteed all citizens a set of "privileges" and "immunities" that pre-Civil War judicial decisions indicated could be far-reaching. The Fifteenth Amendment reinforced this conclusion by protecting voting.
- *All US lands other than Washington, DC, were current or future states.* The expectation that all territories would become states was codified during the founding era in the Northwest Ordinance. The Supreme Court's decision in *Dred Scott v. Sandford* (1857)[15] reinforced this principle: "There is certainly no power given by the Constitution to the federal government to establish or maintain colonies . . . permanently." Today, the decision is infamous for declaring that African Americans could not be citizens. But while the Civil War and Fourteenth Amendment reversed that result, neither necessarily undermined its anticolonial reasoning.

By 1898, the bundle of constitutional consequences that accompanied annexation had grown brittle. Citizens such as African Americans faced disfranchisement and severe discrimination. Territorial residents such as Mormons had little defense against federal authority. With New Mexico entering its sixth decade as a territory, it appeared that eventual statehood could be withheld indefinitely. Democrats had once feared national power as a threat to their control of Southern politics. That opposition had also contributed to the stability of US borders. But as their grip on the former Confederacy tightened, overseas acquisitions looked less like threats to white supremacy than new fields for its operation. Anti-imperial constitutional principles still held, but perhaps only as long as US officials had no compelling reason to challenge them.

Making the Constitution Safe for Empire

The impetus for constitutional change came in 1898 when the United States went to war with the long-declining Spanish Empire. The United States quickly annexed Hawai'i, which had a port that would be valuable to the war effort. Then the United States routed Spain and forced it to cede Guam, Puerto Rico, and the Philippines. Suddenly, US sovereignty stretched across millions of people of African, Asian, and indigenous Pacific Islander descent. Consistent with the widely shared racism of the day, US officials opposed extending blanket citizenship, rights, and statehood to these new Americans. Instead, they favored governing them as colonial subjects, even though it would mean contravening the Constitution as it was then understood.

Rather than forthrightly violate or amend the Constitution, US officials from all branches of government reconciled Constitution and empire by reinterpreting the former. Together, they spent a quarter century developing and implementing constitutional doctrines notable for their vagueness. A federal agency, the War Department, pioneered the approach. In 1900, it still governed Puerto Rico and the Philippines. To establish that the national government could run each as a colony, the agency's top lawyers looked to past Supreme Court decisions. They found many recognizing broad discretion in those governing lands that were not states of the Union and groups that were disfavored, such as African Americans, American Indians, ethnic Chinese, Mormons, and aliens. They concluded that the Constitution did not require citizenship, statehood, or rights for Puerto Rico or the Philippines. Congress agreed, passing legislation that withheld all three legal forms from both places. Attention now shifted toward the courts, and toward the nearby island of Puerto Rico, which the ensuing legislation regularly featured.

The Supreme Court and the Invention of the Unincorporated Territory

The Court gave doctrinal shape to the War Department and Congress's theories through new legal categories: the unincorporated territory and the noncitizen national. The first concept traces to *Downes v. Bidwell* (1901),[16] which presented the question of whether a new tariff on trade between Puerto Rico and New York violated the rule that tariffs be uniform throughout the "United States." The justices answered no but could not agree why.

With no opinion garnering the necessary five of nine votes to become binding doctrine, the most notable writing was Justice Edward Douglass White's concurrence. He proposed a new territorial nonincorporation doctrine in which territories could be acquired by the United States without being incorporated into it. Residents would receive only fundamental constitutional rights, whatever those were.[17] It was unclear whether the Court would continue to follow White's approach.

"American ... Yet Not a Citizen": Isabel Gonzalez and the Supreme Court

Evasion and ambiguity also marked the Court's inching toward agreeing that some Americans were neither Indians nor citizens. *Gonzales v. Williams* (1904)[18] involved a young Puerto Rican woman named Isabel Gonzalez who sought to migrate from Puerto Rico to New York. When she departed San Juan, Puerto Ricans were permitted to land at New York like other Americans. But while she was en route, the agency responsible for immigration changed the rule and told immigration officials to treat Puerto Ricans as aliens. As a result, inspectors at Ellis Island discovered that she was an unmarried mother and also pregnant. They excluded her from the mainland as an undesirable alien.

Gonzalez made a federal case of her predicament. She sued, lost, and appealed to the Supreme Court. Though she married during the litigation, she hid the fact from the courts. Her priority was to win recognition of citizenship for all Puerto Ricans, not to overturn immigration inspectors' impugnation of her individual character. With the help of family already in New York, she was represented by the brilliant constitutional and international law lawyer Frederic Coudert. He reassured the Court that it could recognize Puerto Ricans as US citizens by arguing that the status brought fewer rights than other European empires accorded their colonial subjects. African Americans and US women got very few rights despite undoubtedly being citizens. Coudert, Gonzalez, and her family also drew Puerto Rico's elected representative in Washington into the case as a friend of the Court. He argued that Puerto Ricans should be citizens with full rights because they were the equals of Anglo-Saxon Americans.

During prior disputes over the citizenship of Puerto Ricans, the US attorney general had declared that it was possible to be an "American . . . yet not a citizen."[19] The justices now made this possibility a predicate of their decision. They unanimously decided that Puerto Ricans such as Gonzalez were not aliens. Existing immigration laws applied only to aliens so had no application to Puerto Ricans, who could therefore travel to New York freely. However, by not deciding whether Puerto Ricans were citizens, the Court signaled its openness to the possibility that they were not.

Citizenship Safe for Empire

Congress and the War Department correctly understood that the Court's inability to reach any sweeping unified decision left them with great discretion. The War Department's lead lawyer was future Supreme Court Justice Felix Frankfurter. He told lawmakers that the Court would let them extend or withhold citizenship, rights, statehood, and self-government in whatever mix they chose. They took the advice. In 1916, Congress withheld citizenship, full rights, statehood, and extensive self-government from Filipinos, promising them only independence at some indefinite future date.[20] A year later, Congress eliminated the promise of eventual independence for Puerto Rico and added immediate collective naturalization for Puerto Ricans.[21]

In *Balzac v. Porto Rico* (1922),[22] the Court confirmed Frankfurter's view that citizenship was consistent with colonial subjection. It unanimously and unequivocally declared territorial nonincorporation to be binding doctrine. Puerto Rico would remain unincorporated until Congress said otherwise, never mind that Puerto Ricans were citizens. That meant that Puerto Ricans were citizens with only partial constitutional rights. Their island might never become a state.

The Elusive Benefits of Citizenship for American Indians and Aliens

American Indians experienced an early twentieth-century hollowing out of their US citizenship similar to that in the US colonies. In the late nineteenth century, US officials had envisioned freeing noncitizen Indian wards from federal tutelage by transforming them into rights-bearing, autonomous citizens. Instead, the Supreme Court announced in *United States v. Celestine* (1909)[23] and *United States v. Nice* (1916)[24] that naturalization had no such consequences. Drawing on racist notions of American Indians as dependent people incapable of self-direction, the justices declared that US guardianship over American Indians would continue until Congress expressly stated otherwise. Citizenship was irrelevant. Thus, when long-sought collective naturalization of American Indians finally came with passage of the 1924 Indian Citizenship Act,[25] it produced little excitement.

The racism that lay behind the exclusion of Filipinos from US citizenship also motivated race-based restrictions on immigration. Laws limiting Chinese immigration commenced in 1882[26] and continued for decades. In 1907, President Theodore Roosevelt forged a Gentlemen's Agreement with Japan to limit migration of its people to the United States. Four years later, the congressionally created Dillingham Commission issued a forty-one-volume report identifying dangers of immigration from southern and eastern Europe. Then the 1924 National Origins Act all but ended immigration from Asia and drastically reduced immigration from southern and eastern Europe.[27]

Citizenship Redeemed?

Despite reductions in access to citizenship and rights of citizenship, the promise of citizenship survived. That was evident in the tension between the two trends. If citizenship did not matter, why limit who got it? The answer was that citizenship still mattered, or at least could matter.

For Puerto Ricans, citizenship brought the enduring right to move within the United States. Most Americans of Puerto Rican descent now live on the mainland. Filipinos, by contrast, face a migration regime characterized by exclusion and deportation.

More immediately, citizenship remained associated with voting. Women suffragists made this point to powerful effect. By 1917, eighteen of the forty-eight states permitted women to cast ballots in presidential elections. A constitutional amendment to end sex discrimination in voting was on the horizon.

Many people who sought to benefit from US citizenship between 1877 and 1917 were disappointed. But they still pursued its promise. Citizenship was a basis for making claims. That opportunity grew more valuable as government and corporate power increased. It provided a language for collective action and for individual rights. And it always was capable of being reinvigorated, as had happened before 1877 and as would happen again after 1917.

The Chinese Exclusion Act (and the Anarchist Exclusion Act)—Primary Sources

Political attitudes and forces led Congress to pass the Chinese Exclusion Act in 1882 and to renew it periodically thereafter. The Supreme Court rendered decisions involving Chinese aliens in *Yick Wo v. Hopkins* and *Chae Chan Ping v. United States*. Meanwhile, political pressures also drove Congress to exclude anarchists from entering and remaining in the country—an exclusion upheld by the Court in *Turner v. Williams* and further reinforced during World War I.

Yick Wo v. Hopkins (1886)

In 1880, San Francisco passed a local ordinance, neutral on its face, that required all laundries to obtain a license to operate their business. City authorities proceeded to enforce the law in a discriminatory manner: not a single Chinese-run laundry received a permit. That pattern of discriminatory conduct violated the Constitution, the Supreme Court ruled unanimously.

> The facts shown establish . . . that whatever may have been the intent of the ordinances as adopted, they are applied by the public authorities . . . with a mind so unequal and oppressive as to amount to a practical denial by the state of that equal protection of the laws which is secured to the petitioners, as to all other persons, by the broad and benign provisions of the Fourteenth Amendment. . . . Though the law itself be fair on its face and impartial in appearance, yet if it is applied and administered by public authority with an evil eye and an unequal hand, so as practically to make unjust and illegal discriminations between persons in similar circumstances, . . . the denial of equal justice is still within the prohibition of the Constitution. . . .
>
> Both petitioners [before the Supreme Court] have complied with every requisite deemed by the law [for the safe operation of their laundry]. . . . And while this consent of the supervisors is withheld from them and from two hundred others . . . all of whom happen to be Chinese subjects, eighty others, not Chinese subjects, are permitted to carry on the same business under similar conditions. The fact of this discrimination is admitted. No reason for it is shown, and the conclusion cannot be resisted that no reason for it exists except hostility to the race and nationality to which the petitioners belong and which, in the eye of the law, is not justified. The discrimination is therefore illegal, and the public administration which enforces it is a denial of the equal

protection of the laws and a violation of the Fourteenth Amendment of the Constitution.[28]

The Court emphasized that its holding was unaffected by the fact that Yick Wo himself was not a US citizen.

> The Fourteenth Amendment to the Constitution is not confined to the protection of citizens. It says: "Nor shall any State deprive any person of life, liberty, or property without due process of law; nor deny to any person within its jurisdiction the equal protection of the laws." These provisions are universal in their application to all persons within the territorial jurisdiction, without regard to any differences of race, of color, or of nationality, and the equal protection of the laws is a pledge of the protection of equal laws.[29]

Focusing only on the *Yick Wo* ruling, one might conclude that Chinese nationals in the United States had been the victims of antagonism and prejudice, but that the Supreme Court would step in to prevent any discrimination against them. The first conclusion would be true but not the second.

Edwin Meade Urges Restrictions on Chinese Immigration (1877)

Ever since their arrival in large numbers beginning in the late 1840s, Chinese immigrants to the West Coast faced extraordinary animus because of their impact on the domestic labor market and on racial grounds—animus that, not infrequently, spawned horrific anti-Chinese violence (e.g., lynchings in Los Angeles in 1871 and the Rock Springs (Wyoming) Massacre in 1885). Over the years, calls for their blanket exclusion from the country became more frequent, as exemplified by an 1877 appeal from Edwin Meade, a Democratic congressman from New York.

> [The Chinese immigrant] comes here as a laborer. He personifies the character in its absolutely menial aspect—what the operation of fifty centuries of paganism, poverty, and oppression have made him—a mere animal machine, performing the duties in his accepted sphere, punctually and patiently, but utterly incapable of any improvement. . . . The qualities of [Chinese] labor mentioned, and the fact that it can be secured in any desired amount and discharged without controversy, renders it especially attractive to capitalists and contractors. African slave labor presented to some extent the same features, but in a marked degree [Chinese]

labor is cheaper, and therefore competitive with white labor. . . . It is impossible that the white laborer can exist in the presence of these conditions. . . . The white laborer could not succeed if he would attempt competition with the [Chinese], and will always be driven from his presence, as cheap currency displaces the better. . . .

The [Chinese] entertains a feeling of profound contempt for other civilizations. Founded as our society is upon the Christian religion, he for that reason alone thoroughly rejects it. . . . A republican or even liberal government of any form is to them quite incomprehensible. . . . Their superstitions, prejudices, and opinions have become as fixed as their habits of life. . . . If he seems to conform to our ways it is only to get a better foothold for money-making. . . . Can the injection of such a race into our body politic be viewed by any thinking American without anxiety and alarm? . . . The dignity of American labor and citizenship, the welfare and renown of the white race, and an elevated and Christian civilization, alike demand the exclusion of [Chinese] immigrants.[30]

Chinese Exclusion Act (1882)

In 1875, for the first time in the nation's history, Congress passed an immigration law excluding from entry three categories of persons from "China, Japan, or any Oriental country": women imported for the purpose of prostitution, forced laborers, and alien convicts.[31] Seven years later in the Chinese Exclusion Act, Congress prohibited the admission into the country of every "laborer" of Chinese ethnicity. The law also barred all Chinese immigrants already present in the United States from ever becoming citizens.

Whereas, in the opinion of the government of the United States the coming of Chinese laborers to this country endangers the good order of certain localities within the territory thereof: therefore, be it enacted . . . until the expiration of ten years next after the passage of this act, the coming of Chinese laborers to the United States be, and the same is hereby, suspended; and during such suspension it shall not be lawful for any Chinese laborer to come, or having so come after the expiration of said ninety days, to remain within the United States. . . .

Section 14. That hereafter no state court or court of the United States shall admit Chinese to citizenship. . . .

Section 15. That the words "Chinese laborers" wherever used in this act, shall be construed to mean both skilled and unskilled laborers and Chinese employed in mining.[32]

John Mitchell on the Continuing Chinese Threat (1888)

Even the sweeping provisions of the Chinese Exclusion Act apparently were not sufficient, as nothing in the law forbade the return from China of any workers who had lived and worked in the United States prior to 1882. Senator John Mitchell, a Republican from Oregon, urged that Congress close this loophole, posing the perceived threat in almost-apocalyptic terms.

All Chinese persons of whatever citizenship, save and except perhaps government officials, should be forever excluded from entering this country, whether here formerly or not. . . .

Our soil is again polluted with the curse of human slavery. The domestic tranquility, the public peace, the general welfare are again menaced . . . not this time by a domestic, but a foreign foe, who not only seek to occupy this country as the locusts occupied Egypt, but also aim to establish . . . a system of human bondage more detestable, more degrading, more blighting, and more destructive morally, socially, physically, and politically than was ever that of African slavery in its palmiest days. . . .

In reference to this most herculean of all gigantic evils that is being imposed upon and impressed upon us from the shores of Asia, this evil, which embraces within it explosives more deadly than dynamite, an evil that disposes labor, corrupts morals, debases youth, makes merchandise of personal freedom and female virtue, mocks at justice, defies law, dwarfs enterprise, obstructs development, chains personal liberty, destroys personal freedom, menaces the public peace, invades domestic tranquility, endangers the public welfare, converts whole sections of beautiful American cities . . . into squalid, wretched, crime-smitten, and leprous-spotted habitations of the lowest and most debased classes of the pagan [Chinese]—in reference to all this, in reference to ridding this country of such an evil, for the purpose of saving it from a deadly assault upon its most vital parts and securing it from becoming the pest-house and criminal receptacle of pagan and debauched people of a tabooed race, numbering one-half the population of the globe, the administration, so far as we are advised at present, has made no effort whatever.[33]

The Scott Act (1888)

Congress responded by passing the Scott Act, which retroactively prohibited any Chinese laborer who had left (or intended to leave) the United States from ever returning; any readmission certificates issued previously to such persons were "hereby declared void and of no effect, and the Chinese laborer claiming admission by virtue thereof shall not be permitted to enter the United States."[34]

Grover Cleveland on Chinese Exclusion (1888)

Despite expressing some concern about the impact on foreign relations with China, President Grover Cleveland, in signing the legislation, fully endorsed its domestic objectives.

> The experiment of blending the social habits and mutual race idiosyncrasies of the Chinese laboring classes with those of the great body of the people of the United States has been proved by the experience of twenty years . . . to be in every sense unwise, impolitic, and injurious to both nations. . . . The admitted and paramount right and duty of every government to exclude from its borders all elements of foreign population which for any reason retard its prosperity or are detrimental to the moral and physical health of its people must be regarded as a recognized canon of international law and intercourse.[35]

Chae Chan Ping v. United States (1889)

Only one week after the law was signed and took effect, Chae Chan Ping—who was returning to work in San Francisco after a visit to China—was denied entry under the new law, even though he "[had] in his possession a certificate in terms entitling him to return to the United States." When his case reached the Supreme Court, Justice Stephen Field began his (unanimous) opinion by recounting the historic tensions between Chinese immigrants ("them") and what he termed "our people."

> For some years little opposition was made to them, except when they sought to work in the mines, but, as their numbers increased, they began to engage in various mechanical pursuits and trades, and thus came in competition with our artisans and mechanics, as well as our laborers in the field. The competition steadily increased as the laborers came in crowds on each steamer that arrived from China or Hong Kong, an adjacent English port. They were generally industrious and frugal. Not being accompanied by families, except in rare instances, their expenses were small; and they were content with the simplest fare, such as would not suffice for our laborers and artisans. The competition between them and our people was for this reason altogether in their favor, and the consequent irritation, proportionately deep and bitter, was followed in many cases by open conflicts, to the great disturbance of the public peace. The differences of race added greatly to the difficulties of the situation. . . . They remained strangers in the land, residing apart by themselves, and adhering to the customs and usages of their own country. It seemed impossible for them to assimilate with our people or to make any change in their habits or modes

of living. As they grew in numbers each year the people of the coast saw, or believed they saw, in the facility of immigration and in the crowded millions of China, where population presses upon the means of subsistence, great danger that at no distant day that portion of our country would be overrun by them, unless prompt action was taken to restrict their immigration. The people there accordingly petitioned earnestly for protective legislation.[36]

Having sketched this background, the Court proceeded to uphold Chae Chan Ping's exclusion, concluding that Congress possessed the absolute and unreviewable discretion to exclude foreigners from the country for any reason.

> To preserve its independence and give security against foreign aggression and encroachment is the highest duty of every nation, and to attain these ends nearly all other considerations are to be subordinated. . . . If therefore the government of the United States, through its legislative department, considers the presence of foreigners of a different race in this country, who will not assimilate with us, to be dangerous to its peace and security, their exclusion is not to be stayed because at the time there are no actual hostilities with the nation of which the foreigners are subjects. . . . Its determination is conclusive upon the judiciary. . . .
>
> The power of exclusion of foreigners being an incident of sovereignty belonging to the government of the United States as a part of those sovereign powers delegated by the Constitution, the right to its exercise at any time when, in the judgment of the government, the interests of the country require it, cannot be granted away or restrained on behalf of any one. . . . Whatever license, therefore, Chinese laborers may have obtained, previous to the act of October 1, 1888, to return to the United States after their departure, is held at the will of the government, revocable at any time, at its pleasure.[37]

Nowhere in the *Chae Chan Ping* opinion was there any mention of *Yick Wo v. Hopkins*, much less any effort to attempt to reconcile the two decisions. The Court simply did not discuss the appropriateness of Congress singling out persons of Chinese heritage—alone—for discriminatory treatment. (Or perhaps it believed that any such motivation would be permissible, as "an incident of sovereignty belonging to the government.")

Subsequent Supreme Court Pronouncements on Chinese Exclusion

Congress extended and amended the Chinese Exclusion Act in 1892. Upholding the law in *Fong Yue Ting v. United States*, Justice Horace Gray, writing for the majority, explained that:

the government of the United States was brought to the opinion that the presence within our territory of large numbers of Chinese laborers, of a distinct race and religion, remaining strangers in the land, residing apart by themselves, tenaciously adhering to the customs and usages of their own country, unfamiliar with our institutions, and apparently incapable of assimilating with our people, might endanger good order and be injurious to the public interests.[38]

In a similar vein, Justice John Marshall Harlan, in his dissenting opinion in *Plessy v. Ferguson*, observed: "There is a race so different from our own that we do not permit those belonging to it to become citizens of the United States. Persons belonging to it are, with few exceptions, absolutely excluded from our country. I allude to the Chinese race."[39]

China Objects to Renewal of the Exclusion Act (1901)

When the Chinese Exclusion Act next came up for renewal in 1902, the Imperial Chinese General-Counsel attempted to persuade the United States to lift the prohibition.

> The [Great Wall of China] thrown up by the Mings was intended as a defense against robbers; not as a barrier against those who gave value for value, but one against those who pillaged and slew and ravaged with the sword and the torch. The barricade erected by Congress has no such excuse for being. What are the crimes of which our people are accused that render it needful that we should be treated as hostiles or shunned as those likely to communicate contagion? . . .
>
>   The Chinese exclusion laws are fallacious and a mistake; they are on the statute books unquestionably because the American people do not understand their cause and effect. Moreover, they are a most costly error, not only harmful to China and through China to the world, but visiting upon the United States specifically the most widespread detriment and harm and depriving the country yearly of millions of dollars. It is distinctly a policy of disaster on a scale so vast as to be without comparison in modern times. It is a policy founded in ignorance and arising through passion. . . . One of the greatest and most potential instruments for the creation of wealth is the Chinese laborer. To the unclouded mind it seems preposterous that any people should be shunned and expelled from a country that counts its unused acres by millions, simply because those people are industrious, patient, and frugal laborers who would produce for you at small cost. . . .
>
>   But one count in the indictment remains. It is that the Chinese do not assimilate with the American people and do not adopt American methods and ways. If we would cut our queues, quit shaving our heads, abolish the yungshan, and wear the American coat and vest, this objection would not be raised.

Our people would make as good citizens of the United States as any other for-
eign-born peoples. The average business man among us would vote as intelligently as the average business man among the European foreign element, and
the same may be said of our laborers. This whole trouble has been caused by the
fact that we are not citizens and voters. . . . The evil and loss to which the United
States has been subjected in its relation with China would all have been avoided
had the Chinese been treated the same as any other aliens in the matter of naturalization. With votes in the hands of any considerable number of Chinese the
exclusion laws would never have been possible. What if we do live in colonies?
All your cities are but bunches of colonies. . . . The Chinese gather to themselves
and do not trespass upon the domestic life of your people.[40]

James Phelan Calls for Permanent Exclusion (1901)

In response, James Phelan, the mayor of San Francisco, contended that instead of simply renewing the Chinese Exclusion Act, Congress should make it
permanent.

The Exclusion Acts then passed were limited to ten years' duration. In May next
the latest act will expire by limitation and Congress will be asked to renew it, because until now Chinese exclusion has been regarded in diplomatic circles and
elsewhere as the settled policy of the country. Has there been any change in the
nature of the evil or in the sentiments of the people? Certainly not on the Pacific
coast, where the lapse of time has made still more evident the non-assimilative
character of the Chinese and their undesirability as citizens. The Exclusion Act
has been reasonably effective, although the Chinese, with more or less success,
have employed their well-known cunning in evading its provisions by surrepti-
tiously and fraudulently entering the United States. . . .

To show the unanimity of the people, I may point out that the [California]
legislature submitted by referendum the question of Chinese immigration
to a popular vote. For Chinese immigration 883 votes were polled, and
against Chinese immigration 154,638 votes. In the city of San Francisco,
representing the wealth and intelligence and containing the skilled-labor organizations of the state, only 224 votes were cast in favor of the immigration
and 41,258 votes against it. This result demonstrated clearly that the resident population of California, taking the broad ground of self-preservation,
refused to suffer themselves to be dispossessed of their inheritance by [the]
Chinese. . . .

It is, indeed, generally true to say that the United States must admit its
Chinese population to the right of suffrage and to all the privileges of American
citizenship, if it grants them the privilege of permanent residence. If they are to

be admitted into this country freely they cannot be held as a separate class in a state of quasi-bondage or helotry. They are either desirable as citizens or not desirable at all. They must be admitted as ultimate voters, or excluded as being incapable of wisely using the elective franchise and assuming all the rights, duties, and obligations of citizenship. It is a false position to discuss them simply as laborers, skilled or unskilled. Therefore unless America is prepared to receive them as citizens, the Exclusion Act should be renewed, and we should look to the Caucasian race, as we have in the past, for the upbuilding of our industrial, social, and political fabric. . . .

It is well understood that the invitation of the new republic was addressed to the people of Europe, and that the [Chinese] were not included in it. In interpreting our naturalization laws the federal courts have held that the Caucasian race was alone contemplated by them, and by special exception, the negro race; that exception was the result of political necessity. . . . But the Chinese do not come in the name of liberty as oppressed, nor are they willing to renounce their old allegiance. They are not even bona fide settlers. They do not seek the land of the free for the love of it. On the contrary, they are attached to their own country by a superstitious bond and never think of leaving it permanently. It is also plain that by their mental organization they have no capacity for or appreciation of the blessings of liberty. . . .

The right of a state to exclude an undesirable immigration is fundamental international law. Self-protection yields to no higher law. . . . The Chinese may be good laborers, but they are not good citizens. They may in small numbers benefit individual employers, but they breed the germs of a national disease which spreads as they spread and grows as they grow.[41]

Subsequent Developments

Congress renewed the Chinese Exclusion Act again in 1902; in fact the statute was not repealed until 1943, in the midst of World War II. But by then Congress had amended the immigration laws to prohibit or restrict immigration by other nationalities also. The Immigration Act of 1924 excluded from admission to the United States all Asians, not only the Chinese. Congress also established rigid quotas (in the National Origins Formula) that disproportionately favored northern Europeans over all other immigration applicants.[42]

Angel Island Poetry

Thousands of would-be immigrants crossed the Pacific, only to be denied entry to the United States as a result of the Chinese Exclusion Act. Some of those detained at Angel Island in San Francisco Harbor before being returned to China wrote poems on their cell walls.

> I ate wind and tasted waves for more than twenty days.
> Fortunately, I arrived safely on the American continent.
> I thought I could land in a few days.
> How was I to know I would become a prisoner suffering in the wooden
>   building?

> Imprisoned in the wooden building day after day,
> My freedom withheld; how can I bear to talk about it?
> I look to see who is happy, but they only sit quietly.
> I am anxious and depressed and cannot fall asleep.
> The days are long and the bottle constantly empty;
> My sad mood, even so, is not dispelled.
> Nights are long and the pillow cold; who can pity my loneliness?
> After experiencing such loneliness and sorrow,
> Why not just return home and learn to plow the fields?[43]

Theodore Roosevelt Demands Immigration Restrictions on Anarchists (1901)

Congress also employed its powers over naturalization to exclude immigration on certain political grounds, as exemplified by the Immigration Act of 1903 (sometimes referred to as the Anarchist Exclusion Act). In the last several decades of the 1800s, the country had experienced (or at least perceived that it had experienced) threats and violence from anarchists, culminating in the assassination in 1901 of President William McKinley. The new president, Theodore Roosevelt, reflected on the threat—which he urged Congress to address by amending the immigration laws.

The Congress assembles this year under the shadow of a great calamity. On the sixth of September, President McKinley was shot by an anarchist while attending the Pan-American Exposition at Buffalo. . . . The harm done is so great as to excite our gravest apprehensions and to demand our wisest and most resolute action. This criminal was a professed anarchist, inflamed by the teachings of professed anarchists, and probably also by the reckless utterances of those who, on the stump and in the public press, appeal to the dark and evil spirits of malice and greed, envy and sullen hatred. The wind is sowed by the men who preach such doctrines, and they cannot escape their share of responsibility for the whirlwind that is reaped. . . . The blow was aimed not at this president but at all presidents; at every symbol of government. . . .

On no conceivable theory could the murder of the president be accepted as due to protest against "inequalities in the social order." . . . Anarchy is no more an expression of "social discontent" than picking pockets or wife beating. The anarchist, and especially the anarchist in the United States, is merely one type of criminal, more dangerous than any other because he represents the same depravity in a greater degree. . . . The anarchist is a criminal whose perverted instincts lead him to prefer confusion and chaos to the most beneficent form of social order. His protest of concern for workingmen is outrageous in its impudent falsity. . . . The anarchist is everywhere not merely the enemy of system and of progress, but the deadly foe of liberty. . . . Anarchistic speeches, writings, and meetings are essentially seditious and treasonable.

I earnestly recommend to the Congress that in the exercise of its wise discretion it should take into consideration the coming to this country of anarchists or persons professing principles hostile to all government and justifying the murder of those placed in authority. . . . They and those like them should be kept out of this country; and if found here they should be promptly deported to the country whence they came; and far-reaching provision should be made for the punishment of those who stay. No matter calls more urgently for the wisest thought of the Congress.[44]

Immigration Act (1903)

Congress responded by passing the Immigration Act of 1903, which, for the first time since the Alien Act of 1798, injected questions of political ideology into immigration and naturalization decisions. The 1903 statute—in addition to barring beggars, prostitutes, "idiots," insane persons, polygamists, and epileptics—provided for the exclusion, and potential deportation, of so-called anarchists.

Section 2. That the following classes of aliens shall be excluded from admission into the United States: . . . anarchists, or persons who believe in or advocate the overthrow by force or violence of the government of the United States or of all government or of all forms of law, or the assassination of public officials. . . .

Section 21. That in case the secretary of treasury shall be satisfied that an alien has been found in the United States in violation of this Act he shall cause such alien, within the period of three years after landing or entry therein, to be taken into custody and returned to the country whence he came. . . .

Section 38. That no person who disbelieves in or who is opposed to all or-ganized government, or who is a member of or affiliated with any organiza-tion entertaining and teaching such disbelief in or opposition to all organized government, or who advocates or teaches the duty, necessity, or propriety of the unlawful assaulting or killing of any officer . . . of the government of the United States or of any other organized government because of his or their offi-cial character, shall be permitted to enter the United States.[45]

The *New York Times* Calls for Deporting Anarchists (1903)

When the government made its initial attempt under the new law to deport an-archist John Turner, the *New York Times* was wildly enthusiastic in its support.

The law of 1903 declares that no person shall be permitted to enter the United States "who disbelieves in or who is opposed to all organized govern-ment." . . . Turner manifestly falls within this prohibition. He disbelieves in or-ganized government. . . .

For ourselves, we do not believe that the American people sympathize with Turner or want him set free to preach anarchy among us. No foreigner comes here as a matter of right. It is a privilege which we may extend or withhold and to which we may attach conditions. There being a prevalent belief that we have admitted quite enough anarchists already, the national legislature enacted that the privilege of coming should be withdrawn from men who teach or practice anarchistic doctrines. . . .

It is a travesty upon reason, it is the very height of unreason, to talk of liberty and freedom of speech in discussing the case of Turner. We are an organized society governed in accordance with certain well-tried and accepted principles. We are no more bound to extend the hospitable welcome to men who come to preach the destruction of those principles and the overthrow of our govern-ment than a church is bound to extend the hospitality of its pulpit to a blatant atheist. . . .

If all who hear [Turner] were Americans in fact and spirit, his prating would be neither heard nor heeded. We might let him prate on, unless he made a nuisance of himself. But we have received abundant warning that there are those who not only hear but heed. That fact gives us the right—in the belief of Congress and of many, probably of most Americans, it makes it our duty—to exclude him. We already have quite enough incendiaries.[46]

Turner v. Williams (1904)

Turner's case eventually reached the Supreme Court, which, in an opinion written by Chief Justice Melville Fuller, upheld his deportation as an anarchist.

> It is contended that the act of March 3, 1903, is unconstitutional because . . . no power is delegated by the Constitution to the general government . . . over the beliefs of citizens, denizens, sojourners, or aliens. . . . Repeated decisions of this Court have determined that Congress has the power to exclude aliens from the United States; to prescribe the terms and conditions of which they may come in; to establish regulations for sending out of the country such aliens as have entered in violation of law; and to commit the enforcement of such conditions and regulations to executive officers. . . .
>
>   But it is said that the act violates the First Amendment. . . . We are at a loss to understand in what way the act is obnoxious to this objection. . . . It is, of course, true that if an alien is not permitted to enter this country, or having entered contrary to law is expelled, he is in fact cut off from worshipping or speaking or publishing or petitioning in the country; but that is merely because of his exclusion therefrom. He does not become one of the people to whom these things are secured by our Constitution by an attempt to enter, forbidden by law. To appeal to the Constitution is to concede that this is a land governed by that supreme law, and as under it the power to exclude has been determined to exist, those who are excluded cannot assert the rights in general obtaining in a land to which they do not belong as citizens or otherwise.
>
>   [Turner's] contention really comes to this: that the act is unconstitutional so far as it provides for the exclusion of an alien because he is an anarchist. The argument seems to be that, conceding that Congress has the power to shut out any alien, the power nevertheless does not extend to some aliens, and that if the act includes all alien anarchists, it is unconstitutional because some anarchists are merely political philosophers whose teachings are beneficial rather than otherwise. . . . [The] government has the power to exclude an alien who believes in or advocates the overthrow of the government or of all governments by force or the assassination of officials. To put that question is to answer it. . . .
>
>   We are not to be understood as depreciating the vital importance of freedom of speech and of the press, or as suggesting limitations on the spirit of liberty, in itself unconquerable, but this case does not involve those considerations. The flaming brand which guards the realm where no human government is needed

still bars the entrance, and as long as human governments endure, they cannot be denied the power of self-preservation.[47]

Alien Anarchist Act (1918)

More than a decade later, and shortly after the United States entered World War I, Congress passed the Espionage Act, which punished certain conduct and "seditious" speech. At the same time, Congress enhanced the antianarchist provisions of the immigration laws.

> Aliens who are anarchists; aliens who believe in or advocate the overthrow by force or violence of the government of the United States or of all forms of law; aliens who disbelieve in or are opposed to all organized government; aliens who advocate or teach the assassination of public officials; aliens who advocate or teach the unlawful destruction of property; aliens who are members of or affiliated with any organization that entertains a belief in, teaches, or advocates the overthrow by force or violence of the government of the United States or of all forms of law, or that entertains or teaches disbelief in or opposition to all organized government . . . shall be excluded from admission into the United States.
>
> Any alien who at any time after entering the United States is found to have been at the time of entry, or to have become thereafter, a member of any one of the classes of aliens [listed above] . . . shall . . . be taken into custody and deported.[48]

Armed with these powers, government officials deported hundreds of "radicals" during the Red Scare of 1918–20, including, most prominently, anarchist agitator Emma Goldman.[49]

Roosevelt and Wilson Denounce "Hyphenated" Americans (1915, 1919)

The Chinese Exclusion Act and the program to exclude radicals were far from aberrations; both efforts reflected the spirit of the age. Theodore Roosevelt and Woodrow Wilson agreed on little and eventually became hardened political adversaries. But the two men shared a conviction that immigrants to America needed to put America first (to use modern parlance). And they shared a fear of the dangers that would result if, rather, immigrants clung to their ancestral heritage.

Theodore Roosevelt: There is no place here for the hyphenated American, and the sooner he returns to the country of his allegiance, the better. . . . When I refer to hyphenated Americans I do not refer to naturalized Americans. Some of the very best Americans I have ever known were naturalized Americans born abroad. But a hyphenated American is not an American at all. The one absolutely certain way of bringing this nation to ruin . . . would be to permit it to become a tangle of squabbling nationalities, an intricate knot of German-Americans,   Irish-Americans,   English-Americans,   French-Americans, Scandinavian-Americans, or Italian-Americans, each preserving its separate nationality, each at heart feeling more sympathy with Europeans of that nationality than with the other citizens of the American republic.[50]

Woodrow Wilson: Any man who carries a hyphen about with him carries a dagger that he is ready to plunge into the vitals of this republic whenever he gets ready. If I can catch any man with a hyphen in this great contest I will know that I have got an enemy of the republic.[51]

Woodrow Wilson: There are a great many hyphens left in America. For my part, I think the most un-American thing in the world is a hyphen. I do not care what it is that comes before the word "American." It may be a German-American, or an Italian-American, a Swedish-American, or an Anglo-American, or an Irish-American. It does not make any difference what comes before the "American," it ought not to be there, and every man who comes to take counsel with me with a hyphen in his conversation I take no interest in whatever. The entrance examination . . . into my confidence is, "Where do you put America in your thoughts? Do you put it first, always first, unquestionably first?"[52]

Discussion Questions

1. What principles guided Congress in setting immigration policies in the past, and what principles should guide it now? Would it be permissible for Congress to exclude certain persons on the basis of any of the following grounds: race, ethnicity, country of origin, religion, gender, sexual orientation, political ideology, socioeconomic status, health, disability, age?

2. Congress and the courts made clear that at least one motivation for enacting, renewing, and upholding the Chinese Exclusion Act was economic: to protect American workers from potential immigrants willing to work for significantly lower wages in the rapidly industrializing United States. What if this had been the only reason for the ban? In other words,

had there been no anti-Chinese animus, would economic self-protection be a legitimate justification for exclusion?

3. Anti-Chinese animus of course did motivate the Chinese Exclusion Act. Indeed, the statements of Congressman Edwin Meade and Senator John Mitchell excerpted above are frankly racist, full of stereotypes, slurs, and prejudices. Is it acceptable for teachers to use speeches such as these in their classrooms? Are they historical documents from which students can learn? Or are they too offensive to reproduce?

4. As Imperial Chinese General-Counsel Ho Yow recognized, the Chinese Exclusion Act was the product of both economic fears and racial prejudice. What are his strongest arguments in response to each objection?

5. One of the grounds repeatedly offered at the time against Chinese immigrants: they don't assimilate. Which should be preferred: melting-pot conformity or cultural pluralism? Which vision is more compatible with democracy?

6. The *New York Times* opined when speaking of anarchists: "No foreigner comes here as a matter of right. It is a privilege which we may extend or withhold and to which we may attach conditions." Agree or disagree? How has this idea been applied at various times in US history?

Territories—Primary Sources

What rules should govern territories held by the United States not destined for statehood? The Supreme Court first confronted the question in *Loughborough v. Blake*, involving the District of Columbia. After the Spanish-American War, the justices rendered a series of decisions, collectively known as the *Insular Cases*, resolving the issue in a novel constitutional manner.

Loughborough v. Blake (1820)

Loughborough v. Blake concerned a less-than-earthshaking issue: whether Congress had the power to impose a tax on the residents of the District of Columbia. Yes, answered Chief Justice John Marshall.

The 8th section of the 1st article [of the Constitution] gives to Congress the "power to lay and collect taxes, duties, imposts and excises" for the purposes thereinafter mentioned. This grant is general, without limitation as to place. . . .

The power then to lay and collect duties, imposts, and excises may be exercised and must be exercised throughout the United States. Does this term designate the whole or any particular portion of the American empire? Certainly this question can admit of but one answer. It is the name given to our great republic, which is composed of states and territories. The District of Columbia, or the territory west of the Missouri, is not less within the United States than Maryland or Pennsylvania, and it is not less necessary, on the principles of our Constitution, that uniformity in the imposition of imposts, duties, and excises should be observed in the one than in the other.[53]

In other words, the District of Columbia, as a federal territory, formed an integral part of "the United States," in which the Constitution applied in its entirety.

Background to the *Insular Cases*

Fast-forward eighty years. A combination of factors—a weakened Spanish Empire; independence movements in Cuba that attracted American sympathy and support; a worldwide spirit of imperialism, from whose contagion the United States was far from immune; and theories of Social Darwinism and corresponding widespread belief in Anglo-Saxon racial superiority—led the United States to go to war with Spain in 1898, and thereby to acquire territories that literally spanned the globe (Puerto Rico, Guam, and the Philippines). The ultimate decision to retain territories obtained after the Spanish-American War was far from uncontroversial. President William McKinley professed uncertainty as to how to proceed (especially regarding the Philippines); the Senate ratified the peace treaty with Spain (which awarded Puerto Rico, Guam, and the Philippines to the United States) by the barest of margins; and the wisdom and legitimacy of "American imperialism" became the subject of intense battles during the election campaign of 1900. But constitutional issues were also involved. Were these newly acquired territories part of "the United States," no less than *Loughborough* had concluded with respect to Washington, DC? Did the residents of those territories become citizens, fully clothed with the same constitutional rights as residents of "Maryland or Pennsylvania"? Put differently, did the Constitution follow the flag? In a series of early twentieth-century decisions collectively known as the *Insular Cases*, the Supreme Court answered these questions quite differently than had Chief Justice Marshall.[54] Indeed, it was the Supreme Court's conclusions in the *Insular Cases* that prompted "Mr. Dooley" to quip, "no matter whether the Constitution follows the flag or not, the Supreme Court follows the election returns."[55]

Downes v. Bidwell—Justice White Plurality Opinion (1901)

Article IX of the treaty between Spain and the United States provided: "The civil rights and political status of the native inhabitants of the territories hereby ceded to the United States shall be determined by the Congress."[56] Relying on this treaty language, a narrow (5–4) Supreme Court majority in *Downes v. Bidwell* (the first of the *Insular Cases*) determined that it was solely up to Congress to decide how Puerto Rico and, by extension, the other newly acquired territories were to be treated under the Constitution. Justice (later Chief Justice) Edward White flatly rejected the argument that a territory automatically became fully part of the United States—and its residents fully entitled to rights under the Constitution— as soon as it was acquired by treaty. Instead, writing for a plurality of the Court, White announced a (constitutionally new) distinction between "incorporated" entities—such as the existing states, or territories destined for statehood (e.g., Alaska), where the Constitution fully applied—and so-called "unincorporated" territories, subject to governance under whatever rules Congress chose to impose.

The Constitution has undoubtedly conferred on Congress the right to create such municipal organizations as it may deem best for all the territories of the United States, whether they have been incorporated or not, to give to the inhabitants as respects the local governments such degree of representation as may be conducive to the public wellbeing, to deprive such territory of representative government if it is considered just to do so, and to change such local governments at discretion....

There can ... be no controversy as to the right of Congress to locally govern the island of Puerto Rico as its wisdom may decide, and in so doing to accord only such degree of representative government as may be determined on by that body....

It seems to me impossible to conceive that the treaty-making power, by a mere cession, can incorporate an alien people into the United States without the express or implied approval of Congress.... If the treaty-making power can absolutely, without the consent of Congress, incorporate territory, and if that power may not insert conditions against incorporation, it must follow that the treaty-making power is endowed by the Constitution with the most unlimited right, susceptible of destroying every other provision of the Constitution—that is, it may wreck our institutions. If the proposition be true, then millions of inhabitants of alien territory, if acquired by treaty, can, without the desire or consent of the people of the United States speaking through Congress, be immediately and irrevocably incorporated into the United States, and the whole structure of the government be overthrown....

Where [as here] a treaty contains no conditions for incorporation and, above all, where it not only has no such conditions but expressly provides to the contrary, incorporation does not arise until, in the wisdom of Congress, it is deemed that the acquired territory has reached that state where it is proper that it should enter into and form a part of the American family.[57]

Downes v. Bidwell—Justice Brown Opinion (1901)

A separate opinion authored by Justice Henry Brown—which arrived at the same outcome but for different reasons—was freighted with race-based anxieties.

The Constitution is applicable to territories acquired by purchase or conquest only when and so far as Congress shall so direct. . . . The power to acquire territory by treaty implies not only the power to govern such territory, but to prescribe upon what terms the United States will receive its inhabitants, and what their status shall be in what Chief Justice Marshall termed the "American empire." There seems to be no middle ground between this position and the doctrine that, if their inhabitants do not become, immediately upon annexation, citizens of the United States, their children thereafter born, whether savages or civilized, are such and entitled to all the rights, privileges, and immunities of citizens. If such be their status, the consequences will be extremely serious. Indeed, it is doubtful if Congress would ever assent to the annexation of territory upon the condition that its inhabitants, however foreign they may be to our habits, traditions, and modes of life, shall become at once citizens of the United States. . . . It is obvious that in the annexation of outlying and distant possessions, grave questions will arise from differences of race, habits, laws, and customs of the people and from differences of soil, climate, and production which may require action on the part of Congress that would be quite unnecessary in the annexation of contiguous territory inhabited only by people of the same race or by scattered bodies of native Indians. . . .

In passing upon the questions involved in this and kindred cases, we ought not to overlook the fact that while the Constitution was intended to establish a permanent form of government for the states which should elect to take advantage of its conditions and continue for an indefinite future, the vast possibilities of that future could never have entered the minds of its framers. . . . Had the acquisition of other territories been contemplated as a possibility, could it have been foreseen that within little more than one hundred years we were destined to acquire not only the whole vast region between the Atlantic and Pacific Oceans, but the Russian possessions in America and distant islands in the Pacific, it is incredible that no provision should have been made for them, and the question whether the Constitution should or should not extend to them have been definitely settled. . . .

Patriotic and intelligent men may differ widely as to the desirableness of this or that acquisition, but this is solely a political question. We can only consider this aspect of the case so far as to say that no construction of the Constitution should be adopted which would prevent Congress from considering each case upon its merits, unless the language of the instrument imperatively demands it. A false step at this time might be fatal to the development of what Chief Justice Marshall called the American empire. Choice in some cases, the natural gravitation of small bodies towards large ones in others, the result of a successful war in still others, may bring about conditions which would render the annexation of distant possessions desirable. If those possessions are inhabited by alien races, differing from us in religion, customs, laws, methods of taxation, and modes of thought, the administration of government and justice according to Anglo-Saxon principles may for a time be impossible, and the question at once arises whether large concessions ought not to be made for a time, that ultimately our own theories may be carried out and the blessings of a free government under the Constitution extended to them. We decline to hold that there is anything in the Constitution to forbid such action.[58]

Downes v. Bidwell—Chief Justice Fuller Dissent (1901)

Four justices dissented. Chief Justice Melville Fuller objected to the Court's creation, out of whole cloth, of two distinct categories of territories ("incorporated" vs. "unincorporated").

The contention seems to be that if an organized and settled province of another sovereignty is acquired by the United States, Congress has the power to keep it, like a disembodied shade, in an intermediate state of ambiguous existence for an indefinite period and, more than that, that after it has been called from that limbo, commerce with it is absolutely subject to the will of Congress, irrespective of constitutional provisions. . . . Great stress is thrown upon the word "incorporation," as if possessed of some occult meaning, but I take it that the act under consideration made Puerto Rico, whatever its situation before, an organized territory of the United States. . . . That theory assumes that the Constitution created a government empowered to acquire countries throughout the world to be governed by different rules than those obtaining in the original states and territories, and substitutes for the present system of republican government a system of domination over distant provinces in the exercise of unrestricted power. . . .

Again, it is objected on behalf of the government that the possession of absolute power is essential to the acquisition of vast and distant territories, and that
we should regard the situation as it is today, rather than as it was a century ago.
"We must look at the situation as comprehending a possibility—I do not say a
probability, but a possibility—that the question might be as to the powers of this
government in the acquisition of Egypt and the Sudan, or a section of Central
Africa, or a spot in the Antarctic Circle, or a section of the Chinese Empire."
But it must be remembered that, as [Chief Justice] Marshall and [Justice] Story
declared, the Constitution was framed for ages to come, and that the sagacious
men who framed it were well aware that a mighty future waited on their work.[59]

Downes v. Bidwell—Justice Harlan Dissent (1901)

Justice John Marshall Harlan filed a separate dissent which directly took aim
at the ethnic stereotypes and prejudices prevalent in the country (and, it must
be added, among his colleagues) at the time. In his view, the Constitution
fully applied throughout "the United States"—including its territories and
possessions. Any lesser standard meant, in effect, that the United States—like
other European imperialist powers—was simply establishing its own "colonial
system."

The Constitution speaks not simply to the states in their organized capacities,
but to all peoples, whether of states or territories, who are subject to the authority of the United States. . . .

If the principles thus announced [in Justice Brown's opinion] should ever
receive the sanction of a majority of this Court, a radical and mischievous
change in our system of government will be the result. We will in that event
pass from the era of constitutional liberty guarded and protected by a written
Constitution into an era of legislative absolutism. Although from the foundation of the government this Court has held steadily to the view that the government of the United States was one of enumerated powers, and that no one of
its branches, nor all of its branches combined, could constitutionally exercise
powers not granted, or which were not necessarily implied from those expressly
granted, we are now informed that Congress possesses powers outside of the
Constitution, and may deal with new territory, acquired by treaty or conquest,
in the same manner as other nations have been accustomed to act with respect
to territories acquired by them.

In my opinion, Congress has no existence and can exercise no authority outside of the Constitution. Still less is it true that Congress can deal with new territories just as other nations have done or may do with their new territories. This

nation is under the control of a written Constitution, the supreme law of the land and the only source of the powers which our government, or any branch or officer of it, may exert at any time or at any place. . . . The idea that this country may acquire territories anywhere upon the earth, by conquest or treaty, and hold them as mere colonies or provinces—the people inhabiting them to enjoy only such rights as Congress chooses to accord to them—is wholly inconsistent with the spirit and genius, as well as with the words, of the Constitution. . . .

The glory of our American system of government is that it was created by a written Constitution which protects the people against the exercise of arbitrary, unlimited power, and the limits of which instrument may not be passed by the government it created, or by any branch of it, or even by the people who ordained it, except by amendment or change of its provisions. . . .

Whether a particular race will or will not assimilate with our people, and whether they can or cannot with safety to our institutions be brought within the operation of the Constitution, is a matter to be thought of when it is proposed to acquire their territory by treaty. . . . When the acquisition of territory becomes complete by cession, the Constitution necessarily becomes the supreme law of such new territory, and no power exists in any department of the government to make "concessions" that are inconsistent with its provisions. . . . The Constitution is supreme over every foot of territory wherever situated under the jurisdiction of the United States, and its full operation cannot be stayed by any branch of the government in order to meet what some may suppose to be extraordinary emergencies. . . .

We heard much in argument about the "expanding future of our country." It was said that the United States is to become what is called a "world power," and that if this government intends to keep abreast of the times and be equal to the great destiny that awaits the American people, it must be allowed to exert all the power that other nations are accustomed to exercise. My answer is that the fathers never intended that the authority and influence of this nation should be exerted otherwise than in accordance with the Constitution. If our government needs more power than is conferred upon it by the Constitution, that instrument provides the mode in which it may be amended and additional power thereby obtained. The people of the United States who ordained the Constitution never supposed that a change could be made in our system of government by mere judicial interpretation.[60]

Balzac v. Porto Rico (1922)

Downes v. Bidwell (like Loughborough v. Blake) concerned Congress's power to tax. It soon became evident that the majority's conclusion that the Constitution would not apply to the peoples of Puerto Rico and the other territories (unless Congress so determined) also affected more fundamental protections. In *Balzac v. Porto Rico*, the issue was whether Puerto Ricans were entitled to the jury trial rights of the Constitution (under Article III and the Sixth and Seventh Amendments). Chief Justice William Howard Taft answered this question in the negative. To be sure, Congress had made Puerto Ricans citizens of the United States in the Jones Act of 1917. But in so doing, the majority concluded, Congress had not intended to disturb the "unincorporated" status of the island—particularly if those islanders, in the Court's opinion, might not be fully capable of serving as "responsible" jurors. In other words, Congress was free to pick and choose which portions of the Constitution would, or would not, apply to Puerto Rico (and all other territories).

It is well settled that these provisions for jury trial in criminal and civil cases apply to the territories of the United States. . . . But it is just as clearly settled that they do not apply to territory belonging to the United States which has not been incorporated into the Union. . . . Neither the Philippines nor Puerto Rico was territory which had been incorporated in the Union or become a part of the United States, as distinguished from merely belonging to it. . . .

[Congress passed the Jones Act in response to] a yearning of the Puerto Ricans to be American citizens. . . . What additional rights did it give them? It enabled them to move into the continental United States and becoming residents of any state there, to enjoy every right of any other citizen of the United States, civil, social, and political. . . . In Puerto Rico, however, the Puerto Rican cannot insist upon the right of trial by jury except as his own representatives in his legislature shall confer it on him. . . . The United States has been liberal in granting to the islands acquired by the Treaty of Paris most of the American constitutional guaranties, but has been sedulous to avoid forcing a jury system on a Spanish and civil law country until it desired it. . . .

The jury system needs citizens trained to the exercise of the responsibilities of jurors. In common law countries, centuries of tradition have prepared a conception of the impartial attitude jurors must assume. The jury system postulates a conscious duty of participation in the machinery of justice which it is hard for people not brought up in fundamentally popular government at once to acquire. . . . Congress has thought that a people like the Filipinos, or the Puerto Ricans, trained to a complete judicial system which knows no juries, living in compact and ancient communities, with definitely formed customs and political conceptions, should be permitted themselves to determine how far they wish to adopt this institution of Anglo-Saxon origin, and when.[61]

Conclusion

As commentators have pointed out, Justice Harlan's dissent in *Downes v. Bidwell* echoed his earlier dissent in *Plessy v. Ferguson*.[62] In both instances, Harlan insisted on the equal application of the Constitution's provisions to all—regardless of race (in *Plessy*) and regardless of territorial status (in *Downes*). The synchronicity is not exact, however: *Plessy* was eventually overturned by the Supreme Court, but *Downes*, *Balzac*, and the rest of the *Insular Cases* remain the law of the land to this day.

Discussion Questions

1. The fight over the retention of the Philippines demonstrates that fundamental issues regarding the content and the application of the Constitution can be addressed by the executive branch (President McKinley debating whether to hold onto the Philippines); Congress (Senate treaty ratification); courts (the *Insular* decisions); voters (as William Jennings Bryan made anti-imperialism one of his main issues in the 1900 election); and government agencies (including the War Department, as advised by future Justice Felix Frankfurter). Is it wrong to think of courts as the primary means of resolving constitutional questions?

2. Many of Justice Field's concerns about Chinese immigration in *Chae Chan Ping v. United States* were echoed in Justice Brown's opinion in *Downes v. Bidwell*. What were the similarities and differences between the debates over the Chinese Exclusion Act and US territorial policy?

3. The justices in *Downes v. Bidwell* confronted a constitutional dilemma: How should the Constitution be interpreted and applied to a situation that the framers never contemplated? This question is practically as old as the Constitution itself (did the Constitution permit a National Bank?; was Jefferson's acquisition of the Louisiana Territory constitutional?), and is very much still with us (is cell phone tracking a "search"?; does the Constitution vest the president with sole authority to use nuclear weapons?). What rules should be used by Supreme Court justices in interpreting the Constitution in such situations?

4. It is sometimes argued that one virtue of the "incorporation" approach adopted in the *Insular Cases* is that it permits "unincorporated" territories to follow local traditions. Chief Justice Taft contended that forcing Puerto Rico to adopt jury trials would be inconsistent with its "customs and political conceptions"? By way of further example, as of this writing same-sex marriage is not recognized in American Samoa. But should constitutional

rights otherwise available throughout the nation be absent in jurisdictions belonging to and administered by the United States?

5. To what extent are inhabitants today of Puerto Rico, the United States Virgin Islands, Guam, the Northern Mariana Islands, and American Samoa fully part of "We the People"? Consider, for example, that nearly four million residents of these territories are US citizens, yet none can vote for president and none is represented by a voting member in Congress. Explain why that is, or is not, an acceptable situation.

6. Residents of the District of Columbia also lack voting representation in Congress (although they can cast ballots for president, courtesy of the Twenty-third Amendment). Congress, according to Article I, Section 8, enjoys the "exclusive" power to legislate for the "Seat of Government" (i.e., the national capital) "in all cases whatsoever." Washington, DC, residents argue that they, like the British colonists, face "taxation without representation"—indeed, that is stamped on their license plates. Are they right to make such a claim?

Additional Primary Source Documents

Primary source document excerpts covering the following topics are located on the website accompanying this book:

Birthright Citizenship—including the Fourteenth Amendment; *United States v. Wong Kim Ark*, 169 U.S. 649 (1898); and present-day controversy.

Native Americans—including 1867 Peace Commission; Dawes Act; *United States v. Kagama*, 118 U.S. 375 (1886); *Lone Wolf v. Hitchcock*, 187 U.S. 553 (1903); *Elk v. Wilkins*, 112 U.S. 94 (1884); and Indian Citizenship Act.

Other "Constitutional Moments" during this Era

- Regulation of businesses and corporations—including *Munn v. Illinois*, 94 U.S. 113 (1876) (state police power over private industries); *Wabash, St. Louis & Pacific Railway Co. v. Illinois*, 118 U.S. 557 (1886) (state regulation of interstate commerce); *Lochner v. New York*, 198 U.S. 45 (1905) (maximum work law unconstitutional); *Muller v. Oregon*, 208 U.S. 412 (1908) (maximum work law for women constitutional); Keating-Owen Child Labor Act (1916); *Hammer v. Dagenhart*, 247 U.S. 251 (1918) (child labor law unconstitutional).

- Regulation of labor unions—including *Commonwealth v. Hunt*, 45 Mass. 111 (1842); Haymarket trial; *In re Debs*, 158 U.S. 564 (1895) (upholding labor inunction).
- Antitrust enforcement—including Sherman Act (1890); *United States v. E.C. Knight Co.*, 156 U.S. 1 (1895); *Northern Securities Co. v. United States*, 193 U.S. 197 (1904); *Standard Oil Co. of New Jersey v. United States*, 221 U.S. 1 (1911); Clayton Act (1914).
- Income tax—including *Pollock v. Farmers' Loan & Trust Co.*, 157 U.S. 429 (1895) (striking down income tax); Sixteenth Amendment (1913).
- Other constitutional issues—including *Bailey v. Alabama*, 219 U.S. 219 (1911) (peonage statute violated Thirteenth Amendment); *Weeks v. United States*, 232 U.S. 383 (1914) (exclusionary rule).

Notes

1. Stephen Field, Chae Chan Ping v. United States, 130 U.S. 581 (1889).
2. 98 U.S. 145 (1879).
3. 140 U.S. 453 (1891).
4. 130 U.S. 581 (1889).
5. 149 U.S. 698 (1893).
6. 169 U.S. 649 (1898).
7. 118 U.S. 375 (1886).
8. Dawes Act (An Act to provide for the allotment of lands in severalty to Indians on the various reservations), ch. 199, 24 Stat. 388 (February 8, 1887), govtrackus. s3.amazonaws.com/legislink/pdf/stat/24/STATUTE-24-Pg387.pdf.
9. 163 U.S. 537 (1896).
10. 189 U.S. 475 (1903).
11. 118 U.S. 394 (1886).
12. 129 U.S. 26 (1889).
13. 158 U.S. 564 (1895).
14. Alfred T. Mahan, *The Interest of America in Sea Power, Present and Future* (Boston: Little, Brown, 1918), 257.
15. 60 U.S. 393 (1857).
16. 182 U.S. 244 (1901).
17. *Id.* (White, J., concurring).
18. 192 U.S. 1 (1904).
19. Philander C. Knox to Secretary of the Treasury, May 13, 1902, in *Official Opinions of the Attorneys General of the United States* (Washington, DC: Government Printing Office, 1903), 24:40.
20. An act to declare the purpose of the people of the United States as to the future political status of the people of the Philippine Islands, ch. 416, 39 Stat. 545 (August 29, 1916), govtrackus.s3.amazonaws.com/legislink/pdf/stat/39/STATUTE-39-Pg545.pdf.

21. Jones Act (An act to provide a civil government for Porto Rico), ch. 145, 39 Stat. 951 (March 2, 1917), govtrackus.s3.amazonaws.com/legislink/pdf/stat/39/STATUTE-39-Pg951.pdf.

22. 258 U.S. 298 (1922).

23. 215 U.S. 278 (1909).

24. 241 U.S. 591 (1916).

25. An Act to authorize the Secretary of the Interior to issue certificates of citizenship to Indians, ch. 233, 43 Stat. 253 (June 2, 1924), govtrackus.s3.amazonaws.com/legislink/pdf/stat/43/STATUTE-43-Pg253a.pdf.

26. Chinese Exclusion Act (An Act to execute certain treaty stipulations relating to Chinese), ch. 126, 22 Stat. 58 (May 6, 1882), govtrackus.s3.amazonaws.com/legislink/pdf/stat/22/STATUTE-22-Pg58c.pdf.

27. Immigration Act of 1924 (An Act to limit the immigration of aliens into the United States, and for other purposes), ch. 190, 43 Stat. 153 (May 26, 1924), govtrackus.s3.amazonaws.com/legislink/pdf/stat/43/STATUTE-43-Pg153a.pdf.

28. Yick Wo v. Hopkins, 118 U.S. 356 (1886).

29. Id.

30. Edwin R. Meade, *The Chinese Question: A Paper Read at the Annual Meeting of the Social Science Association of America* (New York, 1877), 7–12, 20.

31. Immigration Act of 1875 (An Act supplementary to the acts in relation to immigration), ch. 141, 19 Stat. 477 (March 3, 1875), govtrackus.s3.amazonaws.com/legislink/pdf/stat/18/STATUTE-18-Pg477.pdf.

32. Chinese Exclusion Act (An Act to execute certain treaty stipulations relating to Chinese), ch. 126, 22 Stat. 58 (May 6, 1882), govtrackus.s3.amazonaws.com/legislink/pdf/stat/22/STATUTE-22-Pg58c.pdf.

33. John Mitchell, "Coming of Chinese," Senate Debate, Cong. Rec., 50th Cong., 1st Sess. 406–07 (January 12, 1888), www.govinfo.gov/content/pkg/GPO-CRECB-1888-pt1-v19/pdf/GPO-CRECB-1888-pt1-v19-19-1.pdf.

34. Scott Act (An Act a supplement to an act entitled "An act to execute certain treaty stipulations Relating to Chinese"), ch. 1064; 25 Stat. 504 (October 1, 1888), govtrackus.s3.amazonaws.com/legislink/pdf/stat/25/STATUTE-25-Pg504a.pdf.

35. Grover Cleveland, "Special Message to Congress" (October 1, 1888), www.presidency.ucsb.edu/documents/special-message-1066.

36. Chae Chan Ping v. United States, 130 U.S. 581 (1889).

37. Id.

38. Fong Yue Ting v. United States, 149 U.S. 698 (1893).

39. Plessy v. Ferguson, 163 U.S. 537 (1896) (Harlan, J., dissenting).

40. Ho Yow, "Chinese Exclusion, a Benefit or a Harm?" *The North American Review* 173, no. 538 (September 1901): 314–30, www.jstor.org/stable/pdf/25105211.pdf?refreqid=excelsior%3Ab1ca15fad921fb70951a51e0fe49f18b.

41. James D. Phelan, "Why the Chinese Should Be Excluded," *The North American Review* 173, no. 540 (November 1901): 663–76, www.jstor.org/stable/pdf/25105245.pdf?refreqid=excelsior%3A487adfe0445da755e7f5fd5e1e2d6e8e.

42. Immigration Act of 1924 (An Act to limit the immigration of aliens into the United States, and for other purposes), ch. 190, 43 Stat. 153 (May 26, 1924), govtrackus. s3.amazonaws.com/legislink/pdf/stat/43/STATUTE-43-Pg153a.pdf. See generally Daniel Okrent, *The Guarded Gate: Bigotry, Eugenics, and the Law That Kept Two Generations of Jews, Italians, and Other European Immigrants Out of America* (New York: Scribner, 2019).

43. Him Mark Lai, Genny Lim, and Judy Yung, *Island: Poetry and History of Chinese Immigrants on Angel Island, 1910-1940*, 2nd ed. (Seattle: University of Washington Press, 2014). Reprinted with permission of University of Washington Press. See also "Chinese Poetry of the Detention Barracks," Angel Island Immigration Station Foundation, www.aiisf.org/poetry-4?rq=chinese%20poetry%20of%20the%20 detention%20barracks.

44. Theodore Roosevelt, "First Annual Message to Congress" (December 3, 1901), millercenter.org/the-presidency/presidential-speeches/december-3-1901-first-annual-message.

45. An Act to regulate the immigration of aliens into the United States, ch. 1012, 32 Stat. 1213, (March 3, 1903), govtrackus.s3.amazonaws.com/legislink/pdf/stat/32/STATUTE-32-Pg1213.pdf.

46. "In Defense of Anarchy," *New York Times*, December 5, 1903, timesmachine.nytimes. com/timesmachine/1903/12/05/105068311.pdf.

47. United States *ex rel.* Turner v. Williams, 194 U.S. 279 (1904).

48. An Act to exclude and expel from the United States aliens who are members of the anarchistic and similar classes, ch. 186, 40 Stat. 1012 (October 16, 1918), govtrackus. s3.amazonaws.com/legislink/pdf/stat/40/STATUTE-40-Pg1012.pdf.

49. Alexander Berkman and Emma Goldman, *Deportation: Its Menace and Meaning* (New York: Ellis Island, 1919), babel.hathitrust.org/cgi/pt?id = miua. 2917032.0001.001&view = 1up&seq = 1.

50. Theodore Roosevelt (speech to Knights of Columbus, New York, October 12, 1915), in "Roosevelt Bars the Hyphenated," *New York Times*, October 13, 1915, timesmachine. nytimes.com/timesmachine/1915/10/13/105042745.pdf.

51. Woodrow Wilson, "Address at the City Hall Auditorium" (speech, Pueblo, CO, September 25, 1919), www.presidency.ucsb.edu/documents/address-the-city-hall-auditorium-pueblo-colorado.

52. Woodrow Wilson, "Address at the St. Paul Auditorium," (speech, St. Paul, MN, September 9, 1919), www.presidency.ucsb.edu/documents/address-the-st-paul-auditorium-st-paul-minnesota.

53. Loughborough v. Blake, 18 U.S. 317 (1820).

54. See generally Sam Erman, *Almost Citizens: Puerto Rico, the U.S. Constitution, and Empire* (Cambridge, UK: Cambridge University Press, 2019).

55. Finley Peter Dunne, *Mr. Dooley at His Best* (New York: Charles Scribner's Sons, 1938), 77.

56. Treaty of Peace between the United States of America and the Kingdom of Spain, 30 Stat. 1754 (December 10, 1898), avalon.law.yale.edu/19th_century/sp1898.asp.

57. Downes v. Bidwell, 182 U.S. 244 (1901) (White, J., concurring).

58. *Id.* (Brown, J., announcing the judgment).
59. *Id.* (Fuller, C.J., dissenting).
60. *Id.* (Harlan, J., dissenting).
61. Balzac v. Porto Rico, 258 U.S. 298 (1922).
62. See Juan R. Torreulla, "Ruling America's Colonies: The *Insular Cases*," *Yale Law and Policy Review* 32 (2013): 57–95, digitalcommons.law.yale.edu/cgi/viewcontent.cgi?article = 1652&context = ylpr.

6

The Constitution during War and Peace
(1917–45)

When comparisons are made between the two most significant Progressive-era constitutional amendments, the resulting narrative can be predictable: How could "We the People" get things so right—with passage of the Nineteenth Amendment, finally recognizing the right to vote for women—and yet, simultaneously, so wrong—with the Eighteenth Amendment's blunderbuss and failed attempt to banish alcohol? But the Eighteenth and Nineteenth Amendments were of similar political provenance and of equal constitutional importance. Both Amendments were intended to achieve social transformations. And yet these Amendments met very different historical fates—fates that offer history teachers and students opportunities to reflect on the purposes, as well as the limitations, of constitutional reformation. Such opportunities for discussion are magnified when one considers that this era also witnessed other major but unsuccessful movements for constitutional change. The Equal Rights Amendment, advanced by a coalition of feminist reformers similar to the one that championed Prohibition, would never be enacted. Nor would a proposed amendment banning child labor that emerged from Congress but was never ratified by the states.

That the Great Depression gave rise to an extraordinary, transformative burst of new regulatory powers on the part of the national government is a major constitutional story in its own right. But the New Deal State engineered by Franklin Delano Roosevelt and Congress, the antagonistic reception it received from a conservative Supreme Court, and the Court's dramatic, dynamic shift in ideology in reaction to FDR's "court-packing" threat occupy familiar terrain. Less well known is the outsized role played by the Eighteenth Amendment in securing outsized authority for the federal government. The now-despised Prohibition Amendment served as the intellectual and political forerunner of a multitude of subsequent attempts by Washington to ameliorate social ills in ways never before imagined.

This era of profound constitutional change was bookended by two world wars—each of which revealed that the emergence of a stronger national government would be accompanied by constitutional disquietudes. Both wars were fought overseas but brought about substantial curtailments of civil liberties at home. Opponents of World War I experienced suppression of their speech rights

With Liberty and Justice for All?. Edited by Steven A. Steinbach, Maeva Marcus, and Robert Cohen, Oxford University Press. © Oxford University Press 2022. DOI: 10.1093/oso/9780197516317.003.0006

courtesy of the Wilson administration, a new law that criminalized sedition, and a Supreme Court that consistently backed up the government's prosecutions. The possibility of a constitutional standard somewhat more protective of free speech emerged only after the war, and only then in the opinions of dissenting justices.

During World War II, political repression melding with prejudice and xenophobia resulted in the internment of 120,000 Americans of Japanese ancestry, citizens and legal residents alike—and was blessed by the Supreme Court on the spurious grounds of "military necessity." Again, constitutional attitudes eventually shifted—indeed, in 2018, the Supreme Court labeled these detention centers "concentration camps"—but only after many years had passed and much harm had been done. In the meantime, the New Deal State had transformed itself into the National Security State, creating a host of continuing constitutional tensions involving due process and First Amendment liberties.

During the interwar years, the Supreme Court also upheld the eugenics practices pursued over several decades by various states—an episode too little studied in constitutional history, as well as in conventional political history. The forced sterilization of Carrie Buck—no less than the imprisonment of Eugene Debs and the conviction of Fred Korematsu—raised unsettling questions about the fragility of the protections provided by the Bill of Rights. Such questions are of no less importance today than a century ago.

Democracy at Home: Prohibition, War, and Women's Suffrage

Julie Suk

Professor of Law, Fordham University School of Law

World War I ushered in two major amendments to the Constitution: the Eighteenth Amendment, prohibiting the sale and manufacture of alcoholic beverages, and the Nineteenth Amendment, securing the rights of women to vote. Both of these amendments were introduced in Congress four decades earlier, but it was not until the United States entered World War I that these proposals advanced politically to meet the Constitution's demanding requirements for amendment. These amendments attempted to use the Constitution to implement grand social transformations in American society. They were adopted and ratified as the nation prepared to rebuild itself after the war. The era of implementation was a decade of unprecedented prosperity, when, in the words of President Calvin Coolidge, "the chief business of the American people [was] business."[1]

But by 1933, another constitutional amendment repealed the Prohibition Amendment, declaring the encroachment of the Constitution into the social and economic sphere of alcohol consumption to be a failed experiment. Nonetheless, the Great Depression led the American people to look to the powers of government to provide, as President Franklin Roosevelt put it, "security against the hazards and vicissitudes of life."[2] As the nation got embroiled in another global war, the 1940s tested its constitutional vision of "We the People" yet again, as fears of enemy nations led to the restriction of civil liberties of American citizens. The constitutional changes that took place between World War I and World War II reenvisioned who was included in "We the People" and what kind of government "We the People" would embrace.

The Constitutional Ambitions of Prohibitionists and Suffragists

The Eighteenth Amendment declared, "After one year from the ratification of this article the manufacture, sale, or transportation of intoxicating liquors within, the importation thereof into, or the exportation thereof from the United States and all territory subject to the jurisdiction thereof for beverage purposes is hereby prohibited." It was adopted by both houses of Congress in December 1917, and ratified by three-fourths of the states, as required by Article V of the Constitution, on January 16, 1919. By its own terms, it went into effect a year later, on January 17, 1920.

One hundred years after the fact, Prohibition appears to be the constitutional mistake of the century. The idea of outlawing booze may strike the twenty-first-century observer as a terrible idea, and to do so in the Constitution—rather than through ordinary laws—seems to misapprehend what constitutions are for. But the story of how Prohibition became a constitutional issue, building up for decades before Congress adopted it, with a strong political boost from World War I, also helps to explain other constitutional change. The Nineteenth Amendment, which secured women's right to vote, was not the only constitutional amendment driven by women and their grievances against the existing legal system. The Prohibition Amendment succeeded when it did in part because of the emerging voice of women in American constitution-making.

Both amendments were reactions to the constitutional impediments to democratic change at the state level. By the time the Eighteenth Amendment was ratified, some states, such as Kansas, already had Prohibition amendments in their state constitutions and others attempted to ban or regulate alcohol by statute. But Prohibition states could not fully enforce their own constitutions as long as alcohol from other states entered their borders through interstate commerce, which only Congress had the constitutional power to restrict. And before the Nineteenth Amendment secured the right of citizens to vote without abridgment on account of sex, states such as Wyoming already allowed women to vote. But other states had constitutional provisions limiting the vote to male citizens only. Like slavery in the nineteenth century, such fundamental differences between the states with regard to defining "We the People" proved unsustainable for a nation at war to make the world safe for democracy.

Although the women's suffrage amendment was not ratified until 1920, the first hearings on such an amendment took place in Congress in 1878. Elizabeth Cady Stanton recited the Preamble to the Constitution, beginning with the words, "We the People." She then asked, "Does anyone pretend to say that men alone constitute races and peoples? When we say parents, do we not mean mothers as well as fathers? When we say children, do we not mean girls as well as boys? When we say people, do we not mean women as well as men?"[3]

By then, women had been politically active, not only in advocating for their right to vote but also in crusading against the alcohol industry. The Woman's Christian Temperance Union was formed in 1874, and by the end of the nineteenth century, it was the largest women's organization in America, with more than ten times as many members as the largest women's suffrage organization. The women's temperance movement protested the social problems caused by alcohol, both as a beverage and as a set of institutions. Women bore the brunt of men's excessive drinking, particularly because the legal system made women powerless against these harms. Women lacked legal status and could not vote, own property in their own name, exercise parental authority over their own children, or own their own earnings if they worked outside the home.

Saloons were institutions where men spent away their time and wages on drinks, leaving less time and money for their families. Saloons were supplied, and sometimes owned, by corporate brewers and manufacturers. When drunk men managed to make it home, domestic violence was not uncommon. When drunk men did not make it home, they were sometimes permanently injured or dead, which then deprived their wives and children of their wage-earning breadwinner. When women's temperance crusaders tried to shut down saloons, the alcohol industry asserted its business and property rights, sometimes grounding these rights in the Constitution. Notwithstanding the Supreme Court's 1873 decision in *Bradwell v. Illinois* (1873),[4] upholding Illinois's exclusion of women from the legal profession (and implicitly from the protections of the Fourteenth Amendment), the first women lawyers to be admitted to practice law in other Midwestern states began to envision a federal constitutional amendment prohibiting the sale and manufacture of alcohol as the way to stop saloons from ruining the lives of women and families.

They simultaneously advocated for women's suffrage. Empowering women through the ballot would lead to "home protection." If enfranchised, women would be able to vote for laws that regulated saloons—and for other legal reforms that would give women more avenues for supporting themselves and their families if their lives were ruined by a drunk husband, such as parental rights over their own children and the right to keep their own earnings.

A movement for Prohibition grew for four decades. Temperance women joined forces with the Anti-Saloon League and religious zealots, participating in politically expedient anti-immigrant rhetoric along the way. World War I provided the final push for a constitutional amendment. After the United States entered into the war in 1917, the federal government engaged in campaigns to persuade the American people to reduce their food consumption to help win the war. Then, on the floor of the Senate that year, as the Prohibition amendment was debated, one Prohibitionist asked, "Will a sober nation not win the war quicker than a drunken nation?" and "When there is a shortage of labor in the important and necessary work to carry on the war, why waste labor in making booze?"[5] By the end of the year, both houses of Congress adopted the Prohibition Amendment and sent it to the states for ratification, which was completed in January 1919.

Women and the Reproduction of the Nation

Meanwhile, the labor shortages occasioned by war created a significant demand for women's work outside the home, adding fuel to the intensifying campaign for the suffrage amendment. "The women of this country are being called upon for every conceivable kind of service," said Mabel Vernon, representing the National Woman's Party at a suffrage hearing that was held in Congress a month after the United States entered into World War I. "We women know that during the very next few months probably we are going to be called upon to perform duties which we never have performed before." Of wartime necessity, women were taking on men's work to enable the nation's survival. Did that not entitle them to vote on the composition of the government? "The women of this country feel that when the government calls upon them for their services and places upon them the responsibility of government, it must also give to them, in decency—that is all it is—the privileges of government."[6]

Anna Howard Shaw, who had retired as president of the National American Woman Suffrage Association, told Congress in 1918 that women were "part of the people, part of the government which claims to be a democracy," and therefore the women's suffrage amendment should be passed "in order that this country may stand clean-handed before the nations of the world, and that when they go out to make the world safe for democracy they may make it safe for democracy at home." Shaw pointed out that after the war, "many women of this country will become both father and mother to fatherless children."[7] Mothers would be essential to the postwar reconstitution of the American nation, and the government could not be democratic without their votes.

"Democracy at home" referred not only to democracy within our own national borders but also to the suffragists' broader vision of the home as a space where democratic values such as equal citizenship could reshape family life. The struggle for suffrage went far beyond votes for women and included claims for justice related to women's role in reproduction.[8] Suffragists challenged the legal order that gave men complete control over their wives' bodies, earnings, and their children. The legal order that deprived women of the vote simultaneously deprived women of freedom to choose whether to engage in sexual relations that could result in pregnancy and motherhood, how many children to have, how to raise the children, and how to allocate the family's resources. Women and children increasingly participated in work outside the home for wages, which husbands and fathers owned.

The legal landscape created by the Supreme Court at the dawn of the twentieth century was hostile to laws regulating labor and burdening business interests. The Supreme Court spent the first two decades of the twentieth century striking down labor legislation that protected workers, such as minimum wage or maximum hour requirements. In *Lochner v. New York* (1905),[9] the Court held that such laws violated the freedom of contract of both worker and business owner. But in *Muller v. Oregon* (1908), the Court made an exception for women workers. Because women did not have the vote or the power to form unions and were thought to be naturally weaker owing to their capacity to bear children, the Supreme Court held that state laws that imposed maximum hours or minimum wages for women's work were constitutionally permitted. The Court reasoned that "as healthy mothers are essential to vigorous offspring, the physical well-being of woman becomes an object of public interest and care in order to preserve the strength and vigor of the race."[10] Nonetheless, in 1918, the Supreme Court struck down a federal law that regulated child labor, on the grounds that Congress lacked the power to enact such laws under its authority to regulate interstate commerce, since not all child labor involved products sold in interstate commerce.[11]

The Eighteenth and Nineteenth Amendments were adopted in this constitutional context. The Nineteenth Amendment guaranteed, "The right of citizens of the United States to vote shall not be denied or abridged by the United States or by any State on account of sex." Although it referenced only the right to vote, the Supreme Court invoked the newly minted amendment to end the prior exception it had recognized in *Muller* for the constitutionality of labor legislation protecting women only. Now recognized as voting citizens, women would no longer need special protection. In *Adkins v. Children's Hospital* (1923), the Court struck down a minimum wage law for women workers in the District of Columbia, concluding that it violated the freedom of contract that all workers possessed by virtue of the Fourteenth Amendment's Due Process Clause. The

Court also invoked the newly ratified Nineteenth Amendment to suggest that women now enjoyed equal status to men and therefore no longer required any special labor protections. "In view of the great—not to say revolutionary—changes which have taken place . . . in the contractual, political, and civil status of women, culminating in the Nineteenth Amendment, it is not unreasonable to say that these differences have now come almost, if not quite, to the vanishing point."[12] With that, the Court struck down minimum wage requirements for women, and women's wages plummeted.

The *Adkins* decision drew mixed reactions from the suffragists who had worked so hard to get the Nineteenth Amendment ratified. Some of them applauded the decision and believed that special protections for women workers constituted sex discrimination. Led by uncompromising suffragist Alice Paul, the National Woman's Party supported the Equal Rights Amendment (ERA) to the Constitution, which was introduced in Congress that same year. They wanted the ERA to strike down every law that treated women as less than fully equal citizens, such as laws that made fathers the sole legal guardians of children and laws that prevented married women from controlling their own earnings, owning property, entering contracts, or exercising a profession. Other women's organizations that had worked for suffrage denounced the *Adkins* decision and opposed the ERA, believing that women workers were more likely to be exploited and therefore required special protection to achieve real equality. The Nineteenth Amendment left a divided legacy concerning the question of government's role in overcoming disadvantages women sustained by virtue of their role in reproduction. Mothers bore the primary burdens of childbearing and childrearing. Should government facilitate, and thereby regulate, women's reproductive lives, or leave women as free as men to fend for themselves?

Some of the advocates for working women sought a constitutional amendment to increase federal governmental authority to protect another class of vulnerable persons: children. In response to the Supreme Court's invalidation of federal child labor legislation in 1918, the Child Labor Amendment proposed to give Congress the power to limit, regulate, and prohibit the labor of persons under the age of eighteen. The Child Labor Amendment had more success than the Equal Rights Amendment. Whereas the ERA did not get a vote during this period, both houses of Congress adopted the Child Labor Amendment by two-thirds majorities in 1924. But the Child Labor Amendment got only twenty-eight state ratifications before the Supreme Court overruled its prior rulings on federal power over child labor, making the amendment unnecessary.[13]

Notwithstanding its rejection of women's minimum wage laws in the 1923 *Adkins* decision, the Supreme Court established the authority of the state to regulate at least some women's reproductive lives in the case of *Buck v. Bell* (1927). The state of Virginia sterilized a mother who was deemed to be "feeble-minded" and who had birthed two illegitimate children. A Virginia statute authorized the sterilization of institutionalized persons as long as the superintendent of the institution deemed that it was for the best interest of the patients and of society. The Supreme Court upheld the constitutionality of the Virginia law, with Justice Oliver Wendell Holmes noting, "The principle that sustains compulsory vaccination is broad enough to cover cutting the Fallopian tubes. Three generations of imbeciles are enough."[14] In saying that it was within the legitimate power of the state to sterilize women deemed unfit for reproduction, *Buck v. Bell* maintained the constitutional validity of state control over reproduction and women's bodies during an era when state control over business and labor of male citizens was in question.

Prohibition and the Enlargement of Federal Power

Meanwhile, against the backdrop of the Supreme Court's hostility to laws regulating labor and business, the Prohibition Amendment brought about unprecedented governmental intrusion on business prerogatives, albeit only with regard to the alcohol industry. The Eighteenth Amendment is the only constitutional provision that actively required the federal government—and possibly also the states—to eradicate an entire industry within a prescribed time frame. By its own terms, the Eighteenth Amendment became effective one year after the date of ratification, so that the nation could prepare for the seismic shift that Prohibition would require. Congress enacted the National Prohibition Act, known as the Volstead Act,[15] which criminalized the sale and manufacture of alcohol, and enlarged the federal government's role in enforcing the criminal law.

The Volstead Act went into effect on January 17, 1920. By then, World War I had already enlarged federal power. In *Schenck v. United States* (1919), the Supreme Court observed that "When a nation is at war, many things that might be said in time of peace are such a hindrance to its effort that their utterance will not be endured so long as men fight."[16] Shortly after adopting the Prohibition Amendment and sending it to the states for ratification, Congress enacted the Sedition Act of 1918, which made it a criminal offense to "willfully utter, print, write, or publish any disloyal, profane, scurrilous, or abusive language about the form of the government of the United States" or to "willfully urge, incite, or advocate any curtailment of the production" of the things "necessary or essential to the prosecution of the war."[17] The Sedition Act was in effect only for two years, but it produced over eight hundred criminal convictions and two Supreme Court decisions that upheld the constitutionality of the law. Pacifist socialist labor leader Eugene Debs was convicted for delivering a public speech opposing the war, espousing socialist principles, and defending specific individuals who had encouraged draft avoidance or obstructed enlistment. Sentenced to ten years in prison, Debs challenged his conviction in *Debs v. United States* (1919),[18] claiming that the Sedition Act violated the First Amendment's protection of free speech. But the Supreme Court upheld his conviction. In *Abrams v. United States* (1919),[19] a few months later, the Supreme Court upheld the Sedition Act again in a case involving the conviction of defendants who had published circulars criticizing the hypocrisy of the United States in sending troops to Russia and expressing solidarity with workers fighting for freedom in Russia.

Although an armistice ended World War I at the end of 1918 and the Sedition Act was repealed in 1920, Prohibition led to a "war on alcohol."[20] The Prohibition Amendment did not prohibit the consumption of alcohol by individuals, and the Volstead Act did not criminalize home production and consumption of alcoholic beverages, but the enforcement of Prohibition against bootleggers empowered federal law enforcement authorities to invade the home as never before. In *Olmstead v. United States* (1928),[21] federal law enforcement officers had unearthed a large-scale alcohol smuggling operation by tapping the telephone lines of the accused conspirators in their homes and offices. The accused conspirators included bootleggers as well as local police officers who were profiting from the illegal liquor trade. The Supreme Court held that this extensive wiretapping by the federal government was constitutionally permitted. In a dissenting opinion, Justice Louis Brandeis argued that the government's wiretapping of home telephone conversations violated the Fourth Amendment right of people to be secure in their persons, houses, papers, and effects against unreasonable searches and seizures. Justice Brandeis proclaimed "the right to be let alone—the most comprehensive of rights and the right most valued by civilized men" and urged that wiretapping was a crime, even when carried out by law enforcement.[22]

Olmstead v. United States came at a time when political support for Prohibition was waning. The proponents of Prohibition had hoped that the Amendment would halt the liquor traffic and thereby eliminate many of society's other ills, including crimes stemming from drunkenness and domestic violence. But they did not anticipate the growth of organized crime to supply illegal liquor, the violence of organized crime groups, and the corruption of some public officials who profited from facilitating the illegal liquor trade. Within the first decade of the Eighteenth Amendment's ratification, an expansive and expensive law enforcement infrastructure emerged to counter these new vices. *Olmstead* demonstrated that the invasion of law enforcement into the private sphere of the home could now become a normal part of life under Prohibition. The very home that Prohibitionists sought to protect was under siege. By the end of the 1920s, the Association against the Prohibition Amendment amplified its campaign against Prohibition, and the Women's Organization for National Prohibition Reform was established. The movement to repeal Prohibition emphasized Prohibition's negative effects on the rule of law, as exemplified by both the local police involvement in the liquor trade and federal law enforcement's use of wiretapping and other privacy violations.

The Prohibition Amendment became the only amendment to be repealed by another amendment adopted under Article V. But although the Eighteenth Amendment was repealed in its entirety, Section 2 of the Twenty-first Amendment preserved one aspect of Prohibition by empowering states to regulate or prohibit alcohol within their territory. The other unique feature of the Twenty-first Amendment was that Congress provided for its ratification in Section 3 by conventions convened in each state for the purpose of ratifying (or rejecting) the amendment, rather than by state legislatures. Article V authorizes Congress to choose "one or the other Mode of Ratification," and the Twenty-first Amendment is the only amendment to have been added to the Constitution by conventions in the states rather than by state legislatures. The convention method was advocated by the Women's Organization for National Prohibition Reform to liberate the ratification process from the undue influence of pressure groups on state legislators.

Protecting Workers: The Constitutionality of New Deal Legislation

Even though the Twenty-first Amendment repealed the prohibition of the sale and manufacture of alcoholic beverages, it could not put the genie of an enlarged federal government back into the bottle. When Prohibition was repealed in 1933, the nation was in the midst of the Great Depression, with an unemployed and destitute citizenry crying out for any available help. The growth of government power during Prohibition set the stage for the New Deal, which legitimized expanded roles for federal and state governments in regulating business and the labor of all workers, including men as well as women and children.

The Fair Labor Standards Act of 1938[23] imposed a federal minimum wage and adopted a forty-hour workweek, requiring employers to pay overtime rates for work exceeding that limit. The Fair Labor Standards Act also prohibited most forms of child labor. Invoking the Supreme Court's precedents, opponents challenged the constitutionality of these laws, claiming that Congress lacked power under the Commerce Clause to enact such federal legislation. But in *United States v. Darby Lumber Company* (1941),[24] the Court switched course and upheld the constitutionality of the federal law requiring minimum wages and prohibiting child labor.

By 1937, the Supreme Court had overruled *Adkins v. Children's Hospital*, concluding that states could constitutionally limit the freedom of contract by enacting a minimum wage for women in order to promote the public welfare. In *West Coast Hotel v. Parrish* (1937), the Court held that the legislature was entitled to consider the situation of women in employment, "the fact that they are in the class receiving the least pay, that their bargaining power is relatively weak, and that they are the ready victims of those who would take advantage of their necessitous circumstances." That decision spoke in broader-brush terms about the legislature's entitlement to "reduce the evils of the 'sweating system,' the exploiting of workers at wages so low as to be insufficient to meet the bare cost of living."[25] By then, the Prohibition Amendment had enlarged the role of the state and federal governments in addressing social ills, and the Nineteenth Amendment began to orient judges and lawmakers toward women as full citizens, worthy of the governmental protection from exploitation that all workers deserved.

World War II and the Discriminating State

The entry of the United States into World War II raised new questions about whether and how this stronger national government would protect the rights and freedoms of its citizens. After the United States declared war on Japan, Executive Order 9066[26] and a 1942 act of Congress[27] authorized the Secretary of War to exclude residents from any area as necessary, in his judgment, to the successful prosecution of war. Military orders then evicted more than one hundred thousand American citizens with Japanese ancestry from the West Coast of the United States, removed them from their homes, and held them in detention camps. Those who violated these military orders were subject to criminal punishment.

Fred Korematsu, a US citizen of Japanese ancestry whose loyalty to the United States was never in question, was convicted of violating the relocation order. When his case reached the Supreme Court, he argued unsuccessfully that Congress, the president, and the military authorities had exceeded their war powers. In upholding the order excluding American citizens of Japanese ancestry from their homes, the Supreme Court reasoned in *Korematsu v. United States* (1944), "We are not unmindful of the hardships imposed by it upon a large group of American citizens." To justify the greater burden on Japanese Americans, the Court noted that "citizenship has its responsibilities as well as its privileges, and in time of war the burden is always heavier." While acknowledging the severity of "compulsory exclusion of large groups of citizens from their homes," the Court concluded that the government's "power to protect must be commensurate with the threatened danger."[28] Thus, if the danger knew no limits, neither would the power of the carceral state.

Fred Korematsu's conviction was overturned forty years later, and today's constitutional experts tend to agree with the three dissenting justices in *Korematsu*, who viewed the military orders excluding and detaining American citizens of Japanese ancestry as racial discrimination in violation of the Constitution's Equal Protection Clause. The *Korematsu* case introduced the analytical framework by which "all legal restrictions which curtail the civil rights of a single racial group are immediately suspect," subject to "the most rigid scrutiny," a test which is still utilized by courts today. Yet, the *Korematsu* Court found the restriction of Japanese Americans' civil liberties to be constitutionally permitted due to "pressing public necessity" and insisted that the government could impose tremendous responsibilities on some groups of citizens without such exercise of coercive state power amounting to racial antagonism. Decades later, as global instability, violence, and migration introduce new claims of pressing public necessity, the *Korematsu* framework will require more demanding scrutiny.

From World War I to World War II, the constitutional order changed considerably. The Nineteenth Amendment expanded the definition of "We the People" by enfranchising women. The Prohibition Amendment and its implementation led to an unprecedented expansion of governmental power, which did not shrink when Prohibition was repealed by the Twenty-first Amendment. Between the end of Prohibition and the onset of World War II, constitutional law secured the role of government in protecting citizens from the hazards of life and work. As "We the People" expanded to include women, immigrants, people of color, and the poor, enlarging the government's power in the postwar period carried great promise but also introduced great peril. The growing stakes of global warfare awakened deep challenges with which we continue to grapple today.

The Nineteenth Amendment and the Equal Rights Amendment—Primary Sources

In 1848, conventioneers meeting in Seneca Falls, New York, issued a manifesto demanding the franchise for women, among other reforms. A quarter century later, however, Susan B. Anthony was arrested for attempting to vote, and the Supreme Court in *Minor v. Happersett* (1875) made clear that states were perfectly free to permit only men to cast ballots. The suffrage movement finally resulted in passage of the Nineteenth Amendment. But the debate over the place of women in the constitutional scheme then shifted to the proposed Equal Rights Amendment.

Declaration of Sentiments (1848)

The foremost demand of the "Declaration of Sentiments" issued by the Seneca Falls convention concerned voting rights for women. The delegates particularly complained of the "entire disfranchisement of one-half the people of this country."

> We hold these truths to be self-evident; that all men and women are created equal; that they are endowed by their Creator with certain inalienable rights; that among these are life, liberty, and the pursuit of happiness; that to secure these rights governments are instituted, deriving their just powers from the consent of the governed. Whenever any form of government becomes destructive of these ends, it is the right of those who suffer from it to refuse allegiance to it and to insist upon the institution of a new government. . . . When a long train of abuses and usurpations, pursuing invariably the same object, evinces a design to reduce them under absolute despotism, it is their duty to throw off such government and to provide new guards for their future security. Such has been the patient sufferance of the women under this government, and such is now the necessity which constrains them to demand the equal station to which they are entitled.
>
> The history of mankind is a history of repeated injuries and usurpations on the part of man toward woman, having in direct object the establishment of an absolute tyranny over her. To prove this, let facts be submitted to a candid world.
>
> He has never permitted her to exercise her inalienable right to the elective franchise.
>
> He has compelled her to submit to laws, in the formation of which she had no voice.
>
> He has withheld from her rights which are given to the most ignorant and degraded men—both natives and foreigners.
>
> Having deprived her of this first right of a citizen, the elective franchise, thereby leaving her without representation in the halls of legislation, he has oppressed her on all sides. . . .
>
> We insist that [women] have immediate admission to all the rights and privileges which belong to them as citizens of these United States.[29]

Susan B. Anthony Protests Denial of the Vote (1873)

In the aftermath of the Civil War, the Constitution was amended to prohibit denial of the franchise to any citizen "on account of race, color, or previous condition of servitude" (Fifteenth Amendment). The Fourteenth Amendment had already prohibited the United States or any state from "abridg[ing] the privileges or immunities of citizens of the United States" or "deny[ing] to any person within its jurisdiction the equal protection of the laws." Relying on these twin constitutional provisions, Susan B. Anthony and other women activists attempted to cast ballots in the 1872 election—an act for which Anthony was prosecuted and convicted.[30] "Is it a crime to vote?" Anthony asked in a series of lectures she gave prior to her trial.

> Friends and fellow citizens: I stand before you tonight under indictment for the alleged crime of having voted at the last presidential election, without having a lawful right to vote. It shall be my work this evening to prove to you that in thus voting, I not only committed no crime, but instead simply exercised my citizen's right, guaranteed to me and all United States citizens by the national Constitution, beyond the power of any state to deny. . . .
>
> It was we, the people, not we, the white male citizens, nor yet we, the male citizens; but we, the whole people, who formed this Union. And we formed it not to give the blessings of liberty, but to secure them; not to the half of ourselves and the half of our posterity, but to the whole people—women as well as men. And it is downright mockery to talk to women of their enjoyment of the blessings of liberty while they are denied the use of the only means of securing them provided by this democratic-republican government—the ballot. . . .
>
> The only question left to be settled now is: Are women persons? And I hardly believe any of our opponents will have the hardihood to say they are not. Being persons, then, women are citizens, and no state has a right to make any new law or to enforce any old law that shall abridge their privileges or immunities. Hence, every discrimination against women in the constitutions and laws of the several states is today null and void, precisely as is every one against Negroes. Is the right to vote one of the privileges or immunities of citizens? I think the disfranchised ex-rebels and the ex-state prisoners will agree with me, that it is not only one of them, but the one without which all the others are nothing. Seek thee first the kingdom of the ballot, and all things else shall be given thee, is the political injunction. . . .
>
> We no longer petition legislature or Congress to give us the right to vote. We appeal to the women everywhere to exercise their too long neglected "citizen's right to vote."[31]

Minor v. Happersett (1875)

But in 1875, the Supreme Court concluded that because voting was not one of the "privileges or immunities" of citizenship, it was perfectly permissible for states to deny the franchise to women. Chief Justice Morrison Waite wrote for a unanimous Court.

The question is presented in this case, whether, since the adoption of the Fourteenth Amendment, a woman who is a citizen of the United States and of the state of Missouri is a voter in that state, notwithstanding the provision of the constitution and laws of the state, which confine the right of suffrage to men alone. . . . It is contended that the provisions of the constitution and laws of the state of Missouri which confine the right of suffrage and registration therefor to men, are in violation of the Constitution of the United States, and therefore void. . . .

There is no doubt that women may be citizens. They are persons, and by the Fourteenth Amendment "all persons born or naturalized in the United States and subject to the jurisdiction thereof" are expressly declared to be "citizens of the United States and of the State wherein they reside." . . . Sex has never been made one of the elements of citizenship in the United States. In this respect men have never had an advantage over women. The same laws precisely apply to both. . . . If the right of suffrage is one of the necessary privileges of a citizen of the United States, then the constitution and laws of Missouri confining it to men are in violation of the Constitution of the United States, as amended, and consequently void. The direct question is therefore presented whether all citizens are necessarily voters.

The Constitution does not define the privileges and immunities of citizens. . . . In this case we need not determine what they are, but only whether suffrage is necessarily one of them. It certainly is nowhere made so in express terms. . . . The Constitution has not added the right of suffrage to the privileges and immunities of citizenship. . . . Certainly, if the courts can consider any question settled, this is one. For nearly ninety years the people have acted upon the idea that the Constitution, when it conferred citizenship, did not necessarily confer the right of suffrage. . . .

We have given this case the careful consideration its importance demands. If the law is wrong, it ought to be changed, but the power for that is not with us. . . . No argument as to woman's need of suffrage can be considered. We can only act upon her rights as they exist. It is not for us to look at the hardship of withholding. Our duty is at an end if we find it is within the power of a state to withhold.

[We are] unanimously of the opinion that the Constitution of the United States does not confer the right of suffrage upon any one, and that the constitutions and laws of the several states which commit that important trust to men alone are not necessarily void.[32]

Carrie Chapman Catt on the Inevitability of Women's Suffrage (1917)

Over the subsequent decades, even as suffragists obtained the right for women to vote in more than a score of states, they attempted to secure passage of a national constitutional amendment. Carrie Chapman Catt, who served as president of the National American Woman Suffrage Association and later founded the League of Women Voters, delivered this appeal to Congress in 1917.

Woman suffrage is inevitable.... Three distinct causes made it inevitable.

1. The history of our country.... With such a history behind it, how can our nation escape the logic it has never failed to follow, when its last un-enfranchised class calls for the vote? Behold our Uncle Sam floating the banner with one hand, "Taxation without representation is tyranny," and with the other seizing the billions of dollars paid in taxes by women to whom he refuses "representation." Behold him again welcoming the boys of twenty-one and the newly made immigrant citizen to "a voice in their own government," while he denies that fundamental right of democracy to thousands of women public school teachers from whom many of these men learn all they know of citizenship and patriotism, to women college presidents, to women who preach in our pulpits, interpret law in our courts, preside over our hospitals, write books and magazines, and serve in every uplifting moral and social enterprise. Is there a single man who can justify such inequality of treatment, such outrageous discrimination? ...

2. The suffrage for women already established in the United States [in many states] makes woman suffrage for the nation inevitable.... It is too obvious to require demonstration that woman suffrage, now covering half our territory, will eventually be ordained in all the nation. No one will deny it. The only question left is when and how will it be completely established.

3. The leadership of the United States in world democracy compels the enfranchisement of its own women. The maxims of the Declaration were once called "fundamental principles of government." They are now called "American principles" or even "Americanisms." They have become the slogans of every movement toward political liberty the world around, of every effort to widen

the suffrage for men or women in any land. . . . Do you realize that in no other country in the world with democratic tendencies is suffrage so completely denied as in a considerable number of our own states?

"There is one thing mightier than kings and armies"—aye, than Congresses and political parties—"the power of an idea when its time has come to move." The time for woman suffrage has come.[33]

Opposition: Women's Suffrage Unnecessary (1917)

But suffrage advocates faced substantial opposition. Some groups, such as the National Association Opposed to Woman Suffrage, argued, among other things, that voting by women would simply be duplicative of male votes.

Votes of women can accomplish no more than votes of men. Why waste time, energy, and money without result?

Vote no on woman suffrage: because 90 percent of the women either do not want it or do not care; because it means competition of women with men instead of cooperation; because 80 percent of the women eligible to vote are married and can only double or annul their husband's votes; because it can be of no benefit commensurate with the additional expense involved; because in some states more voting women than voting men will place the government under petticoat rule; because it is unwise to risk the good we already have for the evil which may occur.[34]

Opposition: Women's Suffrage
Harmful (1917)

The Women Voters Anti-Suffrage Party of New York contended that the suffrage campaign undermined American military efforts during World War I—in part out of concern that women voters might support pacifist candidates.

Whereas, this country is now engaged in the greatest war in history, and

Whereas, the advocates of the federal amendment, though urging it as a war measure, announce . . . that its passage "means a simultaneous campaign in forty-eight states. It demands organization in every precinct; activity, agitation, education in every corner. Nothing less than this nationwide, vigilant, unceasing campaign will win the ratification."

Therefore be it resolved, that our country in this hour of peril should be spared the harassing of its public men and the distracting of its people from work for the war, and further

Resolved, that the United States Senate be respectfully urged to pass no measure involving such a radical change in our government while the attention of the patriotic portion of the American people is concentrated on the all-important task of winning the war, and during the absence of over a million men abroad.[35]

Opposition: Southern Race-Based Concerns (1915)

Some Southerners opposed women's suffrage out of fear it would set a precedent for additional voting and social changes, as revealed in this 1915 appeal from the Georgia Association Opposed to Woman's Suffrage.

Vote against woman suffrage—
   Because the women of Georgia do not want the vote. . . .
   Because universal suffrage wipes out the disenfranchisement of the negro by state law.
   Because of the danger to farmers' families if negro men vote in addition to two million negro women. . . .
   Because the South has been notified that federal authorities will supervise elections.
   Because white supremacy must be maintained.[36]

Opposition: States' Rights Concerns (1920)

Still others—including, in this instance, the Maryland state legislature, which refused to ratify the proposed amendment—objected that the Constitution permitted no interference with a state's determination of eligibility for voting.

Be it resolved by the General Assembly of Maryland, That we deny that the Congress of the United States has any lawful right or power to propose such an amendment to the Constitution. . . .
   The right of a state to determine for itself by the vote of its own people who shall vote at its own state, county, and municipal elections is one of those functions . . . essential to their separate and independent existence as states. . . .
   When we surrender to any outside power the right to say who shall vote at our state elections, we surrender the right to determine who shall govern the state, and, without the right of local self-government, we cease to become a state and become a mere province, with far less power to determine our own destiny than we had prior to the American Revolution under that charter granted by the British Crown.[37]

Nineteenth Amendment (1920)

Despite such various appeals, in August 1920, following ratification by three fourths of the states, the Constitution was amended to provide for voting rights for women. The language of the Nineteenth Amendment paralleled the voting rights provisions of the Fifteenth Amendment. Interestingly, there has been no significant resistance to or litigation challenging the application of the Nineteenth Amendment, in stark contrast to the Fifteenth Amendment.

Rights for Women beyond Voting

In the Declaration of Sentiments, the delegates to the Seneca Falls convention had called for far more than equality of voting rights. What about equal rights with respect to property ownership, marriage, divorce, inheritance, education, employment, jury service, etc.? In *Martin v. Commonwealth of Massachusetts* (1805), the Supreme Judicial Court of Massachusetts ruled, for example, that married women had no political rights of their own, but rather a "duty, which by the laws of their country and the laws of God [they] . . . owed to their husbands."[38]

Crystal Eastman: Voting Is Not Enough (1920)

Some suffragists, including Crystal Eastman, an attorney and a socialist, argued that passage of the Nineteenth Amendment should serve as the beginning of the story of equality for women, not its end.

> Most women will agree that August 23, the day when the Tennessee legislature finally enacted the federal suffrage amendment, is a day to begin with, not a day to end with. Men are saying perhaps, "Thank God, this everlasting woman's fight is over!" But women, if I know them, are saying, "Now at last we can begin." In fighting for the right to vote most women have tried to be either non-committal or thoroughly respectable on every other subject. Now they can say what they are really after; and what they are after, in common with all the rest of the struggling world, is freedom. . . .
>
> What is the problem of women's freedom? It seems to me to be this: how to arrange the world so that women can be human beings, with a chance to exercise their infinitely varied gifts in infinitely varied ways, instead of being destined by the accident of their sex to one field of activity—housework and child-raising. And second, if and when they choose housework and child-raising, to have that occupation recognized by the world as work, requiring

a definite economic reward and not merely entitling the performer to be dependent on some man. . . .

Freedom of choice in occupation and individual economic independence for women: How shall we approach this next feminist objective? By breaking down all remaining barriers, actual as well as legal, which make it difficult for women to enter or succeed in the various professions, to go into and get on in business, to learn trades and practice them, to join trades unions. Chief among these remaining barriers is inequality in pay.[39]

Proposed Equal Rights Amendment (1923)

If the Nineteenth Amendment, echoing the Fifteenth, prohibited denial of the franchise on the basis of gender no less than on race, what about the Fourteenth Amendment's protection of equal rights regardless of race? Should not similar constitutional language provide for equality of rights regardless of gender? Many women thus began advocating for a companion constitutional provision, which eventually became known as the Equal Rights Amendment, first proposed in 1923 by Alice Paul, head of the National Woman's Party. "Men and women shall have equal rights throughout the United States and every place subject to its jurisdiction."[40]

Doris Stevens Supports the Equal Rights Amendment (1924)

Many feminists and women's organizations welcomed the additional proposed amendment, including Doris Stevens of the National Woman's Party.

When women finally got the right to vote, after seventy-five years of agitation in the United States, many good citizens sighed with relief and said, "Now that's over. The woman problem is disposed of." But was it? Exactly what do women want now? Just this. They ask the same rights in law and in custom with which every man is now endowed through the accident of being born a male. Frail and inadequate as these rights may be compared to those rights we would like to see enjoyed by all men, women are nevertheless still deprived of many of them. To establish equality between men and women in law and in custom is the task undertaken by the National Woman's Party, an organization composed of women diverse in political, religious, and economic faith, but united on the platform of improving the position of women. There is not a single state in the Union in which men and women live under equal protection of the law. . . . Woman is still conceived to be in subjection to and under the control of the husband, if married, or of the male members of the family, if unmarried. In most of the states the father and mother have been made equal guardians of their children, but many of these states still deny the mother equal rights to the earnings and services of the children.... In New York, fathers are preferred to mothers as controllers of the services, earnings, and real estate of the children.... In forty states the husband owns the services of his wife in the home.... More than half the states do not permit women to serve on juries.... In only a third of the states is prostitution a crime for the male as well as the female.

With the removal of all legal discriminations against women solely on account of sex, women will possess with men: equal control of their children; equal control of their property; equal control of their earnings; equal right to make contracts; equal citizenship rights; equal inheritance rights; equal control of national, state, and local government; equal opportunities in schools and universities; equal opportunities in government service; equal opportunities in professions and industries; equal pay for equal work....

The final objection says: Grant political, social, and civil equality to women, but do not give equality to women in industry. Here lies the heart of the whole controversy. It is not astonishing, but very intelligent indeed, that the battle should center on the point of woman's right to sell her labor on the same terms as man. For unless she is able equally to compete, to earn, to control, and to invest her money, unless in short woman's economic position is made more secure, certainly she cannot establish equality in fact. She will have won merely the shadow of power without essential and authentic substance. Those who would limit only women to certain occupations and to certain restricted hours of work base their program of discrimination on two points, the "moral hazard" to women and their biological inferiority. It is a philosophy which would penalize all women because some women are morally frail and physically weak.[41]

Alice Hamilton Opposes the Equal Rights Amendment (1924)

At the time, though, other prominent women's and labor organizations opposed the amendment, believing that it would deny to women various special protections they had earlier won in legislatures and courts. For example, in *Muller v. Oregon*, the Supreme Court upheld the constitutionality of a law limiting women factory workers to ten-hour workdays.[42] Alice Hamilton, a physician and the first woman appointed to Harvard University's faculty, argued against the proposed amendment in order not to lose such "protective laws."

There is a difference of opinion between two groups of women in this country with regard to the best way to secure for women freedom from discriminatory laws which hamper them as women and which serve as anachronisms in a modern society. The goal of all feminists is the same, the securing for women of as great a degree of self-determination as can be enjoyed in complex community life without detriment to others, and freedom from handicaps in the industrial struggle. The method whereby this is to be secured is the point of controversy.... If no legislation is to be permitted except it apply to both sexes, we shall find it impossible to regulate by law the hours or wages or conditions of work of women and that would be, in my opinion, a harm far greater than the good that might be accomplished by removing certain antiquated abuses and injustices which, bad as they are, do not injure nearly so many women as would be affected if all protective laws for working women were rendered unconstitutional.

It is not really accurate to call this an amendment for "equal rights" for both sexes, when practically it forbids one sex to proceed along lines already tried and approved unless the other sex will come too. Organized working men in the United States long since adopted the policy of seeking improvement in hours, wages, and conditions of work through their unions and not by legislation. Women, whose labor organizations are young and feeble, have sought to secure reforms through legislation. This amendment would make it impossible for them to do so. ...

The belief in the "equality of the sexes," interpreted to mean their essential identity, is very attractive to many people. When I first entered the labor field my inclination was in that direction, for I come of a family of suffragists; my grandmother was a close friend of Susan B. Anthony, and I had certainly never wished for any sort of privilege or special protection during my own career as a professional woman. ... [But] I must, as a practical person, familiar with the great, inarticulate body of working women, reiterate my belief that they are largely helpless, that they have very special needs which unaided they cannot attain, and that it would be a crime for the country to pass legislation which would not only make it impossible to better their lot in the near future but would even deprive them of the small measure of protection they now enjoy.[43]

Equal Rights Amendment Approved by Congress (1972)

In 1972, Congress finally passed the Equal Rights Amendment and sent it to the states for ratification.

Equality of rights under the law shall not be denied or abridged by the United States or by any state on account of sex. The Congress shall have the power to enforce, by appropriate legislation, the provisions of this article.[44]

US Commission on Civil Rights Supports the ERA (1978)

Proponents of the ERA argued that a constitutional amendment was necessary to obtain full legal equality between men and women. In a 1978 report, the United States Commission on Civil Rights concluded:

> Discrimination on the basis of sex continues to be a major national problem al-most seven years after Congress proposed the Equal Rights Amendment. A re-cent Civil Rights Commission review of statistical measurements of equality provides clear documentation of continuing and serious problems of sex-based inequality in employment, education, and housing. These inequities exist de-spite the passage of federal and state legislation to combat certain forms of sex discrimination. . . . [It is a] myth that women already have equality under law. In federal statutes alone, the Civil Rights Commission has identified over eight hundred sections of the US Code containing examples of substantive sex bias or sex-based terminology that are inconsistent with a national commitment to equal rights, responsibilities, and opportunities. . . .
>
> The Fifth and Fourteenth Amendments have never been interpreted to pro-hibit all discrimination against women as a class. . . . Ratification of the Equal Rights Amendment will set a standard for review of sex discrimination claims that clearly goes beyond current interpretations of the Fifth and Fourteenth Amendments in such cases. The ERA standard would prohibit sex-based classifications, except where the constitutional right to privacy or physical char-acteristics unique to one sex are concerned. The amendment will provide a firm root for the doctrine of equal protection for women and men under the law.[45]

Phyllis Schlafly Opposes the ERA (1972)

But substantial opposition to the ERA soon developed, spearheaded by Phyllis Schlafly, a conservative constitutional lawyer who founded an organization called STOP ERA. Schlafly (and others) argued that the proposed amendment would bring about unwelcome and unintended societal consequences.

> In the last couple of years, a noisy movement has sprung up agitating for "women's rights." Suddenly, everywhere we are afflicted with aggressive females

on television talk shows yapping about how mistreated American women are, suggesting that marriage has put us in some kind of "slavery," that housework is menial and degrading, and—perish the thought—that women are discriminated against. New "women's liberation" organizations are popping up, agitating and demonstrating, serving demands on public officials, getting wide press coverage always, and purporting to speak for some one hundred million American women. It's time to set the record straight. The claim that American women are downtrodden and unfairly treated is the fraud of the century. The truth is that American women never had it so good. Why should we lower ourselves to "equal rights" when we already have the status of special privilege?

The proposed Equal Rights Amendment states: "Equality of rights under the law shall not be denied or abridged by the United States or by any state on account of sex." So what's wrong with that? Well, here are a few examples of what's wrong with it. This amendment will absolutely and positively make women subject to the draft. Why any woman would support such a ridiculous and un-American proposal as this is beyond comprehension. Why any congressman who had any regard for his wife, sister, or daughter would support such a proposition is just as hard to understand. Foxholes are bad enough for men, but they certainly are not the place for women—and we should reject any proposal which would put them there in the name of "equal rights." . . .

Another bad effect of the Equal Rights Amendment is that it will abolish a woman's right to child support and alimony and substitute what the women's libbers think is a more "equal" policy, that "such decisions should be within the discretion of the court and should be made on the economic situation and need of the parties in the case." Under present American laws, the man is always required to support his wife and each child he caused to be brought into the world. Why should women abandon these good laws—by trading them for something so nebulous and uncertain as the "discretion of the court"? The law now requires a husband to support his wife as best as his financial situation permits, but a wife is not required to support her husband (unless he is about to become a public charge). A husband cannot demand that his wife go to work to help pay for family expenses. He has the duty of financial support under our laws and customs. Why should we abandon these mandatory wife-support and child-support laws so that a wife would have an "equal" obligation to take a job? By law and custom in America, in case of divorce the mother always is given custody of her children unless there is overwhelming evidence of mistreatment, neglect, or bad character. This is our special privilege because of the high rank that is placed on motherhood in our society. Do women really want to give up this special privilege and lower themselves to "equal rights" so that the mother gets one child and the father gets the other? I think not. . . .

Women's libbers do not speak for the majority of American women. American women do not want to be liberated from husbands and children. We do not want to trade our birthright of the special privileges of American women—for the mess of pottage called the Equal Rights Amendment.[46]

In the end, the proposed Equal Rights Amendment failed to secure ratification from three-fourths of the states in a timely manner, and thus has not been added—at least yet—to the Constitution.

Discussion Questions

1. Julie Suk directly ties together the Eighteenth (Prohibition) and Nineteenth (women's suffrage) Amendments, and places them both in the larger context of World War I (making the world "safe for democracy"). Her argument reminds us how important it is not to look at constitutional change (such as suffrage) in a vacuum. What are the merits of her point that the temperance and Prohibition movements deserve far less criticism because they got women involved in political activity and ultimately secured for them the right to vote?

2. In rejecting the right of women to vote, the Supreme Court in *Minor v. Happersett* observed that voting is not a "privilege and immunity" of citizenship. It still is not. Even now, there is no explicit constitutional right to vote (which explains why, under certain circumstances, the vote can be denied to felons, those who fail to register in advance or present proper identification at the polls, etc.). Should voting be a fundamental, constitutional right—and why or why not?

3. Often overlooked in considering the history of the Nineteenth Amendment is the fact that by the time the amendment was ratified in 1920, almost thirty states (beginning with Wyoming in 1869) had already granted women the vote, either in all or some elections. What conclusions can be drawn about the place of federalism in our system of government from the fact that so many states granted women the right to vote before the Constitution was amended?

4. Given the length of time it took to secure passage of Nineteenth Amendment and the failure of the Equal Rights Amendment to attain ratification (not to mention the lack of any new amendment on any subject since 1992), the question arises: Is it too difficult to amend the Constitution? Or is the constitutional system safeguarded somehow by the fact that great consensus apparently is required before the Constitution can be changed?

5. Many Black soldiers who fought in World War I returned home to face continued segregation (or worse) in the South and continued discrimination in the North, the armed forces, and government service. If, as Suk suggests, the war led to more rights for women, why was the same not true for African Americans?

6. Why were feminists and women's groups split in the 1920s, and again in the 1970s, over the wisdom of and the need for an Equal Rights Amendment? Why did the Nineteenth Amendment leave a "divided legacy" for women's groups?

7. As Suk notes, the air went out of the proposed child labor amendment after the Supreme Court upheld federal statutes prohibiting underage workers. Beginning in the early 1970s, the Supreme Court struck down as a denial of "equal protection" various state and federal laws that treated men and women disparately. In light of these decisions, coupled with federal civil rights legislation regarding employment (Title VII) and athletics (Title IX), is passage of an Equal Rights Amendment still necessary? Why or why not?

8. When Congress sent the ERA to the states in 1972, it specified a seven-year window (later extended by Congress until 1982) by which time three-quarters of the states were required to ratify the amendment. But only thirty-five (of the necessary thirty-eight) states had ratified the amendment before the time expired—and five of those states, in the meantime, had rescinded their earlier ratifications. In the past several years, however, several additional state legislatures have approved the ERA, and in 2020 Virginia became the thirty-eighth state to ratify the amendment, which raises a number of unprecedented constitutional issues: Is Congress permitted to place a time limit on an amendment's ratification? (Article V of the Constitution mentions nothing about a time limit for ratification.) Could Congress now pass legislation retroactively eliminating the ratification deadline? May a state rescind its earlier ratification of a federal constitutional amendment? And who is ultimately responsible for determining whether a new amendment to the Constitution has been ratified or not?

Confinement of Japanese Americans during World War II—Primary Sources

Just as had been true for those of Chinese ancestry, Japanese persons in the United States faced substantial discrimination and segregation in the early decades of the twentieth century. By 1924, Congress had forbidden further immigration to the country by persons of Japanese descent, as well as any path to citizenship for those already present. As military and economic tensions between the United States and the Empire of Japan rose during the 1930s, persons of Japanese ancestry experienced increased harassment, particularly on the west coast.[47] In the wake of Japan's attack on Pearl Harbor, more than one hundred thousand persons of Japanese ancestry residing in the United States—the majority of them US citizens—were confined by the Army in detention centers throughout most of World War II.

Executive Order 9066 (1942)

Once the United States entered the war, military officials responsible for defending the west coast against possible enemy sabotage or invasion urged that all persons of Japanese ancestry be relocated from their homes and neighborhoods in certain areas of California, Oregon, and Washington to government-run confinement camps. Responding to this request, President Franklin Roosevelt issued Executive Order 9066 in February 1942. The order referred generically to the exclusion of "any or all persons" designated by the military, without specifically acknowledging that only persons of Japanese ancestry were intended to be affected.

> Whereas, the successful prosecution of the war requires every possible protection against espionage and against sabotage to national-defense material, national-defense premises, and national-defense utilities....
>
> Now, therefore, by virtue of the authority vested in me as President of the United States, and Commander in Chief of the Army and Navy, I hereby authorize and direct the Secretary of War and the military commanders whom he may from time to time designate, whenever he or any designated commander deems such actions necessary or desirable, to prescribe military areas in such places and of such extent as he or the appropriate military commander may determine, from which any or all persons may be excluded, and with such respect to which the right of any person to enter, remain in, or leave shall be subject to whatever restrictions the Secretary of War or the appropriate military commander may impose in his discretion. The Secretary of War is hereby authorized to provide for residents of any such area who are excluded therefrom such transportation, food, shelter, and other accommodations as may be necessary, in the judgment of the Secretary of War or the said military commander, and until other arrangements are made, to accomplish the purpose of this order.[48]

Congress contemporaneously made violation of a military exclusion order a criminal offense.[49]

The Army's Evacuation Order (1942)

Acting pursuant to this authority, the US Army subsequently ordered that "all persons of Japanese ancestry" evacuate from certain designated areas and assemble at "reception centers" in order to be relocated.

Instructions to all persons of Japanese ancestry living in the following area: all that portion of the city and county of San Francisco, lying generally west of the of the north-south line established by Junipero Serra Boulevard, Worchester Avenue, and Nineteenth Avenue [etc.]. . . .

All Japanese persons, both alien and non-alien, will be evacuated from the above designated area by 12:00 o'clock noon Tuesday, April 7, 1942. . . .

The Civil Control Station is equipped to assist the Japanese population affected by this evacuation in the following ways: 1. Give advice and instructions on the evacuation. 2. Provide services with respect to the management, leasing, sale, storage, or other disposition of most kinds of property including real estate, business and professional equipment, household goods, boats, automobiles, livestock, etc. 3. Provide temporary residence elsewhere for all Japanese in family groups. 4. Transport persons and a limited amount of clothing and equipment to their new residence as specified below.

The following instructions must be observed: 1. A responsible member of each family, preferably the head of the family or the person in whose name most of the property is held, and each individual living alone must report to the civil control station to receive further instructions. . . . 2. Evacuees must carry with them on departure for the reception center the following property: a. bedding and linens (no mattress) for each member of the family. b. toilet articles for each member of the family. c. extra clothing for each member of the family. d. sufficient knives, forks, spoons, plates, bowls, and cups for each member of the family. e. essential personal effects for each member of the family. . . . 4. Each family, and individual living alone, will be furnished transportation to the reception center. . . .

J. L. DeWitt Lieutenant General, US Army, Commanding[50]

Thereupon followed the largest forced migration—and resulting confinement—in the history of the country, exceeding (at least in numbers) even the Trail of Tears. Approximately 120,000 persons were interned, well more than half of whom were citizens of the United States.

Final Report of the Army (1943)

In order to defend against various court challenges to its evacuation and detention policies, the Army eventually prepared a four-hundred-page *Final Report: Japanese Evacuation from the West Coast 1942* that justified its actions on the grounds of "military necessity."

In the Monterey area in California a Federal Bureau of Investigation spot raid made about February 12, 1942, found more than sixty thousand rounds of ammunition and many rifles, shotguns and maps of all kinds. These raids had not succeeded in arresting the continuance of illicit signaling. . . . It became increasingly apparent that adequate security measures could not be taken unless the federal government placed itself in a position to deal with the whole problem.

The Pacific coast had become exposed to attack by enemy successes in the Pacific. The situation in the Pacific theatre had gravely deteriorated. There were hundreds of reports nightly of signal lights visible from the coast, and of intercepts of unidentified radio transmissions. Signaling was often observed at premises which could not be entered without a warrant because of mixed occupancy. The problem required immediate solution. It called for the application of measures not then in being.

Further, the situation was fraught with danger to the Japanese population itself. The combination of spot raids revealing hidden caches of contraband, the attacks on coastwise shipping, the interception of illicit radio transmissions, the nightly observation of visual signal lamps from constantly changing locations, and the success of the enemy offensive in the Pacific had so aroused the public along the west coast against the Japanese that it was ready to take matters into its own hands. Press and periodical reports of the public attitudes along the west coast from December 7, 1941, to the initiation of controlled evacuation clearly reflected the intensity of feeling. Numerous incidents of violence involving Japanese and others occurred. . . .

Because of the ties of race, the intense feeling of filial piety, and the strong bonds of common tradition, culture, and customs, this population presented a tightly knit racial group. It included in excess of 115,000 persons deployed along the Pacific coast. Whether by design or accident, virtually always their communities were adjacent to very vital shore installations, war plants, etc. While it is believed that some were loyal, it was known that many were not. To complete the situation no ready means existed for determining the loyal and the disloyal with any degree of safety. It was necessary to face the realities—a positive determination could not have been made.

It could not be established, of course, that the location of thousands of Japanese adjacent to strategic points verified the existence of some vast conspiracy to which all of them were parties. Some of them doubtless resided there through mere coincidence. It seems equally beyond doubt, however, that the presence of others was not mere coincidence. . . .

It was certainly evident that the Japanese population of the Pacific coast was, as a whole, ideally situated with reference to points of strategic importance to carry into execution a tremendous program of sabotage on a mass scale should any considerable number of them have been inclined to do so. . . .

It was, perforce, a combination of factors and circumstances with which the commanding general had to deal. Here was a relatively homogeneous, unassimilated element bearing a close relationship through ties of race, religion, language, custom, and indoctrination to the enemy.[51]

Korematsu v. United States—Majority Opinion (1944)

In *Korematsu v. United States* (1944), the Supreme Court by a 6–3 vote affirmed the criminal conviction of Fred Korematsu, an American citizen of Japanese descent who had been charged with remaining in a "military area" contrary to an exclusion order. The majority opinion, written by Justice Hugo Black, deferred to the government's invocation of "military necessity."

We are unable to conclude that it was beyond the war power of Congress and the executive to exclude those of Japanese ancestry from the west coast war area at the time they did. . . . Exclusion from a threatened area, no less than curfew, has a definite and close relationship to the prevention of espionage and sabotage. The military authorities charged with the primary responsibility of defending our shores concluded that curfew provided inadequate protection and ordered exclusion. . . . We cannot reject as unfounded the judgment of the military authorities and of Congress that there were disloyal members of that population, whose number and strength could not be precisely and quickly ascertained. We cannot say that the war-making branches of the government did not have ground for believing that in a critical hour such persons could not readily be isolated and separately dealt with, and constituted a menace to the national defense and safety which demanded that prompt and adequate measures be taken to guard against it. . . .

We uphold the exclusion order as of the time it was made and when the petitioner violated it. In doing so, we are not unmindful of the hardships imposed by it upon a large group of American citizens. But hardships are part of war, and war is an aggregation of hardships. All citizens alike, both in and out of uniform, feel the impact of war in greater or lesser measure. Citizenship has its responsibilities as well as its privileges, and in time of war the burden is always heavier. Compulsory exclusion of large groups of citizens from their homes, except under circumstances of direst emergency and peril, is inconsistent with our basic governmental institutions. But when, under conditions of modern warfare, our shores are threatened by hostile forces, the power to protect must be commensurate with the threatened danger. . . .

It is said that we are dealing here with the case of imprisonment of a citizen in a concentration camp solely because of his ancestry, without evidence or inquiry concerning his loyalty and good disposition towards the United States. Our task would be simple, our duty clear, were this a case involving the imprisonment of a loyal citizen in a concentration camp because of racial prejudice. Regardless of the true nature of the assembly and relocation centers—and we deem it unjustifiable to call them concentration camps, with all the ugly connotations that term implies—we are dealing specifically with nothing but an exclusion order. To cast this case into outlines of racial prejudice, without reference to the real military dangers which were presented, merely confuses the issue. Korematsu was not excluded from the military area because of hostility to him or his race. He was excluded because we are at war with the Japanese Empire, because the properly constituted military authorities feared an invasion of our west coast and felt constrained to take proper security measures, because they decided that the military urgency of the situation demanded that all citizens of Japanese ancestry be segregated from the west coast temporarily, and finally, because Congress, reposing its confidence in this time of war in our military leaders—as inevitably it must—determined that they should have the power to do just this. There was evidence of disloyalty on the part of some, the military authorities considered that the need for action was great, and time was short. We cannot—by availing ourselves of the calm perspective of hindsight—now say that at that time these actions were unjustified.[52]

Korematsu v. United States—Murphy Dissent (1944)

Justices Frank Murphy, Owen Roberts, and Robert Jackson dissented. Justice Murphy concluded that the military's detention order unconstitutionally discriminated on the basis of race.

This exclusion of "all persons of Japanese ancestry, both alien and non-alien," from the Pacific coast area on a plea of military necessity in the absence of martial law ought not to be approved. Such exclusion goes over "the very brink of constitutional power" and falls into the ugly abyss of racism.

In dealing with matters relating to the prosecution and progress of a war, we must accord great respect and consideration to the judgments of the military authorities who are on the scene and who have full knowledge of the military facts. The scope of their discretion must, as a matter of necessity and common sense, be wide. And their judgments ought not to be overruled lightly by those whose training and duties ill-equip them to deal intelligently with matters so vital to the physical security of the nation.

At the same time, however, it is essential that there be definite limits to military discretion, especially where martial law has not been declared. Individuals must not be left impoverished of their constitutional rights on a plea of military necessity that has neither substance nor support. Thus, like other claims conflicting with the asserted constitutional rights of the individual, the military claim must subject itself to the judicial process of having its reasonableness determined and its conflicts with other interests reconciled.

"What are the allowable limits of military discretion, and whether or not they have been overstepped in a particular case, are judicial questions." The judicial test of whether the government, on a plea of military necessity, can validly deprive an individual of any of his constitutional rights is whether the deprivation is reasonably related to a public danger that is so "immediate, imminent, and impending" as not to admit of delay and not to permit the intervention of ordinary constitutional processes to alleviate the danger. Civilian Exclusion Order No. 34, banishing from a prescribed area of the Pacific coast "all persons of Japanese ancestry, both alien and non-alien," clearly does not meet that test. Being an obvious racial discrimination, the order deprives all those within its scope of the equal protection of the laws as guaranteed by the Fifth Amendment. It further deprives these individuals of their constitutional rights to live and work where they will, to establish a home where they choose, and to move about freely. In excommunicating them without benefit of hearings, this order also deprives them of all their constitutional rights to procedural due process. Yet no reasonable relation to an "immediate, imminent, and impending" public danger is evident to support this racial restriction, which is one of the most sweeping and complete deprivations of constitutional rights in the history of this nation in the absence of martial law.

It must be conceded that the military and naval situation in the spring of 1942 was such as to generate a very real fear of invasion of the Pacific coast, accompanied by fears of sabotage and espionage in that area. The military command was therefore justified in adopting all reasonable means necessary to combat these dangers. In adjudging the military action taken in light of the then apparent dangers, we must not erect too high or too meticulous standards; it is necessary only that the action have some reasonable relation to the removal of the dangers of invasion, sabotage, and espionage. But the exclusion, either temporarily or permanently, of all persons with Japanese blood in their veins has no such reasonable relation. And that relation is lacking because the exclusion order necessarily must rely for its reasonableness upon the assumption that all persons of Japanese ancestry may have a dangerous tendency to commit sabotage and espionage and to aid our Japanese enemy in other ways. It is difficult to believe that reason, logic, or experience could be marshalled in support of such an assumption.[53]

Korematsu v. United States—Jackson Dissent (1944)

Justice Robert Jackson filed a separate dissent in which he argued that courts should not become involved in reviewing and enforcing military orders, lest claims of "military necessity" end up swallowing constitutional principles.

Much is said of the danger to liberty from the Army program for deporting and detaining these citizens of Japanese extraction. But a judicial construction of the due process clause that will sustain this order is a far more subtle blow to liberty than the promulgation of the order itself. A military order, however unconstitutional, is not apt to last longer than the military emergency. Even during that period, a succeeding commander may revoke it all. But once a judicial opinion rationalizes such an order to show that it conforms to the Constitution, or rather rationalizes the Constitution to show that the Constitution sanctions such an order, the Court for all time has validated the principle of racial discrimination in criminal procedure and of transplanting American citizens. The principle then lies about like a loaded weapon, ready for the hand of any authority that can bring forward a plausible claim of an urgent need. . . .

I should hold that a civil court cannot be made to enforce an order which violates constitutional limitations even if it is a reasonable exercise of military authority. . . . My duties as a justice, as I see them, do not require me to make a military judgment as to whether General DeWitt's evacuation and detention program was a reasonable military necessity. I do not suggest that the courts should have attempted to interfere with the Army in carrying out its task. But I do not think they may be asked to execute a military expedient that has no place in law under the Constitution. I would reverse the judgment and discharge the prisoner.[54]

Gerald Ford Rescinds Executive Order 9066 (1976)

The verdict of history has not been kind to the military's exclusion orders and the *Korematsu* decision. In 1976 President Ford formally rescinded Executive Order 9066.

In this Bicentennial year, we are commemorating the anniversary dates of many great events in American history. An honest reckoning, however, must include a recognition of our national mistakes as well as our national achievements. Learning from our mistakes is not pleasant, but as a great philosopher once admonished, we must do so if we want to avoid repeating them.

February 19th is the anniversary of a sad day in American history. It was on that date in 1942, in the midst of the response to the hostilities that began on December 7, 1941, that Executive Order 9066 was issued, subsequently enforced by the criminal penalties of a statute enacted March 21, 1942, resulting in the uprooting of loyal Americans. Over one hundred thousand persons of Japanese ancestry were removed from their homes, detained in special camps, and eventually relocated. . . .

We now know what we should have known then—not only was that evacuation wrong, but Japanese Americans were and are loyal Americans. On the battlefield and at home, Japanese Americans . . . have been and continue to be written in our history for the sacrifices and the contributions they have made to the well-being and security of this, our common nation.

Now, therefore, I, Gerald R. Ford, President of the United States of America, do hereby proclaim that all authority conferred by Executive Order 9066 terminated upon the issuance of Proclamation 2714, which formally proclaimed the cessation of hostilities of World War II on December 31, 1946.

I call upon the American people to affirm with me this American promise— that we have learned from the tragedy of that long-ago experience forever to treasure liberty and justice for each individual American, and resolve that this kind of action shall never again be repeated.[55]

Fred Korematsu's Conviction Vacated by a Federal Court (1984)

Decades after Korematsu's conviction, archival research revealed that Justice Department officials had concluded at the time that many of the specific allegations contained in the Army's *Final Report* were exaggerated or even false. Nonetheless, succumbing to pressure from the War Department, government attorneys did not apprise the Supreme Court of their concerns about the integrity of the military's proffered evidence.[56] Fred Korematsu's criminal conviction eventually was vacated by a federal district court in 1984 on the grounds that the government had wrongly withheld information from the Supreme Court about the veracity of the *Final Report*.

The record is replete with protestations of various Justice Department officials that the government had the obligation to advise the courts of the contrary facts and opinions. . . . In fact, several Department of Justice officials pointed out to their superiors and others the "wilful historical inaccuracies and intentional falsehoods" contained in the DeWitt report.

These omissions are critical. In the original proceedings, before the district court, and on appeal, the government argued that the actions taken were within the war-making powers of the executive and legislative branches and, even where the actions were directed at a particular class of persons, they were beyond judicial scrutiny so long as they were reasonably related to the security and defense of the nation and the prosecution of the war. . . . The facts which the government represented it relied upon and provided to the courts were those contained in a report entitled *Final Report, Japanese Evacuation from the West Coast* (1942), prepared by General DeWitt. His evaluation and version of the facts informed the courts' opinions. Yet, omitted from the government's representations was any reference to contrary reports which were considered reliable by the Justice Department and military officials other than General DeWitt. . . .

Whether a fuller, more accurate record would have prompted a different decision [by the Supreme Court in *Korematsu*] cannot be determined. Nor need it be determined. Where relevant evidence has been withheld, it is ample justification [that] . . . the conviction should be set aside. . . .

Korematsu remains on the pages of our legal and political history. As a legal precedent it is now recognized as having very limited application. As historical precedent it stands as a constant caution that in times of war or declared military necessity our institutions must be vigilant in protecting constitutional guarantees. It stands as a caution that in times of distress the shield of military necessity and national security must not be used to protect governmental actions from close scrutiny and accountability. It stands as a caution that in times of international hostility and antagonisms our institutions, legislative, executive and judicial, must be prepared to exercise their authority to protect all citizens from the petty fears and prejudices that are so easily aroused.[57]

Civil Liberties Act (1988)

In 1988, Congress passed the Civil Liberties Act, which ultimately provided modest monetary reparations for more than eighty thousand persons of Japanese ancestry detained by the US government during the war.

The Congress recognizes that . . . a grave injustice was done to both citizens and permanent resident aliens of Japanese ancestry by the evacuation, relocation, and internment of civilians during World War II. . . . These actions were carried out without adequate security reasons and without any acts or espionage or sabotage . . . and were motivated largely by racial prejudice, wartime hysteria, and a failure of political leadership. The excluded individuals of Japanese ancestry suffered enormous damages, both material and intangible, and there were incalculable losses in education and job training, all of which resulted in significant human suffering for which appropriate compensation has not been made. For these fundamental violations of the basic civil liberties and constitutional rights of these individuals of Japanese ancestry, the Congress apologizes on behalf of the nation.[58]

Fred Korematsu Receives the Medal of Freedom (1997)

A decade later, in 1997, President Bill Clinton awarded the Presidential Medal of Freedom (the nation's highest civilian honor) to Fred Korematsu.

In 1942, an ordinary American took an extraordinary stand. Fred Korematsu boldly opposed the forced internment of Japanese Americans during World War II. After being convicted for failing to report for relocation, Mr. Korematsu took his case all the way to the Supreme Court. The high court ruled against him. But thirty-nine years later, he had his conviction overturned in federal court, empowering tens of thousands of Japanese Americans, and giving him what he said he wanted most of all: a chance to feel like an American once again. In the long history of our country's constant search for justice, some names of ordinary citizens stand for millions of souls. Plessy, Brown, Parks. To that distinguished list, today we add the name of Fred Korematsu.[59]

Korematsu v. United States Overruled (2018)

Finally, in 2018, the Supreme Court formally overturned the *Korematsu* decision.

The dissent invokes *Korematsu v. United States*. Whatever rhetorical advantage the dissent may see in doing so, *Korematsu* has nothing to do with this case. The forcible relocation of US citizens to concentration camps, solely and explicitly on the basis of race, is objectively unlawful and outside the scope of presidential authority. . . . The dissent's reference to *Korematsu*, however, affords this Court the opportunity to make express what is already obvious: *Korematsu* was gravely wrong the day it was decided, has been overruled in the court of history, and—to be clear—"has no place in law under the Constitution."[60]

Discussion Questions

1. Of what use is the Bill of Rights during moments of crisis (often war-time)? Are rights least honored when they are most needed? Eventually, the worst violations are repudiated—dissents provide initial guidance, and amends sometimes come to be made (by Congress; by presidents; by the Supreme Court). But that did not do Dred Scott or Homer Plessy much good—or, in this instance, Fred Korematsu. Is the Bill of Rights sometimes no more than a "parchment barrier," to use James Madison's phrase?

2. The *Korematsu* Court afforded great deference to the judgment of the military, particularly in times of war. When might it be wise to respect the doctrine of "military necessity"? When might it be problematic and dangerous? Do the tensions in the Preamble of the Constitution between national security ("provide for the common defence") and civil liberties ("secure the Blessings of Liberty") make conflict inevitable?

3. In evaluating the legality and legitimacy of internment orders issued to persons of Japanese ancestry at the outset of World War II, should the Supreme Court have taken any of the following into account? (a) The government did not order mass detentions of persons of German and Italian ancestry living in the country, even though the United States was also at war with those two nations. (b) All Hawaiians lived under martial law during most of the war, but persons of Japanese descent in the islands were not confined in camps, in part because they were indispensable to the local economy. (c) The military asserted in its *Final Report* that Japanese Americans needed to be isolated to protect them from harm from an "aroused public . . . ready to take matters into its own hands." (d) Evidence suggests that Roosevelt kept the camps open throughout 1944 (an election year) for political reasons, despite military advice that they were no longer necessary.

4. In the wake of Pearl Harbor, what *should* have been done by civilian and military authorities, consistent with constitutional values, to prevent the homeland from experiencing additional catastrophic surprise attacks?[61]

5. "*Korematsu* was gravely wrong the day it was decided," declared a majority of the Supreme Court in 2018.[62] To be sure, from time to time precedents are overruled because the Supreme Court changes its interpretation of the Constitution. But what does it mean when a subsequent Supreme Court declares that one of its earlier decisions was "wrong the day it was decided"? That the earlier justices were simply ignorant (or worse) about the meaning of the Constitution?[63]

Additional Primary Source Documents

Primary source document excerpts covering the following topics are located on the website accompanying this book:

Free Speech During World War I—including Woodrow Wilson; Committee on Public Information; Espionage Act of 1917; Sedition Act of 1918; *Debs v. United States*, 249 U.S. 211 (1919); *Schenck v. United States*, 249 U.S. 47 (1919).

Eugenics—including Woodrow Wilson; Theodore Roosevelt; Madison Grant; Virginia Sterilization Act; *Buck v. Bell*, 274 U.S. 200 (1927); Human Betterment Foundation.

Other "Constitutional Moments" during this Era

- Growth and regulation of the administrative state—including the New Deal; Second New Deal; *A.L.A. Schechter Poultry Corp. v. United States*, 295 U.S. 495 (1935) (invalidating New Deal legislation); Franklin Roosevelt court-packing plan; *West Coast Hotel Co. v. Parrish*, 300 U.S. 379 (1937) (upholding minimum wage law; "switch in time saves nine"); *National Labor Relations Board v. Jones & Laughlin Steel Corp.*, 301 U.S. 1 (1937) (upholding NLRA); *Wickard v. Filburn*, 317 U.S. 111 (1942) (Commerce Clause authority of Congress).
- Foreign policy—including Treaty of Versailles debate; *Missouri v. Holland*, 252 U.S. 416 (1920) (treaty power); *United States v. Curtiss-Wright Export Corp.*, 299 U.S. 304 (1936) (presidential foreign affairs authority); Neutrality Acts.
- Civil rights—including proposed antilynching legislation; *Buchanan v. Warley*, 245 U.S. 60 (1917) (striking down discriminatory housing ordinance); *Missouri ex rel. Gaines v. Canada*, 305 U.S. 337 (1938) (right to equal educational access); Executive Order 8802 (establishing Fair Employment Practice Committee); *Smith v. Allwright*, 321 U.S. 649 (1944) (striking down whites-only primary voting).
- Other constitutional issues—including Seventeenth Amendment (direct election of senators); *Meyer v. Nebraska*, 262 U.S. 390 (1923) (education); *Village of Euclid v. Ambler Realty*, 272 U.S. 365 (1926) (zoning and economic regulation); *Pierce v. Society of Sisters*, 268 U.S. 510 (1925) (education); *Near v. Minnesota*, 283 U.S. 697 (1931) (freedom of press); *Palko v. Connecticut*, 302 U.S. 319 (1937) (incorporation of Bill of Rights); *De Jonge v. Oregon*, 299

U.S. 353 (1937) (freedom of assembly); *Minersville School District v. Gobitis*, 310 U.S. 586 (1940); and *West Virginia Board of Education v. Barnette*, 319 U.S. 624 (1943) (compelled student speech—Pledge of Allegiance).

Notes

1. Calvin Coolidge, "The Press under a Free Government" (speech, Washington, DC, January 17, 1925), www.presidency.ucsb.edu/documents/address-the-american-society-newspaper-editors-washington-dc.
2. Franklin D. Roosevelt, "Message to Congress on the Objectives and Accomplishments of the Administration" (June 8, 1934), www.presidency.ucsb.edu/documents/message-congress-the-objectives-and-accomplishments-the-administration.
3. *Prohibiting the Several States from Disfranchising United States Citizens on Account of Sex: Hearing before the Senate Comm. on Privileges and Elections*, 45th Cong. 5 (1878) (statement of Elizabeth Cady Stanton), crowd.loc.gov/campaigns/elizabeth-cady-stanton-papers/Speeches-and-writings/mss412100137/mss412100137-7/.
4. 83 U.S. 130 (1873).
5. William S. Kenyon, Senate Debates, Cong. Rec. 55:5639. (August 1, 1917), www.govinfo.gov/app/details/GPO-CRECB-1917-pt8-v55/GPO-CRECB-1917-pt8-v55-7.
6. *Woman Suffrage: Hearings before the House Comm. on the Judiciary*, 65th Cong. 214 (1917) (statement of Mabel Vernon).
7. *Extending the Right of Suffrage to Women: Hearing on H.R.J. Res. 200 before the House Comm. on Woman Suffrage*, 65th Cong. 9 (1918) (statement of Anna Howard Shaw).
8. See generally Reva B. Siegel, "The Nineteenth Amendment and the Democratization of the Family," *Yale Law Journal Forum* 129 (2020): 450-95, www.yalelawjournal.org/forum/the-nineteenth-amendment-and-the-democratization-of-the-family.
9. 198 U.S. 45 (1905).
10. Muller v. Oregon, 208 U.S. 412 (1908).
11. Hammer v. Dagenhart, 247 U.S. 251 (1918).
12. Adkins v. Children's Hosp., 261 U.S. 525 (1923).
13. United States v. Darby Lumber Co., 312 U.S. 100 (1941).
14. Buck v. Bell, 274 U.S. 200 (1927).
15. Volstead Act (An act to prohibit intoxicating beverages, and to regulate the manufacture, production, use, and sale of high-proof spirits for other than beverage purposes), ch. 85, 41 Stat. 305 (October 28, 1919), govtrackus.s3.amazonaws.com/legislink/pdf/stat/41/STATUTE-41-Pg305a.pdf.
16. Schenck v. United States, 249 U.S. 47 (1919).
17. An Act to amend section three [of the Espionage Act of 1917], ch. 75, 40 Stat. 553 (May 16, 1918), govtrackus.s3.amazonaws.com/legislink/pdf/stat/40/STATUTE-40-Pg553.pdf.
18. 249 U.S. 211 (1919). Debs received a pardon in 1921 from President Warren Harding.
19. 250 U.S. 616 (1919).
20. See generally Lisa McGirr, *The War on Alcohol: Prohibition and the Rise of the American State* (New York: W.W. Norton, 2015).
21. 277 U.S. 438 (1928).

22. *Id.* (Brandeis, J., dissenting).
23. An act to provide for the establishment of fair labor standards in employments in and affecting interstate commerce, ch. 676, 52 Stat. 1060 (June 25, 1938), govtrackus. s3.amazonaws.com/legislink/pdf/stat/52/STATUTE-52-Pg1060.pdf.
24. 312 U.S. 100 (1941).
25. West Coast Hotel v. Parrish, 300 U.S. 379 (1937).
26. Exec. Order No. 9066 (February 19, 1942); www.ourdocuments.gov/doc.php?flash= false&doc=74&page=transcript.
27. An Act to provide a penalty for violation of restrictions or orders with respect to persons entering, remaining in, leaving, or committing any act in military areas or zones, ch. 191, 56 Stat. 173 (March 21, 1942), govtrackus.s3.amazonaws.com/legislink/pdf/ stat/56/STATUTE-56-Pg173b.pdf.
28. Korematsu v. United States, 323 U.S. 214 (1944).
29. "Declaration of Sentiments," Seneca Falls Convention (July 29, 1848), www.nps.gov/ wori/learn/historyculture/declaration-of-sentiments.htm.
30. See Douglas O. Linder, "The Trial of Susan B. Anthony: An Account," in *Famous Trials*, www.famous-trials.com/anthony/444-home.
31. Susan B. Anthony, "Is It a Crime for a U.S. Citizen to Vote?" (speech, Washington, DC, January 16, 1873), in *Against an Aristocracy of Sex, 1866 to 1873*, Vol. 2, The Selected Papers of Elizabeth Cady Stanton and Susan B. Anthony, ed. Ann D. Gordon (New Brunswick, NJ: Rutgers University Press, 2000), 554–83, susanb.org/wp-content/uploads/2018/12/Susan-B-Anthony-1872-1873.pdf.
32. Minor v. Happersett, 88 U.S. 162 (1875).
33. Carrie Chapman Catt, "Address to the United States Congress" (speech, Washington, DC, November 1917), susanbanthonyhouse.org/blog/wp-content/uploads/2017/07/ Carrie-Chapman-Catt-Washington-DC-1917.pdf.
34. Jewish Women's Archive, "Pamphlet distributed by the National Association Opposed to Woman Suffrage" (n.d.), jwa.org/media/pamphlet-distributed-by-national-association-opposed-to-woman-suffrage.
35. Petition from the Women Voters Anti-Suffrage Party of New York to the US Senate (1917), Petitions and Memorials, Resolutions of State Legislatures, and Related Documents, 65th Cong., Records of the U.S. Senate, National Archives Identifier: 7452146, www.docsteach.org/documents/document/ petition-antisuffrage-ny.
36. Georgia Association Opposed to Woman Suffrage Card (ca. 1915), Records of the U.S. House of Representatives, National Archives Identifier: 119222090, www.docsteach. org/documents/document/ga-opposed-woman-suffrage-card.
37. Joint Resolution of the Senate and House of Delegates of Maryland Rejecting and Refusing to Ratify an Amendment to the Constitution of the United States, March 26, 1920, Records of the U.S. House of Representatives, National Archives, www.docsteach.org/documents/document/resolution-legislature-maryland-rejecting-19th-amendment.
38. Martin v. Commonwealth, 1 Mass. Reports 348 (1805); see Linda K. Kerber, "The Paradox of Women's Citizenship in the Early Republic: The Case of *Martin v. Massachusetts*, 1805," *American Historical Review* 97, no. 2 (April 1992): 349–78, www.jstor.org/stable/2165723. See generally Linda K. Kerber, *No Constitutional*

Right to Be Ladies: Women and the Obligations of Citizenship (New York: Hill and Wang, 1998).

39. Crystal Eastman, "Now We Can Begin," *The Liberator* 3, no. 12 (December 1920): 23–24, www.marxists.org/history/usa/culture/pubs/liberator/1920/12/v3n12-w33-dec-1920-liberator.pdf.

40. Alice Paul Institute, "The History of the Equal Rights Amendment," www.alicepaul.org/equal-rights-amendment-2/.

41. Doris Stevens, "Suffrage Does Not Give Equality," *The Forum* 72, no. 2 (August 1924): 124–52.

42. Muller v. Oregon, 208 U.S. 412 (1908).

43. Alice Hamilton, "Protection for Women Workers," *The Forum* 72, no. 2 (August 1924): 152–60.

44. H.J. Res. 208, Proposed Amendment to the US Constitution, 92d Cong. (1972), www.govinfo.gov/content/pkg/STATUTE-86/pdf/STATUTE-86-Pg1523.pdf.

45. US Commission on Civil Rights, *Statement on the Equal Rights Amendment* 5, 16–18 (December 1978), babel.hathitrust.org/cgi/pt?id=ucl.31210023598095&view=1up&seq = 1. See also US Commission on Civil Rights, *The Equal Rights Amendment: Guaranteeing Equal Rights for Women under the Constitution* (June 1981), www2.law.umaryland.edu/marshall/usccr/documents/cr11068.pdf.

46. Phyllis Schlafly, "What's Wrong with 'Equal Rights' for Women?" *The Phyllis Schlafly Report* 5, no. 7 (February 1972), eagleforum.org/publications/psr/feb1972.html. Reprinted with permission of Eagle Forum Education and Legal Defense Fund.

47. See generally Greg Robinson, *By Order of the President: FDR and the Internment of Japanese Americans* (Cambridge, MA: Harvard University Press, 2001); Greg Robinson, *A Tragedy of Democracy: Japanese Confinement in North America* (New York: Columbia University Press, 2009).

48. Exec. Order No. 9066 (February 19, 1942); www.ourdocuments.gov/doc.php?flash=false&doc=74&page=transcript.

49. An Act to provide a penalty for violation of restrictions or orders with respect to persons entering, remaining in, leaving, or committing any act in military areas or zones, ch. 191; 56 Stat. 173 (March 21, 1942), govtrackus.s3.amazonaws.com/legislink/pdf/stat/56/STATUTE-56-Pg173b.pdf.

50. Western Defense Command and Fourth Army Wartime Civil Control Administration, "Instructions to All Persons of Japanese Ancestry" (April 1, 1942), www.sfmuseum.net/hist9/evacorder.html.

51. Headquarters Western Defense Command and Fourth Army, *Final Report, Japanese Evacuation from the West Coast 1942* (Washington, DC: Government Printing Office, 1943), 8–10, 15, www.collections.nlm.nih.gov/ext/dw/01130040R/PDF/01130040R.pdf.

52. Korematsu v. United States, 323 U.S. 214 (1944).

53. *Id.* (Murphy, J., dissenting).

54. *Id.* (Jackson, J., dissenting).

55. Gerald R. Ford, Proclamation 4417, "Confirming the Termination of the Executive Order Authorizing Japanese-American Internment during World War II" (February 19, 1976), www.fordlibrarymuseum.gov/library/speeches/760111p.htm.

56. See Peter Irons, *Justice at War: The Story of the Japanese American Internment Cases* (Berkeley: University of California Press, 1983).

57. Korematsu v. United States, 584 F. Supp. 1406 (N.D. Cal. 1984), law.justia.com/cases/federal/district-courts/FSupp/584/1406/2270281/.

58. An Act to implement recommendations of the Commission on Wartime Relocation and Internment of Civilians, Pub. L. No. 100-383, 102 Stat. 903 (August 10, 1988), www.govinfo.gov/content/pkg/STATUTE-102/pdf/STATUTE-102-Pg903.pdf.

59. Bill Clinton, "Remarks at Presentation of Presidential Medals of Freedom" (January 15, 1997), www.c-span.org/video/?c4660995/fred-korematsu-awarded-presidential-medal-freedom.

60. Trump v. Hawaii, 585 U.S. ___ (2018).

61. Similar questions were asked in the aftermath of the September 11 attacks in 2001. Fred Korematsu himself filed an amicus brief with the Supreme Court in several post-9/11 cases, where he argued that "to avoid a repetition of past mistakes, this Court should closely scrutinize the government's claims of 'military necessity' . . . to ensure that civil liberties are not unnecessarily restricted." See Brief of Amicus Curiae Fred Korematsu in Support of Petitioners, *Al Odah, et al. v. United States*, No. 03-343 (October 3, 2003); ccrjustice.org/sites/default/files/attach/2015/05/2003-10-03_Rasul_AmicusBriefSupportCert_Fred_Korematsu.pdf.

62. In Lawrence v. Texas, 539 U.S. 558 (2003), the Supreme Court similarly said that Bowers v. Hardwick, 478 U.S. 186 (1986), "was not correct when it was decided, and it is not correct today."

63. In a related vein, see Justice William Brennan's statement in New York Times v. Sullivan, 376 U.S. 254 (1964), that "the attack upon [the validity of the Sedition Act of 1798] has carried the day in the court of history."

7

The Constitution in the Postwar World
(1945–74)

The civil rights story is not ordinarily told as constitutional history (apart, of course, from the celebrated case of *Brown v. Board of Education*). From Montgomery to Birmingham-Selma to Memphis, the focus is largely on protests in the streets rather than progress in the courts—civil disobedience that flouts the law rather than counts on it. The decade's most eloquent words on racial justice came not in court but from Martin Luther King Jr.'s "I Have a Dream" speech at the March on Washington. But throughout this era, constitutional law too played a crucial role. It hardly undercuts the sacrifices of the bus boycotters to point out that their struggle culminated with a victory in the Supreme Court, *Gayle v. Browder*, outlawing segregation in public transportation.[1] Nor does it devalue the valor of the Freedom Riders to note that their very purpose in boarding buses was to add teeth to the Court's decision in *Boynton v. Virginia*.[2] In fact, the civil rights story is a chronicle of judicial rulings and congressional laws, no less than of activism and protest. Its martyr-heroes won and lost battles in courtrooms and Congress, no less than in jails and on the streets. And focusing on the workings, unpredictability, and limitations of constitutional change highlights what is arguably the era's crowning achievement: the awakening of the sleeping giants of the Fourteenth and Fifteenth Amendments.

With respect to racial equality, the 1950s and 1960s witnessed profound constitutional challenges—and even more profound constitutional changes. The post-*Plessy* era commenced with a landmark Supreme Court ruling that overturned the doctrine of "separate but equal" for the nation's public schools; it concluded with several landmark civil rights statutes from Congress. Jim Crow laws for public accommodations were legislated out of existence in the Civil Rights Act of 1964. Voting rights were dramatically expanded, initially by a series of "one person, one vote" rulings from the Court; then by the Voting Rights Act of 1965 and the Twenty-fourth and Twenty-sixth Amendments. *Brown v. Board of Education*, the Civil Rights Act of 1964, and the Voting Rights Act of 1965 revolutionized the nation's constitutional legacy.

With Liberty and Justice for All?. Edited by Steven A. Steinbach, Maeva Marcus, and Robert Cohen, Oxford University Press. © Oxford University Press 2022. DOI: 10.1093/oso/9780197516317.003.0007

But constitutional revolutions do not simply fall from the skies, and they certainly are not dinner parties. The *Brown* ruling was the subject of intense controversy at the time it was issued; furious segregationists even compared the decision to *Dred Scott* and urged defiance of and "massive resistance" to it. *Brown* thus raises important teaching questions that are no less relevant in today's times: What happens when the Court leaps ahead of prevailing sentiment on an issue (in this instance, race)? Realistically, how much enforcement power do courts actually have—or, for that matter, how relevant are constitutional rulings generally—in achieving fundamental social, behavioral, and attitudinal change? While the dynamics that propel constitutional developments sometimes flow from the top—and sometimes arise from below—and sometimes involve (or require) both street protests and adversarial courtroom engagement—change is far from inevitable. The civil rights saga, then, provides an unparalleled opportunity to dig much deeper in the effort to explain constitutional evolution.

This historical period also encompasses the transformational role played by the justices of the Warren Court in creating new constitutional rights by expanding the reach and effect of a variety of constitutional provisions relating to speech, religion, due process, criminal protections, and student rights. Once again, this was not without controversy, ranging from condemnations of "activist" courts to an unsuccessful effort to impeach Chief Justice Earl Warren. Regardless of ideological perspective, observers cannot help but reflect on the extent to which all of this was surprising, appropriate, laudable, or lasting.

Another watershed moment in the struggle for constitutional rights was McCarthyism. The relevant issues can be framed not simply in terms of international Cold War tensions or domestic political pressures but also in terms of the amount of existential dissent permitted (or tolerable) within our constitutional system. It does little good to pillory the excesses of Joseph McCarthy and his allies without at least pausing to ponder whether anyone, under any circumstances, should be permitted to voice any political opinion. To what extent should the American public be willing to give those it considers its most ardent and abhorrent adversaries rights under the Constitution to promote views that, by their very nature, seem to threaten constitutional liberties for all? The Cold War may be over, but can the same be said of intolerance? And in the final analysis, what good are "rights" anyway? To what extent can the Bill of Rights—or the courts—or the Constitution—be expected to protect civil liberties and minority rights in times of war and national stress? Such questions are hardly time bound to the 1950s and 1960s.

The Warren Court and Constitutional Liberalism

Laura Kalman

Distinguished Research Professor, University of California, Santa Barbara

The August 15, 1945, banner headlines shouted "PEACE!" Instead, communism emerged as America's greatest existential threat. The Cold War and the ideal of democracy would provide the impetus for expanding and contracting liberty and equality between World War II and the twin traumas of Vietnam and Watergate, and the period would prove anything but peaceful.

Almost as soon as the war ended, the Soviet Union turned from ally to antagonist. There was reason for concern. Some US citizens in government service had become Soviet spies before and during the war. The trials of Julius and Ethel Rosenberg for conspiracy to commit espionage, the Soviet Union's demonstration of an atomic bomb and the fall of mainland China to the communists in 1949, and North Korea's 1950 invasion of South Korea understandably alarmed Americans. Just as obviously, Republicans exploited the fear because they saw the "Red Scare" as a political winner. In 1950, an obscure Wisconsin Republican, Senator Joe McCarthy, would win acclaim by falsely charging that the Democratic-run State Department swarmed with communists. A wave of anticommunism, "McCarthyism," swept the country, and few remained above suspicion.

In such a climate, President Harry Truman had to crack down on domestic subversion or risk impeachment. His dismal solution was to mount the most sweeping inquiry into employee loyalty in history. Truman directed each executive branch department and agency to establish a board to investigate employees and dismiss anyone of doubtful loyalty. The program proved a bust. Of the three million employees screened by 1950, only 468 were declared ineligible for government employment, and no espionage plots had been uncovered. The Truman loyalty program, however, provided the template for McCarthyism in two ways. First, it imposed political tests and economic sanctions for failing them, and universities, schools, Hollywood, and many others followed suit. Second, in another move others copied, the program denied accused individuals the basic ingredients of due process—the right to know the charges against them and to confront and cross-examine their accusers. Though by the 1950s the loyalty program's constitutionality had twice been challenged, the Supreme Court let it stand. Truman's successor, Republican Dwight Eisenhower, would make the program more restrictive and precipitate a "Lavender Scare" by rooting gays and lesbians out of government as "security risks."

The Truman administration also contributed to the Cold War by prosecuting Eugene Dennis, who headed the Communist Party, and other communist leaders for violating the 1940 Smith Act. That legislation made it a crime to teach or advocate the violent overthrow of the US government or to belong to a group engaged in such advocacy.[3] It represented a departure from the modern civil libertarian position of prohibiting only utterances that represented (in the words of Justice Oliver Wendell Holmes) a "clear and present danger"[4] to the American people. Though Dennis and his colleagues never publicly advocated violence, the government made the case against them by presenting books such as *The Communist Manifesto* and claiming that by teaching them, the defendants did. Hysteria about communism preordained a guilty verdict. When the defendants appealed and the case reached the Supreme Court, Chief Justice Fred Vinson explained in *Dennis v. United States* (1951) that the Smith Act did not infringe on the First Amendment because it outlawed "advocacy, not discussion."[5] He reformulated the clear and present danger test as clear and probable danger: the government need not show that that speech posed an immediate, imminent danger before prohibiting it. "Public opinion being what it now is," Justice Hugo Black said in dissent, "few will protest the conviction of these communist petitioners," but perhaps "in calmer times, when present pressures, passions, and fears subside," the Court would "restore the First Amendment liberties to the high preferred place where they belong in a free society."[6]

"Calmer times" arrived in 1957, when the Court gutted *Dennis*, one of its worst Cold War decisions. In *Yates v. United States* (1957), it set aside the Smith Act conviction of fourteen midlevel communist leaders. Distinguishing between advocacy of belief and action, the majority maintained that the Smith Act did not prohibit advocating and teaching the violent overthrow of government in the abstract.[7] So, too, the government lost ten other cases before the Court that year involving communist activities or investigations of them. Changed personnel on the Court helped explain the shift toward civil libertarianism. Chief Justice Earl Warren had replaced Vinson in 1953, and two justices had taken the spots of another two in the *Dennis* majority. Further, McCarthy had overreached by implausibly charging that there were communists in the US Army. The Cold War had thawed, but it had not disappeared. During the 1960s it would flare into hot war in Vietnam.

Like its response to Japanese American internment, the Court's record during the early Cold War makes for disappointment among those who count on it to protect the minority rights and civil liberties frequently suppressed by the executive and legislative branches in wartime. Yet the Cold War also provided the impetus for expanding civil liberties and rights. Defense spending, along with consumer spending on capitalist comforts, created a booming economy that could promote reform. The Cold War also made it crucial to publicize American democracy. How could the United States burnish its global image for those whose hearts and minds it sought when the Soviet Union would publicize every lynching of an African American?

The National Association for the Advancement of Colored People (NAACP) underlined the point in a 1947 United Nations petition: white supremacy in Mississippi, more than the Soviet Union, endangered the United States. Many powerful whites agreed. "The number one question at any press conference or forum was, 'What about America's treatment of the Negro?'" lamented the US ambassador to India.[8] To be sure, the Cold War also narrowed the civil rights movement's options by discouraging mass action, which suddenly sounded too radical, and shifting the NAACP's attention from economic inequality to fighting state-sponsored school segregation. Yet the latter task was also a worthy one. With their schools segregated by law, Southern states devoted woefully few resources to the "separate but equal" schools they had created for African Americans.

Thanks to the brilliant litigation strategy of the NAACP's Thurgood Marshall and Warren's politicking, a unanimous Court declared school segregation laws an unconstitutional violation of the Fourteenth Amendment's Equal Protection Clause in the 1954 case of *Brown v. Board of Education*.[9] The ruling did not touch school segregation in the North and West, often then wrongly assumed to reflect residential patterns and economic inequality and not officials' deliberative intent. But *Brown* seemed to promise an end to educational apartheid in the South. Warren's opinion rested on the claim that education was the most important function of state and local governments and on social science data suggesting that segregation made African American children feel inferior. He deliberately kept it short so it could be read on Voice of America.

Open almost any American history textbook today, and you will find a triumphal narrative suggesting that the decision lit the spark that kindled the modern civil rights movement. At the time, many African Americans did consider it their greatest victory since Emancipation. Yet *Brown* and *Brown II* (1955),[10] which demanded only that desegregation proceed "with all deliberate speed," have always been controversial.

Martin Luther King Jr. worried that attacking discrimination and segregation in the courts distracted attention from grass-roots organizing, and there is little evidence that *Brown* inspired the revival of mass action in the 1955 Montgomery bus boycott. Some African Americans on the right and left now believe that the Court would have served them better had it used *Brown* to direct that the "separate" schools receive a financial infusion that made them truly "equal" to those for whites. Then there is *Brown*'s legal fuzziness. The opinion stressed the special place of public education in American society. But the Warren Court then struck down state-sponsored segregation in cases involving parks, beaches, golf courses, and buses in short opinions that included no legal reasoning beyond a citation to *Brown*, while dodging a decision on the constitutionality of laws barring interracial marriage. (Only later did it unanimously strike down state-sponsored antimiscegenation laws in *Loving v. Virginia* (1967).[11])

Then there are *Brown* and *Brown II*'s results. Ironically, *Brown* triggered "massive resistance" among white Southerners at the same time that *Brown II* and the Court's acceptance of token desegregation efforts ensured that just one in a hundred African Americans attended desegregated Southern schools in 1964. Small wonder that some disillusioned liberals now grieve that *Brown* spawned the "hollow hope" that the Supreme Court could remedy injustice.[12] Meanwhile, some further left blame *Brown* for exposing the peril of the larger rights consciousness the Court made possible: In declaring rights, whose exercise it then deferred, the Warren Court just duped subordinated classes into believing in the fairness of the legal system. Surely Earl Warren is spinning in his grave at the contemporary reception of his proud achievement.

Still, for all their criticisms, most legal scholars and judges consider his handiwork in *Brown* sacred. Conservatives critical of the Warren Court's activist "social engineering" insulate *Brown* from their imprecations. Confirmation hearings feature Supreme Court nominees ritualistically swearing fealty to *Brown*. The decision reminded Americans of their collective aspirations for racial justice and equality and inspired a generation of baby boomers to become lawyers. That seemed a considerable accomplishment, since the Eisenhower administration and Congress often blocked social change.

Its prospects became brighter in the mid-1960s. Prodded by a vigorous civil rights movement whose members boycotted white supremacy and braved violence at the hands of made-for-TV white Southern racists who increased sympathy for the cause in the North and West, all three branches of government worked in tandem. For a time, liberalism—which coupled a global anticommunist crusade aimed at spreading capitalism and democracy with domestic reform designed to strengthen them by reducing racial and economic inequality—became Washington's watchword. President Lyndon Johnson's Great Society embodied it, as did legal liberalism, trust in the potential of the federal courts, particularly the Warren Court, to produce change for the disempowered.

At Martin Luther King Jr.'s urging, LBJ, a master legislative strategist, broke a filibuster to ram the 1964 Civil Rights Act[13] through Congress. It authorized the attorney general to bring school desegregation suits. By this time, the Warren Court, like the Johnson administration and much of Congress, had lost patience with the slow pace of school desegregation. As a result, the desegregation of Southern schools seemed nearly complete at *Brown*'s twentieth anniversary—for a moment.

The Civil Rights Act of 1964 also battled segregation elsewhere by banning discrimination and segregation in employment on the basis of race, religion, sex, national origin, or color and creating the Equal Employment Opportunity Commission (EEOC) to enforce the legislation. The EEOC made few inroads in the fight against employment-related racial discrimination in the 1960s, but in *Griggs v. Duke Power Company* (1971), the Court invalidated even apparently neutral tests and practices, regardless of the employer's intent in using them, that had no relationship to employment, maintained the effects of past discrimination, and had a disparate impact on minorities.[14] Then, after the EEOC's obvious lack of interest in attacking sex discrimination prompted feminists to create the National Organization for Women, the agency launched an investigation of AT&T, the nation's largest private employer. It resulted in a historic 1973 consent decree prohibiting the telephone company from using discriminatory recruitment, hiring, and promotion practices and providing millions in back pay for women and minorities.

In another, more immediately successful section of the Civil Rights Act, Congress used its Commerce Clause power to justify banning discrimination and segregation in accommodations open to the public—restaurants, motels, bowling alleys, and so on. Predictably, objections that some public accommodations were not "in interstate commerce" followed. No matter: the Court unanimously upheld the act as applied to an Atlanta motel that attracted some interstate travelers in *Heart of Atlanta Motel v. United States* (1964).[15] The same day, in *Katzenbach v. McClung* (1964), the Court unanimously did so again for Ollie's Barbecue, a Birmingham restaurant that catered to a local clientele and used supplies purchased locally.[16] Ollie McClung spoke for conservatives and many white Southerners when he declared himself "shocked and sad at heart" at the Court's infringement on his liberty and private property and its "gross misinterpretation of the United States Constitution."[17]

Goaded by a vibrant civil rights movement, however, Johnson, Congress, and the Warren Court pressed onward. The voting system in the United States made a mockery of its democratic pretensions. The Constitution awarded every state two senators and at least one representative, while providing for the apportionment of states according to the census. That meant Wyoming, with its 330,000 residents in 1960, possessed one member of the 435 in the House of Representatives, while California, with its nearly sixteen million, got thirty-five. Just as inequitably, some state legislatures charged with reapportionment for state and federal elections according to census results routinely privileged rural over urban and suburban voters. In California, for example, one state senator represented Los Angeles County, with its population of more than six million, but the senator from the remote eastern Sierras spoke for just fourteen thousand residents. Other states reapportioned districts rarely: like Tennessee, Alabama had not done so since 1901. Over the objections of Justices Felix Frankfurter and John Marshall Harlan that reapportionment presented a nonjusticiable political question, the Court threw open the doors of the federal courts to those challenging legislative apportionment in *Baker v. Carr* (1962).[18] In *Gray v. Sanders* (1963), the Court relied on the Equal Protection Clause to announce that "the conception of political equality from the Declaration of Independence, to Lincoln's Gettysburg Address, to the Fifteenth, Seventeenth, and Nineteenth Amendments can mean only one thing—one person, one vote,"[19] a principle it applied to congressional districting in *Wesberry v. Sanders* (1964),[20] and to state legislative districting in *Reynolds v. Sims* (1964). "Legislators represent people, not trees or acres," Warren wrote, and "in a free and democratic society . . . the right to elect legislators in a free and unimpaired fashion is a bedrock of our political system."[21]

Democratic rhetoric, all-important when the United States was escalating its involvement in Vietnam, meant little as long as African Americans could not vote in the South, where whites maintained their order by disfranchisement— sometimes by requiring payment of poll taxes; sometimes by imposing literacy tests on African Americans administered by hostile local registrars, while exempting whites whose grandfathers had voted; and sometimes by savage violence. The Constitution's Twenty-fourth Amendment (1964) prohibited the use of poll taxes in federal elections. After "Bloody Sunday" in March 1965—when Alabama police brutally beat hundreds of civil rights protesters attempting to march from Selma to Montgomery to challenge the disfranchisement of African Americans—LBJ appeared before Congress to plead for voting rights legislation. "I speak tonight for the dignity of man and the destiny of democracy," the Texan said in saluting "the effort of American Negroes to secure for themselves the full blessings of American life." Despite a century of promises, African Americans still lacked freedom and equality, and "all of us . . . must overcome the crippling legacy of bigotry and injustice." Making the mantra of the civil rights movement his own, Johnson left many in tears when he stressed, "and we shall overcome."[22] Congress enacted the Voting Rights Act of 1965,[23] which gave teeth to the Fifteenth Amendment, and LBJ vowed to move swiftly in enforcing it.

He and the Supreme Court did. Directed at states that employed tests or other devices to determine voter eligibility and had less than 50 percent of the population registered to vote in national elections, the Voting Rights Act empowered federal officials to register African Americans to vote. Southern states decried the act as a violation of federalism, but the Warren Court upheld the legislation in *South Carolina v. Katzenbach* (1966) as a legitimate exercise of Congress's power to enforce the Fifteenth Amendment when it confronted "an insidious and pervasive evil which had been perpetuated in certain parts of our country through unremitting and ingenious defiance of the Constitution."[24] The same year, the Court ruled in *Harper v. Virginia State Board of Elections* (1966) that the use of poll taxes in state elections violated the Equal Protection Clause.[25] In *Katzenbach v. Morgan* (1966), it also sustained one of the few Voting Rights Act sections that targeted the Northeast by providing that no one who had graduated from a Puerto Rican elementary school could be denied the right to vote because of English illiteracy.[26]

Just as the Voting Rights Act guaranteed the voting rights of mainland Puerto Ricans, it transformed the South. African Americans would wryly observe that in giving them the vote, the act turned Southern politicians from segregationist demagogues into celebrants of their "Black brothers and sisters."[27] That metamorphosis did not fully occur until the 1970s, and the legislation also increased pressure on Democratic lawmakers, who still dominated the region, to reassure conservative white constituents they supported the Southern way of life. Signs of change, however, appeared everywhere. By 1966, the percentage of African Americans registered to vote in the Deep South had nearly doubled, rising to 46 percent.

The civil rights movement's emphasis on equality (along with the Cold War) also prompted reconsideration of American immigration policies. Hitler's *Mein Kampf* celebrated the 1924 Immigration Act,[28] which restricted the annual quota of immigrants to 150,000. Its national origins system favored immigration from northern and northwest Europe by allotting immigrant quotas to countries outside the Western Hemisphere on the basis of their representation in the 1890 census, before Jews and Catholics began pouring in from southern and eastern Europe. The 1924 act prohibited Asian immigration. Presidents Truman, Eisenhower, and Kennedy worked to reform immigration with limited success. Stressing that residents of Germany, Ireland, and the United Kingdom received 70 percent of the visas, LBJ urged Congress to develop opportunity for those "seeking the promise of America" by designing "an immigration law based on the work a man can do and not where he was born or how he spells his name."[29]

The Immigration and Nationality Act of 1965[30] established a system of preferred categories. It prioritized family reunification and welcomed those with needed skills, such as professionals, and refugees who fled communism. Abolishing the old national origins system, the 1965 act created an annual ceiling of 170,000 for countries outside the Western Hemisphere, with per-country limits of up to 20,000—a boon for Greece, Armenia, and Egypt, previously restricted to under 125; African countries other than Egypt, which had been limited to 1,100; and all Asia. Over administration objections, the legislation established an immigration quota for all Western Hemispheric countries of 120,000 annually without per-country limits, not counting those who were spouses, unmarried children, and parents of American citizens or resident aliens. Lesbians, gays, bisexuals, and transsexuals from anywhere were barred.

The House and Senate overwhelmingly approved the act. A 1965 Harris poll suggested that by more than two to one, a less enthusiastic public opposed allowing more people to enter the United States. It also strongly preferred Canadians and northern and northwest European immigrants over those from elsewhere.

In the face of such objections, the act's promoters insisted that it would change little and that foreign policy considerations and the American commitment to racial equality required it. "The national origins system is discriminatory, and it gives a bad image to our friends overseas," one member of Congress stressed,[31] while others pointed to the annual quota of one hundred for South Vietnam before 1965. Were Americans fighting and dying for people with whom they refused to live? LBJ, who signed the immigration bill into law at the base of the Statue of Liberty, claimed that it was "not . . . revolutionary" and "will not reshape the structure of our daily lives," but it performed the vital task of repairing a system that had been "un-American" and "untrue to the faith that brought thousands to these shores even before we were a country."[32] So, too, Senator Ted Kennedy maintained that the cities would not be "flooded" with immigrants and that "the ethnic mix of this country will not be upset."[33] Whether or not enthusiasts knew otherwise and deliberately misled is still debated. In any event, the bill did prove revolutionary and created a multiracial America rooted in Africa, Asia, and Latin America, as well as Europe. Whether or not that was a blessing is still debated too.

Though no significant cases involving the Immigration and Nationality Act came before the Supreme Court during the 1960s, it joyously participated in the realization of Great Society and legal liberalism. After Frankfurter retired in 1962 because of a stroke he blamed on *Baker v. Carr*, and Kennedy successfully nominated Arthur Goldberg, the bloc comprised of Earl Warren, William J. Brennan, William O. Douglas, and Hugo Black won the crucial fifth vote for change. In its heyday between 1962 and Warren's retirement in 1969, the Court largely adopted LBJ's politics. Johnson strengthened the liberal bloc by substituting his intimate adviser, Abe Fortas, for Goldberg in 1965 and by naming *Brown*'s architect, Thurgood Marshall, as the first African American justice in 1967.

Without a doubt, the Warren Court was the most liberal Supreme Court in history. Until the crisis of the 1930s, the protection of property had preoccupied the justices. The new constitutional order after 1937 authorized administrative agencies and legislatures to resolve economic issues and made federal courts guardians of individual and civil rights and liberties. The Warren Court went into mission overdrive after 1962, and its expansion of rights and freedoms made sense during a period in which liberals and conservatives shared an anticommunist consensus and liberals also wanted to enfranchise previously sidelined outsiders. So while the Soviet Union was consigning religious dissidents to the Gulag, the Warren Court, for example, protected religious minorities. It declared school-sponsored prayer and state-sponsored Bible reading and Arkansas legislation barring the teaching of evolution unconstitutional violations of the First Amendment's Establishment Clause.[34]

Yet many public schools, particularly in the South, defiantly continued beginning the day with a prayer or Bible reading and, doubtless, continued to teach creationism too. And the Warren Court majority's attempt to realize long-standing ideals did not stop the Court from becoming a lightning rod for those who disagreed with its decisions on religion, communism, civil rights, reapportionment, privacy, and criminal procedure. Nor did it appease those, such as Justice Harlan, who contended that the overly "activist" majority was treating the Constitution as "a panacea for every blot upon public welfare" and transforming "this Court, ordained as a judicial body" into "a general haven for reform movements."[35] Others protested the Court's creation of constitutional rights. For example, it discovered a right to privacy, about which the Constitution said not one word, in *Griswold v. Connecticut* (1965),[36] which subsequently became the basis for a constitutional right to abortion in *Roe v. Wade* (1973).[37] Further, changing laws on the books turned out to be, relatively speaking, easy, and did not always transform American hearts. It developed that there were limits to the liberalism of LBJ and the Warren Court.

In foreign policy matters, as in domestic ones, the Warren Court sided with LBJ. Like Nixon after him, Johnson rested his authority to wage the Vietnam War on congressional approval of the 1964 Gulf of Tonkin Resolution after the North Vietnamese allegedly assaulted two US Navy destroyers. It authorized the president to "take all necessary measures to repel any armed attack against the forces of the United States and to prevent further aggression."[38] That Congress never formally declared war became a matter of mounting concern as the number of American soldiers coming home in body bags rose. Did Presidents Johnson and Nixon violate the Constitution by fighting the Vietnam War? Asked to consider the question ten times between 1967 and 1969, the Warren Court repeatedly refused, often over the objection of Justice Douglas, who publicly declared the war unconstitutional. That some justices either sided with Johnson on the war, which represented the culmination of the Cold War and liberal commitment to the containment of communism, and/or feared endangering their relationship with the president by expressing doubts, is clear. Moreover, historically, the Court had not significantly interfered with any war in progress. Yet the Warren Court decided many matters its predecessors had left to other branches of government.

Perhaps it missed an opportunity. Had the Court taken a case and decided against the government, it surely would not have ordered relief endangering deployed American soldiers. It could, however, have halted the induction of a few soldiers, while ruling the war unconstitutional. That symbolic victory for the antiwar movement might have helped persuade the administration to negotiate a settlement in Vietnam instead of pressing on for a victory in a war that LBJ knew was unwinnable. But the Warren Court, like the Burger Court afterward, ducked the issue. (The war did, however, bring some constitutional change: it sparked the enactment of the Twenty-sixth Amendment in 1971, which reduced the voting age from twenty-one to eighteen, on the rationale that those old enough to fight were old enough to vote.)

The Warren Court's sympathy for antiwar movement tactics was questionable. The Court's First Amendment record was often strong: in *New York Times v. Sullivan* (1964), it extended constitutional protection to newspapers and others badmouthing public officials by ruling that the officials could recover damages only if they showed the criticism had been made with false or reckless disregard of the truth, a blessing for those who reported on the civil rights movement and would have been deluged with libel or defamation suits from angry Southern officials otherwise.[39] And in *Brandenburg v. Ohio* (1969), the Court said that a Ku Kluxer's speech could be prohibited only if it is "directed to inciting or producing imminent lawless action and is likely to incite or produce such action."[40] That was a huge step beyond *Dennis v. United States* and a big one beyond "clear and present danger." But what about "symbolic speech"? Were nonverbal acts that communicated ideas entitled to the protection of the First Amendment?

No and yes. Consider two examples. The United States had long possessed legislation penalizing anyone who did not carry his draft card, but in 1965 Congress enacted an additional measure making knowingly destroying or mutilating it a separate offense. Prosecuted for dramatizing his disagreement with the war by publicly setting his card afire, David O'Brien claimed that the 1965 legislation infringed on his First Amendment rights. A lower federal court agreed, powerfully arguing that Congress had unconstitutionally targeted "symbolic speech." The Supreme Court did not. "We cannot accept the view that an apparently limitless variety of conduct can be labeled 'speech' whenever the person engaging in the conduct intends thereby to express an idea," Earl Warren wrote for the majority in *United States v. O'Brien* (1968). Even if it were, he added, government regulation of symbolic speech was justified "if it is within the constitutional power of the government; if it furthers an important or substantial governmental interest; if the governmental interest is unrelated to the suppression of free expression; and if the incidental restriction on alleged First Amendment freedoms is no greater than is essential to the furtherance of that interest."[41]

The following year, in *Tinker v. Des Moines* (1969), the Court sustained the First Amendment rights of junior high and secondary school students who protested the war by wearing black armbands in classrooms in defiance of school policy. The landmark opinion declared students did not "shed their constitutional rights to freedom of speech or expression at the schoolhouse gate."[42] *Tinker* repeatedly emphasized the peaceful, nondisruptive nature of the conduct and the fact that students were permitted to wear other political symbols, including the Nazi Iron Cross. It gave neither policymakers nor students as much guidance about acceptable symbolic speech as *O'Brien*, perhaps one reason for

Tinker's subsequent erosion. And in the context of "the sixties," which were all about disruption, *Tinker* represented no celebration of "student power." As one commentator observed, the justices had obviously decided "when they extended the First Amendment's free speech right to children that it would have to be a child-sized First Amendment."[43]

One can imagine Lyndon Johnson and other liberals nodding approvingly at the Court's disposition of *O'Brien* and *Tinker*, though. The opinions stressed hard-won constitutional ideals and the difference between the United States and its communist foes by permitting protest—up to a point. The president and others proved less comfortable with the Warren Court's record on crime.

Like so much else of its work, the Court's interest in reforming criminal procedure stemmed from its civil rights commitment: poor people of color received the short end of the stick from law enforcement. A 1961 opinion threw its criminal procedure work into high gear. *Mapp v. Ohio* (1961) held evidence obtained through an illegal search of the residence of Dollree Mapp, an African American who became known as "the Rosa Parks of the Fourth Amendment,"[44] inadmissible in state, as well as federal, criminal prosecutions.[45] A torrent of other opinions followed, but none caused as much consternation as *Miranda v. Arizona* (1966), ruling that police must advise all criminal suspects in custody of their rights to remain silent and to a court-appointed attorney.[46] The dissent complained the majority went "too far too fast."[47]

Today, some would disagree. By ensuring that police must generally acquire valid search warrants before they entered homes, *Mapp* encouraged officials to replace searches of private spaces with detested "stop and frisk" tactics, sanctioned by the Warren Court in *Terry v. Ohio* (1968), which targeted people of color in public places.[48] So, too, officials had feared a decision that went much farther than *Miranda*, possibly one forbidding interrogation in the absence of counsel, and were surely relieved by the ruling, which was not retroactive. The state still possessed sufficient evidence to justify a guilty verdict for Ernesto Miranda when it retried him without the tainted confession. Moreover, enough officials, including the FBI, already used "*Miranda* warnings" to know that suspects frequently waived their rights, especially when officials read them in a monotone suggesting their worthlessness and promised more favorable treatment if suspects did not "lawyer up."

In fact, in retrospect, it seems that the Warren Court's attempts to reduce the gulf between rich and poor defendants actually swelled it. Its efforts launched an army of overworked public defenders who relegated indigent clients, a disproportionate number of them Black or Brown, to mass incarceration by prompting them to plead guilty and by concentrating on cutting the time spent there, rather than obtaining acquittals. The Warren Court added procedural bells and whistles to safeguard defendant rights in criminal trials, but the rush toward plea bargaining made them less frequent. The Court's focus on policing also moved crime to the center of politics and prompted legislators competing for the "tough on crime" moniker to define crimes and sentences more punitively and in such a way that caused the mass incarceration of people of color and/or the poor.

But crime was increasing in the 1960s. Exactly why is still debated. And at the time, the media and pollsters fueled the impression that it was growing not alongside Warren Court decisions but because of them and their concern for people of color.

The explosion of northern and western inner cities during the "long hot summers" of the sixties, beginning with Harlem in 1964—two weeks after LBJ signed the Civil Rights Act—also meant that minority rage, often sparked by complaints about police mistreatment, was spreading outside the South. Five days after the Voting Rights Act became law in 1965, African Americans rose up in Los Angeles, leaving thirty-four dead. "We've got riots in all the major cities, and it's knocked our polls down by 15 percent," Johnson complained in 1966 to Justice Fortas while pushing his friend to persuade the justices "to do some-thing on law and order . . . and tell these fellows that they got to quit turning over cars and stuff."[49] Other especially deadly riots and rebellions occurred in Detroit and Newark in 1967 and in Washington, DC, in 1968. Whereas earlier in the 1960s, civil rights provided justification for changing the criminal justice system by causing many to equate Los Angeles cops with the redneck officials who brutalized protesters in Selma, now even some liberals, including the pres-ident and some justices, began to see people of color as part of the problem. The liberal interracialism of the early 1960s was crumbling. White supremacy had morphed into "law and order," though the transformation preserved the under-lying racism.

Republican presidential candidate Richard Nixon became one of the most en-thusiastic champions of "law and order" in 1968. Nixon allowed his audiences to create their own nightmare of disorderliness. Who needed to shape up? Perhaps antiwar protesters, inner-city people of color, school desegregation proponents, criminals "coddled" by the Warren Court, or all four. Enthusiastic audiences heard Nixon vow to unleash the "peace forces" against the lawless ones, espe-cially criminals, and to appoint "strict constructionists" of the Constitution to the Supreme Court. Such assurances, along with his unkept promise to end the Vietnam War, enabled him to eke out a narrow victory in 1968.

President Nixon continued condemning some Warren-era school desegrega-tion and crime decisions when as president he confronted a House and Senate still dominated by a healthy majority of Democrats and a Republican Party that still included liberals and moderates. He received a rare prize, four Supreme Court vacancies. Though he presided over a remarkably sloppy nominating process, he successfully made Warren Burger the new chief justice, and Harry

Blackmun, Lewis Powell, and William Rehnquist associate justices. Despite his acrid rhetoric, Nixon remained most invested in the Court for strategical political reasons and the opportunity it offered to make the GOP the new majority party by wooing white ethnics in the Northeast and Midwest and Southern whites away from the Democrats. Beyond that, he cared about the Supreme Court very little, if at all. So, although it was ironic that the Court Nixon created ended his presidency in *United States v. Nixon* (1974),[50] was it so startling that it upheld busing as a means of achieving racial balance in Southern schools in *Swann v. Charlotte-Mecklenburg Board of Education* (1971)?[51]

Like the Warren Court and LBJ, the Burger Court and Nixon look different with hindsight. During the 1960s, most, except for a few on the left, found the Warren Court almost revolutionary. Today it seems to fit comfortably within the mainstream of "sixties liberalism" that remained popular at least through 1965. Vilified by the left for a war he had inherited during the 1960s, LBJ now elicits praise from scholars for his domestic achievements. So, too, historians divide about the significance of Nixon's presidency. Some maintain that the sixties ended with his election, while others equally persuasively contend that the sixties continued into the early 1970s and that Nixon's presidency constituted a liberal high-water mark. As usual, what one sees depends on where one looks. Nixon scorned the Warren Court, but, thanks to federal spending, the poverty rate fell to its lowest point in recent history in his first term. And where constitutional experts in the 1980s portrayed the Burger Court as "the counter-revolution that wasn't" because it did not roll back Warren-era jurisprudence,[52] equally distinguished ones today emphasize the "stark . . . contrast" between the Warren and Burger Courts.[53] They point to the erosion of equality underlying Warren Court opinions during the Burger years and argue that despite its sanctioning of busing to achieve racial balance in the South, the Burger Court chomped, rather than nibbled, on its predecessor's school desegregation and criminal procedure decisions and lay the foundation for the infusion of "dark money" into political campaigns by protecting corporate "speech."

But almost all would stress the importance of placing the events between World War II and Watergate within Cold War parameters. They would also say that our continuing disagreements invigorate our teaching and scholarship. The disputes remind us that there is no historical "truth" and that each generation must write its own history. And they keep us all employed.

McCarthyism—Primary Sources

What eventually came to be known as McCarthyism, or the Second Red Scare, certainly did not originate with—and in fact involved far more than—the persona of Joe McCarthy. Indeed, the United States experienced its first "Red Scare" in reaction to the 1917 Bolshevik Revolution in tsarist Russia. In 1938, years before the start of the Cold War, the House of Representatives established a Committee on Un-American Activities (HUAC), which was charged with investigating "the extent, character, and objects of un-American propaganda activities in the United States [and] the diffusion within the United States of subversive and un-American propaganda that is instigated from foreign countries or of a domestic origin and attacks the principle of the form of government as guaranteed by our Constitution."[54] Over the course of more than two decades, HUAC subjected many witnesses—from Hollywood, academia, and leftist political organizations—to its most infamous interrogatory: "Are you now or have you ever been a member of the Communist Party?" Folk singer Pete Seeger (to pick only one example among many) was convicted of contempt by a court for refusing to answer the committee's questions about his political associations and beliefs (including whether he was "a member of the Communist Party"), as well as about various musical audiences before which he had performed.[55]

Smith Act (1940)

By 1940, even before the nation entered World War II, Congress had passed legislation, popularly referred to as the Smith Act (named after its chief author, Rep. Howard W. Smith, a Democrat from Virginia), which criminalized efforts to teach or advocate the overthrow of the government.

It shall be unlawful for any person—
(1) to knowingly or willfully advocate, abet, advise, or teach the duty, necessity, desirability, or propriety of overthrowing or destroying any government in the United States by force or violence or by the assassination of any officer of any such government;
(2) with the intent to cause the overthrow or destruction of any government in the United States, to print, publish, edit, issue, circulate, sell, distribute, or publicly display any written or printed matter advocating, advising, or teaching the duty, necessity, desirability, or propriety of overthrowing or destroying any government in the United States by force or violence;
(3) to organize or help to organize any society, group, or assembly of persons who teach, advocate, or encourage the overthrow or destruction of any government in the United States by force or violence; or to be or become a member of or affiliate with any such society, group, or assembly of persons, knowing the purposes thereof.[56]

"Loyalty" Reviews (1947)

During the late 1940s, a host of international tensions (e.g., the Berlin crisis, spying scandals, the Soviet acquisition of the atomic bomb, the "fall" of China to communism, and (soon) the stalemated conflict in Korea) caused many Americans to question the potential loyalty of some within their midst. Such concerns resonated even at the highest levels of government. In 1947, President Harry Truman issued an executive order establishing detailed procedures designed to assess the "loyalty" of current and prospective government employees.

> Whereas each employee of the government of the United States is endowed with a measure of trusteeship over the democratic processes which are the heart and sinew of the United States; and whereas it is of vital importance that persons employed in the federal service be of complete and unswerving loyalty to the United States; and whereas, although the loyalty of by far the overwhelming majority of all government employees is beyond question, the presence within the government service of any disloyal or subversive person constitutes a threat to our democratic processes; and whereas maximum protection must be afforded the United States against infiltration of disloyal persons into the ranks of its employees. . . .
>
> Part I—Investigation of applicants. There shall be a loyalty investigation of every person entering the civilian employment of any department or agency of the executive branch of the federal government. . . .
>
> Part II—Investigation of employees. The head of each department and agency in the executive branch of the government shall be personally responsible for an effective program to assure that disloyal civilian officers or employees are not retained in employment in his department or agency. . . . The head of each department and agency shall appoint one or more loyalty boards . . . for the purpose of hearing loyalty cases arising within such department or agency and making recommendations with respect to the removal of any officer or employee of such department or agency on grounds relating to loyalty.[57]

As a result of loyalty reviews during the Truman years, several hundred federal employees were dismissed from government service (and several thousand others resigned). In the next administration, President Dwight Eisenhower further expanded the criteria under which federal government employees and applicants could be reviewed: in addition to being "of complete and unswerving loyalty to the United States," were they also "reliable, trustworthy, [and] of good conduct and character"?[58] In what historians refer to as the "Lavender Scare," these so-called suitability reviews were often used to investigate and dismiss homosexuals, on the grounds that (in the words of the chairman of the

Republican Party) "sexual perverts who have infiltrated our government in recent years" were "perhaps as dangerous as the actual communists."[59]

Subversive Activities Control Act (1950)

Further evidence of how concerns about possible communist infiltration came to dominate the domestic political scene in the early Cold War years can be found in the Subversive Activities Control Act of 1950 (more commonly known as the McCarran Internal Security Act). The law required any "communist-action organization" or "communist-front organization" to register with the attorney general on an annual basis and to provide detailed reports about its leadership, membership, and finances. Failure to register (along with a host of other acts and omissions) subjected the offenders to criminal penalties. A newly established Subversive Activities Control Board was empowered to conduct investigations, issue subpoenas, and hold public hearings on the activities of such organizations and their members. The legislation was necessary, according to Congress, because:

> There exists a world communist movement which, in its origins, its development, and its present practice, is a world-wide revolutionary movement whose purpose it is, by treachery, deceit, infiltration into other groups (governmental and otherwise), espionage, sabotage, terrorism, and any other means deemed necessary, to establish a communist totalitarian dictatorship in the countries throughout the world through the medium of a world-wide communist organization. . . .
>
> The communist movement in the United States is an organization numbering thousands of adherents, rigidly and ruthlessly disciplined. Awaiting and seeking to advance a moment when the United States may be so far extended by foreign engagements, so far divided in counsel, or so far in industrial or financial straits that overthrow of the government of the United States by force and violence may seem possible of achievement, it seeks converts far and wide by an extensive system of schooling and indoctrination. . . . The communist organization in the United States, pursuing its stated objectives, the recent successes of communist methods in other countries, and the nature and control of the world communist movement itself present a clear and present danger to the security of the United States and to the existence of free American institutions, and make it necessary that Congress, in order to provide for the common defense, to preserve the sovereignty of the United States as an independent nation, and to guarantee to each state a republican form of government, enact appropriate legislation recognizing the existence of such worldwide conspiracy and designed to prevent it from accomplishing its purpose in the United States.[60]

McCarthy's "List" (1950)

Into this fertile mix stepped the junior senator from Wisconsin, Joseph McCarthy, who in early 1950 delivered largely unscripted remarks before the Republican Women's Club of Wheeling, West Virginia.

> Today we are engaged in a final, all-out battle between communistic atheism and Christianity. The modern champions of communism have selected this as the time, and ladies and gentlemen, the chips are down—they are truly down. . . . Ladies and gentlemen, can there be anyone tonight who is so blind as to say that the war is not on? . . . Six years ago . . . there was within the Soviet orbit, 180,000,000 people. Lined up on the antitotalitarian side there were in the world at that time, roughly 1,625,000,000 people. Today, only six years later, there are 800,000,000 people under the absolute domination of Soviet Russia— an increase of over 400 percent. On our side, the figure has shrunk to around 500,000,000. In other words, in less than six years, the odds have changed from nine-to-one in our favor to eight-to-five against us. This indicates the swiftness of the tempo of communist victories and American defeats in the cold war. As one of our outstanding historical figures once said, "When a great democracy is destroyed, it will not be from enemies from without, but rather because of enemies from within." . . .
>
> The reason why we find ourselves in a position of impotency is not because our only powerful potential enemy has sent men to invade our shores . . . but rather because of the traitorous actions of those who have been treated so well by this nation. It has not been the less fortunate or members of minority groups who have been traitorous to this nation, but rather those who have had all the benefits that the wealthiest nation on earth has had to offer . . . the finest homes, the finest college education, and the finest jobs in government we can give. This is glaringly true in the State Department. There the bright young men who are born with silver spoons in their mouths are the ones who have been most traitorous. . . .
>
> I have here in my hand a list of 205 . . . a list of names that were made known to the secretary of state as being members of the Communist Party and who nevertheless are still working and shaping policy in the State Department.[61]

In an "official" transcript of the speech he later submitted to the *Congressional Record*, McCarthy revised his specific allegation:

> In my opinion the State Department, which is one of the most important government departments, is thoroughly infested with communists. I have in my hand fifty-seven cases of individuals who would appear to be either card

carrying members or certainly loyal to the Communist Party, but who nevertheless are still helping to shape our foreign policy.[62]

Two days after his Wheeling remarks, McCarthy released a telegram he had written to President Truman. Any failure by Truman to investigate and remove the "nest of communists and communist sympathizers who are helping to shape our foreign policy," McCarthy contended, would "label the Democratic Party of being the bedfellow of international communism."[63] Over the next several years, he hurled highly publicized accusations—and launched numerous intrusive investigations—of alleged communist infiltration of public entities and government agencies, including the State Department, the White House, and the Army.

Margaret Chase Smith's "Declaration of Conscience" (1950)

Despite his prominence and power, McCarthy was not without his opponents. Perhaps foremost among them was a fellow Republican, Sen. Margaret Chase Smith of Maine. In June 1950, shortly after McCarthy's talk in Wheeling, Smith delivered a Senate speech that she referred to as a "Declaration of Conscience."

> I speak as a Republican. I speak as a woman. I speak as a United States senator. I speak as an American. The United States Senate has long enjoyed worldwide respect as the greatest deliberative body in the world. But recently that deliberative character has too often been debased to the level of a forum of hate and character assassination sheltered by the shield of congressional immunity. . . .
>
> Those of us who shout the loudest about Americanism in making character assassinations are all too frequently those who, by our own words and acts, ignore some of the basic principles of Americanism. The right to criticize. The right to hold unpopular beliefs. The right to protest. The right of independent thought. The exercise of these rights should not cost one single American citizen his reputation or his right to a livelihood nor should he be in danger of losing his reputation or livelihood merely because he happens to know someone who holds unpopular beliefs. Who of us does not? . . . The American people are sick and tired of being afraid to speak their minds lest they be politically smeared as "Communists" or "Fascists" by their opponents. Freedom of speech is not what it used to be in America. It has been so abused by some that it is not exercised by others. The American people are sick and tired of seeing innocent people smeared and guilty people whitewashed. . . .
>
> Surely it is clear that this nation will continue to suffer so long as it is governed by the present ineffective Democratic administration. Yet to displace it with a Republican regime embracing a philosophy that lacks political integrity or

intellectual honesty would prove equally disastrous to the nation. The nation sorely needs a Republican victory. But I do not want to see the Republican Party ride to political victory on the Four Horsemen of Calumny: Fear, Ignorance, Bigotry, and Smear.[64]

Dennis v. United States (1951)

Dozens of individuals and groups were eventually prosecuted under the Smith Act during the Cold War years, including, in 1949, eleven leaders of the American Communist Party. In *Dennis v. United States*, the Supreme Court upheld their criminal convictions, in an opinion written by Chief Justice Fred Vinson.

> [The Court of Appeals] held that the record in this case amply supports the necessary finding of the jury that petitioners, the leaders of the Communist Party in this country, were unwilling to work within our framework of democracy, but intended to initiate a violent revolution whenever the propitious occasion appeared. . . .
>
> The obvious purpose of the [Smith Act] is to protect existing government not from change by peaceable, lawful, and constitutional means, but from change by violence, revolution, and terrorism. That it is within the power of the Congress to protect the government of the United States from armed rebellion is a proposition which requires little discussion. Whatever theoretical merit there may be to the argument that there is a "right" to rebellion against dictatorial governments is without force where the existing structure of the government provides for peaceful and orderly change. . . .
>
> Congress did not intend to eradicate the free discussion of political theories, to destroy the traditional rights of Americans to discuss and evaluate ideas without fear of governmental sanction. Rather Congress was concerned with the very kind of activity in which the evidence showed these petitioners engaged. . . .
>
> In this case, we are squarely presented with the application of the "clear and present danger" test. . . . Overthrow of the government by force and violence is certainly a substantial enough interest for the government to limit speech. Indeed, this is the ultimate value of any society, for if a society cannot protect its very structure from armed internal attack, it must follow that no subordinate value can be protected.[65]

Dennis v. United States—Dissent (1951)

Two justices dissented from the Court's ruling, including William O. Douglas:

> Free speech has occupied an exalted position because of the high service it has given our society. Its protection is essential to the very existence of a democracy.

The airing of ideas releases pressures which otherwise might become destructive. When ideas compete in the market for acceptance, full and free discussion exposes the false, and they gain few adherents. Full and free discussion even of ideas we hate encourages the testing of our own prejudices and preconceptions. Full and free discussion keeps a society from becoming stagnant and unprepared for the stresses and strains that work to tear all civilizations apart. Full and free discussion has indeed been the first article of our faith. We have founded our political system on it.... We have deemed it more costly to liberty to suppress a despised minority than to let them vent their spleen....

There comes a time when even speech loses its constitutional immunity. Speech innocuous one year may at another time fan such destructive flames that it must be halted in the interests of the safety of the republic. That is the meaning of the clear and present danger test. When conditions are so critical that there will be no time to avoid the evil that the speech threatens, it is time to call a halt.... Yet free speech is the rule, not the exception. The restraint to be constitutional must be based on more than fear, on more than passionate opposition against the speech, on more than a revolted dislike for its contents. There must be some immediate injury to society that is likely if speech is allowed....

As a political party, [communists] are of little consequence. Communists in this country have never made a respectable or serious showing in any election. I would doubt that there is a village, let alone a city or county or state, which the communists could carry. Communism in the world scene is no bogeyman; but communism as a political faction or party in this country plainly is. Communism has been so thoroughly exposed in this country that it has been crippled as a political force. Free speech has destroyed it as an effective political party. It is inconceivable that those who went up and down this country preaching the doctrine of revolution which petitioners espouse would have any success.... How it can be said that there is a clear and present danger that this advocacy will succeed is, therefore, a mystery....

Free speech—the glory of our system of government—should not be sacrificed on anything less than plain and objective proof of danger that the evil advocated is imminent.... Our faith should be that our people will never give support to these advocates of revolution, so long as we remain loyal to the purposes for which our nation was founded.[66]

Yates v. United States (1957)

Eventually (although not until 1954), McCarthy's influence waned, to the point of being censured by his colleagues for conduct unbecoming a senator.[67] And eventually the Supreme Court came to adopt a far more tolerant judicial attitude toward the ideas and actions of communist sympathizers within the United States—and, in the process, a far more expansive reading of the First

Amendment. In *Yates v. United States*, the Court was forced to strain, intellectually and legally, to distinguish the case before it from the facts of the *Dennis* precedent. But the Court's volte-face led to the reversal of criminal convictions under the Smith Act of more than a dozen Communist Party "organizers." *Dennis* was effectively overruled, albeit not in so many words.

> We are thus faced with the question whether the Smith Act prohibits advocacy and teaching of forcible overthrow as an abstract principle, divorced from any effort to instigate action to that end, so long as such advocacy or teaching is engaged in with evil intent. We hold that it does not....
>
> The essence of the *Dennis* holding was that indoctrination of a group in preparation for future violent action, as well as exhortation to immediate action, by advocacy found to be directed to "action for the accomplishment" of forcible overthrow, to violence as "a rule or principle of action," and employing "language of incitement," is not constitutionally protected when the group is of sufficient size and cohesiveness, is sufficiently oriented towards action, and other circumstances are such as reasonably to justify apprehension that action will occur. This is quite a different thing from the view of [the trial court] that mere doctrinal justification of forcible overthrow, if engaged in with the intent to accomplish overthrow, is punishable per se under the Smith Act. That sort of advocacy, even though uttered with the hope that it may ultimately lead to violent revolution, is too remote from concrete action....
>
> The Smith Act does not denounce advocacy in the sense of preaching abstractly the forcible overthrow of the government.... The Smith Act reaches only advocacy of action for the overthrow of government by force and violence. The essential distinction is that those to whom the advocacy is addressed must be urged to *do* something, now or in the future, rather than merely to *believe* in something.[68]

Communist Control Act (1954)

The Supreme Court's decision in *Yates* reflected the tenor of the times, no less than had its earlier ruling in *Dennis*. Although the Cold War continued for more than three decades, by the late 1950s Americans (at least most of them) had learned to live (at least for the most part) with the "threat" of communism at home. Yet even today, more than three decades after the fall of the Berlin Wall, the Communist Control Act, passed in 1954, remains part of the federal code.

The Communist Party of the United States, or any successors of such party regardless of the assumed name, whose object or purpose is to overthrow the government of the United States, or the government of any state, territory, district, or possession thereof, or the government of any political subdivision therein by force and violence, are not entitled to any of the rights, privileges, and immunities attendant upon legal bodies created under the jurisdiction of the laws of the United States or any political subdivision thereof; and whatever rights, privileges, and immunities which have heretofore been granted to said party or any subsidiary organization by reason of the laws of the United States or any political subdivision thereof are terminated.[69]

Discussion Questions

1. Is it good or bad that Supreme Court decisions often reflect the tenor of their times—as (arguably) demonstrated by the very different outcomes reached by the Court several years apart in *Dennis* and *Yates*?

2. Should it be a crime to advocate "overthrowing or destroying any government in the United States by force or violence or by the assassination of any officer of any such government" (Smith Act)? If not, why not? How confident are we that "full and free discussion" will expose the "false" ideas of those unwilling to abide by democratic norms, as Justice Douglas maintained in his *Dennis* dissent? Should the Constitution permit communists (or Nazis; or white supremacists) to have the same free speech rights as everyone else?

3. Is it possible, as *Dennis* and *Yates* suggested, to draw lines between permissible speech and impermissible action?

4. Some would argue that McCarthyism, far from being an aberration, was part of a consistent pattern in American history of imposing restrictions on civil liberties and the rights of political minorities during times of war and national tension—for example, consider the Alien and Sedition Acts during the Quasi-War with France; the Sedition Act during World War I and the "Red Scare" immediately thereafter; and the internment of Japanese Americans during World War II. Is this a fair criticism of US history?

5. McCarthyism often involved the use and abuse of sensitive, confidential, nonpublic information about a person's past—for example, statements they made or wrote; organizations to which they belonged or supported, and so on. Especially given the massive amounts of information available about people nowadays on the internet and social media, should more

steps be taken to protect personal privacy or prevent the use and abuse of such information?

Civil Rights: School Desegregation—Primary Sources

In *Brown v. Board of Education* (1954), the Supreme Court unanimously rejected its nearly unanimous and utterly antithetical ruling in *Plessy v. Ferguson* (1896). Homer Plessy had no right to ride in a train carriage reserved by Louisiana law for "the white race" to which "he did not belong." The Fourteenth Amendment "could not have been intended to abolish distinctions based upon color," said the Court, and thus the Constitution was not offended by "equal but separate" accommodations.[70] As a result of the ruling, "Jim Crow" segregation laws proliferated throughout the South. And *Plessy* remained the law of the land for more than half a century—that is, until *Brown* struck down segregation laws in the nation's elementary and secondary public schools.

Brown did not come out of nowhere. In earlier decisions, the Supreme Court had deemed unconstitutional an all-white primary voting scheme[71] and racially discriminatory housing ordinances and covenants.[72] And in several successful lawsuits prior to *Brown*, lawyers from the NAACP, led by Thurgood Marshall, chipped away at *Plessy* by building factual records demonstrating, for example, the lack of "equal" educational opportunities at graduate and professional schools.[73] By the early 1950s, Marshall and his fellow advocates went for the jugular: they attacked the "separate but equal" doctrine root and branch.

John W. Davis Argument in *Brown* (1953)

During oral argument before the Supreme Court, John W. Davis, who had been the unsuccessful Democratic nominee for president in 1924, represented South Carolina, one of several states whose education segregation laws were under review. Davis maintained that "the overwhelming preponderance of the evidence demonstrate[d]" that desegregation of the public schools had never been envisioned by the authors of Fourteenth Amendment. In any event, a system of "separate" but "equal" education facilities was perfectly permissible under the Constitution.

> We are not concerned here with the mandate of the Constitution that the Negro, as well as the white, shall enjoy the equal protection of the laws. The question with which Your Honors are confronted is: Is segregation in schools a denial of equality where the segregation runs against one race as well as against the other,

and where, in the eye of the law, no difference between the educational facilities of the two classes can be discerned? . . .

It was not the understanding of the framers of the Amendment that future Congresses might . . . abolish segregation in public schools. And . . . it was not the understanding of the framers of the Amendment that it would be within the judicial power, in light of future conditions, to construe the Amendment as abolishing segregation in public schools of its own force. . . .

If [desegregation] is done on the mathematical basis [in the schools of Clarendon, South Carolina, for example], . . . you would have twenty-seven Negro children and three whites in one school room. Would that make the children any happier? Would they learn any more quickly? Would their lives be more serene? . . . Would the terrible psychological disaster being wrought, according to some of these witnesses, to the colored child be removed if he had three white children sitting somewhere in the same school room? Would white children be prevented from getting a distorted idea of racial relations if they sat with twenty-seven Negro children? . . . You say that is racism. Well, it is not racism. Recognize that for sixty centuries and more humanity has been discussing questions of race and race tension, not racism. . . .

Let me say this for the state of South Carolina. . . . It believes that its legislation is not offensive to the Constitution of the United States. It is confident of its good faith and intention to produce equality for all of its children of whatever race or color. It is convinced that the happiness, the progress, and the welfare of these children is best promoted in segregated schools, and it thinks it a thousand pities that by this controversy there should be urged the return to an experiment which gives no more promise of success today than when it was written into their Constitution during what I call the tragic era [of Reconstruction].[74]

Thurgood Marshall Argument in *Brown* (1952, 1953)

Thurgood Marshall—who himself would later (from 1967 to 1991) serve as a justice of the Supreme Court—argued in response:

Witnesses testified that segregation deterred the development of the personalities of these children. Two witnesses testified that it deprives them of equal status in the community, that it destroys their self-respect. Two other witnesses testified that it denies them full opportunity for democratic social development. Another witness said that it stamps him with a badge of inferiority. The summation of that testimony is that the Negro children have road blocks put up in their minds as a result of this segregation, so that the amount of education that they take in is much less than other students take in. . . .

In each instance where these matters come up in [a] "sensitive" field [such as] civil rights, freedom of speech, etc., at all times they have this position: The majority of the people wanted the statute; that is how it was passed. There are always respectable people who can be quoted as in support of a statute. But in each case, this Court has made its own independent determination as to whether that statute is valid. Yet in this case, the Court is urged to give blanket approval that this field of segregation and, if I may say, this field of racial segregation, is purely to be left to the states, the direct opposite of what the Fourteenth Amendment was passed for.[75]

The same argument has been made in every case that has come up to this Court: . . that you should leave this because it has been longstanding, the "separate but equal" doctrine, and there are so many states involved. . . . You leave it to the states, they say; and then they say that the states haven't done anything about it in a hundred years. . . . The argument of judicial restraint has no application in this case. . . . The duty of following the Fourteenth Amendment is placed upon the states. The duty of enforcing the Fourteenth Amendment is placed upon this Court. . . . We hereby charge them with making the same argument that was made before the Civil War, . . . the same argument that was made during the period between the ratification of the Fourteenth Amendment and the *Plessy v. Ferguson* case. . . .

I understand them to say that it is just a little feeling on the part of Negroes: They don't like segregation. As Mr. Davis said yesterday, the only thing the Negroes are trying to get is prestige. Exactly correct. Ever since the Emancipation Proclamation, the Negro has been trying to get . . . the same status as anybody else regardless of race. . . . They can't take race out of this case. . . . [School segregation laws] are Black Codes. . . . The only way to [defend these laws] is to find that for some reason Negroes are inferior to all other human beings. . . . [There must be some] reason why, of all of the multitudinous groups of people in this country, you have to single out Negroes and give them this separate treatment. . . . The only thing [it] can be is an inherent determination that the people who were formerly in slavery, regardless of anything else, shall be kept as near that stage as is possible; and now is the time, we submit, that this Court should make it clear that that is not what our Constitution stands for.[76]

Brown v. Board of Education (1954)

The unanimous opinion of the Supreme Court in *Brown v. Board of Education* was delivered by Chief Justice Earl Warren in May 1954.

There are findings below that the Negro and white schools involved have been equalized, or are being equalized, with respect to buildings, curricula, qualifications and salaries of teachers, and other "tangible" factors. Our decision, therefore, cannot turn on merely a comparison of these tangible factors in the Negro and white schools involved in each of the cases. We must look instead to the effect of segregation itself on public education.

In approaching this problem, we cannot turn the clock back to 1868, when the Amendment was adopted, or even to 1896, when *Plessy v. Ferguson* was written. We must consider public education in the light of its full development and its present place in American life throughout the nation. Only in this way can it be determined if segregation in public schools deprives these plaintiffs of the equal protection of the laws.

Today, education is perhaps the most important function of state and local governments. Compulsory school attendance laws and the great expenditures for education both demonstrate our recognition of the importance of education to our democratic society. . . . It is the very foundation of good citizenship. . . . In these days, it is doubtful that any child may reasonably be expected to succeed in life if he is denied the opportunity of an education. Such an opportunity, where the state has undertaken to provide it, is a right which must be made available to all on equal terms.

We come then to the question presented: Does segregation of children in public schools solely on the basis of race, even though the physical facilities and other "tangible" factors may be equal, deprive the children of the minority group of equal educational opportunities? We believe that it does. . . . To separate [students] from others of similar age and qualifications solely because of their race generates a feeling of inferiority as to their status in the community that may affect their hearts and minds in a way unlikely ever to be undone. . . . Segregation of white and colored children in public schools has a detrimental effect upon the colored children. The impact is greater when it has the sanction of the law, for the policy of separating the races is usually interpreted as denoting the inferiority of the Negro group. A sense of inferiority affects the motivation of a child to learn. . . .

We conclude that in the field of public education, the doctrine of "separate but equal" has no place. Separate educational facilities are inherently unequal.[77]

Criticism of *Brown* (1955)

Brown v. Board of Education is now accorded almost iconic status in American constitutional law; it is a judicial opinion that rarely gets criticized. But at the time, not all African Americans were supportive; some questioned the supposed benefits of integration; others envisioned (correctly) that the ruling would lead many Black teachers to lose their jobs. Consider this 1955 public letter from novelist and anthropologist Zora Neale Hurston.

> How much satisfaction can I get from a court order for somebody to associate with me who does not wish me near them? . . . If there are not adequate Negro schools in Florida, and there is some residual, some inherent and unchangeable quality in white schools, impossible to duplicate anywhere else, then I am the first to insist that Negro children of Florida be allowed to share this boon. But if there are adequate Negro schools and prepared instructors and instructions, then there is nothing different except the presence of white people. For this reason, I regard the ruling of the US Supreme Court as insulting rather than honoring my race. Since the days of the never-to-be-sufficiently deplored Reconstruction, there has been current the belief that there is no great[er] delight to Negroes than physical association with whites. . . . Meanwhile, personally, I am not delighted. . . . Negro schools in the state are in very good shape and on the improve.[78]

Southern Manifesto (1956)

Less surprising, *Brown* was denounced by many white Southerners, who vowed to "resist" the Court's desegregation decrees by any and all available means. Nineteen senators and eighty-two representatives (all hailing from states of the former Confederacy) signed what became known as the *Southern Manifesto* in 1956.

> The unwarranted decision of the Supreme Court in the public school cases is now bearing the fruit always produced when men substitute naked power for established law. The Founding Fathers gave us a Constitution of checks and balances because they realized the inescapable lesson of history that no man or group of men can be safely entrusted with unlimited power. They framed this Constitution with its provisions for change by amendment in order to secure the fundamentals of government against the dangers of temporary popular passion or the personal predilections of public officeholders. We regard the decisions of the Supreme Court in the school cases as a clear abuse of judicial power. It climaxes a trend in the federal judiciary undertaking to legislate, in derogation of the authority of Congress, and to encroach upon the reserved rights of the states and the people.
>
> The original Constitution does not mention education. Neither does the Fourteenth Amendment nor any other amendment. The debates preceding the submission of the Fourteenth Amendment clearly show that there was no

intent that it should affect the system of education maintained by the states. The very Congress which proposed the amendment subsequently provided for segregated schools in the District of Columbia. . . .

In the case of *Plessy v. Ferguson* in 1896, the Supreme Court expressly declared that under the Fourteenth Amendment no person was denied any of his rights if the states provided separate but equal facilities. This decision has been followed in many other cases. It is notable that the Supreme Court, speaking through Chief Justice Taft, a former President of the United States, unanimously declared in 1927 in *Lum v. Rice*[79] that the "separate but equal" principle is "within the discretion of the state in regulating its public schools and does not conflict with the Fourteenth Amendment." This interpretation, restated time and again, became a part of the life of the people of many of the states and confirmed their habits, traditions, and way of life. It is founded on elemental humanity and common sense, for parents should not be deprived by government of the right to direct the lives and education of their own children. Though there has been no constitutional amendment or act of Congress changing this established legal principle almost a century old, the Supreme Court of the United States, with no legal basis for such action, undertook to exercise their naked judicial power and substituted their personal political and social ideas for the established law of the land.

This unwarranted exercise of power by the Court, contrary to the Constitution, is creating chaos and confusion in the states principally affected. It is destroying the amicable relations between the white and Negro races that have been created through ninety years of patient effort by the good people of both races. It has planted hatred and suspicion where there has been heretofore friendship and understanding. Without regard to the consent of the governed, outside mediators are threatening immediate and revolutionary changes in our public school systems. If done, this is certain to destroy the system of public education in some of the states.

With the gravest concern for the explosive and dangerous condition created by this decision and inflamed by outside meddlers: We reaffirm our reliance on the Constitution as the fundamental law of the land. We decry the Supreme Court's encroachment on the rights reserved to the states and to the people, contrary to established law and to the Constitution. We commend the motives of those states which have declared the intention to resist forced integration by any lawful means. We appeal to the states and people who are not directly affected by these decisions to consider the constitutional principles involved against the time when they, too, on issues vital to them may be the victims of judicial encroachment. . . . We pledge ourselves to use all lawful means to bring about a reversal of this decision which is contrary to the Constitution and to prevent the use of force in its implementation.[80]

Cooper v. Aaron (1958)

One year after *Brown*, the Supreme Court directed that school desegregation proceed "with all deliberate speed."[81] But resistance continued—most prominently requiring President Eisenhower to send federal troops to Little Rock, Arkansas. In 1958, in the face of continued recalcitrance, the Supreme Court explained why state and local officials were obligated to follow *Brown* even if they disagreed with its holding.

> As this case reaches us, it raises questions of the highest importance to the maintenance of our federal system of government. It necessarily involves a claim by the governor and legislature of a state that there is no duty on state officials to obey federal court orders resting on this Court's considered interpretation of the United States Constitution. Specifically, it involves actions by the governor and legislature of Arkansas upon the premise that they are not bound by our holding in *Brown v. Board of Education*. . . .
>
> The constitutional rights of [school children] are not to be sacrificed or yielded to the violence and disorder which have followed upon the actions of the governor and legislature. As this Court said some forty-one years ago in a unanimous opinion in a case involving another aspect of racial segregation: "It is urged that this proposed segregation will promote the public peace by preventing race conflicts. Desirable as this is, and important as is the preservation of the public peace, this aim cannot be accomplished by laws or ordinances which deny rights created or protected by the federal Constitution." Thus, law and order are not here to be preserved by depriving the Negro children of their constitutional rights. . . .
>
> We should answer the premise of the actions of the governor and legislature that they are not bound by our holding in the *Brown* case. It is necessary only to recall some basic constitutional propositions which are settled doctrine. Article VI of the Constitution makes the Constitution the "supreme Law of the Land." In 1803, Chief Justice Marshall, speaking for a unanimous Court, referring to the Constitution as "the fundamental and paramount law of the nation," declared in the notable case of *Marbury v. Madison* . . . that "it is emphatically the province and duty of the judicial department to say what the law is." This decision declared the basic principle that the federal judiciary is supreme in the exposition of the law of the Constitution, and that principle has ever since been respected by this Court and the country as a permanent and indispensable feature of our constitutional system. It follows that the interpretation of the Fourteenth Amendment enunciated by this Court in the *Brown* case is the supreme law of the land, and Article VI of the Constitution makes it of binding

effect on the states "any Thing in the Constitution or Laws of any State to the Contrary notwithstanding." . . .

It is, of course, quite true that the responsibility for public education is primarily the concern of the states, but it is equally true that such responsibilities, like all other state activity, must be exercised consistently with federal constitutional requirements as they apply to state action. The Constitution created a government dedicated to equal justice under law. The Fourteenth Amendment embodied and emphasized that ideal. State support of segregated schools through any arrangement, management, funds, or property cannot be squared with the Amendment's command that no state shall deny to any person within its jurisdiction the equal protection of the laws.[82]

Resistance to desegregation continued nonetheless—and even sixty-plus years later, the debate continues as to the decision's actual effectiveness in achieving integration in the nation's public schools. But there can be no doubt that as a matter of constitutional law, *Brown*'s long-term significance, no less than its immediate holding, was profound and transformative.

Discussion Questions

1. Compare and contrast the successes and limitations of achieving significant constitutional change through the courts (as in *Brown*), or through legislation (as with the Civil Rights Act of 1964 and the Voting Rights Act of 1965), or through citizen protest and activism (as during the Montgomery bus boycott, sit-ins, Selma, etc.).

2. Does the Equal Protection Clause at issue in *Brown* concern equality only of opportunities or also of outcomes? Political equality only or also social and economic equality? And equality between/among which persons and/or groups?

3. The government treats people "unequally" all the time: by building a road in one neighborhood but not another; by spending money to eradicate one disease but not another; by prohibiting some pollutants but not every pollutant; by imposing a higher tax rate on some people compared to others. Broadly speaking, courts have held that such legislation is permissible as long as the government does not treat individuals or groups unequally because of, or on the basis of, their race, ethnicity, religion, gender, and sexual orientation. Why are distinctions made with respect to these categories somehow more "suspect" than others? Separately, should it ever be permissible for the government to draw distinctions on the basis of race or

gender (for instance, in the context of affirmative action or to redress past wrongs)?

4. What were the competing arguments of John W. Davis and Thurgood Marshall about the effects of school segregation? Why did the Supreme Court conclude that "separate educational facilities are inherently unequal"?

5. In footnote 11 of its opinion in *Brown*, the Supreme Court invoked social science studies in support of a conclusion that segregation stigmatized Black schoolchildren. What are the reasons the Supreme Court should or should not rely on such evidence in interpreting the Constitution?

6. The *Southern Manifesto* complained that "though there has been no con-stitutional amendment or act of Congress changing this established legal principle almost a century old, the Supreme Court of the United States, with no legal basis for such action, undertook to exercise their naked ju-dicial power and substituted their personal political and social ideas for the established law of the land." How valid is this objection to the *Brown* decision?

7. In *Cooper v. Aaron*, the Supreme Court declared that "the federal judiciary is supreme in the exposition of the law of the Constitution." The Abraham Lincoln who contested the *Dred Scott* decision would not have agreed with the Court being the "ultimate interpreter" of the Constitution. To what extent is the Court's constitutional primacy mandated by (or not), and consistent with (or not) (a) the text of Article III of the Constitution; (b) the Supreme Court's decision in *Marbury v. Madison*; and (c) the Supreme Court's role and powers—and resistance to its role and powers— throughout the nation's history?

Civil Rights: Public Accommodations—Primary Sources

If *Brown* represented the culmination of years of sophisticated legal attacks on *Plessy* and school segregation, it could also be viewed as only the opening scene in what became a decade-long drama known as the modern civil rights move-ment. *Brown*—at least on paper—ended the doctrine of "separate but equal" for public schools, but by its terms, it had no direct bearing on the countless Jim Crow laws littered throughout the South—laws that affected not only schools but virtually every aspect of public life. Public facilities—restaurants, hotels, buses and streetcars, bathrooms, barber shops, drinking fountains, waiting rooms, telephone booths, libraries, parks, swimming pools, beaches, even cemeteries— remained segregated by race as a matter of law.

In 1905, the City of Ensley, Alabama, required all barbers to use separate razors, brushes, linens, and chairs for black and white patrons, while the City of Birmingham outlawed interracial games of pool, cards, dice, dominoes, checkers, and billiards. Arkansas and Florida segregated black and white prisoners, and in 1939, Louisiana required circuses to maintain separate, racially segregated tent entrances and ticket booths. Hospitals, public transportation, and public schools were segregated throughout the South.[83]

Appeal for Human Rights (1960)

The struggle for civil rights after *Brown* played out in venues far beyond the courts: on the pavement of Montgomery, as bus boycotters walked to work for a year after the arrest of Rosa Parks; at segregated lunch counters and hundreds of public facilities, as students engaged in provocative "sit-ins"; on interstate bus lines, especially during the dramatic Freedom Rides; in the streets of Albany, Georgia, and Birmingham, Alabama, and elsewhere, as thousands upon thousands (including young children) marched for their rights in the face of intimidation, violence, and imprisonment. Fundamentally, the struggle over civil rights was a constitutional struggle: One full century after ratification of the Fourteenth Amendment, how could "equal protection of the laws" be guaranteed to every "person," regardless of race?

Shortly after the sit-in protests began, a group of students from historically-Black colleges in Atlanta attempted to address that question. In March 1960, they published *An Appeal for Human Rights* in local newspapers. Their professed goal was to gain "those rights which are inherently ours as members of the human race and as citizens of these United States"—especially with respect to education, jobs, housing, voting, access to public facilities, and law enforcement.

> The students who instigate and participate in these sit-down protests are dissatisfied not only with the existing conditions, but with the snail-like speed at which they are being ameliorated. . . . We do not intend to wait placidly for those rights which are already legally and morally ours to be meted out to us one at a time. Today's youth will not sit by submissively while being denied all of the rights, privileges, and joys of life. . . .
>
> We hold that:
>
> (1) The practice of racial segregation is not in keeping with the ideals of Democracy and Christianity.
> (2) Racial segregation is robbing not only the segregated but the segregator of his human dignity. Furthermore, the propagation [of] racial prejudice is unfair to the generations yet unborn.
> (3) In times of war, the Negro has fought and died for his country; yet he still has not been accorded first-class citizenship.

(4)   In spite of the fact that the Negro pays his share of taxes, he does not enjoy participation in city, county, and state government at the level where laws are enacted.

(5)   The social, economic, and political progress of Georgia is retarded by segregation and prejudices.

(6)   America is fast losing the respect of other nations by the poor example which she sets [in] the area of race relations.

It is unfortunate that [the] Negro is being forced to fight, in any way, for what is due him and is freely accorded other Americans. It is unfortunate that even today some people should hold to the erroneous idea of racial [superiority], despite the fact that the world is fast moving toward an integrated humanity.... We plan to use every legal and non-violent means at our disposal to secure full citizenship rights as members of this great democracy of ours.[84]

Opposition to Civil Rights Protests (1963)

Not everyone welcomed the "civil disobedience" approach of sit-ins, street marches, and boycotts. In early 1963, as Martin Luther King Jr. brought his civil rights campaign to Birmingham, a group of white clergymen issued an appeal for "law and order and common sense." The religious leaders condemned "defiance, anarchy, and subversion," and "urge[d] those who strongly oppose desegregation to pursue their convictions in the courts, and in the meantime peacefully to abide by the decisions of those same courts."[85] Several months later, local officials in Birmingham obtained a state court injunction prohibiting further demonstrations, which King and other civil rights leaders defied, leading to their arrests. The Birmingham clergy issued a second appeal, this time directing their focus more pointedly at King and his fellow protesters.

We are now confronted by a series of demonstrations by some of our Negro citizens, directed and led in part by outsiders. We recognize the natural impatience of people who feel that their hopes are slow in being realized. But we are convinced that these demonstrations are unwise and untimely....

Just as we formerly pointed out that "hatred and violence have no sanction in our religious and political traditions," we also point out that such actions as incite to hatred and violence, however technically peaceful those actions may be, have not contributed to the resolution of our local problems....

We further strongly urge our own Negro community to withdraw support from these demonstrations and to unite locally in working peacefully for a better Birmingham. When rights are consistently denied, a cause should be pressed in the courts and in negotiations among local leaders, and not in the streets. We appeal to both our white and Negro citizenry to observe the principles of law and order and common sense.[86]

It was in response to this "appeal" from the city's religious leaders that King wrote his "Letter from Birmingham Jail," which outlined his justification for civil disobedience against "unjust" and "morally wrong and sinful" segregation laws.

John F. Kennedy Civil Rights Speech (1963)

After the highly publicized and visibly disturbing events in Birmingham and other efforts by state and local officials to resist integration, President John F. Kennedy, putting aside previous hesitations, called for national civil rights legislation.

We are confronted primarily with a moral issue. It is as old as the scriptures and is as clear as the American Constitution. The heart of the question is whether all Americans are to be afforded equal rights and equal opportunities, whether we are going to treat our fellow Americans as we want to be treated. . . .

We preach freedom around the world and we mean it, and we cherish our freedom here at home, but are we to say to the world, and much more importantly to each other, that this is the land of the free except for the Negroes; that we have no second-class citizens except Negroes; that we have no class or caste system, no ghettoes, no master race except with respect to Negroes?

Now the time has come for this nation to fulfill its promise. The events in Birmingham and elsewhere have so increased the cries for equality that no city or state or legislative body can prudently choose to ignore them. . . . We face, therefore, a moral crisis as a country and a people. It cannot be met by repressive police action. It cannot be left to increased demonstrations in the streets. It cannot be quieted by token moves or talk. It is a time to act in the Congress . . .

I am therefore asking the Congress to enact legislation giving all Americans the right to be served in facilities which are open to the public—hotels, restaurants, theaters, retail stores, and similar establishments. This seems to me to be an elementary right. Its denial is an arbitrary indignity that no American in 1963 should have to endure, but many do.[87]

But despite Kennedy's appeal—and despite the March on Washington shortly thereafter, at which Dr. King delivered his dramatic "I Have a Dream" speech—civil rights legislation faltered in Congress.

Lyndon Johnson Civil Rights Speech (1963)

Five days after President Kennedy's assassination, the new president, Lyndon Johnson, appeared before a joint session of Congress and reiterated the call for civil rights legislation.

> No memorial oration or eulogy could more eloquently honor President Kennedy's memory than the earliest possible passage of the civil rights bill for which he fought so long. We have talked long enough in this country about equal rights. We have talked for one hundred years or more. It is time now to write the next chapter, and to write it in the books of law.[88]

Johnson and civil rights leaders then led aggressive efforts to secure congressional passage of an antisegregation law.

Strom Thurmond Opposes Civil Rights Legislation (1964)

By early 1964, the House of Representatives had passed a civil rights bill by a nearly two-to-one margin. In the Senate, however, progress stalled, as debates and filibusters stretched on for more than sixty days. In a television appearance at the time, Senator Strom Thurmond, a Democrat (although later a Republican) from South Carolina, attacked the proposed legislation.

> This bill, in order to bestow preferential rights on a favored few who vote en bloc, would sacrifice the constitutional rights of every citizen and would concentrate in the national government arbitrary powers, unchained by laws, to suppress the liberty of all. This bill makes a shambles of constitutional guarantees and the Bill of Rights. . . . It empowers the national government to tell each citizen who must be allowed to enter upon and use his property without any compensation or due process of law as guaranteed by the Constitution. This bill would take away the rights of individuals and give to government the power to decide who is to be hired, fired, and promoted in private businesses. . . . This bill would abandon the principle of a government of laws in favor of a government of men. It would give the power in government to government bureaucrats to decide what is discrimination. . . .
>
> It is because of these and other radical departures from our constitutional system that the attempt is being made to railroad this bill through Congress without following normal procedures. . . . The issue is whether the Senate will pay the high cost of sacrificing a precious portion of each and every individual's constitutional rights in a vain effort to satisfy the demands of the mob. The

choice is between law and anarchy. What shall rule these United States, the Constitution or the mob? . . .

This title is entirely a misnomer. It's not public accommodations, it's invasion of private property. This will lead to integration of private life. The Constitution says that a man shall not be deprived of life, liberty, or property. We should observe the Constitution. . . . We live in a country of freedom—and under our Constitution a man has a right to use his own private property as he sees fit.[89]

Everett Dirksen Supports Civil Rights Legislation (1964)

Senate Minority Leader Everett Dirksen, a Republican from Illinois—one of more than 150 Republicans in Congress who ultimately voted for civil rights legislation—argued in favor of the law.

It is said that on the night he died, [French novelist] Victor Hugo wrote in his diary substantially this sentiment: Stronger than all the armies is an idea whose time has come. The time has come for equality of opportunity in sharing in government, in education, and in employment. It will not be stayed or denied. It is here. The problem began when the Constitution makers permitted the importation of persons to continue for another twenty years. That problem was to generate the fury of civil strife seventy-five years later. Out of it was to come the Thirteenth Amendment ending servitude, the Fourteenth Amendment to provide equal protection of the laws and dual citizenship, the Fifteenth Amendment to prohibit government from abridging the right to vote. Other factors had an impact. Two and three-quarter million young Negroes served in World Wars I, II, and Korea. Some won the Congressional Medal of Honor and the Distinguished Service Cross. Today they are fathers and grandfathers. They brought back impressions from countries where no discrimination existed. These impressions have been transmitted to children and grandchildren. Meanwhile, hundreds of thousands . . . have become teachers and professors, doctors and dentists, engineers and architects, artists and actors, musicians and technicians. They have become status minded. They have sensed inequality. . . . They feel that the time has come for the idea of equal opportunity. . . .

The issue which is before us . . . is essentially moral in character. . . . Nor is it the first time in our history that an issue with moral connotations and implications has swept away the resistance, the fulminations, the legalistic speeches, the ardent but dubious arguments, the lamentations, and the thought patterns of an earlier generation and pushed forward to fruition. More than sixty years ago came the first efforts to secure federal pure food and drug legislation. The speeches made on this floor against this intrusion of federal power sound fantastically incredible today. But it would not be stayed. Its time had come.... When the first efforts were made to ban the shipment of goods in interstate commerce made with child labor, it was regarded as quite absurd.... More than eighty years ago came the first efforts to establish a civil service and merit system to cover federal employees. The proposal was ridiculed and drenched with sarcasm.... Fifty years ago, the Constitution was amended to provide for the direct election of senators. Its time had come. Ninety-five years ago came the first endeavor to remove the limitation on sex in the exercise of the franchise. The comments made in those early days sound unbelievably ludicrous. But on and on went the effort and became the Nineteenth Amendment to the Constitution. Its time had come....

These are but some of the things touching closely the affairs of the people which were met with stout resistance, with shrill and strident cries of radicalism, with strained legalisms, with anguished entreaties that the foundations of the republic were being rocked. But an inexorable moral force which operates in the domain of human affairs swept these efforts aside and today they are accepted as parts of the social, economic, and political fabric of America. Pending before us is another moral issue. . . . It deals with equality of opportunity in exercising the franchise, in securing an education, in making a livelihood, in enjoying the mantle of protection of the law.[90]

Clarence Mitchell Eyewitness Account (1964)

Eventually, the Civil Rights Act of 1964 passed the Senate (by a final vote of 73–27) and was signed by President Johnson. But it would be a mistake to view this triumph solely through the lens of debates and votes and compromises in Congress and the executive branch. Instead, the comprehensive and sweeping desegregation legislation that ultimately became the law of the land resulted from years of courageous struggle by civil rights advocates and strategists, leaders and foot soldiers alike. As Clarence Mitchell, Director of the Washington Bureau of the NAACP, observed at the time:

In a jammed chamber of the US Senate there came the solemn moment on Friday, June 19, when the . . . civil rights bill was approved. . . . This letter is written . . . following a conversation with a daily newspaperman. He admitted that they had agreed that their news reporting in the Senate would focus on the role of Senator Dirksen and, in effect, ignore any other forces that may have had an effect upon approval of the bill.

However, the facts of history cannot be changed. It is a fact that the passage of the civil rights bill has come about because of the tremendous and consistent work that you [the NAACP] and others have done to make it possible. It is true that there have been some magnificent contributions by Senate leaders in this fight, but it was also you and the people that you represent who used your resources to make it possible for us to get a successful vote.[91]

Civil Rights Act of 1964

By its terms, the Civil Rights Act of 1964 prohibited all discrimination on the basis of race—or on the basis of national origin or religion—with respect to any public accommodations involved in interstate commerce. In one blow, Jim Crow statutes throughout the nation were nullified.

Section 201. (a) All persons shall be entitled to the full and equal enjoyment of the goods, services, facilities, privileges, advantages, and accommodations of any place of public accommodation, as defined in this section, without discrimination or segregation on the ground of race, color, religion, or national origin.

(b) Each of the following establishments which serves the public is a place of public accommodation within the meaning of this title if its operations affect commerce, or if discrimination or segregation by it is supported by state action:

(1) any inn, hotel, motel, or other establishment which provides lodging to transient guests, other than an establishment located within a building which contains not more than five rooms for rent or hire and which is actually occupied by the proprietor of such establishment as his residence; (2) any restaurant, cafeteria, lunchroom, lunch counter, soda fountain, or other facility principally engaged in selling food for consumption on the premises, including but not limited to any such facility located on the premises of any retail establishment; or any gasoline station; (3) any motion picture house, theater, concert hall, sports arena, stadium, or other place of exhibition or entertainment. . . .

Section 202. All persons shall be entitled to be free at any establishment or place from discrimination or segregation of any kind on the ground of race, color, religion, or national origin, if such discrimination or segregation is or purports to be required by any law, statute, ordinance, regulation, rule, or order of a state or any agency or political subdivision thereof.[92]

Prohibition on Employment Discrimination (1964)

The 1964 Act gave significant new powers to the attorney general and the Department of Justice to strengthen federal oversight of school desegregation and voting. The law also mandated nondiscrimination in all federal programs and established a new Commission on Civil Rights. Additionally, the legislation prohibited discrimination in employment on the basis of both race and sex, and it established the Equal Employment Opportunity Commission, which was charged with preventing, investigating, and punishing racial and gender discrimination in most workplaces.

Section 703. (a) It shall be an unlawful employment practice for an employer:

(1) to fail or refuse to hire or to discharge any individual, or otherwise to discriminate against any individual with respect to his compensation, terms, conditions, or privileges of employment, because of such individual's race, color, religion, sex, or national origin; or (2) to limit, segregate, or classify his employees in any way which would deprive or tend to deprive any individual of employment opportunities or otherwise adversely affect his status as an employee, because of such individual's race, color, religion, sex, or national origin.[93]

The Supreme Court and the Civil Rights Act

In a pair of opinions delivered later the same year, the Supreme Court unanimously upheld the 1964 Civil Rights Act against a host of constitutional challenges.[94] As a result of the civil rights revolution, Linda Brown was able to walk to and attend her neighborhood elementary school in Topeka, Kansas— and Ollie's Barbecue, "a family owned restaurant in Birmingham, Alabama, specializing in barbecued meats and homemade pies,"[95] was no longer permitted to serve only white diners. Important and dramatic changes had come to the nation. Indeed, from a constitutional perspective, the transformation that occurred between *Brown* and *McClung* was no less important, and no less dramatic, than what had taken place between the *Dred Scott* decision and the passage of the Fourteenth Amendment.

Discussion Questions

1. In a nation pledged to the rule of law, is civil disobedience ever justified? That was at least one objection raised by the Birmingham clergy (although they likely had other motivations). How did King's refusal to obey an "unjust" or "immoral" law differ from Southern segregationists who refused to follow the Supreme Court's ruling in *Brown*?

2. What were the strongest arguments offered against civil rights legislation? To what extent were those arguments legitimately couched in terms of important constitutional principles—for example, federalism and states' rights; the preservation of "liberty"; the protection of private property—as opposed to appeals to discrimination and racism? Was the Civil Rights Act of 1964 a "radical departure from our constitutional system" (Senator Thurmond) or the fulfillment of the principles of the Thirteenth, Fourteenth, and Fifteenth Amendments (Senator Dirksen)? Indeed, the premise of Dirksen's speech—that "the time had come" for civil rights legislation—all but conceded that the meaning of the Constitution shifts (and should shift) over time. How can both sides appeal to the same Constitution yet disagree so profoundly about its meaning and applicability?

3. The Warren Court aligned itself squarely with the ideology and objectives of Lyndon Johnson and his Great Society programs. The contrast with Franklin Roosevelt's struggles with the Supreme Court—"the crisis of the New Deal"—could not be more striking. Is it healthier under our constitutional system for the Supreme Court to act in harmony or in tension with the political branches?

Additional Primary Source Documents

Primary source document excerpts covering the following topics are located on the website accompanying this book:

Voting Rights—including "one person, one vote"; Twenty-fourth Amendment; Voting Rights Act of 1965; Twenty-sixth Amendment; *Shelby County v. Holder*, 570 U.S. 529 (2013); *Brnovich v. Democratic National Committee*, 594 U.S. ___ (2021).

Student Speech Rights—including *Tinker v. Des Moines Independent Community School District*, 393 U.S. 503 (1969); *Morse v. Frederick*, 551 U.S. 393 (2007); *Mahanoy Area School District v. B.L.*, 594 U.S. ___ (2021).

Other "Constitutional Moments" during this Era

- Presidential powers during wartime—including the firing of General Douglas MacArthur; *Youngstown Sheet & Tube Co. v. Sawyer*, 343 U.S. 579

(1952) (steel seizure case); rise during the Cold War of unfettered presidential power, especially over nuclear weapons; Gulf of Tonkin Resolution; Warren Court decisions regarding the Vietnam War; War Powers Resolution.

- Warren Court criminal law decisions—including *Mapp v. Ohio*, 367 U.S. 643 (1961) (excluding evidence from search that violated the Fourth Amendment); *Gideon v. Wainwright*, 372 U.S. 335 (1963) (Sixth Amendment right to counsel); *Miranda v. Arizona*, 384 U.S. 436 (1966) (police warnings on the right to remain silent); *Terry v. Ohio*, 392 U.S. 1 (1968) (authorizing "stop and frisk").

- Warren Court First Amendment decisions—including *Roth v. United States*, 354 U.S. 476 (1957) (defining obscenity); *Engel v. Vitale*, 370 U.S. 421 (1962) (prohibiting compelled prayer in public schools); *Abington School District v. Schempp*, 374 U.S. 203 (1963) (prohibiting mandatory Bible reading in public schools); *NAACP v. Button*, 371 U.S. 415 (1963) (recognizing litigation as a form of public expression); *Epperson v. Arkansas*, 393 U.S. 97 (1968) (striking down ban on teaching evolution).

- Freedom of the press—including *New York Times v. Sullivan*, 376 U.S. 254 (1964) (protecting press from libel suits); *New York Times v. United States*, 403 U.S. 713 (1971) (Pentagon Papers case); *Branzburg v. Hayes*, 408 U.S. 665 (1972) (confidential sources).

- Public education funding—including *San Antonio Independent School District v. Rodriguez*, 411 U.S. 1 (1973) (the poor are not a specially protected constitutional class).

- Holding a president accountable—including executive privilege; *United States v. Nixon*, 418 U.S. 683 (1974) (Watergate tapes case); Gerald Ford's pardon of Richard Nixon.

Notes

1. Gayle v. Browder, 352 U.S. 903 (1956).
2. Boynton v. Virginia, 364 U.S. 454 (1960).
3. Alien Registration Act of 1940 (An Act to prohibit certain subversive activities [etc.]), ch. 439, 54 Stat. 670 (June 28, 1940), govtrackus.s3.amazonaws.com/legislink/pdf/stat/54/STATUTE-54-Pg670.pdf.
4. Schenck v. United States, 249 U.S. 47 (1919).
5. Dennis v. United States, 341 U.S. 494 (1951).
6. *Id.* (Black, J., dissenting).
7. Yates v. United States, 354 U.S. 298 (1957).
8. Chester Bowles, *Ambassador's Report* (New York: Harper, 1954), 31.
9. 347 U.S. 483 (1954).
10. Brown v. Bd. of Educ. (II), 349 U.S. 294 (1955).
11. 388 U.S. 1 (1967).

12. See generally Gerald N. Rosenberg, *The Hollow Hope: Can Courts Bring about Social Change?*, 2nd ed. (Chicago: University of Chicago Press, 2008).

13. Civil Rights Act of 1964 (An Act to enforce the constitutional right to vote, to confer jurisdiction upon the district courts of the United States to provide injunctive relief against discrimination in public accommodations [etc.]), Pub. L. No. 88-352, 78 Stat. 241 (1964), www.govinfo.gov/content/pkg/STATUTE-78/pdf/STATUTE-78-Pg241.pdf#page=1.

14. Griggs v. Duke Power Co., 401 U.S. 424 (1971).

15. 379 U.S. 241 (1964).

16. Katzenbach v. McClung, 379 U.S. 294 (1964).

17. "Warns Court Opens Door to Socialist U.S.," *Chicago Tribune*, December 15, 1964.

18. 369 U.S. 186 (1962).

19. Gray v. Sanders, 372 U.S. 368 (1963).

20. 376 U.S. 1 (1964).

21. Reynolds v. Sims, 377 U.S. 533 (1964).

22. Lyndon Johnson, "Special Message to the Congress: The American Promise" (March 15, 1965), www.presidency.ucsb.edu/documents/special-message-the-congress-the-american-promise.

23. Voting Rights Act of 1965 (An Act to enforce the Fifteenth Amendment to the Constitution of the United States), Pub. L. No. 89-110, 79 Stat. 437 (August 6, 1965), www.govinfo.gov/content/pkg/STATUTE-79/pdf/STATUTE-79-Pg437.pdf.

24. South Carolina v. Katzenbach, 383 U.S. 301 (1966).

25. Harper v. Va. State Bd. of Elections, 383 U.S. 663 (1966).

26. Katzenbach v. Morgan, 384 U.S. 641 (1966).

27. Andrew Young, quoted in "Out of a Cocoon," *Time*, September 27, 1976, www.content.time.com/time/subscriber/article/0,33009,918352,00.html.

28. Immigration Act of 1924 (An Act to limit the immigration of aliens into the United States, and for other purposes), ch. 190, 43 Stat. 153 (May 26, 1924), govtrackus.s3.amazonaws.com/legislink/pdf/stat/43/STATUTE-43-Pg153a.pdf.

29. Lyndon Johnson, "Annual Message to Congress on the State of the Union" (January 4, 1965), www.presidency.ucsb.edu/documents/annual-message-the-congress-the-state-the-union-26.

30. An Act to amend the Immigration and Nationality Act, Pub. L. No. 89-236, 79 Stat. 911 (October 3, 1965), www.govinfo.gov/content/pkg/STATUTE-79/pdf/STATUTE-79-Pg911.pdf.

31. Joseph Addabbo, H.R. Debates, 89th Cong., 1st Sess., Cong. Rec. 111:21,768 (August 25, 1965), www.govinfo.gov/app/details/GPO-CRECB-1965-pt25/GPO-CRECB-1965-pt25-1.

32. Lyndon Johnson, "Remarks at the Signing of the Immigration Bill" (October 3, 1965), www.lbjlibrary.org/lyndon-baines-johnson/timeline/lbj-on-immigration.

33. *To Amend the Immigration and Naturalization Act: Hearing on S. 500 before the Subcomm. on Immigration and Naturalization of the Comm. on the Judiciary*, 89th Cong. 1–3 (February 10, 1965) (opening statement of Sen. Edward Kennedy), acsc.lib.udel.edu/items/show/301.

34. Engel v. Vitale, 370 U.S. 421 (1962); School Dist. of Abington Twp., Pa. v. Schempp, 374 U.S. 203 (1963); Epperson v. Arkansas, 393 U.S. 97 (1968).

35. Reynolds v. Sims, 377 U.S. 533 (1964) (Harlan, J., dissenting).

36. 381 U.S. 479 (1965).

37. 410 U.S. 113 (1973).

38. Joint Resolution to promote the maintenance of international peace and security in Southeast Asia, Pub. L. No. 88-408, 78 Stat. 384 (August 10, 1964), www.govinfo.gov/content/pkg/STATUTE-78/pdf/STATUTE-78-Pg384.pdf#page=1.

39. 376 U.S. 254 (1964).

40. 395 U.S. 444 (1969).

41. United States v. O'Brien, 391 U.S. 367 (1968).

42. Tinker v. Des Moines, 393 U.S. 503 (1969).

43. Fred Graham, "Freedom of Speech, But Not License," New York Times, March 2, 1969, timesmachine.nytimes.com/timesmachine/1969/03/02/90056961.pdf?pdf_redirect = true&ip = 0.

44. Ken Armstrong, "Dollree Mapp, 1923-2014: 'The Rosa Parks of the Fourth Amendment,'" The Marshall Project, December 8, 2014, www.themarshallproject.org/2014/12/08/dollree-mapp-1923-2014-the-rosa-parks-of-the-fourth-amendment.

45. Mapp v. Ohio, 367 U.S. 643 (1961).

46. Miranda v. Arizona, 384 U.S. 436 (1966).

47. Id. (Clark, J., dissenting).

48. Terry v. Ohio, 392 U.S. 1 (1968).

49. Lyndon Johnson to Abe Fortas, October 3, 1966, 8:16 a.m., WH6610.2, PNO 1, #10912, Miller Center, University of Virginia, millercenter.org/the-presidency/secret-white-house-tapes/conversation-abe-fortas-october-3-1966-1 (at 6:36-7:55).

50. 418 U.S. 683 (1974).

51. 402 U.S. 1 (1971).

52. Vincent Blasi, ed., The Burger Court: The Counter-Revolution That Wasn't (New Haven, CT: Yale University Press, 1986).

53. Michael Graetz and Linda Greenhouse, The Burger Court and the Rise of the Judicial Right (New York: Simon and Schuster, 2016), 341.

54. H.R. Res. 282, 75th Cong., 3d Sess. (1938), archive.org/details/investigationofu193801unit/page/n5.

55. Investigation of Communist Activities, New York Area: Hearings before the House Comm. on Un-American Activities, 84th Cong. 2447–60 (August 18, 1955) (testimony of Peter Seeger), archive.org/stream/investigationofc557unit/investigationofc557unit_djvu.txt.

56. Alien Registration Act of 1940 (An Act to prohibit certain subversive activities [etc.]), ch. 439, 54 Stat. 670 (June 28, 1940), govtrackus.s3.amazonaws.com/legislink/pdf/stat/54/STATUTE-54-Pg670.pdf.

57. Exec. Order No. 9835, 12 Fed. Reg. 1935 (March 25, 1947), cdn.loc.gov/service/ll/fedreg/fr012/fr012059/fr012059.pdf.

58. Exec. Order No. 10,450, 18 Fed. Reg. 2489 (April 27, 1953), www.archives.gov/federal-register/codification/executive-order/10450.html.

59. "Perverts Called Government Peril," *New York Times*, April 19, 1950, www.nytimes. com/1950/04/19/archives/perverts-called-government-peril-gabrielson-gop-chief-says-they-are.html.

60. Subversive Activities Control Act of 1950 (An Act to protect the United States against certain un-American and subversive activities by requiring registration of Communist organizations, and for other purposes), ch. 1024, 64 Stat. 987 (September 23, 1950), govtrackus.s3.amazonaws.com/legislink/pdf/stat/64/STATUTE-64-Pg987.pdf.

61. Joseph McCarthy, "Address to the League of Women Voters" (speech, Wheeling, WV, February 9, 1950), teachingamericanhistory.org/library/document/address-to-the-league-of-women-voters-wheeling-west-virginia-2/.

62. Joseph McCarthy, Senate Debate, Cong. Rec. 1956 (February 20, 1950), www.govinfo. gov/content/pkg/GPO-CRECB-1950-pt2/pdf/GPO-CRECB-1950-pt2-12-1.pdf.

63. Joseph McCarthy, Senate Debate, at 1953.

64. Margaret Chase Smith, "Declaration of Conscience," Senate Debate, Cong. Rec. 7894 (June 1, 1950), www.senate.gov/artandhistory/history/resources/pdf/SmithDeclaration. pdf.

65. Dennis v. United States, 341 U.S. 494 (1951).

66. *Id.* (Douglas, J., dissenting).

67. S. Res. 301, 83d Cong., 2d Sess. 16392 (December 2, 1954), www.govinfo.gov/content/pkg/GPO-CRECB-1954-pt12/pdf/GPO-CRECB-1954-pt12-15.pdf.

68. Yates v. United States, 354 U.S. 298 (1957).

69. 50 U.S.C. § 842, www.law.cornell.edu/uscode/text/50/842.

70. Plessy v. Ferguson, 163 U.S. 537 (1896).

71. Smith v. Allwright, 321 U.S. 649 (1944).

72. Buchanan v. Warley, 245 U.S. 60 (1917); Shelley v. Kraemer, 334 U.S. 1 (1948).

73. Missouri ex rel. Gaines v. Canada, 305 U.S. 337 (1938); Sweatt v. Painter, 329 U.S. 629 (1950); McLaurin v. Oklahoma State Regents, 339 U.S. 637 (1950).

74. John W. Davis, Transcript of Oral Argument, Briggs v. Elliott (December 7, 1953), in Philip B. Kurland and Gerhard Casper, eds., *Landmark Briefs and Arguments of the Supreme Court of the United States: Constitutional Law*, Vol. 49A (Frederick, MD: University Publications of America, 1975), 483, 488, 490–92.

75. Thurgood Marshall, Transcript of Oral Argument, *Briggs v. Elliott* (December 9, 1952), in Kurland and Casper, *Landmark Briefs and Arguments of the Supreme Court of the United States*, 310–12.

76. Marshall, Transcript of Oral Argument, in Kurland and Casper, *Landmark Briefs and Arguments of the Supreme Court of the United States*, 518–23.

77. Brown v. Bd. of Educ., 347 U.S. 483 (1954). See generally Richard Kluger, *Simple Justice: The History of* Brown v. Board of Education *and Black America's Struggle for Equality*, rev. ed. (New York: Vintage, 2004).

78. Zora Neale Hurston, letter to the editor, *Orlando Sentinel*, August 11, 1955; teachingamericanhistory.org/library/document/letter-to-the-orlando-sentinel/.

79. 275 U.S. 78 (1927).

80. "Declaration of Constitutional Principles," Cong. Rec. 4515–16 (March 12, 1956), www.govinfo.gov/content/pkg/GPO-CRECB-1956-pt4/pdf/ GPO-CRECB-1956-pt4-3-2.pdf.

81. Brown v. Bd. of Educ. (II), 349 U.S. 294 (1955).

82. Cooper v. Aaron, 358 U.S. 1 (1958). See generally Tony A. Freyer, *Little Rock on Trial: Cooper v. Aaron and School Desegregation* (Lawrence: University Press of Kansas, 2011).

83. Equal Justice Initiative, "From Slavery to Segregation," *Segregation in America* (2018), segregationinamerica.eji.org/report/from-slavery-to-segregation.html. See also National Park Service, "Jim Crow Laws" (April 17, 2018), www.nps.gov/malu/learn/ education/jim_crow_laws.htm.

84. Willie Mays et al., *An Appeal for Human Rights* (March 9, 1960), en.wikisource.org/ wiki/An_Appeal_for_Human_Rights.

85. "An Appeal for Law and Order and Common Sense," *Birmingham News*, January 17, 1963, reprinted in S. Jonathan Bass, *Blessed Are the Peacemakers: Martin Luther King Jr., Eight White Religious Leaders, and the "Letter from Birmingham Jail"* (Baton Rouge: Louisiana State University Press, 2001), App. 1.

86. "White Clergymen Urge Local Negroes to Withdraw from Demonstrations," *Birmingham News*, April 13, 1963, bplonline.contentdm.oclc.org/digital/collec-tion/p4017coll2/id/746/; and "Demonstrators Called 'Unwise and Untimely,'" *Birmingham Post-Herald*, April 13, 1963, bplonline.contentdm.oclc.org/digital/ collection/p4017coll2/id/7072/rec/3, reprinted in S. Jonathan Bass, *Blessed Are the Peacemakers: Martin Luther King Jr., Eight White Religious Leaders, and the "Letter from Birmingham Jail"* (Baton Rouge: Louisiana State University Press, 2001), App. 2, also reprinted in Cong. Rec. A4409 (App.), 88th Cong., 1st Sess. (July 15, 1963).

87. John F, Kennedy, "Radio and Television Report to the American People on Civil Rights" (June 11, 1963), www.presidency.ucsb.edu/documents/ radio-and-television-report-the-american-people-civil-rights.

88. Lyndon Johnson, "Address before a Joint Session of the Congress" (November 27, 1963), www.presidency.ucsb.edu/documents/address-before-joint-session-the-congress-0.

89. Strom Thurmond, *CBS Reports*, March 18, 1964, reprinted in Cong. Rec. 6428–29 (Senate), (March 26, 1964), www.senate.gov/artandhistory/history/resources/pdf/ CivilRightsFilibuster_HumphreyThurmondDebate.pdf.

90. Everett Dirksen, Senate Debate, Cong. Rec. 13,319–320 (June 10, 1964), www.senate. gov/artandhistory/history/resources/pdf/CivilRights_DirksenSpeechJune101964. pdf.

91. Clarence Mitchell to Roy Wilkins, June 20, 1964, www.loc.gov/exhibits/civil-rights-act/civil-rights-act-of-1964.html#obj193. Reprinted with permission of Denton Watson, Project Director of the Papers of Clarence Mitchell Jr. Project.

92. Civil Rights Act of 1964 (An Act to enforce the constitutional right to vote, to confer jurisdiction upon the district courts of the United States to provide injunctive relief against discrimination in public accommodations [etc.]), Pub. L. No. 88-352, 78 Stat. 241 (July 2, 1964), www.govinfo.gov/content/pkg/STATUTE-78/pdf/STATUTE-78-Pg241.pdf#page=1.

93. Civil Rights Act of 1964 (An Act to enforce the constitutional right to vote, to confer jurisdiction upon the district courts of the United States to provide injunctive relief against discrimination in public accommodations [etc.]), Pub. L. No. 88-352, 78 Stat. 241 (July 2, 1964), www.govinfo.gov/content/pkg/STATUTE-78/pdf/STATUTE-78-Pg241.pdf#page=1.

94. Heart of Atlanta Motel v. United States, 379 U.S. 241 (1964); Katzenbach v. McClung, 379 U.S. 294 (1964).

95. *Katzenbach*, 379 U.S. 294 (1964).

8

Constitutionalism
in Contemporary America

US history *is* constitutional history—and never has this been more apparent than in recent times. Twenty-first-century politics is frequently driven by—riven by—debates over "rights." To be sure, national disputes are still resolved through elections or economic forces. But increasingly Americans have turned to the courts—and to the Constitution—to debate and resolve their political, social, ideological, and even religious disagreements. As a result, both major political parties have become far more focused on the judicial confirmation process, for both the Supreme Court and lower federal courts, reflecting an increased consciousness of the crucial role that judges play in interpreting and applying the Constitution. And as the courts, particularly the Supreme Court, whether by happenstance or design, have been increasingly perceived as more "political" in their reach and effect, they have been variously applauded or condemned, defended or denounced, as "activist" or "reactionary" or both, depending on the outcome of any particular case.

In many ways, once-arcane constitutional theory has become a central part of American political life and disputation. It is difficult to navigate twenty-first-century politics without a firm grounding in the Constitution: what it is, what it means, who it includes, and what rights it secures. It is similarly not possible to appreciate everyday public affairs without grasping the importance of litigants, lawyers, academics, protest movements, legislators, policymakers, and judges who participate in the ongoing dance of constitutional law.

As Americans fight out their policy disagreements over abortion, women's rights, gay rights, affirmative action, immigration, guns, and private property, they increasingly turn to the courts—at a minimum for political leverage, but ideally for slam-dunk victories in the form of new constitutional rights. Those with opposing political views strategically resort to the same judicial fora in the hope of achieving opposite outcomes. To be sure, the judiciary is not being asked (or being expected) to resolve all policy disputes, such as charting a carbon-free future or overhauling the healthcare system. But recent years have witnessed the steady evolution of the Constitution's potential reach in highly charged matters

With Liberty and Justice for All?. Edited by Steven A. Steinbach, Maeva Marcus, and Robert Cohen, Oxford University Press. © Oxford University Press 2022. DOI: 10.1093/oso/9780197516317.003.0008

involving privacy, gender, sexuality, security, and inclusivity—as more and more Americans have attempted to secure, through the judicial branch, "the Blessings of Liberty."

Few decisions of the Supreme Court have divided the nation so profoundly and for so long as *Roe v. Wade*. In holding that abortion was a matter best left to a woman and her physician (at least during the early stages of pregnancy), the Court invoked the constitutional principle of "privacy," which itself had been rather newly minted. *Roe*—and the countless laws and court cases it has spawned—generated polarization not only over highly charged questions involving religion, morality, autonomy, and identity but also over the appropriate role for the judiciary within a democratic frame of government. *Roe* formed part of a much larger narrative, as the nation's women sought an equal place at the nation's table. That transformation, too, had its distinct constitutional moments: Beginning in the early 1970s, the Supreme Court, reversing nearly a century of its own precedents, struck down a number of laws that differentiated—irrationally, the Court determined—between the genders. The privacy and women's rights revolution in turn inspired advocates of gay rights to advance analogous constitutional claims—claims that eventually, but over a longer timeline, were embraced by the Supreme Court, albeit not without substantial dissent.

To a quite discernable extent, then, the course of American history over the last quarter of the twentieth century and the first quarter of the next was determined by lawsuits, courts, activists, and constitutional strategists, no less than by legislators, public servants, and voters. In fact, the national political agenda has become focused on the Constitution to an extent arguably not experienced since the Civil War. Bitter judicial confirmation battles attest to that reality, as does the fact that virtually everything—college admissions, gun possession, real estate development, and immigration policies—has become "constitutionalized." For better or for worse, the justices of the Supreme Court have become almost household names; for better or for worse, they adjudicate in the spotlight glare of the front pages of our newspapers and the home pages of our websites.

Whether all this is a good thing or not is subject to dispute. It is not out of bounds to ask big-picture questions: Is modern constitutional law driven more by the ideal of impartial justice or the reality of partisan politics? Have the Supreme Court and its role in interpreting the Constitution fallen into fatal dysfunction? Should the entire constitutional system be reimagined? More than two centuries after Philadelphia, the debate over the Constitution continues.

The Rights Revolution and the Modern Supreme Court

Melissa Murray

Frederick I. and Grace Stokes Professor of Law, New York University Law School

As the tumult of the 1960s gave way to the 1970s, much had changed in American constitutional law. In 1965, the Supreme Court announced its decision in *Griswold v. Connecticut* (1965),[1] a challenge to Connecticut's contraception ban. Enacted in 1879, the ban prohibited the use and distribution of contraception— even to married couples. For years, birth control activists had sought repeal of the law through the political process, with no success. When a legal challenge to the law failed in Connecticut's highest court, birth control advocates, led by the Planned Parenthood League of Connecticut (PPLC), turned their attention to a federal challenge arguing that the Connecticut law violated the US Constitution.

PPLC envisioned a new legal challenge that would focus both on doctors who wished to advise patients about birth control and on married couples for whom pregnancy would entail serious health risks and complications. The case—*Poe v. Ullman* (1961)[2]—argued that the Connecticut contraceptive ban violated the patients' and physicians' due process rights under the Fourteenth Amendment. In making this claim, PPLC relied on arguments that the American Civil Liberties Union (ACLU) first made in the context of the rights of criminal defendants. In these earlier cases, the ACLU had argued that individuals maintained a zone of privacy against unwarranted state intrusion and interference. Now, in the context of birth control, PPLC and its lawyers argued that the logic of privacy prevented the state from criminally proscribing the use of birth control.

In the end, the Supreme Court dismissed the claim in *Poe* on jurisdictional grounds, concluding that the case was not yet ripe for review because the Connecticut contraception ban had not actually been enforced against the plaintiffs. Still, the privacy argument that the *Poe* plaintiffs raised resonated with Justice William O. Douglas. In an impassioned dissent, he observed that "full enforcement of the law . . . would reach the point where search warrants issued and officers appeared in bedrooms to find out what went on." Such an intrusion into "the innermost sanctum of the home" constituted, in Douglas's view, "an invasion of the privacy that is implicit in a free society."[3]

Still eager for the Court to consider the merits of the law's constitutionality, PPLC sought an opportunity to bring a live case and controversy before the Court. To do so, PPLC Executive Director Estelle Griswold opened a birth control clinic in New Haven, which immediately drew law enforcement attention. In just a few days, Griswold was arrested and charged with violating the Connecticut law, setting the stage for *Griswold v. Connecticut*.

As in *Poe v. Ullman*, the logic of privacy loomed large in *Griswold*. PPLC argued that the Constitution afforded individuals some degree of privacy against undue government interference in the most intimate aspects of their lives. A majority of the Court agreed. In a 7–2 decision authored by Justice Douglas, the Court struck down the Connecticut contraceptive ban, and in so doing announced a right to privacy that was implicit in the "penumbras" of "specific guarantees in the Bill of Rights." Critically, Douglas specifically tethered the privacy right to marriage—the Connecticut law had gone too far, inviting the state to police "the sacred precincts of marital bedrooms."[4] Going forward, married couples would enjoy a constitutional right to privacy that allowed them to make decisions about contraception and family planning.

If the *Griswold* Court's understanding of privacy allowed married couples the autonomy to make decisions about contraceptive use, it was silent on whether the unmarried enjoyed the same right. Seven years later, in *Eisenstadt v. Baird* (1972), the Court would take up the question, striking down a Massachusetts statute that prohibited unmarried persons from using birth control. As the Court reasoned, "If the right of privacy means anything, it is the right of the individual, married or single, to be free from unwarranted governmental intrusion into matters so fundamentally affecting a person as the decision whether to bear or beget a child."[5]

A year later, in *Roe v. Wade* (1973),[6] the Court would further elaborate the individual's right to privacy in the context of criminal abortion laws. Throughout the United States, criminal abortion laws forced women to leave the country in order to safely terminate a pregnancy. Those without the means for international travel resorted to black market abortion procedures that were unregulated and unsafe. These realities fueled grass-roots efforts to liberalize—or even repeal—state laws criminalizing abortion, with uneven results. In four jurisdictions, abortion laws were repealed entirely. In a handful of other jurisdictions, the repeal effort faltered and gave way to liberalization as legislatures relaxed their abortion restrictions to allow women to obtain an abortion if they secured the approval of a panel of physicians. While the liberalization effort was, for some, a step in the right direction, for others it echoed the logic of the underlying laws by divesting women of the autonomy to decide for themselves whether or not to carry a pregnancy to term.

In 1969, a young Texas woman named Norma Jean McCorvey found herself pregnant for the third time. She had carried her previous two pregnancies to term, surrendering one child for adoption and letting her mother raise her daughter. Resolved to terminate this pregnancy, she soon learned that Texas's criminal abortion ban prevented her from doing so. After a failed attempt to obtain an illegal abortion from an underground clinic, McCorvey went to see Henry McCluskey, a Dallas adoption lawyer. Recognizing that McCorvey had little interest in carrying the pregnancy to term and surrendering the child for adoption, McCluskey referred her to two young attorneys, Linda Coffee and Sarah Weddington, who were hoping to mount a legal challenge to Texas's abortion law. McCorvey agreed to serve as plaintiff in the case, although she later maintained that neither Coffee nor Weddington advised her that the litigation would take a long time, making McCorvey's prospects for a legal abortion in Texas unlikely and forcing her to carry the pregnancy to term. Indeed, she eventually delivered and surrendered the child for adoption. According to McCorvey, she was merely a "pawn" in Coffee and Weddington's grand plan to challenge the constitutionality of criminal abortion laws.

If McCorvey failed to obtain her desired outcome, Coffee and Weddington were more fortunate, bringing their legal challenge to the Texas abortion law to the Supreme Court. The case, *Roe v. Wade*, resulted in a 7–2 decision, written by Nixon-appointee Harry A. Blackmun, which struck down the Texas law. In doing so, the *Roe* Court acknowledged that an unwanted pregnancy "may force upon the woman a distressful life and future," including physical and psychological harm. In view of these burdens to women and their families, the majority concluded that "[the] right of privacy . . . is broad enough to encompass a woman's decision whether or not to terminate her pregnancy."

Critically, *Roe* consigned the abortion decision to "the woman and her responsible physician" and made clear that the right to choose was rooted in values of liberty and autonomy, rather than in a principle of sex equality. In a line of other cases, the Burger Court would explicitly consider whether the Constitution protected women as equal citizens under law. The question of women's equality had emerged from the ashes of the Civil War as part of the residue of abolition. Were women citizens in their own right, on par with newly freed African American men? Or were they merely appendages of their husbands or fathers, as slaves had been appendages to their masters? Reconstruction offered women an opportunity and a vernacular to extend the protections of the Fourteenth Amendment to their own circumstances. In *Bradwell v. Illinois* (1873), Myra Bradwell argued that Illinois's refusal to admit her to the bar as a practicing attorney violated the Privileges or Immunities Clause of the Fourteenth Amendment.[7] The Court disagreed, citing the *Slaughter-House Cases* (1873),[8] which just a day earlier had rejected the right to pursue a particular profession as one of the privileges or immunities of citizenship. Associate Justice Joseph Bradley agreed with the majority's decision but drafted a separate concurrence in which he offered an alternative rationale for denying Bradwell's claims. Instead of relying on the logic of constitutional text to defeat Bradwell's claims, Bradley relied on "the Constitution of the family organization." On Bradley's logic, though women were citizens, their "natural and proper timidity and delicacy" better equipped them for "the noble and benign offices of wife and mother" than for "the occupations of civil life."[9]

Bradley's logic reverberated in the Court's decision in *Muller v. Oregon* (1908), a challenge to an Oregon law that limited the number of hours that women could work in laundries. Just a few years earlier, in *Lochner v. New York* (1905),[10] the Court had invalidated a similar maximum-hours law on the ground that it undermined freedom of contract. In *Muller*, however, the Court had little concern for the contractual freedom of female laundry workers. It upheld the challenged law as a permissible exercise of state police power necessary to protect the health and safety of vulnerable women workers. Because "healthy mothers are essential to vigorous offspring, the physical wellbeing of woman becomes an object of public interest and care in order to preserve the strength and vigor of the race."[11] The *Muller* Court's logic—that "woman's physical structure, and the functions she performs" justified sex-differentiated laws—would undergird the Court's approach to sex equality until the 1970s.

If the Civil War and abolition had shaped first-wave feminists' efforts to secure women's rights during Reconstruction, then the legal successes of the civil rights movement informed second-wave feminists as they pursued sex equality claims a century later. In particular, the Court's jurisprudence striking down racially discriminatory laws prompted an important question: Could the logic of equal protection extend further to dismantle laws that distinguished on the basis of sex? In *Reed v. Reed* (1971),[12] the Court confronted the question. Under the challenged Idaho probate law, "males must be preferred to females" in appointing administrators of estates. Accordingly, an Idaho probate court appointed Cecil Reed as the executor of his deceased son's estate over the objections of Sally Reed, the boy's mother and Cecil's estranged wife. Sally challenged Cecil's appointment, arguing that the Equal Protection Clause of the Constitution prohibited such discrimination based on sex.

As the case made its way to the Supreme Court, the ACLU joined Sally Reed's cause. Together, Melvin Wulf, the ACLU's legal director, and Ruth Bader Ginsburg, a Rutgers law professor who would go on to found the ACLU's Women's Rights Project (WRP), wrote Sally Reed's brief to the Court. Wulf and Ginsburg built on the work of pioneering women's rights advocates Dorothy Kenyon and Pauli Murray to argue that sex, like race, was a suspect classification, and that Idaho's use of sex to appoint executors was neither justified by any compelling state purpose nor rationally related to any legitimate state interest. The Court agreed, striking down the Idaho law and concluding that Idaho's mandatory preference in favor of male executors was "the very kind of arbitrary legislative choice forbidden by the Equal Protection Clause of the Fourteenth Amendment."

Using *Reed* as a foundation, Ginsburg and the WRP initiated a series of lawsuits aimed at dismantling "Jane Crow"—sex-based legal impediments—and establishing gender as a suspect classification that, like race, was subject to the most rigorous constitutional scrutiny. In *Frontiero v. Richardson* (1973), Ginsburg challenged a US military regulation that allowed servicemen to claim their wives as dependents and receive benefits for them automatically, while requiring servicewomen to prove that their husbands were dependent on them for more than half their support. Relying on *Reed*, the Court struck down the challenged regulation, but a majority could not agree on the appropriate standard of review to apply to sex-based classifications.[13]

The issue surfaced again two years later in *Stanton v. Stanton* (1975), a challenge to a Utah law which, on the assumption that women "matured faster and married earlier" than men, prescribed twenty-one as the age of majority for men and eighteen as the age of majority for women. The Court invalidated the law, noting its roots in gendered stereotypes that consigned women to "the home and the rearing of the family" and men to "the marketplace and the world of ideas." Indeed, because the Utah law was rooted in outdated gender stereotypes, it was easy for the Court to strike it down "under any test—compelling state interest, or rational basis, or something in between."[14] But what about those cases where the challenged law or regulation was not so obviously unconstitutional? Should sex-based classifications be subject to strict scrutiny, as race-based classifications were, or the more deferential rational basis review, or "something in between"?

In *Craig v. Boren* (1976), the Court finally settled the issue. Drawing on the *Stanton* Court's notion of "something in between" strict scrutiny and rational basis review, the Court identified a new standard of review for sex-based classifications: intermediate scrutiny. Under this new standard, a sex-based classification could be upheld only if it was "substantially related to an important governmental purpose."[15]

For almost twenty years, the formulation of intermediate scrutiny was used to evaluate whether a sex-based classification survived equal protection scrutiny. However, in 1996 when the Court took up a challenge to the Virginia Military Institute's (VMI) male-only admissions policy, one of its newest members, Ruth Bader Ginsburg, who had co-written the brief in *Reed* and argued for the application of strict scrutiny in *Frontiero*, took the opportunity to inject more rigor into the intermediate standard of review.

The facts of *United States v. Virginia* (1996)[16] were an especially compelling canvas for Ginsburg's efforts. Seeking to maintain its "adversative method" of military education, VMI refused to admit women to its undergraduate program. When a lower court ruled the male-only admissions policy unconstitutional, it concluded that Virginia could remedy the constitutional injury by creating a parallel educational program for women. Accordingly, when the case finally arrived at the Court, the questions presented were twofold: whether the male-only admissions policy was constitutional; and if not, whether the creation of the Virginia Women's Institute for Leadership at Mary Baldwin College (VWIL) was an adequate remedy. In a 7–1 opinion (Justice Clarence Thomas recused himself from the case because his son was a student at VMI), Justice Ginsburg, writing for the majority, concluded that the admissions policy was unconstitutional, and that VWIL was insufficient as a constitutional remedy, as the "parallel program" was a "pale shadow" of the VMI experience.

In reaching these conclusions, Justice Ginsburg traced the development of the Court's sex equality jurisprudence, from cases upholding the benign paternalism of *Muller* to the repudiation of this logic in *Reed* and *Craig v. Boren*'s articulation of intermediate scrutiny. Applying these precedents to the facts of the case, Ginsburg observed that "the Commonwealth has shown no exceedingly persuasive justification for withholding from women qualified for the experience premier training of the kind VMI affords." Ginsburg's demand for an "exceedingly persuasive justification" appeared to subtly transform the Court's approach to sex-based classifications. Though less rigorous than strict scrutiny, Ginsburg's vision of "skeptical scrutiny," in which the state must present an exceedingly persuasive justification for its actions, appeared more searching and less deferential than traditional intermediate scrutiny—indeed, it seemed more in keeping with the exacting standard of review that Ginsburg had argued for years earlier as an advocate.

The Court's struggle to identify the appropriate standard of review for sex-based discrimination reflected, to some degree, a discomfort with treating sex like race for purposes of equal protection. That said, there were also reasons to believe that treating sex like race could lead to unintended and undesirable outcomes. By the 1970s, it had become clear that applying strict scrutiny to race-based classifications was something of a double-edged sword. While strict scrutiny dismantled Jim Crow's racial classifications, it also called into question the benign use of race in government policies, including affirmative action policies. Launched in an effort to provide racial minorities and women greater access to careers and educational opportunities that they had previously been denied, affirmative action policies quickly drew fire as "reverse racism" that disadvantaged nonminorities and men.

Those who opposed affirmative action argued that under the rigorous strict scrutiny standard, such race-based programs, even if intended to remedy past discrimination, could not withstand constitutional review. Recognizing that the application of strict scrutiny could doom affirmative action policies, some members of the Court, including Thurgood Marshall, the first African American justice, argued that benign racial classifications should be subjected to a less exacting standard of review. In a series of cases involving government-sponsored employment preferences for women and minorities, the Court rejected this view and insisted that strict scrutiny would apply to all racial classifications.

Still, there was flexibility in practice. If strict scrutiny was applied, then racial classifications could only survive review if they were justified by a compelling state interest. In *Regents of the University of California v. Bakke* (1978),[17] the Court had the opportunity to consider what sorts of state interests might justify the use of a racial classification. Allan Bakke, a former Marine officer and engineer, sought admission to medical school but was rejected by several due in part to his age—he was in his early thirties and some medical schools considered him too old. After twice being rejected by the medical school at the University of California, Davis, Bakke filed suit in California state court challenging the constitutionality of Davis's affirmative action program, which set aside a certain number of seats for racial minorities in the hopes that these students would graduate and practice medicine in underserved minority communities. Despite the medical school's lofty intentions, the California Supreme Court struck down the program on the ground that it violated the rights of white applicants. The University of California appealed the decision to the US Supreme Court, which accepted the case.

The Court's consideration of *Bakke* was extremely fractured, producing no fewer than six different opinions. Justice Lewis F. Powell wrote the Court's judgment, with two different blocs of four justices joining various parts. Powell concluded that, as a general matter, affirmative action was constitutionally permissible, though Davis's program went too far and functioned as an unconstitutional quota. Colleges and universities could consider race in admissions if done to foster "diversity" in the educational experience. The state's interest in promoting diversity in higher education, Powell concluded, was sufficient to justify the consideration of race in the admissions process. But because the Court's decision had been so fractured and there was no clear majority opinion, questions remained as to whether *Bakke* was a binding precedent. The Court later made clear that diversity was a compelling state interest in *Grutter v. Bollinger* (2003), a decision upholding the University of Michigan's law school admissions policy, which considered race as one of many characteristics in the school's "holistic" evaluation of each applicant.[18]

Although much of the Court's jurisprudence during this period considered the rights of racial minorities and women, other underrepresented groups also sought constitutional recognition. The 1969 Stonewall Riots in New York City, when gays and lesbians spontaneously pushed back against police harassment, ushered in the gay rights movement. Soon enough, the question of whether the Constitution's commitment to equal protection of the laws also applied to sexual minorities made its way to the Court. In *Bowers v. Hardwick* (1986), the Court considered a challenge to a Georgia law prohibiting sodomy. The facts of the case were compelling: law enforcement officers had entered Michael Hardwick's home and found him engaged in a sexual act with another man. Hardwick was arrested and charged with violating Georgia's sodomy ban. Hardwick challenged the law, arguing that it violated his right to privacy. A majority of the Court disagreed, concluding that the privacy right protected in *Griswold* and its progeny did not go so far as to protect a "claimed constitutional right of homosexuals to engage in acts of sodomy." According to the Court, crediting Hardwick's privacy claim would effectively create a new fundamental right—something the Court was "quite unwilling to do" because it would result in "judge-made constitutional law having little or no cognizable roots in the language or design of the Constitution."[19]

In the end, the Court upheld the sodomy law under rational basis review, noting that the law's enactment reflected "the presumed belief of a majority of the electorate in Georgia that homosexual sodomy is immoral and unacceptable." But the question of whether a majority of the electorate could render unequal the status of gay men and lesbians again found its way to the Court. In 1992, Colorado voters approved by ballot initiative Amendment 2, which amended the state constitution to withdraw all state-level antidiscrimination protections for lesbians, gays, and bisexuals (LGB) and forbid the enactment of any future laws that treated LGB persons as a protected class.

The case, *Romer v. Evans* (1996), reached the Supreme Court, where, in a 6–3 decision authored by Justice Anthony Kennedy, it struck down Amendment 2 as a violation of the Equal Protection Clause. In doing so, the majority did not denominate LGB persons a suspect class entitled to strict scrutiny or intermediate scrutiny, as is the case for racial minorities and women. Instead, Justice Kennedy concluded that the challenged amendment failed the rational basis test. As Kennedy explained, the amendment "identifies persons by a single trait and then denies them protection across the board," raising "the inevitable inference that the disadvantage imposed is born of animosity toward the class of persons affected." Such a "bare . . . desire to harm a politically unpopular group cannot constitute a legitimate governmental interest."[20]

The favorable decision in *Romer* augured well for the effort to secure greater civil rights for LGB persons. A number of state legislatures repealed their laws criminalizing consensual adult sodomy; while in other states, antisodomy laws lingered on the books but were infrequently enforced. While many understood *Romer* as signaling a softening in the Court's approach to homosexuality, *Bowers* and its defense of sodomy bans continued to haunt the legal treatment of gays and lesbians, signaling that the law still condoned homophobia and antigay sentiment.

All of this changed, however, with the 1998 arrest and conviction of John Geddes Lawrence and Tyron Garner for violating Texas's antisodomy law. The pair challenged their convictions on the ground that the law violated their right to privacy. Recognizing that *Bowers v. Hardwick* foreclosed privacy protection for homosexual acts, they further argued that the 1986 decision should be overruled. In a 6–3 decision in *Lawrence v. Texas* (2003), the Supreme Court agreed. Writing for the majority, Justice Kennedy first addressed *Bowers*. In concluding that the right to privacy did not protect acts of sodomy, the *Bowers* Court had emphasized the long history of criminal laws prohibiting sodomy in the United States. Relying on an amicus brief filed by prominent historians, Kennedy questioned the veracity of *Bowers*'s historical claims. As Kennedy explained, historically the criminalization of sodomy was not intended to punish homosexuality but rather to prohibit nonprocreative sexual acts. Indeed, it was not until the 1970s—and the rise of the gay rights movement—that states, including Texas, modified their sodomy prohibitions to "single out same-sex relations for criminal prosecution." Because "the historical grounds relied upon in *Bowers* [were] more complex than the majority opinion" appreciated, and noting "an emerging awareness" in the United States and elsewhere "that liberty gives substantial protection to adult persons in deciding how to conduct their private lives in matters pertaining to sex," the *Lawrence* majority determined that "*Bowers* was not correct when it was decided, and it . . . should be . . . overruled."[21]

Having consigned *Bowers* to the anticanon of overruled precedents, Kennedy squarely confronted the question of whether the state could impose majoritarian sexual mores on all of its citizens through the criminal law. While acknowledging that the state could use the criminal law to prohibit sex acts that posed harm to third parties, the *Lawrence* Court noted that harm to vulnerable persons was not an issue in the case at hand. Instead, the facts concerned "two adults who, with full and mutual consent from each other, engaged in sexual practices common to a homosexual lifestyle." In striking down the sodomy law, the Court made clear that the right to liberty enshrined in the Fourteenth Amendment's Due Process Clause gave Lawrence and Garner "the full right to engage in their conduct without intervention of the government," and there was "no legitimate state interest which can justify [the state's] intrusion into the personal and private life of the individual."[22]

Lawrence was a landmark decision for gay rights, allowing gay men and lesbians to emerge from the closet, secure in the knowledge that their private sexual conduct would not be criminalized. But for other members of the Court, the majority's decision decriminalizing sodomy gestured toward more than simply welcoming gay men and women into public life. In a vigorous dissent, Justice Antonin Scalia insisted that in overruling *Bowers*, the majority "called into question" all other criminal morals legislation, including "state laws against bigamy, same-sex marriage, adult incest, prostitution, masturbation, adultery, fornication, bestiality, and obscenity." More importantly, in Scalia's view, the decriminalization of sodomy would lead inexorably to the legalization of same-sex marriage. Although Justice Kennedy had insisted that the decriminalization of sodomy did not implicate the fraught question of "whether the government must give formal recognition to any relationship that homosexual persons seek to enter," Justice Scalia remained unconvinced. As he explained, the majority's opinion "dismantles the structure of constitutional law that has permitted a distinction to be made between heterosexual and homosexual unions, insofar as formal recognition in marriage is concerned."[23]

Scalia's logic proved prescient. Just a few months after the *Lawrence* decision was announced, the Massachusetts Supreme Judicial Court, the state's highest court, issued a decision, based on the state constitution, legalizing same-sex unions. Similar decisions in a handful of other states soon followed. And in 2013, just ten years after *Lawrence*, the Supreme Court, in an opinion authored by Justice Kennedy, struck down the federal Defense of Marriage Act, allowing the recognition of same-sex unions for purposes of federal law in *United States v. Windsor* (2013).[24] Two years later, in *Obergefell v. Hodges* (2015), the Court took up the very question that had vexed Justice Scalia in *Lawrence*: Did the Constitution's guarantee of liberty encompass an individual right to marry a person of the same sex? In a sweeping opinion that drew on the history of marriage and its importance in "shap[ing] an individual's destiny," the *Obergefell* majority concluded that it did.[25]

The *Obergefell* decision was hailed as a civil rights victory, but it also inspired critiques and backlash. Some religious conservatives took solace in *Obergefell*'s acknowledgment that those "who deem same-sex marriage to be wrong reach that conclusion based on decent and honorable religious or philosophical premises." And indeed, in *Obergefell*'s wake, those in various faith communities filed legal challenges rooted in the First Amendment's religion clauses seeking religious accommodations from laws that mandated that clergy perform same-sex marriages or the equal treatment of LGBTQ persons in places of public accommodation.

The collision between the First Amendment's commitment to religious liberty and the Fourteenth Amendment's commitments to equal protection and due process was not confined to questions of gay rights. These questions also punctuated broader issues of immigration policy and national security in *Trump v. Hawaii* (2018),[26] a challenge to a presidential proclamation restricting foreign nationals from select Muslim-majority nations from entering the United States without certain travel documents. Hawaii and several other states and groups challenged the so-called travel ban (and two earlier executive orders) on constitutional and statutory grounds. Relying on a variety of statements by President Donald Trump and officials in his administration, plaintiffs maintained that the travel ban and its predecessor orders were motivated by anti-Muslim animus.

A federal district court issued a preliminary injunction preventing the ban from taking effect, concluding that plaintiffs were likely to succeed on their argument that the travel ban violated the First Amendment and exceeded the president's powers under federal immigration laws. An intermediate appellate court agreed, ruling that the proclamation likely violated federal immigration law. The Supreme Court, however, disagreed, reversing the lower court decision in a 5–4 ruling. The Court concluded that plaintiffs were unlikely to succeed on the merits on either their statutory or constitutional claims. Written by Chief Justice John Roberts, the majority decision emphasized deference to the executive branch in matters of national security and immigration. Meaningfully, the decision also disavowed the Court's 1944 decision in *Korematsu v. United States* (1944),[27] which upheld a World War II executive order establishing internment camps for Japanese Americans. In a vigorous dissent, Justice Sonia Sotomayor acknowledged the Court's repudiation of *Korematsu* but observed that the majority's decision upholding the travel ban "redeploys the same dangerous logic underlying *Korematsu* and merely replaces one gravely wrong decision with another."[28]

Beyond the First Amendment, other provisions of the Bill of Rights also became legal flashpoints, particularly for those who espoused a more conservative ethos. Antipathy for government regulation and state enactment of more restrictive gun control legislation sparked interest in the Second Amendment. Washington, DC's Firearms Control Regulations Act of 1975, which had been enacted and amended to address the growing problem of gun violence in the nation's capital, restricted residents from owning handguns. The law also required that all firearms including rifles and shotguns be kept "unloaded and disassembled or bound by a trigger lock." Six DC residents filed suit challenging the law on the ground that it violated the Second Amendment's individual right to "to keep and bear arms." The District argued that the firearms law was constitutionally permissible because the Second Amendment protected only the collective right of states to maintain militias and the individual's right to keep and bear arms in connection with militia service.

When the case, *District of Columbia v. Heller* (2008),[29] reached the Supreme Court, it was the first time that the Court had considered the breadth and scope of the Second Amendment since 1939. In *United States v. Miller*, the Court had unanimously upheld a federal law requiring the registration of sawed-off shotguns on the ground that such weapons did not have a "reasonable relationship to the preservation or efficiency of a well-regulated militia."[30]

In *Heller*, however, the Court's approach to the Second Amendment took an abrupt turn. In a 5–4 decision, the Court struck down the DC law, rejecting the "collective-right" theory of the Second Amendment credited in *Miller*, in favor of an individual-right theory that located the Second Amendment's command that "the right of the people to keep and bear Arms, shall not be infringed" in the English common law and the 1689 English Bill of Rights. According to this logic, the Second Amendment's preamble, "A well-regulated Militia, being necessary to the security of a free State," did not restrict the right to bear arms to militia service, as *Miller* had maintained. Instead, the preamble was best understood as reflecting the framers' belief that the most effective way to destroy a citizens' militia and facilitate government tyranny was to disarm citizens. Further, because the framers understood the right of self-defense to be "the central component" of the right to keep and bear arms, the *Heller* majority concluded that the Second Amendment implicitly protected the individual's right "to use arms in defense of hearth and home."[31]

The Court's interest in vindicating individual rights in the face of state efforts to restrict their exercise would also surface in the context of property rights. Seeking to revitalize the Fort Trumbull area of New London, Connecticut, the New London Development Corporation (NLDC), a private corporation operating with the approval of state and local governments, produced a development plan to build housing, office space, and other facilities in the area. Upon redevelopment, Fort Trumbull would support a new and expanded corporate headquarters for Pfizer, a prominent pharmaceutical company. Indeed, Pfizer had worked closely with NLDC to plan and create the proposed development.

In order to implement the plan, NLDC sought to purchase property from Fort Trumbull homeowners. Although many agreed to the sale of their property, some owners refused. To counter these recalcitrant owners, NLDC, working with the city and the state, deployed the power of eminent domain to condemn the holdout properties and proceed with the development plan. Under eminent domain, governments and their agents may expropriate private property for public use, with payment of compensation. According to NLDC, the use of eminent domain to acquire the holdout properties would serve an important public use—the revitalization project, which would bring jobs, new services, and increased tax revenue to New London and its citizens.

Hoping to use political pressure to thwart NLDC's plans, the objecting homeowners formed the Coalition to Save Fort Trumbull. These efforts attracted the attention of the Institute for Justice, a libertarian public interest law firm, which agreed to represent the homeowners in a constitutional challenge against the city. In *Kelo v. City of New London* (2005),[32] they argued that the NLDC's use of eminent domain constituted an unconstitutional "taking" in violation of the Fifth and Fourteenth Amendments. Specifically, the homeowners maintained that NLDC, a private entity, could not deploy the state's power of eminent domain to acquire private property. They also maintained that even if NLDC's use of eminent domain was permissible, economic revitalization was not an appropriate "public use" sufficient to justify the use of eminent domain.

Not surprisingly, the case—and the residents' arguments—drew considerable public attention. Throughout the country, many homeowners were surprised to learn that state and local governments could deploy the power of eminent domain to seize properties that were not blighted or in decay. At the Supreme Court, more than twenty-five "friend of the court" briefs were filed in support of the homeowners, reflecting a diverse coalition of libertarian, economic justice, and racial justice groups and interests.

But if public opinion favored the residents, the Supreme Court did not. Noting that Connecticut law "specifically authorizes the use of eminent domain to promote economic development," the Court upheld NLDC's use of eminent domain in a 5–4 decision. In so doing, the Court concluded that NLDC, though nominally a private entity, was operating as an agent of the city. Further, although New London was "not confronted with the need to remove blight in the Fort Trumbull area," its "determination that the area was sufficiently distressed to justify a program of economic rejuvenation is entitled to our deference." Meaningfully, the Court's decision did not preclude "any state from placing further restrictions on its exercise of the takings power." In *Kelo*'s wake, a number of states enacted legislation to limit the use of eminent domain.

In these and other decisions, the modern Supreme Court has attempted to strike a delicate balance between equality and liberty, deference to government and skepticism of government action, collective interests and individual autonomy, and private interests and the public good. In the years to come, the Court will face innumerable challenges and difficult questions—but perhaps none more difficult than its perennial challenge of striking these balances in a way that avoids the appearance of partisan politics and maintains its position as a neutral arbiter of law and constitutional values.

Privacy and Abortion—Primary Sources

This group of sources explores the constitutional right to abortion, first recognized by the Supreme Court in *Roe v. Wade*. That decision was preceded by *Griswold v. Connecticut*, which established a constitutional right to "privacy" in the context of reproductive activity. But the right identified in *Roe* was far from unlimited—and far from uncontroversial. Twenty years thereafter, the Court in *Planned Parenthood v. Casey* both reaffirmed and narrowed *Roe*. And in the years since *Casey*, state legislatures and the Supreme Court have engaged in what effectively amounts to a constitutional colloquy over the availability and regulation of abortion. Few constitutional issues have divided the nation as much as the half-century controversy over abortion. The precise contours of the abortion right—and the role of the Supreme Court in establishing such a right—remain the subject of intense political, moral, and legal debate.

Griswold v. Connecticut (1965)

The "right to privacy" determined by the Court in *Roe* to encompass abortion was based on an earlier watershed decision involving contraceptives. Connecticut had passed a statute preventing the use, sale, or advocacy (including counseling) of birth control.[33] Estelle Griswold, who headed New Haven's Planned Parenthood center, was arrested for providing advice and prescriptions to married couples "for the purpose of preventing conception." In *Griswold v. Connecticut*, the Court concluded that the Constitution prohibited the government from interfering with "the notions of privacy surrounding the marriage relationship." Although the seven justices in the majority disagreed as to the textual source of this privacy right—pointing, variously, to a handful of constitutional clauses (such as the Ninth Amendment); other constitutional doctrines (such as "substantive due process" under the Fourteenth Amendment); and constitutional "penumbras" ("formed by emanations" from the First, Third, Fourth, and Fifth Amendments)—they generally agreed that "the right of privacy which presses for recognition here is a legitimate one."

> Would we allow the police to search the sacred precincts of marital bedrooms for telltale signs of the use of contraceptives? The very idea is repulsive to the notions of privacy surrounding the marriage relationship. We deal with a right of privacy older than the Bill of Rights—older than our political parties—older than our school system. Marriage is a coming together for better or for worse, hopefully enduring, and intimate to the degree of being sacred. It is an association that promotes a way of life, not causes; a harmony in living, not political faiths; a bilateral loyalty, not commercial or social projects. Yet it is an association for as noble a purpose as any involved in our prior decisions.[34]

In striking down Connecticut's law on the grounds of privacy, the justices relied on earlier decisions recognizing similar constitutional rights not necessarily grounded in explicit textual provisions, including, for example, the right to educate a child consistent with parental choice;[35] the freedom to associate with others and the "privacy in one's associations";[36] and the right to teach certain subjects in school.[37]

Griswold v. Connecticut—Dissent (1965)

Justices Potter Stewart and Hugo Black, who dissented, shared the majority's disdain for the Connecticut law but were stymied by a substantial problem: no right to privacy—no expression of the importance of personal and relational autonomy—appears in the Constitution.

Since 1879, Connecticut has had on its books a law which forbids the use of contraceptives by anyone. I think this is an uncommonly silly law. As a practical matter, the law is obviously unenforceable, except in the oblique context of the present case. As a philosophical matter, I believe the use of contraceptives in the relationship of marriage should be left to personal and private choice, based upon each individual's moral, ethical, and religious beliefs. As a matter of social policy, I think professional counsel about methods of birth control should be available to all, so that each individual's choice can be meaningfully made.

But we are not asked in this case to say whether we think this law is unwise, or even asinine. We are asked to hold that it violates the United States Constitution. And that I cannot do.[38]

Texas Antiabortion Statute (1961)

Eight years later, the Supreme Court decided *Roe v. Wade*, building on the privacy right first recognized in *Griswold*. At the time, the vast majority of states prohibited women from obtaining abortions in all or most circumstances. At issue was one such law from Texas.

If any person shall designedly administer to a pregnant woman or knowingly procure to be administered with her consent any drug or medicine, or shall use towards her any violence or means whatever externally or internally applied, and thereby procure an abortion, he shall be confined in the penitentiary not less than two nor more than five years; if it be done without her consent, the punishment shall be doubled. By "abortion" is meant that the life of the fetus or embryo shall be destroyed in the woman's womb or that a premature birth thereof be caused....

Nothing in this chapter applies to an abortion procured or attempted by medical advice for the purpose of saving the life of the mother.[39]

Roe v. Wade—The Court Begins with History (1973)

The Court did not address the abortion question in a vacuum. In the same year that Pope Paul VI had condemned "all direct abortion, even for therapeutic reasons,"[40] the National Organization for Women had issued a call for "the right of women to control their own reproductive lives by removing from penal codes . . . laws governing abortion."[41] Justice Harry Blackmun, writing for the majority, more or less proceeded from first principles, beginning with a panoramic survey of abortion practices down through the ages (covering Persia, ancient Greece and Rome, and medieval and common law England, as well earlier legislation in the United States); he also canvassed the views of the American Medical Association, the American Public Health Association, and the American Bar Association. Justice Blackmun explained why his opinion devoted so much attention to what might be considered extralegal perspectives.

> We forthwith acknowledge our awareness of the sensitive and emotional nature of the abortion controversy, of the vigorous opposing views, even among physicians, and of the deep and seemingly absolute convictions that the subject inspires. One's philosophy, one's experiences, one's exposure to the raw edges of human existence, one's religious training, one's attitudes toward life and family and their values, and the moral standards one establishes and seeks to observe, are all likely to influence and to color one's thinking and conclusions about abortion. In addition, population growth, pollution, poverty, and racial overtones tend to complicate and not to simplify the problem. Our task, of course, is to resolve the issue by constitutional measurement, free of emotion and of predilection. We seek earnestly to do this, and, because we do, we have inquired into, and in this opinion place some emphasis upon, medical and medical-legal history and what that history reveals about man's attitudes toward the abortion procedure over the centuries.[42]

Roe v. Wade—The Court Rejects Proffered Justifications for Abortion Restrictions (1973)

Antiabortion laws had historically been justified on three grounds, only the last of which the Court found to be potentially persuasive.

> [First] to discourage illicit sexual conduct.... This is not a proper state purpose at all and ... if it were, the Texas statutes are overbroad in protecting it since the law fails to distinguish between married and unwed mothers.
>
> [Second, when] most criminal abortion laws were first enacted, the procedure was a hazardous one for the woman.... Thus, it has been argued that a state's real concern in enacting a criminal abortion law was to protect the pregnant woman.... Modern medical techniques have altered this situation.
>
> The third reason is the state's interest—some phrase it in terms of duty—in protecting prenatal life.... Logically, of course, a legitimate state interest in this area need not stand or fall on acceptance of the belief that life begins at conception or at some other point prior to live birth. In assessing the state's interest, recognition may be given to the less rigid claim that as long as at least *potential* life is involved, the state may assert interests beyond the protection of the pregnant woman alone.[43]

Roe v. Wade—The Court's Holding (1973)

Having surveyed the possible justifications for abortion restrictions, the Court then proceeded to enunciate its central holding. In doing so, it relied in large measure on *Griswold v. Connecticut* and its earlier privacy-related decisions.

> The Constitution does not explicitly mention any right of privacy. In a line of decisions, however . . . the Court has recognized that a right of personal privacy, or a guarantee of certain areas or zones of privacy, does exist under the Constitution. . . . This right of privacy . . . is broad enough to encompass a woman's decision whether or not to terminate her pregnancy. The detriment that the state would impose upon the pregnant woman by denying this choice altogether is apparent. Specific and direct harm medically diagnosable even in early pregnancy may be involved. Maternity or additional offspring may force upon the woman a distressful life and future. Psychological harm may be imminent. Mental and physical health may be taxed by child care. There is also the distress for all concerned associated with the unwanted child, and there is the problem of bringing a child into a family already unable, psychologically and otherwise, to care for it. . . .
>
> On the basis of elements such as these, [Roe and others] argue that the woman's right is absolute and that she is entitled to terminate her pregnancy at whatever time, in whatever way, and for whatever reason she alone chooses. With this we do not agree. [Roe's] arguments that Texas either has no valid interest at all in regulating the abortion decision, or no interest strong enough to support any limitation upon the woman's sole determination, are unpersuasive. The Court's decisions recognizing a right of privacy also acknowledge that some state regulation in areas protected by that right is appropriate. As noted above, a state may properly assert important interests in safeguarding health, in maintaining medical standards, and in protecting potential life. At some point in pregnancy, these respective interests become sufficiently compelling to sustain regulation of the factors that govern the abortion decision. The privacy right involved, therefore, cannot be said to be absolute . . . and must be considered against important state interests in regulation.[44]

The Court finished its opinion by announcing a so-called trimester policy, permitting virtually no limitations on the constitutional right to an abortion during the first three months of pregnancy, consistent with the determination of medical professionals ("the abortion decision and its effectuation must be left to the medical judgment of the pregnant woman's attending physician"). After fetal "viability," which the Court equated with the last three months of pregnancy, states were allowed to regulate and even prohibit all abortions (save when a mother's life or health was in danger). That left the middle months subject to (somewhat undefined) "regulat[ion] of the abortion procedure."

Doe v. Bolton—Dissent (1973)

Justice Byron White, joined by Justice (later Chief Justice) William Rehnquist, filed a dissenting opinion (in Doe v. Bolton, the companion case decided jointly with Roe v. Wade).

At the heart of the controversy in these cases are those recurring pregnancies that pose no danger whatsoever to the life or health of the mother but are, nevertheless, unwanted for any one or more of a variety of reasons—convenience, family planning, economics, dislike of children, the embarrassment of illegitimacy, etc. The common claim before us is that for any one of such reasons, or for no reason at all, and without asserting or claiming any threat to life or health, any woman is entitled to an abortion at her request if she is able to find a medical advisor willing to undertake the procedure. The Court for the most part sustains this position. During the period prior to the time the fetus becomes viable, the Constitution of the United States values the convenience, whim, or caprice of the putative mother more than the life or potential life of the fetus; the Constitution, therefore, guarantees the right to an abortion as against any state law or policy seeking to protect the fetus from an abortion not prompted by more compelling reasons of the mother.

With all due respect, I dissent. I find nothing in the language or history of the Constitution to support the Court's judgment. The Court simply fashions and announces a new constitutional right for pregnant mothers and, with scarcely any reason or authority for its action, invests that right with sufficient substance to override most existing state abortion statutes. The upshot is that the people and the legislatures of the fifty states are constitutionally disentitled to weigh the relative importance of the continued existence and development of the fetus, on the one hand, against a spectrum of possible impacts on the mother, on the other hand. As an exercise of raw judicial power, the Court perhaps has authority to do what it does today; but, in my view, its judgment is an improvident and extravagant exercise of the power of judicial review that the Constitution extends to this Court. . . . This issue, for the most part, should be left with the people and to the political processes the people have devised to govern their affairs.[45]

Roe v. Wade Is Affirmed in *Planned Parenthood v. Casey* (1992)

Roe v. Wade launched years of political struggle, as state legislatures and Congress grappled with the extent to which abortions could be regulated or even prohibited, consistent with constitutional limitations—and also years of judicial uncertainty, as each new law was inevitably challenged in the federal courts. In 1992, the Supreme Court squarely rejected a request that it overturn *Roe v. Wade.* In an unusual joint opinion (by Justices Sandra Day O'Connor, Anthony Kennedy, and David Souter, each of whom had been appointed by a Republican president), the Court chose instead to reaffirm what it described as *Roe's* "essential [three-part] holding," which the Court now cloaked in the constitutional language of "liberty" as well as privacy.

> First is a recognition of the right of the woman to choose to have an abortion before viability and to obtain it without undue interference from the state. Before viability, the state's interests are not strong enough to support a prohibition of abortion or the imposition of a substantial obstacle to the woman's effective right to elect the procedure. Second is a confirmation of the state's power to restrict abortions after fetal viability, if the law contains exceptions for pregnancies which endanger the woman's life or health. And third is the principle that the state has legitimate interests from the outset of the pregnancy in protecting the health of the woman and the life of the fetus that may become a child. These principles do not contradict one another, and we adhere to each. . . .
>
> Our law affords constitutional protection to personal decisions relating to marriage, procreation, contraception, family relationships, child rearing, education, [and] . . . the decision whether to bear or beget a child. . . . These matters, involving the most intimate and personal choices a person may make in a lifetime, choices central to personal dignity and autonomy, are central to the liberty protected by the Fourteenth Amendment. At the heart of liberty is the right to define one's own concept of existence, of meaning, of the universe, and of the mystery of human life.[46]

Roe v. Wade Is Reformulated in *Planned Parenthood v. Casey* (1992)

At the same time, though, the splintered Court in *Planned Parenthood v. Casey* afforded legislators significantly greater leeway to impose abortion restrictions nominally designed to advance two important state interests—as long as those restrictions did not place an "undue burden" or a "substantial obstacle in the path of a woman seeking an abortion before the fetus attains viability."

[First,] the state is [not] prohibited from taking steps to ensure that [a woman's] choice is thoughtful and informed. Even in the earliest stages of pregnancy, the state may enact rules and regulations designed to encourage her to know that there are philosophic and social arguments of great weight that can be brought to bear in favor of continuing the pregnancy to full term and that there are procedures and institutions to allow adoption of unwanted children as well as a certain degree of state assistance if the mother chooses to raise the child herself. The Constitution does not forbid a state or city, pursuant to democratic processes, from expressing a preference for normal childbirth. . . .

[Second,] the state has an interest in protecting the life of the unborn. . . . To promote the state's profound interest in potential life, throughout pregnancy the state may take measures to ensure that the woman's choice is informed, and measures designed to advance this interest will not be invalidated as long as their purpose is to persuade the woman to choose childbirth over abortion. . . . Subsequent to viability, the state in promoting its interest in the potentiality of human life may, if it chooses, regulate, and even proscribe, abortion.[47]

Justice Blackmun's Separate Opinion in *Planned Parenthood v. Casey* (1992)

The *Planned Parenthood v. Casey* decision, too, generated vigorous disagreement—this time from both sides of the judicial spectrum. Justice Blackmun, the author of *Roe*, concurred in the reaffirmance of *Roe* but objected to the Court's more restrictive approach to abortion; he also expressed great fear for the overall future of reproductive rights.

Five members of this Court today recognize that the Constitution protects a woman's right to terminate her pregnancy in its early stages. . . . I do not underestimate the significance of today's joint opinion. Yet I remain steadfast in my belief that the right to reproductive choice is entitled to the full protection afforded by this Court [in *Roe v. Wade*]. And I fear for the darkness as four justices anxiously await the single vote necessary to extinguish the light. . . .

While there is much to be praised about our democracy, our country since its founding has recognized that there are certain fundamental liberties that are not to be left to the whims of an election. A woman's right to reproductive choice is one of those fundamental liberties. Accordingly, that liberty need not seek refuge at the ballot box.

In one sense, the Court's approach is worlds apart from that of the Chief Justice and Justice Scalia [who dissented]. And yet, in another sense, the distance between the two approaches is short—the distance is but a single vote. I am eighty-three years old. I cannot remain on this Court forever, and when I do step down, the confirmation process for my successor well may focus on the issue before us today. That, I regret, may be exactly where the choice between the two worlds will be made.[48]

Chief Justice Rehnquist Dissent in *Planned Parenthood v. Casey* (1992)

Four justices, led by Chief Justice Rehnquist, would have expressly overruled *Roe v. Wade*, which they declared had been "wrongly decided" in the first place.

We think, therefore, both in view of this history and of our decided cases dealing with substantive liberty under the Due Process Clause, that the Court was mistaken in *Roe* when it classified a woman's decision to terminate her pregnancy as a "fundamental right." . . . The Court is most vulnerable and comes nearest to illegitimacy when it deals with judge-made constitutional law having little or no cognizable roots in the language or design of the Constitution. . . . The Court in *Roe* reached too far when it analogized the right to abort a fetus to the rights involved in [other decisions, including] *Griswold*, and thereby deemed the right to abortion fundamental.[49]

Justice Scalia Dissent in *Planned Parenthood v. Casey* (1992)

Justice Antonin Scalia wrote an additional (and fiery) opinion on behalf of the four dissenters.

The states may, if they wish, permit abortion on demand, but the Constitution does not *require* them to do so. The permissibility of abortion, and the limitations upon it, are to be resolved like most important questions in our democracy: by citizens trying to persuade one another and then voting. . . . The issue in [abortion cases is] not whether the power of a woman to abort her unborn child is a "liberty" in the absolute sense; or even whether it is a liberty of great importance to many women. Of course it is both. The issue is whether it is a liberty protected by the Constitution of the United States. I am sure it is not. I reach that conclusion not because of anything so exalted as my views concerning the "concept of existence, of meaning, of the universe, and of the mystery of human life." Rather, I reach it for the same reason I reach the conclusion that bigamy is not constitutionally protected—because of two simple facts: (1) the Constitution says absolutely nothing about it, and (2) the longstanding traditions of American society have permitted it to be legally proscribed. . . .

There comes vividly to mind a portrait by Emanuel Leutze that hangs in the Harvard Law School: Roger Brooke Taney, painted in 1859, the eighty-second year of his life, the twenty-fourth of his chief justiceship, the second after his opinion in *Dred Scott*. He is all in black, sitting in a shadowed red armchair, left hand resting upon a pad of paper in his lap, right hand hanging limply, almost lifelessly, beside the inner arm of the chair. He sits facing the viewer and staring straight out. There seems to be on his face, and in his deep-set eyes, an expression of profound sadness and disillusionment. Perhaps he always looked that way, even when dwelling upon the happiest of thoughts. But those of us who know how the luster of his great chief justiceship came to be eclipsed by *Dred Scott* cannot help believing that he had that case—its already apparent consequences for the Court and its soon-to-be-played-out consequences for the nation—burning on his mind. . . .

It is no more realistic for us in this litigation than it was for him in that, to think that an issue of the sort they both involved—an issue involving life and death, freedom and subjugation—can be "speedily and finally settled" by the Supreme Court. . . . Quite to the contrary, by foreclosing all democratic outlet for the deep passions this issue arouses, by banishing the issue from the political forum that gives all participants, even the losers, the satisfaction of a fair hearing and an honest fight, by continuing the imposition of a rigid national rule instead of allowing for regional differences, the Court merely prolongs and intensifies the anguish. We should get out of this area, where we have no right to be, and where we do neither ourselves nor the country any good by remaining.[50]

State Abortion Statutes

In other words, *Planned Parenthood v. Casey* came nowhere close to resolving the constitutional disputation over abortion that had been initiated two decades earlier by *Roe v. Wade*. During the thirty years that have followed *Planned Parenthood v. Casey*, the abortion debates have continued unabated. State legislatures have imposed more and more (and more creative) restrictions on access to abortions. By way of representative examples:

Physician and Hospital Requirements: 36 states require an abortion to be performed by a licensed physician. 19 states require an abortion to be performed in a hospital after a specified point in the pregnancy, and 17 states require the involvement of a second physician after a specified point.

Gestational Limits: 43 states prohibit abortions after a specified point in pregnancy, with some exceptions provided. . . .

Public Funding: 33 states and the District of Columbia prohibit the use of state funds [for abortion] except . . . where the patient's life is in danger or the pregnancy is the result of rape or incest. . . .

Refusal: 45 states allow individual health care providers to refuse to participate in an abortion. . . .

State-Mandated Counseling: 18 states mandate that individuals be given counseling before an abortion. . . .

Waiting Periods: 25 states require a woman seeking an abortion to wait a specified period of time, usually 24 hours, between when they receive counseling and the procedure is performed. . . .

Parental Involvement: 37 states require some type of parental involvement in a minor's decision to have an abortion. 27 states require one or both parents to consent to the procedure, while 10 require that one or both parents be notified.[51]

Supreme Court Abortion Decisions

Inevitably, each of these restrictions gets litigated in the federal courts. Consequently, the Supreme Court over the years has developed its own extensive abortion-related jurisprudence. Again, by way of representative examples:

Can a state refuse to fund public facilities to perform abortions? Yes.[52]
Are states required to fund abortions for the indigent? No.[53]
Can "partial-birth" abortions be banned? Initially, no;[54] subsequently, yes.[55]
May a state unduly restrict access to abortion clinics and services? No.[56]
Can a state require spousal consent prior to an abortion? No.[57]
When minors seek an abortion, can a state require parental notification and/or consent? Yes, provided a judicial bypass option is made available and parents do not have an absolute veto.[58]

Coda

The nation remains divided along political, moral, gender, regional, religious, and legal lines; prolife and prochoice camps inhabit two sides of an almost unbridgeable schism; abortion is often mentioned as a "litmus test" for judicial nominees; and whether or not *Roe v. Wade* will be reversed is the topic of endless discussion. The abortion debates are, of course, about what laws and restrictions, if any, should apply to a woman's termination of her pregnancy. But the abortion debates are also about who should be setting the nation's abortion rules: whether these matters are best addressed and resolved by elected representatives in the legislative crucible, or whether the courts are responsible for defining and protecting abortion rights no less than any other constitutional entitlement.

To close with two vignettes, the first of which captures the significance of the abortion controversy. "When asked to name a case that the Supreme Court has decided, most Americans who can name one point to *Roe v. Wade*—a case that they are eight times more likely to name than *Brown v. Board of Education*."[59] The second vignette elucidates the ambivalence surrounding abortion and involves Norma McCorvey—the real name of "Jane Roe," whose inability to obtain an abortion under Texas law eventually led to the landmark Supreme Court case. Over the years, McCorvey changed her mind about the morality of abortion and joined the prolife movement. In 2003, McCorvey returned to court in an attempt to get *Roe v. Wade* overturned. Her lawsuit was dismissed.[60]

Discussion Questions

1. Is the "right of privacy" justly implied from the Fourth, Ninth, and Fourteenth Amendments? Who had the better of the argument in *Griswold*: the majority, which fashioned privacy protections out of the implications (and "penumbras") of other constitutional values, or the dissenters? Did the justices inject their own personal values into the debate over privacy rights?

2. Melissa Murray makes clear that the evolution of constitutional law is often far from accidental. Outcome-oriented attorneys and litigants purposely brought legal challenges in *Poe*, *Griswold*, *Roe*, and *Eisenstadt* after efforts to change laws through the political process had failed. A similar resort to the courts was employed to provide expanded constitutional protections for women and for LGBTQ persons. What are the arguments for and against relying on the judicial branch, as opposed to elected lawmakers, to settle issues like privacy and abortion?

3. In *Planned Parenthood v. Casey*, Justice Blackmun observed that "the distance between the [majority and dissenting] approaches is short—the distance is but a single vote." Does constitutional history depend, at least in part, on which "side" has the most votes? Does the significance of a single vote on the Supreme Court explain the intense focus on ideology and the use of "litmus tests" for prospective justices? Is this a positive development or a necessary evil?

4. Once one admits the possibility of identifying a "privacy" or "liberty" or "autonomy" interest in the Constitution, where does one draw the line? Does a right to use contraceptives in the "sacred precincts of marital bedrooms" (quoting *Griswold*) necessarily imply similar protected liberty interests in other contexts—for example, contraceptive use by unwed persons? (Answer: Yes, said the Court in *Eisenstadt v. Baird* (1972).[61]) What about contraceptive use by underage teens? (Answer: Yes, said the Court in *Carey v. Population Services International* (1977).[62]) Is there a right to private consensual same-sex activity? (The Court first said no in *Bowers v. Hardwick* (1986),[63] but then changed its mind in *Lawrence v. Texas* (2003).[64]) Should our society rely on the Supreme Court or the political process to determine other "liberty" rights, such as the "right" for a terminally ill person to die? To conscientiously object to the draft? To marry more than one person? To engage in prostitution? Is it a fault or genius that the Constitution did not enumerate all the imaginable rights individuals might claim?

Women's Rights—Primary Sources

Traditionalism and paternalism dominated attitudes—certainly constitutional attitudes—toward women well into the second half of the twentieth century. Questions about the status of women had been wholly ignored at the Constitutional Convention in Philadelphia. During the Reconstruction era, the word "male" was included three times in the Fourteenth Amendment, and nothing was said about voting by women in the Fifteenth Amendment. Despite eventual passage of the Nineteenth Amendment prohibiting gender-based voting discrimination, a proposed Equal Rights Amendment floundered. And throughout these years, in interpreting the Constitution, courts were unwilling either to guarantee equal rights for women or to doubt that they needed "benevolent" protections.

Bradwell v. Illinois—Concurrence (1873)

As an example of traditionalism, consider *Bradwell v. Illinois* (1873). Illinois did not permit women to become lawyers, and the Supreme Court found this to be perfectly acceptable under the Constitution, given that the "privileges or immunities" of national citizenship did not include any right to practice a profession. In a concurring opinion that was joined by two of his colleagues, however, Justice Joseph Bradley went further.

The claim of [Myra Bradwell], who is a married woman, to be admitted to practice as an attorney and counselor at law is based upon the supposed right of every person, man or woman, to engage in any lawful employment for a livelihood....

But the civil law as well as nature herself has always recognized a wide difference in the respective spheres and destinies of man and woman. Man is, or should be, woman's protector and defender. The natural and proper timidity and delicacy which belongs to the female sex evidently unfits it for many of the occupations of civil life. The Constitution of the family organization, which is founded in the divine ordinance as well as in the nature of things, indicates the domestic sphere as that which properly belongs to the domain and functions of womanhood. The harmony, not to say identity, of interest and views which belong, or should belong, to the family institution is repugnant to the idea of a woman adopting a distinct and independent career from that of her husband....

It is true that many women are unmarried and not affected by any of the duties, complications, and incapacities arising out of the married state, but these are exceptions to the general rule. The paramount destiny and mission of woman are to fulfill the noble and benign offices of wife and mother. This is the law of the Creator. And the rules of civil society must be adapted to the general constitution of things, and cannot be based upon exceptional cases....

It is within the province of the legislature to ordain what offices, positions, and callings shall be filled and discharged by men, and shall receive the benefit of those energies and responsibilities and that decision and firmness which are presumed to predominate in the sterner sex.[65]

Muller v. Oregon (1908)

Consistent with the then-perceived wisdom recognizing certain fundamental differences between men and women, Supreme Court jurisprudence also permitted the government to craft legislation that provided special protections for (or benefits to) women as a class. In fact, achieving restrictions on the abuse of women in the workplace had been one of the foremost goals of Progressive-era reformers. In *Muller v. Oregon*, the Supreme Court unanimously upheld a state law mandating that women (but not men) could not work in laundries or factories more than ten hours a day. Justice David Brewer rejected a claim brought by a laundry owner who challenged the law as violating the Fourteenth Amendment. The Court began by acknowledging "a widespread belief that woman's physical structure, and the functions she performs in consequence thereof, justify special legislation restricting or qualifying the conditions under which she should be permitted to toil."

> That woman's physical structure and the performance of maternal functions place her at a disadvantage in the struggle for subsistence is obvious. This is especially true when the burdens of motherhood are upon her. Even when they are not, by abundant testimony of the medical fraternity, continuance for a long time on her feet at work, repeating this from day to day, tends to injurious effects upon the body, and, as healthy mothers are essential to vigorous offspring, the physical wellbeing of woman becomes an object of public interest and care in order to preserve the strength and vigor of the race.
>
> Still again, history discloses the fact that woman has always been dependent upon man. He established his control at the outset by superior physical strength, and this control in various forms, with diminishing intensity, has continued to the present. As minors, though not to the same extent, she has been looked upon in the courts as needing especial care that her rights may be preserved. Education was long denied her, and while now the doors of the schoolroom are opened and her opportunities for acquiring knowledge are great, yet, even with that and the consequent increase of capacity for business affairs, it is still true that in the struggle for subsistence she is not an equal competitor with her brother. Though limitations upon personal and contractual rights may be removed by legislation, there is that in her disposition and habits of life which will operate against a full assertion of those rights. She will still be where some legislation to protect her seems necessary to secure a real equality of right. . . .
>
> The limitations which this statute places upon her contractual powers, upon her right to agree with her employer as to the time she shall labor, are not imposed solely for her benefit, but also largely for the benefit of all. Many words cannot make this plainer. The two sexes differ in structure of body, in the functions to be performed by each, in the amount of physical strength, in the capacity for long-continued labor, particularly when done standing, the influence of vigorous health upon the future well-being of the race, the self-reliance which enables one to assert full rights, and in the capacity to maintain the struggle for subsistence. This difference justifies a difference in legislation and upholds that which is designed to compensate for some of the burdens which rest upon her.[66]

Reed v. Reed (1971)

Such remained the state of constitutional law with respect to gender roles and equality until the early 1970s. As a result, for example, the Supreme Court upheld laws preventing women from serving in various jobs such as working in restaurants at night[67] or bartending, which might give rise to "moral and social problems."[68] The Court also unanimously endorsed a state law that required men to serve on juries, but accepted women jurors only if they volunteered, in part because a "woman is still regarded as the center of home and family life."[69]

All this changed quite suddenly with a series of decisions starting with *Reed v. Reed*, where the Supreme Court began to require more compelling justifications for unequal treatment of men and women by the government. *Reed* concerned an Idaho law that required that "males must be preferred to females" in making appointments to serve as administrators of estates. The justices found no "rational reason" for such a gender-based distinction and—for the first time in the country's history—struck down as unconstitutional a law that treated men and women differently. Chief Justice Warren Burger wrote for the (unanimous) Court.

This Court has consistently recognized that the Fourteenth Amendment does not deny to states the power to treat different classes of persons in different ways. The Equal Protection Clause of that Amendment does, however, deny to states the power to legislate that different treatment be accorded to persons placed by a statute into different classes on the basis of criteria wholly unrelated to the objective of that statute. A classification "must be reasonable, not arbitrary, and must rest upon some ground of difference having a fair and substantial relation to the object of the legislation, so that all persons similarly circumstanced shall be treated alike." The question presented by this case, then, is whether a difference in the sex of competing applicants for letters of administration bears a rational relationship to a state objective. . . .

Clearly the objective of reducing the workload on probate courts by eliminating one class of contests [when two persons are both seeking an appointment to be the administrator] is not without some legitimacy. The crucial question, however, is whether [Idaho's law] advances that objective in a manner consistent with the command of the Equal Protection Clause. We hold that it does not. To give a mandatory preference to members of either sex over members of the other, merely to accomplish the elimination [of proceedings to select an administrator], is to make the very kind of arbitrary legislative choice forbidden by the Equal Protection Clause of the Fourteenth Amendment; and whatever may be said as to the positive values of avoiding intrafamily controversy, the choice in this context may not lawfully be mandated solely on the basis of sex.[70]

Ruth Bader Ginsburg on the Strategy for Achieving Gender Equality (2006)

A series of similar decisions—with similar outcomes—followed in rapid succession. In *Stanton v. Stanton* (1975), the Court ruled that it was unconstitutional for Utah to establish a different age of majority for boys versus girls.[71] In *Craig v. Boren* (1976), it was similarly unconstitutional for Oklahoma to set different minimum drinking ages based on gender.[72] Federal statutes that treated men and women differently for dependent's and survivor's benefits were struck down in *Frontiero v. Richardson* (1973) and *Weinberger v. Wiesenfeld* (1975).[73] Ruth Bader Ginsburg, who served as founder of the Women's Rights Project of the American Civil Liberties Union, argued before the Supreme Court or helped write the legal briefs in almost all of these (and other) lawsuits. After Ginsburg herself became a justice, she reflected on her strategy and goals in bringing gender discrimination challenges.

> In one sense, our mission in the 1970s was easy: the targets were well defined. There was nothing subtle about the way things were. Statute books in the states and nation were riddled with what we then called sex-based differentials. Illustrative laws were set out in an appendix to a brief the ACLU filed in the Supreme Court in the summer of 1971 in [*Reed v. Reed*]. . . .
>
> Judges and legislators in the 1960s, and at least at the start of the 1970s, regarded differential treatment of men and women not as malign, but as operating benignly in women's favor. Legislators and judges, in those years, were overwhelmingly white, well-heeled, and male. Men holding elected and appointed offices generally considered themselves good husbands and fathers. Women, they thought, had the best of all possible worlds. Women could work if they wished; they could stay home if they chose. They could avoid jury duty if they were so inclined, or they could serve if they elected to do so. They could escape military duty or they could enlist.
>
> Our mission was to educate, along with the public, decision-makers in the nation's legislatures and courts. We tried to convey to them that something was wrong with their perception of the world. As Justice [William] Brennan wrote in . . . *Frontiero v. Richardson*. . . . "Traditionally, [differential treatment on the basis of sex] was rationalized by an attitude of 'romantic paternalism' which, in practical effect put women not on a pedestal, but in a cage." . . .
>
> The US Supreme Court in the 1970s, as I see it, effectively carried on in the gender discrimination cases a dialogue with the political branches of government. The Court wrote modestly, it put forth no grand philosophy. But by propelling and reinforcing legislative and executive branch re-examination of sex-based classifications, the Court helped to ensure that laws and regulations would "catch up with a changed world."[74]

J.E.B. v. Alabama (1994)

Over time, the Supreme Court came to require a heightened showing—a "substantial relation" or an "exceedingly persuasive justification"—in order to sustain a law or practice that treated men and women differently, particularly if based on stereotypes or generalizations. For example, in 1994, the Court held that it was unconstitutional for trial lawyers to pick or reject potential jurors on the basis of their gender.

> Whether the trial is criminal or civil, potential jurors, as well as litigants, have an equal protection right to jury selection procedures that are free from state-sponsored group stereotypes rooted in, and reflective of, historical prejudice. . . . Our nation has had a long and unfortunate history of sex discrimination, a history which warrants the heightened scrutiny we afford all gender-based classifications today. Under our equal protection jurisprudence, gender-based classifications require "an exceedingly persuasive justification" in order to survive constitutional scrutiny. . . .
>
> Discrimination in jury selection, whether based on race or on gender, causes harm to the litigants, the community, and the individual jurors who are wrongfully excluded from participation in the judicial process. . . . When [lawyers pick jurors] in reliance on gender stereotypes, they ratify and reinforce prejudicial views of the relative abilities of men and women.[75]

United States v. Virginia (1996)

Sandra Day O'Connor, the first woman appointed to the Supreme Court, wrote the 5–4 majority opinion in *Mississippi University for Women v. Hogan* (1982),[76] which struck down as unconstitutional a female-only nursing school established by the state of Mississippi. Fourteen years later, the Court ruled 7–1, in an opinion written by Justice Ginsburg, that the males-only admissions policy of the Virginia Military Institute (VMI) discriminated on the basis of gender.

> VMI has notably succeeded in its mission to produce leaders; among its alumni are military generals, members of Congress, and business executives. The school's alumni overwhelmingly perceive that their VMI training helped them to realize their personal goals. VMI's endowment reflects the loyalty of its graduates; VMI has the largest per-student endowment of all public undergraduate institutions in the nation. Neither the goal of producing citizen-soldiers nor VMI's implementing methodology is inherently unsuitable to women. And the school's impressive record in producing leaders has made admission desirable to some women. Nevertheless, Virginia has elected to preserve exclusively for men the advantages and opportunities a VMI education affords. . . . We conclude that Virginia has shown no "exceedingly persuasive justification" for excluding all women from the citizen-soldier training afforded by VMI. . . .

A prime part of the history of our Constitution . . . is the story of the extension of constitutional rights and protections to people once ignored or excluded. VMI's story continued as our comprehension of "We the People" expanded. There is no reason to believe that the admission of women capable of all the activities required of VMI cadets would destroy the Institute rather than enhance its capacity to serve the "more perfect Union."[77]

Current Status

Congress has passed legislation specifically targeted at ending the discriminatory and disparate treatment of women, including the Equal Pay Act (1963); Title VII of the Civil Rights Act (1964) (prohibiting sex discrimination in employment); Title IX of the Education Amendments (1972) (prohibiting sex discrimination in educational programs or activities); and the Pregnancy Discrimination Act (1978). At the same time, not all laws that distinguish between the sexes have been treated as constitutionally suspect by the courts. Gender-based classifications have been permitted "to compensate women for particular economic disabilities they have suffered"[78] and "to promote equal employment opportunity."[79] And, in *Rostker v. Goldberg* (1981), the Court upheld (by a vote of 6–3) a law that required only men to register for the draft under the Military Selective Service Act, because "Congress acted well within its constitutional authority" in concluding that men and women were not "similarly situated" for purposes of combat duties[80]—although subsequent executive orders and congressional legislation have led to far more gender equality in the armed forces. Overall, the past fifty years have witnessed a sea change in the Constitution's (in)tolerance of gender-based disparities—to the point where some commentators maintain that the Equal Rights Amendment, although never ratified by the states, has effectively been added by the Supreme Court to the Constitution.

Discussion Questions

1. Do the courts tend to be out in front on social change? Or do they lag behind? Why did Thurgood Marshall's historic court victories for racial equality come decades before Ruth Bader Ginsburg's victories for gender equality?[81]

2. What do you think of the argument that in light of *Reed* and subsequent decisions striking down a host of gender-based distinctions as a denial of equal protection, an Equal Rights Amendment is not necessary?[82]

3. Were an Equal Rights Amendment to pass, would single-sex colleges or dorms, gender-segregated bathrooms, or separate-sex sports teams be threatened? Should laws continue to differentiate between men and women with respect to matters relating to reproduction and pregnancy? Could Congress continue to treat women and men differently for purposes of the military draft?

4. Given the modern critique of binary gender distinctions, what rights should belong to those persons who decline to categorize themselves as either male or female? Is it wrong for the government to permit only the designation of "M" or "F" on passports and driver's licenses? To what extent should schools and government agencies accommodate self-identification other than male and female? Is it constitutional to disfavor the use of gender-neutral pronouns? Is it constitutional to prohibit transgender athletes from competing in women's sports?

Same-Sex Relationships—Primary Sources

In *Griswold v. Connecticut*, *Roe v. Wade*, and related cases, the Supreme Court announced a right of privacy (or "liberty") that broadly protected intimate sexual relationships and permitted individuals to control their reproductive decisions without government interference. These rights, however, did not extend to gays and lesbians. Indeed, the Court declared in *Bowers v. Hardwick* (1986) that recognizing a constitutional right to same-sex activity would be "facetious."[83] To the same effect, even though in *Loving v. Virginia* (1967) the Court had declared unconstitutional a dozen-plus state laws that prohibited interracial marriage,[84] more than a generation later no state permitted persons of the same gender to wed. But after the early years of the twenty-first century, same-sex activity had been protected by the Supreme Court, same-sex marriages were recognized nationwide, gays could serve in the military without fear of being discharged, federal laws defining marriage as between a man and a woman had been struck down—and the president in an Inaugural Address referred to Stonewall in the same breath as Seneca Falls and Selma.[85]

Bowers v. Hardwick (1986)

None of this could be foreseen in the mid-1980s, when *Bowers v. Hardwick* made its way to the nation's highest court. At the time, more than two dozen states criminalized sodomy—including Georgia, where Michael Hardwick had been arrested for participating in consensual sexual activity with a fellow adult male.

A lower court had concluded that homosexual behavior constituted intimate associational activity covered by the privacy/liberty doctrine. The Supreme Court reversed, with Justice Byron White writing the majority (5–4) opinion.

This case does not require a judgment on whether laws against sodomy between consenting adults in general, or between homosexuals in particular, are wise or desirable. It raises no question about the right or propriety of state legislative decisions to repeal their laws that criminalize homosexual sodomy, or of state court decisions invalidating those laws on state constitutional grounds. The issue presented is whether the federal Constitution confers a fundamental right upon homosexuals to engage in sodomy, and hence invalidates the laws of the many states that still make such conduct illegal and have done so for a very long time. The case also calls for some judgment about the limits of the Court's role in carrying out its constitutional mandate....

We first register our disagreement ... that the Court's prior cases [including *Griswold* and *Roe*] have construed the Constitution to confer a right of privacy that extends to homosexual sodomy and, for all intents and purposes, have decided this case.... We think it evident that none of the rights announced in those cases bears any resemblance to the claimed constitutional right of homosexuals to engage in acts of sodomy that is asserted in this case. No connection between family, marriage, or procreation, on the one hand, and homosexual activity, on the other, has been demonstrated....

Precedent aside, however, [Hardwick] would have us announce ... a fundamental right to engage in homosexual sodomy. This we are quite unwilling to do.... The Court has [previously] sought to identify the nature of the rights qualifying for heightened judicial protection: ... those fundamental liberties that are "implicit in the concept of ordered liberty," such that "neither liberty nor justice would exist if [they] were sacrificed," [and] ... that are "deeply rooted in this nation's history and tradition." ... It is obvious to us that neither of these formulations would extend a fundamental right to homosexuals to engage in acts of consensual sodomy. Proscriptions against that conduct have ancient roots.... In 1868, when the Fourteenth Amendment was ratified, all but five of the thirty-seven states in the Union had criminal sodomy laws. In fact, until 1961, all fifty states outlawed sodomy, and today, twenty-four states and the District of Columbia continue to provide criminal penalties for sodomy performed in private and between consenting adults.... Against this background, to claim that a right to engage in such conduct is "deeply rooted in this nation's history and tradition" or "implicit in the concept of ordered liberty" is, at best, facetious.[86]

Justice Lewis Powell, who joined the Court's majority in *Bowers*, later stated, "I think I probably made a mistake in that one." He also acknowledged having switched his vote to uphold Georgia's law, after having initially decided to strike down the statute.[87]

Bowers v. Hardwick—Dissent (1986)

Justice Harry Blackmun (the author of *Roe v. Wade*) wrote the dissenting opinion on behalf of himself and three fellow justices in *Bowers v. Hardwick*.

> This case is [not] about "a fundamental right to engage in homosexual sodomy," as the Court purports to declare. . . . Rather, this case is about "the most comprehensive of rights and the right most valued by civilized men," namely, "the right to be let alone." . . .
>
> Our cases long have recognized that the Constitution embodies a promise that a certain private sphere of individual liberty will be kept largely beyond the reach of government. . . . [The Court] has recognized a privacy interest with reference to certain decisions that are properly for the individual to make. . . . [The Court has also] recognized a privacy interest with reference to certain places without regard for the particular activities in which the individuals who occupy them are engaged. . . .
>
> Only the most willful blindness could obscure the fact that sexual intimacy is a sensitive, key relationship of human existence, central to family life, community welfare, and the development of human personality. The fact that individuals define themselves in a significant way through their intimate sexual relationships with others suggests, in a nation as diverse as ours, that there may be many "right" ways of conducting those relationships, and that much of the richness of a relationship will come from the freedom an individual has to choose the form and nature of these intensely personal bonds. . . . The Court claims that its decision today merely refuses to recognize a fundamental right to engage in homosexual sodomy; what the Court really has refused to recognize is the fundamental interest all individuals have in controlling the nature of their intimate associations with others. . . .
>
> I can only hope that . . . the Court soon will reconsider its analysis and conclude that depriving individuals of the right to choose for themselves how to conduct their intimate relationships poses a far greater threat to the values most deeply rooted in our nation's history than tolerance of nonconformity could ever do.[88]

Lawrence v. Texas (2003)

Justice Blackmun eventually got his wish: Seventeen years later, the Supreme Court overruled *Bowers* in *Lawrence v. Texas.*[89] John Geddes Lawrence and his male partner were arrested by Houston police for engaging in "deviate" sexual activity with "another person of the same sex," in violation of Texas law. Rather than following *Bowers* as a precedent, or somehow attempting to distinguish it, the 6–3 majority, led by Justice Anthony Kennedy, flatly rejected it.

> We conclude the case should be resolved by determining whether the petitioners were free as adults to engage in the private conduct in the exercise of their liberty under the Due Process Clause of the Fourteenth Amendment to the Constitution. For this inquiry we deem it necessary to reconsider the Court's holding in *Bowers.* . . .
>
> To say that the issue in *Bowers* was simply the right to engage in certain sexual conduct demeans the claim the individual put forward, just as it would demean a married couple were it to be said marriage is simply about the right to have sexual intercourse. The laws involved in *Bowers* and here are, to be sure, statutes that purport to do no more than prohibit a particular sexual act. Their penalties and purposes, though, have more far-reaching consequences, touching upon the most private human conduct, sexual behavior, and in the most private of places, the home. The statutes do seek to control a personal relationship that, whether or not entitled to formal recognition in the law, is within the liberty of persons to choose without being punished as criminals. . . .
>
> *Bowers* was not correct when it was decided, and it is not correct today. It ought not to remain binding precedent. *Bowers v. Hardwick* should be and now is overruled.[90]

Justice Kennedy then defined the scope of the "liberty interest" that protected Lawrence's adult, consensual, nonharmful, and private activities and relationships.

> Liberty protects the person from unwarranted government intrusions into a dwelling or other private places. In our tradition the state is not omnipresent in the home. And there are other spheres of our lives and existence, outside the home, where the state should not be a dominant presence. Freedom extends beyond spatial bounds. Liberty presumes an autonomy of self that includes freedom of thought, belief, expression, and certain intimate conduct. . . .

[This case involves] two adults who, with full and mutual consent from each other, engaged in sexual practices common to a homosexual lifestyle. The petitioners are entitled to respect for their private lives. The state cannot demean their existence or control their destiny by making their private sexual conduct a crime. Their right to liberty under the Due Process Clause gives them the full right to engage in their conduct without intervention of the government. . . .

Had those who drew and ratified the Due Process Clauses of the Fifth Amendment or the Fourteenth Amendment known the components of liberty in its manifold possibilities, they might have been more specific. They did not presume to have this insight. They knew times can blind us to certain truths and later generations can see that laws once thought necessary and proper in fact serve only to oppress. As the Constitution endures, persons in every generation can invoke its principles in their own search for greater freedom.[91]

Lawrence v. Texas—Dissent (2003)

Justice Antonin Scalia dissented, along with Chief Justice William Rehnquist and Justice Clarence Thomas. They found no compelling reason "to reconsider a decision rendered a mere seventeen years ago in Bowers v. Hardwick."

The Texas statute undeniably seeks to further the belief of its citizens that certain forms of sexual behavior are "immoral and unacceptable"—the same interest furthered by criminal laws against fornication, bigamy, adultery, adult incest, bestiality, and obscenity. Bowers held that this was a legitimate state interest. The Court today reaches the opposite conclusion. The Texas statute, it says, "furthers no legitimate state interest which can justify its intrusion into the personal and private life of the individual." . . . This effectively decrees the end of all morals legislation. If, as the Court asserts, the promotion of majoritarian sexual morality is not even a legitimate state interest, none of the above-mentioned laws can survive. . . . Texas's prohibition of sodomy neither infringes a "fundamental right" (which the Court does not dispute), nor is unsupported by a rational relation to what the Constitution considers a legitimate state interest, nor denies the equal protection of the laws.[92]

Justice Scalia and his colleagues also spoke more generally about what they believed to be the limited role of courts in deciding the sorts of issues raised in Lawrence.

It is clear . . . that the Court has taken sides in the culture war, departing from its role of assuring, as neutral observer, that the democratic rules of engagement are observed. Many Americans do not want persons who openly engage in homosexual conduct as partners in their business, as scoutmasters for their children, as teachers in their children's schools, or as boarders in their home. They view this as protecting themselves and their families from a lifestyle that they believe to be immoral and destructive. The Court views it as "discrimination" which it is the function of our judgments to deter. . . .

Let me be clear that I have nothing against homosexuals, or any other group, promoting their agenda through normal democratic means. Social perceptions of sexual and other morality change over time, and every group has the right to persuade its fellow citizens that its view of such matters is the best. That homosexuals have achieved some success in that enterprise is attested to by the fact that Texas is one of the few remaining states that criminalize private, consensual homosexual acts. But persuading one's fellow citizens is one thing, and imposing one's views in absence of democratic majority will is something else. I would no more *require* a state to criminalize homosexual acts—or, for that matter, display *any* moral disapprobation of them—than I would *forbid* it to do so. What Texas has chosen to do is well within the range of traditional democratic action, and its hand should not be stayed through the invention of a brand-new "constitutional right" by a Court that is impatient of democratic change. It is indeed true that "later generations can see that laws once thought necessary and proper in fact serve only to oppress," and when that happens, later generations can repeal those laws. But it is the premise of our system that those judgments are to be made by the people, and not imposed by a governing caste [of judges] that knows best.[93]

At the conclusion of his dissent in *Lawrence*, Justice Scalia warned that the Court's principles, taken to their logical extreme, would inevitably require the constitutional recognition of same-sex marriage. ("If moral disapprobation of homosexual conduct is no legitimate state interest for purposes of proscribing that conduct, . . . what justification could there possibly be for denying the benefits of marriage to homosexual couples exercising 'the liberty protected by the Constitution'?") His prediction turned out to be correct.

Defense of Marriage Act (1996)

At the beginning of the twenty-first century, no state legally permitted same-sex couples to wed. To the contrary, the majority of states either expressly outlawed

same-sex marriages or else (to the same effect) defined marriage as a legal relationship between a man and a woman. Indeed, in 1996, Congress had passed,
and President Bill Clinton had signed, legislation known as the Defense of
Marriage Act.

> Section 2. Powers reserved to the states. . . . No state . . . shall be required to give
> effect to any public act, record, or judicial proceeding of any other state . . . re-
> specting a relationship between persons of the same sex that is treated as a mar-
> riage under the laws of such other state. . . .
>   Section 3. Definition of marriage. . . . In determining the meaning of any
> act of Congress, or of any ruling, regulation, or interpretation of the various
> administrative bureaus and agencies of the United States, the word "marriage"
> means only a legal union between one man and one woman as husband and
> wife.[94]

United States v. Windsor (2013)

In *United States v. Windsor*, the Court struck down the Defense of Marriage Act
as unconstitutional. The marriage of Edith Windsor and Thea Spyer, performed
in Canada, was legally recognized under the laws of New York in 2008. When
Spyer died, Windsor sought the same federal estate tax exemption to which she
would have been entitled had she married a man. The Defense of Marriage Act
made that impossible. In a complicated 5–4 ruling, the Supreme Court majority
determined that the Defense of Marriage Act discriminated against same-sex
couples validly married under state law, by denying to them the advantages (in
this case, under federal tax law) otherwise available to fellow state residents who
had entered into heterosexual marriages.

> The responsibility of the states for the regulation of domestic relations is an
> important indicator of the substantial societal impact the state's classifications
> have in the daily lives and customs of its people. [The Defense of Marriage
> Act's] unusual deviation from the usual tradition of recognizing and accepting
> state definitions of marriage here operates to deprive same-sex couples of the
> benefits and responsibilities that come with the federal recognition of their
> marriages.[95]

Congress offended the equal protection standards of the Fifth and Fourteenth
Amendments to the extent its law upset "the long-established precept that the
incidents, benefits, and obligations of marriage are uniform for all married
couples within each state." Put differently, the federal statute "interfer[ed] with

the equal dignity of same-sex marriages, a dignity conferred by the states in the exercise of their sovereign power."[96]

Background to *Obergefell v. Hodges*

In 2004, Massachusetts became the first state to recognize same-sex marriage, as a result of a decision by its highest court (based on interpretation of the state's constitution). At the time *Windsor* was decided in 2013, a dozen states permitted same-sex marriages—but nothing in *Windsor* affected the remaining states one way or the other. By 2015, though, courts and legislatures in more than thirty states had legalized gay marriage. At the same time, however, other states had expressly rejected same-sex marriage by statute or referendum.[97] Such was the checkerboard legal background against which the Supreme Court decided *Obergefell v. Hodges*, where the Court found a constitutional right to same-sex marriage, applicable nationwide.

For more than a century, the Supreme Court had afforded the institution of marriage special protection under the Constitution. Marriage constituted "the most important relation in life, as having more to do with the morals and civilization of a people than any other institution."[98] Liberty, as protected under the Constitution, included the right to "marry, establish a home, and bring up children," the Court had said previously.[99] Marriage was "fundamental to the very existence and survival of the race."[100]

Loving v. Virginia (1967)

The justices had relied upon these precedents about marriage in striking down Virginia's miscegenation law in 1967. Virginia, along with fifteen other states, forbade interracial marriages. The Court held that such a prohibition infringed upon the "fundamental freedom" of Mildred and Richard Loving.

> The freedom to marry has long been recognized as one of the vital personal rights essential to the orderly pursuit of happiness by free men. Marriage is one of the "basic civil rights of man," fundamental to our very existence and survival. To deny this fundamental freedom on so unsupportable a basis as the racial classifications embodied in these statutes, classifications so directly subversive of the principle of equality at the heart of the Fourteenth Amendment, is surely to deprive all the state's citizens of liberty without due process of law. The Fourteenth Amendment requires that the freedom of choice to marry not be restricted by invidious racial discriminations. Under our Constitution, the

freedom to marry, or not marry, a person of another race resides with the individual, and cannot be infringed by the state.[101]

Obergefell v. Hodges (2015)

By the time the same-sex marriage issue reached the Supreme Court, many states had already recognized such relationships. The question in *Obergefell* was whether all remaining states would be required to do so—essentially, whether the last sentence of *Loving* should be rewritten as follows: "Under our Constitution, the freedom to marry, or not marry, a person of *the same gender* resides with the individual, and cannot be infringed by the state." Which is exactly what the Court decided, by a vote of 5–4, with Justice Kennedy writing for the majority.

The centrality of marriage to the human condition makes it unsurprising that the institution has existed for millennia and across civilizations. Since the dawn of history, marriage has transformed strangers into relatives, binding families and societies together. . . . That history is the beginning of these cases. The respondents [opponents of same-sex marriage] say it should be the end as well. To them, it would demean a timeless institution if the concept and lawful status of marriage were extended to two persons of the same sex. Marriage, in their view, is by its nature a gender-differentiated union of man and woman. This view long has been held and continues to be held in good faith by reasonable and sincere people here and throughout the world. . . . Far from seeking to devalue marriage, the petitioners seek it for themselves because of their respect and need for its privileges and responsibilities. And their immutable nature dictates that same-sex marriage is their only real path to this profound commitment. . . .

The nature of injustice is that we may not always see it in our own times. The generations that wrote and ratified the Bill of Rights and the Fourteenth Amendment did not presume to know the extent of freedom in all of its dimensions, and so they entrusted to future generations a charter protecting the right of all persons to enjoy liberty as we learn its meaning. When new insight reveals discord between the Constitution's central protections and a received legal stricture, a claim to liberty must be addressed. . . .

[An analysis of the Court's previous decisions] compels the conclusion that same-sex couples may exercise the right to marry. The four principles and traditions to be discussed demonstrate that the reasons marriage is fundamental under the Constitution apply with equal force to same-sex couples. A first premise of the Court's relevant precedents is that the right to personal choice regarding marriage is inherent in the concept of individual autonomy. . . . A second principle in this Court's jurisprudence is that the right to marry is fundamental because it supports a two-person union unlike any other in its importance to the committed individuals. . . . A third basis for protecting the right to marry is that it safeguards children and families and thus draws meaning from related rights of childrearing, procreation, and education. . . . As all parties agree, many same-sex couples provide loving and nurturing homes to their children, whether biological or adopted. . . . Fourth and finally, this Court's cases and the nation's traditions make clear that marriage is a keystone of our social order. . . . There is no difference between same- and opposite-sex couples with respect to [these principles]. . . . It demeans gays and lesbians for the state to lock them out of a central institution of the nation's society. Same-sex couples, too, may aspire to the transcendent purposes of marriage and seek fulfillment in its highest meaning. . . .

These [and other] considerations lead to the conclusion that the right to marry is a fundamental right inherent in the liberty of the person, and under the Due Process and Equal Protection Clauses of the Fourteenth Amendment couples of the same sex may not be deprived of that right and that liberty. The Court now holds that same-sex couples may exercise the fundamental right to marry. No longer may this liberty be denied to them. . . .

The dynamic of our constitutional system is that individuals need not await legislative action before asserting a fundamental right. The nation's courts are open to injured individuals who come to them to vindicate their own direct, personal stake in our basic charter. An individual can invoke a right to constitutional protection when he or she is harmed, even if the broader public disagrees and even if the legislature refuses to act. The idea of the Constitution "was to withdraw certain subjects from the vicissitudes of political controversy, to place them beyond the reach of majorities and officials, and to establish them as legal principles to be applied by the courts."[102]

Obergefell v. Hodges—Dissent (2015)

Four justices dissented, each writing a separate dissenting opinion. The dissent authored by Chief Justice John Roberts (and joined by Justices Scalia and Thomas) focused as much on the proper role of courts in a democracy (in Roberts's view) as it did on the status of same-sex relationships.

Petitioners make strong arguments rooted in social policy and considerations of fairness. They contend that same-sex couples should be allowed to affirm their love and commitment through marriage, just like opposite-sex couples. That position has undeniable appeal; over the past six years, voters and legislators in eleven states and the District of Columbia have revised their laws to allow marriage between two people of the same sex.

But this Court is not a legislature. Whether same-sex marriage is a good idea should be of no concern to us. Under the Constitution, judges have power to say what the law is, not what it should be. . . . Although the policy arguments for extending marriage to same-sex couples may be compelling, the legal arguments for requiring such an extension are not. The fundamental right to marry does not include a right to make a state change its definition of marriage. And a state's decision to maintain the meaning of marriage that has persisted in every culture throughout human history can hardly be called irrational. In short, our Constitution does not enact any one theory of marriage. The people of a state are free to expand marriage to include same-sex couples, or to retain the historic definition.

Today, however, the Court takes the extraordinary step of ordering every state to license and recognize same-sex marriage. Many people will rejoice at this decision, and I begrudge none their celebration. But for those who believe in a government of laws, not of men, the majority's approach is deeply disheartening. Supporters of same-sex marriage have achieved considerable success persuading their fellow citizens—through the democratic process—to adopt their view. That ends today. Five lawyers have closed the debate and enacted their own vision of marriage as a matter of constitutional law. . . .

The majority's decision is an act of will, not legal judgment. The right it announces has no basis in the Constitution or this Court's precedent. . . . The Court invalidates the marriage laws of more than half the states and orders the transformation of a social institution that has formed the basis of human society for millennia, for the Kalahari Bushmen and the Han Chinese, the Carthaginians and the Aztecs. Just who do we think we are? . . .

A much different view of the Court's role is possible. That view is more modest and restrained. It is more skeptical that the legal abilities of judges also reflect insight into moral and philosophical issues. It is more sensitive to the fact that judges are unelected and unaccountable, and that the legitimacy of their power depends on confining it to the exercise of legal judgment. It is more attuned to the lessons of history, and what it has meant for the country and Court when justices have exceeded their proper bounds. And it is less pretentious than to suppose that while people around the world have viewed an institution in a particular way for thousands of years, the present generation and the present Court are the ones chosen to burst the bonds of that history and tradition.

If you are among the many Americans—of whatever sexual orientation—who favor expanding same-sex marriage, by all means celebrate today's decision. Celebrate the achievement of a desired goal. Celebrate the opportunity for a new expression of commitment to a partner. Celebrate the availability of new benefits. But do not celebrate the Constitution. It had nothing to do with it.[103]

Conclusion

The Supreme Court's recognition of same-sex marriage formed only part of a much larger gay rights mosaic. In the 1980s, the government's neglectful response to the AIDS pandemic galvanized the LGBTQ community into political and social action. Until very late in the twentieth century, homosexuals were not allowed in—and could be discharged from—the armed forces; in 1993, the "don't ask, don't tell" policy permitted gays to continue to serve in the military, as long as they were not open about their sexual orientation; by 2011, all such restrictions had been lifted. Congress and state legislatures, especially after the shocking murder of Matthew Shepard in Wyoming in 1998, passed "hate crime" laws, providing enhanced penalties for criminal acts committed with antihomosexual animus. Public opinion polls in the country showed a steady progression of support for LGBTQ rights over time, particularly regarding same-sex marriage. And with respect to same-sex marriage, it was the work of many—ordinary citizens and activists alike—that wrought changes through political processes in state after state. So, the story of the fifty years after Stonewall involved far more than courts and rulings and legislatures and laws. But the saga also entailed the transformation of constitutional law.

Discussion Questions

1. Over time, the Supreme Court evolved in its attitude toward protecting same-sex activity from "facetious" to a constitutional right; a similar evolution occurred regarding same-sex marriage. With respect to same-sex relationships, the same question could be asked as with respect to women's rights: on matters of social change, do the courts lead, or do they follow?
2. Compare the underlying premises and the arguments of Justices Blackmun and White in *Roe/Doe* and Justice Kennedy and Chief Justice Roberts in *Obergefell* about the relationship between the courts and the democratic process. What role should courts play in securing rights in addition to—or in the absence of—legislation and constitutional amendment?
3. Title VII of the Civil Rights Act of 1964 prohibits employers from discriminating on the basis of "race, color, religion, sex, or national origin." The Supreme Court recently held that discrimination on the basis of "sex" includes firing an employee merely for being gay or transgender.[104] But to date the Supreme Court has not interpreted the Fourteenth Amendment to

treat sexual identity, like race, as a "suspect" classification requiring equal treatment in all situations absent a "compelling governmental interest" justifying a "narrowly tailored" law. To what extent do existing Supreme Court decisions suggest that LGBTQ Americans are entitled to equal treatment in situations that might occur in daily life?

4. A highly publicized controversy involved the First Amendment religious-based claim of a Colorado baker who refused to sell one of his specialty cakes to a to-be-married same-sex couple.[105] To what extent should deeply held religious beliefs be a factor in determining LGBTQ rights?

Additional Primary Source Documents

Primary source document excerpts covering the following topics are located on the website accompanying this book:

Affirmative Action and Diversity—including Lyndon Johnson's "War on Poverty"; Executive Orders on affirmative action; *Adarand Constructors, Inc. v. Pena*, 515 U.S. 200 (1995); *Regents of University of California v. Bakke*, 438 U.S. 265 (1978); *Parents Involved in Community Schools v. Seattle*, 551 U.S. 701 (2007); *Fisher v. University of Texas*, 579 U.S. ___ (2016).

"New" Rights: Guns and Property—including the Second Amendment; *District of Columbia v. Heller*, 554 U.S. 570 (2008); National Rifle Association; Giffords Law Center; Fifth Amendment; *Kohl v. United States*, 91 U.S. 367 (1876); *Kelo v. New London*, 545 U.S. 469 (2005).

Immigration—including Immigration and Nationality Act of 1965; Deferred Action for Childhood Arrivals (DACA); "Travel Ban"; *Trump v. Hawaii*, 585 U.S. ___ (2018).

Other "Constitutional Moments" during this Era

- First Amendment, free speech and press—including *Federal Communications Commission v. Pacifica Foundation*, 438 U.S. 726 (1978) (indecency standards); *Richmond Newspapers, Inc. v. Virginia*, 448 U.S. 555 (1980) (public criminal trials); *Texas v. Johnson*, 491 U.S. 397 (1989) (flag burning); *Virginia v. Black*, 538 U.S. 343 (2003) (cross burning); *Doe v. Reed*, 561 U.S. 186 (2010) (confidentiality of petitions); *Snyder v. Phelps*, 562 U.S. 443 (2011) (funeral protests); *Matal v. Tam*, 582 U.S. ___ (2017)

(disparaging trademarks); *Iancu v. Brunett*, 588 U.S. ___ (2019) (scandalous and immoral trademarks).

- First Amendment, religion—including *Wallace v. Jaffree*, 472 U.S. 38 (1985) (school prayer); *Edwards v. Aguillard*, 482 U.S. 578 (1987) (teaching of creationism); Religious Freedom Restoration Act (1993); *City of Boerne v. Flores*, 521 U.S. 507 (1997) (striking down RFRA's application to the states); *Towne of Greece v. Galloway*, 572 U.S. 565 (2014) (public prayer).

- Criminal law—including *Strickland v. Washington*, 466 U.S. 668 (1984) (ineffective assistance of counsel); *Batson v. Kentucky*, 476 U.S. 79 (1986) (race and jury selection); *United States v. Jones*, 565 U.S. 400 (2012) (warrantless surveillance); *Carpenter v. United States*, 585 U.S. ___ (2018) (cell phone tracking).

- Death penalty cases—including *Furman v. Georgia*, 408 U.S. 238 (1972) (death penalty unconstitutional); *Gregg v. Georgia*, 428 U.S. 153 (1976) (death penalty upheld); *McCleskey v. Kemp*, 481 U.S. 279 (1987) (death penalty and race); *Atkins v. Virginia*, 536 U.S. 304 (2002) (intellectual disabilities); *Roper v. Simmons*, 543 U.S. 551 (2005) (juveniles); *Kennedy v. Louisiana*, 554 U.S. 407 (2008) (nonmurder crimes).

- Assisted suicide and the "right to die"—including *Cruzan v. Director, Missouri Department of Health*, 497 U.S. 261 (1990); *Washington v. Glucksberg*, 521 U.S. 702 (1997); *Gonzalez v. Oregon*, 546 U.S. 243 (2006).

- Commerce clause powers—including *United States v. Lopez*, 514 U.S. 549 (1995) (guns near schools); *United States v. Morrison*, 529 U.S. 598 (2000) (Violence against Women Act); *National Federation of Independent Business v. Sebelius*, 567 U.S. 519 (2012) (Affordable Care Act).

- National security and presidential power—including Authorization for Use of Military Force (2001); USA PATRIOT Act (2001); "enhanced interrogation"/"torture" practices; *Hamdi v. Rumsfeld*, 542 U.S. 507 (2004); *Rasul v. Bush*, 542 U.S. 466 (2004); *Hamdan v. Rumsfeld*, 548 U.S. 557 (2006); and *Boumediene v. Bush*, 553 U.S. 723 (2008) (status of and constitutionality of government policies at Guantanamo).

- Presidential accountability—including *Clinton v. Jones*, 520 U.S. 681 (1997); Clinton impeachment; Trump impeachment; *Trump v. Vance*, 591 U.S. ___ (2020); *Trump v. Mazars USA, LLP*, 591 U.S. ___ (2020); second Trump impeachment.

- Constitutional structure—including *Immigration and Naturalization Service v. Chadha*, 462 U.S. 919 (1983) (one-house legislative veto); *U.S. Term Limits, Inc. v. Thornton*, 514 U.S. 779 (1995) (congressional term limits); *Printz v. United States*, 521 U.S. 898 (1997) (Tenth Amendment); *Clinton v. City of New York*, 524 U.S. 417 (1998) (line-item veto); *National*

Labor Relations Board v. Noel Canning, 573 U.S. 513 (2014) (recess appointments).
- Politics, elections, and voting—including Twenty-fifth Amendment; *Buckley v. Valeo*, 424 U.S. 1 (1976) (campaign finance); *Bush v. Gore*, 531 U.S. 98 (2000) (election of 2000); *Crawford v. Marion County Election Board*, 553 U.S. 181 (voter identification) (2008); *Citizens United v. Federal Election Commission*, 558 U.S. 310 (2010) (campaign finance); *Rucho v. Common Cause*, 588 U.S. ___ (2019) (gerrymandering).

Notes

1. 381 U.S. 479 (1965).
2. 367 U.S. 497 (1961).
3. *Id.* (Douglas, J., dissenting).
4. Griswold v. Connecticut, 381 U.S. 479 (1965).
5. Eisenstadt v. Baird, 405 U.S. 438 (1972).
6. 410 U.S. 113 (1973).
7. Bradwell v. Illinois, 83 U.S. 130 (1873).
8. *Id.*
9. *Id.* (Bradley, J., concurring).
10. 198 U.S. 45 (1905).
11. Muller v. Oregon, 208 U.S. 412 (1908).
12. 404 U.S. 71 (1971).
13. Frontiero v. Richardson, 411 U.S. 677 (1973).
14. Stanton v. Stanton, 421 U.S. 7 (1975).
15. Craig v. Boren, 429 U.S. 190 (1976).
16. 518 U.S. 515 (1996).
17. Regents of the University of California v. Bakke, 438 U.S. 265 (1978).
18. Grutter v. Bollinger, 539 U.S. 306 (2003).
19. Bowers v. Hardwick, 478 U.S. 186 (1986).
20. Romer v. Evans, 517 U.S. 620 (1996).
21. Lawrence v. Texas, 539 U.S. 558 (2003).
22. *Id.*
23. *Id.* (Scalia, J., dissenting).
24. United States v. Windsor, 570 U.S. 744 (2013).
25. Obergefell v. Hodges, 576 U.S. 644 (2015).
26. Trump v. Hawaii, 585 U.S. ___ (2018).
27. 323 U.S. 214 (1944).
28. *Trump*, 585 U.S. ___ (Sotomayor, J., dissenting).
29. 554 U.S. 570 (2008).

30. United States v. Miller, 307 U.S. 174 (1939).
31. *Heller*, 554 U.S. 570.
32. 545 U.S. 469 (2005).
33. Gen. Stat. Conn., § 53-32 (1958 rev.) ("Any person who uses any drug, medicinal article or instrument for the purpose of preventing conception shall be fined not less than fifty dollars or imprisoned not less than sixty days nor more than one year or both fined and imprisoned."), quoted in Griswold v. Connecticut, 381 U.S. 479 (1965).
34. *Griswold*, 381 U.S. 479.
35. Pierce v. Society of Sisters, 268 U.S. 510 (1925).
36. NAACP v. Alabama, 357 U.S. 449 (1958).
37. Meyer v. Nebraska, 262 U.S. 390 (1923).
38. *Griswold*, 381 U.S. 479 (Stewart, J., dissenting).
39. 2A Tex. State Pen. Code, arts. 1191, 1196 (1961), law.jrank.org/pages/11631/Brief-Appellant-STATUTES-INVOLVED.html.
40. Paul VI, Encyclical Letter, *Humanae Vitae*, July 25, 1968, w2.vatican.va/content/paul-vi/en/encyclicals/documents/hf_p-vi_enc_25071968_humanae-vitae.html.
41. National Organization for Women, *Bill of Rights in 1968*, en.wikisource.org/wiki/N.O.W._Bill_of_Rights.
42. Roe v. Wade, 410 U.S. 113 (1973). See generally David J. Garrow, *Liberty and Sexuality: The Right of Privacy and the Making of* Roe v. Wade (New York: Macmillan, 1994).
43. *Roe*, 410 U.S. 113.
44. *Id.*
45. Doe v. Bolton, 410 U.S. 179 (1973) (White, J., dissenting).
46. Planned Parenthood of Se. Pa. v. Casey, 505 U.S. 833 (1992).
47. *Id.*
48. *Id.* (Blackmun, J., concurring and dissenting).
49. *Id.* (Rehnquist, C.J., concurring and dissenting).
50. *Id.* (Scalia, J., concurring and dissenting).
51. Guttmacher Institute, "An Overview of Abortion Laws," *State Law and Policies* (December 1, 2021), www.guttmacher.org/state-policy/explore/overview-abortion-laws. The Supreme Court has agreed to consider the constitutionality of pre-viability prohibitions on elective abortions—and possibly the fate of *Roe v. Wade* as well—in *Dobbs v. Jackson Women's Health Organization* (forthcoming).
52. Webster v. Reprod. Health Servs., 492 U.S. 490 (1989).
53. Harris v. McRae, 448 U.S. 297 (1980).
54. Stenberg v. Carhart, 530 U.S. 914 (2000).
55. Gonzales v. Carhart, 550 U.S. 124 (2007).
56. Whole Woman's Health v. Hellerstedt, 579 U.S. ___ (2016); June Med. Servs. v. Russo, 591 U.S. ___ (2020).
57. Planned Parenthood v. Danforth, 428 U.S. 52 (1976).
58. Bellotti v. Baird, 443 U.S. 622 (1979).
59. Linda Greenhouse and Reva B. Siegel, "Before (and After) *Roe v. Wade*: New Questions about Backlash," *Yale Law Journal* 120 (2011): 2028–87, www.yalelawjournal.org/feature/before-and-after-roe-v-wade-new-questions-about-backlash.

60. McCorvey v. Hill, 385 F.3d 846 (5th Cir. 2004), law.justia.com/cases/federal/appellate-courts/F3/385/846/582508/. Shortly before she died, McCorvey stated that she had been paid to profess antiabortion views. See Norma McCorvey, interview, *AKA Jane Roe*, FX, 2020; Jenny Gross and Aimee Ortiz, "Roe v. Wade Plaintiff Was Paid to Switch Sides, Documentary Says," *New York Times*, May 19, 2020.

61. 405 U.S. 438 (1972).

62. 431 U.S. 678 (1977).

63. 478 U.S. 186 (1986).

64. 539 U.S. 558 (2003).

65. Bradwell v. Illinois, 83 U.S. 130 (1873) (Bradley, J., concurring).

66. Muller v. Oregon, 208 U.S. 412 (1908).

67. Radice v. New York, 264 U.S. 292 (1924).

68. Goesaert v. Cleary, 335 U.S. 464 (1948).

69. Hoyt v. Florida, 368 U.S. 57 (1961).

70. Reed v. Reed, 404 U.S. 71 (1971).

71. Stanton v. Stanton, 421 U.S. 7 (1975).

72. Craig v. Boren, 429 U.S. 190 (1976).

73. Frontiero v. Richardson, 411 U.S. 677 (1973); Weinberger v. Wiesenfeld, 420 U.S. 636 (1975).

74. Ruth Bader Ginsburg, "Advocating the Elimination of Gender-Based Discrimination: The 1970s New Look at the Equality Principle" (speech, Cape Town, South Africa, February 10, 2006), www.supremecourt.gov/publicinfo/speeches/viewspeech/sp_02-10-06.

75. J.E.B. v. Alabama, 511 U.S. 127 (1994).

76. 458 U.S. 718 (1982).

77. United States v. Virginia, 518 U.S. 515 (1996).

78. Califano v. Webster, 430 U.S. 313 (1977).

79. California Fed. Sav. & Loan Ass'n v. Guerra, 479 U.S. 272 (1987).

80. Rostker v. Goldberg, 453 U.S. 57 (1981).

81. Excerpted from Robert Cohen and Laura J. Dull, "Teaching about the Feminist Rights Revolution: Ruth Bader Ginsburg as 'The Thurgood Marshall of Women's Rights,'" *The American Historian* (November 2017):13–17, www.oah.org/tah/issues/2017/november/teaching-about-the-feminist-rights-revolution-ruth-bader-ginsburg-as-the-thurgood-marshall-of-womens-rights/.

82. Here is one person's opinion: "I would like to be able to take out my pocket Constitution and say that the equal citizenship stature of men and women is a fundamental tenet of our society like free speech." Ruth Bader Ginsburg (remarks, Aspen, CO, May 30, 2017), www.aspeninstitute.org/blog-posts/justice-ruth-bader-ginsburg-road-womens-rights/.

83. 478 U.S. 186 (1986).

84. Loving v. Virginia, 388 U.S. 1 (1967).

85. Barack Obama, Second Inaugural Address (January 21, 2013), www.presidency.ucsb.edu/documents/inaugural-address-15.

86. *Bowers*, 478 U.S. 186.

87. Ruth Marcus, "Powell Regrets Backing Sodomy Law," *Washington Post*, October 26, 1990, www.washingtonpost.com/archive/politics/1990/10/26/powell-regrets-backing-sodomy-law/a1ae2efc-bec6-47ec-bfb6-1c098e610c5b/.

88. *Bowers*, 478 U.S. 186 (Blackmun, J., dissenting).

89. Arguably, the stage had been set for *Lawrence* by Romer v. Evans, 517 U.S. 620 (1996), where the Supreme Court by a vote of 6–3 struck down an antigay provision in Colorado's state constitution as a violation of the Equal Protection Clause of the Fourteenth Amendment.

90. Lawrence v. Texas, 539 U.S. 558 (2003). See generally Dale Carpenter, *Flagrant Conduct: The Story of* Lawrence v. Texas (New York: W.W. Norton, 2012).

91. *Lawrence*, 539 U.S. 558.

92. *Id.* (Scalia, J., dissenting).

93. *Id.*

94. An Act to define and protect the institution of marriage, Pub. L. No. 104-199, 110 Stat. 2419 (September 21, 1996), www.congress.gov/bill/104th-congress/house-bill/3396/text.

95. United States v. Windsor, 570 U.S. 744 (2013).

96. *Id.*

97. "Same-Sex Marriage, State by State," Pew Research Center, June 26, 2015; www.pewforum.org/2015/06/26/same-sex-marriage-state-by-state/. See generally Kenji Yoshino, *Speak Now: Marriage Equality on Trial* (New York: Penguin Random House, 2015).

98. Maynard v. Hill, 125 U.S. 190 (1888).

99. Meyer v. Nebraska, 262 U.S. 390 (1923).

100. Skinner v. Oklahoma *ex rel.* Williamson, 316 U.S. 535 (1942).

101. Loving v. Virginia, 388 U.S. 1 (1967).

102. Obergefell v. Hodges, 576 U.S. 644 (2015).

103. *Id.* (Roberts, C.J., dissenting).

104. Bostock v. Clayton Cnty., 590 U.S. ___ (2020).

105. Masterpiece Cakeshop, Ltd. v. Colorado Civ. Rts. Comm'n, 584 U.S. ___ (2018); see also Fulton v. Philadelphia, 593 U.S. ___ (2021) (city violated Free Exercise Clause by refusing to contract with foster-care provider that objected to certifying same-sex couples as foster parents). See generally William N. Eskridge, Jr. and Robin Fretwell Wilson, eds., *Religious Freedom, LBGT Rights, and the Prospects for Common Ground* (Cambridge, UK: Cambridge University Press, 2018).

Debating the Constitution

Over the years, admirers and critics from across the political spectrum have offered contrasting perspectives on the Constitution. This collection of provocative quotations enables teachers and students to continue the debate in their classrooms. What arguments resonate, and why? How have the Constitution's supporters and its critics been vindicated (or not) by important events in the country's history? To what extent has the Constitution helped to achieve—or served to hinder—"liberty and justice for all"?

The federal constitution, which has lately been proposed by the convention of the states . . . is calculated to increase the influence, power, and wealth of those who have any already. If the Constitution be adopted it will be a grand point gained in favor of the aristocratic party.
John Quincy Adams, 1787[1]

The warmest friends and the best supporters the Constitution has do not contend that it is free from imperfections. . . . I think the people (for it is with them to judge) can, as they will have the advantage of experience on their side, decide with as much propriety on the alterations and amendments which are necessary as ourselves. I do not think we are more inspired, have more wisdom, or possess more virtue, than those who will come after us.
George Washington, 1787[2]

Would it be wonderful if under the pressure of all these difficulties, the convention should have been forced into some deviations from that artificial structure and regular symmetry, which an abstract view of the subject might lead an ingenious theorist to bestow on a constitution planned in his closet or in his imagination? The real wonder is that so many difficulties should have been surmounted; and surmounted with a unanimity almost as unprecedented as it must have been unexpected. It is impossible for any man of candor to reflect on this circumstance without partaking of the astonishment. It is impossible for the man of pious reflection not to perceive in it a finger of that Almighty hand which has been so frequently and signally extended to our relief in the critical stages of the revolution.
James Madison, 1788[3]

The establishment of a constitution, in time of profound peace, by the voluntary consent of a whole people, is a prodigy, to the completion of which I look forward with trembling anxiety.
Alexander Hamilton, 1788[4]

'Tis really astonishing that the same people who have just emerged from a long and cruel war in defense of liberty should now agree to fix an elective despotism upon themselves and their posterity!
Richard Henry Lee (Virginia Antifederalist), 1788[5]

No society can make a perpetual constitution, or even a perpetual law. The earth belongs always to the living generation. . . . Every constitution then, and every law, naturally expires at the end of nineteen years. If it be enforced longer, it is an act of force and not of right.

 Thomas Jefferson, 1789[6]

In examining the Constitution of the United States, which is the most perfect federal constitution that ever existed, one is startled . . . at the variety of information and the excellence of discretion which it presupposes in the people whom it is meant to govern. . . . The Constitution of the United States is like those exquisite productions of human industry which ensure wealth and renown to their inventors, but which are profitless in any other hands.

 Alexis de Tocqueville, 1835[7]

[The Constitution is] the source and parent of all the other atrocities—a covenant with death, and an agreement with hell.

 William Lloyd Garrison, 1854[8]

The federal Constitution is a perfect and entire thing, an edifice put together not for the accommodation of a few persons, but for the whole human race; not for a day or a year, but for many years, perhaps a thousand, perhaps many thousand. . . . It is the grandest piece of moral building ever constructed; I believe its architects were some mighty prophets and gods.

 Walt Whitman, 1856[9]

The American government and the American Constitution . . . are entirely distinct from each other and totally different. In regard to the question of slavery . . . they are as distinct from each other as the compass is from the ship—as distinct from each other as the chart is from the course which a vessel may be sometimes steering. . . . If the American government has been mean, sordid, mischievous, devilish, it is no proof whatever that the Constitution of government has been the same.

 Frederick Douglass, 1860[10]

The preamble of the federal Constitution says: We the People of the United States . . . not, we, the white male citizens; nor yet we, the male citizens; but we, the whole people, who formed the union. And we formed it, not to give the blessings of liberty, but to secure them; not to the half of ourselves and the half of our posterity, but to the whole people—women as well as men. And it is a downright mockery to talk to women of their enjoyment of the blessings of liberty while they are denied . . . the ballot.

 Susan B. Anthony, 1873[11]

You are putting a Wall Street lawyer in a helluva box, but if it is a question of safety of the country, [or] the Constitution of the United States, why, the Constitution is just a scrap of paper to me.

 Assistant Secretary of War John J. McCloy, 1942[12]

We were interviewed by an FBI agent at some point after being arrested. He wanted to know, "Why are you doing this?" I said something about defending . . . the Fourteenth Amendment. . . . He said, "Don't you know nobody believes in those things anymore?"

 Peggi Oakley (Freedom Rider), 1961[13]

Here's my problem, Governor [Ross Barnett of Mississippi]. Listen, I didn't put him [James Meredith] in the university [as its first African American student]. But under the Constitution I have to . . . carry that order out, and I don't want to do it in any way that causes difficulty to you or to anyone else. But I've got to do it. Now, I'd like to get your help in doing that.

John F. Kennedy, 1962[14]

By our courage . . .by dignity in the face of unprovoked violence, by the insatiable adherence to principle of the students on this campus . . . we've shown ourselves guilty of one thing—of passionately entering into a conspiracy to uphold the First and Fourteenth Amendments.

Mario Savio (student activist), 1964[15]

All we say to America is, "Be true to what you said on paper." If I lived in China or even Russia, or any totalitarian country, maybe I could understand the denial of certain basic First Amendment privileges, because they hadn't committed themselves to that over there. But somewhere I read of the freedom of assembly. Somewhere I read of the freedom of speech. Somewhere I read of the freedom of the press. Somewhere I read that the greatness of America is the right to protest for right.

Martin Luther King Jr., 1968[16]

My faith in the Constitution is whole; it is complete; it is total.

Congresswoman Barbara Jordan, 1974[17]

I can't help but muse on the genius of our founders. . . . They created, with a sureness and originality so great and pure that one inescapably perceives the guiding hand of God, the first political system that made it clear that power flows from the people to the state—and not the other way around.

Ronald Reagan, 1985[18]

The genius of the Constitution rests not in any static meaning it might have had in a world that is dead and gone, but in the adaptability of its great principles to cope with current problems and current needs.

Justice William Brennan Jr., 1985[19]

I do not believe the meaning of the Constitution was forever "fixed" at the Philadelphia Convention. Nor do I find the wisdom, foresight, and sense of justice exhibited by the framers particularly profound. To the contrary, the government they devised was defective from the start, requiring several amendments, a civil war, and momentous social transformation to attain the system of constitutional government, and its respect for the individual freedoms and human rights, we hold as fundamental today. When contemporary Americans cite "The Constitution," they invoke a concept that is vastly different from what the framers barely began to construct two centuries ago.

Justice Thurgood Marshall, 1987[20]

The United States, as a true nation, was conceived in Philadelphia in the summer of 1787, but it was not yet born until the document was ratified.

Chief Justice Warren Burger, 1988[21]

[In 1987] the newspapers carried large advertisements for "The Constitution Bowl," announced by the official Commission on the Bicentennial, to be made of "Lenox fine ivory China" showing the official flowers of the thirteen original states, and "bordered with pure twenty-four-karat gold . . . a masterpiece worthy of the occasion." . . . A beautiful bowl indeed. And it was a perfect representation of the Constitution—elegant, but empty, capable of being filled with good or bad by whoever possessed the power and the resources to fill it.

Professor Howard Zinn, 1991[22]

The whole purpose of the Constitution is to prevent a future society from doing whatsoever it wants to do. To change, to evolve, you don't need a constitution. All you need is a legislature, as well as a ballot box. Things will change as fast as you want. You want to create new rights and/or destroy old ones? A legislature and the electoral franchise are all that you need. The only reason you need a constitution is because there are some things which you don't want a majority to be able to change.

Justice Antonin Scalia, 1996[23]

As the Constitution endures, persons in every generation can invoke its principles in their own search for greater freedom.

Justice Anthony Kennedy, 2003[24]

The outlines of Madison's constitutional architecture are so familiar that even schoolchildren can recite them: not only rule of law and representative government, not just a bill of rights, but also the separation of the national government into three coequal branches, a bicameral Congress, and a concept of federalism that preserved authority in state governments, all of it designed to diffuse power, check factions, balance interests, and prevent tyranny by either the few or the many. . . . Conservative or liberal, we are all constitutionalists.

Barack Obama, 2006[25]

The Constitution [places] almost insurmountable barriers in the way of any acceptable notion of democracy. . . . [Because] the Constitution is both insufficiently democratic, in a country that professes to believe in democracy, and significantly dysfunctional in terms of the quality of government we receive, then it follows that we should no longer express our blind devotion to it.

Professor Sanford Levinson, 2006[26]

Our Founding Fathers fought and bled for freedom and then crafted the most miraculous political document ever conceived, our Constitution.

Senator Ted Cruz, 2012[27]

Like all American children, I recited the pledge to the flag every morning. I must tell you, however, that I had to question whether those inspiring words "liberty and justice for all" included little Elijah.

Congressman Elijah Cummings, 2019[28]

Notes

1. John Quincy Adams, October 12, 1787, in *The Adams Papers, Diary of John Quincy Adams, vol. 2, March 1786–December 1788*, ed. Robert J. Taylor and Marc Friedlaender (Cambridge, MA: Harvard University Press, 1981), 302–03, founders. archives.gov/documents/Adams/03-02-02-0002-0010-0012.

2. George Washington to Bushrod Washington, November 9, 1787, in *The Papers of George Washington*, Confederation Series, Vol. 5, ed. W.W. Abbot (Charlottesville: University of Virginia Press, 1997), 420–25, founders.archives.gov/documents/Washington/04-05-02-0388.

3. The Federalist No. 37 (James Madison) (January 11, 1788), guides.loc.gov/federalist-papers/text-31-40#s-lg-box-wrapper-25493391.

4. The Federalist No. 1 (Alexander Hamilton) (October 27, 1787), guides.loc.gov/federalist-papers/text-1-10#s-lg-box-wrapper-25493264.

5. Richard Henry Lee to John Lamb, June 27, 1788, in *The Letters of Richard Henry Lee, Volume 2, 1779-1794*, ed. James Curtis Ballagh (New York: Macmillan, 1914), 474–76, leefamilyarchive.org/papers/letters/transcripts-ballagh/b375.html.

6. Thomas Jefferson to James Madison, September 6, 1789, founders.archives.gov/documents/Madison/01-12-02-0248.

7. Alexis de Tocqueville, *Democracy in America*, Vol. 1 (1835), www.gutenberg.org/files/815/815-h/815-h.htm.

8. William Lloyd Garrison (speech, Framingham, MA, July 4, 1854), www.masshist.org/object-of-the-month/objects/a-covenant-with-death-and-an-agreement-with-hell-2005-07-01.

9. Walt Whitman, "The Eighteenth Presidency" (1856), in *Walt Whitman: Complete Poetry and Collected Prose*, ed. Justin Kaplan (New York: Library of America, 1982), 1318.

10. Frederick Douglass, "The American Constitution and the Slave" (speech, Glasgow, March 26, 1860), in *The Speeches of Frederick Douglass: A Critical Edition*, ed. John R. McKivigan, Julie Husband, and Heather L. Kaufman (New Haven, CT: Yale University Press, 2018), 159–60.

11. Susan B. Anthony, "Is It a Crime for a U.S. Citizen to Vote?" (speech, Washington, DC, January 16, 1873), in *Against an Aristocracy of Sex, 1866 to 1873, Vol. 2: The Selected Papers of Elizabeth Cady Stanton and Susan B. Anthony*, ed. Ann D. Gordon (New Brunswick, NJ: Rutgers University Press, 2000), 554–83, susanb.org/wp-content/uploads/2018/12/Susan-B-Anthony-1872-1873.pdf.

12. John J. McCloy quoted in Kai Bird, *The Chairman: John J. McCloy: The Making of the American Establishment* (New York: Simon & Schuster, 1992), 149–50).

13. Peggi Oakley, quoted in Eric Etheridge, *Breach of Peace: Portraits of the 1961 Mississippi Freedom Riders* (Nashville, TN: Vanderbilt University Press, 2018), 188–89.

14. John F. Kennedy and Governor Ross Barnett, transcript of telephone call (September 22, 1962), in Ted Widmer, *Listening In: The Secret White House Recordings of John F. Kennedy* (New York: Hyperion, 2012), 101–06, americanradioworks.publicradio.org/features/prestapes/jfk_rb_092962_2pm.html.

15. Mario Savio (speech, Berkeley, CA, October 16, 1964), in Mario Savio, *The Essential Mario Savio: Speeches and Writings That Changed America*, ed. Robert Cohen (Oakland: University of California Press, 2014), vii.

16. Martin Luther King Jr., "I've Been to the Mountaintop" (speech, Memphis, TN, April 3, 1968), reprinted by arrangement with The Heirs to the Estate of Martin Luther King Jr., care of Writers House as agent for the proprietor, New York, NY. Copyright © 1968 by Dr. Martin Luther King Jr. Renewed © 1996 by Coretta Scott King.

17. Statement of Barbara Jordan, House Judiciary Committee (July 24, 1974), millercenter.org/the-presidency/impeachment/my-faith-constitution-whole-it-complete-it-total.

18. Ronald Reagan, "Presidential Article: 200th Anniversary of the Republic," *Parade Magazine* (draft), June 26, 1985, www.reaganlibrary.gov/public/digitallibrary/smof/counsel/roberts/box-005/40-485-6908381-005-014-2017.pdf.

19. William J. Brennan, Jr., "To the Text and Teaching Symposium, Georgetown University" (speech, Washington, DC, October 12, 1985), in *The Great Debate: Interpreting Our Written Constitution* (Washington, DC: Federalist Society, 1986), fedsoc.org/commentary/publications/the-great-debate-justice-william-j-brennan-jr-october-12-1985.

20. Thurgood Marshall, "The Constitution's Bicentennial: Commemorating the Wrong Document?" *Vanderbilt Law Review* 40, no. 6 (November 1987): 1337–42, scholarship.law.vanderbilt.edu/cgi/viewcontent.cgi?article = 2686&context = vlr.

21. Warren E. Burger, "Foreword," in *The Constitution and the States: The Role of the Original Thirteen in the Framing and Adoption of the Federal Constitution,* ed. Patrick T. Conley and John P. Kaminski (Madison, WI: Madison House, 1988), vii.

22. Howard Zinn, *Declarations of Independence: Cross-Examining American Ideology* (New York: HarperCollins, 1990), thirdworldtraveler.com/Zinn/FreeSpeech_DI.html.

23. Antonin Scalia, "Judicial Adherence to the Text of Our Basic Law: A Theory of Constitutional Interpretation" (speech, Washington, DC, October 18, 1996), www.proconservative.net/PCVol5Is225ScaliaTheoryConstlInterpretation.shtml.

24. Lawrence v. Texas, 539 U.S. 558 (2003).

25. Barack Obama, *The Audacity of Hope: Thoughts on Reclaiming the American Dream* (New York: Crown, 2006), 87–88.

26. Sanford Levinson, *Our Undemocratic Constitution: Where the Constitution Goes Wrong (and How We the People Can Correct It)* (New York: Oxford University Press, 2006), 6, 9.

27. Ted Cruz, "Speech at the Republican National Convention" (speech, Tampa, FL, August 29, 2012), www.texasgopvote.com/2012-elections/video-and-transcript-ted-cruz-speech-2012-republican-national-convention-004545.

28. Elijah Cummings, quoted in Astead W. Herndon, "Elijah Cummings," *New York Times Magazine*, December 23, 2019, www.nytimes.com/interactive/2019/12/23/magazine/elijah-cummings-death.html.

Other Ideas for Teaching Constitutional History

This book has focused on a textual approach to the Constitution, involving scholarly essays and primary source documents. But there are other creative ways that teachers can use to explore the Constitution in their classrooms. We offer here a range of suggestions.

Breaking Free of Chronology

The chronological approach to history in traditional textbooks—as well as in this book—can sometimes fragment history and serve as an obstacle to exploring larger themes. Because constitutional issues often play out over long spans of time, they can be profitably used by teachers to reach across the centuries. For example, one can readily compare free speech issues—laws, court decisions, and constitutional principles—in the context of the Alien and Sedition Acts, World War I, the Cold War (McCarthyism), and the more recent War on Terror. The same is true of constitutional controversies involving race, gender, and immigration, among other matters.

Is Biography Destiny?

Chief Justices John Marshall and Roger Taney owned slaves; to what extent might that have influenced their decisions, especially Taney's *Dred Scott* opinion? Prior to joining the Court, Justice Louis Brandeis was a Progressive-era reformer, having authored a brief to the Supreme Court (in *Muller v. Oregon*) in support of the constitutionality of protective legislation for women. Before becoming a justice, Hugo Black had once been a member of the Ku Klux Klan (although one would be hard pressed to find any influence of that background in his judicial opinions). Chief Justice Earl Warren's political skills—he had been governor of California and ran for president in 1948 and 1952—are often invoked when explaining how the Supreme Court achieved unanimity in *Brown v. Board of Education*. Justice Thurgood Marshall had served for decades as a constitutional litigator for the NAACP. In addition to Thurgood Marshall, only one other African American (Clarence Thomas) has served on the Court. To what extent might Justices Sandra Day O'Connor, Ruth Bader Ginsburg, Sonia Sotomayor, Elena Kagan, and Amy Coney Barrett arguably bring a different perspective to the Court than their 110 male predecessors and colleagues? To date, only one justice has been of Hispanic heritage—Justice Sotomayor (who years before her Supreme Court nomination had suggested that the life experiences of a "wise Latina" might enrich her judging). No person of Asian descent has yet served on the Court. Most (although not all) justices have come from affluent, non-working-class backgrounds. None has been openly gay. Although most justices have been WASPs, more recently the Court has been dominated by Catholic and Jewish justices. How relevant is the background of a justice?

The Supreme Court in Real Time

Teachers and students may wish to follow significant constitutional controversies as they unfold during the course of the school year. In addition to keeping abreast of coverage of the Supreme Court in the *New York Times* and other media outlets, information about pending cases, oral arguments, and recent decisions can be found on the SCOTUSblog website.[1] The Supreme Court's official website publishes opinions and, on a slightly delayed basis, transcripts and audio recordings of oral arguments.[2] In this connection, students might consider whether Supreme Court proceedings should be televised.

Debating Judicial Reform

Whether or not the judiciary is (per Alexander Hamilton) the "least dangerous" branch, is it not surely the least democratic? Federal judges are not elected. By contrast, about half the states hold elections for judges. Is it better or worse for judges to be isolated from the political processes? Moreover, Supreme Court justices and other federal judges serve for life, not for a fixed term. Should federal judges be subject to term limits, or recall elections (as in some states), or mandatory retirement ages? Under the Constitution, Congress determines the number of justices, which over the course of the nation's history has ranged from five to ten but has been fixed at nine since 1869; proposals have recently been advanced to expand the number of Supreme Court seats. Other suggested Supreme Court-related reforms include giving each president an automatic appointment every two years; establishing staggered terms for justices of anywhere from nine to eighteen years; requiring an up or down vote by the Senate on every submitted nominee; enlarging the number of justices to fifteen, with five permanent justices affiliated with each political party in turn being required to select, unanimously, an additional five "moderate" colleagues to serve for fixed terms; and choosing justices by lottery from among sitting appellate judges.[3] Still other suggestions for court reform include Congress using its authority under Article III to remove certain issues from judicial oversight, requiring a supermajority of justices to declare a law unconstitutional (as do several states), and amending the Constitution to permit congressional override of Supreme Court constitutional rulings. President Joseph Biden established a special presidential commission to consider and evaluate these and other potential judicial reforms.[4]

Revising and Rewriting the Constitution

The Twenty-seventh Amendment was ratified in May 1992. Students could be asked to propose a new constitutional amendment(s). If it were possible to wave a magic wand, what would be the Twenty-eighth Amendment? In other words, what's wrong with or missing from the current Constitution?[5] Or, venturing out even more boldly, what about a rewrite of the entire document? A group of scholars—including several contributors to this book—recently engaged in just such an exercise, with fascinating insights, disagreements, and results.[6]

Other Constitutions

The United States has not one but fifty-one constitutions. State constitutions offer a wide array of structures, powers, rights, and limitations—and state governments, as well as state courts, profoundly affect the rights and duties of citizens and residents. Interesting and instructive comparisons can be made between state constitutions and the US Constitution.[7] Students might also profit from comparing the Constitution with models from other nations. Not all constitutional regimes are democracies by any means, and students may wish to reflect on the relationship between written constitutions, government authority, and personal liberties.[8] Justice Ginsburg once observed:

> If I were drafting a constitution . . . I might look at the constitution of South Africa. That was a deliberate attempt to have a fundamental instrument of government that embraced basic human rights, had an independent judiciary. . . . Canada has a Charter of Rights and Freedoms. . . . You would almost certainly look at the European Convention on Human Rights. Yes, why not take advantage of what there is elsewhere in the world?[9]

Oral History

Many significant constitutional events have occurred in recent decades, making them highly appropriate subjects for oral history interviews by students of family members and acquaintances. Such interviews might cover key court rulings or constitutional controversies, but they could also include judicial confirmation battles, "culture wars," free speech controversies (e.g., on college campuses), criminal law reform, social justice issues, and the like.

Field Trips

Whether visited in person or virtually, a number of historic sites and museums are broadly focused on the Constitution, including the National Archives, the Supreme Court, and the United States Capitol (all in Washington, DC) and Independence Hall and the National Constitution Center (both in Philadelphia). More specific constitutional issues are often addressed at locations and websites maintained by the National Park Service as National Historical Parks and National Historical Sites. Notable examples include Birmingham Civil Rights Institute National Monument (Alabama); *Brown v. Board of Education* National Historic Site (Kansas); Frederick Douglass National Historic Site (Washington, DC); Gateway Arch National Park—Old Courthouse (*Dred Scott* case) (Missouri); Martin Luther King Jr. National Historical Park (Georgia); Little Rock Central High School National Historic Site (Arkansas); Manzanar National Historic Site (Japanese American internment) (California); Selma to Montgomery National Historic Trail

(Alabama); Stonewall National Monument (New York); Harriet Tubman Underground Railroad National Historical Park (Maryland); Women's Rights National Historical Park (New York). Scores of private historical museums abound, and students can also research and visit sites of local and community history.

The Arts and Popular Culture

Artistic works can be useful in providing unique, creative perspectives on the Constitution and its history.[10] Some examples:

Movies: *On the Basis of Sex* (2018); *The Post* (2017); *Marshall* (2017); *Selma* (2014); *Lincoln* (2012); *Amistad* (1997); *Inherit the Wind* (1960); *Twelve Angry Men* (1957).

Plays and musicals: Heidi Schreck, *What the Constitution Means to Me* (2017); Lin-Manuel Miranda, *Hamilton* (2015); John Strand, *The Originalist* (2015); Robert Schenkkan, *All the Way* (2012); Arthur Miller, *The Crucible* (1953).

Opera: Derrick Wang, *Scalia/Ginsburg* (2015).

Graphic arts: Morgan O'Hara's "Handwriting the Constitution" project;[11] Sam Fink, *The Constitution of the United States of America* (New York: Random House, 1985).

Other arts: Photographs of billboards in the South urging the impeachment of Chief Justice Warren, Hale Woodruff's *Amistad* murals, Kerry James Marshall's paintings, political cartoons, and bobblehead dolls of various justices.

Notes

1. SCOTUSblog, www.scotusblog.com/.
2. Supreme Court of the United States, www.supremecourt.gov/.
3. See generally Daniel Epps and Ganesh Sitaraman, "How to Save the Supreme Court," *Yale Law Journal* 129 (2019): 148–206; papers.ssrn.com/sol3/papers.cfm?abstract_id=3288958.
4. Presidential Commission of the Supreme Court of the United States, Final Report (December 2021); https://www.whitehouse.gov/wp-content/uploads/2021/12/SCOTUS-Report-Final-12.8.21-1.pdf.
5. By way of example, the *New York Times* asked seven writers and legal scholars to "update" the Constitution. See "We the People," *New York Times*, August 4, 2021, www.nytimes.com/interactive/2021/08/04/opinion/us-constitution-amendments.html?searchResultPosition=4; see also Letters to the Editor, "Ideas for New Amendments to the Constitution," *New York Times*, August 14, 2021; www.nytimes.com/2021/08/14/opinion/letters/constitution-amendments.html.
6. "A New Constitution for the United States," *Democracy: A Journal of Ideas*, no. 61 (Summer 2021); democracyjournal.org/magazine/61/a-new-constitution-for-the-united-states/; see also "Symposium: The Democracy Constitution," *Democracy: A Journal of Ideas*, no. 61 (Summer 2021), democracyjournal.org/category/magazine/61/.

7. Links to various state constitutions can be found at constitution.org/1-Constitution/cons/usstcons.htm and www.stateconstitutions.umd.edu/index.aspx. See also Sanford Levinson, *Framed: America's 51 Constitutions and the Crisis of Governance* (New York: Oxford University Press, 2012).

8. The text of many foreign constitutions can be found at www.constituteproject.org/. Linda Colley, *The Gun, the Ship, and the Pen: Warfare, Constitutions, and the Making of the Modern World* (New York: Liveright, 2021), provides a global historical survey of the constitution-making era.

9. Ruth Bader Ginsburg, interview by *Al-Hayat TV*, January 30, 2012, www.memri.org/tv/us-supreme-court-justice-ruth-bader-ginsburg-egyptians-look-constitutions-south-africa-or-canada.

10. For two academic studies of the relationship between popular culture, the law, and the Supreme Court, see Maxwell Bloomfield, "The Supreme Court in American Popular Culture," *Journal of American Culture* 4 (1981): 1–13, scholarship.law.edu/cgi/viewcontent.cgi?article = 1810&context = scholar, and David Ray Papke, "The Impact of Popular Culture on American Perceptions of the Courts," *Indiana Law Journal* 82, no. 5 (2007): 1225–34; www.repository.law.indiana.edu/cgi/viewcontent.cgi?article=1514&context=ilj.

11. See news.artnet.com/art-world/morgan-ohara-handwriting-constitution-1018610.

Further Reading

Books about the Constitution and Constitutional History

Amar, Akhil Reed. *America's Constitution: A Biography*. New York: Random House, 2005.

Amar, Akhil Reed. *America's Unwritten Constitution: The Precedents and Principles We Live By*. New York: Basic Books, 2012.

Amar, Akhil Reed. *The Bill of Rights: Creation and Reconstruction*. New Haven, CT: Yale University Press, 1998.

Amar, Akhil Reed. *The Words That Made Us: America's Constitutional Conversation, 1760–1840*. New York: Basic Books, 2021.

Bodenhamer, David J. *Our Rights*. New York: Oxford University Press, 2007.

Bodenhamer, David J. *The U.S. Constitution: A Very Short Introduction*. New York: Oxford University Press, 2018.

Farrand, Max. *The Records of the Federal Convention of 1787*, 4 vols., rev. ed. New Haven, CT: Yale University Press, 1966.

Hamilton, Alexander, James Madison, and John Jay. *The Federalist*, ed. Benjamin Fletcher Wright. Cambridge, MA: Harvard University Press, 1961.

Levinson, Cynthia, and Sanford Levinson. *Fault Lines in the Constitution: The Framers, Their Fights, and the Flaws That Affect Us Today*. Atlanta, GA: Peachtree, 2019.

Levinson, Sanford. *An Argument Open to All: Reading* The Federalist *in the 21st Century*. New Haven, CT: Yale University Press, 2015.

Lipsky, Seth. *The Citizen's Constitution: An Annotated Guide*. New York: Basic Books, 2009.

National Archives. *Our Documents: 100 Milestone Documents from the National Archives*. New York: Oxford University Press, 2003.

Rakove, Jack. *The Annotated U.S. Constitution and Declaration of Independence*. Cambridge, MA: Harvard University Press, 2009.

Raphael, Ray. *The U.S. Constitution: Explained Clause by Clause for Every American Today*. New York: Penguin Random House, 2016.

Ritchie, Donald A., and JusticeLearning.org. *Our Constitution*. New York: Oxford University Press, 2006.

Books about the Supreme Court

Greenhouse, Linda. *The U.S. Supreme Court: A Very Short Introduction*, 2nd ed. New York: Oxford University Press, 2020.

Hall, Kermit. *The Oxford Companion to the Supreme Court of the United States*, 2nd ed. New York: Oxford University Press, 2005.

Hall, Kermit, and John J. Patrick. *The Pursuit of Justice: Supreme Court Decisions that Shaped America*. New York: Oxford University Press, 2006.

Irons, Peter. *May It Please the Court: The Most Significant Oral Arguments Made before the Supreme Court since 1955*. New York: New Press, 2007.

Irons, Peter. *A People's History of the Supreme Court*, rev. ed. New York: Penguin Books, 2006.

Rosen, Jeffrey. *The Supreme Court: The Personalities and Rivalries That Defined America*. New York: Times Books, 2006.

Urofsky, Melvin, and Paul Finkelman. *Documents of American Constitutional and Legal History*, 2 vols. 3rd ed. New York: Oxford University Press, 2008.

Books about Specific Supreme Court Cases

Carpenter, Dale. *Flagrant Conduct: The Story of* Lawrence v. Texas. New York: W.W. Norton, 2012.

Cohen, Adam. *Imbeciles: The Supreme Court, American Eugenics, and the Sterilization of Carrie Buck*. New York: Penguin Press, 2016.

Fehrenbacher, Don E. *The* Dred Scott *Case: Its Significance in American Law and Politics*. New York: Oxford University Press, 1978.

Freyer, Tony A. *Little Rock on Trial:* Cooper v. Aaron *and School Desegregation*. Lawrence: University Press of Kansas, 2011.

Garrow, David J. *Liberty and Sexuality: The Right of Privacy and the Making of* Roe v. Wade. New York: Macmillan, 1994.

Hall, Kermit L., and Melvin I. Urofsky. New York Times v. Sullivan: *Civil Rights, Libel Law, and the Free Press*. Lawrence: University Press of Kansas, 2011.

Johnson, John W. *The Struggle for Student Rights:* Tinker v. Des Moines *and the 1960s*. Lawrence: University Press of Kansas, 1997.

Kluger, Richard. *Simple Justice: The History of* Brown v. Board of Education *and Black America's Struggle for Equality*, rev. ed. New York: Vintage, 2004.

Labbe, Ronald M., and Jonathan Lurie, *The* Slaughterhouse Cases: *Regulation, Reconstruction, and the Fourteenth Amendment*. Lawrence: University Press of Kansas, 2003.

Lendler, Marc. Gitlow v. New York: *Every Idea an Incitement*. Lawrence: University Press of Kansas, 2012.

Lewis, Anthony. *Gideon's Trumpet*. New York: Random House, 1964.

Oshinsky, David M. *Capital Punishment on Trial:* Furman v. Georgia *and the Death Penalty in Modern America*. Lawrence: University Press of Kansas, 2010.

Strum, Philippa. *Speaking Freely:* Whitney v. California *and American Speech Law*. Lawrence: University Press of Kansas, 2015.

Tanenhaus, David S. *The Constitutional Rights of Children:* In re Gault *and Juvenile Justice*. Lawrence: University Press of Kansas, 2011.

Books by Supreme Court Justices

One comprehensive study (Ronald Collins, "353 Books by Supreme Court Justices," SCOTUSblog, November 7, 2012, www.scotusblog.com/2012/03/351-books-by-supreme-court-justices/) identified more than 350 books penned by the justices themselves. Many of these works cover arcane legal topics, but some are aimed at general audiences, including accounts rich in autobiographical detail.

Websites

Educating for American Democracy, a comprehensive report released in 2021 by a national network of educators and scholars, proposes an integrated and blended approach to the study of US history and constitutional literacy, consistent with the themes and goals of this book. See generally Educating for American Democracy (EAD), March 2, 2021, *Educating for American Democracy: Excellence in History and Civics for All Learners* (report) and *Roadmap to Educating for American Democracy*, www.educatingforamericandemocracy.org/.

Other websites explore constitutional issues and contain a wealth of primary source materials, including:

Annenberg Classroom, www.annenbergclassroom.org/
iCivics, www.icivics.org/
Library of Congress, guides.loc.gov/constitution
National Archives, www.archives.gov/founding-docs/constitution
National Constitution Center, constitutioncenter.org/
NYU Steinhardt, steinhardt.nyu.edu/social-studies-collaborative
The Quill Project, www.quillproject.net/library/
Teaching American History, teachingamericanhistory.org/
University of Missouri, Kansas City School of Law, law2.umkc.edu/faculty/
    projects/ftrials/conlaw/home.html

Acknowledgments

The Editors wish to express their profound appreciation to the constitutional scholars who contributed the essays that anchor this volume. Of course, we bear sole responsibility for all sins of commission or omission in this book.

Stacie Brensilver Berman (Instructor, NYU teacher residency program), Ryan Mills (Assistant Principal, Edward R. Murrow High School, New York), Samuel Moore (The George Washington University Law School), Sonia Murrow (Professor, Brooklyn College), David Steinbach, and Alison Steinbach reviewed various portions of the work and provided valuable suggestions for its improvement. Julie Silverbrook (with the Constitutional Sources Project and then iCivics) assisted immeasurably throughout this endeavor.

We are deeply grateful to all those at Oxford University Press who worked on this book and its companion website—but especially to our virtuoso editor, Nancy Toff. Her involvement dates to the inception of this project, when we first collectively discussed the need for a constitutional history resource for classroom teachers, and she has been with us every step of the way thereafter, dispensing support, guidance, feedback, and wisdom. We were extraordinarily fortunate to have been under Nancy's care.

Special thanks to Lucille Werlinich, whose generosity made this book possible and who has enabled us to conduct constitutional history teacher workshops that inform this work.

The Editors acknowledge the assistance and generosity of our friends and colleagues at the educational institutions where we teach. At New York University, thanks go to NYU Steinhardt's former Dean Dominic Brewer, current Dean Jack Knott, Jeannine Starr of the NYU Steinhardt Development office, NYU School of Law Dean Trevor Morrison, NYU Teaching and Learning Department Chairs Catherine Milne and Diana Turk, and department finance officer Cherrelle Hall. The George Washington University Law School has supported the Institute for Constitutional Studies and numerous constitutional history seminars over the years. At Sidwell Friends School, enthusiastic encouragement and support was provided by Head of School Bryan Garman and Upper School Principal Mamadou Guéye, among many others.

The editors are particularly indebted to their wonderful students, who, in count-less classes over many years, have provided invaluable feedback about the ideas and sources that resulted in this book.

Robby and Steve would especially like to thank Maeva for being that rarest of constitutional historians and law professors who has worked brilliantly and tire-lessly to enhance high school teacher knowledge of the Constitution. This book is a testament to that work.

Index

For the benefit of digital users, indexed terms that span two pages (e.g., 52–53) may, on occasion, appear on only one of those pages.

Printed in the USA/Agawam, MA
April 29, 2022

792370.029